HEBREW–ENGLISH LEXICON
OF THE BIBLE

HEBREW–ENGLISH LEXICON
OF THE BIBLE

CONTAINING ALL THE HEBREW AND ARAMAIC

WORDS IN THE HEBREW SCRIPTURES,

WITH THEIR MEANINGS IN ENGLISH

SCHOCKEN BOOKS · NEW YORK

First SCHOCKEN PAPERBACK edition 1975
Second Printing, 1978

Library of Congress Cataloging in Publication Data

Hebrew-English lexicon.

  Originally published by S. Bagster, London.
  1. Hebrew language—Dictionaries—English.
  2. Aramaic language—Dictionaries—English.
  PJ4833.H4 1975   492.4′3′21   74-26705

Manufactured in the United States of America

PUBLISHER'S PREFACE

HERE is a handy, concise, and practical dictionary to assist the student reading Scripture in the original Hebrew and Aramaic. This manual is based on Ernst Friedrich Leopold's *Lexicon Hebraicum et Chaldiacum in Veteris Testamenti, ordine etymologico compositum* (Leipzig, 1832) which, in turn, goes back to the standard works of Wilhelm Gesenius and Georg Benedict Winer.

Gesenius' *Hebräisch-deutsches Handwörterbuch* first appeared in 1810–1812; an expanded second edition came out in 1815; various scholars reworked and revised later editions. The sixteenth edition (1915) was translated into English; a corrected impression of this latter version appeared in 1952.

Winer issued a *lexicon manuale* to the Hebrew Bible in Leipzig in 1828; an English version appeared in London in 1832.

The original preface of the present lexicon stated that it "is specially designed to put into the hands of the English [predominantly Christian] student in a compressed and compendious form, the contributions of modern philology to the interpretation of the

Hebrew Scriptures." Wherever the learning of the time did not succeed in elucidating a given phrase, the compiler offered the rendering in the Authorized English Version rather than indulging in uncertain speculations.

The last generation of biblical scholarship has added much to our knowledge. Comparative Semitic linguistics, form criticism, the writings of Ugarit have greatly enriched the field of biblical studies. But more time is needed until these insights will find their way into a student's dictionary. Until then this little manual will be of good service to a student.

April, 1974

ABBREVIATIONS OF GRAMMATICAL TERMS
USED IN THE LEXICON.

———◇———

m.	masculine.	pl.	plural.	
f.	feminine.	Niph.	Niphal form of verb.	
s.	substantive.	Hiph.	Hiphil ,, .	
pa.	particle.	Hith.	Hithpael ,,	
part.	participle.	Pi.	Piel ,, ,,	
denom.	denominative ; that is, a verb derived imme-diately from a noun (*de nomine*).	Pu.	Pual ,, ,,	
		Po.	Poel *or* Polel ,,	
		Hoth.	Hothpael ,,	
		Ith.	Ithpael ,, ,,	
patron.	patronymic: a pro-per name derived from that of the father of the individual.	imp.	imperative mood.	
		const.	construct state of noun.	
sing.	singular.	emph.	emphatic state of noun.	

אָב m. (const. אֲבִי and אַב‏, Gen. 17:4,
5; with suff. אָבִי‏, אָבִיךְ‏, אֲבִיכֶם‏;
pl. אָבוֹת‏).—I. *a father.*—II. *a pro-
genitor, ancestor;* used generally
for any senior male relative.—III.
an originator, inventor, Gen. 10:21,
&c.—IV. *a head, chief,* or *ruler;*
applied to kings, prophets, priests,
&c.; אָב לְפַרְעֹה *a father,* that
is, a counsellor *to Pharaoh,* Gen.
45:8.

אַב m. Ch. (with suff. אֲבִי‏, אֲבוּךְ‏,
אֲבוּהִי‏, pl. אֲבָהָן‏), *a father.*

אָבַב not used.

אֵב m., *greenness, freshness,* אִבִּים
green herbs.

אֵב m., Ch. *fruit;* אִבֵּהּ for אִנְבֵּהּ‏, *his
fruit.*

אָבִיב m.—I. *a green ear of corn,* Lev.
2:14.—II. *shooting into the ear;*
spoken of barley, Ex. 9:31. Hence
חֹדֶשׁ הָאָבִיב *the month Abib,* the
name of the month in which the
barley shoots into ear, corresponding partly with our March, partly
with April, otherwise called נִיסָן‏.

אַבַגְתָא p.n., one of the chamberlains
of King Ahasuerus, Est. 1:10.

אָבַד (inf. אֲבֹד‏, אָבֹד‏, fut. יֹאבַד and
יֹאבֵד‏).—I. *strayed, lost.*—II. *was
ruined, perished* (const. with לְ or
מִן‏); part. אֹבֵד *one about to perish,
a wretch;* Pi. אִבַּד‏, and Hiph.
הֶאֱבִיד *made to stray, dispersed,
laid waste, ruined, destroyed.*

אֲבַד Ch. (fut. יֵאבַד‏), *perished;* Aph.
הוֹבֵד *destroyed;* Hoph. הוּבַד *was
destroyed.*

אֹבֵד m., *perishing, ruin.*

אֲבֵדָה f., *something lost, the grave;*
see following word.

אֲבַדּוֹן *extermination, destruction, the
grave,* the place where the body
decays after death, opposed to
שְׁאוֹל the place of the soul after
death, Pro. 15:11, &c.; see the
word.

וָאֲבַדְךָ‏, אֲבַדְּךָ for וָאֲאַבֶּדְךָ‏, Pi. fut.
with suff.

אַבְדָן m., *extermination, ruin,* Est. 9:
5; אָבְדָן the same, Est. 8:6.

אָבָה (fut. יֹאבֶה‏), in Kal only, *desirous, willing;* const. mostly with
the neg. לֹא and with or without לְ‏.

אֵבֶה m., *a reed, rush;* אֳנִיּוֹת אֵבֶה
vessels made of reeds, Job 9:26.

אָבוּא for אָבוּ pret. pl.

אֶבְיוֹן m., *wishing, desiring;* hence, *destitute, poor, miserable.*

אֶבְיוֹנָה f., *desire,* Eccl. 12:5.

אֲבוֹי (lit. *misery), alas!* Pro. 23:29.

אָבוֹשׁ fut.; see בּוּשׁ.

אֲבַח ,אִבְחָה f., אִבְחַת חֶרֶב, *the resting, descent of the sword;* according to others, *the threatening of the sword,* or, *the drawn sword.* Ezek. 21:20.

אֲבַטִּיחִים m. pl., *melons,* Nu. 11:5; see טבח.

אָבִי for אָבִיא Hiph. fut. 1 pers.; see בּוֹא, 1 Ki. 21:29; Mic. 1:15.

אֲבִי (*my father*), p. n., the mother of King Hezekiah, 2 Kings 18:2.

אֹבִידָה for אַאֲבִידָה Hiph. fut. 1. pers.; see אבד.

אֲבִיאֵל (*the divine Father*), p. n.—I. the grandfather of Saul, 1 Sa. 9:1.—II. one of David's generals.

אֲבִיאָסָף ,אֶבְיָסָף (*father of gathering, collector*),p.n.,one of the Korahites.

אֲבִינָיִל,אֲבִינַל (*she whose father rejoiceth,* or, *the dancer*), p. n.—I. the wife of Nabal, afterwards of David.—II. the sister of David, 1 Chron. 2:16.

אֲבִידָן (*the father of judgment, the judge*) p. n., one of the princes of Benjamin, Nu. 1:11, &c.

אֲבִיהוּ,אֲבִיָּה (*he whose father is Jehovah*), see אָבִים; p. n.—I. of a man.—II. of a woman

אֲבִיהוּא p. n., a son of Aaron.

אֲבִיחוּד (*the father of glory,* πατροκλος) p. n. of a man.

אֲבִיחַיִל (*the father of artifices, he who is skilful*), p. n. of a man.

אֲבִיחַיִל (the same), p. n. of a woman.

אֲבִיטוּב (*father of goodness*), p. n. of a man.

אֲבִיטַל (*father of dew, vigorous*), p.n., a wife of David.

אֲבִים (*the sailor*), p. n. of a man; the same as אֲבִיָהוּ, and probably an error of some transcriber.

אֲבִימָאֵל p. n. of a man.

אֲבִימֶלֶךְ (*father of a king*), p. n.—I. a king of the Philistines, Gen. c. 20, perhaps the common name of the kings of that country.—II. name of a man, Jud. 8:31, &c.

אֲבִינָדָב (*father of willingness*), p. n. of a man.

אֲבִינֹעַם (*father of pleasantness*), p. n. of a man.

אֲבִינֵר ,אַבְנֵר (*father of light*), p.n., one of Saul's generals.

אֲבִיעֶזֶר (*father of help*), p. n. of a man.

אֲבִי-עַלְבוֹן m. (*violator*), p.n. of a man.

אָבִיר ,אַבִּיר *mighty;* see אבר.

אֲבִירָם m. (*father of pride, a proud one*), p. n. of a man.

אֲבִישַׁג f. p. n., one of David's concubines, 1 Kings 1:15, &c.

אֲבִישׁוּעַ (*father of salvation*), p. n. of a man.

אֲבִישׁוּר (*father of song, singer*), p. n. of a man, 1 Chron. 2:28.

אֲבִישַׁי ,אַבְשַׁי (*father of gifts, generous*), p. n. of a man.

אֲבִישָׁלוֹם (*father of peace*), the grandfather of Abijam king of Judah, 1 Kings 15:2.

אֶבְיָתָר (*a father of excellence, he who excels*), *Abiathar,* the son of Ahimelech, a high priest in David's time, 1 Sa. 22:20

אָבַךְ Hith. only. יִתְאַבְּכוּ "they swell with a rolling motion like volumes of smoke," Isa. 9:17.

I. אָבַל (fut. יֶאְבַּל), *mourned, lamented;* const. with עַל; Hiph. הֶאֱבִיל *made* or *caused to mourn;* Hith. הִתְאַבֵּל *grieved, betook himself to mourn;* const. with אֶל or עַל.

אָבֵל m. (const. אָבֶל-,אֲבֶל; pl. אֲבֵלִים), אֲבֵלָה f. *mourning;* אֵבֶל m. (with suff. אֶבְלִי) the same, *grief, howling.*

אָבֵל מִצְרַיִם (*the mourning of Egypt*), p.n., a place beyond Jordan, where the children of Israel mourned for their father when they carried him forth to his burial; Gen. 50:11.

II. אָבֵל not used (Arab. *fresh, green, grass*).

אָבֵל *a grassy place, field;* hence the following names of places.—I. 'א הַגְּדוֹלָה *the greater Abel,* a district of the Philistines, 1 Sa. 6:18.—II. 'א בֵּית־מַעֲכָה a large city in the land of the tribe of Manasseh, called 'א מַיִם, 2 Chron. 16:4.—III. 'א הַשִּׁטִּים a place in the land of Moab.—IV. 'א כְּרָמִים a village of the Ammonites.—V.'א מְחוֹלָה a village in the land of Issachar; hence the appellation מְחֹלָתִי; see the word.

III. אֲבָל adv., *certainly, but, indeed.* אוּבָל,אֲבָל; see יבל.

אֶבֶן f., I. *a stone, rock* (pl. אֲבָנִים; אַבְנֵי) לְאֶבֶן *like a stone;* אֶבֶן יָד a stone which may be thrown with the hand; (אֲבָנִים גְּדֹלוֹת) 'א בָּרָד hail stones.—II. *precious stones, jewels;* אַבְנֵי־אֵשׁ *shining stones.*

—III. *a weight;* אֶבֶן וָאֶבֶן *divers weights.*—IV. *a plummet.*

אֶבֶן עֶזֶר (*stone of help*), p. n. of a place, 1 Sa. 7:12.

אֶבֶן הָאֵזֶל (*stone of departure*), p. n. of a place.

אֶבֶן f. Ch. emph. state אַבְנָא; *a stone.*

אֹבֶן m., dual אָבְנָיִם.—I. "potter's wheel," Jer. 18:3.—II. "upon the stools," Ex. 1:16; Eng. Ver. The true meaning is uncertain.

אֲבָנָה p. n., a river of Damascus, 2 Ki. 5:12.

אַבְנֵט see בנט.

אֲבִינֵר p. n. of a man ; see אֲבִינֵר.

אָבַס, part. אָבוּס *fattened.*

אֵבוּס m. (pl. אֲבוּסִים) *a crib or stall* in which animals are fed; מַאֲבוּס m., *barn, granary,* Jer. 50:26.

אֲבַעְבֻּעוֹת *ulcers;* see בוע.

אֶבֶץ p.n. of a city in the tribe of Issachar.

אִבְצָן (*he who is shining, famous*), p. n., a judge of Israel.

אָבָק m., *fine dust, powder;* אֲבָקָה f., אֲבַקַת רוֹכֵל *aromatic dust, powdered perfume;* "powder of the merchant," Cant. 3:6, Eng. Ver.; נֶאֱבַק Niph. *wrestled* (because the ancient wrestlers covered their bodies with dust before they began to wrestle).

אָבַר Kal, not used, *was strong;* Hiph. הֶאֱבִיר *flew, soared.*

אֵבֶר m., *quill, wing-feather.*

אֶבְרָה f., the same.

אַבִּיר,אָבִיר m.—I. *mighty* (an epithet of God).—II. *strong, valiant, noble;* אַבִּירִים *strong bulls,* or *horses;* אַבִּיר הָרֹעִים *the prince of the shepherds.*

אַבְרָם (*exalted father*), p. n., Abram; אַבְרָהָם (*father of a multitude*), p. n., the patriarch *Abraham*.

אַבְרֵךְ Gen. 41:43, "bow the knee," Eng. Ver. The true meaning is uncertain.

אֲבָרְכְכָה Pi. fut. with suff.; see ברך.

אֲבִישַׁי p.n., see אבישי.

אַבְשָׁלוֹם (*father of peace*), p. n., *Absalom*, the son of David.

אָגָא (*fugitive*), p. n. of a man.

אֶנְאָלָתִי Hith. pret. 1. pers. for הִנְאָלְתִּי; see גאל.

אֲגַג p.n., a king of the Amalekites.

אֲגָגִי *Agagite*, a title of Haman, Est. 3:1.

אָגַר not used (Ch. and Arab. *bound in a mass*).

אֲגֻדָּה f.—I. *a bunch* or *bundle* (of hyssop).—II. *a band* or *body of men*; אֲגֻדָּתוֹ *his church, people*, Am. 9:6. —III. *knots, bindings*, Isa. 58:6.

אֱגוֹז m., *a nut*, Cant. 6:11.

אָגוּר (*companion*), p. n. of a woman.

אֲגוֹרָה *wages*; see אגר.

אָגַל not used (Arab. *gathered together, collected*).

אֵגֶל m., אֶגְלֵי טַל *drops of dew*, Job 38:28.

אֶגְלַיִם (*two fountains*), p. n., a village of the Moabites, Isa. 15:8.

אָגַם not used (Arab. *was hot*).

אָגַם Ch., *was stagnant* (of water); see עגם.

אֲגַם m. (pl. אֲגַמִּים, אַגְמֵי).—I. *a pool, pond, marsh*.—II. *flags, reeds*.

אָגֵם m., *sorrowful*.

אַגְמוֹן m.—I. *a reed, rush*.—II. *a rope of rushes*.—III. *a cauldron, kettle*,

---

Job 41:12, this is however doubtful. See Lee in loco.

אַגָּן (Arab. *a bason*); אַגָּן m., אַגָּנָה f., (pl. אַגָּנוֹת), *a bason* or *bowl*.

אַגָּף or אֲגַף m., pl. אֲגַפִּים *hosts, armies*; see גַּף.

אָגַר (fut. יֶאֱגֹר), *he laid up provision*.

אֲגוֹרָה f., *a small coin*; ὀβολός, 1 Sa. 2:36; see גרה.

אִגְּרָא f. Ch. emph. state אִגַּרְתָּא; same as the following word.

אִגֶּרֶת f. (pl. אִגְּרוֹת), *letter, edict*.

אֲגַרְטָל *a dish* or *bason*, Ezr. 1:9.

אֶגְרוֹף *the fist*; see גרף.

אֵד *mist, vapour*; see אוד.

אָדַב Kal, not used, Hiph. *he languished, was fatigued*; לְהַאֲדִיב for לַאֲדִיב inf.).

אַדְבְּאֵל (*the finger of God*), p.n. of a man.

אֶדְרָה for אֶתְדָּרָה Hith. fut.; with suff. אֶדְּדָם; see דרה.

אַדָּד (*long-lived*), p. n. of a man.

אַדּוֹ p. n. of a man.

אָדוֹן, אֲדֹנָי *Lord*; see אֶדֶן.

אֲדוֹרַיִם (*two hills*), p. n., a city of Judah.

אֲדוֹרָם p. n. of a man.

אֱדַיִן Ch. adv., *then*; בֵּאדַיִן *at that very time*; מִן אֱדַיִן *from that time*.

אַדְקֵם Hiph. fut. with suff. for אֲדִיקֵם; see דקק.

אַדִּיר *great*; see אדר.

אֲדַלְיָה (*Jehovah's righteousness*), p. n. of a man.

אָדַם *was red, reddish brown*; Pu. part. מְאָדָם *growing, turning red*; Hiph. *be red*; Hith. *grow red*.

דָּם m.(const. דַּם; with suff. דָּמוֹ; pl. דָּמִים, דְּמֵי).—I. *blood*; דָּם נָקִי

innocent blood; אִישׁ דָּמִים a man of bloods, i.e. cruel.—II. slaughter, murder; גֹּאֵל הַדָּם avenger of blood; אֵין לוֹ דָם blood is not on him, i.e. he has done no murder; בֵּית הַדָּמִים a bloody house.—III. דַּם עֲנָבִים blood of grapes, wine; see דמה.

אָדָם m., man (in general); כָּל־אָדָם all men; אָדָם a man, as distinguished from a woman; בֶּן־אָדָם mortal man.

אָדָם p.n.—I. Adam, the first man.—II. a city on Jordan, Jos. 3:16.

אָדֹם, אֲדַמָּה m., f., red, reddish brown.

אֱדֹם (red), p.n., one of the names of Esau.

אֱדֹם p.n., the land of Edom; אֲדֹמִי an Edomite.

אֹדֶם m., a ruby, or carnelion.

אָדַם, וְאָדֹם Kal fut.; see דמם.

אֲדַמְדָּמֹת m.; f. אֲדַמְדֶּמֶת; pl. אֲדַמְדָּם very red, glowing.

אֲדָמָה f.—I. ground, soil; אֹהֵב אֲ given to agriculture, lit. loving the ground.—II. fruit, produce.—III. region, country, the whole earth.—IV. p.n., a city of the tribe of Naphtali.

אֲדָמָה p.n., one of the cities of the plain.

אֲדָמָה for אֶתְדַּמֶּה Hith. fut. 1. pers.; see דמה.

אֲדָמִים p.n. of a place.

אַדְמוֹנִי red haired, πυῤῥάκης.

אֲדָמִי p.n., a city of the tribe of Naphtali.

אַדְמָתָא (land), p.n. of a man.

אֶדֶן m. (pl. אֲדָנִים)—I. the base of a column.—II. any foundation.

אַדֹּן, אֲדֹן p.n. of a man.

אָדֹון m. (from אדן, pl. אֲדוֹנִים), proprietor, master, lord.

אֲדֹנָי m., the Lord, exclusively applied to God.

אֲדֹנִי בֶזֶק (lord of Bezek), p.n., a king of the Canaanites, Jud. 1:5.

אֲדֹנִי צֶדֶק (righteous lord), p.n., Canaanitish king of Jerusalem, Jos. 10:1.

אֲדֹנִיָּה (the Lord is my Lord), p.n. of a m.

אֲדֹנִיָּהוּ p.n. of a man.

אֲדֹנִיקָם (the Lord confirmeth), p.n. of a m.

אֲדֹנִירָם (the Lord exalteth), p. n. of a man, 1 Ki. 4:6.

אָדַר does not occur in Kal; Niph. part. נֶאְדָּר, with Jod parag. נֶאְדָּרִי, it hath become glorious; Hiph. (fut. יַאְדִּיר) he made glorious.

אַדִּיר great, powerful, glorious, majestic.

אַדִּיר m., a prince

אֶדֶר m.—I. a cloak; see אַדֶּרֶת.—II. amplitude, splendour.

אַדֶּרֶת f. (with suff. אַדַּרְתּוֹ).—I. a cloak; אֲ שִׁנְעָר a Babylonish garment; אֲ שֵׂעָר a hair cloak.—II. magnificence.

אֲדַרְגָּזְרִין Ch. pl., officers of the court at Babylon, Dan. 3:2, 3, the nature of their office unknown.

אַדָּר p.n.—I. a place in the tribe of Judah.—II. of a man.

אָדַר threshing-floor; see נדר.

אֲדָר m., the twelfth month of the Hebrew year, corresponding with our February and March.

אָדְרַזְדָּא Ch., quickly, diligently.

דַּרְכְּמוֹן, אֲדַרְכֹּן, δαρεικὸς, a Persian gold coin.

אַדְרַמֶּלֶךְ (the exalted Moloch), p. n.—I. an idol of the Sepharvites, 2 Ki. 17:31.—II. a son of Sennacherib, Isa. 37:38, &c.

אֶדְרָע arm; see דרע.

אֶדְרֶעִי (planting), p. n.—I. the city of Og, Deu. 1:4.—II. a city of the tribe of Naphtali.

אִדְרָשׁ for הִדָּרֵשׁ Niph. inf. abs.; see דרש.

אָדֹשׁ (inf. אָדוֹשׁ the same as דּוּשׁ), threshing, beating out corn with the wheel, Isa. 28:28.

אָהֵב, אָהַב (inf. const. אַהֲבָה, אֲהֹב; imp. אֱהַב; fut. יֶאֱהַב; p. 1. אֹהַב and אֵהַב), loved, desired, delighted in; part. אֹהֵב (pl. אֹהֲבִים, f. אֹהֶבֶת) a friend; Niph. part. pl. נֶאֱהָבִים loved, amiable; Pi. part. מְאַהֵב lover.

אֵהַב Kal fut. 1. pers.

אַהֲבָה f., love, beloved.

אֲהָבִים m. pl. (sing. אַהַב), amours, loves, love-gifts.

אֹהָבִים m. pl. (sing. אֹהַב), the same.

אֹהַד (strength), p. n., one of the sons of Simeon.

אֲהָהּ ah! alas! an exclamation of sorrow.

אַהֲוָא p. n.—I. of a country.—II. of a river.

אֵהוּד (he who is powerful), p. n. of a man.

אֹהִדֶנּוּ(for אוֹרִדֶנּוּ)Hiph. fut. 1. pers. with suff.; see ידה.

אֱהִי the same as אֵי where?

אֱהִי probably for אַיֵּה where? which see: Hos. 13:10.

אֱהִי fut. apoc. 1. pers.; see היה.

אָהַל (fut. יֶאֱהַל), pitched a tent, lived in tents; Pi. fut. יַהֵל for יְאַהֵל the same; יַאֲהִיל shone, Job 25:5; see הלל to shine.

אֹהֶל m. (with ה parag. אֹהֱלָה; with suff. אֹהֱלֶךָ, אֹהֱלָךְ, Syr. אֹהֱלֵךְ; pl. אֹהָלִים, Syr. אֹהֱלֵי, אֹהֱלִים).—I. tabernacle, tent, habitation.—II. p. n. of a man, 1 Chron. 3:20.

אֹהֱלָה (her tent), p. n., allegorical name of Samaria, Eze. 23:4.

אֹהֱלִיאָב (tent of her father), p. n. of a m.

אֹהֱלִיבָה (my tent with her), p. n., allegorical name of Jerusalem, Eze. 23:4.

אֹהֱלִיבָמָה (my tent a high place), p. n. of a wife of Esau.

אֲהָלִים m. pl., אֲהָלוֹת f., ξυλαλόη, ἀγάλλοχον, lign-aloes, a perfumed wood.

אֶהֱמָיָה fut. with ה parag. for אֶהֱמֶה, see המה.

אַהֲרֹן p. n., Aaron, the brother of Moses; בֵּית א׳, בְּנֵי א׳ Aaronites.

אוֹ conj.—I. or, either; יָמִים אוֹ עָשׂוֹר ten days at least.—II. for אוֹ כִּי but if.—III. אוֹ....אוֹ, whether....or.

אַו desire; see אוה.

אוּאֵל p. n. of a man.

אוֹב not used.

אוֹב m. (pl. אֹבוֹת).—I. a spirit of divination, or necromancy.—II. νεκρόμαντις, a necromancer, one who calls up spirits from the abyss to foretel future events.—III. the art of necromancy.

אוֹבוֹת I. skins used as bottles for wine, Job 32:19.—II. p. n. of a place in the wilderness.

אוֹבִיל (he that causeth joy), p. n. of a man, 1 Chron. 27:30.

אוּבָל ; see יבל

אוּד not used (Arab. bent, crooked; also wood); etymology doubtful.

אֵד m., smoke, mist.

אוּד m., smoking firebrand.

אוֹדוֹת f. pl., projects, means, cause; עַל אוֹדוֹת (and אֶל for עַל) because of; עַל אֲדוֹתִי on my account; עַל אֲדוֹתֶיךָ because of thee.

אוֹדְךָ, with נ epenth. אוֹדֶךָ Hiph. fut. 1. pers. with suff.; see ידה.

אֵיד m., calamity, destruction.

מְאֹד m.—I. power, might, excess; בְּכָל־ מְאֹדְךָ with all thy might; בִּמְאֹד מְאֹד in great excess; עַד מְאֹד even to excess, exceedingly.—II. adv. exceedingly.

אָוָה not used (Arab. desired); Pi. אִוָּה (fut. יְאַוֶּה), desired, longed for, const. with ב and ל; Hith. הִתְאַוָּה (fut. apoc. יִתְאָו), desired, coveted, claimed; וְהִתְאַוִּיתֶם לָכֶם and claim for yourselves, Nu.34:10.

אַו or אָו m., desire, Pro. 31:4.

אַוָּה f.—I. natural desire for food.—II. lust.

מַאֲוַי m. (pl. מַאֲוַיִּים), desires, Ps. 140:9.

תַּאֲוָה f.—I. desire, lust.—II. an object of desire; see תאה

אוֹחִילָה, Kri אוֹחִילָה Hiph.fut. 1.pers.; see חול

אוֹי, אוֹיָה I. alas! expression of grief.—II. ho! expressing anger.

אוֹת com. (pl. אֹתוֹת).—I. mark, memorial, warning.—II. sign, portent, miracle.

אָת Ch. (pl. אָתִין), the same.

אִי m. (pl. אִיִּים).—I. habitable land, continent, island.—II. shore, coast, countries on the coast; אִיֵּי הַגּוֹיִם and אִיֵּי הַיָּם isles of the Gentiles, isles of the West, countries little known to the Hebrews.—III. אִיִּים savage land animals, Is. 13:22, hence:—IV. interj. woe! horror! see און

אוֹיֵב enemy; see איב

אוּנִי p. n. of a man.

אֻנְגָּל p. n. of a city in Arabia; probably Senaar, the capital of Arabia Felix, Gen. 10:27.

אֱוִי p. n. of a king of Midian.

אוֹבִיל Hiph. fut. 1. pers.; see אכל

אוֹכַל Kal fut. 1. pers.; see אכל

אוֹל root not used; same as יאל.

אֱוִיל a fool, an impious person.

אֱוִיל־מְרֹדַךְ p. n., a king of Babylon, descendant of Nebuchadnezzar, 2 Ki. 25:27.

אֱוִילִי, same as אֱוִיל

אִוֶּלֶת f. (with suff. אִוַּלְתִּי), folly, sin.

I. אוּל (Arab. to dispose, govern aright); root not used.

אוּל m.—I. a prince.—II. administration.—III. body, Ps. 73:4.

אוּלַי adv.—I. perhaps, unless.—II. p.n of a river, Dan. 8:2.

אֻלָם (pl. אֵלַמִּים).—I. m., an entrance hall, vestibule.—II. pa. but; nevertheless.—III. p. n. of a man.

II. אוּל (Arab. grew thick, of fluids); root not used.

אַיִל m. (const. אֵיל ; pl. אֵילִים).—I. a ram.—II. lintel, arch over a door or window.

אַיִל m., *strength, force.*

אֱיָלוּת f., *the same.*

אַיָּל com., *an antelope, gazelle.*

אַיָּלָה f. (pl. אַיָּלוֹת; const. אַיְלוֹת),
female antelope.

אַיֶּלֶת הַשַּׁחַר f., *the same;* the
name of the tune to which the
Psalm is to be sung, Ps. 22.

אַיִל m. (pl. אֵילִים, אֵלִים).—I. *hero,
mighty man.*—II. *the pine or terebinth* (a tall thick tree).

אֵילִים p. n. of one of the stations of the
Israelites in the wilderness, Ex.c.15.

אֵל (with suff. אֵלִי; pl. אֵלִים, אֵלִם).—
I. *hero, man of might.*—II. *power;*
יֶשׁ לְאֵל יָדִי *it is in the power of
my hand,* i. e. I am able.—III. *God*
(the true God); בְּנֵי אֵלִים *the
sons of God,* i. e. *the angels.*—IV.
an epithet denoting excellence;
אַרְזֵי אֵל *cedars of God,* i. e. lofty,
well grown.—V. *an idol, false god.*

אֵלָה f., *terebinth;* see אַיִל, אַלָּה, &c.

אַלּוֹן m.—I. *oak, lofty tree;* compare
preceding word.—II. p. n. of a man.
—III. of a city.

אַיִל, אֵילָם, אֻלָם m., *a lintel;* see אוּלָם I.

אִילָן m. Ch., *a tree.*

וָאֵלֶךְ, אוֹלִיךְ Hiph. fut. 1. pers.; see
הלך, ילך.

אוֹמָר p. n. of a man.

אָוֶן or אִין root not used; (Arab. *time,
a fit time).*

אָוֶן m. (with suff. אוֹנְךָ, אוֹנִי; pl.
אוֹנִים).—I. *vanity, falseness, that
which is nothing,* hence:—II. *an
idol;* בֵּית אָוֶן *house of idols;*
בִּקְעַת אָוֶן *valley of idols* (a valley
near Damascus, now *Un,* Am. 1:5).
—III. *sin, wickedness.*—IV. *sorrow,*

distress; בֶּן־אוֹנִי *the son of my sorrow;* לֶחֶם אוֹנִים *bread of affliction;* see אנן.

אוֹן m. (with suff. like אָוֶן).—I. *power.*
—II. *manhood;* רֵאשִׁית הָאוֹן *first-
born.*—III. *wealth, riches.*

אַיִן const. אֵין I. *non-existence;* אֵין
בַּבּוֹר *he was not in the pit;*
אֵין יֹצֵא וְאֵין בָּא *there was neither
going out nor coming in;* אֵין לִי *I
have not,* lit. *there is nothing to me;*
אֵין לָבוֹא "none might enter," Eng.
Ver., Est. 4:2; אֵין דָּבָר, מְאוּמָה
nothing; אֵין כֹּל *absolutely nothing;*
אֵינֶנּוּ *it is not.*—II. with personal
pronoun אֵינֶנּוּ, אֵינְךָ, אֵינֵךְ, אֵינֶנִּי,
אֵינֵימוֹ אֵינָם, אֵינְכֶם, אֵינֶנָּה and *I
am, was, not, shall not be, thou art
not, &c.*—III. with prepositions,
בְּאֵין *in not being, before, without,*
כְּאֵין *like not being, nearly,* Ps.73:2;
לְאֵין *to him who has not,* Is. 40:29;
מֵאַיִן (poetic only), *not,* absolute
negation; מֵאֵין יוֹשֵׁב *no inhabitant,* Jer. 33:10.

אִין same as אַיִן, 1 Sa. 21:9.

אִי (perhaps from אַיִן), *not,* Job c. 22;
אִי־כָבוֹד (*ignoble*), p. n. of a man.

תְּאֵנָה f. (pl.תְּאֵנִים, *fig* (tree and fruit);
יָשַׁב תַּחַת תְּאֵנָתוֹ *he sat under
his fig-tree,* i. e. *he lived* peace-
fully and prosperously.

תְּאֵנִים m. pl., *vexation, vanity, falsehood,* Eze. 24:12.

אוֹן I. (*strength*), p. n. of a man.—II.
אֹן, אוֹן *Heliopolis,* a city of Lower
Egypt.

אוֹנוֹ (*strong*), p. n. of a city in the tribe
of Benjamin.

אוֹנָם (the same), p. n. of a man.

אוֹנָן (*vigorous*), p. n., one of the sons of Judah.

אוּפָז p. n., a country where gold was found (perhaps the same as the following word).

אוֹפִיר, אוֹפַר p. n., a country abounding in gold, gems, and perfumed wood.

אוֹפָן *a wheel*; see אפן.

אוּץ *pressed, was urgent upon*; const. with בְּ, לְ, מִ; Hiph. *pressed, hastened*; const. with בְּ, לְ.

אוֹצָר *treasure*; see אצר.

אוֹצְרָה Hiph. fut. 1. pers. with ה parag.; see רצא.

אוֹר I. *became light, shone, enlightened.*—II. *prospered*; imperat. אוֹרִי f. *shine thou*, Isa. 60:1. Niph. נָאוֹר (fut. יֵאוֹר), *become bright*; part. נָאוֹר *illustrious.* Hiph. הֵאִיר (fut. apoc. יָאֵר).—I. *enlighten, illuminate, kindle.*—II. פְּנֵי עֵינַי פ' ה' *cheer up, exhilarate*, lit. *enlighten the eyes*, or *face*; פָּנִין (const. with עַל, לְ, בְּ, אֶת, אֶל).—III. *instruct, inform* (illuminate the mind), Ps. 119:130.

אוֹר m. (f. Job 36:32).—I. *light, brightness, lightning, luminary*; אוֹר חַיִּים *the light of life*; א' פָּנִים *light of the face*, i. e. *cheerfulness, good will*; pl. אוֹרִים *stars*, i. e. *luminaries*, Ps. 136:7.—II. metaph. *prosperity.*—III. *knowledge.*

אוּר I. *fire, the light of fire.*—II. p. n. of a man.—III. (אוּרִים וְתֻמִּים) אֻרִים LXX. δήλωσις καὶ ἀλήθεια, "Urim and Thummim," Eng. Ver., a part of the high-priest's breast-plate; meaning uncertain.—IV. אֻרִים

(*lights*), p. n. of a country.—V. אוּר כַּשְׂדִּים p. n., *Ur of the Chaldeans*, a place in Mesopotamia.

אוֹרָה f. (pl. אוֹרוֹת).—I. *light*, Ps. 139: 12.—II. *prosperity, joy*, Est. 8:16.—III. טַל אוֹרוֹת *light reflecting dew*, Isa. 26:19; אוֹרוֹת *herbs*, 2 Kings 4:39.

אוֹרוּ imp. pl.; see ארר.

מָאוֹר m.—I. *light*; מְאֹרֹת *stars; luminaries.*—II. *candlestick*; מְנוֹרַת הַמָּאוֹר *the candlestick in the tabernacle*, lit. *place of light.*

מְאוּרָה f., *den, hole, of a serpent*, Isa. 11:8.

אֲוֵרוֹת *stables*; see ארה.

אוּרִי (*fiery*), p. n. of a man.

אוּרִיאֵל (*fire of God*), p. n. of a man.

אוּרִיָּה (the same), p. n.—I. the husband of Bathsheba.—II. a priest in the reign of Ahaz.

אוֹת *sign*; see אָוָה.

נָאוֹת or אוֹת, אוּת; Niph. (fut. pl. p. 1. נֵאוֹת, p. 3. יֵאוֹתוּ), *consenting to, agreeing.*

אוֹתִיּוֹת part. f. pl.; see אתה.

אָז adv., *then, at that time* (used with either tense); (מֵאָז, מִן אָז).—I. *from that time, of old, before.*—II. *whence*; מֵאָז אַפֶּךָ *whence thine anger* (was kindled); מֵאָז בָּאתִי *whence I came*; with infin. מ' דַּבְּרָךְ *whereof thou hast spoken.*

אָזַי *then*, Ps. 124:3,4,5.

אֲזָא or אֲזָה Ch., *he kindled.*

אָזַב, root not used; Arab. the same meaning.

אֵזוֹב m., *hyssop.*

אֶזְבַּי p. n. of a man.

אֲזַד Ch., *went forth, departed.*

אֵזוֹר belt; see אזר.

אֵזִין for אַאֲזִין Hiph. fut. 1. pers.; see אזן.

אַזְכָּרָה memorial; see זכר.

אָזַל he went away, departed; מֵאֻזָּל from אוּזָל Uzal (see the word), Ez. 27:19, taken by mistake for Pu. part. of this verb. See Rosenmüller on the passage.

אֲזַל Ch., the same.

אָזֵל m., departure, 1 Sa. 20:19, (some call it a p. n.).

אֲזַל Ch. imp. for אֲזֵל. Syr. for אֲזֵל; see אזל.

אָזַן, Pi. אִזֵּן attended to and investigated, Ecc. 12:9. Hiph. הֶאֱזִין heard, attended; const. with אֶל, לְ, עַד, עַל: of God, he hearkened, heard prayer; of man, he obeyed.

מֹאזְנַיִם dual, the balance, lit. having two dishes, bilanx.

מֹאזְנַיִן Ch., the same.

אֹזֶן f. (with suff. אָזְנִי; dual אָזְנַיִם), the ear; בְּאָזְנֵי פ' in the ears (that is, the hearing), of any one.

אַזְנוֹת־תָּבוֹר p. n. of a city in the tribe of Naphtali.

אָזְנִי (he who hearkens), p. n. of a man, Nu. 26:16.

אֲזַנְיָה (whom the Lord hears), p. n. of a man.

אֹזֶן שְׁאֵרָה p. n. of a place.

אֵזֵן m. (pl. אֲזֵנִים), "weapons," Deu. 23:14, Eng. Ver.; meaning uncertain.

אֲזִקִּים chains; see זקק.

אָזַר (imp. אֱזֹר; fut. יֶאְזֹר; with suff. יַאַזְרֵנִי), bound, girt, clothed himself; trop. אָזְרוּ חַיִל they clothed themselves with strength; const. with

בְּ. Niph. part. נֶאְזָר girded; const. with בְּ. Pi. sense as Kal. Hith. became bound, armed himself.

אֵזוֹר m.—I. a belt, girdle.—II. fetters.

אֶזְרוֹעַ arm, same as זְרוֹעַ; see זרע.

אֶזְרָחִי, אֶזְרָח native; see זרח.

אָח m., (const. אֲחִי; with suff. אָחִי, אֲחִיכֶם, אָחִיךָ, אָחִינוּ; pl. אַחִים, אֲחִי; with suff. אֲחִינוּ, אַחַי, אֶחָיו, אָחִיו (אֲחֵיכֶם).—I. a brother.—II. a relative.—III. a fellow countryman.—IV. a friend.—V. any person or thing like another.—VI. a term of affection; אִישׁ מֵעַל אָחִיו one from the other; אִישׁ אֶל אָחִיו one from the other.

אַח Ch., a brother.

אַחֲוָה f., fraternity.

אָחוֹת f. (with suff. אֲחוֹתִי; pl. אֲחָיוֹת, with suff. אֲחוֹתֵךְ, אַחְיוֹתַי).—I. sister.—II. used as אָח V., which see; אִשָּׁה אֶל אֲחוֹתָהּ one from the other (of persons or things fem.).

אָח interj., alas! exclamation of grief.

אָחַח not used; οἰμώζειν, to howl; whence is derived:—

אֹחִים m. pl., howlings, or howling animals (it is uncertain which), Isa. 13:21.

אָח f., a pot filled with hot coals to warm rooms in winter, Jer. 36:22, 23.

אַחְאָב (brother of the father), p.n., Ahab, king of Israel.

אֶחָב p. n. of the same king.

אַחְבָּן p. n. of a man.

אֶחָד const. אַחַד m., אַחַת with the pause, אֶחָת f.—I. one.—II. the first (used with days of the month); בְּאֶחָד לַחֹדֶשׁ *on the first day of the month;* שְׁנַת אַחַת *the first year.*— III. *alone, a single one;* לֹא אֵין, אֶחָד *not a single one, no one.*—IV. *a certain one* (τις); *it has the power of the ind. article a, an;* הָעָם אֶ' *one of the people, a person;* נְבִיא אֶ', προφήτης τις, *a certain prophet.*— V. *the same one, the same;* אַחַת, (פַּעַם) בְּאַחַת, *at the same time, together;* כְּאֶחָד as כְּאִישׁ אֶחָד *one man, together;* pl. אֲחָדִים *the same, united into one, a few.*

אָחַד Hith., *take hold of, unite thyself;* see יָחַד.

חַד Ch., *one, first, any one,* same as אֶחָד.

אָחוּ m., *the bulrush, reed,* an Egyptian word; Copt. *āχι.*

אֱחוּד (*union*), p. n. of a man.

אֲחֲוָה and אָחוֹת; see אָח.

אַחֲוָה; see חוה.

אֲחִיָּה, אֲחוֹת p.n. of a man; patr. אֲחֹחִי.

אַחֲוֶּךָ, with נ epenth. אֲחַוְּךָ, Pi. fut. 1. pers. with suff.; see חוה.

אֲחוּמַי p. n. of a man.

אָחוֹר *after;* see אחר.

אָחַז (inf. c. אֱחֹז; with pref. בֶּאֱחֹז; imper. אֱחֹז; fut. יֹאחֵז and יֶאֱחֹז).— I. *seized* (fear, terror); const. with בְּ.—II. *caught* (i.e. in hunting). —III. *took hold of, seized;* const. with בְּ of the part seized.—IV. *held, kept.*—V. *joined, united.*—VI. *locked up,* Neh. 7:3.—VII. *covered, overlaid, veneered,* 1 Ki. 6:10.— VIII. *drew by lot.* Niph.—I. *was*

caught, Ecc. 9:12.—II. *was held,* Gen. 22:13. Pi. מֵאָחֵז *shut up* (same as Kal VI.), Job 26:9. Hoph. מֵאָחֵז *joined, united* (same as Kal V.), 2 Chron. 9:18.

אָחָז p.n.—I. *Ahaz,* king of Judah.— II. of a man.

אֲחֻזָּה fut. apoc. in pause for אֶאֱחֹז, אַחַז; see חזה.

אֲחֻזָּה f., *possession, tenure.*

אֲחַזַּי p. n. of a man.

אֲחַזְיָה and אֲחַזְיָהוּ p.n.—I. of the son of Ahab king of Israel.—II. of the son of Joram king of Judah.

אֲחֻזָּם p. n. of a man.

אֲחֻזַּת p. n. of a man.

אֶחֱטֶנָּה Pi. fut. 1. pers. with suff. for אֲחַטְּאֶנָּה; see חטא.

אֲחִי p. n. of a man.

אֲחִירָה; see חוּד.

אֲחִיָּה (*friend of God*), p. n. of a man.

אֲחִיהוּד (*friend of the Jews*), p.n. of a m.

אֲחִיו p. n. of a man.

אֲחָיוֹת *sisters;* see אָחוֹת, in אָח.

אֲחִיחֻד and אֲחִיחֻר p. n. of a man.

אֲחִיטוּב (*loving good*), p. n. of a man.

אֲחִילוּד (*brother's son*), p. n. of a man.

אֲחִימוֹת (*brother of death*), p. n. of a m.

אֲחִימֶלֶךְ (*brother of a king*), p.n. of a m.

אֲחִימָן (*brother of gifts*), p. n. of a man.

אֲחִימַעַץ (*brother of anger*); p.n. of a m.

אֲחִין (*brotherly*) p. n. of a man.

אֲחִינָדָב (*brother of good will*), p. n. of a man.

אֲחִינֹעַם (*brother of delight*), p.n. of a w.

אֲחִיסָמָךְ (*brother of defence*), p.n. of a m.

אֲחִיעֶזֶר (*brother of help*), p. n. of a man.

אֲחִיקָם (*brother of enmity*), p.n. of a m.

אֲחִירָם (*exalted brother*), p. n. of a m.

אֲחִירַע (*evil brother*), p. n. of a man.

אֲחִישַׁחַר (*brother of the morning*), p. n. of a man.

אֲחִישָׁר (*brother of song*), p. n. of a man.

אֲחִיתֹפֶל (*foolish brother*), p.n. of a m.

אָחֵל Hiph. fut. 1. pers., אָחֵל with dag. forte imp.; see חלל.

אַחְלָב (*fecundity*), p. n. of a place in the tribe of Asher.

אַחְלַי (*would that!*) p.n.—I. of a man.— II. of a woman.

אַחֲלַי, אַחֲלִי *would that! I wish!* see חלה.

אַחְלָמָה *amethyst*; see חלם.

אֲחַסְבַּי p. n. of a man.

אַחְמְתָא p. n., *Ecbatana*, a city of Media, Ezr. 6:2.

אָחַר root not used; fut. 1. pers. pl. אֵחַר, Gen. 32:5. Pi. אִחַר (fut. יְאַחֵר), *delayed, waited, deferred* (Arab. the same); see יָחַר.

אָחוֹר m. (pl. אַחֹרִים).—I. *the but-end of a spear*, 2 Sa. 2:23.—II. *the west, westward.* Adv. *behind, after;* מֵאָחוֹר, לְאָחוֹר, בְּאָחוֹר *behind;* לְאָחוֹר *hereafter,* Isa. 41:23.

אַחֵר m., אַחֶרֶת f. (pl. אֲחֵרִים, אֲחֵרוֹת). —I. *another;* אֱלֹהִים א' *other gods, idols.*—II. p. n. of a man.

אַחַר *the hinder part.* Adv. of time and place, *behind, afterwards.* Prep. *behind, after;* הָלַךְ א' *follow;* א' הַדְּבָרִים הָאֵלֶּה *after these things, afterwards;* א' דִּבֶּר פ' *after he had spoken;* pl. const. אַחֲרֵי (with suff. אַחֲרַי, אַחֲרָיו, אַחֲרֶיךָ), *behind, after;* א' אֲשֶׁר כֵּן *after;* אַחֲרֵי כֵן *afterwards;* with prefixes מֵאַחַר, מֵאַחֲרֵי *after something past, after that;* מֵאַחֲרֶיךָ מֵא' כֵן *afterwards;* מֵאַחֲרֶיךָ *behind him;* עַל א' אַחֲרֵי *after;* אֶל א' *behind.*

אֶחֱרוּ Pi. pret. pl. for אֶחֱרוּ; see אחר.

אַחֲרוֹן m., אַחֲרוֹנָה f.—I. *the hinder part, the back part.*—II. *the latter day,* or *time.*—III. *the west;* הַיָּם הָא' *the Mediterranean sea.*—IV. *posterity;* דּוֹר א' *the generation to come;* אַחֲרֹנִים *successors;* לָאַחֲרוֹנָה, בָּאַחֲרוֹנָה *afterwards.*

אָחֳרִי Ch. adj. f., *another.*

עַד־אָחֳרֵין Ch., *at last, at length.*

אַחֲרִית f.—I. *the last, the latter time;* א' הַיָּמִים *the latter days.*—II. *the end;* א' הַשָּׁנָה *end of the year.*— III. *posterity.*

אָחֳרָן Ch. m., *another.*

אֲחֹרַנִּית adv., *backwards.*

אֲחַרַח (*after his brother?*) p.n. of a man.

אֲחַרְחֵל (*behind a wall?*) p. n. of a man.

אֲחַשְׁדַּרְפְּנִים m. pl., *chief satraps,* or *doorkeepers,* officers of the Persian court. אֲחַשְׁדַּרְפְּנַיָּא Ch., the same.

אֲחַשְׁוֵרוֹשׁ a title common to all the kings of Persia. It is spelt *Chosroes* by the later Greek and Latin historians.

אֲחַשְׁרשׁ the same.

אֲחַשְׁתָּרִי p.n. of a man; see next word.

אֲחַשְׁתְּרָנִים m. pl., *mules.*

אַחַת f., *one;* see אֶחָד.

אַחֵת Ch. Aph. imp.; see נחת.

אֵחָתֶה Niph. fut. 1. pers. with ה parag.; see חתת.

אַט Hiph. fut. apoc. 1. pers. for אַטֶּה; see נטה.

אָטָד m., *black thorn; rhamnus paliurus* (Linn.).

אָטָד p.n., a place beyond Jordan, where was a threshing-floor; afterwards Abel-mizraim, Gen. 50:10, 11.

אֵטוּן m., *linen* (of Egypt) ὀθόνιον, probably an Egyptian word, Pro. 7:16.

אָטַט not used; (Arab. *uttered a low sound*).

אַט m. (pl. אַטִּים).—I. *necromancers, enchanters.*—II. *gentle, soft.* Adv. לְאַט, לָאַט softly, *slowly*; לְאִטִּי *at my convenience.*

אָטַם *shut up, closed.* Hiph. the same; יַאֲטֵם אָזֶן *he closes* (his) *ear.*

אָטַר with עַל *shut*; fut. יֶאֱטָר, Ps. 69:16.

אִטֵּר *maimed*; אִ׳ יַד יְמִינוֹ lit. *having his right hand bound* (left-handed).

אִטֵּר (*he that halteth*), p. n. of a man.

אִי; see אָוָה and אָן.

אִי *where?* with suff. אַיֶּכָּה *where art thou?* אַיּוֹ *where is he?* אַיָּם *where are they?* also with pronouns and adverbs, אֵי זֶה *who? what? where?* אֵי מִזֶּה *whence?* אֵי לָזֹאת *wherefore? why?* with ה demonst. אַיֵּה *where?*

אֵיכָה *where? how?*

אֵיךְ (apoc.) *how?*

אֵיכֹה (Kri אֵיכוֹ) *where?* 2 K. 6:13.

אֵיכָכָה *how?*

אַיִן *always in comp.*; מֵאַיִן *whence?* (for another meaning see אָן).

אֵיפֹה *where? how?*

אָן (contract. from אַיִן), *where? whither?* מְאָן *whence?* עַד־אָן *until*; with the paragogic ה, אָנָה *whither? whereunto? where?* עַד־אָנָה *how long?* אָנָה וָאָנָה *hither and thither,* 1 K. 2:36, 42.

אָיַב *hated, was an enemy,* Ex. 23:22. אוֹיֵב m., *enemy*; אוֹיֶבֶת f., the same. אֵיבָה f., *enmity.*

אֵיד *calamity*; see אוּד.

אַיֵּה *where?* see אִי.

אַיָּה f.—I. name of a bird of prey; "vulture, kite," Eng. Ver.; LXX. ἰκτίν; Vulg. *vultur.*—II. p. n. of a man.

אִיּוֹב (*miserable*), p.n., *Job,* the patriarch.

אִיזֶבֶל p. n., *Jezebel,* the wife of Ahab.

אַיֶּכָּה, אֵיךְ; see אִי.

אִי־כָבוֹד (*where is the glory?* i.e. without glory); p. n. of a man.

אַיֶּכָּה *where art thou?* אֵי with suff. and נ epenth.

אַיָל, אֵיל, אֱיָל, &c.; see אוּל.

אַיָּלוֹן (*oak*), p. n.—I. of a city.—II. of a man.

אַיָּלוֹן (*place of hinds*), p. n. of a city.

אֵלְכָה for אֵלְכָה Kal fut. 1. pers. with ה parag.; see הלך, ילך.

אֵילִים (*grove of oaks*), p. n. of a place.

אֵילַת (*tree*), אֵילוֹת (*trees*), p.n., *Elath,* a city on the eastern gulf of the Red Sea, now Akabah.

אַיֶּלֶת *a gazelle*; see אוּל.

אָיַם root not used, *was terrible*; Ch. Pa. *frightened.*

אֵימָה, אֵים m., *terrible,* Hab. 1:7.

אֵימָה f. (pl. אֵימוֹת; with ה parag. אֵימָתָה) *terror*; pl. אֵמִים, אֵימִים.—I. *terrible things.*—II. *idols,* Jer. 50:38.—III. p.n. of one of the tribes of the Moabites.

אַיִן; see אָן and אִי.

אֵינֵימוֹ *they are not*; see אַיִן with suff.

אִיעֶזֶר (*helpless*), p.n. of a man.

אֵפָה, אֵיפָה f., *Ephah,* a corn measure, capacity unknown; אֵיפָה וְאֵיפָה *divers measures*; אֵ׳ שְׁלֵמָה *just measure.*

אֵיפֹה ; see אֵי.

אֵיפֹוא same as אֵפֹוא.

אִישׁ m. (pl. אֲנָשִׁים ,אַנְשֵׁי ; see אֱנושׁ; three times אִישִׁים).—I. *a man*, as distinguished from a woman.—II. *a husband*.—III. *a male*.—IV. used collectively for the inhabitants of a country; אִישׁ יִשְׂרָאֵל *the Israelites*.—V. used to denote the qualifications of men; אִי מִלְחָמָה *a warrior*; אִי אֱמֶת *a faithful man*; אִי שָׂדֶה *a husbandman*.—VI. any one; אִישׁ...אִישׁ *one...another*.—VII. *every man*; opposed to אָח, וַיֵּלְכוּ אִישׁ לִמְקֹמוֹ ;רֵעַ עָמִית *they went every one to his place*; כָּל־אִישׁ *every one*.—VIII. *every thing*, Ex. 25:20.—IX. impers., כֹּה אָמַר הָאִישׁ *thus it was said.*

אִישׁ, Hith. הִתְאֹשֵׁשׁ (ἀνδρίζεσθαι, 1 Cor. 16:13); pl. הִתְאֹשֵׁשׁוּ *become ye men*, i. e. be courageous, Isa. 46:8.

אִישׁוֹן m., lit. *little man*, i. e. the small image of one's self seen in the eye of another.—I. אִי בַּת עַיִן ,אִי עַיִן *pupil of the eye*; hence:—II. אִי חֹשֶׁךְ לַיְלָה lit. *pupil*, i. e. *middle, of the night, midnight.*

אִשָּׁה or אֵשֶׁת f. (with suff. אִשְׁתִּי, אִשְׁתְּךָ and אִשְׁתֵּךְ), I.—*woman*.—II. *wife*.—III. *concubine*.—IV. opposed to אָחוֹת and רְעוּת, like אִישׁ—V. *any one, every one*.—VI. applied to men by way of reproach.

אִישׁ־בֹּשֶׁת p. n. of a son of Saul.

אִישְׁהוֹד (*man of vigour*), p.n. of a man.

אִישַׁי (*manly*), p. n. of a man.

אִיתַי Ch., same as יֵשׁ *he is*; אִיתֶיךָ

thou art; אִיתוֹהִי *he is*; אִיתָנָא *we are*; אִיתֵיכוֹן *ye are.*

אִיתַי p.n. of a man.

אִיתִיאֵל (*God with me*), p. n. of a man.

אִיתָם for אַתֶּם Kal fut. 1. pers.; see תמם.

אִיתָמָר (*place of palm trees*), p. n. of one of the sons of Aaron.

אֵיתָן p. n. of a man; see יתן.

אַךְ adv., *only, alone, except*; אַךְ שָׂמֵחַ *only* (i. e. nothing else but) *rejoicing*, Deu. 16:15; אַךְ חֹשֶׁךְ *only* (nothing but) *darkness*, Ps. 139:11; אַךְ טָרֹף טֹרָף *he is only torn in pieces*, i. e. nothing else has happened to him, Gen. 44:28.

אַכַּד (*fortress*), p. n. of a city built by Nimrod, Gen. 10:10.

אַכּוֹת Kal fut. 1. pers.; see כתת.

אַכְזִיב p. n.—I. of a city in the tribe of Asher, Greek ἔκδιππα, now *Zib*. —II. of a city in the tribe of Judah.

אַכְזָר ,אַכְזְרִיּוּת; see כזר.

אָכִישׁ (*Ethiopian*), p. n. of a king of the Philistines.

אָכַל (inf. אָכוֹל ; const. אֲכָל; with pref. לֶאֱכֹל ; with suff. אָכְלְךָ, אָכְלוֹ ; imper. אֱכֹל; with ה parag. אָכְלָה ; fut. יֹאכַל and יֹאכֵל).—I. *ate*.—II. *devoured*, spoken of men or things; joined to the accusative with בְּ, אָכַל לֶחֶם ,מִן: *feasted*; בְּלֶחֶם and אָכַל לֶחֶם פּ׳, אִי לֶחֶם עַל שֻׁלְחַן פּ׳ *to be the guest, inmate, of any one*; אָכַל לִפְנֵי יְהֹוָה *ate that which was offered in sacrifice*; אָכַל בִּשַׂר פּ׳ *ate his flesh*, i. e. injured him, Ps. 27:2 ; Niph. נֶאֱכַל, part. f. נֶאֱכֶלֶת *is, may be*, eaten. Pu. אֻכַּל *devoured, consumed.* Hiph. הֶאֱכִיל (fut. יַאֲכִיל; inf. הַאֲכִיל) *gave, made, caused, to eat, devour.*

אֲכַל Ch., the same.

אֹכֶל m., *food;* with suff. אָכְלוֹ.

אָכְלָה f., *meat, food,* Gen. 1 : 29, 30

אֲכִילָה f., *meat, feast,* 1 K. 19 : 8.

מַאֲכָל m., *food,* that which may be eaten; עֵץ מ׳ *fruit tree;* צֹאן מַאֲכָל *cattle to be slaughtered for the table.*

מַאֲכֹלֶת, מַאֲכֶלֶת f., *food.*

מַאֲכֶלֶת f., *slaughtering knife,* lit. *devourer;* pl. מַאֲכָלוֹת.

אֻכָל (*eaten, consumed*), p. n. of a man.

אֲכַל, וָאֲכַל Pi. fut. apoc. 1. pers.; see כלה.

אֲכַלֶּךָ Ex. 33 : 3, Pi. fut. 1. pers. with suff. for אֲכַלְךָ; see כלה.

אָכֵן *truly;* see כון.

אַכֶּנּוּ Hiph. fut. 1. pers. with suff.; see נכה.

אָכַף *compel, bow down to,* Pro. 16 : 26.

אֶכֶף m. (with suff. אַכְפִּי), *palm of the hand,* Job 33 : 7.

אֶכַּף for אֶכָּף Niph. fut. 1. pers.; see כפף.

אָכַר *root not used;* (Arab. *digged*).

אִכָּר m., *ploughman, husbandman.*

אַכְשָׁף (*city of magicians*), p. n. of a city in the tribe of Asher.

אַל *not, &c.;* see אלל.

אֵל *God;* see אול.

אֶל, אֶל־ prep. (with suff. אֵלַי, אֵלֶיךָ, אֵלַיִךְ, אֵלָיו, אֵלֶיהָ, אֵלֵינוּ, אֲלֵיכֶם, אֲלֵיהֶן, אֲלֵיהֶם; poet. אֵלֵימוֹ; pl. poet. אֱלֵי).—I. *sign of the dative,* like ל.—II. *to, towards.*—III. *unto,*

at.—IV. *of, concerning.*—V. *in, into.* —VI. *among.*—VII. *by, through.*— VIII. *for, on account of;* the original meaning is *to, towards,* variously modified by the context; אֶל־פִּי יְהֹוָה *according to the command* (*mouth*) *of God;* אֶל־אַמָּה *a cubit,* i. e. according to the measure of a cubit, Gen. 6 : 16; וַיֹּאמֶר אֶל־ שָׂרָה *he said concerning* (*relative to*) *Sarah;* וַיֵּלֶךְ אֶל־נַפְשׁוֹ *he went, having regard to his life,* i. e. to save his life; אֶל־בְּאֵר הַמַּיִם *near* (i. e. *towards*) *the well;* יֵשֶׁב אֶל־ הַשֻּׁלְחָן *he sat at* (i. e. *to*) *the table.* —IX. used with other particles; אֶל־מֵחוּץ ל *behind me;* אֶל־אַחֲרֵי *without;* אֶל־תַּחַת *a pleonasm,* same as תַּחַת.

אֵל, with article הָאֵל אֵלֶּה pron., *these, those;* אֵלֶּה וְאֵלֶּה oi μὲν— oi δὲ, *these—those;* Ch., the same.

אֵלָא (*terebinth*), p. n. of a man; see אלה.

אֶלְגָּבִישׁ m., *hail;* see גבש.

אַלְגֻמִּים name of a tree; see אַלְמֻגִּים.

אֶלְדָּד (*beloved of God*), p. n. of a man.

אֶלְדָּעָה (*called of God*), p. n. of a man.

אָלָה I. *lay under a curse, imprecate.* —II. *howl,* see ילל. Hiph. *swore, execrated, laid under a curse;* fut. apoc. וַיֹּאֶל.

אָלָה f.—I. *oath, imprecation;* בֹּא בְאָלָה *come into the terms of the oath, agree by oath,* Neh. 10 : 30; הֵבִיא בְאָלָה *make one swear,* Eze. 17 : 13; נָשָׂא אָלָה בְּ *lay an oath upon any one.*—II. *curse, cursing;* הָיָה לְאָלָה *he was for a curse;* נָתַן לְאָלָה *he gave over unto cursing*

תַּאֲלָה f., *cursing.*

אֱלָהּ m. Ch., *God.*

אֱלוֹהַּ m., *God* (pl. אֱלֹהִים).—I. *God, the true God.*—II. *false gods,* idols; followed by the verb in the sing., very rarely in the pl.; אִישׁ א׳ *a man of God;* בְּנֵי א׳ *sons of God,* i. e. they that loved and served God; with pref. בֵּאלֹהִים, לֵאלֹהִים; const. אֱלֹהֵי.

אַלָּה *gazelle;* see אוּל.

אֵלָה *terebinth;* see אלל.

אֲלוּ Ch., *behold!* same as אֲרוּ.

אִלּוּ for אִם־לוּ, *otherwise, unless,* Ecc. 6:6, Est. 7:4.

אֱלוּל m.—I. *vanity;* same as אֱלִיל; see אלל.—II. *Elul,* the sixth month of the Hebrew year, answering nearly to our September, Neh. 6:15.

אַלּוֹן *oak;* see אוּל אֵלוֹן the same; in אלל

אַלּוּף *friend;* see אלף.

אֵלוּשׁ (*lion's den*), p. n., one of the encampments of the Israelites.

אֶלְזָבָד (Θεοδῶρος), p. n. of a man.

אָלַח, Niph. נֶאֱלַח *was corrupt, base.*

אֶלְחָנָן (*gift of God*), p. n. of a man.

אֱלִיאָב (*who has God for his father*), p.n. of a man.

אֱלִיאֵל (*strong in God*), p.n. of a man.

אֱלִיאָתָה or אֱלִיָּתָה (*to whom God comes*), p.n. of a man.

אֶלְדָּד (*beloved of God*), p.n. of a prince of the Benjamites.

אֶלְדָּע (*known of God*), p.n. of a man.

אַלְיָה f. (Arab. the same), *the fat tail of the sheep in the East.*

אֵלִיָּה, אֵלִיָּהוּ (*the Lord he* IS *God*), p.n., *Elijah* ('Ηλίας), the prophet.

אֵלִיָּהוּא, אֵלִיָּהוּ (the same), p.n. of one of Job's friends.

אֶלְיְהוֹעֵינַי, אֶלְיְהוֹעֵינַי (*mine eyes* ARE *unto the Lord*), p.n. of a man.

אֱלִיחְבָּא (*hidden of God*), p.n. of one of David's generals.

אֱלִיחֹרֶף (*God* IS *his avenger*), p. n. of a man.

אֱלִיל *vanity;* see אלל.

אֱלִימֶלֶךְ (*God* IS *king*), p.n. of a man.

אִלֵּן, אִלֵּין pron. pl. Ch., *these, those.*

אֶלְיָסָף (*increased of God*), p. n. of a prince of the Gadites.

אֱלִיעֶזֶר (*holpen of God*), p.n. of a man.

אֱלִיעֵינַי (*God is mine eye,* i. e. directs me), p. n. of a man.

אֶלְיָעָם (*people of God*), p. n. of a man.

אֱלִיפַז (*God is precious*), p.n.—I. of a son of Esau.—II. of one of Job's friends.

אֱלִיפָל (*my God* IS *strong*), p.n. of a man.

אֱלִיפְלֵהוּ (*whom God makes famous*), p.n. of a man.

אֱלִיפֶלֶט (*God* IS *his help*), p.n. of a m.

אֱלִיצוּר (*God* IS *his rock*), p.n. of a man.

אֶלְצָפָן or אֱלִיצָפָן (*whom God protects*), p.n. of a man.

אֱלִיקָא p.n. of a man.

אֶלְיָקִים (*whom God makes strong*), p. n.—I. of the house-steward of Hezekiah.—II. of a king of Judah, afterwards changed to יְהוֹיָקִים (*Jehovah makes strong*).

אֱלִישֶׁבַע (*vowed to God*), p.n., *Elishebah* ('Ελισάβετ), the wife of Aaron.

אֱלִישָׁה p.n. of a place on the shores of the Mediterranean.

אֱלִישׁוּעַ (*whose salvation is God*), p.n. of a son of David.

אֶלְיָשִׁיב (whom God pardons), p.n. of a man.

אֱלִישָׁמֵע (whom God hears), p.n. of a m.

אֱלִישָׁע (whose salvation is God), p.n., Elisha (Ἐλισσαῖος), the prophet.

אֱלִישָׁפָט (God is the judge), p.n. of a m.

אֱלִיָתָה p.n.; see אֱלִיאָתָה.

אֵלֶּךְ pron. m. pl. Ch.; same as Heb. אֵלֶּה those, Dan. 3:12, 13.

אֵלֵךְ with ה parag. אֵלְכָה, וָאֵלֵךְ Kal fut. 1. pers.; see הָלַךְ, יֵלֵךְ.

אָלַל root not used (Arab. passed away quickly).

אַל s., nothing, Job 24:25.; adv. not; with the fut. אַל־תִּירָאוּ fear not; אַל־נָא do not (I beseech you), Gen. 19:18.

אֱלִיל vain things, vanity; אֱלִילִים idols, lit. vain things.

אַלְלַי woe is me! see יָלַל.

אֵלָה f., terebinth, Jos. 24:26; see אוּל.

אַלּוֹן m.—I. oak.—II. p.n. of a man; see אוּל.

אָלַם not used in Kal either in Heb. or Arab. Niph. נֶאֱלַם was dumb, silent, lit. tongue-tied. Pi. bound, like sheaves of corn, Gen. 37:7.

אֵלֶם m., silence; אֵלֶם צֶדֶק is justice silent? Ps. 58:2; יוֹנַת אֵלֶם the dove of silence, title to Ps. 56.

אִלֵּם m., dumb person; pl. אִלְּמִים.

אֲלֻמָּה f. (pl. אֲלֻמִּים and אֲלֻמּוֹת), a sheaf of corn.

אַלְמֹן m., widowhood, Isa. 47:29.

אַלְמָן m., a widower, Jer. 51:5.

אַלְמָנָה f., a widow.

אַלְמְנוֹת for אַרְמְנוֹת palaces, Isa. 13:22.

אַלְמָנוּת f., widowhood; pl. אַלְמְנוּתִים.

אַלְמֹנִי m., some one, a certain one, lit. one not to be named; always joined with פְּלֹנִי, which see.

אֻלָם and אֻלָּם; see אוּל.

אַלְגֻּמִּים a resinous and odoriferous wood, not the produce of Canaan; perhaps the red sandal-wood, 1 Ki. 10:11, &c.; in 2 Chron. 2:7, it is transposed to אַלְגּוּמִּים.

אַלְמוֹדָד p.n. of one of the descendants of Shem, Gen. 10:26.

אַלַּמֶּלֶךְ (the king's oak), p.n. of a place in the tribe of Asher.

אַלְמָן, אַלְמֹן, אַלְמָנָה, אַלְמָנוּת, אַלְמֹנִי; see אָלַם.

אֶלְנַעַם (God is his delight), p.n. of a man.

אֶלְנָתָן (given of God), p.n. of a man.

אֶלָּסָר p.n. of a city.

אֶלְעָד (God is his help), p.n. of a man.

אֶלְעָדָה (whom God adorns), p.n. of a m.

אֶלְעוּזַי (God my strength), p.n. of a m.

אֶלְעָזָר (God is his helper), p.n. of a m.

אֶלְעָלָא, אֶלְעָלֵה p.n. of a town in the tribe of Reuben.

אֶלְעָשָׂה (made of God), p.n. of a man.

אָלַף learnt; fut. יֶאֱלַף. Pi. taught. Hiph. part. f. מַאֲלִיפוֹת (from אֶלֶף), producing a thousand, Ps. 144:13.

אֶלֶף m., a thousand; dual אַלְפַּיִם two thousand; pl. אֲלָפִים thousands; שְׁלֹשֶׁת אֲלָפִים three thousand; אַרְבָּעִים אֶלֶף forty thousand; מֵאָה אֶלֶף a hundred thousand; אֶלֶף אֲלָפִים a thousand thousands; אַלְפֵי רְבָבָה 10,000,000; אֶלֶף s.—I. a chiliad (a troop of 1000 soldiers); שַׂר הָאֶלֶף, χιλίαρχος, commander of a chiliad.—II. a nation,

tribe (i.e. *many persons*).—III. pl.
אֲלָפִים *oxen*; see below.—IV. p.n.
of a city in the tribe of Benjamin,
Jos. 18:28.

אֶלֶף, אֲלַף Ch., *a thousand*.

אַלּוּף adj., *familiar, tame*, Jer. 11:19.
s.—I. *a friend.*—II. *an ox (a tame animal).*—III. *head of a tribe or family*, φύλαρχος.

אֶלְפֶּלֶט (*God the deliverer*), p.n. of a m.
אֶלְפַּעַל (*God who performeth*), p.n. of a man.

אֶלְצָפָן p.n. of a man; see אֶלִיצָפָן.

אָלַץ (Syr. *he urged*). Pi. אִלֵּץ *pressed, urged on*, Jud. 16:16.

אַלְקוּם m., Prov. 30:31, מֶלֶךְ אַלְקוּם עִמּוֹ *a king who is irresistible;* "against whom there is no rising up," Eng.Ver.; meaning uncertain.

אֶלְקָנָה (*for whom God cared*), p. n. of a man.

אֶלְקֹשִׁי p.n. of a people.

אֶלְתּוֹלַד p.n. of a city; same as תּוֹלַד.

אֶלְתְּקֵה, אֶלְתְּקֵא p. n. of a city of the Levites in the tribe of Dan.

אֶלְתְּקֹן p.n. of a city in the tribe of Judah.

אֵם f. (with suff. אִמִּי; pl. אִמּוֹת).—I.
a mother.—II. *a grand-mother.*—III. *a step-mother.*—IV. *metropolis, chief city;* אֵם הַדֶּרֶךְ *mother*, i.e. *head of two ways*, Ez. 21:26.—V *nation, entire people*.

אַמָּה f.—I. *fore arm*, hence:—II. *a cubit*, measure of 21·888 inches; dual אַמָּתַיִם *two cubits;* עֶשֶׂר אַמּוֹת *ten cubits;* שְׁלֹשׁ מֵאוֹת אַמָּה *three hundred cubits.*—III. *a basis or pedestal*, Isa. 6:4.—IV. p.n. of a hill, 2 Sa. 2:24.

אַמָּה f. Ch., *cubit*.

אֻמָּה f. (pl. אֻמּוֹת, אֻמִּים), *families, tribes.*

אֻמָּה f. Ch., the same.

אִם cond. pa.—I. *surely, truly*, this is its radical meaning, hence:—II. *if;* אִם...אִם *whether...or;* עַד־אִם, עַד־אֲשֶׁר־אִם *whilst, until.*—III. *if? whether?* אִם...אִם, הֲ...אִם, הֲ...וְאִם *whether?...or?*—IV. used as an asseveration אִם has the power of denial, אִם־לֹא of affirmation; אֶעֱשֶׂה אִם *let me be accursed if I do it*, i.e. I will not do it.—V. in comp. הַאִם same as הֲלֹא *is not?* אִם־לֹא *unless.*

אֲמַאסְאָךְ Hos. 4:6; perhaps for אֶמְאָסְךָ i.e. אֶמְאָסְאָךְ Kal fut. 1. pers. with suff.; see מאס.

אָמָה f. (with suff. אֲמָתִי; pl. אֲמָהוֹת; const. אֲמָהוֹת), *maid-servant;* בֶּן אָמָה *servant*.

אֲמָהוֹת pl.; see אָמָה.

אֵמָה, אַמָּה; see אֵם.

אֲמֻנָה, אָמוֹן, אָמוֹן; see אמן.

אָמוֹץ (*strong*), p.n. of the father of Isaiah, Isa. 1:1.

אָמִי p.n. of a man.

אֵמִים p.n. of one of the giant races in Canaan.

אָמִיץ *strong;* see אמץ.

אָמִיר *top;* see אמר.

אָמַל root not used; *was sick.* Pul. אֻמְלַל *sick, wasting, declining.*

אֲמֵלָה f., *pained, sick*, Eze. 16:30.

אֻמְלַל m., *wasting with disease*, Ps. 6:3.

אֻמְלָל m. (pl. אֻמְלָלִים), *wasted, feeble men*, Neh. 3:34.

אֲמָם p. n. of a city.

אָמַן I. *was true, faithful*; part. אֱמוּנִים *the faithful*.—II. *nursed, brought up*; part. אֹמֵן *foster-father, nurse*. Niph. נֶאֱמַן.—I. *was sure.*—II. *was enduring, durable*; בַּיִת נֶאֱמָן *an enduring house*.—III. *was faithful*.—IV. *was carried* (as a child), Isa. 60:4. Hiph. הֶאֱמִין *confided, entrusted, believed, relied on*, followed by בְּ, לְ with inf.

אֲמַן Ch. Aph. הֵימִן *entrusted*.

אָמָן m., *artificer*, Cant. 7:2.

אֹמֶן m.—I. *a true thing, truth*; אֱלֹהֵי א' *the God of truth*.—II. formula of acquiescence, *Amen, so be it*.

אָמוֹן m.—I. *constant, unvarying*, Pro. 8:30.—II. same as הָמוֹן *the multitude*, Jer. 52:15.—III. p. n. of an Egyptian idol *Amoun* in נֹא אָמוֹן, which see.—IV. p. n. of a king of Judah.

אֵמוּן m.—I. *a faithful, true, sincere one*.—II. *educated, brought up*, Lam. 4:5.

אֹמֶן m., *faith*; adv. *truly*.

אֲמָנָה f., *beam, lintel*, 2 Kings 18:16.

אֱמוּנָה I. f. of אָמוּן; אֱמוּנָה וַיְהִי יָדָיו *his hands were made steady, true*.—II. *faithfulness*.—III. *truth*. Pl. אֱמוּנוֹת.

אֲמָנָה f.—I. *covenant, contract*, Neh. 11:23.—II. p. n. of a river near Damascus.—III. of a region.

אָמְנָה I. adv., *truly, indeed*.—II. f., *education, nursing*, Est. 2:20.

אָמְנָם, אֻמְנָם adv., *certainly, verily*; הַאֻמְנָם *indeed?* 1 Kings 8:27.

אֱמֶת f. (with suff. אֲמִתּוֹ).—I. *per-*

manency, durability.—II. *truth*, especially religious truth; used for truthfulness in God, and piety in man.

אֲמִינוֹן, אַמְנוֹן (*faithful*), p. n. of a son of David.

אָמֵץ (imp. אֱמַץ; fut. יֶאֱמַץ), *was powerful, courageous*; with מִן *prevailed, was mightier than*.—Pi. I. *strengthen*, Job 4:1.—II. *repair* (a house), 2 Chro. 24:13.—III. *fasten, secure*, Pro. 8:28.—IV. *encourage.*—V. א' לֵב פ' *harden the heart*. Hiph. *strengthen, confirm*. Hith. *acquired power, took courage*.

אַמִּיץ *strong, prevailing*.

אֹמֶץ m., *vigour*, Job 17:9.

אָמֹץ m., *powerful, vigorous* (of horses); pl. אֲמֻצִּים Zec. 6:3.

אַמְצָה f., *strength*, Zec. 12:5.

אֲמַצִי (*strong*), p. n. of a man.

אֲמַצְיָהוּ, אֲמַצְיָה (*strengthened of God*), p. n., *Amaziah* king of Judah.

מַאֲמַצִּים m. pl.; מַאֲמַצֵּי כֹחַ *confirmers of power*, Job 36:19.

אָמַר I. *he said* (to any one, with אֶל, לְ; of any one, with לְ and accus.); sometimes same as דִּבֶּר *he spoke*; inf. לֵאמֹר *saying*.—II. *commanded.*—III. *he thought*, lit. *he spake inwardly*, Gen. 44:28, Ex. 2:14, &c. &c. בִּלְבָבוֹ, בְּלִבּוֹ. Niph. *was said of or concerning any one* (with לְ); impers. יֵאָמֵר *it is said*; with לְ *it is said to some one*. Hiph. *made declared*, "avouched," Eng. Ver., Deu. 26:17, 18. Hith. *were declared, published, made famous*.

אֲמַר Ch., *he said, commanded*.

אֹמֶר m.—I. same as דָּבָר *a discourse*,

speech; אִמְרֵי אֵל the words of God.
—II. an appointment, declaration,
Job 20:29; with suff. אִמְרִי; pl.
אֲמָרִים.

אֹמֶר m., enunciation, expression, saying; same as דָּבָר a thing, a
matter.

אֵמֶר (tall), p. n. of a man.

אִמַּר Ch., a lamb, Ezr. 6:9,17, &c.

אִמְרָה f., word, declaration, discourse;
pl. אֲמָרוֹת.

אֶמְרָה f., the same.

אָמִיר m., the pod which contains
the fruit of the palm tree, Isa.
17:6.

מַאֲמָר m., edict, command, Ezr. 1:
15, &c.

מֵאמַר m. Ch., the same.

אִמְרִי (eloquent), p. n. of a man.

אֱמֹרִי the Amorite; LXX.'Αμορραῖος.

אֲמַרְיָה and אֲמַרְיָהוּ p. n. of a man.

אַמְרָפֶל p. n. of the king of Shinar,
Gen. 14:1, 9.

אֶמֶשׁ yesterday, lit. the day before
last night.

אֱמֶת truth; see אמן.

אַמְתַּחַת sack; see מתח.

אֲמִתַּי (truth-teller), p. n. of the father
of the prophet Jonah, Jon. 1:1.

אָן אָנָה אָנֶה; see אי.

אֹן Heliopolis; see און.

אָנָא אֲנָה Ch., pers. pron. I.

אָנָּא interj., gently, I pray, &c.

אִנְבֶּה Ch., for אִבֶּה; see אָב in אבב.

אֲנְדַּע; see ינדע.

אָנָה he suffered, Isa. 3:19. Pi. אִנָּה
he caused pain, Ex. 21:13. Pu.
was made to suffer, Pro. 12:21,
Ps. 91:10. Hith. part. מִתְאַנֶּה

affecting irritation, seeming to be
irritated, followed by לְ.

אֲנָחֲרָה p. n. of a city.

אֲנִיָּה f., suffering, pain, Isa. 29:2.

תַּאֲנִיָּה f., the same, Lam. 2:5.

אֳנִי com., a ship; collectively, a fleet.

אֳנִיָּה f., a ship.

תַּאֲנָה f., sexual impulse, Jer. 2:24.

תֹּאֲנָה f. opportunity, revenge, Jud. 14:4.

אֲנוּ com., we, Jer. 42:6; see אָנֹכִי.

אִנּוּן אִנִּין f. pron. pl. Ch., these,
those.

אֱנוֹשׁ p. n.; see אנשׁ.

אָנַח. Niph. נֶאֱנַח he sighed (the things
sighed for preceded by מִן עַל).

אֲנָחָה f., sighing, sobbing.

אֲנִי I; see אָנֹכִי.

אֳנִי; see אֲנִיָּה אָנֳיָה אֳנִי; see אנה.

אֲנִיעָם (mourning of the people), p.n. of
a man.

אֲנָךְ m.—I. lead.—II. a plummet, Am.
7:7, 8.

אָנֹכִי (contr. אֲנִי; with the pause אָנִי),
pers. pron. I; pl. אֲנַחְנוּ, sometimes
נַחְנוּ (אָנוּ Jer. 42:6), we.

אָנַן. Hith. הִתְאוֹנֵן he groaned, Nu.
11:1, Lam. 3:39.

אָנַס urge, force, Est. 1:8.

אֲנַס Ch., the same; trouble, Dan. 4:6.

אָנַף (fut. יֶאֱנַף), breathe through the
nose, snort; hence was irritated,
angry (with בְּ). Hith. הִתְאַנַּף
became angry.

אַף m. (with suff. אַפִּי).—I. nose; גְּבַהּ
אַף disdainful, haughty, lit. turned
up of nose, Ps. 10:4.—II. anger;
dual אַפַּיִם I. nostrils by synecd.—
II. face, countenance; לְאַפֵּי same

as לִפְנֵי *in the sight of, before;* מָנָה אַחַת אַפָּיִם *one of two persons,* i. e. a double portion, 1 Sa. 1:5.— III. *anger,* אֶרֶךְ אַ' *slow to anger;* קְצַר אַ' *quick to anger, hasty.*

אַף *also;* see in its place.

אֲנַף Ch., dual, *nostrils, face.*

אֲנָפָה f., name of an unclean bird, "heron," Eng. Ver.; LXX. χαρα- δριός; Lev. 11:19, Deu. 14:18.

אָנַק *cry out for pain;* inf. אֲנֹק; fut. יֶאֱנַק. Niph. נֶאֱנַק *lament.*

אֲנָקָה const. אַנְקַת f.—I. *crying out for pain.*—II. name of a reptile so called from its cry, Lev. 11:30.

אָנַשׁ root not used. (אֲנַס Ch., *compress, compel).* Part. אָנוּשׁ m., אֲנוּשָׁה f. *incurable* (of a wound), *grievous, mortal, unlucky* (of a day), *ma- lignant* (of a disposition); Niph. *he became mortally sick,* 2 Sa. 12:15.

אֱנוֹשׁ m.—I. *man* (as mortal and miserable). — II. *mankind.* — III. *plebeian, low person;* pl. אֲנָשִׁים (const. אַנְשֵׁי; with suff. אֲנָשֶׁיךָ, אַנְשֵׁיהֶם), *man, men;* see אִישׁ.— IV. אֱנוֹשׁ p. n. of a son of Seth.

אֱנָשׁ, אֲנָשׁ Ch., *man.*

אַנְתָּה Ch., pers. pron. m., *thou.*

אָסָא (*healing*), p. n. of a king of Judah.

אָסוּךְ *cup;* see סוּךְ.

אָסִיר, אָסֻר, אָסוּר *bound;* see אסר.

אָסִיף *harvest;* see אסף.

אָסָם m., pl. אֲסָמִים *store-houses, granaries;* LXX. ταμεῖα.

אָסַן root not used; (Arab. *death, des- truction).*

אָסוֹן m., *injury, death by accident.*

אָסְנָה p. n. of a man.

אָסְנַפַּר p. n. of an Assyrian general.

אָסְנַת (*belonging to Neith*), p. n. of the wife of Joseph.

אַסְעָרֵם Syr. for אֲסָעֲרֵם Pi. fut. 1. pers. with suff.; see סער.

אָסַף (inf. אָסֹף; const. אֱסֹף; with suff. אָסְפְּךָ; fut. יֶאֱסֹף, with suff. יַאַסְפֵנִי; 1. pers. אֶאֱסֹף and אֹסֵף).— I. *collected, gathered* (with אֶל and עַל before the place in which). —II. *take away, take off, destroy;* נַפְשׁוֹ אַ' *he deprived himself of life.* Niph. נֶאֱסַף I. *was gathered, received.*—II. *was taken away, ceased.* — III. *perished,* Hos. 4:3, (with אֶל, לְ, עַל; נ' אֶל־עַמּוֹ; עַמָּיו, אֲבוֹתָיו, *was gathered to his people, fathers,* i. e. was buried; used in this sense alone נֶאֱסַף Nu. 20:26.—Pi. I. *gather, receive.*— II. *close the rear of a march,* Nu. 10:25, Jos. 6:9, 13. Pu. *was gathered.* Hith. הִתְאַסֵּף *gather themselves together,* Deu. 33:5.

אָסָף (*collector*), p. n. of a man.

אֹסֶף m., *ingathering, harvest of fruits.*

אָסִיף m., *harvest of apples.*

אֲסֵפָה f., *collection, gathering,* Isa. 24:22.

אֲסָפִים m. pl., *collection of stores or money, storehouses.*

אֲסֻפּוֹת f. pl., the same.

אֹסְפְּךָ Kal fut. 1. pers. with suff. 1 Sa. 15:6; Kal part. with suff. 2 Ki. 22:20; see אסף.

הָאסַפְסֻף אֲסַפְסֻף m., with the article *mixed multitude,* Nu. 11:4.

אָסְפַּרְנָא Ch. adv., *exactly, carefully, quickly.*

אַסְפָּתָא p. n. of a son of Haman.

אָסַר (fut. יַאְסֹר and יֶאְסֹר).—I. he tied, bound, followed by לְ ; אֱ הַמֶּרְכָּבָה yoking the horses to the chariot.— II. אֱ מִלְחָמָה he kept together the battle, i. e. made his troops attack closely and continuously. — III. אָסַר אִסָּר עַל־נַפְשׁוֹ he bound himself by an oath; part. אָסוּר captive, prisoner. Niph. becoming bound. Pu. taken, reduced to bondage.

אָסוּר m., chain; pl. אֲסוּרִים ; בֵּית הָאֵסוּר prison.

אֱסוּר Ch., the same.

אָסִיר m., a captive.

אַסִּיר m.—I. captive.—II. p.n. of a man.

אֱסָר m., an obligation.

אֱסָר m. Ch., the same.

אִסָּר m., the same.

מוֹסֵר m.; see in its place.

אֵסַר־חַדֹּון p. n., Esar-haddon king of Assyria, the successor of Sennacherib; LXX. Ἀσορδὰν.

אֶפְרֵם Kalfut.1.pers.with suff.; see יסר.

אֶסְתֵּר (star), p. n., Esther queen of Persia; her name before was הֲדַסָּה Est. 2:7.

אָע m. Ch., same as Heb. עֵץ wood.

אַף nose; see אָנַף.

אַף part., also, moreover, nay, indeed; אַף כִּי אָמַר indeed, truly; אַף כִּי hath (God) indeed said, Gen. 3:1.

אַף Ch., the same.

אֲפָאֵיהֶם Hiph. fut. 1. pers. with suff.; see פאה.

אָפַד he put on the Ephod, Ex. 29:5, Lev. 8:7 (with לְ of the person, and בְּ of the thing).

אֵפוֹד m.—I. Ephod, a garment worn

bythe priesthood; נָשָׂא אֵ he wore the ephod, i. e. he fulfilled the priest's office.—II. perhaps the name of an idol, Jud. 8:27, &c.

אֲפֻדָּה f., made like an ephod; probably the dress of an idol.

אֵפֹד p. n. of a man.

אַפֶּדֶן camp; see פדן.

אָפָה baking. Niph. baked.

אֹפֶה m., a baker; pl. אֹפִים.

אֹפָה f., the same; pl. אֹפוֹת.

מַאֲפֶה m., bakemeat.

אֵפוּ Syr. for אֵפוֹ imp. pl. of the verb אפה.

אֵפוֹ, אֵפוֹא pa., οὖν, δή, now, then; אִם כֵּן אֵ if then it be so; אַיֵּה אֵ where then? מָה אֵ what then? דְּעוּ אֵ γινώσκετε οὖν l know then!

אֵפוֹד ephod; see אפד.

אֲפִיחַ p. n. of a man.

אַפַּיִם p. n. of a man.

אָפִיק swelling; see אפק.

אָפַל root not used (Arab. set as the sun).

אָפִיל m., אֲפִילָה f.—I. concealed.— II. very dark.

אֹפֶל m., obscure.

אֹפֶל m., thick darkness; more intense than חֹשֶׁךְ.

אֲפֵלָה f., darkness; חֹשֶׁךְ אֵ thick darkness.

מַאֲפֵל m., darkness.

מַאְפֵלְיָה f., extreme darkness, Jer. 2:31.

אֶפְלָל (judgment), p. n. of a man.

אָפַן root not used; same as פָּנָה turn, roll.

אוֹפָן m., wheel; const. אֹפַן ; pl. אֹפַנִּים.

אֹפֶן *season* (περίοδος); דָּבָר עַל־אָפְנָיו *a word in season*, Pro. 25:11.

אֶפֶס m.—I. *termination, extremity;* אַפְסֵי אֶרֶץ *ends of the earth;* dual אֲפָסִים *two extremities*, i.e. of both feet; *the soles* or *ankles*, Eze. 47:3. —II. *deficiency, wanting;* בְּאֶפֶס *without*, lit. *in there not being*, followed by the genitive of the thing; עַד אֵ֫ין *until there is none;* אַפְסִי *besides me;* מֵאֶפֶס *without;* בְּאֶפֶס *of, from nothing;* אֶפֶס כִּי *except, unless.*

אֶפֶס דַּמִּים p.n. of a town in the tribe of Judah, 1 Sa. 17:1; see פַּס דַּמִּים

אֶפַע m., *an adder*, Isa. 41:24; see פָּעָה

אֶפְעֶה *adder;* see פָּעָה

אָפַף *enclose, hem in;* pret. pl. אֲפָפוּ; with suff. אֲפָפוּנִי

אָפַק Kal, root not used; (Arab. *visited many countries*). Hith. הִתְאַפֵּק I. *went on, proceeded.*—II. *restrained himself from proceeding*, Gen. 45:1, &c.; LXX. ἀνέχομαι, ἐγκρατεύομαι.

אָפִיק m. adj.—I. *mighty, eminent man*, Job 12:21.—II. *river, torrent.*—III. *the bosses of a shield*, Job 41:7.—IV. *swellings of the sea.*— V. p.n. of a city in the tribe of Asher, Jud. 1:31, same as:—

אָפֵק p.n.—I. of a city in the tribe of Asher.—II. of a city in the tribe of Issachar.

אֲפֵקָה p. n. of a town in the mountains of Judah, Jos. 15:53.

אָפַר root not used; (Arab. *casting away*).

אֵפֶר m.—I. *ashes.*—II. *any thing worthless.*

אוֹפִיר p. n. of a kingdom; see in its place.

אֲפֵר m. (transpos. of פְּאֵר), *a tiara, crown*, 1 Ki. 20:38, 41.

אֶפְרֹחַ *chicken;* see פרח

אַפִּרְיוֹן m., LXX. φορεῖον, *car, sedan*, Cant. 3:9, 10.

אֶפְרַיִם p.n.—I. *Ephraim*, the younger son of Joseph.—II. the tribe that descended from him.—III. afterwards, the kingdom formed by the ten tribes that revolted from the house of David.

אֶפְרָתָה, אֶפְרָת p.n.—I. of a city in the tribe of Judah: called also אֶפְרַיִם,—II. same as בֵּית־לֶחֶם Ps. 132:6.

אֶפְרָתִי I. *an Ephraimite.*—II. an inhabitant of Ephratah.

אֲפָרְסָיֵא p.n. of an unknown people, Ezr. 4:9.

אֲפַרְסְכָיֵא p.n., as above, Ezr. 5:6.

אֲפַרְסַתְכָיֵא p. n. of the inhabitants of a city in Assyria, Ezr. 4:9.

וָאֶפָּת, אֶפָּת Niph. fut. apoc. 1. pers. for אֶפָּתֶה; see פתה

אַפְתֹם pa., *thus then, then moreover.* Ezr. 4:13.

אֶצְבּוֹן p. n. of a man.

אֶצְבַּע *finger;* see צבע

אַצִּיעָה Hiph. fut. 1. pers. with ה parag.; see יצע

אֵצֶל I. *holding back, withholding*, with מִן.—II. *laying up with one's self*, with לְ. Niph. *contracted*, Eze. 42:6. Hiph. *withhold;* fut. וַיָּאצֶל, Nu. 11:25.

אָצִיל m. (Arab. *rooted, firm*).—I. *nobleman*, Eze. 24:11.—II. *end, extremity*, Isa. 41:9.

אַצִּיל m. *joint, suture*; אַצִּילֵי יָדָיִם *the wrists*.

אָצֵל p. n.—I. of a man.—II. of a place near Jerusalem, Zec. 14:5.

אֵצֶל prep., *near*; מֵאֵצֶל *near*; מֵאֶצְלוֹ *near him*.

אֲצַלְיָה p. n. of a man.

אֹצֶם p. n. of a man.

אֶצְעָדָה *bracelet*; see צעד.

אָצַק Kal fut. 1. pers. of the verb; see יצק.

אָצַר *treasured*. Niph. *laid up*, Isa. 23:1,18. Hiph. הוֹצֵר *appoint as treasurer*, Neh. 13:13, with עַל; fut. with ה parag. אוֹצְרָה.

אוֹצָר m. (pl. אוֹצָרוֹת).—I. *treasury*.—II. *treasure*; בֵּית הָא׳ I. *treasure-house*.—II. *warehouse*.

אֶצֶר p. n. of a man.

אֶצְרְךָ Kri, Jer. 1:5, Kal fut. 1. pers. with suff.; see יצר.

אֶקְדָּח *carbuncle*; see קדח.

אַקּוֹ m., *gazelle*, Deu. 14:5.

אֶקַּח Kal·fut. 1. pers. of the verb לקח.

אֶקְחָה for אֶקְחָה Isa. 56:12, Kal fut. 1. pers. with ה parag., from לקח.

אֶקְרָאָה Kal fut. 1. pers. with ה parag., from קרא.

אֹר *light*; see יאור.

אֲרָא p. n. of a man.

אֵרֶא וָאֵרָא Niph. fut. apoc., from ראה.

אֲרִאֵל אֲרִאֵלִי *name of Jerusalem*; see ארה.

אָרַב *lying in wait, ambush*; with לְ, עַל; fut. יֶאֱרֹב, part. אוֹרֵב *ambus-*

cader. Pi. part. pl. מְאָרְבִים *lying in wait*. Hiph. *he places an ambush*, 1 Sa. 15:5.

אֲרָב p. n. of a town in the tribe of Judah.

אַרְבִּי a native of Arabia.

אֶרֶב m., *lying in wait, place of ambush*, Job 37:8, 38:40.

אֹרֶב m., the same; with suff. אָרְבּוֹ.

אָרְבָּה f., the same; pl. אֲרָבוֹת; const. אָרְבוֹת.

אַרְבֶּה m., a species of *locust*, from רָבָה *was many*.

אֲרֻבָּה f.—I. *net* or *wicker work* to cover windows: hence,—II. *window*.—III. *pigeon-holes*, Isa. 60:8. IV. applied to the visible heavens, Gen. 7:11, 8:2.—V. a *chimney*, Hos. 13:3.

אֲרֻבּוֹת (*plots*), p. n. of a place in the tribe of Judah.

מַאֲרָב m., *ambush, ambuscade*.

אַרְבֵּאל p. n. of a place, Hos. 10:14; see בֵּית.

אַרְבַּע p. n. of a giant.

אַרְבַּע *four*; see רבע.

אָרַג I. *plaiting the hair*, Jud. 16:13.—II. *weaving*, Isa. 59:5; part. אֹרֵג *a weaver*, f. אֹרְגָה.

אֶרֶג m.—I. *texture, web*, Job 7:6.—II. *weaver's comb*, Jud. 16:14.

אַרְגֹּב p. n.—I. of the district of Og.—II. of a man.

אַרְגְּוָן Ch., *purple*, same as אַרְגָּמָן.

אַרְגָּז *bag*; see רגז.

אַרְגָּמָן m., *purple*.

אַרְדְּ p. n. *Ard*, a son of Benjamin; אַרְדִּי patronymic of Ard.

אַרְדּוֹן p. n. of a man.

אָרָה I. *pluck fruit*, Ps. 80:13.—II. *gather*.

אָרֵה Nu. 22:6, imp. with ה parag.; see ארר.

אֻוְרוֹת f. pl., *stables, stalls for beasts*, 2 Chron. 32:28.

אֲרָווֹת f. pl., const. אַרְווֹת.
אֲרָיוֹת f. pl., const. אַרְיוֹת.—I. *stalls*.—II. *stable*.

אֲרִי m., *a lion*; pl. אֲרָיִים and אֲרָיוֹת.
אַרְיֵה m., *a lion*.

אַרְיֵה m. Ch., *a lion*; pl. אַרְיָוָן.

אֲרֶיוּךְ Isa. 16:9, transpos. for אֲרַיְוֵךְ or אַרְיָוֵךְ (same as רָיְוָה). Pi. fut. 1. pers. with suff.; see רוה.

אֲרִיאֵל, אֲרִאֵל (*lion of God*).—I. a name of the altar of burnt-offering.—II. a name for Jerusalem.—III. p. n. of a man.

אֲרְאֵל (the same), p. n. of a man.

אַרְאֵלִי (the same), p. n. of a man.

אֶרְאֶלָם m., "their valiant ones," Isa. 33:7, Eng. Ver.; probably for אֵרָאֶה לָהֶם *I will appear unto them* (Lee).

אָרוֹן com.—I. *ark, chest*; אֲרוֹן הַבְּרִית, אֱלֹהִים, הָעֵדוּת, *the ark of the covenant*.—II. *coffin, mummy-case*, Gen. 50:26.

אֲרוּ Ch., *behold! see!*

אַרְוָד p. n., *Aradus*, a city and district on the coast of Phœnicia.

אֲרוֹדִי, אֲרוֹד p. n. of a man.

אֲרוּכָה *repairing*; see ארך.

אֲרוּמָה p. n. of a city.

אֲרוֹמִים *Syrians*; see ארם, אֲרַמִּי.

אֲרוֹמַם for אֶתְרוֹמָם Hith. fut. 1. pers.; see רום.

אָרַז *was firm, closely packed*; part אֲרֻזִים.

אֶרֶז m., *cedar*; pl. אֲרָזִים, const. אַרְזֵי.

אַרְזָה f., *cedar wainscot*, Zep. 2:14.

אָרַח *he goeth to herd with*, Job 34:8; part. אֹרֵחַ *traveller*.

אֶרַח (*wanderer*), p. n. of a man.

אֹרַח com. (with suff. אָרְחִי; pl. אֳרָחוֹת; const. אָרְחוֹת; with suff. אָרְחֹתָם and אָרְחֹתָ/י (אָר).—I. *way, road, path*.—II. *mode or manner*; א יְהוָֹה *way of the Lord*, i. e. the way that pleases the Lord; א חַיִּים *the way of life*, i. e. that leads to life; א עוֹלָם *the old path*, i. e. the manners of ancient times.—III. *wayfaring man*.

אֹרַח m. Ch., the same; pl. אָרְחָן.

אֹרְחָה f.—I. *step, progress*.—II. *travelling company, caravan*.

אֲרֻחָה f.—I. *fixed portion, ration*.—II. *portion generally*.

אֲרִיאֵל, אֲרָיוֹת, אַרְיֵה, אֲרִי; p. n.; see ארה.

אֲרִידַי p. n. of a son of Haman, Ἀριδαῖος.

אֲרִידָתָא (*strong*), p. n. of a man.

אַרְיוֹךְ p. n.—I. of a king of Ellasar, Gen. 14:1.—II. of a Chaldean.

אֲרִיסַי p. n. of a son of Haman.

אָרַךְ (fut. יַאֲרַךְ; pl. יַאַרְכוּ), *was long, became or was made long*; אָרְכוּ־ לוֹ הַיָּמִים *he had tarried there many days*, Gen. 26:8. Hiph. הֶאֱרִיךְ trans. *make long, prolong*; ה' יְמֵי פ' *lengthen his days, prolong life*; ה' אַפּוֹ, נַפְשׁוֹ *was long-suffering, patient*.

אֲרֻכָּה, אֲרֵכָה f.—I. *lengthening out*.

—II. *repairing, restoring, healing;* (Arab. the same).

אֲרַךְ Ch. (part. אֲרִיךְ), *becoming, suitable.*

אָרֵךְ (const. אֶרֶךְ), *long;* אֶבְרָ אִ with *long pinions,* Ecc. 7:8; אַפַּיִם אִ *slow to anger;* רוּחַ אִ μακρόθυμος, *long-suffering.*

אֶרֶךְ p. n. of a city of Shinar, Gen. 10:10; hence אַרְכְּוָיֵא an inhabitant of Erech; אַרְכִּי the same.

אֹרֶךְ m., *length* (of time and space); with suff. אָרְכּוֹ.

אָרֹךְ m., אֲרֻכָּה f., *long, lasting long.*

אַרְכָא ,אַרְכָה f. Ch., *time, duration.*

אַרְכֻּבָּה *the knee,* Dan. 5:6; see בְּרַךְ.

אֲרָם f.(const. אֲרַם), p.n., *Aramea;* the region of Damascus and Syria to the Orontes and Mesopotamia; אִ פַּדַּן אֲרָם נַהֲרַיִם *Mesopotamia;* אִ צוֹבָה *Padan Aram;* אִ צוֹבָה part of *Syria;* אִ דַּמֶּשֶׂק *Syria of Damascus;* אִ מַעֲכָה the region beyond Jordan at the foot of Anti-Libanus; אִ בֵּית־רְחוֹב part of *Syria;* see רְחֹב.

אֲרַמִּי m., *Syrian* (f. אֲרַמִּיָּה; pl. אֲרַמִּים and אֲרוֹמִים).

אֲרָמִית adv., *in Syriac, in the language of Syria.*

אַרְמוֹן m. (pl. const. אַרְמְנוֹת), *palace.*

אַרְמֹנִי p.n. of one of the sons of Saul.

אֹרֶן m., *the mountain ash,* Isa. 44:14; LXX. πίτυς; Vulg. *pinus.*

אֹרֶן p. n. of a man.

אֹרֶן p. n. of a man.

אַרְנֶבֶת f., *the hare,* Lev. 11:6, Deu. 14:17; (Arab. the same).

אַרְנוֹן (*sounding,* see רָנַן), p. n., *Arnon,*

a river which bounded the land of Israel to the east.

אַרְנָן p. n. of a man.

אֲרַנְיָה (אַרְנָן 2 Sa. 24:15). p. n., *Araunah,* the Jebusite.

אֲרַע ,אַרְעָא m. Ch.—I. *the earth.* —II. an epithet: *low, inferior,* followed by מִן.

אַרְעִית f. Ch., *low, mean.*

אַרְפָּד p. n. of a city of Syria.

אַרְפַּכְשַׁד p.n. of a son of Shem.

אֶרֶץ f., sometimes m. (with art. הָאָרֶץ; with suff. אַרְצוֹ; pl. אֲרָצוֹת).—I. *earth.*—II. *the world.*—III. *the ground;* אַרְצָה *on the ground.*— IV. *region, province.* Pl. אֲרָצוֹת I. *lands, countries.*—II. *heathen nations.*

אַרְעָא p. n. of a man.

אֲרַק f. Ch., *the earth,* Jer. 10:11.

אָרַר (imp. אֹר; with ה parag. אָרָה; pl. אוֹרוּ; fut. יָאֹר), *denounce, curse.* Niph. part. pl. נְאָרִים *denounced, cursed.* Pi. אֵרַר *denounce, bring on a curse;* part.pl. מְאָרְרִים. Hoph. fut. יוּאָר *is made accursed.*

מְאֵרָה f., *cursing.*

אֲרָרָט p. n., *Ararat,* a mountain in Armenia.

אֲרָרִי same as הֲרָרִי *Ararite.*

אָרַשׂ. Pi. אֵרַשׂ ,אֵרֵשׂ (with accusative אִשָּׁה) *espouse a wife* by entering into a contract under a fine; with בְּ of the sum mulcted. Pu. pret. f. אֹרָשָׂה *espoused;* part. f. מְאֹרָשָׂה.

אָרַשׁ root not used; (Arab. *he desired*).

אֲרֶשֶׁת f., *petition;* LXX. δέησις, Ps. 21:3.

אַרְתַּחְשַׁשְׁתָּא ,אֲרְתַּחְשַׁשְׁתָּא } Arta-
אַרְתַּחְשַׁשְׁתְּא } xerxes,
king of Persia.

אֶשְׂרָאֵל (same as אֶסְרָאֵל), p.n. of a m.
אַשְׂרִיאֵל p.n. of a man; ־ִי patronymic
of above.

אֵשׁ f., sometimes m. (with suff. אִשּׁוֹ,
אִשְּׁכֶם, אִשָּׁם).—I. fire.—II. lightning; אֵשׁ אֱלֹהִים lightning.—III.
heat of the sun, Joel 1:19, 20.—
IV. appearance of God.—V. God's
fierce anger.—VI. ardour of mind.
—VII. great tribulations.

אֶשָּׁא com. Ch., emph. state אֶשָּׁא fire.

אִשֶּׁה m.(const. אִשֵּׁה; pl. אִשִּׁי, אִשִּׁים).
—I. burnt-offering. — II. incense-
offering.

אֶשֶּׁה f.(אֶשְׁתָּם Jer. 6:29), for אֵשׁ תָּם
(by) fire is consumed.

אַשְׁבֵּל p. n. of a son of Benjamin; ־ִי
patronymic of the same.

אֶשְׁבָּן p.n. of a man.

אֶשְׁבֵּעַ p. n. of a son of Saul.

אֶשְׁבַּעַל p. n. of a son of Saul.

אָשַׁד root not used; (Arab. he rushed).

אֶשֶׁד m., bed of a river or brook; אֶ
הַנְּחָלִים bed of the torrents, Nu.
21:15.

אַשֵּׁדָה foot, base of a mountain; pl.
אַשְׁדוֹת; const. אַשְׁדוֹת.

אַשְׁדּוֹד (from שָׁדַד), p.n. Ashdod ("Αζω-
τος), a city of the Philistines;
אַשְׁדּוֹדִי an Ashdodite; ־ִית I. a
woman of Ashdod.—II. in the language of Ashdod.

אִשָּׁה woman; see אנשׁ.

אֲשִׁיָּה f., foundation, Jer. 50:15; from
שׁוּת.

אֲשׁוּר ,אַשּׁוּר ,אַשּׁוּרִי footstep; see אשׁר.

אַשְׁחוּר p. n. of a man.

אֲשִׁימָא p.n. of a god of the Hamathites.

אֲשֵׁרָה erection; see אֲשֵׁרָה.

אָשִׁישׁ foundation, Isa. 16:7, see אשׁשׁ,
perhaps for אִישֵׁי men, as Jer.
48:31.

אֲשִׁישָׁה ,אִשְׁין food; see אשׁשׁ.

אֶשֶׁךְ m., testicles, Lev. 21:20.

אֶשְׁכֹּל Eshcol; from שׁכל.

אֶשְׁכִּים Ch. Hiph. inf. abs.; from שׁכם.

אַשְׁכְּנַז p. n. of a people of North Asia.

אֶשְׁכָּר a rich gift, Eze. 27:15, Ps. 72:
14; from שׁכר.

אֵשֶׁל m., the tamarisk, a middle-sized
thorny tree; tamarix orientalis
(Linn.).

אָשַׁם and אָשֵׁם (fut. יֶאְשַׁם).—I. was
guilty, sinned (when against any
one, with לְ; when in any thing,
with בְּ and לְ).—II. was conscious
of guilt.—III. suffered for sin, Ps.
34:22, &c. Niph. suffered the consequences of sin, Joel 1:18; Hiph.
bring on the consequences of guilt,
Ps. 5:11.

אָשֵׁם m., guilty.

אָשָׁם m.—I. guilt, i.e. the consequence of sin.—II. a sacrifice to
expiate it.

אַשְׁמָה f.—I. (inf. of אָשַׁם, אֲשֹׁם),
בָהּ to trespass therein, Lev. 5:26;
לְאַשְׁמַת הָעָם so that the people
trespass.—II. guilt, trespass.—III.
a trespass-offering, Lev. 6:5.

אַשְׁמַנִּים m., "desolate places," Eng.
Ver., Isa. 59:10; meaning uncertain.

אַשְׁמֻרָה f., the three watches into which
the night was divided; root שׁמר.

אֶשְׁנָב m., *a latticed window*, Jud. 5: 28, Pro. 7:6.

אַשְׁנָה p. n. of two cities in the tribe of Judah.

אֶשְׁעָן (*a prop*), p. n. of a city in the tribe of Judah.

אַשָּׁף m. Heb. and Ch. (pl. אַשָּׁפִים), *an enchanter.*

אַשְׁפָּה f., *quiver;* בְּנֵי א' *sons of the quiver, arrows*, Lam. 3:13.

אַשְׁפּוֹת f. pl., *dung, dung heap.*

אַשְׁפַּתּוֹת f. pl., *the same.*

אַשְׁפְּנַז p. n. of one of the eunuchs of Nebuchadnezzar.

אֶשְׁפָּר *measure, cup,* 2 Sa. 6:10, 1 Chron. 6:3.

אַשְׁקְלוֹן p. n. of a city of the Philistines.

אָשַׁר *went straight on, walked along.* —Pi. I. *guide, lead aright.*—II. *consider, pronounce good, happy;* Pu. אוּשַּׁר, אָשַׁר—I. *was guided.*—II. *was esteemed happy.*

אָשֵׁר p. n. of one of the sons of Jacob; אָשֵׁרִי I. *an Asherite.*—II. p. n. of a city near Sichem, Jos. 17:7.

אֶשֶׁר m., *happiness;* only in the const. pl. as אַשְׁרֵי הָאִישׁ *blessed is the man*, Ps. 1:1; אַשְׁרֶיךָ *blessed art thou*, Deu. 33:29.

אֹשֶׁר m., *happiness*, Gen. 30:13; with suff. אָשְׁרִי.

אָשׁוּר f.—I. *a step.*—II. *wood of the box tree*, Eze. 27:6.

אַשּׁוּר f.—I. *step*, Job 31:7.—II. p.n.f., *Assyria, kingdom of;* m., *an Assyrian;* דֶּרֶךְ א' *into Assyria;* אַשּׁוּרָה *the way of Assyria.*—III. אַשּׁוּרִים *a race of Ishmaelites*, Gen. 25:3.

אַשּׁוּר p. n. of a man.

אֲשַׁרְנָא m. Ch., *wall, building,* Eze. 5:3.

תְּאַשּׁוּר m., *the box tree*, Isa. 41:19, 60:13.

אֲשֶׁר I. relat. pron. of every gender and number; *he who, she who, it which, &c.*—II. note of the relative when it comes before pronouns and adverbs; אֲשֶׁר הוּא חַי *he who lives;* א' אֶת־עָפָר *which is dust;* א' לוֹ, לֹה *to whom,* sing.; א' לָהֶם, *to whom, which,* pl.; א' אֹתוֹ, *whom, which,* sing.; א' אֹתָם, *whom, which,* pl.; אֲשֶׁר־לְשֹׁנוֹ *whose tongue;* א' בּוֹ, בָּהּ *in whom, which;* א' בְּאַרְצָם *in whose land;* א' מִמֶּנּוּ *from whom;* א' שָׁם *where;* א' מִשָּׁם *whence;* א' שָׁמָּוֹ *whither;* א' תַּחַת כְּנָפָיו *under whose wings.*—III. precedes pron. of the 1. and 2. pers.; א' מְכַרְתֶּם אֹתִי *(ye) who have sold me;* א' בָּחַרְתִּיךָ *thee whom I have chosen.*—IV. compounded with preps.; אֶת־אֲשֶׁר *him whom;* בַּאֲשֶׁר *where;* כַּאֲשֶׁר *according to, as if, because, when;* מֵאֲשֶׁר *from thence, whence.*—V. preceded by adverbs; אַחַר, בַּעֲבוּר, תַּחַת, עַל, עַד, יַעַן connecting them with the following words.—VI. אֲשֶׁר לְ note of the genitive; לָאֲבִיהָ הַצֹּאן א' *her father's cattle;* אֲשֶׁר conj. ὅτι, *because, that;* ἵνα with fut.; *since, when,* ὅτε; ὡς *as,* with כֵּן.

שֶׁ with dag. forte (sometimes שְׁ) same as אֲשֶׁר relat. pron. and in its other significations; שֶׁשָּׁם *where;* שֶׁל *of, whose;* בְּשֶׁ *because;* כְּמַעַט שֶׁ *almost;* עַד־שֶׁ *until.* For אֲשֶׁר and שֶׁ; see Noldii Concordantiæ, and Prof. Lee's Grammar

בְּשֶׁל because, on account of; בְּשֶׁלְמִי for my sake; בְּשֶׁלְמִי on whose account? בְּשֶׁל אֲשֶׁר, whatever.

אֲשַׂרְאֵלָה (from אֲשֶׁר and אֵל), p. n. of a man.

אֲשֵׁירָה, אֲשֵׁרָה (probably m. of עַשְׁתֹּרֶת), p. n. of a deity of the Syrians; pl. אֲשֵׁרִים and אֲשֵׁרוֹת images of this idol.

אֲשַׁרְנָא buildings; see אשר.

אָשֵׁשׁ root not used. Hith. הִתְאֹשֵׁשׁ be men; see אִישׁ.

אָשִׁישׁ m. pl., const. אֲשִׁישֵׁי foundations; see in its place.

אֲשִׁישָׁה f., cake, pancake; pl. ־ים and אֲשִׁישׁוֹת.

אָשִּׁין m. pl. Ch., foundations.

אֵשֶׁת woman; see אנש.

אֶשְׁתִּיו Ch. pret. pl. with א prosthet., from שתה.

אֶשְׁתָּאֹל p. n. of a town of the Danites.

אֶשְׁתַּדּוּר Hith. of שדר.

אֶשְׁתּוֹן p.n. of a man.

אֶשְׁתְּמֹעַ and אֶשְׁתְּמֹה p.n. of a town in the tribe of Judah.

אָת sign; see אוה.

I. אֵת m., ploughshare; pl. אִתִּים and אֵתִים 1 Sa. 13:21; with suff. אִתֵּיכֶם.

II אֵת־, אֶת note of:—I. the accus. —II. the nom. with verbs passive and neuter; יִקְרֵא אֶת־שְׁמֶךָ thy name shall be called; with suff. אֹתְךָ, אֹתִי, אֵתִי me (with pause אֹתָךְ; with ה parag. אֹתְכָה, אֹתְכָה) m., אֹתָךְ f., thee; אֹתוֹ him; אֹתָהּ her; אֹתָנוּ us; אֶתְכֶם, אֶתְכֶן, אֹתָם, אֶתְהֶם, אוֹתָם you;

ה with אֹתָן, m.; אוֹתְהֶם them, m.; parag. אֹתְהֶנָה, אֹתָנָה them, f.

III. אֵת־, אֶת prep. with, by, on, besides, towards; אֶת־פְּנֵי פ׳ before some one; with suff. אִתִּי with me; אִתְּךָ (with pause אִתָּךְ) m., אִתָּךְ f., with thee; אִתּוֹ with him; אִתָּהּ with her; אִתָּנוּ with us; אִתְּכֶן, אִתְּכֶם with you; אִתָּם with them (sometimes מֵאֵת, אֹתוֹ, אֹתִי, &c.).; denotes separation, from; מֵאִתִּי, מֵאִתְּךָ, מֵאוֹתָם from me; מֵאוֹתִי from me, &c.

אֶתְבַּעַל p.n. of a king of Sidon.

אַתָּה (sometimes אַתְּ m.; אַתְּ, with pause אָתָּ, sometimes אַתִּי f.), pers. pron. thou; אַתֶּם m., אַתֵּן, אַתֵּנָה f., ye.

אָתָה (אָתָא Isa. 21:12), came; pret. pl. אָתָנוּ; imper. pl. אֵתָיוּ; fut. וַיֵּאת, וַיֵּאתָא, תֵּאתָה, יֶאֱתֶה pl. יֶאֱתָיוּ. Hiph. imper. pl. הֵתָיוּ bring ye.

אֲתָה Ch., came. Aph. הַיְתִי brought. Hoph. was brought.

אִיתוֹן m., entrance, Eze. 40:15.

אֶתְוַדַּע Hith. fut. 1. pers., from ידע.

אַתּוּן com. Ch., furnace, Dan. 3:6, 11, 15.

אַתִּיק, אַתּוּק m., gallery, Eze. 41: 3, 15.

אַתַּי p. n. of a man.

אֵתָיו Syr. for אֱתָיו which is for אֱתוּ imp. pl., from אתה.

אֲתָיו for אֲתָאנוּ pret. pl. 1. pers., from אָתָה. אָתָא.

אַתֶּן, אַתֶּם you; see אַתָּה.

אֵתָם p. n. of a place in the desert.

אִתְמוֹל, אֶתְמוּל, אֶתְמוֹל *yesterday;* same as תְּמוֹל.

אָתַן root not used (Arab. *stepping shortly, she-ass*).

אָתוֹן f., *she-ass.*

אֶתְנַן, אֶתְנָה *gift;* see יתן.

אֶתְנִי (*gift*), p. n. of a man.

אֶתְּקֶנְךָ Kal fut. 1. pers. with suff. and נ epenth., from נתק.

אֲתַר m. Ch., *place;* אֲתַר דִּי *in that place, where;* בָּאתַר *after;* בָּתְרָךְ *after thee.*

אֲתָרִים m., *places;* or p. n. according to others Nu. 21:1.

ב

בְּ prep.—I. of place: *in, among, with, near, before;* never motion either to or in a place.—II. of time: *in, within.*—III. used of the means or instrument: *by, with.*—IV. of the cause: *for, because.*—V. of the rule: *according to.*—VI. *by* (in an oath).—VII. often prefixed to the inf. of verbs, translated by *in* or *when;* with suff. בִּי; בְּךָ m. (with the pause בָּךְ); בָּהּ, בּוֹ, בָּךְ f.; בָּנוּ; בָּהֵן and בָּם, בָּהֶן, בָּכֶם.

בֹּאָה imp. with ה parag.; בָּאַי, בָּאִים part. pl.; בָּאֲכָה inf. with suff.; בָּאת and בָּאת pret. f. 2. pers., from בּוֹא.

בֹּאָה *entrance;* see בּוֹא.

בָּאוֹשׁ *wicked;* see באש.

בֵּאֵר, בָּאַר Pi.—I. *dig, cut upon or into, define well;* with עַל.—II. *make clear, publish,* Deu. 1:5.

בְּאֵר f. (pl. const. בְּאֵרוֹת).—I. *well, cistern.*—II. p. n. of one of the stations in the desert.—III. p.n. of

a town in the tribe of Judah. בְּאֵר אֵלִים (*the well of heroes*), p. n. of a well. בְּאֵר לַחַי רֹאִי (*the well of the living God that seeth me*), p. n. of a well in the desert. בְּאֵר שֶׁבַע (*well of the oath*), p. n. of a city in the tribe of Simeon. בְּאֵרוֹת p. n. of a city in the tribe of Benjamin; בְּאֵרֹתִי בְּרֹתִי, epithet of an inhabitant of *Beeroth.* בְּאֵרוֹת בְּנֵי יַעֲקָן (*wells of the sons of Iaachan*), p. n. of a station in the desert.

בְּאֵר often, בּוֹר m.—I. *well of water; well of bitumen,* Gen. 14:10.—II. *pit* or *dungeon in which prisoners were kept;* בֵּית הַבּוֹר *prison house.*—III. *grave, sepulchre;* יֹרְדֵי בוֹר *they that go down into the pit,* i. e. the dead; עַד בּוֹר *even to the grave;* with ה *den, place,* בֹּרָה, pl. בְּאֵרוֹת, בֹּרוֹת.

בְּאֵרָא p. n. of a man.

בְּאֵרָה p. n. of a man.

בְּאֵרִי p. n.—I. of the father of Hosea.—II. of the father-in-law of Esau.

בָּאַשׁ (fut. יִבְאַשׁ) *emitted an ill savour, stank.* Niph. *became fetid, in ill odour,* i.e. *hateful;* (with בְּ, אֶת). Hiph. הִבְאִישׁ *rendered, made bad,* i. e. *odious;* (with בְּ); int. *stank,* Ex. 16:24; *did wickedly, became bad;* (with עִם), 1 Chron. 19:6.

בְּאֵשׁ Ch., *was evil;* (with עַל), Dan. 6:15.

בְּאֹשׁ m.—I. *stench;* with suff. בָּאְשׁוֹ בְּאָשְׁם.—II. *evil, affliction.*

בָּאְשָׁה f., *poisonous herb,* probably hemlock, Job 31:40.

בָּאֻשִׁים m. pl., *wild, sour grapes,* Is 5:2, 4.

בְּאוּשׁ m. Ch., *bad, wicked;* f. emph.
בְּאוּשְׁתָּא.

בָּאתַר *after;* see אָתַר.

בָּבָה *pupil of the eye;* see בּוּב.

בֵּבַי p.n. of a man.

בָּבֶל p.n.f.—I. *Babylon;* with ה, signifying place, בָּבֶלָה.—II. *the kingdom of Babylon.*

בַּבְלִי Ch. *Babylonish;* pl. const. בַּבְלָיֵא.

בָּג m., לְבַג, Eze. 23:7, a wrong reading; Kri לְבַז "for a spoil," Eng.
Ver.

בָּגַד (fut. יִבְגַּד, יִבְגֹּד; inf. בָּגוֹד; const.
בְּגוֹד; with suff. בִּגְדוֹ), *dissem-
bled, acted perfidiously, cheated,*
with בְּ and מִן; part. בֹּגֵד *a perfidious person.*

בֶּגֶד m.(f. Lev. 6:20; with suff. בִּגְדִי,
בִּגְדוֹ; pl. בְּגָדִים; const. בִּגְדֵי,
בְּגָדוֹתֶיךָ, Ps. 45:9).—I. *wrapper,
coverlet.*—II. *cloak, garment.*—III.
dissimulation, perfidy.—IV. *rapine,
violence.*

בֹּגְדוֹת f. pl., *great perfidy,* Zep. 3:4.

בָּגוֹד m., בֹּגֵדָה f., *perfidious,* Jer. 3:
7, 10.

בִּגְוַי p.n. of a man.

בִּגְלַל *because;* see גלל.

בִּגְתָא p.n. of a eunuch of Ahasuerus.

בִּגְתָן p.n. of a eunuch of Ahasuerus.

בַּד m., *fine linen;* בַּדִּים *linen garments;* see also בַּד under בדד.

בָּרָא *originated, innovated;* part. with
suff. בֹּדְאָם Syr. for בְּדָאָם.

בָּדַד, part. בּוֹדֵד *separate, solitary
person.*

בַּד m., *being alone, separate, apart;*
pl בַּדִּים.—I. *shoots, branches.*—II.

staves of wood.—III. *limbs, members of the body.*—IV. *defences,* i.e.
princes, Hos. 11:6, &c.—V. *lies,* Is.
16:6, &c.

לְבַד adv., *alone, separate, only;* אָנֹכִי
לְבַדִּי *I alone;* אַתָּה לְבַדְּךָ *thou
alone;* לְבַדְּךָ *to thee alone;* לְבַדּוֹ
he alone; מִלְּבַד מִן and לְבַד *and
besides;* מִלְּבַד אֲשֶׁר *beside that
which;* לְבַד עַל *the same.*

לְבָדָד m., *separate, alone, solitary;*
and בָּדָד adv. *apart, separate.*

בְּדַד p.n. of the father of Hadad
king of Edom.

בְּדֵי *same as* בְּ; see דִּי.

בְּדֵיָה p.n. of a man.

בָּדַל Niph. *was separated;* with לְ it
signifies, *unto something;* with מִן,
from something; with אֶל, *he separated himself unto one thing
alone.* Hiph. הִבְדִּיל I. *made,
caused division,* const. with מִן and
מֵעַל.—II. *distinguished, divided,*
with בֵּין...לְ, בֵּין, בֵּין...וּבֵין.
—III. *designed,* with לְ.

בָּדָל m., בְּדַל אֹזֶן *portion of the ear,*
Amos 3:12.

בְּדִיל m., *tin;* אֶבֶן הַבְּדִיל *the weight
at the plumb-line, the plummet.*

מִבְדָּלוֹת f. pl., *separations, separate
places,* Jos. 16:9.

בְּדֹלַח m. *bdellium,* a translucent and
odoriferous gum; according to Lee,
a precious stone, either *the crystal*
or *the beryl,* Gen. 2:12, Num. 11:7.

בְּדָן p.n.—I. of a judge, perhaps the
same as בָּרָק, 1 Sam. 12:11.—II.
of another man, 1 Chron. 7:17.

בָּדַק (Arab. *tear, rend*); inf. בְּדוֹק

repairing injury, decay, 2 Chron. 34:10.

בֶּדֶק injury, decay in a building; with suff. בִּדְקֵךְ.

בִּדְקַר p. n. of a man.

בְּדַר Ch. same as Heb. בָּזַר; Pa. imper. בַּדְּרוּ sprinkle.

בָּהָה (Arab. void).

בֹּהוּ m., emptiness, destitution.

בַּהַט m., marble, Est. 1:6.

בָּהַל Niph.—נִבְהַל—I. was terrified, astonished.—II. cast down, ruined, with לְ at, מִ from. Pi. בִּהֵל—I. cause to hurry, hasten.—II. astonish, confound, ruin; fut. יְבַהֵל. Pu. part. מְבֹהָל hurried, gotten too speedily. Hiph. הִבְהִיל same as Pihel.

בְּהַל Ch., Pa. affrighted. Ithp. part. alarmed.

בֶּהָלָה f., fear, terror, ruin; pl. בֶּהָלוֹת.

בְּהִילוּ f. Ch., hurry, haste, Ezr. 4:23.

הִתְבַּהֲלָה f. Ch., haste.

בָּהַם root not used; (Arab. was dumb).

בְּהֵמָה f. (const. בֶּהֱמַת; with suff. בְּהֶמְתְּךָ).—I. cattle.—II. wild beast; בֶּהֱמַת יַעַר, הָאָרֶץ, הַשָּׂדֶה, wild beasts; pl. בְּהֵמוֹת; const. בַּהֲמוֹת, Job 40:15, name of some stupendous quadruped.

בֹּהֶן m.—I. the thumb.—II. the great toe; pl. בְּהֹנוֹת.

בֹּהַן (thumb), p. n. of a son of Reuben; אֶבֶן בֹּהַן p. n. of a place in the tribe of Judah.

בָּהַק root not used; (Arab. was shining).

בֹּהַק m., LXX. ἀλφὸς, a white scurf, cicatrix on the skin, Lev. 13:39.

בָּהַר root not used; Ch. he shone.

בָּהִיר m., breaking through the clouds (of light), Job 37:21.

בַּהֶרֶת f., the white spot covered with hair which was the sure symptom of leprosy; pl. בֶּהָרוֹת, Lev. c. 13

בְּהֵרָג for בְּהֵהָרֵג Niph. inf. with the pref. בְּ from הרג.

בְּהִשַּׁמָּה for בְּהִשַּׁמָּה Hoph. inf. with suff. and pref. from שמם.

בּוֹא (fut. יָבֹא, וַיָּבֹא; part. pl. בָּאִים, בָּאֵי), entered, came or went in, to, for, &c., with יָצָא, לְ, בְּ, אֶל, וּבָא same as הָלַךְ, he went in and out, i. e. he lived familiarly; with לִפְנֵי הָעָם to go before, lead the people; בּוֹא בְרִית he entered into covenant; בּוֹא אֶל אִשָּׁה with had connection with a woman; שֶׁמֶשׁ בָּאָה the sun was setting; const. also with עַד, עַל, לְ, בְּ, אֶל; בּוֹא בַיָּמִים advanced in years; with אֵת, עִם, אֶת went with, had intercourse with, Ps. 26:4, Pro. 22:24. Hiph. הֵבִיא (with suff. הֱבִיאוֹ); imper. הָבִי, הָבֵא; fut. יָבִיא, (וַיָּבֵא) caused, made, induced to enter, come in; with אֶל, לְ, עַל. Hoph. הוּבָא brought in.

בָּאָה f., entrance.

מָבוֹא m., entrance, porch; מְבוֹא הַשֶּׁמֶשׁ place of sunset. Pl. מְבוֹאִים, const. מְבוֹאֵי and מְבֹאוֹת.

מוֹבָא m., entrance, 2 Sa. 3:25, Ez. 43:11.

תְּבוּאָה f.—I. income.—II. store.—III. profit.—IV. produce; pl. תְּבוּאוֹת.

תְּבוּאָה f., Job 22:21; תְּבוּאָתְךָ from בּוֹא, fut. Kal with ה parag.

בּוּב Niph. part. נָבוּב.—I. proud, insolent, Job 11:12.—II. hollow.

בָּבָה f., apple of the eye, pupil; בָּבַת עַיִן pupil, Zec. 2:12.

בּוּז (fut. יָבוּז), despised, neglected; with ל comp. בוז, בזה.

בּוּז m.—I. contempt.—II. p. n. of a brother of Abraham, and of the nation he founded in Arabia Deserta; בּוּזִי a Buzite.—III. p.n. of a man, 1 Chron. 5:14.

בּוּזָה f., contempt, contemptible thing.

בָּנִי p. n. of a man.

בּוּךְ Niph. נָבוּךְ confused, perplexed, Ex. 14:3, Est. 3:15.

מְבוּכָה f., confusion, perplexity, Isa. 22:5; Mic. 7:4.

בּוֹכִיָה Kal, part. from בכה.

בּוּל increase, same as יְבוּל; see יבל.

בּוּן and בִּין.—I. distinguished, discerned.—II. perceived, understood, with בְּ, אֶל, ל, עַל; part. בָּנִים prudent persons; pret. בַּנְתָּ, בָּן, and בִּינוֹתִי, בִּין; fut. יָבִין. Niph. נָבוּן became discerning; part. נָבוּן wise; נ' דָּבָר wise in word, eloquent. Pil. בּוֹנֵן made him discerning, Deu. 32:10. Hiph. הֵבִין.—I. taught, explained, with ל, בְּ, אֶל.—II. understood, was wise; part. מֵבִין skilful, learned; imper. הָבֵן and הָבִין; with suff. הֲבִינֵנִי; fut. יָבִין, וַיָּבֶן. Hith. הִתְבּוֹנֵן same as Niph.; with עַד, בְּ, אֶל, עַל.

בֵּין const. בֵּין s.—I. interval, midst; dual אִישׁ בֵּנַיִם man of two intervals, i. e. between the two armies,

1 Sam. 17:4.—II. prep. between, among, within; בֵּין...לְ, בֵּין...וּבֵין, בֵּין...לְבֵין between...and (whether... or, Lev. 27:12); with suff. בֵּינְךָ, בֵּינִי; with pause בֵּינֶךָ; בֵּינוֹ; with suff. pl. בֵּינֵיכֶם, בֵּינֵינוּ and בֵּינֵיכֶם; בֵּינֵיהֶם; fem. אֶל־בֵּין־בֵּינוֹתָם among; בֵּינוֹתֵינוּ the same; אֶל־בֵּנוֹת לְ the same; מִבֵּין from between; מִבֵּינוֹת the same; עַל־בֵּין up among; בַּבֵּין in the midst.

בֵּין Ch., among; pl. with suff. בֵּינֵיהוֹן.

בִּינָה f., intelligence, discernment, prudence; Ch. the same.

תָּבוּן m., תְּבוּנָה f., understanding, prudence; pl. תְּבוּנוֹת.

בּוּנָה (intelligence), p. n. of a man.

בּוּנִי from בָּנָה, p. n. of a man.

בּוּס (fut. יָבוּס and יָבוּס; part. pl. בּוֹסִים) trampled, trod upon, despised. Pil. בּוֹסֵס trod down (profaned holy place). Hoph. part. מוּבָס trodden down. Hith. part. f. מִתְבּוֹסֶסֶת become trodden down, Eze. 16:6, 22.

מְבוּסָה f., treading upon.

תְּבוּסָה f., destruction, 2 Chron. 22:7.

בּוּעַ root not used, Ch. was boiling.

אֲבַעְבֻּעוֹת f. pl., spots on the skin.

בּוּץ root not used; (Arab. fine linen).

בּוּץ, בֵּץ m., βύσσος, linen, fine linen.

בֵּיץ m., or בֵּיצָה f., pl. בֵּיצִים eggs.

בּוֹצֵץ (shining), p. n. of a rock near Gibeah.

בּוּק root not used; (Arab. heavy rain; see בקק).

בּוּקָה f., emptiness, devastation, Neh. 2:11.

מְבוּקָה f., emptiness; the same.

בּוֹר well, same as בְּאֵר; see בָּאַר.

בוּר (same as בָּרַר), *explored*.

בּוֹשׁ (pret. בֹּשְׁנוּ, בּוֹשׁוּ, בֹּשְׁתָּ, בּוֹשׁ; fut. יֵבוֹשׁ, (אֵבוֹשׁ) *ashamed, put to shame, blushed*, with מִן and לְ; עַד־בּוֹשׁ *until they were ashamed.* Pil. בֹּשֵׁשׁ *put to a stand, delayed*, Jud. 5:28, Ex. 32:30. Hiph. הֵבִישׁ and הוֹבִישׁ (from cognate יבשׁ) *brought to shame, confusion*; part. מֵבִישׁ *bringing, causing shame, wicked.* Hith. הִתְבֹּשֵׁשׁ *become ashamed*, Gen. 2:25.

בּוּשָׁה f., *shame, ignominy.*

בָּשְׁנָה f., *the same*, Hos. 10:6.

בֹּשֶׁת f.—I. *shame, blushing.*—II. *ignominy.*—III. *an idol.*

מָבוּשׁ m., pl. מְבֻשִׁים *secret parts*, Deu. 25:11.

בֹּשְׁתְּכֶם Po. inf. with suff. from בשׁ

בּוּת Ch.; בָּת *passed the night*, Dan. 6:19.

בַּיִת m. (const. בֵּית; with suff. בֵּיתְךָ, בֵּיתוֹ; pl. בָּתִּים, const. בָּתֵּי), *habitation.*—I. *temple* of God or idols.—II. *palace.*—III. *house, tent, cave;* אֲשֶׁר עַל בַּיִת *mayor of the palace;* בֶּן or יְלִיד בַּיִת *household-slave*).—IV. *sepulchre.* — V. *receptacle of anything;* בָּתֵּי נֶפֶשׁ *perfume boxes*, Isa. 3:20.—VI. *family, race.* With ה parag. בַּיְתָה, const. בֵּיתָה, adv. *inwards;* מִבֵּית *within;* מִבַּית לְ, בֵּית לְ, לְמִבֵּית לְ, מִבֵּית לְ *within.*

בַּיִת m. Ch., *house, palace, temple.*

בִּיתָן m., *great house, palace*, Est. 1: 5; 7:7, 8.

The p.n. of many towns are compounds of בַּיִת; בֵּית אָוֶן in the tribe of Benjamin; בֵּית־אֵל between Jerusalem and Sichem; בֵּית הָאֱלִי a *Bethelite;* בֵּית אֶצֶל in Samaria; בֵּית אַרְבֵּאל *Arbela* in Galilee; בַּעַל מְעוֹן, בֵּי בַּעַל מְעוֹן and בֵּית מְעוֹן in the tribe of Reuben; בֵּי בָּרָה (ferry-house) Βηθαβαρὰ, near Jordan; בֵּי בִּרְאִי in the tribe of Simeon; בֵּי גָּדֵר in the tribe of Judah; בֵּי הַגִּלְגָּל same as גִּלְגָּל, see גָּלַל; בֵּי גָּמוּל (see גָּמַל) in the land of Moab; בֵּי דָּגוֹן; בֵּי דִּבְלָתַיִם, see דִּבְלָתַיִם (temple of Dagon), in the tribe of Judah, also in the tribe of Asher; בֵּי הָרָם and הָרָן in the tribe of Gad; בֵּי חָגְלָה (place of partridges), town of the Benjamites in the tribe of Judah; בֵּי חָנָן (house of mercy), in the tribe of Judah or Dan; בֵּי חֹרוֹן two towns in the tribe of Ephraim; בֵּי הַיְשִׁימוֹת town of the Reubenites on the shore of the Red Sea; בֵּי בַּר a strong place of the Philistines in the tribe of Judah; בֵּי הַכֶּרֶם (house of vineyards), in the tribe of Judah; בֵּי לְבָאוֹת (place of lionesses), in the tribe of Simeon; בֵּי לֶחֶם (house of bread) Βηθλεὲμ, in the tribe of Judah, see אֶפְרָתָה; another town in the tribe of Zebulun; בֵּי הַלַּחְמִי a *Bethlehemite;* בֵּי מִלּוֹא, see עַפְרָה; בֵּי לְעַפְרָה see מִלּוֹא; בֵּי מַעֲכָה a town at the foot of Hermon; בֵּי הַמֶּרְחָק (from רָחַק), on the banks of Kedron; בֵּי הַמַּרְכָּבוֹת (house of chariots), in the tribe of Simeon; בֵּי נִמְרָה (place of pure water), in the tribe of Gad; בּ׳ עֶדֶן (*pleasant place*), a town near Damascus; בּ׳ הָעֵמֶק, see עַזְמָוֶת; בּ׳ עַזְמָוֶת (*house of the valley*), in the tribe of Asher; בּ׳ עֲנוֹת (*place of echo*), in the tribe of Judah; בּ׳ עֲנָת (the same), in the tribe of Naphtali; בּ׳ עֵקֶד הָרֹעִים (*place where shepherds bind their sheep*), near Samaria; בּ׳ הָעֲרָבָה (*place in the desert*), on the confines of Judah and Benjamin; בּ׳ פֶּלֶט (*place of flight*), in the tribe of Judah; בּ׳ פְּעוֹר (see פְּעוֹר), in the land of Moab, not far from Jordan; בּ׳ פַּצֵּץ (*place of dispersion*), in the tribe of Issachar; בּ׳ צוּר (*house of the rock*), in the mountains of Judah; בּ׳ רְחֹב (see רְחֹב, אֲרָם), a city of Syria; בּ׳ שֵׁן, שָׁן, בּ׳ שְׁאָן (*house of sleep*), in the tribe of Manasseh, beyond Jordan; בּ׳ הַשִּׁטָּה (see שִׁטָּה), a town on Jordan; בּ׳ שֶׁמֶשׁ (*house of the sun*), name of several towns: *a.* of the Levites in the tribe of Judah; בֵּירת־הַשִּׁמְשִׁי *inhabitant of....; β.* in the tribe of Naphtali; *γ.* in the tribe of Issachar or Zebulon; *δ.* same as אוֹן in Egypt; בּ׳ תַּפּוּחַ; תַּנְרְמָה, בּ׳ תּוֹנַרְמָה, see תַּנְרְמָה (*place of apple trees*), in the tribe of Judah.

בֻּז from בָּזַז for בַּז, Zec. 4:10; see בּוּז. בִּזָּה בַּז *spoiled;* see בזז.

בָּזָא, בָּזְאוּ Isa. 18:2, *have spoiled.*

בָּזָה same as בּוּז *despised, spurned;* const. with לְ, עַל. Niph. part. נִבְזֶה *despised;* pl. נִבְזִים. Hiph. inf. הַבְזוֹת *make despised,* Est. 1:17.

בָּזֹה inf., *despised,* Isa. 49:7.

בִּזָּיוֹן m., *great contempt,* Est. 1:18.

בִּזְיוֹתְיָה (*despised of the Lord*), p. n. of a town in the tribe of Judah.

נִמְבְזָה *contemptible,* 1 Sa. 15:9.

בָּזַז *took the spoil or prey;* part. pl. בֹּזְזִים *spoilers;* pret. pl. בָּזַזְנוּ, בָּזְזוּ and בַּזּוֹנוּ; inf. בֹּז; fut. יָבֹז. Niph. נָבֹז, and Pu. בֻּזַּז *were spoiled,* Jer. 50:37.

בַּז m. (with suff. בִּזָּהּ), *spoil;* הָיָה לָבַז *was for a spoil;* נָתַן לָבַז *gave for a spoil.*

בִּזָּה f., *booty.*

בָּזָק m., *lightning,* Eze. 1:14.

בֶּזֶק p.n. of a town to the southward of Bethshan, Βεζέκ.

בָּזַר (fut. יִבְזֹר), *dispersed,* Dan. 11:24; Pi. בִּזַּר the same, Ps. 68:31.

בִּזְתָּא p.n. of a eunuch of Ahasuerus.

בָּחַל *was greedy, niggard;* with בְּ, Zec. 11:8. Pu. part. f. מְבֹחֶלֶת *coveted, gotten by covetousness,* Pro. 20:21.

בָּחַן (imper. בְּחַן; with suff. בְּחָנֵנִי, בְּחָנוּנִי; fut. יִבְחַן).—I. *tried, tested* (metals with fire).—II. *tried* (men with affliction).—III. *tried* (God.... the heart). Niph. *be tried.*

בֹּחַן m., *examination, trial,* Isa. 28:16, Eze. 21:18.

בַּחַן m., *watch-tower,* Isa. 32:14.

בָּחוֹן m., *mound, watch-tower,* Isa. 23:14.

בָּחֻן m., *trial, experiment.*

בָּחַר (fut. יִבְחַר), *chose;* with בְּ, לְ, עַל; בָּחַר לוֹ *he chose for himself;* with מִן *preferred;* part. בָּחוּר

chosen, excellent. Niph. chosen; part. נִבְחָר elect, excellent; with מִן better.

בָּחִיר m., elect; (ἐκλεκτὸς τοῦ Θεοῦ the elect of God).

בָּחוּר m., a youth; pl. בַּחוּרִים youths, liable to be chosen (balloted) for military service.

בְּחוּרִים m. pl., youth.

בְּחוּרוֹת f. pl., the same.

בַּחֻרִים p. n. of a town in the tribe of Benjamin; בַּרְחֻמִי and בַּחֲרוּמִי an inhabitant of Bachurim.

מִבְחָר ,מִבְחוֹר m.—I. the choice, the best.—II. p. n. of a man.

מִבְחוֹר m., the same, 2 Ki. 3:19; 19:23.

בָּטָא and בָּטָה speaks wrongfully, falsely, Pro. 12:18; part. בּוֹטֶה. Pi. בִּטֵּא spake falsely.

מִבְטָא m., rashness in speaking; מִ' שְׂפָתַיִם, Nu. 30:7,9.

בָּטַח (inf. בְּטוֹחַ; with suff. בִּטְחֲךָ; imper. בְּטַח; fut. יִבְטַח; pl. f. תִּבְטַחְנָה), trusted in, to, on; with בְּ, אֶל ,עַל ,לְ, Job 6:20; impers. was for a confidence; part. בָּטוּחַ trusted, was confident, incautious; part. בֹּטֵחַ secure, confiding. Hiph. הִבְטִיחַ made to confide, trust; with עַל and אֶל.

בֶּטַח m., confidence, security; בֶּטַח and לְבֶטַח adv. confidently, securely, safely.

בֶּטַח p. n. of a town of Aram Zobah, 2 Sam. 8:8.

בִּטְחָה f., confidence, Isa. 30:15.

בִּטָּחוֹן m., the same, Isa. 36:4, Ecc. 9:4.

בַּטֻּחָה f., the same; pl. בַּטֻּחוֹת, Job 12:6.

מִבְטָח m. (with suff. מִבְטַחִי ,מִבְטָחֶה, pl. מִבְטָחִים (מִבְטַחִים), trust, confidence; metonym. he in whom trust is reposed.

אֲבַטִּיחִים see טבח.

בָּטֵל cease, fail, Ecc. 12:3.

בְּטֵל Ch., ceased, Ezr. 4:24. Pa. בַּטֵּל caused to cease, hindered.

בֶּטֶן f. (with suff. בִּטְנִי).—I. belly.—II. womb; פְּרִי בֶטֶן fruit of the womb, offspring; מִבֶּטֶן ,מִן־הַבֶּטֶן, מִבֶּטֶן אִמִּי ἐκ γαστρὸς, the same.—III. ἡ κοιλία the inner man, seat of thought, feelings.—IV. the projecting part of the chapter of a column, 1 Ki. 7:20.—V. p. n. of a town in the tribe of Asher.

בָּטְנִים m. pl., nuts, Gen. 43:11. Pistachia vera (Lin.), a tree abounding in Palestine, but unknown in Egypt.

בְּטֹנִים p. n. of a town in the tribe of Gad.

בִּי pa. of supplication (always with אֲדֹנָי or אֲדֹנִי), Lord, I pray thee; ah, Lord!

בִּינָה ,בֵּין ,בִּין understand; see בּוּן.

בֵּיצִים eggs; see בּוּץ.

בִּיקְרוֹתֶיךָ f. pl., with suff., pref., and dag. euphon. see יָקַר.

בַּיִר well; same as בְּאֵר.

בִּירָה f.—I. palace.—II. the temple.

בִּירָה f. Ch., the same.

בִּירָנִיּוֹת f. pl., palaces; sing. never occurs.

בַּיִת ,בִּיתָן house, &c.; see בּוּת.

בָּכָה (fut. יִבְכֶּה ,וַיֵּבְךְ; inf. בָּכֹה and בָּכֹה).—I. wept.—II. mourned;

with אֶת. בְּ, עַל, ל, אֶל Pi. *de-plored*, with עַל.

בָּךְ m.—I. *the Baka shrub*, Amyris Gileadensis (Linn.); pl. בְּכָאִים —II. עֵמֶק הַבָּכָא (*valley of weeping*), p.n. of a valley in Palestine, Ps. 84:7.

בֶּכֶה m., *weeping*, Eze. 10:1.

בָּכוֹ inf. abs. from בכה.

בָּכוּת and בְּכִית f., *weeping*, Gen. 50:4.

בְּכִי m. (with pause בֶּכִי; with suff. בִּכְיִי).—I. *weeping.*—II. *dropping of water in wells*, Job, 28:11.

בֹּכִים p.n. of a town near Gilgal.

בָּכַר Kal, root not used; (Arab. *early*). Pi. בִּכֵּר.—I. *brought forth early fruits.*—II. *was the first-born*, Deu. 21:16. Pu. passive of Pi., Lev. 27:26. Hiph. *brought forth her first-born*, Jer. 4:13.

בְּכוֹר m., *first-born*; בְּכֹרוֹת pl., *the first-born of brutes*, Gen. 4:4, Deu. 12:17. Trop. בְּכוֹר מָוֶת *the worm*, Job 18:13; בְּכוֹרֵי דַלִּים *the first-born of the poor, the poorest*.

בְּכוֹרָה f., *primogeniture*.

בְּכוֹרַת p.n. of a man, 1 Sa. 9:1.

בְּכִירָה f., *eldest, first-born daughter*.

בִּכְרוּ (same as בֶּכֶר הֻוא), p.n. of a man.

בִּכְרִי (*my first-born*), p.n. of a man.

בֶּכֶר m., *a young camel*, Isa. 60:6; בִּכְרָה f. *a young she-camel*, Jer. 2:23.

בֶּכֶר, בַּכְרִי p.n.—I. of a son of Ephraim.—II. of a son of Benjamin.

בִּכּוּר m., pl. בִּכּוּרִים and בִּכֻּרִים *first-fruits*; יוֹם הַבִּכֻּרִים *feast of first-fruits, Pentecost*, Nu. 28:26.

תְּאֵנֵי בַכֻּרוֹת f., *the early fig*; בִּכּוּרָה *early figs*.

בְּכוֹרַת p.n. of a man.

בַּל; see בלה.

בֵּל Bel, same as בַּעַל.

בְּלָא destroy; see בָּלָה.

בַּלְאֲדָן (*whose lord is Baal*), p.n. of a king of Babylon; see מְרֹדָךְ.

בָּלַג Kal, root not used (Arab. *opened, shone*).—Hiph. הִבְלִיג with עַל I. *made to rise*, Am. 5:9.—II. *made glad*, Ps. 39:14.

בִּלְגָּה (*joy*), p.n. of a priest.

מַבְלִיגִית f., *exhilaration*, Jer. 8:18.

בִּלְדַּד p.n. of one of Job's friends.

בָּלָה (fut. יִבְלֶה).—I. *grew old.*—II. *perished*; with מֵעַל *worn off*, spoken of clothes. Pi. בִּלָּה. *made cold.*

בְּלָא Ch. form. Pa. *destroy, make to disappear*, Dan. 7:25; see בלה Pi.

בָּלֶה m., בָּלָה f., *old, effete, worn out*, Jos. 9:4, 5, Eze. 23:43.

בָּלָה p.n. of a city.

בְּלוֹיִם and בְּלֹאִים m. pl., *old, worn*, Jer. 38:11, 12.

בְּלוֹ m. Ch., *custom, tax*.

תַּבְלִית f., *destruction*, Isa. 10:26.

בָּל m. Ch., *the heart, mind*, Dan. 6:15.

בַּל (*wanting*); adv., *not, nothing*.

בְּלִי I. *loss, destruction*, Isa. 38:17.—II. *wanting, without* (written בִּבְלִי and בְּלִי); בְּלִי דַעַת *without knowledge*; לִבְלִי *without*; מִבְּלִי *from want of.*—III. adv., same as לֹא *not*; הֲמִבְּלִי אֵין *is it not because there is not?* מִבְּלִי אֲשֶׁר לֹא *excepting that not*, Ecc. 3:11; עַד בְּלִי *until the ceasing of*, Mal. 3:10; עַל בְּלִי *because not*, Gen. 31:20.

בְּלִימָה (compounded of בְּלִי and מָה), *nothing*, Job 26:7.

בְּלִיַּעַל (compounded of בְּלִי and יַעַל).—I. *uselessness.*— II. *wickedness, sin;* אִישׁ בּ׳ *a wicked man.*—III. *injury, destruction;* נַחֲלֵי בּ׳ *destructive torrents,* i.e. overwhelming oppressions, Ps. 18:5.

בַּלְעֲדֵי and בִּלְעֲדֵי (compounded of בַּל and עֲדִי).—I. *besides, without.*—II. *not concerning, nothing to;* בִּלְעֲדָי *nothing to me;* מִבַּלְעֲדֵי *the same.*

בֵּלֶת *consumption;* used only with the parag. jod, בִּלְתִּי.—I. *without.* —II. *besides, except.*—III. *adv., not;* with suff. בִּלְתִּי *besides me,* בִּלְתֶּךָ *besides thee;* לְבִלְתִּי *not, that it may not,* with a verb; מִבַּלְתִּי with inf., *because it is not;* עַד־בִּלְתִּי *until it is not.*

בָּלָה Pi. בִּלָּה same as בָּהַל, *harassing,* Ezr. 4:4.

בַּלָּהָה f.—I. *terror.*—II. *calamity.*

בִּלְהָה p. n.—I. of the handmaid of Rachel.—II. of a town in the tribe of Simeon.

בִּלְהָן p. n. of a man.

בְּלוֹאִים ,בְּלֹו; see בָּלָה.

בֵּלְטְשַׁאצַּר p. n., Chaldee name of Daniel.

בְּלִי ,בְּלִימָה ,בְּלִיַּעַל; see בָּלָה.

בָּלַל (fut. יָבֹל).—I. *suffused,* Ps. 92:3. —II. *confounded,* const. with בְּ. Hith. *become confounded,* Hos. 7: 8, with בְּ.—III. from בְּלִיל; *gave fodder,* Jud. 19:21.— IV. *fade, wither,* Isa. 64:5.

בְּלִיל m., *fodder for cattle,* lit. *mixture.*

תֶּבֶל m., *unnatural intercourse,* Lev. 18:23, 20:12.

תְּבַלֻּל m., *a disease in the eye,* Lev. 21:20; תּ׳ בְּעֵינוֹ *confused* (i. e. indistinct for vision) *in his eye.*

בָּלַם *bound, bridled,* Ps. 32:8.

בָּלַס *pluck figs,* Am. 7:14.

בָּלַע I. *swallowed.* — II. *destroyed;* עַד־בִּלְעִי רֻקִּי *until I have swallowed my spittle;* i. e. in a moment, Job 7:19. Niph. *be swallowed up, lost;* with מִן הַיַּיִן *immersed in wine,* Isa. 28:7. Pi. as Kal; (כְּבַלַּע *as in a moment*). Pu. *was swallowed up.* Hith. as Niph., Ps. 107:27.

בֶּלַע m.—I. *swallowing up.*—II. *destruction;* with suff. בִּלְעוֹ.—III. p.n. of a town on the Dead Sea.—IV. of a man; בַּלְעִי m., *inhabitant of Bela.*

בְּלָה. see בִּלְעֲדֵי ,בַּלְעֲדֵי *besides.*

בִּלְעָם (*stranger*).—I. p.n. of the prophet Balaam.—II. same as יִבְלְעָם.

בָּלַק *make waste,* Isa. 24:1. Pu. part. f. מְבֻלָּקָה *desolate,* Nah. 2:11.

בָּלָק p.n. of a king of Moab.

בֵּלְאשַׁצַּר and בֵּלְשַׁאצַּר p.n. of the last king of the Chaldees (Nabonnedus or Labynetus).

בִּלְשָׁן p.n of a man.

בִּלְתִּי *not;* see בֵּלֶת under בָּלָה.

בָּמָה f. (pl. בָּמוֹת, const. בָּמֳתֵי [בָּמֳתֵי] Kri] with suff. בָּמוֹתֶיךָ [בָּמֹתֵי].— I. *high place for idolatrous worship;* רָכַב עַל בָּמֳתֵי אָרֶץ *he rode upon the high places of the earth,* i.e. he conquered. — II. *places for true worship.*—III. *fortresses, places of strength;* דָּרַךְ עַל בּ׳ *he rode upon the high places,* i. e. he subdued.—IV. *waves of the sea*, Job 9:8.—V. *clouds*, Isa. 14:14. בָּתֵּי הַבָּמוֹת same as בָּמוֹת *idol temples*; כֹּהֲנֵי הַבָּמוֹת *idolatrous priests*.

בָּמוֹת and בַּעַל בָּמוֹת p. n. of a town in Moab on the Arnon.

בְּמִהָל (*son of circumcision*), p.n. of a m.

בְּמוֹ same as בְּ; see מוֹ, מָה.

בָּמֹתֵי pl. const. from בָּמָה.

בָּנָה בָּנָה (inf. בְּנֹה; const. בְּנוֹת; fut. יִבְנֶה, וַיִּבֶן).—I. *built*, really.—II. *built*, metaphorically, i. e. raised, increased in family; const. with בְּ, עַל, לְ אֶת־הָהָר בּ *he built upon the hill*, 1 Ki. 16:24; בַּיִת לְ בּ *he raised up a house to*.—Niph. I. *was built*.—II. *was raised up*, as a house, family.

בְּנָא, בְּנָה Ch., *built*. Ithp. *was built*.

בֵּן m. (const. בֶּן, sometimes בָּן; with suff. בְּנוֹ, בְּנִי, בִּנְךָ; pl. בָּנִים).—I. *son*; בְּנֵי בָנִים *grandsons, posterity*; בְּנֵי עַמּוֹן *Ammonites*; אִישׁ מִבְּנֵי יִשְׂרָאֵל *an Israelite*; בְּנֵי צִיּוֹן *inhabitants of Zion*; בְּנֵי נְבִיאִים *sons*, i.e. *disciples of the prophets*.—II. used metaphorically; בֶּן־עַוְלָה *son of perverseness*, i. e. perverse person; בֶּן־מָוֶת *son of death*, i.e. a person guilty of a capital crime; בֶּן־קֶשֶׁת *son of the bow*, i.e. arrow, Job 41:20.—III. used with numerals; בֶּן־שְׁמוֹנִים שָׁנָה *one eighty years old, octogenarian*; בֶּן־שָׁנָה *yearling*.—IV. *the young of brutes*; בֶּן־יוֹנָה *young dove*.—V. *young shoots of trees*; בֶּן־פֹּרָת *twig of a fruit tree*.

בֵּן p. n. of a Levite, 1 Chron. 15:18.

בֵּן m. Ch., *son*; pl. בְּנִין, בְּנַיָּא.

בֶּן־אוֹנִי (*son of my sorrow*), p.n. given to Benjamin by his mother.

בֶּן־הֲדַד p.n. of the kings of Damascus.

בִּנּוּי p. n. of a man.

בֶּן־חַיִל (*strong*), p.n. of a man.

בֶּן־חָנָן (*son of mercy*), p.n. of a man.

בָּנִי (*built up*), p.n. of a man.

בֻּנִּי (*built up*), p. n. of two men.

בְּנֵי בְרַק p. n. of a town in the tribe of Dan.

בְּנֵי יַעֲקָן p.n. of a place.

בִּנְיָה f., *building*, Eze.41:13.

בְּנָיָה (*built up of God*), p.n. of a man.

בְּנָיָהוּ the same.

בִּנְיָמִין (*son of my right hand*), p. n., Benjamin, the son of Jacob; and אִישׁ־יְמִינִי, בֶּן־הַיְמִינִי, בֶּן־יְמִינִי *a Benjamite*; pl. בְּנֵי יְמִינִי; אֶרֶץ־יְמִינִי *land of the Benjamites*.

בֶּן־יָמִין I. same as בִּנְיָמִין.—II. p. n. of a man, 1 Sa. 9:1.

בִּנְיָן m., *building*, Eze. 40:5.

בְּנֵינוּ (*our son*), p.n. of a man.

בָּאנוּ for בָּנוּ Kal pret. pl. 1. pers., from בּוֹא.

בְּנֹתֶךָ for בְּנוֹתֵךְ Kal inf. with suff., from בנה.

בַּת f. (with suff. בִּתִּי; pl. בָּנוֹת; const. בְּנוֹת).—I. *daughter*.—II. *niece*.—III. the female inhabitants of any place; בְּנוֹת צִיּוֹן *the daughters of Zion*, Isa. 3:17; בְּנוֹת יִשְׂרָאֵל *daughters of Israel*.—IV. used for the inhabitants of any place collectively; בַּת צֹר *the Tyrians*, Ps. 45:12; בַּת מִצְרַיִם *the Egyptians*.—V. בְּנוֹת הָעִיר *smaller cities*

dependent upon larger ones.—VI.
used with numerals in the age of
women: בַּת תִּשְׁעִים שָׁנָה *a woman
of ninety* (see בֶּן III.).—VII. used
metaph.: בְּנוֹת הַשִּׁיר *daughters of
song*, i.e. singers; בַּת עַיִן *pupil of
the eye* (see בֶּן II.).—VIII. applied
to the produce of animals, trees, or
places; בַּת הַיַּעֲנָה *female ostrich, &c.*

בַּת f. Ch., the same; pl. בַּתִּין.

בַּת־רַבִּים (*daughter of multitudes*),
p. n. of the gate of Heshbon.

בַּת־שֶׁבַע (*daughter of an oath*), p. n.
of the wife of Uriah.

בַּת־שׁוּעַ the same.

מִבְנֶה m., *building*, Eze. 40:2.

תַּבְנִית f.—I. *model*, πρωτότυπον.—II.
form, resemblance.—III. *building.*

בָּנַט, Pers. *bando*; Sansc. *bandha*;
Eng. *band.*

אַבְנֵט m., *a girdle* (a foreign word).

בְּנַס Ch., *was angry*, Dan. 2:12.

בִּנְעָא, בִּנְעָה p. n. of a man.

בְּסוֹדְיָה (*in the council of the Lord*),
p. n. of a man.

בְּסַי p. n. of a man.

בֹּסֶר root not used; (Arab. *unripe date*).

בֶּסֶר m., *unripe, sour grape*, Job 15:33.

בֹּסֶר m., the same.

בְּעָא; see בעה.

בְּעַד root not used; (Arab. *after*).

בְּעַד prep., *after, behind*, as to time
or place; with suff.בַּעֲדִי and בַּעֲדִי,
בַּעֲדֵינוּ, בַּעֲדֵנוּ ,בַּעֲדוֹ, בַּעֲדֵךְ and
בַּעֲדְכֶם; מִבַּעַד לְ *behind*, Cant.
4:1, &c.

בָּעָה I. *pressed forward, ran over*, Isa.
64:1.—II. *requested, importuned*;

fut. pl. תִּבְעָיוּן; imp. pl. בְּעָיוּ. Niph.
—I. *become obtruded, swelled out*,
Isa. 30:13.—II. *being sought*, Obad.
v. 6.

בְּעָה and בְּעָא Ch., *requested, prayed*,
with מִן and מִן קֳדָם.

בָּעוּ f. Ch., *petition*, Dan. 6:8, 14.

בֶּעִי m., *prayer*, Job 30:24.

בְּעוֹן *habitation*; same as מְעוֹן.

בְּעוֹר p. n. of the father of Balaam.

בֹּעַז p. n.—I. the husband of Ruth.—
II. name of one of the pillars in
Solomon's temple.

בָּעַט I. *trample upon, kick at:* hence,
—II. *despise, reject.*

בְּעִי *building*; see בָּעָה.

בְּעָיוּ Kal imper. pl. with pause, from
בעה.

בְּעִיר *beast*; see בער.

בָּעַל I. *possess, govern.*—II. *marry a
wife*; part. pl. majest. בְּעָלַיִךְ *thy
husband*; בְּעֻלָה and בַּעֲלַת־בַּעַל
married. — III. (with בְּ) *despised*,
Jer. 3:14; 31:32. Niph. *be married*

בַּעַל m. (suff. בַּעֲלִי, בַּעֲלָהּ, בַּעֲלֵיהֶם)
—I. *lord.*—II. *husband.*—III. *owner,
possessor*, that wherein any one
excels; בַּ' הַחֲלֹמוֹת *dreamer*; בַּעֲלֵי
שְׁכֶם *the Shechemites, &c.*; pl.
בְּעָלִים (const. בַּעֲלֵי; with suff. בְּעָלָיו,
בְּעָלֶיהָ) often used of one only.—
IV. הַבַּעַל p. n., *Baal*, name of a
Phenician god; הַבְּעָלִים *statues of
Baal.*—V. p. n. of a man.—VI.
compounded in the names of many
towns: בַּעַל גָּד a town on the
borders of Palestine, to the north;
בַּ' הָמוֹן at the foot of Lebanon; בַּ'
חָצוֹר in the tribe of Ephraim;

חֶרְמוֹן בּ׳ one of the peaks of Mount Hermon; a town near it; בֵּת מָעוֹן and בּ׳ מְעוֹן in the tribe of Reuben; בּ׳ פְּרָצִים (*place of slaughter*) where the Philistines were routed by David; בּ׳ צְפוֹן in Egypt; בּ׳ שָׁלִשָׁה in Mount Ephraim; בּ׳ תָּמָר (*place of palms*) not far from Gibeah; בַּעֲלֵי יְהוּדָה Jews.

בְּעֵל m. Ch., *lord.*

בַּעֲלָה f.—I. *lady.*—II. used collectively (like בַּת) *a city.*—III. p. n. of a city in the north of Judah; otherwise קִרְיַת־בַּעַל and יְעָרִים.—IV. another city in Judah; otherwise בָּלָה and בִּלְהָה.

בַּעֲלַת p. n. of a city in the tribe of Dan.

בַּעֲלוֹת p. n. of a city in the tribe of Judah.

בְּעֶלְיָדָע (*whom Baal knows*), same as אֶלְיָדָע

בְּעַלְיָה (*in whom the Lord rules*), p. n. of a man.

בַּעַל־חָנָן (*the Lord of grace*), p. n. of a king of Edom.

בַּעֲלִים p. n. of a king of the Ammonites.

בַּעֲנָא (*son of misery*), p. n. of a man.

בַּעֲנָה (the same), p. n. of a man.

בָּעַר *injure, consume.*—I. *by fire.*—II. *with anger.*—III. *burn.*—IV. *that which injures, is brutish* (from בְּעִיר); part. בֹּעֲרִים *cattle, beasts.* Niph. *become brutish.* Pi. בֵּעֵר.—I. *injured, destroyed.*—II. *consumed with fire;* with בְּ, מִן and אַחֲרֵי. Pu. part. f. מְבֹעֶרֶת *burnt.* Hiph. same as Pi.

בְּעִיר m.—I. *beast, cattle generally.*—II. *beast of burden.*

בַּעַר m., *stupid, brutish.*

בְּעֵרָה f., *burning,* Ex. 22:5.

בְּעֵרָא p. n. of a man.

תַּבְעֵרָה p.n. of a place in the desert.

בַּעֲשֵׂיָה (*work of God*), p.n. of a man.

בַּעְשָׁא p. n. of a king of Israel, son of Ahijah.

עַשְׁתֹּרֶת an idol; see בַּעֲשְׁתְּרָה.

בָּעַת. Niph. נִבְעַת *was terrified.* Pi. בִּעֵת.—I. *alarmed.*—II. *excited, came suddenly upon;* fut. יְבַעֵת; part. f. with suff. מְבַעִתֶּךָ.

בְּעָתָה f., *terror,* Jer. 8:15; 14:19.

בְּעוּתִים m. pl., *terrors,* Ps. 88:17.

בֹּץ בָּצָה *mud;* see בצץ.

בְּצֹאתָו for בְּצֹוֹתָיו pl. with suff. from בצץ or בָּצָה.

בְּצִי (same as בֶּסִי), p. n. of a man.

בָּצִיר *vintage;* see בצר.

בָּצָל m., *onion,* Nu. 11:5.

בַּצְלִית, בַּצְלוּת p.n. of a man.

בָּצַע I. *cut off parts, pieces.*—II. *acquire gain.* Pi. בִּצַּע I. *cutting off* (as the weaver his web from the loom): hence,—II. *finish, complete.*—III. *acquired filthy lucre,* Eze. 22:12.

בֶּצַע m. (with suff. בִּצְעָם).—I. *gain.*—II. *filthy lucre;* מַה־בֶּצַע *what gain?*

בָּצֵן root not used; (Arab. *run slowly*).

בֹּץ m., *mud, mire,* Jer. 38:22.

בָּצָה f., the same; pl. with suff. בְּצֹאתָו for בְּצֹוֹתָיו.

בָּצֵק *swelled* (of the foot), Deu. 8:11, Neh. 9:21.

בָּצֵק m., *dough* (from its swelling in fermenting).

בָּצְקַת p. n. of a town in the tribe of Judah.

בָּצַר I. *cut, cropped off*: hence,—II. *pruned the vine.*—III. *gathered the vintage*, Ps. 76:13; part. בֹּצֵר *vintage-gatherer*; trop. *remorseless enemy*; part. בָּצוּר *inaccessible*, lit. *cut off from access*; בְּצֻרוֹת *hidden, incomprehensible*, Jer. 33:3. Niph. *cut off, prohibited*, with מִן. Pi. *fortified* (of cities).

בָּצִיר m., *vintage*; adj., same as בָּצוּר *fortified*, Zec. 11:2.

בֶּצֶר m., *gold*; perhaps *wealth*, Job 36:19.

בֶּצֶר m.—I. the same, Job 22:24, 25. —II. p. n. of a city in the tribe of Reuben.—III. p. n. of a man.

בָּצְרָה f.—I. *fold for cattle*, Mic. 2: 12.—II. p. n. of a city of Edom, Βόστρα.—III. of a city of Moab.

בִּצָּרוֹן m., *fortified place*, Zec. 9:12.

בַּצֹּרֶת f., and pl. בַּצָּרוֹת *withholding of rain, drought*, Jer. 14:1; 17:8.

מִבְצָר m.—I. *fortification*; עִיר מ׳ *fortified town*; pl. מִבְצָרִים and מִבְצָרוֹת—II. p. n. of a chief of the Edomites.

בְּקִי, בַּקְבּוּק, &c.; see בקק.

בָּקַע with בְּ.—I. *cut, cleft, divided.*— II. *laid open*, i. e. subdued, took (of fortified places).—III. *let go* (as young birds from eggs, or water from a dam).—Niph. I. *became cleft, destroyed.*—II. *laid open, subdued.*—III. *let go* (as young birds or water). Pi. *same*

as Kal. Pu. pass. of Pi. Hiph. I. *cause to be subdued*—II. *sent forth*, with אֶל. Hoph. *was broken up*, Jer. 39:2. Hith. as Niph. I., Jos. 9:13, Mic. 1:4.

בָּקִיעַ m., *fissure*, Isa. 22:9, Am. 6:11.

בֶּקַע m. (*cutting*), half a shekel, Gen. 24:22, Ex. 38:26.

בִּקְעָה f., *valley, plain*; pl. בְּקָעוֹת; בִּקְעַת הַלְּבָנוֹן *valley of Lebanon*, between Anti-Libanus and Hermon, κοιλή ἡ Συρία, Cœle-Syria, Jos. 11:37, 12:7; בִּקְעַת אָוֶן, see אָוֶן.

בָּקַק I. *threw, cast off, out* (as fruit from a tree); with אֶת־עֵצָה *I will cast off* (*deprive of*) *counsel*, Jer. 19:7.—II. *make empty, void*, Isa. 24:1. Niph. נָבַק (inf. הִבּוֹק, fut. יִבּוֹק) *become void*, Isa. 19:3; 24:3. Pi. fut. יְבַקְקוּ *make empty, void*, Jer. 51:2.

בַּקְבּוּק I. *bottle, narrow-necked vase*; the word expresses the sound of a fluid issuing from it.—II. p. n. of a man.

בַּקְבֻּקְיָה p. n. of a man.

בַּקְבַּקַּר p. n. of a man.

בֻּקִּי p. n. of a man.

בֻּקִּיָּהוּ p. n. of a man.

בָּקַר *cut, laid open*; not in use: hence, Pi.—I. *look, inquire after.*—II. *observe.*—III. *care for*, with לְ and בֵּין...לְ.

בַּקַּר Pa. Ch., *inquired*. Ithpa. *was sought*.

בַּקָּרָה f., *inquiring after, seeking*, Ezr. 34:12.

בִּקֹּרֶת f., *observation, chastisement*, Lev. 19:20.

בָּקָר (from the plough which *cleaves* the earth).—I. *oxen* used in ploughing, Job. 1:14.—II. *oxen* generally; עֲלוֹת ב' *milch cows*; בֶּן בָּקָר *steer*; seldom pl. בְּקָרִים *oxen*.

בּוֹקֵר m., *herdsman*, Am. 7:14.

בֹּקֶר m. (pl. בְּקָרִים).—I. *dawn, morning*; לַבֹּקֶר ,בַּבֹּקֶר ,בֹּקֶר *in the morning*; לַבְּקָרִים ,בַּבֹּקֶר בַּבֹּקֶר *every morning*; עַד הַבֹּקֶר *to-morrow morning.* — II. לַבֹּקֶר *early, soon*, Ps. 49:15, &c.

בָּקַשׁ. Pi. בִּקֵּשׁ *sought, sought out, after* or *into*, with עַל ,מִן ,לְ or אֶל *according to the sense*; ב' אֶת־יְהוָֹה or אֶת־פְּנֵי יְהוָֹה *he sought the Lord*; ב' נֶפֶשׁ פ' *the soul, life of any one, to injure destroy it*; ב' דָּם פ'...*his blood.*

בַּקָּשָׁה f., *petition*, Est. 5:3; 7:3, Ezr. 7:6.

בַּר ,בֹּר ,ברר *son*, &c.; see ברא and ברר.

בָּרָא (inf. בְּרֹא; with suff. בָּרַאֲךָ; imp. בְּרָא; fut. יִבְרָא).—I. *created, formed, made.*—II. same as בָּרָה *he ate.* Niph. *was created, born, produced.* Pi. בֵּרֵא — I. *cut*, as with a sword or axe.—II. *make, form.* Hiph. הִבְרִיא *fatten*, 1 Sa. 2:29.

בְּרִיאָה f., *a wonderful, new thing.*

בַּר m., *son*; with suff. בְּרִי; another meaning, see in ברר.

בַּר m. Ch.—I. *son.*—II. *grandson*; with suff. בְּרֵהּ.

בְּרָאיָה (*created of God*), p. n. of a m.

בְּלַאדַךְ; see מְרֹאדַךְ.

בַּרְבֻּרִים *fed beasts*; see ברר.

בָּרַד *hailed*, Isa. 32:19.

בָּרָד m., *hail.*

בָּרֹד m. (pl. בְּרֻדִּים), *spotted*, "grisled," Eng. Ver.

בֶּרֶד p.n.—I. of a place in the wilderness of Shur.—II. of a man.

בָּרָה I. *ate.*—II. same as בָּרַר *chose.* Pi. inf. בָּרוֹת *eating.* Hiph. *give food.*

בָּרִיא m., בְּרִיאָה f., *fat*; see another meaning above.

בְּרִי m., בְּרִיָה f., *fat*, Eze. 34:20.

בִּרְיָה f., *food*, 2 Sa. 13:5, 7, 10.

בָּרוּת f. *food*, Ps. 69:22.

בְּרִית f.—I. *any agreement*; בַּעֲלֵי ב' *united in covenant*, Gen. 14:13.—II. the covenant made by God with the patriarchs, and ratified in the person of Jesus Christ.—III. the sign of that covenant (circumcision), Gen. 17:13; מַלְאַךְ הַבְּרִית μεσίτης, *the angel of the covenant, Messiah*; בַּעַל בְּרִית a name of Baal.

בָּרוּךְ *blessed*; see ברך.

בְּרוֹמִים *costly clothing*; see ברם.

בְּרוֹשׁ m.—I. *fir-tree*; עֲצֵי בְרוֹשִׁים *instruments of fir-wood*, 2 Sa. 6:5.—II. *staves of lances made of fir-wood*, Nah. 2:4.

בְּרוֹת m. the same, Cant. 1:17.

בֵּרוֹתַי ,בְרוֹתָה p. n. of a city in Syria of Zobah.

בָּרוֹת *eating*; see ברה.

בִּרְזִית p. n. of a woman.

בַּרְזֶל m. (with suff. בַּרְזִלּוֹ).—I. *iron.* —II. *hard as iron.*—III. *instrument of iron.*

בַּרְזִלַּי p. n. of a man.

בָּרַח (fut. יִבְרַח; part. m. בֹּרֵחַ,f.בֹּרַחַת).—I. *pass on.*— II. *fly*, with מִן,

בְּרַח לְךָ ;אַחֲרֵי ,מִפְּנֵי ,מֵאַת ;imper. flee away.—IV. pass through, Ex. 36:33. Hiph. made to pass, fly.

בָּרִחַ ,בָּרַח m.—I. a fugitive.—II. p. n. of a man.

בְּרִיחַ m.—I. transverse bar.—II. bars or bolts for fastening the gates of a city; בְּרִיחֶהָ, Isa. 15:6, "her fugitives" as above, not "her princes" i. e. bars, defences.

מִבְרָח m., fugitive, Eze. 40:2.

בְּרִי ,בָּרִיא ,בְּרִיָה; see ברה.

בְּרִי (same as בְּאֵרִי my well), p. n. of a man.

בְּרִיאָה; see ברא.

בְּרִיעָה p. n. of a man.

בְּרִית covenant; see ברה.

בֹּרִית soap; see ברר.

בֶּרֶךְ f., knee; dual בִּרְכַּיִם both knees.
בְּרַךְ ,בֶּרֶךְ f. Ch., the same.

בָּרַךְ (fut. יְבָרֵךְ; inf. abs. בָּרוֹךְ).—I. knelt.—II. worshipped, blessed; בָּרוּךְ יְהֹוָה and בָּרוּךְ לַיהֹוָה blessed of the Lord; בָּרוּךְ יְהֹוָה blessed be the Lord. Niph. be blessed. Pi. בֵּרַךְ ,בֵּרֵךְ pronounced, made, blessed, with בְּשֵׁם יְהֹוָה ,לְ. Pu. בֹּרַךְ be or become blessed. Hiph. הִבְרִיךְ made kneel down, Gen. 24: 11. Hith. הִתְבָּרֵךְ be made blessed, Gen. 22:18, &c.; account oneself blessed, Deu. 29:18, &c.

בְּרַךְ Ch., knelt. Pa. blessed.

בָּרוּךְ p. n. of the friend of Jeremiah.

בֶּרֶכְאֵל (blessed of God), p.n. of a man.

בְּרָכָה f. (בֶּרֶכָה Gen. 27:38; const. בִּרְכַּת; pl. בְּרָכוֹת, const. בִּרְכוֹת).—I. blessing, ascription of praise to God.—II. the same received

from God.—III. favour, pr. —IV. p. n. of a man.

בְּרֵכָה f., pool, fish-pond.

בֶּרֶכְיָה and בֶּרֶכְיָהוּ (blessed of the Lord), p.n. of a man.

אַבְרֵךְ; see in its place.

אַרְכּוּבָה f. Ch., knee.

בָּרַם Ch. pa. of confirmation, but.

בָּרַם root not used; (Arab. garment adorned with gems).

בְּרוֹמִים m. pl., costly raiment, Eze. 27:24.

לִבְרֹם ,בָּרֹם Kal inf. with pref. and suff., from ברר.

בִּרְנֵעַ (fountain of delight), p. n. of a place in the wilderness, written קָדֵשׁ־בַּ, which see.

בֶּרַע p.n. of a king of Sodom.

בִּרְעָה p. n. of a man.

בָּרַק lightened, Ps. 144:6.

בָּרָק m. (pl. בְּרָקִים).—I. lightning.—II. glitter of a sword.—III. p. n. of the captain who defeated the Canaanites, Jud. 4:6, &c.

בָּרֶקֶת f., carbuncle.

בַּרְקָנִים m. pl., threshing waggons, having sharp iron teeth, Jud. 8: 7,16.

בַּרְקוֹס p. n. of a man.

בָּרַר I. examined, tested, Ecc. 3:18.— II. separated, selected, chose, Eze. 20:38, with מִן and לְ; part. בָּרוּר pure, chaste. Niph. נָבַר became pure; part. נָבָר pure Pi. purify, Dan. 11:35. Hiph. make clean, polish. Hith. become, appear pure.

בַּר m., בָּרָה f.—I. beloved, Cant. 6:9. — II. pure, clean.—III. empty, void, Pro. 14:4.

בַּר, בַּר m.—I. *corn*, purified from the chaff.—II. *growing corn;* see another meaning in בֹרא.

בַּר m., *field, open plain*, Job 39:4.

בַּר m. Ch., the same.

בֹּר m.—I. *pureness.*—II. same as בְּרִית.

בֹּרִית f., *soap*, Jer. 2:22, Mal. 3:2.

בַּרְבֻּרִים m., *stalled cattle*, 1 Ki. 5:3.

בִּרְשַׁע p. n. of king of Gomorrah.

בְּשׂוֹרָה, בְּשׂוֹר *good news;* see בשׂר.

בֶּשֶׂם m. (Anyrum opobalsamum), *the balsam tree*, an aromatic shrub.

בֶּשֶׂם and בֹּשֶׂם m. (pl. בְּשָׂמִים).—I. *the odour of perfumes.*—II. *the perfumes themselves.*

בָּשְׂמַת I. p. n. of the wife of Isaiah. —II. of the daughter of Solomon.

מִבְשָׂם p. n. of a man.

בָּשַׂר Pi. בִּשֵּׂר I. *announce, declare.* —II. *tell glad tidings.* Hith. *was, became informed,* 2 Sa. 18:31.

בְּשׂוֹרָה and בְּשׂרָה f.—I. *good tidings,* 2 Sa. 18:22, 27.—II. *the reward of good tidings,* 2 Sa. 4:10.

בְּשׂוֹר p. n. of a river near Gaza.

בָּשָׂר m.—I. *flesh.*—II. *body.*—III. כָּל־בָּשָׂר *all living creatures.*—IV. עַצְמִי וּבְשָׂרִי *my bone and flesh, kinsman;* also בְּשָׂר *kinsman,* Lev. 15:2, &c.—V. *secret parts* (male).

בְּשַׂר m. Ch.—I. *flesh.*—II. *mankind.*

בָּשַׁל I. *ripened*, Joel 4:13.—II. *boiled, cooked*, Eze. 24:5. Pi. *boiled, cooked;* part. pl. מְבַשְּׁלִים *cooked*, Eze. 46:24. Pu. *was cooked.* Hiph. *matured, ripened*, Gen. 40:10.

בָּשֵׁל m., בְּשֵׁלָה f., *cooked.*

מְבַשְּׁלוֹת f. pl., *boilers*, Eze. 46:23.

בִּשְׁלָמִי, בִּשְׁלָמִי; see שֶׁל in אֲשֶׁר.

בִּשְׁלָם p. n. of a man.

בָּשָׁן p.n., *Batanea*, the region beyond Jordan, between Hermon and the brook of Jabbok.

בָּשְׁנָה *shame;* see בּוּשׁ.

בָּשַׁס. Po. בּוֹשֵׁס same as בּוֹסֵס *trampling on, injuring*, Am. 5:11.

בֹּשֶׁת *shame;* see בּוּשׁ.

בַּת *daughter;* see בנה.

בַּת *measure;* see בתת.

בָּתָה and בַּתָּה; see בתת.

בְּתוּאֵל p.n.—I. of the father of Laban. —II. same as בָּתוּל name of a place.

בְּתַיָּה p. n. of a man.

בָּתִּים *houses;* see בַּיִת, בּוּת.

בָּתַל root not used; (Arab. *separated*).

בְּתוּלָה f. (pl. בְּתוּלוֹת, בְּתֻלוֹת).—I. *a virgin.*—II. used for *nation, city, people*, like בַּת, which see.

בְּתוּלִים m. pl., *tokens of virginity.*

בָּתַק. Pi. בִּתֵּק *cut, pierce*, Eze. 16:40.

בָּתַר. Pi. בִּתֵּר *dissect, cut in two*, Gen. 15:10.

בֶּתֶר m. (with suff. בִּתְרוֹ).—I. *part, piece.*—II. *separation*, Cant. 2:17.

בָּתַר Ch., same as בָּאתַר *after;* see אָתַר.

בִּתְרוֹן p.n. of a place on Jordan.

בָּתַת root not used; (Arab. *cut, cleft*).

בַּת m. (f. Isa. 5:10), *Bath;* a liquid measure, the tenth part of a Homer.

בַּת m. Ch., the same.

בַּתָּה f., *desolation, excision*, Isa. 5:6.

בַּתָּה f. (pl. בְּתּוֹת), Isa. 7:19, *clefts, fissures.*

ג

גָּאָה (fut. יִגְאֶה).—I. *grew high* (as a plant), Job 8:11; (as water,) Ezr. 47:5.— II. *becoming lofty, powerful, proud.*

גֵּא m., *proud*, Isa. 16:6.

גֵּאֶה m.—I. *elevated.*—II. *proud, arrogant;* pl. גֵּאִים.

גַּאֲוָה f., *pride, arrogance*, Pro. 8:13.

גַּאֲוָה f.—I. *excellency, majesty.*—II. *pride, arrogance.*

גְּאוּאֵל (*the divine majesty*), p. n. of a man.

גָּאוֹן m.—I. *excellency, glory.*—II. *pride;* pl. גְּאוֹנִים.

גֵּאוּת f.—I. *ascent*, Isa. 9:17.—II. *sublimity, excellency.*—III. *pride, arrogance.*

גַּאֲיוֹן m., *proud*, Ps. 123:4.

גֵּוָה f. (for גַּאֲוָה).—I. *elevation, victory*, Job 22:29.—II. *pride*, Job 33:17.

גֵּוָה f. Ch., the same, Dan. 4:34.

גֵּאָיוֹת *valleys;* see גֵּוָה.

גָּאַל (fut. יִגְאַל).—I. *redeem by paying value for.*—II. *retribute, avenge.*—III. *pollute;* part. גֹּאֵל *redeemer, avenger, relative,* to whom the duty of avenging the death of any one was assigned; part. pass. גְּאוּלִי, גְּאוּלִים *redeemed, set at liberty.* Niph. נִגְאַל, נִגְאַל *was redeemed, liberated, polluted.* Pi. גֵּאַל *polluted*, Mal. 1:7. Pu. *was polluted.* Hiph. אֶגְאָלְתִּי *contaminate*, Isa. 63:1. Hiph. *polluted himself*, Dan. 1:8.

גֹּאֵל m., *pollution;* pl. const. גָּאֳלֵי, Neh. 13:29.

גְּאֻלָּה f.—I. *relationship.*—II. *right, duty of redemption.*—III. *price of redemption.*—IV. *thing redeemed.*

מֹגְאָל m., *next of kin after the Goel.*

גֹּב *locust;* see גּוּב.

גָּבָא root not used; (Arab. *gathered together*).

גֶּבֶא m., *cistern, pit.*

גָּבַב root not used.

גַּב m. (with suff. גַּבִּי; pl. גַּבִּים, גַּבּוֹת).—I. *back.*—II. *defence, mound.*—III. *vaults.*—IV. *arch of the eyebrow*, Lev. 14:9; גַּב מָגֵן *the boss of a shield*, Job 15:26.

גַּב m. Ch., *back.*

גֹּב m. Ch., *well;* emph. גֻּבָּא.

גּוֹב m., *locust;* pl. גּוֹבַי.

גֵּב m. (pl. גֵּבִים), *locusts.*

גָּבַהּ (fut. יִגְבַּהּ; inf. גָּבְהָה).—I. *was high, lofty,* with עַל; when with מִן *was higher than.*—II. *exalted;* גָּבַהּ לִבּוֹ *his heart was lifted up;* or merely גָּבַהּ *lifted up.* Hiph. *raise, exalt.*

גָּבֹהַּ m. (const. גְּבֹהַּ; f. גְּבֹהָה).—I. *high, tall.*—II. *haughty, proud.* Subst. *height*, 1 Sa. 16:7.

גָּבֹהַּ; const. גְּבֹהַּ m.—I. *high.*—II. *arrogant, proud.*

גֹּבַהּ m. (with suff. גָּבְהוֹ; pl. const. גָּבְהֵי).—I. *height.*—II. *majesty*, Job 40:10.—III. *arrogance;* גֹּבַהּ אַף *insolence*, Ps. 10:4.

גַּבְהוּת m., *pride*, Isa. 2:11, 17.

גְּבוּלָה, גְּבוּל *border;* see נבל.

גְּבוּרָה, גִּבּוֹר *mighty;* see גבר.

גִּבֵּחַ m., *bald*, Lev. 13:41.

גַּבַּחַת f.—I. *baldness.*—II. *loss of knap* (in cloth), Lev. 13:55.

גַּבַּי p. n. of a man.

גֵּבִים (see גֵּב), p. n. of a place not far from Jerusalem.

גְּבִינָה cheese; see נבן.

גָּבִיעַ cup; see נבע.

גְּבִירָה‎, גְּבִיר master; see נבר.

גְּבִישׁ; see נבש.

גָּבַל limited; with בְּ and אֶת. Hiph. set bounds to.

גְּבָל p.n. of a Phenician city; גִּבְלִי an inhabitant of Gebal.

גְּבָל p. n. of a mountainous district beyond Jordan, Ps. 83:8.

גְּבוּל‎, גְּבֻל m.—I. limit, boundary.— II. space or country limited.

גְּבֻלָה‎, גְּבוּלָה f.,pl. גְּבוּלוֹת boundaries, lands.

גַּבְלוּת f., artificial work, device, Ex. 28:22; 37:15.

מִגְבָּלָה f. (pl. מִגְבָּלוֹת), the same, Ex. 28:14.

גָּבַן root not used; (Syr. curdled).

גְּבִינָה f., cheese, 2 Sa. 16:2.

גִּבֵּן m., hunchback, Lev. 21:20.

גַּבְנֻנִּים m. pl., risings, mounds; הַר גּ‎ a hill of mounds, i. e. made up of other hills.

גָּבִיעַ m. (with suff. גְּבִיעִי; pl. גְּבִיעִים). —I. a cup or vase.—II. flower, the calix of an artificial flower.

גֶּבַע p. n. of a town in the tribe of Benjamin.

גֻּבְעָא p. n. of a man.

גִּבְעָה f., a hill; pl. גְּבָעוֹת.

גִּבְעַת אֱלֹהִים p.n. of a place.

גִּבְעַת בְּנֵי בִנְיָמִין p.n. of a city in the tribe of Benjamin.

גִּבְעַת פִּינְחָס p. n. of a city.

גִּבְעַת שָׁאוּל p. n. of a hill.

גִּבְעָתִי inhabitant of Gibeah.

גִּבְעוֹן p.n. of a city in the tribe of Benjamin.

מִגְבָּעָה f. (pl. מִגְבָּעוֹת), the mitre or bonnet of the priests.

גִּבְעֹל flowering (of flax), Ex. 9:31

גָּבַר and גָּבֵר (fut. יִגְבַּר).—I. was powerful, mighty.—II. conquered, (prevailed), with מִן or עַל. Pi. made strong. Hiph.—I. was powerful, Ps. 12:5.— II. confirm, Dan. 9:27. Hith. became powerful, victorious.

גֶּבֶר m.—I. man, husband, hero; pl. גְּבָרִים; לִגְבָרִים manfully.—II. p. n. of a man, 1 Ki. 4:19.

גְּבַר m., Ch. the same; pl. גֻּבְרִין.

גֶּבֶר m. (same as Ch.), man, Ps.18:26.

גְּבִיר m., lord, Gen. 27:29, 37.

גְּבִירָה f., lady, queen.

גְּבֶרֶת f. (with suff. גְּבִרְתִּי), the same.

גִּבּוֹר‎, גִּבֹּר m.—I. mighty, brave.—II. renowned; גִּבּוֹר חַיִל renowned for wealth, rich.

גִּבָּר m. Ch.—I. brave, strong, heroic. —II.p.n.same as גִּבְעוֹן, Ezr.2:20.

גְּבוּרָה f.—I. power.—II. courage.— III.acts of courage, power; גְּבוּרוֹת יְהֹוָה acts of God, i.e. miracles.

גְּבוּרָה f. Ch. the same.

גַּבְרִיאֵל p.n. of an archangel.

גָּבַשׁ root not used; (Arab. congelation).

גָּבִישׁ m., crystal (lit. ice), Job 28:18.

גִּבְּתוֹן p. n. of a town of the Philistines in the tribe of Dan.

גָּג m. (with suff. גַּגּוֹ; pl. גַּגּוֹת).—I. roof of a house.—II. covering, grate of the altar.

גַּד‎, גַּד; see נדד.

גִּזְבְּרִין m. pl. Ch., *treasures*, Dan. 3: 2,3; same as גִּזְבָּר.

גְּדֵרָה p. n. of a place in the Arabian desert.

גָּדַד *assault, attack* (as an army). Hith. הִתְגֹּדֵד I. *cutting, making incisions.*—II. *attacking, assembling to attack.*

גְּדַד Ch., *cut down* (of a tree), Dan. 4:11,20.

גְּדוּד m. (pl. גְּדוּדִים, גְּדֻדוֹת).—I. *cutting*, Jer. 48:37.—II. *furrow*, Ps. 65:11.—III. *section, detachment of an army.*

גַּד m., *coriander seed*, Ex. 16:31, Nu. 11:7.

גַּד m., *good fortune;* בְּגַד *prosperously*, Gen. 30:11.

גַּד nom., p. n. of an idol, Isa. 65:11.

גַּד p. n. *Gad.*—I. one of the sons of Jacob.—II. the tribe descended from him; גָּדִי *a Gadite.*

גַּדִּי p. n. of a man, Nu. 13:11.

גַּדִּיאֵל p. n. of a man.

גָּדָה root not used; (Syr. *leaping*).

גְּדִי m., *a kid;* pl. גְּדָיִים; const. גְּדָיֵי.

גְּדִיָּה f., pl. גְּדִיּוֹת *female kids*, Cant. 1:8.

גָּדָה f., const. pl. גְּדוֹת *banks of a river.*

גְּדוּד, גְּדִי; see נדד.

גָּדוֹל, גְּדוּלָה, גְּדִילִים *great*; see גדל.

גְּדוּף, גְּדוּפָה *reproach;* see נדף.

גְּדִי, גְּדִיָּה; see גדה.

גָּדִישׁ *heap*; see נדש.

גָּדַל and גָּדֵל (fut. יִגְדַּל), *was or grew great* (in anything), with עַד, מִן, לְ, בְּ, אֶת. Pi. I. גִּדֵּל *made* or *pronounced great:* hence,

—II. *trained, educated.* Hiph. I. *became great.*—II. *made great, high;* הִגְדִּיל אֶת פִּיו *he spake insolently.* Hith. *showed himself great.*

גָּדֵל m., pl. const. גְּדֻלֵי, *great ones,* Eze. 16:26.

גָּדוֹל m. (const. גְּדוֹל and גְּדָל; f. גְּדוֹלָה (גְּדֹלָה), *great* (in anything); גְּדוֹלִים *nobles;* גְּדָל חָסֶד *great in mercy;* עוֹד הַיּוֹם גָּדוֹל *it is yet high day,* i. e. early, Gen. 29:7; pl. גְּדוֹלוֹת *great* (i. e. proud) *things*, Ps. 12:4.

גֹּדֶל m. (with suff. גָּדְלוֹ, גָּדְלוֹ), *greatness, magnificence, pride.*

גְּדֻלָּה, גְּדוֹלָה f.—I. *great* (act or deed). —II. *greatness;* pl. גְּדֻלוֹת *great things.*

גְּדִילִים m. pl., *platted chain-work*, 1 Ki. 7:17.

גִּדֵּל p. n. of a man.

גְּדַלְיָהוּ, גְּדַלְיָה *Gedaliah,* p. n. of a man.

גְּדַלְתִּי p. n. of a man, 1 Ch. 25:4, 29.

מִגְדָּל (pl. מִגְדָּלִים, מִגְדָּלוֹת).—I. *tower, castle.*—II. *pulpit,* Neh. 8:4.—III. artificial *mound,* in a garden covered with sweet flowers, Cant. 5:13.

מִגְדּוֹל, מִגְדֹּל p. n. of a city in Egypt.

מִגְדַּל־אֵל p. n. of a fortress in the tribe of Naphtali.

מִגְדַּל־גָּד p. n. of a place in the tribe of Judah.

מִגְדַּל עֵדֶר p. n. of a place near Bethlehem.

גָּדַע I. *cut off* or *down.*—II. *broke.* Niph. *became cut off, down.* Pi. *broke.* Pu. *was cut down,* Isa. 9:9.

גִּדְעָם p. n. of a place in the tribe of Benjamin.

גִּדְעוֹן p. n. of a judge of Israel.

גִּדְעֹנִי p. n. of a man.

גָּדַף. Pi. גִּדֵּף blasphemed.

גִּדּוּף m., pl. גִּדּוּפִים, גִּדּוּפוֹת reproaches, Isa. 43:28; 51:7.

גְּדוּפָה f., reproach, Zep. 2:8.

גָּדַר walled, fenced up; part. גֹּדֵר fencer.

גָּדֵר com. (const. גְּדֶר; with suff. גְּדֵרוֹ; pl. גְּדֵרִים).—I. wall, fence. —II. fenced place.

גְּדֵרָה f.—I. wall.—II. fence, hurdle.— III. same as בֵּית גָּדֵר p.n. of a town in the tribe of Judah; גְּדֵרָתִי a Gederite.—IV. גְּדֵרוֹת and גְּדֵרוֹתַיִם p.n. of places in the tribe of Judah.

גְּדֶרֶת f., a fence, Eze. 42:12.

גֶּדֶר p.n. of a city of the Canaanites.

גְּדֹר p.n. of a town in the tribe of Judah.

גְּדֵרִי an inhabitant of בֵּית גָּדֵר.

גָּדַשׁ root not used; Ch. heaped up.

גָּדִישׁ m.—I. sepulchral mound.—II. heap of corn.

גֵּה for זֶה, Eze. 47:13.

גָּהָה raise up, Hos. 5:12.

גֵּהָה f., relief, healing, Pro. 17:22.

גָּהַר bowed, bent downwards.

גּוֹ, גֵּו, גַּו; see נוה.

גּוּב cut, cleft; part. גֹּבִים ploughers.

גֵּב m.—I. board, plank.—II. well; see another meaning in גֵּבָה.

גּוֹב (cistern), p.n. of a place; see another meaning in גֵּבָה.

גּוֹג p.n. of the king of Magog; see מָגוֹג.

גּוּד, יְגוּדֶנּוּ, see גָּדַד; shall rush upon him, Gen. 49:19; Hab. 3:16.

גָּוָה root not used.

גּוֹ, גַּו, גּוֹא m. Ch., middle.

גַּו m. Ch.—I. middle; with suff. גַּוֵּהּ. —II. Heb. back; with suff. גַּוִּי.

גַּו m.—I. back.—II. middle; with suff. גַּוִּי.

גֵּוָה f., a body, Job 20:25; see another meaning under גַּאֲוָה.

גְּוִיָּה f.—I. body, person.—II. dead body, carcase of men or animals.

גּוֹי m. (with suff. גּוֹיִי; pl. גּוֹיִם, גּוֹיֵי, with suff. גּוֹיֵךְ, גּוֹיֵהֶם).—I. generally people, Israelites as well as foreigners.—II. specially, foreign nations.—III. multitudes of locusts, Joel 1:6; of animals, Zep. 2:14.

גַּיְא com. (const. גֵּיא; pl. גֵּיאוֹת), valley.

גֵּיא, גֵּא the same.

גַּי m. (const. גֵּי), the same.

גֵּאָיוֹת f. pl., valleys.

גּוּז pass over, Ps. 90:10; fut. apoc. וַיָּגָז, Nu. 11:31.

גּוֹזָל young bird; see נזל.

גּוֹזָן p.n., a district in North Mesopotamia, between the rivers Chaboras and Saocoras, the Γαυζανῖτις of Ptolemy.

גּוּחַ break forth; see גִּיחַ.

גְּוִיָּה, גּוֹי; see גוה.

גּוּל rejoice; see גִּיל.

גּוֹלָן, גּוֹלָה; see גלה.

גּוּמָץ pit; see נמץ.

גּוּנִי p.n. of a man.

גָּוַע (fut. יִגְוַע; inf. גֹּוֵעַ; const. גְּוַע and גֹּוֵעַ), expire, die.

גּוּף Kal, root not used; (Arab. shut up). Hiph. fut. pl. יָגִיפוּ let (them) shut, Neh. 7:3.

גּוּפָה f., dead body; (Arab. the same).

גּוּר I. sojourned, dwelt, with בְּ, עִם.

אֵת; part. גָּר dwelling with; גָּרַת בֵּיתָהּ her inmate.—II. avoided, feared, with מִן and מִפְּנֵי.—III. congregated, come together, with עַל; see גָּרָה. Hith. הִתְגּוֹרֵר—I. withdraw.—II. dwell, 1 Ki. 17:20.—III. violent destroying, Jer. 30:23.

גֵּר (גֵּיר, 2. Ch. 2:16), m., sojourner, stranger.

גֵּרוּת f., sojourning, residing, Jer. 41:17.

גּוּר m.—I. lion's whelp; גּוּר אַרְיֵה, Gen. 49:9, &c.—II. jackall, 2 Sa. 4:3.

גֹּר m. the same; f. pl. גֹּרוֹת.

גּוּר בַּעַל (dwelling of Baal), p. n. of a town in Arabia.

מָגוּר m.—I. sojourning.—II. residence, habitation.—III. human life; sojourn on earth.

מָגוֹר m., fear, terror; pl. מְגוּרִים.

מְגוֹרָה f., fear; pl. מְגוֹרוֹת.

מְגוּרָה f.—I. granary.—II. fear, terror; pl. מְגוּרוֹת.

מַמְּגֻרָה f. (pl. מַמְּגֻרוֹת), granaries, Joel 1:17.

גּוֹרָל lot; see גרל.

גּוּשׁ m., clod, Job 7:5.

גֵּישָׁן p. n. of a man.

גֵּז fleece; see נזז.

גִּזְבָּר treasurer, Ezr. 1:8; pl. גִּזְבָּרִין, Ezr. 7:21, and גְּדָבְרִין, Dan.3:2,3.

גָּזָה (Arab. bring forth); part. גּוֹזִי, lit. "he who brought me forth," Ps. 71:6.

גָּזִית f.—I.lit. cutting, hewing: hence,—II. hewn stones.

גָּזַז (fut. יָגֹז; inf. גֹּז and גְּזֹז).—I. shear, cut off hair, wool, &c.; part. גּוֹזְזִים

shavers.—II. drive away (of quails), Nu. 11:31. Niph. pret. pl. נָגֹזּוּ were cut off.

גֵּז m. (pl. const. גִּזֵּי).—I. shearing of sheep: hence,—II. the fleece.—III. young grass after mowing.

גִּזָּה f., fleece, Jud. 6:39, 40.

גָּזֵז (barber), p. n. of a man.

גָּזַל I. cut off.—II. snatch away, injure. Niph. was taken away, Pro. 4:16.

גָּזֵל m., const. גֵּזֶל rapine, plunder.

גְּזֵלָה f., the same.

גּוֹזָל m., young pigeon, Gen. 15:9; Deu. 32:11.

גָּזַם root not used; (Arab. destruction).

גָּזָם m., a species of locust.

גִּזָּם p.n. of a man.

גִּזּוֹנִי m., an inhabitant of Gizon.

גָּזַע root not used; (Arab. cutting off)

גֶּזַע m. (with suff. גִּזְעָם), stock; trunk of a tree.

גָּזַר I. cut off, down.—II. in two parts divided. — III. decided, as judgment. Niph. was cut off, with מִן; was decided, Est. 2:1.

גְּזַר Ch., decided, determined the fate of others by astrology; part. pl. גָּזְרִים soothsayers.

גֶּזֶר I. division, section; pl. גְּזָרִים.—II. p. n. of a city on the western frontier of the tribe of Ephraim, Γάζηρα.

גְּזֵרָה (גְּזֵירָה) f., place cut off, separated, Lev. 16:22.

גְּזֵרָה f. Ch., decision. Dan. 4:14,21.

גִּזְרָה f.—I. cut, polish (of precious stones), Lam. 4:7.—II. insulated, separated (of a certain enclosure of the temple), Eze. 41:42.

מַגְזֵרָה f., *axe*, 2 Sa. 12:31.

גִּזְרִי inhabitant of *Gezer*.

גָּחוֹן *belly*; see גחן.

גֵּיחֲזִי ,גֵּחֲזִי p. n. of a servant of the prophet Elisha.

גָּחַל root not used; (Arab. *to burn*).

גֶּחָל m. (pl. גֶּחָלִים ,גַּחֲלֵי).—I. *burning coals.*—II. *thunderbolts.*

גַּחֶלֶת f., *the same*; with suff. גַּחַלְתִּי.
גַּחַם p. n. of a man.

גָּחַן root not used; Ch. גְּחַן *bowed down.*

גָּחוֹן m., *belly of a serpent*, Lev. 11:42; with suff. גְּחֹנְךָ, Gen. 3:14.

גֵּי ,גַּיְא ,גֵּיא ,גַּי; see גוה.
גַּחַר p. n. of a man.

גִּיד m., *sinew, nerve.*

גִּיחַ and גּוּחַ (fut. יָגִיחַ; part. גָּח).—
I. *drew out.* — II. *extended, elongated.* Hiph. *drew out.*

גִּיחַ or גּוּחַ Ch. Aph. *rushed forth.*

גִּיחַ p. n. of a place near Gibeon, 2 Sa. 2:24.

גִּיחוֹן I. p. n. of a river of Paradise, Gen. 2:13.—II. of an aqueduct near Jerusalem; otherwise שִׁלֹחַ.

גִּיל and גּוּל (fut. יָגִיל) *leap, exult, rejoice*, with בְּ, עַל, לְמַעַן.

גִּיל m., *exultation, rejoicing.*

גִּיל m. Ch., *equal in age, rank, &c.*, Dan. 1:10.

גִּילָה f., *exultation.*

גִּילֹנִי; see גלה in נלה.

גִּינַת; see גנן.

גִּיר (גִּר) m., *burnt lime-stone*, Isa. 27:9.

גִּיר m. Ch., *plaster of lime*, Dan. 5:5.

גֵּיר *stranger*, same as גֵּר; see גור.

גֵּישׁ *clod*, same as גּוּשׁ.

גֵּישָׁן p. n. of a man.

גָּל for גֹּל Kal imper. from גָּלַל Ps. 119: 12. Pi. imper. apoc. from גָּלָה, Ps. 119:18.

גְּלָא Ch., *reveal*; see נלה.

גָּלַב root not used; (Arab. *drew, shaved*).
גַּלָּב m., *barber*, Eze. 5:1.

גִּלְבֹּעַ p. n., *Gilboa*, hills in the tribe of Issachar.

גֻּלְגֹּלֶת ,גֻּלְגַּל ,גַּלְגַּל; see גלל.

גֶּלֶד m., *skin*; with suff. גִּלְדִּי *my skin*, Job 16:15.

גֻּלָּה *bowl*; see גלל.

גָּלָה (fut. יִגֶל ,יַגְלֶה; inf. גָּלֹה ,גָּלוֹת).—
I. *laid bare, disclosed, opened.*—II. *depopulated a country*, i. e. *led into captivity, migrated*; part. m. גּוֹלֶה, f. גּוֹלָה *migrated, gone into captivity*; גָּלוּי *opened, proclaimed, published* (of an edict). Niph. נִגְלָה (fut. יִגָּל ,יִגָּלֶה; inf. abs. נִגְלֹה, נִגְלוֹת).—I. *was uncovered, exposed, revealed.*— II. *migrated, went into captivity*, Isa. 38:12; part. f. pl. נִגְלֹת *revealed*, Deu. 29:29. Pi. גִּלָּה (fut. יְגַל ,יְגַלֶּה).—I. *uncovered, made naked.*— II. *had carnal connexion with*, with אֶל and עַל. Pu. גֻּלָּה *was uncovered*; part. f. מְגֻלָּה *openly said.* Hiph. הִגְלָה ,הֶגְלָה *led captive* (fut. וַיֶּגֶל ,וַיַּגְלֶה). Hoph. הָגְלָה *was made captive.* Hithp. הִתְגַּלָּה *made himself naked*; fut. apoc. וַיִּתְגַּל, Gen. 9:21.

גְּלָא Ch., *revealed.* Piel גַּלִּי ,גַּלָּא *revealed.* Aph. הַגְלִי *carried captive*, Ezr. 4:10, 12.

גָּלָה p. n. of a city in the mountains

of Judah; its inhabitants were styled גִּילֹנִי.

גּוֹלָה, גֹּלָה f.—I. *captivity.*—II. *captive, troop of captives.*

גּוֹלָן p.n. of a city of Batanea, Γαυλών.

גֹּלָת, גֹּלֶת f., *captive;* as גּוֹלָה.

גָּלוּת f. Ch., the same.

גִּלָּיוֹן m., *tablet, book,* Isa. 8:1; pl. גִּלְיוֹנִים *mirrors,* Isa. 3:23. Writing tablets and mirrors were both, in ancient times, plates of metal.

גָּלְיָת p. n., *Goliath,* the giant whom David slew.

גַּלִּים, גְּלִלָה, גָּלִיל, גַּלְגַּלִּים; see גלל.

גֹּלוּם; see גלם.

גָּלַח. Pi. גִּלַּח—I. *shaved head* or *beard.* II. *devastated by war,* Isa. 7:20. Pu. *was shaven,* Ju. 16:17, 22; Jer. 41:5. Hithp. *shave himself.*

גִּלֹּה p.n. of a city.

גָּלְיָת, גִּלְיוֹן; see גלה.

גָּלַל (sing. p. 1. גַּלּוֹתִי, pl. גַּלְלוּ; inf. גֹּל, גּוֹל; imp. גַּל, גֹּל).—I. *roll* (as a stone).—II. with מֵעַל *roll away,* used metaphorically of things morally heavy. — III. with אֶל עַל, גּוֹל עַל יְיָ *commit to,* lit. *roll upon;* גֹּל אֶל דַּרְכֶּךָ *commit thy way unto the Lord,* Ps. 37:5. Niph. נָגֹל *were rolled up,* Isa. 34:4; *rolled away,* Am. 5:24. Pil. גִּלְגֵּל *roll off,* Jer. 51:25. Hithpal. *roll, rush in violently,* Job 30:14. Hiph. הֵגֵל *roll,* Gen. 29:10. Po. גּוֹלֵל *roll about in,* Isa. 9:4. Hithpo. הִתְגּוֹלֵל *rolled in, weltered in,* 2 Sa. 20:12.—II. *fall upon,* with עַל, Gen. 43:18.

גָּלָל m.—I. *dung.*—II. בִּגְלַל *because, for the sake of;* בִּגְלָלְךָ *for thy sake.*—III. p. n. of a man.

גְּלָל m. Ch., *great, heavy,* (of stones).

גֵּל m. (with suff. גֶּלְלוֹ; pl. גְּלָלִים; const. גֶּלְלֵי) *dung.*

גַּלָּל p.n. of a man.

גִּלּוּלִים m. pl., *idols.*

גָּלִיל m.—I. *that which can be turned on hinges,* 1 Ki. 6:34.—II. *ring,* Cant. 5:14.—III. *circuit, tract of country;* הַגָּלִילָה and הַגָּלִיל p.n. of a region in the tribe of Naphtali, *Galilee.*

גְּלִילָה f. *circuit, region.*

גַּל m. (pl. גַּלִּים).—I. *a heap* (of stones, &c.).—II. *spring, fountain.*—III. pl. *waves, breakers.*

גַּלִּים p.n. of a town in the tribe of Benjamin; 1 Sa. c. 25; Jos. c. 10.

גֹּל m., *oil jar,* Zec. 4:2.

גֻּלָּה f.—I. same as גַּל (pl. גֻּלּוֹת) *well,* Jos. 15:10; Jud. 1:15.—II. const. גֻּלַּת *oil jar* or *vessel.*—III. vase-like ornaments, or flowers on the capitals of columns.

גַּלְגַּל m.—I. *wheel;* pl. גַּלְגַּלִּים.—II. *whirlwind.*—III. *chaff* (as driven by the wind).

גַּלְגַּל m. Ch., *wheel,* Dan. 7:9.

גִּלְגָּל m.—I. *cart wheel,* Isa. 28:28.—II. p. n. of a city between Jericho and Jordan.

גֻּלְגֹּלֶת f.—I. *skull.*—II. used in numbering men, as we say, *head of cattle;* with suff. גֻּלְגָּלְתּוֹ; pl. with suff. גֻּלְגְּלֹתָם.

מְגִלָּה f., *volume, roll, book.*

מְגִלָּה f. Ch., the same.

גָּלַם *wrapped together* (as a mantle), 2 Ki. 2:8.

גְּלוֹם m., *cloak, mantle,* Eze. 27:24.

גֹּלֶם m., embryo, fœtus, Ps. 139:16.

גַּלְמוּד m., hard, barren, fruitless.

גָּלַע. Hithp. הִתְגַּלַּע intermeddle, be impudent.

גִּלְעָד I. p.n., Gilead, the son of Machir, grandson of Manasseh: hence,—II. p.n. of a hill and town near Lebanon.—III. of a region beyond Jordan ; גִּלְעָדִי a Gileadite.

גַּלְעֵד (heap of witness), p. n. of the heap of stones erected by Laban and Jacob, Gen. 31:47, 48.

גָּלַשׁ "appear," Cant. 4:1; 6:5, Eng. Ver.; meaning uncertain.

גֵם; see גמם.

גָּמָא Pi. drink in, Job 29:24. Hiph. give to drink, Gen. 24:17.

גֹּמֶא m., the paper reed; תֵּבַת גֹּמֶא an ark of reeds, and כְּלֵי גֹ' a boat of reeds.

גֶּמֶר m., pruning knife, short-sword, Ju. 3:16.

גְּמָדִים m. pl., short-swordsmen, Eze. 27:11.

גִּמְזוֹ p.n. of a town in the tribe of Judah.

גָּמַל (fut. יִגְמֹל).—I. recompense, repay, with לְ and עַל.—II. mature, ripen.—III. wean as a child. Niph. was weaned.

גְּמוּל recompence, retribution, either of good or bad actions.

גְּמוּל p. n. of a man.

גְּמוּלָה f., recompence, retribution.

גַּמְלִיאֵל (God my restorer), p.n. of a man.

תַּגְמוּל m., retribution, kindness, Ps. 116:12.

גָּמָל com., camel; pl. גְּמַלִּים.

גְּמַלִּי p. n. of a man.

גָּמַם (Arab. filled up, desired).

גַּם moreover, also; הֲגַם is it not also? גַּם...גַּם and...also; גַּם כִּי but if, although.

מְגַמָּה f., desire, object, Hab. 1:9.

גֶּמֶץ (Syr. a well).

גּוּמָץ m., a well or pit, Ecc. 10:8.

גָּמַר (fut. יִגְמֹר).—I. bring to pass.—II. finish, fail.

גְּמַר Ch., complete, learned, Eze. 7:12.

גְּמַרְיָה and גְּמַרְיָהוּ p.n. of a man.

גֹּמֶר p.n.—I. of a northern race of people, perhaps the Cymri.—II. of the wife of Hosea.

גַּן garden; see גנן.

גָּנַב he stole, with or without violence; with לֵב, Gen. 31:20, 26, 27, "stole away unawares." Niph. stolen. Pi. secretly; Ex. 22:11. Pu. steals, was stolen. Hith. stole themselves away.

גַּנָּב m., a thief.

גְּנֵבָה f., stolen thing, Ex. 22:2, 3.

גְּנֻבַת p.n. of a man.

גַּנָּה ,גִּנָּה; see גנן.

גָּנַז root not used; (Arab. covered).

גֶּנֶז m., pl. גְּנָזִים; const. גִּנְזֵי treasures.

גֶּנֶז or גְּנַז m. Ch., pl. גִּנְזִין treasures.

גִּנְזַךְ m., treasury, 2 Ch. 28:11.

גָּנַן guard, protect, with עַל, אֶל. Hiph. the same.

גַּן com. (with suff. גַּנִּי, pl. גַּנִּים) a garden.

גַּנָּה f., a garden ; pl. גַּנּוֹת.

גִּנָּה f., the same.

גִּינַת p. n. of a man.

גִּנְּתוֹי, גִּנְּתוֹן p. n. of a man.

מָגֵן m. (suff. מָגִנִּי, pl. מָגִנִּים) shield, fig., *God the protector*, Gen. 15:10; מָגִנֵּי־אָרֶץ *shields of the earth*, i.e. princes, Ps. 47:10., &c.

מְגִנָּה f., with לֵב *veiling, covering of heart*, Lam. 3:65.

גָּעָה *lowed* (as oxen), Job 6:5.

גֹּעָה p. n. of a place near Jerusalem.

גָּעַל *loathed, abhorred.* Niph. *was rejected, cast away*, 2 Sa. 1:21. Hiph. *cast* (brought forth prematurely), Job 21:10.

גֹּעַל m., *loathing*, Eze. 16:5.

גַּעַל p. n. of a man.

גָּעַר (fut. יִגְעַר) *rebuked, reproved*, with בְּ.

גְּעָרָה f., *chiding, reproof.*

מִגְעֶרֶת *rebuke, calamity*, Deu. 28:20.

גָּעַשׁ *shook, trembled*, Ps. 18:8. Pu. גֹּעַשׁ *was shaken*, Job 34:20. Hithp. *was moved.* Hithpo. the same, Jer. 25:16.

גַּעַשׁ p. n. of a mountain in the tribe of Ephraim.

גַּעַת Kal. inf. const. from נגע.

גַּעְתָּם p. n. of the son of Eliphaz.

גַּף *body*; see גפה.

גֶּפֶן com.—I. *climbing plant.*—II. *vine.*

גָּפַף root not used; (Arab. *troop of men*).

גַּף m.—I. *person, self*; בְּנַפּוֹ *with himself only*, i.e. *alone*, Ex. 21:3,4.—II. *back*, i.e. *hillock*, Pro. 9:3.

גַּף m. Ch., pl. גַּפִּין *wings.*

גֹּפֶר m., name of a tree; probably, *the pitch-pine*, Gen. 6:14.

גָּפְרִית f., *brimstone.*

גֻּר; see גּוּר and גָּרַר.

גֹּר, גֻּר; see גּוּר.

גֵּרָא (same as גֵּרָה), p. n. of a man.

גָּרַב root not used; like *scratch, scurf*, and many other words in all languages, an imitation of the noise made in *scratching*, &c.

גָּרָב m., *scurf, scurvy.*

גָּרֵב p. n. of one of David's generals.

נַגְרְנוֹת, וַרְגְּנַר; see גרר.

גִּרְגָּשִׁי p. n. of a nation of Canaanites.

גָּרַד Hithp.inf. הִתְגָּרֵד *scrape, scratch*, Job 2:8; see גָּרַב.

גָּרָה Pi. גֵּרָה *produce, kindle strife.* Hithp. *prepare to contend, contend with*; const. with בְּ.

תִּגְרָה f., *attack, stroke*, Ps. 39:11.

גָּרוֹן m., *throat*; see גרר.

גָּרוֹן, גֵּרָה; see גרר.

גֵּרוּת *sojourning*; see גּוּר.

גָּרַז same as גָּזַר. Niph. pret. נִגְרַזְתִּי *I am cut off*, Ps. 31:23; 88:6.

גַּרְזֶן m., *axe.*

גִּרְזִי (גִּרְזִי) p. n. of a nation of Canaanites.

הַר גְּרִזִים p n. of a mountain, *Gerizim.*

גָּרַל root not used; (Arab. *was gravelly, sandy*).

גּוֹרָל m. (pl. גּוֹרָלוֹת).—I. *lot*, lit. *the pebble* by which it was determined.—II. הִפִּיל, הִשְׁלִיךְ, יָדָה, יָרָה, נָתַן הַגּוֹרָל *determined by lot*; הָיָה לוֹ גוֹרָל, עָלָה עָלָיו גוֹרָל i.e. יָצָא *the lot fell.*—III. *the thing obtained by lot.*

גָּרָל (const. גְּרָל) Pro. 19:19; keri גָּדֹל *great.*

גֶּרֶם m. (pl. גְּרָמִים).—I. *bone.*—II. *powerful,* Gen.49:14.—III. *framework, pulpit,* 2 Ki. 9:13.

גֶּרֶם m. Ch., *bone.*

גָּרַם *cut, spoil,* Zep. 3:3. Pi. fut. יְגָרֵם *shall destroy.*

גַּרְמִי p. n. of a man.

גֹּרֶן root not used; (Arab. *place for drying dates*).

גֹּרֶן f. (pl. גְּרָנוֹת; const. גָּרְנוֹת).—I. *open place at the gate of a city, court of justice.*—II. *threshing-floor.*—III. *corn of the floor,* Job 39:12. גֹּרֶן הָאָטָד p. n. of a place beyond Jordan; see אָטָד.

גָּרַס *pained, overwhelmed,* Ps. 119:20. Hiph. fut. וַיַּגְרֵס *and brake, destroyed,* Lam. 3:16.

גֶּרֶשׂ m. (with suff. גִּרְשָׂהּ), *thrashed;* perhaps, *ground corn,* Lev. 2: 14,16.

גָּרַע I. *took away.*—II. *shaved, took away the beard,* Jer. 48:37. Niph. (fut. יִגָּרַע, יִגְרַע) *was taken away.* Pi. *draws off;* fut. יִגְרַע Job 36:27.

מִגְרָעוֹת f. pl., *ledges, steps in buildings,* 1 Ki. 6:6.

גָּרַף *swept away* (as a flood), Jud. 5:21. אֶגְרוֹף m., *fist.*

מְגְרָפָה f., *furrow,* Joel 1:17.

גָּרַר *he drew, dragged;* fut. יִגֹּר. Niph. fut. יִגֹּר *chew the cud.* Po. *sawed,* 1 Ki. 7:9. Hithpo. *swept away,* Jer. 30:23.

גֵּרָה f.—I. *the cud.*—II. *Gerah,* a weight equal to the twentieth part of a shekel.

גַּרְגַּר m., *berry,* Isa. 17:6.

גַּרְגְּרָה f., *throat, front of the neck.*

גָּרוֹן m. (const. גְּרוֹן), *throat.*

מְגֵרָה f., *saw.*

גְּרָר p. n. of a city of the Philistines.

גֶּרֶשׂ *flower;* see נרם.

גָּרַשׁ *put forth, cast forth.* Niph. *was cast, driven, out.* Pi. גֵּרֵשׁ *expel.* Pu. גֹּרַשׁ *was expelled.*

גֶּרֶשׁ m., *produce, fruit,* Deu. 33:14.

גְּרֻשָׁה *expulsion.*

מִגְרָשׁ m.—I. *suburbs.*—II. *pastures, open places.*—III. *lands,* surrounding the cities of the Levites; pl. מִגְרָשׁוֹת, מִגְרָשִׁים.

גֵּרְשֹׁם p. n. of the son of Moses.

גֵּרְשׁוֹן (Gershon), p. n. of a man; גֵּרְשֻׁנִּי a Gershonite.

גַּשׁ, גְּשָׁה, גֶּשׁ Kal imp., from נגשׁ. גְּשׁוּ Kal imp. pl., from נגשׁ.

גְּשׁוּר (bridge), p. n. of three places.— I. the country of the Canaanites to the east of Jordan.—II. of a district in South Palestine.—III. of a district in Syria. גְּשׁוּרִי a Geshurite.

גָּשַׁם Kal, root not used; (Arab. *fatness*). Hiph. part. pl. מַגְשִׁמִים *cause to rain,* Jer. 14:22.

גֶּשֶׁם m., *heavy shower;* pl. גְּשָׁמִים, גִּשְׁמֵי.

גֶּשֶׁם m., the same; with suff. גִּשְׁמָהּ.

גֶּשֶׁם m., *body.*

גֶּשֶׁם, גַּשְׁמוּ p. n. of a man.

גֹּשֶׁן (Goshen), p. n.—I. of the country bordering on Egypt, which was inhabited by the Israelites during the first captivity.—II. of a town in the tribe of Judah.

נִשְׁפָּא I. n. of a man.

גָּשַׁשׁ Pi. fut. with ה parag. נְגַשְׁשָׁה we feel, grope about, Isa. 59:10.

גֶּשֶׁת Kal inf. with suff. גִּשְׁתּוֹ, from נגש.

גַּת f.—I. the vat in which grapes were trodden; pl. גִּתּוֹת.—II. p. n. of a city of the Philistines in the country of Goliath. גַּת הַחֵפֶר p. n. of a town in the tribe of Zebulun; גַּת רִמּוֹן p. n. of cities of the Levites in Dan and Manasseh; גִּתִּי a Gittite.

גִּתַּיִם p. n. of a town in the tribe of Benjamin.

גִּתִּית f., probably the name of a musical instrument; occurs in the titles of certain psalms.

גֶּתֶר p. n. of a people of Syria, Gen. 10:23.

ד

דָּא pron. Ch. f. and neuter, this; דָּא לְדָא together.

דָּאַב same as דוּב was languid.
דְּאָבָה f., pining away, Job 41:14.
דְּאָבוֹן m., extreme languor, fainting; const. דַּאֲבוֹן, Deu. 28:65.

דָּאן fish, same as דָּג; see דָּנָה.

דָּאַג I. grieve, be anxious, with לְ.— II. fear, with מִן.

דֹּאָן (Syr. דֹּוָיֵן), p. n. of a prince of the Edomites.

דְּאָגָה f., anxiety, alarm.

דָּאָה flew; fut. יִדְאֶה. וַיֵּרָא.
דָּאָה f., name of a bird, kite, Lev. 11: 14; LXX. γὺψ; Vulg. milvus; corresponding passage, Deu. 14: 13, רָאָה.

דֹּאר p. n., same as דּוֹר.
דֹּב bear; see דבב.

דָּבָא root not used; (Arab. produced, multiplied).

דֹּבֶא riches, power; LXX. ἰσχύς, Deu. 33:25; with suff. דָּבְאֶךָ.

דָּבַב crept, flowed softly (of wine), Cant. 7:10.
דֹּב m. (pl. דֻּבִּים) a bear.
דֹּב m. Ch., the same.
דִּבָּה f.—I. calumny.—II. calumniator, Pro. 25:10.

דְּבוֹרָה bee; see דבר.

דְּבַח Ch., sacrificed, Ezr. 6:3; see זבח.
דְּבַח m. Ch., sacrifice, Ezr. 6:3.
מַדְבַּח m. Ch., altar, Ezr. 7:17.

דִּבְיוֹנִים m. pl., pigeons' dung, 2 Ki. 6:25.

דְּבִיר oracle; see דבר.

דָּבַל root not used; (Arab. pressed together).

דְּבֵלָה f. (const. דְּבֶלֶת; pl. דְּבֵלִים) παλάθη, cake of dry figs.

בֵּית דִּבְלָתַיִם, דִּבְלָה p. n. of a city of the Moabites.

דִּבְלַיִם p. n. of a man.

דָּבַק and דְּבֵק (fut. יִדְבַּק; inf. דִּבְקָה). —I. adhered, cleft to.—II. reached, attained, with אֶל, לְ, בְּ. Pu. fut. pl. יְדֻבָּקוּ made to adhere. Hiph. (fut. יַדְבִּיק, וַיַּדְבֵּק) joined, caused to stick, attained. Hoph. part. מֻדְבָּק stuck to, Ps. 22:16.

דְּבַק Ch., adhered, Dan. 2:43.
דָּבֵק m., adhering; pl. דְּבֵקִים.
דֶּבֶק m., solder, for joining metals pl. דְּבָקִים rivets (for armour).

דָּבַר not used in the pres. pret.; part. דֹּבֵר *speaking*; דָּבֻר *spoken*; inf. דָּבְרְךָ *thy speaking*. Piel דִּבֵּר, (fut. יְדַבֵּר) *he spoke, uttered words to* or *with any one*, with לְ, עַל, אֶת, עִם, בְּ; *concerning any one*, with בְּ, אֶל, עַל; *against any one*, with עַל, בְּ; *by any one*, with בְּיַד. דִּבֶּר בְּיַד used idiomatically; דִּבְּרִים לַעֲשׂוֹת *he threatened*; דִּ' דְּבָרִים *he uttered words*; דִּ', שָׁלוֹם, with אֵת or עִם *he spoke friendly with any one*; with בְּ the same; דִּ' לְאִשָּׁה *he asked her in marriage.* Pu. *was spoken.* Niph. *became,* i. e. *set about speaking,* with בְּ, עַל. Hiph. *subdued* (with his word); fut. וַיַּדְבֵּר. Hithp. part. מְדַבֵּר *speaking.*

דָּבָר m. (const. דְּבַר, pl. דְּבָרִים, דִּבְרֵי.)—I. *word*; בַּעַל דְּבָרִים אִישׁ *eloquent man.*—II. *thing.*—III. *thing, matter, subject in hand*; דְּבַר יוֹם בְּיוֹמוֹ *the thing* (duty) *of the day in its day*; אַחַר הַדְּבָרִים הָאֵלֶּה *after these things*, μετὰ ταῦτα: לֹא דָבָר *nothing*; אֵין דִּ' *there is nothing*; בְּעַל דִּ' *he who pleads a cause*; עַל דְּבַר and עַל דִּבְרֵי *because*; עַל דְּבַר אֲשֶׁר *because of.*

דֶּבֶר m., *pestilence*; pl. דְּבָרִים.

דְּבִיר m.—I. *the oracle*, i. e. the place in the temple whence responses were given.—II. p. n. of a city in the tribe of Judah.

דֹּבֶר m., *fold, pasture,* Mic. 2:12.

דִּבְרָה f., *cause for adjudication*; עַל דִּבְרַת *because*; with שֶׁ *because that*; עַל דִּבְרָתִי *according to,* after the order of, Ps. 110:4.

דִּבְרָה f. Ch., *cause.*

דְּבוֹרָה f.—I. *a bee*; pl. דְּבֹרִים.—II. p. n. of a woman who judged Israel.

דֹּבְרוֹת f. pl., *floats, rafts,* 1 Ki. 5:23.

דַּבְּרוֹת f. pl., *sayings,* Deu. 33:3.

מִדְבָּר m.—I. any large plain used for pasture.—II. *a desert* or *wilderness*; הַמִּדְבָּר *the desert of Sinai.*—III. *speech, address,* Cant. 4:3.

דְּבַשׁ m. (with suff. דִּבְשִׁי).—I. *honey* of bees.—II. *honey dew,*collected in large quantities in Palestine.

דַּבֶּשֶׁת f.—I. *the hunch,* or more probably, *the pack-saddle of a camel.*—II. p.n. of a place, Jos. 19:11.

דָּגָה *multiplied,* Gen. 48:16.

דָּג (דָּאג) m., *fish*; pl. דָּגִים, דְּגֵי const. דְּנַת f., *a fish, fish* in general.

דָּגוֹן m., p. n. of an idol of the Philistines, probably in the form of a fish.

דָּגָן (const. דְּגַן) m.—I.*bread.*—II. *corn.*

דָּגַל part. דָּגוּל—I. *marked, signalised,* Cant. 5:10.—II.fut. נִדְגֹּל *we will set up our banner,* Ps. 20:6. Niph. part. pl. נִדְגָּלוֹת *having banners,* i.e. *an army,* Cant. 6:4, 10; see next word.

דֶּגֶל m. (with suff. דִּגְלוֹ; pl. דְּגָלִים, דְּגָלַי), *standard, banner.*

דָּגָן com.; see דָּגָה.

דָּגַר *hatch, brood over eggs,* Isa. 34: 15; Jer. 17:11.

דַּד m., dual דַּדַּיִם, דַּדֵּי *the two breasts of a woman.*

דָּדָה. Hith. fut. אֶדַּדֶּה *I will proceed gently, submissively, joyfully.*

דְּדָן (pl. דְּדָנִים), p. n. of the inhabitants of a district in the north of Arabia.

דֹּדָנִים m. pl., p. n. of a people.

דְּהַב m. Ch., *gold.*

מַדְהֵבָה f., an epithet of Babylon, lit. *place of gold,* Isa. 14:4.

דֶּהָיֵא p. n. of a people who were colonised in Samaria, Ezr. 4:9.

דָּהַם. Niph. part. נִדְהָם *reduced, impotent,* Jer. 14:9.

דָּהַר, part. דֹּהֵר *charging, attacking,* Nah. 3:2.

דַּהֲרָה f., *charge of cavalry;* pl. דַּהֲרוֹת, Jud. 5:22.

תִּדְהָר m., name of a tree; Vulg. ulnus; *the elm or box.*

דּוֹב same as דֹּב *bear;* see דבב·

דּוּב same as דָּאַב *wasting.* Hiph. part. pl. מְדִיבוֹת *things wasting,* Lev. 26:16.

דּוּג and **דִּיג** (from דָּג) *he shall fish,* Jer. 16:16.

דַּיָּג, דַּוָּג m., *a fisher.*

דּוּנָה f., *fishing,* Am. 4:2.

דּוּד I. root not used; Ch. *was agitated.*—II. same as יָדַד *he loved.*

דּוּד m.—I. *a pot* or *caldron;* pl. דְּוָדִים·—II. *basket;* pl. דּוּדִים·

דּוּדָאִים m. pl.—I. *baskets.*—II. *mandrakes,* plants used as philtres or love potions.

דּוֹד m. (pl. דֹּדִים).—I. *love.*—II. *offices of love.*—III. *beloved.*—IV. *uncle.*

דּוֹדָה f., *aunt.*

דָּוִיד, דָּוִד p. n., *David* king of Israel.

דָּוָה I. *was sick.*—II. *was unclean, polluted;* inf. דְּוֹתָהּ *her uncleanness* (i. e. the menses), Lev. 12:2.

דָּוֶה m., דָּוָה f., *sick, unclean.*

דְּוַי m., *sickness, disease,* Ps. 40:4.

דַּוָּי m., *habitual* (chronic) *disorder.*

דְּוֹת inf. of דָּוָה, which see.

מַדְוֶה m., *consuming disease.*

דּוּחַ. Hiph. הֵדִיחַ I. *expel,* Jer. 51: 34.—II. *dispel,* i. e. scour clean.

דָּוִיד p.n., same as דָּוִד; see דּוּד·

דּוּךְ same as דָּכַךְ *beat, pounded,* Nu. 11:8.

מְדֹכָה f., *mortar,* Nu. 11:8.

דּוּכִיפַת f., LXX. ἔποψ; Vulg. upupa; *the hoopoe,* Lev. 11:19; Deu. 14:18.

דּוּם root not used, same as דָּמַם *was silent.*

דּוּמָה f.—I. *silent.*—II. *death.*—III. *the grave.*—IV. p. n. of a people of Arabia.

דּוּמִיָּה f.—I. *remaining, abiding.*—II. *quietness, silence.*

דּוּמָם m., *very quiet, silent.*

דּוּמֶשֶׂק p. n., same as דַּמֶּשֶׂק·

דּוֹן; see דּין·

דּוֹנַג, דּוֹנָג m., *wax.*

דּוּץ (fut. יָדוּץ) *leaps, exults,* Job 41:14.

דּוּק Ch., *grind small,* Dan. 2:35.

דָּיֵק m., *entrenchment, foss, dyke,* used in sieges.

דּוּר I. *dwell, reside,* Ps. 84:11.—II *encircle, place round,* Eze. 24:5.

דּוּר Ch., *dwell.*

דּוּר m.—I. *a circle*, Isa. 29:3.—II. *a ball*, Isa. 22:18.

דּוֹר, דֹּר m. (lit. *circle of years*).— I. *age, generation.*—II. *race of men;* עַד דֹּר, לְדֹר דֹּר, לְדֹר וָדֹר, דֹּר וָדֹר, מִדֹּר דֹּר *from generation to generation, for ever;* pl. דּוֹר *eternity;* דֹּרִים *generations of men, posterity.*—III. *habitation* (see דּוּר); with אָבוֹת *sepulchre,* Ps. 49:20.

דָּר m. Ch., *age, generation.*

דֹּאר, דֹּור and דֹ׳ נְפֹת p.n. of a city not far from Mount Carmel.

מְדוֹר m. Ch., *habitation.*

מְדֹר m. Ch., the same.

מְדוּרָה f., *pile of fire.*

בִּתְדִירָא f. Ch., *a revolution;* *continually,* Dan. 6:17, 21.

דּוּרָא p.n. of a valley or plain in Babylonia.

דּוּשׁ and דִּישׁ (fut. יָדוּשׁ).—I. *tread, trample on.*—II. *tread out corn.*— III. metaphorically, *conquer enemies.* Niph. נָדוֹשׁ *was trampled down;* inf. abs. הַדּוֹשׁ. Hoph. fut. יוּדַשׁ *is trodden,* Isa. 28:27.

דּוּשׁ Ch., *is trodden,* Dan. 7:23.

דִּישׁ m., *time of treading out corn,* Lev. 26:5.

מְדוּשָׁה f., with suff. מְדֻשָׁתִי *my treading out,* Isa. 21:10.

דְּוֹת see דָּוָה.

דָּחָה *drive, urge on to fall;* inf. abs. דָּחֹה; part. f. דְּחוּיָה *impelled.* Niph. *urged* or *impelled;* part. pl. נִדְחֵי, נִדְחִים. Pu. pl. דֹּחוּ *are driven.*

דְּחִי m. (with pause דֶּחִי), *impulse, being driven on.*

דַּחֲוָה Ch. f., pl. דַּחֲוָן Dan. 6:19. "instruments of music," Eng. Ver.; meaning uncertain.

מַדְחָה m., *driving out, ruin,* Prov. 26:28.

דָּחַח Niph. fut. pl. יִדָּחוּ, same as דָּחָה Niph., *is urged, impelled.*

דְּחַל Ch., part. דְּחִיל *fearful.* Pa. *affright,* Dan. 4:2.

דֹּחַן m., *millet,* Eze. 4:9.

דָּחַף, part. pl. דְּחוּפִים *hurried, hastened.* Niph. *was hurried.*

מַדְחֵפוֹת f. pl.; לִמְדָּחֵ *swiftly, hastily,* Ps. 140:12.

דָּחַק *press upon,* Joel 2:8; part. דֹּחֵק *oppressor,* Ju. 2:18.

דַּי m. (const. דֵּי, with suff. דַּיִּי), *a sufficiency, enough;* דֵּי הָשִׁיב *as much as shall restore,* Lev. 25:28; דַּיָּם *sufficient for them;* דֵּי חֲלָב *enough of milk,* Pro. 27:27; בְּדֵי same as בְּ; כְּדֵי *as (it were) enough;* מִדֵּי same as מִן; מִדֵּי שָׁנָה בְּשָׁנָה *from year to year, yearly.*

דִּי Ch.—I. the relative pron. *who, which, what,* like אֲשֶׁר.—II. *of,* like the *de* of the modern European languages. — III. conj. like אֲשֶׁר *that.*—IV. same as כִּי, ὅτι. כְּדִי *when, as;* מִן דִּי *from the time when;* עַד דִּי *until.*

דִּי זָהָב (*enough of gold*); p. n. of a place in the desert near Sinai, Deut. 1:1.

דִּיבוֹן p. n.—I. of a town of the Moabites.—II. of a place in the tribe of Judah; same as דִּימוֹנָה.

דַּיָּג, דַּיָּג *fishermen;* see דּוּג.

דָּיָה root not used; Ch. דְּהָא *was black.*

דִּיָּה f., *black vulture, turkey-buzzard;* LXX. ἰκτινος, Vulg. milvus, Deut. 14:13, &c.

דְּיוֹ m., *ink,* Jer. 36:18.

דִּימוֹן same as דִּיבוֹן p. n. of a town of Moab.

דִּימוֹנָה p. n. of a town in the tribe of Judah.

דִּין and דּוּן (pret. and part. דָּן; inf. and imper. דִּין; fut. יָדִין).—I. *judged.*—II. *pleaded, defended.*—III. *punished,* with בְּ.—IV. *contend with one,* with עִם.—V. *govern,* with בְּ. Niph. part. נָדוֹן *contend,* 2 Sa. 19:10.

דִּין and דּוּן Ch., the same.

דִּין (דּוּן Job 19:29.) m.—I. *judgment.*—II. *cause for judgment* (דָּן and דִּין עָשָׂה *he pleaded a cause*).—III. *litigation, strife.*

דִּין m. Ch.—I. *judgment.*—II. *court of judgment.*—III. *punishment.*

דִּינָה p. n. of the daughter of Jacob.

דִּינָיֵא Ch., p. n. of a people of Assyria.

דַּיָּן m., *a judge;* Ch. pl. דַּיָּנִין *judges.*

דָּן p. n., *Dan.*—I. a son of Jacob and his tribe.—II. a city in the north of Palestine.

דָּנִיֵּאל, דָּנִאֵל p. n., *Daniel.*

מָדוֹן m.—I. *dispute, contention;* pl. מְדָנִים, מִדְיָנִים.—II. אִישׁ מָדוֹן *man of height, stature* (see מִדָּה), 2 Sa. 21:20.—III. p. n. of a city of the Canaanites.

מָדָן m. (pl. מְדָנִים).—I. *strifes, disputes.*—II. p. n. of the son of Abraham and Keturah.

מְדָנִי (pl. מְדָנִים) *Midianite;* see מִדְיָנִים.

מְדִינָה f., lit. *jurisdiction:* hence,—I. *province.*—II. *region, country.*

מְדִינָה f. Ch., the same.

דִּיפַת p. n. of a son of Japhet, 1 Ch. 1:6, a wrong reading for רִיפַת, Gen. 10:3.

דָּיֵק *dyke;* see דּוּק.

דָּישׁ *tread;* see דּוּשׁ.

דִּישׁוֹן m.—I. a species of deer, Deut. 14:5.—II. p. n. of a son of Seir and of a district called after him.

דַּךְ *poor;* see דכך.

דֵּךְ Ch. pron., *this, he;* fem. דָּךְ *she.*

דָּכָא. Pi. דִּכָּא.—I. *beat small, break.*—II. *trample on.*—Pu. *was broken, contrite.* Hith. fut. יִדַּכְּאוּ *shall be broken.* Niph. part., *beaten, oppressed,* Isa. 57:15.

דַּכָּא m.—I. *crushed.*—II. *humbled, dejected.*

דָּכָה *is broken,* Ps. 10:10. Niph. *broken, afflicted.* Pi. דִּכִּיתָ *thou hast broken.*

דֳּכִי m., with suff. דָּכְיָם, *their beating, dashing,* Ps. 93:3.

דָּכַךְ root not used, same as דָּכָה and דּוּךְ.

דַּךְ (with pause דָּךְ m.), *poor, mean, afflicted,* Pro. 26:28; יִשְׁאָ דַּכְּיוֹ *makes hateful those whom it has afflicted.*

דַּכָּה f., *bruising,* θλάσις, Deu. 33:2.

דִּכֵּן Ch. pron., *this.*

דְּכַר Ch., same as זָכָר *male.*

דְּכַר m. Ch., *a ram;* pl. דִּכְרִין.

דִּכְרוֹן m. Ch. (emph. státe וְדִכְרוֹנָה), *memorial, record,* Ezr. 6:2.

דָּכְרָן m. Ch., the same, Ezr. 4:15.

דַּל *poor*; see דלה and דלל.

דָּלַג *leaping, skipping.* Pi. the same, with עַל.

דָּלָה I. *draw* (water from a well). Pi. *draw up out of prison*, Ps. 30:2. —II. *totter, vacillate, be lame*; דַּלְיוּ for דָּלְיוּ, Pro. 26:7.

דַּל m. for דֶּלֶת *door*, Ps. 141:3.

דֶּלֶת *gate, door*; dual דְּלָתַיִם, דַּלְתֵי *folding, double doors or gates*; דַּלְתֵי שָׁמַיִם *the doors of heaven* (clouds?); ד' פָּנִים *doors of the face* (jaws), Job 41:6; ד' בֶטֶן *doors of the womb*. Pl. דְּלָתוֹת; const. דַּלְתוֹת f. (m. Neh. 13:19). —I. *doors.*—II. *leaves, valves of gates.*—III. *leaves of a book*, Jer. 36:23.

דְּלִי m., *bucket*, Isa. 40:15.

דָּלְיִי m., dual דָּלְיַיִם (with suff. דָּלְיָו), *his drawings up* or *forth*, Nu. 24:7.

דָּלִית f., pl. דָּלִיּוֹת *boughs, branches.*

דְּלָיָהוּ, דְּלָיָה p. n. of a man.

דַּלָּה *poverty*; see דלל.

דָּלַח *disturb, render muddy* (of water), Eze. 32:2, 13.

דַּלְיוּ for דָּלְיוּ Pi. imp. pl., from דלה.

דָּלַל *wasted, reduced, weakened.* Niph. (fut. וַיִּדַּל) *is wasted, reduced.*

דַּל m. (pl. דַּלִּים; f. דַּלָּה, pl. דַּלּוֹת), *poor, weak.*

דַּלָּה f.—I. *thin thread*, Isa. 38:12.— II. *smallness, poverty.*—III. *hair of the head*, Cant. 7:6; pl. דַּלּוֹת.

דְּלִילָה p. n. of the concubine of Samson.

דִּלְעָן p. n. of a town in the tribe of Judah.

דָּלַף I. *dropped.*—II. *shed tears.*

דֶּלֶף m., *rain drop.*

דַּלְפוֹן p. n. of the son of Haman.

דָּלַק (fut. יִדְלַק).—I. *burning, consuming.*—II. applied metaphorically to *strong mental affections*, with אַחֲרֵי. Hiph. *kindled, inflamed.*

דְּלַק Ch., *burnt*, Dan. 7:9.

דַּלֶּקֶת f., *burning fever*, Deu. 28:22.

דְּלָתַיִם, דְּלָתוֹת; see דלה.

דָּם; see אדם.

דָּמָה I. *was like to, resembled*, with אֶל, לְ. Niph. *was assimilated*, with כְּ. Pi. דִּמָּה.—I. *assimilated, compare*, with אֶל, לְ.—II. *imagined, thought, meditated.* Hithp. fut. אֶדַּמֶּה same as Niph., Isa. 14:14.

דָּמָה II. same as דָּמַם.—I. *silent, quiet.*—II. *ruined, destroyed.* Niph. *was silent, ruined.* Pi. *exterminate, destroy.*

דְּמָה Ch., *be similar, like.*

דְּמוּת f., *similitude, likeness*; כִּדְמוּת (also without כְּ) *as, like.*

דֳּמִי m., *silence, rest.*

דֳּמִי m., the same.

דִּמְיוֹן m., same as דְּמוּת *likeness*, Ps. 17:12.

דָּמַם (pret. pl. דַּמּוּ; imp. and inf. דֹּם; fut. יִדֹּם; pl. יִדְּמוּ) *was dumb, quiet, inactive*, in consequence of some strong affection of the mind, with ד' לַיהֹוָה *to wait silently upon the Lord.* Po. דּוֹמַמְתִּי *made silent*, Ps. 131:2. Hiph. הֵדַם *reduced to silence, ruined*, Jer. 8:14. Niph. נָדַם (fut. תִּדְמִי, יִדְּמוּ) *became silent, destroyed.*

דֻּמָּה f., *cut off, ruined*, Eze. 27:32.

דְּמָמָה f., *silence*, 1 Ki. 19:12.

דֹּמֶן m., *dung*.

דִּמְנָה p.n. of a town in the tribe of Zebulun.

דִּימוֹן p.n. of a town of Moab.

מַדְמֵנָה f.—I. *dung-hill*, Isa. 25:10.— II. p.n. of a town in the tribe of Benjamin.

מַדְמַנָּה p.n. of a town in the tribe of Judah, Jos. 15:31.

דֶּמַע m., lit. *tear* (with suff. דִּמְעֲךָ, Ex. 22:29), *juice of the grape, olive, &c.*

דִּמְעָה f. (pl. דְּמָעוֹת) — I. *tear.*—II. *weeping.*

דּוּמֶשֶׂק, דַּרְמֶשֶׂק, דַּמֶּשֶׂק p.n. —I. *Damascus*, a city of Syria.— II. *a Damascene* (supp. אִישׁ), Gen. 15:2.

דַּמֶּשֶׂק or דְּמֶשֶׂק *damask*, silk cloth made at Damascus.

דָּן, see דִּין.

דֵּן Ch. pron., *this, that*; emph. דְּנָה; כִּדְנָה *thus*; עַל דְּנָה *thereupon*; אַחֲרֵי דְנָה *afterwards.*

דַּנָּה p.n. of a town in the tribe of Judah.

דִּנְהָבָה p.n. of a town in Edom.

דָּנִיֵּאל p.n.; see דִּין.

דָּנַנִּי Kal pret. with suff. and נ epenth., from דִּין.

דֵּעַ, דֵּעָה *knowledge*; see ידע.

דְּעֵה Kal imp. with ה parag., from ידע.

דְּעוּאֵל p.n. of a man.

דָּעַךְ.—I. *put out, extinguish.* — II. *made worse.* Niph. נִדְעֲכוּ *are extinguished*, Job 6:17. Pu. דֹּעֲכוּ the same, Ps. 118:12.

דַּעַת *knowledge*; see ידע.

דָּפָה root not used; (Arab. *slaying*).

דֹּפִי (with pause דֹּפִי m.) *stroke, destruction*, Ps. 50:20.

דָּפַק.—I. *beat, drive* (as cattle), Gen 33:13.—II. *knock at a door*, Cant 5:2. Hith. *knocked*, Judg. 19:22.

דָּפְקָה p.n. of one of the stations of the Israelites in the desert.

דֹּק, דַּקָּה, דָּק; see דקק.

דִּקְלָה p.n. of a district of Joktan in Arabia, Gen. 10:27.

דָּקַק (fut. יָדֹק, with suff. יְדֻקֶּנּוּ) *beat* or *grind small.* Hiph. הֵדַק (fut. with suff. אֲדִיקֵם for אֲדִקֵּם; inf. הָדֵק, also הָדֵק adv., *as fine as dust*, Ex. 30:36), *reduce to powder.* Hoph. fut. יוּדַק *is ground, powdered*, Isa. 28:28.

דְּקַק Ch., *pounded.* Aph. *made small*; see דּוּק.

דַּקָּה m., דַּקָּה f., *small, thin, impalpable*; דַּק s., *small dust.*

דֹּק m., *thin, fine cloth*, Isa. 40:22.

דָּקַר (fut. יִדְקֹר) *pierce, run through.* Niph. fut. יִדָּקֵר *shall be thrust through*, Isa. 13:15. Pu. part. מְדֻקָּרִים—I. *they who are thrust through.*—II. *slain by want*, Lam. 4:9.

דֶּקֶר p.n. of a man.

מַדְקָרוֹת f. pl., *piercings of the sword*, Pro. 12:18.

דַּר *marble*; see דרר.

דֹּר, דָּר *race*; see דּוּר.

דָּרָא root not used; (Arab. *excite evil*).

דְּרָאוֹן m., *abhorring, contempt*, Dan. 12:2.

דְּרָאוֹן m. *abomination*, Isa. 66 : 24.

דָּרַב root not used ; (Arab. *point*.)

דָּרְבָן m. *goad* ; βούκεντρον, 1 Sa. 13 : 21.

דָּרְבוֹנוֹת f. pl. *goads*,. Ecc. 12 : 11.

דָּרַג root not used ; (Arab. *step, stair*).

מַדְרֵגָה f. *steep place, precipice*.

דָּרוֹם ,דַּרְדַּר ,דַּרְדַּע ,דְּרוֹר ; see דרר·

דָּרְיָוֶשׁ p. n. of the kings of Persia.—
—I. *Darius* the Median (Cyaxares II.).—II. *Darius* Hystaspes.—III. *Darius* Nothus.

דָּרַךְ I. *tread* (as grapes), with בְּ, עַל.—II. *bend a bow*, by placing the left foot upon it; דּ׳ חִצִּים *he shot arrows from the bent bow*.—III. *tread down, destroy*.—IV. *enter, pass in*, with בְּ, עַל.—V. *walk in state*.—Hiph. I. *caused to proceed, led*.—II. *bent as a bow*.—III. *trod down*.—IV. *took possession of*.

דֶּרֶךְ com. (with suff. דַּרְכִּי; pl. דְּרָכִים, דַּרְכֵי; dual דְּרָכַיִם).—I. *way, road*; דּ׳ עֵץ *way to the tree*; דּ׳ הַמֶּלֶךְ *king's highway*.—II. *journey*; דּ׳ הַיּוֹם *a day's journey*.—III. *mode, manner, custom*; דּ׳ יְהוָה *God's dealings*.—IV. *the fruits of one's ways*, Isa. 10:24, &c.

מִדְרָךְ m., *foot-prints*, Deu. 2:5.

דַּרְכְּמוֹן *drachm*, same as אֲדַרְכֹּן·

דַּרְמֶשֶׂק *Damascus*, same as דַּמֶּשֶׂק·

דְּרָע com. Ch., *arm*, Dan. 2:32.

אֶדְרָע com. Ch., *arm*, Ezr. 4:23.

דַּרְקוֹן p. n. of a man.

דָּרַר root not used ; (Arab. *flew, went, round*).

דְּרוֹר m.—I. *swallow* or *wild pigeon*.

—II. *spontaneously flowing myrrh*, Ex. 30:23, hence:—III. *liberty*; קָרָא דּ׳ לְ and בְּ *he proclaimed liberty to any one, he manumitted his slave*; שְׁנַת הַדְּרוֹר *the year of Jubilee*, in which all Hebrew slaves were free, Lev. 25:10.

דַּר m., *some unknown kind of marble*, Ezr. 1:6; LXX. πίννινος λίθος.

דַּרְדַּע p. n. of a man.

דַּרְדַּר m., *brambles*.

דָּרוֹם m., *the country south of Judea*

דָּרַשׁ I. *he sought, enquired for, into*, &c., with אֶת, אֶל, לְ, בְּ.—II. *enquired about, concerning*, with עַל; used especially of asking supernatural counsel : with מֵעִם before the person asked; with בְּ, אֶל, לְ before the being from whom the oracle is asked.—III. *demanded, asked, required*: with מִן before the person from whom the demand is made; דָּרַשׁ דָּם with מִן or מֵעִם or מִיָּד *required the blood of one slain*, i. e. avenge his death.—IV. *promoted, sought to accomplish*; דּ׳ רָעַת פ׳ *sought to do him evil*.—V דּ׳ יְהוָה *sought the Lord*, in acts of worship.—VI. *cared for*. Niph. *was sought, enquired after*.

דְּרִישׁ m., *seeking*, Ezr. 10:16.

מִדְרָשׁ m., *book, commentary*, 2 Chron. 13:22.

דָּשָׁא *became grassy*, Joel 2:22. Hiph. *sent forth grass*, Gen. 1:11,12.

דֶּשֶׁא m., *tender herb, first blades of grass*.

דָּשֵׁן *grew fat*, Deu. 31:20.—Pi. דִּשֵּׁן

I. *made, considered fat.*—II. *anoint-ed.*—III. from דֶּשֶׁן *removed ashes.* Pu. *was made fat, satisfied.* Hothpa. pret. הַדֻּשְׁנָה *made fat* (of a sword), Isa. 34:6.

דָּשֵׁן m., *fat, fruitful.*

דֶּשֶׁן m. (with suff. דִּשְׁנִי).—I. *fatness of meat.*—II. *fertility.*—III. *ashes,* specially those of burnt-offerings, &c. which were used for manure.

דָּת f. (pl. דָּתֵי, דָּתִים, *edict, mandate, law.*

דָּת f. Ch. *law, edict.*

דְּתָבַר m. Ch., *judges* or *lawyers,* Dan. 4:12, 20.

דִּתְאָה emph. דִּתְאָא Ch. m., same as Heb. דֶּשֶׁא *grass.*

דֹּתַיִן p.n. of a place north of Samaria.

דָּתָן p.n. of one of the accomplices of Korah.

ה

ה (הָ, הַ).—I. def. art. ὁ, ἡ, τὸ *the.*—II. demon. pron. *this;* הַיּוֹם *this day.*—III. relat. pron. *who, which;* הֶחָלְכוּא *who went,* Jos. 10:24; הָעָלֶיהָ *that which is above her.*—IV. sign of the vocative; הַמֶּלֶךְ O *King!* הַבַּעַל O *Baal!* 1 Ki. 18:26.

ה (הַ, הֲ) pref., sign of an interrogation; הֲשֹׁמֵר אָחִי אָנֹכִי *am I my brother's keeper,* Gen. 4:9.

הָא (הָא Ch.) *behold!*

הָאָח *aha!* exclamation of joy or scorn.

הַאֲזִינוּ for הִזְנִיחוּ Hiph. pret. pl., from זנח.

הַב with ה parag. הָבָה; pl. הָבוּ Kal imper., from יהב.

הָבִיא, הָבֵא Hiph. imper., from בוא.

הֻבָאת Hoph. pret. f., from בוא.

הֹבְאִישׁ for הוֹבִישׁ Hiph., from בוש.

הַבְהָבִים *gifts;* see יהב

הֵבוּ Hos. 4:18, pret. pl. for יְהָבוּ, from יהב.

הַבּוֹק Niph. inf., from בקק.

הָבִי Ruth 3:15, Kal imp. f., from יהב, or Hiph. imp. f. for הָבִיא, from בוא.

הֶבֶל (fut. יֶהְבַּל) *act vainly, sinfully.* Hiph. *cause to act vainly,* Jer. 23:16.

הֶבֶל m. (with suff. הֶבְלִי; pl. הֲבָלִים, הַבְלֵי).—I. *vanity, instability, deception.*—II. *idols.*—III. *abortions,* Ecc. 6:4, and thence, *men in general.*—IV. adv., *vainly, in vain.*—V. p.n., *Abel,* the son of Adam.

הֲבֵל m., *vanity.*

הָבְנִים (הוֹבְנִים) *ebony,* Eze. 27:15.

הָבַר (Arab. *that which cuts*); הֹבְרֵי שָׁמַיִם *they who cut, divide the heavens, astrologers,* Isa. 47:13; Vulg. *augures cœli;* LXX. ἀστρολόγοι τοῦ οὐρανοῦ.

הָבַר Hiph. inf. from בור.

הָגַג root not used; (Syr. *imagined*). הָגִיג m., *deep, ardent meditation.*

הָגָה (fut. יֶהְגֶּה) inf. הָגֹה).—I. *murmur, coo, growl.*—II. *meditate.*—III. *declare one's meditations,* with בְּ—IV. *discern, separate.* Po. inf. הֹגוּ *utter, speak.* Hiph. part. pl. מַהְגִּים *mutterers,* i. e. *enchanters,* Isa. 8:19.

הֶגֶה m.—*murmur, whisper.*—II. *thunder.*

הָגוּת f., meditation, Ps. 49:4.

הִגָּיוֹן (m., a musical stringed-instru-
הִגָּיוֹן (ment or the sound of one.

הֹנֶה 2 Sa. 20:13, for הוֹנֶה Hiph. from
יגה he removed

הָגוֹ Kal inf. abs. from II. הגה.

הֹנּוֹ Po. inf. from הגה.

הָגִין m., הֲגִינָה f., straight, commódi-
ous, Eze. 42:12.

הָגְלָת (Syr. for הָגְלָתָה) Hoph. pret. f.,
from גלה.

הָגָר p.n. of the mother of Ishmael.

הַגְרִיאִים, הַגְרִים p. n. of a people eastward of Gilead.

הַד shout; see הדד.

הַדָּבְרִין m. pl. Ch., title of certain officers in the court of Babylon;
"counsellors," Eng. Ver.

הָדַד root not used; (Arab. shouting).

הֵידָד shouting (of bodies of men).

הַד m., shouting, Eze. 7:7.

הֲדַד p. n. of a king of Edom.

הֲדַדְעֶזֶר p.n. of a king of Syria.

הֲדַדְרִמּוֹן p. n. of a town not far
from Megiddo.

הָדָה guided (his hand), Isa. 11:8.

הֹדוּ (for הִנְדּוּ Hindu), p. n. Hin-
dustan, India.

הֲדוֹרָם p.n. of an Arab tribe, descended from Joktan, Gen. 10:27.

חוֹרִי, הֲדִי p. n. of a man.

הָדַךְ break down, overturn, Job 40:12.

הָדַם root not used; (Arab. destruction).

הֲדֹם m., footstool.

הַדָּם m. Ch., piece, fragment.

הֲדַם m., myrtle; pl. הֲדַסִּים.

הֲדַסָּה p.n. the former name of Esther.

הָדַף (fut. יֶהְדֹּף), thrust out, drive
back.

הָדַר (fut. יֶהְדַּר), honoured, dignified
(in dress), Isa. 63:1 ; with פְּנֵי פ׳
take the part of any one. Niph.
was honoured, Lam. 5:12. Hith.
was glorious, Pro. 25:5.

הֲדַר Ch. Pa. honoured.

הָדָר m., glorious, honourable, dignified.

הֶדֶר m., honour, Dan. 11:20.

הֲדָרָה f. (const. הַדְרַת), honourable (in
apparel).

הָדַּשְׁנָה Hothp. pret. f., from דשׁן.

הָה ah! exclamation of grief.

הוֹ same as הוֹי alas!

הוּא pers. pron. m.—I. he, it.—II.
this, the same.

הֲוָא Ch., was; same as הָוָה.

הֱוֵא for הֱוֵה imp., from הוה.

הוּבַד Hoph. pret., from אבד.

הוֹבָדָה Ch. Aph. inf., from אבד.

הוֹבִישׁ Hiph., from בּוֹשׁ and יָבֵשׁ.

הוֹד glory; see with its comp. in
נהד.

הוֹדָה Hiph. pret. הוֹדוּ ; imp. pl.
הוֹדוֹת ; inf. from ידה.

הָוָה.—I. fell, descended.—II. existed,
was; part. הֹוֶה ; imper. הֱוֵא, הֱוֵה,
f. הֱוִי ; fut. יָהוּא (for יֶהֱוֶה, יְהוּ).
הֲוָא, הֲוָה Ch., was.

הַוָּה f.—I. intense desire, lust.—II. accident, injury, ruin.

הֹוָה f., accident, injury.

הַיָּה f., same as הַוָּה calamity.

יְהֹוָה Jehovah, the name whereby God
would be known to the Hebrews,
Ex. 3:14. Written with prefixes

(like אֲדֹנָי), בֵּיהוָֹה, לַיהוָה, מֵיהוָֹה; with אֲדֹנָי it is written יֱהוִֹה (like אֱלֹהִים).

יָהּ an abbreviated form of יְהוָֹה.

יֵהוּא p. n.—I. *Jehu,* king of Israel.—II. of a man.

יְהוֹאָחָז, יוֹאָחָז p. n.—I. a king of Israel, the son of Jehu.—II. a king of Judah, the son of Josiah.

יְהוֹאָשׁ, יוֹאָשׁ p. n.—I. a king of Judah, the son of Ahaziah.—II. a king of Israel, the son of Joash.

יְהוֹזָבָד p. n. of a man.

יְהוֹחָנָן, יוֹחָנָן (*the Lord is merciful*), Ἰωάννης, p. n. of a man.

יְהוֹיָדָע, יוֹיָדָע p. n. of a man.

יְהוֹיָכִין, יוֹיָכִין, יְכָנְיָהוּ p. n. of a king of Judah, the son of Jehoiakim.

יְהוֹיָקִים, יוֹיָקִים (*the Lord confirmeth*), p. n. of a king of Judah, the son of Josiah.

יְהוֹיָרִיב, יוֹיָרִיב p. n. of a man.

יְהוֹנָדָב, יוֹנָדָב (*the Lord's gift*), p. n. of a man.

יְהוֹנָתָן, יוֹנָתָן (*the Lord giveth,* Θεόδωρος), p. n. of a man.

יְהוֹעַדָּה (*the Lord adorneth*), p. n. of a man.

יְהוֹעַדָּן p. n. of a woman.

יְהוֹצָדָק, יוֹצָדָק (*the Lord is righteous*), p. n. of a man.

יְהוֹרָם, יוֹרָם (*the Lord is exalted*), p. n.—I. a king of Judah, the son of Jehosaphat. — II. a king of Israel, the son of Ahab.

יְהוֹשֶׁבַע (*the Lord hath sworn*), p. n. of a son of king Joram.

יְהוֹשֻׁעַ, יְהוֹשֻׁע (*the Lord saveth*), p. n. of a man, *Joshua.*

יְהוֹשָׁפָט (*the Lord judgeth*), p. n.—I.

of a king of Judah, the son of Asa —II. of many men.

יוֹאָב p. n. of a man.

יוֹאָח p. n. of a man.

יוֹאֵל (*the Lord he is God*), p. n. of man.

יוֹזָבָד p. n. of a man.

יוֹזָכָר p. n. of a man.

יוֹכֶבֶד p. n. of the mother of Moses

יוֹעֵד (*the Lord is witness*), p. n. of man.

יוֹעֶזֶר (*the Lord helpeth*), p. n. of a m.

יוֹעָשׁ p. n. of a man.

יוֹתָם p. n.—I. of a king of Judah, the son of Uzziah.—II. of a man.

יוֹהָם p. n. of a king.

הוֹ, הוֹי interj. of exhortation, threatening, grief, with עַל, אֶל and לְ.

הוּךְ Ch., *proceed, go;* fut. יְהָךְ; inf. מְהָךְ.

הוּבָּה for הֻכָּה Hoph., from נָכָה.

הוּלֶּדֶת, הֻלֶּדֶת Hoph. inf., from יָלַד.

הוּלְלוּ for הֻלְלוּ Pu. pret. pl., from הָלַל; הוֹלֵלוֹת, הוֹלֵלוּת; see הָלַל.

הוּם pret. הָם *perturb, harass,* Deu. 7:23. Niph. *was moved, excited;* fut. f. וַתֵּהֹם. Hiph. *heave, swell, be tumultuous.*

מְהוּמָה f., *perturbation, tumult, vexation.*

תְּהוֹם com. (pl. תְּהֹמוֹת), *the deep, the ocean;* from its tossing and roaring.

הוֹמִיָּה, הוֹמָה part. f., from הָמָה.

הוֹמָם p. n. of a man.

הוּן Kal, root not used; (Arab. *was light*). Hiph. *made light of, despised,* with inf. and לְ.

הוֹן m.—I. *wealth, plenty.*—II. adv. *enough,* Pro. 30:15, 16.

הִין m., a liquid measure containing twelve logs (לג).

הוֹר הֹ־עַד "thy progenitors," Eng. Ver., Gen. 49:26, from הרה.

הֹשֻׁבוֹתִים Zec. 10:6. Hiph. pret. 1. pers., with suff., for הֹשַׁבְתִּים, from ישׁב.

הוֹשָׁמָע (*the Lord heareth*), p. n. of a m.

הוֹשֵׁעַ p. n., name of Joshua, afterwards changed to יְהוֹשֻׁעַ.

הוֹשַׁעְיָה (*the Lord saveth*), p. n. of a m.

הוֹת תְּהוֹתְתוּ Po. fut. *attack unjustly,* Ps. 62:4.

הוּתַל Pu. or Hoph., from התל.

הָזָה *doze, sleep idly,* Isa. 56:10.

הַזְדָּה Ch. Aph. inf., from זוד.

הִזְדְּמִנְתּוּן Ch. Ithp., from זמן.

הֵילִילוּ Hiph. pret. pl., from ילל.

הִזַּכּוּ for הִתְזַכּוּ Hithp. imper. pl., from זכה.

הִזָּרוֹתֵיכֶם for הִזָּרוֹתְכֶם Niph. inf., with suff., from זרה.

הֶחֱבָּאתָה Jos. 6:17. Hiph. pret. fem., with ה parag., for הֶחְבִּיאָה, from חבא.

הֶחָדַלְתִּי Jud. 9:9, 11, 13. for הֶחָדַלְתִּי Kal pret. 1.pers., with ה interrog., from חדל.

הֶחֱטִי הֶחֱטִיא Hiph. pret. for הֶחֱטִי inf. for הַחֲטִיא, from חטא.

הֵחֵל Hiph. pret., Eze. 20. Niph. inf, with suff. and pref. לְהֵחַלּוֹ, Lev. 21:4; see חלל.

הַט Hiph. imp. apoc., from נטה.

הִטַּמָּא Hothp., from טמא.

הִטַּתּוּ Hiph. pret. 3. pers. fem. with suff., from נטה.

הַטֹּתָהּ Hiph. inf. with suff., from נטה.

הִי *lamentation;* see נהה.

הִיא pers. pron. f., *she, this;* see הוּא; with art. הַהִיא *the same, this very* (*woman,* &c.); Ch. the same.

הֵידוֹת f. pl., Neh. 12:8; wrong reading for הוֹדוֹת *dignities;* see in נָהַד.

הֵידָד *shouting;* see הדד.

הָיָה (inf. abs. הָיֹה; const. הֱיוֹת, with pref. בִּהְיוֹת; imper. הֱיֵה f. הֱיִי, pl. הֱיוּ; fut. יִהְיֶה apoc. יְהִי).—I. *came to pass* וַיְהִי, with כְּ and וְ *and it came to pass that.*—II. *was,* i. e. *existed;* never used as the logical copula, *is, was;* const. with לְ *there was to any one,* i. e. *he had;* with לְ and the inf. *was about to, intent upon;* with כְּ *was the same as;* with עִם *was, had communication with.* Niph. *came to be, took effect, had been,* Dan. 2:1; 8:27.

הַיָּה *ruin;* see הוה.

הֵיךְ Ch., same as אֵיךְ *how?*

הֵיכָל m. (pl. הֵיכָלִים, הֵיכָלוֹת).—I. *any great and splendid building, temple, palace,* &c.—II. *the temple of Jehovah built by Solomon.*

הֵיכַל m. Ch.—I. *palace.*—II. *temple.*

הֵילִיכִי Hiph. imp. f., from הלך.

הֵילֵל *glorious;* see הלל.

הֵים *swell;* see הום.

הֵימָן p. n. of a man.

הֵימִן Ch. Aph. pret., from אמן.

הֵימִיר for הֵמִיר Hiph., from מור.

הֵין *light;* see הון.

הַיְתִי Ch. Aph. pret.; הֵיתָיָה inf.; הֵיתָיַת Hoph. pret. f. 3. pers.; הֵיתָיוּ pl., from אתה.

הַךְ Hiph. imp. apoc., from נכה.

הֻכּוּם Hiph. pret. pl., with suff., from נכה.

הַכּוֹת Hiph. inf., from נכה.

הַכּוֹנֵן for הִתְכּוֹנֵן Hithpo., from כּוּן.

הָכִיל Eze. 21:33, for הַאֲכִיל Hiph. inf., from אכל (others make it Hiph., from כּוּל).

הַכֵּנִי Hiph imp., with suff. for הַכֵּנִי, from נכה.

הַכְּךָ Hiph. pret. with suff., from נכה.

הָכְלַמְנוּ for הִכְלַמְנוּ Hiph. pret. pl. 1. pers., from כלם.

הַכֵּם Hiph. pret. with suff., from נכה.

הֲכַנּוּ for הֲכַנֵנוּ Hiph. pret. pl. 1. pers., from כּוּן.

הַכֵּנִי Hiph. pret. with suff., from נכה.

הָכַר, fut. תַּהְכְּרוּ ye contemn, Job 19:3.

הַכָּרָה astonishment; see נכר.

הָל, the ה inter. and the pref. ל written thus, for reverence sake, in the phrase הַל יְיָ Deu. 32:6.

הָלָא. Niph. part. f. נַהֲלָאָה removed, cast away, Mic. 4:7.

הָלְאָ removed; הָלְאָה pa., thence, farther, onward; denotes time and place.

הֶלְאָת for הֶלְאָתָה Hiph. pret. f., from לאה.

הִלּוּ Kal inf. with suff., from הלל.

הִלּוּלִים great praise; see הלל.

הַלֵּזֶה, הַלָּז, הַלֵּזוּ; see זֶה.

הָלַךְ and יָלַךְ (part. הוֹלֵךְ; pl. הֹלְכִים; f. הֹלֶכֶת, הֹלְכָה; inf. הָלוֹךְ; const. לֶכֶת; with suff. לֶכְתְּךָ; imper. לֵךְ, לְכָה; with ה parag. לְכָה; fut. אֵלֵךְ, יֵלֵךְ; poet. יַהֲלֹךְ, וַיֵּלֶךְ; (תְּהֲלָךְ).—I. walked, went, proceeded; const. with many particles which modify the sense, e. g. with אַחֲרֵי followed; with עִם, אֵת

accompanied; with בְּ walked with, i. e. brought, Hos. 5:6.—II. made way, progress; וַיֵּלֶךְ הָלֹךְ וְגָדֵל increased continually.—III. proceeded, went on.—IV. went off, disappeared, i. e. died, Gen. 15:2; Ps. 39:14. Niph. נֶהֱלַכְתִּי I set about departing, Ps. 109:23. Pi. הִלֵּךְ went, proceeded. Hiph. הוֹלִיךְ and הֵילִיךְ.—I. cause to go, lead, conduct.—II. let perish, Ps. 125:5. Hith. הִתְהַלֵּךְ becomewalking, proceed, go on, go about.

הֵלֶךְ m.—I. going, travel, 2 Sa.12:4. —II. a stream, 1 Sa. 14:26.

הֲלַךְ Ch., walked, proceeded. Aph. the same.

הֲלָךְ m. Ch., proceeds of the state, taxation.

הֲלִיךְ m.; הֲלִיכָה f.; pl. הֲלִיכוֹת.—I. step.—II. way.—III. procedure.

מַהֲלָךְ m.—I. walk.—II. journey.

תַּהֲלוּכָה f., procession, Neh. 12:31.

הַהֹלְכוּא, הַהֹלְכוּא who went, Jos.10:24. Kal pret. pl. with א parag. and ה relat., from הלך.

הָלַל shone. Pi. הִלֵּל.—I. praised. — II. gloried. — III. pronounced vain-glorious, foolish, mad; const. with לְ (הַלְלוּ־יָהּ [without dag. forte] praise ye the Lord). Pu. הֻלַּל was praised; part. מְהֻלָּל praised, to be praised. Hiph. הֵלֵל shone. Hith. began to glory, boast. Po. fut. יְהוֹלֵל make a fool, shame. Poal part. מְהוֹלָל mad. Hithpo. became mad.

הֵילֵל m., Lucifer, i.e. the morning star, Isa. 14:12.

הוֹלֵלָה f. (pl. הוֹלֵלוֹת), glory, folly.

הוֹלֵלוּת f., *folly*, Ecc. 10:13.

הִלּוּלִים m. pl.—I. *great praise, subject of praise*, Lev. 19:24.—II. *songs of, feasts of, joy*, Ju. 9:27.

הִלֵּל p.n. of a man.

מַהֲלָל m., *praising*, Pro. 27:21.

מַהֲלַלְאֵל (*the praise of God*), p.n. of a m.

תְּהִלָּה f.—I. *praise*.—II. *hymn of praise*; pl. תְּהִלּוֹת *praises*; pl. m. תְּהִלִּים *the book of Psalms*.

תָּהֳלָה f., *folly, emptiness*, Job 4:18.

הָלַם *struck, beat*.

הֲלֹם adv., *hither*; עַד־הֲלֹם *thus far*.

הֶלֶם (*blow*), p.n. of a man.

הַלְמוּת f., *workman's hammer*, Jud. 5:26.

יַהֲלֹם m., *name of a gem, adamant*.

מַהֲלֻמּוֹת f. pl., *beatings, stripes*.

הָם or הֹם p.n. of an unknown place, Gen. 14:5.

הֵמָּה, הֵם pers. pron. m. pl., *these, they*; with the art. הָהֵמָּה, הָהֵם.

הִמּוֹן Ch., *these, they*.

הַמְּדָתָא p.n. of a man.

הָמָה (inf. const. הָמוֹת; fut. יֶהֱמֶה; part. m. הֹמֶה; f. הוֹמִה).—I. *ferment* (as wine).—II. *moved* (as the bowels with mental emotions).—III. *roar, rage, murmur, moan*; part. f. pl. הוֹמִיּוֹת *noisy*, i.e. full of people, Pro. 1:21.

הָם or הֹם pl. הָמִים; with suff. and pref. מֵהֶמְהֶם *their riches*, Ezr. 7:11.

הֶמְיָה f., *sound of the lute*, Isa. 14:11.

הָמוֹן m. (f. Job 31:34).—I. *emotion*, lit. *moving the bowels*.—II. *musical sounds*.—III. *multitude of men*, &c.

הָמֹן m., *abundance*; with suff. הֲמֹנְכֶם, Eze. 5:7.

הֲמוֹנָה the mystical name of a city, Eze. 39:16; see preceding verse.

הֵימִין for הֵימִן Hiph., from ימן.

הֲמִתִּיו הֲמִתִּיו 1 Sa. 17:35, for הֲמִתִּיו, Hiph. pret. 1. pers. with suff., from מות.

הֻמְכּוּ for הוּמְכּוּ Hoph. pl., from מכך.

הָמַל root not used; (Arab. *rain continually*).

הֲמֻלָּה הֲמֻלָּה f., *commotion, rushing of wings*.

הָמַם (fut. יָהֹם; וַיָּהָם; inf. const. with suff. הֻמָּם).—I. *put in motion, agitated*.—II. *dispersed, put to the rout*.

הָמָן p.n. of a man.

הָמֹן *multitude*; see in הָמָה.

הֲמוּנָךְ or הֲמֹנִיךְ Ch., *collar, bracelet*, Dan. c. 5.

הֻמַּם Niph. inf., from מסס.

הַמְסִיו Ch. for הַמְסוּ Hiph. pl., from מסה.

הֶמֶם m., pl. הֲמָסִים *slight noises*, Isa. 64:1.

הָמַר root not used; (Arab. *poured water*).

מַהֲמֹרוֹת f. pl., *torrents, floods*, Ps. 140:11.

הֲמִרוֹתָם Hiph. inf. with suff. and dag. euphon., from מרה.

הֲמִתָּה Hiph. 2. pers. with ה parag., הֲמִתִּי 1. pers., הֲמִיתָה 1. pers. with suff., הֲמִתֶּם 2. pers. pl., from מות.

הֵנָּה, הֵן pers. pron. f. pl., *they, them*; with art. הָהֵנָּה; adv., *here, hither*; הֵנָּה וָהֵנָּה *hither and thither*, מִמְּךָ וָהֵנָּה *from thee hitherwards*, עַד הֵנָּה *thus far*.

הַנּוּ pers. pron. m. pl. Ch., *he*; f. הִנֵּין *she.*

הֵן, הֶנֵּה, הִנֵּה, הֵן interj., *behold! lo!* with suff. הִנְנִי, הִנֶּנִּי, הִנְנִי *behold me! lo I am here!* הִנְּךָ *behold thou art, &c.*

Ch., *if, whether;* הֵן...הֵן *either... or.*

הַנַח Hiph. imp., from ינח.

הַנִּיחַ Hiph. הַנִּיחַ Hoph., from ינח. הַנָּחָה *rest;* see נוח.

הַנֹּם p. n.; גֵּי בֶּן־הִנֹּם *the valley of the sons of Hinnom* (where Molech was worshipped).

הֵנַע p. n. of a city in Mesopotamia.

הַנְעָלָה Ch. Aph. pret., הַנְעָלָה inf., from עלל.

הַנָּפָה Ch. for הָנִיף Hiph. inf., from נוף.

הָסָה Pi. imp. הַס; with pause הָס *hush! be silent!* pl. הַסּוּ. Hiph. (fut. apoc. וַיַּהַס), *made to be silent,* Nu. 13:30.

הֵסִית for הֵסִית Hiph., from סות.

הַעַל Hiph. imper. apoc., from עלה.

הֶעֱלָה for הֶעֱלָה Hiph., from עלה.

הָעֲלָה for הָעֲלָה Hoph., from עלה.

הֲפָנוֹת *remission;* see פוג.

הַפֹּדֶה part. with suff. and art., from פדה.

הָפַך (fut. יַהֲפֹך; inf. הָפוֹך; const. הֲפֹך; with suff. הָפְכִי).—I. *turn over.* — II. *subvert, ruin.* — III. *change, pervert, convert.* Niph. נֶהְפַּך *was turned, &c.;* with עַל, לְ, *to or into, was ruined.* Hoph. הָהְפַּך *turned upon, against,* Job 30:15. Hith. part. מִתְהַפֵּך *becomes turned about;* f. מִתְהַפֶּכֶת *the*

same; fut. f. תִּתְהַפֵּך *becomes changed,* Job 38:14.

הֶפֶך, הֵפֶך m., *perversion,* Eze. 16:34.

הֲפֵכָה f., *subversion,* Gen. 19:29.

הֲפַכְפַּך m., *turning, tortuous,* Pro. 21:8.

מַהְפֵּכָה f., *overthrow, subversion.*

מַהְפֶּכֶת f., *imprisonment, stocks;* בֵּית הַמַּהְפֶּכֶת *prison-house.*

תַּהְפּוּכָה f. (pl. תַּהְפֻּכוֹת), *perversion, perverseness.*

הַפְרְכֶם Hiph. inf. with suff., from פרר.

הִצְטַמֵּיד Hith. denom., from צַיִד or צוד. הַצָּלָה *deliverance;* see נצל.

הֶצֶן m., *an armament, force,* Eze 23:24.

הַר m. (with art. הָהָר; pl. הָרִים; with art. הֶהָרִים), aff. הֲרָרִי, הֲרָרֵי; pl. הַרְרֵיהָ; also const. הָרְרֵי, הָרֵי,הָרִי.—I. *mountain.*—II. *mountainous district.* — III. *fastness, stronghold.*—IV. *strong men,* Isa. 41:15; with ־ה affix (הֶרָה), *towards the mountain.*

הֲרָרִי *a mountaineer,* 2 Sa. 23:33.

הָרָרִי *the same, v. 11, a title of Shammah.*

הֹר p. n.—I. of the mountain in Edom where Aaron was buried.—II. of a mountain in Palestine.

הַר חֶרֶם p. n. of a mountain in the tribe of Dan, Jud. 1:35.

הָרָא p. n. of a region in Syria.

הַרְאֵל p. n. of the altar of burnt-offering, Eze. 43:15; elsewhere אֲרִיאֵל which see in ארה.

הַרְבֶּה Hiph. imp. apoc., from רבה.

הָרַג (fut. יַהֲרֹג; inf. הָרוֹג; const. הֲרֹג), with לְ, בְּ *kill, slay,* generally with violence. Niph. *was slain.* Pu. הֹרַג *slain.*

הֶרֶג m., | הֲרֵגָה f., } *slaughter, slaying.*

הָרָה (inf. abs. הָרֹה, הָרוֹ; fut. f. תַּהַר, וַתַּהַר).—I. *conceived, became pregnant,* with אֶת, לְ; part. f. הוֹרָה; inf. הֹרוֹ *she that conceiveth.*—II. *conceive in the mind, devise.* Pu. הֹרָה *conceived,* Job 3:3.

הָרָה adj. f., *pregnant;* pl. הָרוֹת.

הָרִיָּה adj. f., pl. with suff. הָרִיּוֹתָיו *her pregnant women.*

הֵרוֹן / הֵרָיוֹן } m., *conception.*

הַרְהֹר m. Ch., *imaginations,* Dan. 4:2, from Pa. Ch. הַרְהֵר.

הֹרָם p.n. of a king of Canaan.

הָרָם p.n. of a man.

הָרְמוּ Niph. imp. pl., from רמם.

הַרְמוֹן m. (same as אַרְמוֹן) *palace,* Am. 4:3.

הָרָן p.n. of a man.

הֹרֵנִי Hiph. pret. with suff., from ירה.

הָרַס (וַהֲרַס) (inf. הָרוֹס, fut. יֶהֱרָס; *broke down.*—1. houses, &c.—2. men, i.e. *put down, reduced.*—3. teeth, Ps. 58:7. Niph. *was broken down.* Pi. *destroyed;* as Kal.

עִיר הַהֶרֶם m., הֶרֶם p.n. of an unknown city in Egypt, Isa. 19:18; "city of destruction," Eng. Ver.; some read חֶרֶם which see.

הֲרִיסָה f., *broken down,* Am. 9:11.

הֲרִיסֻת f., *ruin,* Isa. 49:19.

הֶרֶף Hiph. imp. apoc., from רפה.

הָרְצָה Ch. for הִרְצָתָה Hiph. pret. f. 3. pers., from רצה.

הָרָרִי, הֲרֵר, הָרוּ; see הַר.

Hiph. הָשִׁיב, הָשֵׁב with pause for הָשֵׁב, imp. from שוב.

Hoph. (הֻשַׁמָּה) הָשַׁמָּה (in some editions) inf. with suff., from שמם.

הֻשָׁם p.n. of a man.

הַשְׁמָעוֹת *hearing;* see שמע.

הַשְׁעֵ Ps. 39:14, Hiph. imp., from שעה; Isa. 6:10, Hiph. imp., from שעע.

הִשְׁתַּחֲוָה Hithp., from שחה.

הִשְׁתַּעְשַׁע Hithpa., from שעע.

הִתְאֹשֵׁשׁוּ Hithp., from אוש.

הִתַּבוּתָךְ Ch. Aph. inf. with suff., from תוב.

הִתְגָּר Hithp. imp. apoc., from גרה.

הִתְוַדֵּה Hithp., from ידה.

הִתָּחֵל Hithp. imp. apoc., from חלה.

הָאֵתָיו for הָאָתָיו which is for הֵתָיו, Hiph. imp. pl., from אתה.

הֲתִמְּךָ for הָתַמְּךָ Hiph. inf. with suff., from תמם.

הִתּוּךְ *melting;* see נתך.

הֲתָךְ p.n. of a Persian eunuch.

הָתַל (inf. הָתֵל; Pi. הָתֵל, הִתֵּל; fut. יְהָתֵל; pl. תְּהָתְלוּ, יְהָתְלוּ) *deluded, deceived.* Hoph. הוּתַל *deceived.*

הֲתֻלִים m. pl., *mockeries,* Job 17:2.

מַהֲתַלּוֹת f. pl., *delusions,* Isa. 30:10.

הָתֵל Pi.; see התל.

הִתְנַבּוֹת Hithp. inf., from נבא.

הִתְנַבִּית Hithp. pret., from נבא.

ו

וְ, וּ, וָ conj., used to connect together words, phrases, sentences, &c.; it may be interpreted in modern languages by any of the particles which are applied to the same use: such as *and, but, if, moreover,* &c. according to the context.

וָדָן p.n. of a place in Arabia.

וָהֵב Num. 21:14, probably p. n. of a place or well.

וָו m., pl. וָוִים hooks or pins at the top of the pillars of the tabernacle.

וָזָר loaded; see יזר.

וַיְזָתָא p.n. of a son of Haman.

וָלָד‚ וָלֶד; see ילד.

וַנְיָה p.n. of a man.

וָפְסִי p.n. of a man.

וַשְׁנִי p.n. of a man.

וַשְׁתִּי p.n. of the wife of Ahasuerus.

ז

זְאֵב m.—I. a wolf.—II. p. n. of one of the princes of Midian.

זֹאת demonst. pron. f. of זֶה this, that.

זֹה for זֹאת this.

זוֹ for זֹה relat. pron. this, Ps. 132:12.

זָבַב root not used; (Arab. fly).

זְבוּב m., fly or bee; בַּעַל זְבוּב (fly-god), p. n. Baalzebub, the idol of the Ekronites.

זָבַד hath given, endowed, Gen. 30:20.

זֶבֶד a gift, Gen. 30:20.

זָבָד p.n. of a man.

זַבְדִּי p.n. of a man.

זַבְדִּיאֵל (gift of God), p.n. of a man.

זְבַדְיָה (given of the Lord), p.n. of a man, Ζεβεδαῖος.

וּזְבַדְיָהוּ p.n. of a man.

זָבוּד p.n. of a man.

זַבּוּד p. n. of a man.

זְבִידָה‚ זְבוּדָּה p.n. of a woman

זֻבֹב fly; see זבב.

זְבוּלוּן‚ זְבֻל‚ זֶבֶל; see זבל.

זָבַח (inf. const. זְבֹחַ; fut. יִזְבַּח), slaughtered for sacrifice. Pi. זִבַּח sacrificed.

זֶבַח m. (with suff. זִבְחִי; pl. זְבָחִים [זִבְחֵי, זְבָחוֹת].)—I. slaughter of men or animals.—II. the thing slaughtered.—III. sacrifice.—IV. that which is offered in sacrifice.—V. p. n. of a king of Midian.

מִזְבֵּחַ m. (const. מִזְבַּח; with suff. מִזְבְּחִי, מִזְבַּחֲךָ, pl. מִזְבְּחוֹת‚) altar; הַמִּזְבֵּחָה toward the altar.

זַבַּי p.n. of a man.

זָבַל, fut. with suff. יִזְבְּלֵנִי he will dwell with me, Gen. 30:20.

זֶבֶל‚ זְבֻל m.—I. habitation, place of residence.—II. p. n. of a man.

זְבוּלוּן‚ זְבֻלֻן‚ זְבוּלֹן (residence), p. n. of a son of Jacob; זְבוּלֹנִי a Zebulonite.

זְבַן Ch., gaining (time), Dan. 2:8.

זְבִינָא p.n. of a man.

זָג m., the transparent skin of the grape, Nu. 6:4.

זֵד, זָדוֹן; see זוד.

זֶה demonst. pron., he, it, this, that; with art. הַזֶּה this; זֶה...זֶה the one...the other; זֶה אֶל־זֶה the one to the other; כָּזֶה וְכָזֶה thus and thus; sometimes same as אֲשֶׁר that; זֶה פַעֲמַיִם these two times; בָּזֶה in this place, here, there; מִזֶּה hence; מִזֶּה וּמִזֶּה from this and that part; מַה־זֶּה what is this? לָמָּה־זֶּה where? אֵי־זֶה why?

זוּ com., this; sometimes for אֲשֶׁר.

הַלָּזֶה m.,
הַלֵּזוּ f., } this.
הַלָּז com.,

זָהָב m. (const. זְהַב, זַהֲב.).—I. *gold;* with a numeral preceding, supply שֶׁקֶל : עֲשָׂרָה זָהָב *ten shekels of gold.*—II. perhaps *fair weather,* Job 37:22.

זָהָה root not used; (Syr. *splendour*). זָו m. (*beauty of flowers*), the second month of the Hebrew year, which probably began on the thirty-first day after the sun had entered Aries.

זִיו m. Ch., *majesty, splendour.*

זָהַם. Pi. זִהֵם *abhorred,* Job 33:20. זַהַם p. n. of a man.

זָהַר. Hiph. הִזְהִיר I. *enlighten, give light.*—II. *admonish, warn,* with מִן of the thing to be avoided. Niph. נִזְהַר *was admonished.*

זְהַר Ch., part. זָהִירִין *admonished, cautioned.*

זֹהַר m., *brilliancy.*

זוֹ, זֶה *this;* see זֹאת.

זוּ the same; see זֶה.

זוּ; see זהה.

זוּב.—I. *issue, flow,* as water, blood, &c. — II. *abound, overflow.* — III. *waste away, expire;* part. זָב; f. זָבָה; const. זָבַת.

זוֹב m., *issue, discharge of blood,* &c.

זוּד, זִיד.—I. *boil, seethe,* Gen. 25:29. —II. *swell, behave* or *act insolently,* with אֶל or עַל (fut. with נ parag. יְזִידוּן), Deu. 17:13.

זוּד Ch. Aph., *was proud, haughty,* Dan. 5:20.

זֵד m., *proud, haughty.*

זֵידוֹן m., *overflowing, overwhelming,* Ps. 124:5.

זָדוֹן const. זְדוֹן m., *pride, haughtiness, insolence.*

נָזִיד m. (part. Niph. for נָזוֹד), any viand prepared by boiling.

זָוָה root not used; (Arab. *angle, corner*).

זָוִיָּה or זָוִית f. (pl. זָוִיּוֹת), *angle, corner of a building,* &c.

מְזָוֶה m. (pl. מְזָוִים), *vault for corn, matadore,* Ps. 144:13.

זִין, זוּן root not used; (Arab. *abundance, riches*).

זִין m.—I. *abundance,* Isa. 66:11.— II. זִין שָׂדַי *wealth* (i. e. cattle) *of the fields,* Ps. 50:11; 80:14.

זִיזָא p. n. of a man.

זִיזָה p. n. of a man.

מְזוּזָה f., *doorpost, jamb.*

זוּזִים p. n. of a race of giants.

זוֹחֵת p. n. of a man.

זוּל, part. זָלִים *removing, pouring forth, casting out,* Isa. 46:6.

זוּלָה const. זוּלַת f. (lit. *removal, rejection*), prep. *besides;* with suff. זוּלָתִי *besides me;* זוּלָתְךָ *besides thee,* &c.; with י parag. זוּלָתִי *besides.*

זוּן. Hoph. part. מוּזָנִים *fed, fattened,* Jer. 5:8.

זוּן Ch. Hithp. *nourished, fed,* Dan. 4:9.

מָזוֹן m., *food, meat.*

מָזוֹן m. Ch., *meat.*

זוֹנָה; see זנה.

הוּזָּה, for זָנָה, Pu.; see זנה.

זוּע *moved, was agitated.* Pil. part. מְזַעֲזֵעַ *vexing,* Hab. 2:7.

זוּע Ch., part. pl. זָאֲעִין Dan. 5:19

(זִיעִין) id. 6:27. *moving, in commotion.*

זַוָעָה f., *agitation, commotion.*

זַעֲיָה f., *vexation.*

זֵעָה f., *sweat (as the result of motion),* Gen. 3:19.

זַעֲוָן p.n. of a man.

זִיעַ p.n. of a man.

זוּר (pret. זָר; fut. יָזוּר, וַיָּזַר).—I. *compressed, squeezed.*—II. (same as סוּר *departed*) *departed, receded, was strange, abominable, adulterous;* part. זָר *a stranger, a barbarian, an enemy;* f. זָרָה *strange woman, harlot.* Niph. נָזוֹרוּ *been receding, falling off,* Isa. 1:4. Hoph. part. מוּזָר *made separate,* Ps. 69:9.

זוּרָה m., *pressed together, broken,* Is. 59:5.

מָזוֹר m., *compression of a wound by bandages;* יָשִׂימוּ מִ׳ *they make a binding (wound),* Obad. 7.

זָחַח Niph. *be removed, separated;* fut. יִזַּח.

זָחַל *withdrew, hesitated, delayed,* Job 32:6; part. pl. זֹחֲלֵי עָפָר *fearful things (serpents of the dust).*

זֵידוֹן, זֵיד *pride;* see זוד.

זִיו *splendour;* see זהה.

זִיז, זִיזָא, זִיזָה; see זוז.

זִיף p.n.—I. of a town and desert in the tribe of Judah; זִיפִי *a Ziphite.*—II. p.n. of a man.

זִיקוֹת *ornaments,* &c.; see זנק.

זַיִת const. זֵית m.—I. *olive tree.*—II. *olive;* הַר הַזֵּיתִים *Mount of Olives,* near Jerusalem.

זֵיתָן p.n. of a man.

זָכָה same as זָכַךְ *was pure.* Pi. זִכָּה

cleanse, purify. Hitnp. imp. הִזַּכּוּ (for הִתְזַכּוּ) *be, become, clean,* Isa. 1:16.

זָכוּ f. Ch., *purity, innocence,* Dan. 6:23.

זָכַךְ *was pure, clean.* Hiph. הֲזַךְ *have cleansed,* Job 9:30.

זַךְ m., זַכָּה f.—I. *pure, free from dregs.*—II. *innocent, upright.*

זְכוּכִית f., *glass or crystal,* Job 28:17.

זַכַּי p.n. of a man.

זָכַר (fut. יִזְכֹּר).—I. *remember.*—II. *meditate upon, call to mind,* with בְּ, לְ; part. זָכוּר *remembered.* Niph. נִזְכָּר — I. *be remembered, recollected.*—II. *be born a male,* from זָכָר, Ex. 34:19. — Hiph. הִזְכִּיר *record, commemorate, make mention of;* part. מַזְכִּיר לְבֹנָה *bringing a memorial* or *praise-offering of frankincense,* Isa. 66:3; מַזְכִּיר s., *recorder,* ἱστοριογράφος.

זֵכֶר, זֶכֶר m. (with suff. זִכְרוֹ).—I. *memory.*—II. *memorial.*

זָכָר m., *male.*

זָכוּר m., *male.*

זַכּוּר p.n. of a man.

זִכָּרוֹן m. (const. זִכְרוֹן; pl. זִכְרֹנִים, זִכְרֹנ‎וֹת‎—) *memorial, record.*

זִכְרִי p.n. of a man.

זְכַרְיָהוּ, זְכַרְיָה (*whom the Lord remembers*), Ζαχαρίας, p.n. of a m.

אַזְכָּרָה f., *an offering for a memorial,* Lev. 2:2, &c.

זָלַל *root not used.*

מַזְלֵג m., *a fork with three teeth.*

מִזְלָגָה f., pl. מִזְלָגוֹת *the same.*

זָלַל, part. זוֹלֵל *acting basely, profligately, obscenely.* Hiph. הִזִּיל *debase, defile.* Niph. נָזֹל; pl. נָזֹלּוּ, נָזֹלֵי *were debased.*

זַלּוּת f., *baseness, lightness*, Ps. 12:9.

זַלְזַלִּים m. pl., *tender branches*, Isa. 18:5.

זַלְעָפָה, זִלְעָפָה f.—I. *poisonous wind,* Simoon.—II. *great excitement.*— III. *hunger, famine.*

זִלְפָּה p.n. of the hand-maid of Leah.

זַמְזֻמִּים, זַמָּה, זִמָּה; see זמם.

זָמִיר, זָמִיר, זְמוֹרָה; see זמר.

זַמּוֹתִי Ps. 17:3, for זַמּוֹתִי; see זמה or זמם.

זָמַם (pret. זַמֹּתִי, זָמַמְתִּי; fut. pl. יָזֹמּוּ), *intended, determined;* part. זֹמֵם *determines, plots against.* Ps. 37:12.

זָמָם m., *determination, project*, Ps. 140:9.

זִמָּה f.—I. *intention, imagination.*— II. *sin*, specially *adultery.*—III. p.n. of a man.

זַמָּה f., pl. with suff. זַמּוֹתִי *my meditation* (Gesenius), Ps. 17:3.

זַמְזֻמִּים p. n. of a race of giants, same as זוּזִים, which see.

מְזִמָּה f., *thought, intention, purpose* (for good or evil).

זָמַן Kal, root not used; (Arab. *appointed time*). Pu. part. עִתִּים מְזֻמָּנִים, עִתִּים מְזֻמָּנוֹת *stated times.*

זְמַן Ch. Pa. *appointed, concerted,* or Hith. הִזְדַּמִּן *according to Ketib,* Dan. 2:9.

זְמָן m., *appointed time;* pl. זְמַנִּים.

זְמָן, זִמָּן m. Ch. (pl. זִמְנִין), *appointed time;* זִמְנִין תְּלָתָה *thrice, three times.*

זָמַר (fut. יִזְמֹר), *cut, prune.* Niph. *was cut.* Pi. זִמֵּר *he sang,*

with בְּ; *celebrated the praises of,* with לְ.

זֶמֶר m., *mountain goat*, Deu. 14:5.

זָמִיר m., *pruning time*, Cant. 2:12.

זָמִיר m., *song, hymn;* pl. זְמִירוֹת.

זְמוֹרָה f., *branch, bough;* pl. זְמֹרִים.

זִמְרָת, זִמְרָה, const. זִמְרַת f., *song, praise, music;* זִמְרַת הָאָרֶץ *the cropping, gathering of the earth,* Gen. 43:11.

זִמְרִי p. n. of a man.

זִמְרָן p. n. of a son of Abraham.

זְמָר m. Ch., *sound* (of musical instruments).

זַמָּר m. Ch., *singer*, Ezr. 7:24.

מִזְמוֹר m., *psalm* or *hymn.*

מְזַמֶּרֶת f., pl. מְזַמְּרוֹת *psalteries.*

מַזְמֵרָה f., pl. מַזְמֵרוֹת *pruning instruments.*

זַן, with pause זָן m. (pl. זְנִים), *kind, species.*

זַן m. Ch., the same.

זָנָב m. (pl. זְנָבוֹת; const. זַנְבוֹת), *tail of an animal;*

זִנֵּב Pi., *cut off, smite the rear of an army,* lit. *tail it.*

זָנָה I. *play the whore.*—II. *become, be idolatrous,* with אֶל, בְּ, אַחֲרֵי, מִן, מֵאַחֲרֵי, מִתַּחַת, תַּחַת, מֵעַל; part. f. זוֹנָה *harlot.* Pu. זוּנָּה *committed fornication.* Hiph. הִזְנָה *caused to commit whoredom.*

זְנוּן m., pl. זְנוּנִים.—I. *whoredom.*— II. *idolatry.*

זְנוּת f., *idolatry;* pl. זְנוּתִים.

תַּזְנוּת f., the same; pl. תַּזְנוּתִים.

זָנַח I. *stank*, Hos. 8:5.—II. *rejected, loathed.* Hiph. הִזְנִיחַ.—I. *stank,* Isa. 19:6.—II. *rejected*

זָנוֹחַ p. n. of two towns in the tribe of Judah.

זָנַק. Pi. fut. יְזַנֵּק strikes, restrains, Deu. 33:22.

זֵק f., pl. זִקִּים Pro. 26:18, "fire-brands," Eng. Ver.; arrows tipped with fire; see זקק.

זִיקָה f., pl. זִיקוֹת Isa. 50:11, "sparks," Eng. Ver.; sparkling ornaments, (Lee); meaning uncertain.

זָעַן, זַעֲוָה, זֵעָה; see זוע.

זָעִיר little; see זער.

זָעַךְ. Niph. נִזְעָכוּ "are extinct," Eng. Ver.; are swift (Lee).

זָעַם (imp. זַעֲמָה; fut. אֶזְעָם), was in-dignant, angry, with עַל, אֶת. Niph. part. נִזְעָמִים became indig-nant, angry, Pro. 25:23.

זַעַם m. (with suff. זַעְמִי, זַעַמְךָ), in-dignation, anger.

זָעַף I. was indignant, enraged, with עַל, עָם.—II. part. pl. זֹעֲפִים men-tally excited, wretched, σκυθρωποί.

זָעֵף m., indignant.

זַעַף m. (with suff. זַעְפּוֹ).—I. anger.—II. metaphorically, the raging of the sea.

זָעַק (fut. יִזְעַק; imp. זְעַק; inf. זְעֹק, לִזְעֹק), cry out, shout for help, with אֶל, לְ of the person implored; with עַל, לְ of the cause of suffering. Niph. was crying out. Hiph. הִזְעִיק sum-moned, proclaimed.

זְעַק Ch., called to, Dan. 6:21.

זַעַק m., } a cry, shout for help.
זְעָקָה f., }

זָעַר root not used; (Syr. was little).

זָעִיר m., a little.

זְעֵירָה f. Ch., the same, Dan. 7:8.

מִזְעָר m., a little (of time or number).

זִפְרוֹן p. n. of a town in the north of Palestine, Nu. 34:9.

זֶפֶת f., pitch.

זֵק, זִקִּים; see זנק and זקק.

זָקָן com.—I. the beard.—II. the chin.

זָקֵן was old; fut. יִזְקַן. Hiph. grew old.

זָקֵן m. (const. זְקַן; pl. זְקֵנִים, זִקְנֵי), old, aged, with מִן; pl. heads of tribes or families; f. pl. זְקֵנוֹת old women, Zec. 8:4.

זֹקֶן m., age, old age, Gen. 48:10.

זִקְנָה f., old.

זְקֻנִים m. pl., the same.

זָקַף erected, lifted up.

זְקַף Ch. part. זְקִיף lift up, hang a criminal.

זָקַק pour out, melt, fuse. Pi. זִקַּק fuse as metals, Mal. 3:3. Pu. fused, purified.

זֵק m., pl. זִקִּים bonds, fetters; see also in זנק.

אֲזֵק m., pl. אֲזִקִּים fetters, Jer. 40:1, 4.

זָר, זָרָה; see זור.

זַר; see זרר.

זָרָא part. from זור strange, abominable, Num. 11:20.

זָרַב. Pu. fut. יְזֹרְבוּ they are bound, oppressed, Job 6:17.

זְרֻבָּבֶל p. n.; see זרה.

זֶרֶד p. n. of a valley in the land of Moab.

זָרָה spread, disperse. Niph. was dis-persed. Pi. זֵרָה.—I. disperse.—II. discern, sift. Pu. זֹרָה was dis-persed, spread out.

זְרֻבָּבֶל p. n. of the leader of the Jews on their return from Babylon.

זֶרֶת f., *a span*, a measure of 10·944 inches.

מִזְרֶה m., *winnowing fan*.

מְזָרִים m., Job 37:9, probably the name of some northern constellation.

מַזָּרוֹת Job 38:32, probably the same; but see more under נזל.

זֵרוֹעַ ,זְרוּעַ *seed*; see זרע.

זַרְזִיף *shower*; see זרף.

זַרְזִיר *firm*; see זרר.

זָרַח (fut. יִזְרַח; inf. זְרֹחַ).—I. *rise as the sun*.—II. *give light, glory*.—III. *be white*; hence, *have leprosy*.

זֶרַח m.—I. *rising*.—II. p. n. of one of the sons of Judah, and others; זַרְחִי *a Zarchite*.

זְרַחְיָה ,זְרַחְיָהוּ p. n. of a man.

אֶזְרָח m., *indigenous, home born*, a tree not transplanted, Ps. 37:35.

אֶזְרָחִי (יִזְרַח) p. n., *an Ezrachite*.

מִזְרָח m., *the east*, the quarter of heaven whence the sun rises; מִזְרָחָה (and without ה affix) *towards the east*.

זָרַם *overwhelm*, Ps. 90:5. Po. *made to pour down*, Ps. 77:18.

זֶרֶם m., *inundation*, of rain or otherwise.

זִרְמָה f., *effusion, emission*, Eze. 23:20.

זָרַם Pi. pret. with suff.; see זרה.

זָרַע (fut. יִזְרַע; inf. זְרֹעַ; imp. זְרַע).—I. *sowing* (as seed, &c.).—II. *planting*.—III. metaphorically of righteousness, wickedness, &c. Niph. *was sown, was propagated, was dispersed*, Eze. 36:9. Pu. זֹרָעוּ *shall they be sown*, Isa. 40:24.

Hiph. part. מַזְרִיעַ *producing seed*; fut. תַּזְרִיעַ, Lev. 12:2.

זֶרַע m. (with suff. זַרְעִי ,זַרְעֲךָ; pl. זְרָעִים ,זְרָעִים).—I. *seed*.—II. *seed time*.—III. *semen* (of animals).—IV. *issue, progeny*.

זְרַע m. Ch., *the same*.

זְרֹעַ f., sometimes m. (pl. זְרֹעִים ,זְרֹעֵי, זְרֹעוֹת).—I. *arm*.—II. *fore-leg of an animal*.—III. *strength, power, violence*.

זֵרוּעַ m., *seed corn*; pl. זֵרֻעִים.

זֵרָעִים and זֵרְעֹנִם m. pl., *legumes, vegetables*.

אֶזְרוֹעַ f., same as זְרֹעַ *arm*.

יִזְרְעֶאל p. n.—I. of a town in the tribe of Issachar; m. יִזְרְעֵאלִי; f. יִזְרְעֵאלִית ,יִזְרְעֵאלִת *a Jezreelite*.—II. of a town in the tribe of Judah.—III. of a man.

מִזְרָע m., *sown field*, Isa. 19:7. const. מִזְרַע.

זָרַף root not used.

זַרְזִיף m., *copiously raining*, Ps. 72:6.

זָרַק (fut. יִזְרֹק) *scatter, sprinkle*; with עַל *of grey hairs*, Hos. 7:9. Pu. זֹרַק *was sprinkled*, Nu. 19:13, 20.

מִזְרָק m., *bowl* or *cup*; pl. מִזְרָקִים, מִזְרָקוֹת.

זֵר m., *border, moulding*.

זַרְזִיר m., *firm, compact*, Pro. 30:31.

זֶרֶשׁ p. n. of the wife of Haman.

זֶרֶת *span*; see זרה.

זַתּוּא p. n. of a man.

זֵתָם p. n. of a man.

זֵתַר p. n. of a eunuch of Ahasuerus.

ח

חָבָא Kal, root not used. Niph. נֶחְבָּא *became, was, hidden*; with

בְּ, אֶל followed by inf. with לְ
ἔλαθε, in secret; נַחְבֵּאתָ לִבְרֹחַ
thou fleddest secretly. Pu. חֻבָּא
same as Niph., Job 24:4. Hiph.
הֶחְבִּיא hide, conceal. Hoph.
הָחְבָּא same as Niph., Isa. 42:22.
Hithp. הִתְחַבָּא was, lay, hidden.

מַחֲבֵא m., hiding-place, Isa. 32:2.

מַחֲבֹא m., pl. מַחֲבֹאִים the same,
1 Sa. 23:23.

חָבַב part. חֹבֵב loving, cherishing,
Deu. 33:3.

חֹב m., with suff. חֻבִּי•my bosom, Job
31:33.

חֹבָב p. n. of the father-in-law of
Moses.

חָבָה same as חָבָא hide, be in conceal-
ment; imp. f. חֲבִי. Niph. inf.
הֵחָבֵה lay hidden.

חֲבָיָה p.n. of a man.

חֶבְיוֹן covering, vail, Hab. 3:4.

חוֹבָה p.n.of a place near Damascus,
Gen. 14:15.

נֶחְבִּי p.n. of a man.

חַבּוּרָה, חָבוּר; see חבר.

חָבַט (fut. יַחְבֹּט) beat off, threshed out.
Niph. is beaten out, Isa. 28:27.

I. חָבַל 1. bind; part. חֹבְלִים binders,
bands, Zec.11:7.—2. bind by pledge,
pledge; inf. חָבֹל; imp. חֲבֹל; fut.
יַחְבֹּל יַחֲבֹל. Pi. חִבֵּל brought
forth with pain.

II. חָבַל inflicting pain, oppressing.
Niph. suffer pain, loss, Pro. 13:13.
Pi. injure, corrupt. Pu. חֻבַּל in-
jured, destroyed.

חֲבַל Ch. Pa. injure, destroy. Ithp.
perish.

חֵבֶל m.—I. the throes of child-bearing,

ὠδίς.—II. pains generally, Job 21:
17 ; pl. חֶבְלֵי חֲבָלִים.

חֶבֶל m. (f. Zep. 2:6, with suff. חַבְלִי;
pl. (חֶבְלֵי חַבְלֵי, חֲבָלִים)—I. rope,
cord.— II. measuring line.— III.
tract of land, region, inheritance.
— IV. snare, gin.— V. company,
band of men, I Sa. 10:5, 10.

חֵבֶל m.,
חֲבֹלָה f., } pledge, deposit.

חֲבַל m. Ch.,
חֲבָל m. Ch., } injury, hurt.

חֲבוּלָא f. Ch., corrupt thing, Dan 6:
23.

חִבֵּל m., mast of a ship, Pro. 23:34.

חֹבֵל m., sailor.

תַּחְבֻּלוֹת, תַּחְבּוּלוֹת f.pl.—I. guidance,
direction.—II. rule of action.—III.
wisdom.

חֲבַצֶּלֶת f., bulbous-rooted flower,
lily.

חֲבַצִּנְיָה p. n. of a man.

חָבַק embrace, fold together, with לְ.
Pi. חִבֵּק embraced.

חִבֻּק m., folding of the hands.

חֲבַקּוּק p. n. of a prophet; LXX.
'Αμβακούμ.

חָבַר I. joined, attached, assembled,
with אֶל.—II. charm, bind with a
spell. Pi. חִבֵּר bind, join, with עִם.
Pu. חֻבַּר was joined, with אֶל, לְ,
אַחְבִּירָה Ps. 94:20. Hiph. fut.
I might compose, put together, with
עַל, Job. 16:4. Hithp. be joined.

חָבֵר m., companion; pl. חֲבֵרִים,
חַבְרִי

חֲבֶרֶת f., associate.

חֲבַר m. Ch., companion.

חֲבְרָה f. Ch., the same.

חָבֵר m., pl., חֲבֵרִים associates, Job 40:30.

חֶבֶר m.—I. association.—II. incantation, Isa. 47:9,12; pl. חֲבָרִים.—III. p.n. of a man; חֶבְרִי Heberite, Nu. 26:45.

חֶבְרָה f., association.

חֹבֶרֶת f., coupling, Ex. 26:4, 10.

חָבוֹר p.n. of a river in Mesopotamia, Chaboras.

חֲבוּרָה, חַבֻּרָה f., closing, seam, scar of a wound; with suff. חַבֻּרָתִי; pl. חַבֻּרוֹת, with suff. חַבֻּרוֹתַי.

חֶבְרוֹן p.n.—I. of a town in the tribe of Judah.—II. of a man; חֶבְרֹנִי a Hebronite.

חֲבַרְבֻּרוֹת f. pl., spots of the leopard, Jer. 13:23.

מַחְבֶּרֶת f., joining, seam; with suff. מַחְבַּרְתּוֹ.

מְחַבְּרוֹת f. pl.—I. binders, beams of timber, 2 Chron. 34:11.—II. iron cramps, 1 Chron. 22:3.

הִתְחַבְּרוּת f., league, Dan. 11:23.

חָבַשׁ (inf. חֲבוֹשׁ; fut. יַחְבָּשׁ).—I. bind, gird, with עַל, לְ.—II. govern, restrain. Pi. חִבֵּשׁ restrain, Job 28:11, with מָן Pu. חֻבַּשׁ was bound up.

חָבִית m., pl. חֲבִתִּים pancakes, 1 Chron. 9:31.

מַחֲבַת f., frying pan.

חָגָב.—I. locust.—II. p.n. of a man.

חֲגָבָה p.n. of a man.

חָגַג (fut. יָחֹג), feasting, revelling, specially, keeping the festivals prescribed by law.

חַג m. (const. חַג; with art. הֶחָג;

with suff. חַגֵּנוּ; pl. חַגִּים (חַגִּים), festival under the law.

חָגָא f., refuge, Isa. 19:17.

חַגַּי p.n. of the prophet Haggai; LXX. Ἀγγαῖος.

חַגִּי p.n. of a son of Gad.

חַגִּיָה p.n. of a man.

חַגִּית p.n. of one of the wives of David.

חָגָה root not used; (Syr. a rock).

חֲגָוֵי חֲגָוִים m. pl., fastnesses, clefts.

חֲגוֹרָה,חֲגֹר girdle; see חגר.

חָגְלָה p.n. of a woman.

חָגַר (fut. יַחְגֹּר).—I. gird, attire; with עַל of the part of the body attired; with בְּ of the object put on; part. חָגוּר girt.—II. withhold, restrain.

חֲגוֹר m.,
חֲגוֹר m., } girdle, belt; pl. חֲגֹרוֹת.
חֲגוֹרָה f.,

מַחֲגֹרֶת f., girding, Isa. 3:24.

חַד Ch., a, an, once; see אֶחָד, also חדד.

חָדַד are keen, fierce; pret. חַדּוּ Hab. 1:8. Hiph.fut. יָחַד sharpens, Pro. 27:17. Hoph. הוּחַד sharpened, Eze. 21:14—16.

חַד m., חַדָּה f., sharp.

חַדּוּדֵי,חַדּוּדִים m. pl., very sharp, Job 41:22.

חֲדַד p.n. of a son of Ishmael.

חָדִיד p.n. of a town of the Benjamites.

חָדָה (fut. apoc. יַחַדְּ), rejoice, Ex. 18:9. Pi. fut. with suff. תְּחַדֵּהוּ make glad, Ps. 21:7. Hiph. יָחַד delight, make glad, Pro. 27:17.

חֶדְוָה f. Ch., joy, gladness.

חֲדִין m. pl. Ch., Dan. 2:32, same as Heb. חָזֶה breast.

חָדֵל and חָדַל (inf. חֲדֹל; imp. חֲדַל; fut. יֶחְדַּל) cease, desist, forbear, fail, with מִן.

חָדֵל m., ceasing, wanting, failing. חֶדֶל with pause חָדֵל m., leisure, Isa. 38:11.

חַדְלִי Jud. 5:7, with pause and with dag. euphon. for חָדְלוּ, חָדֵלוּ pret. pl., from חדל.

חַדְלַי p. n. of a man.

הֶחָדַלְתִּי; see חֲדַלְתִּי.

חָדַק root not used; (Arab. melongena spinosa, a thorny shrub).

חֵדֶק and חֶדֶק, with pause חָדֶק m., a species of thorn, Pro. 15:19.

חִדֶּקֶל a river of Mesopotamia, perhaps the Tigris.

חָדַר, part. f. חֹדֶרֶת enclosing, laying siege to, Eze. 21:19.

חֶדֶר m. (const. חֲדַר; with suff. חַדְרוֹ; pl. חֲדָרִים, חַדְרֵי), chamber, inner apartment; fig. חַדְרֵי־תֵמָן the chambers of the south, i. e. the south; חַדְרֵי בֶטֶן the inner parts of the body; חַ מָוֶת the tomb.

חַדְרָךְ p. n. of a part of Syria, near Damascus, Zec. 9:1.

חָדַשׁ. Pi. חִדֵּשׁ renew, restore. Hith. is renewed, Ps. 103:5.

חָדָשׁ m., new, recent, fresh; f. חֲדָשָׁה (pl. חֲדָשׁוֹת).

חֹדֶשׁ m. (with suff. חָדְשׁוֹ; pl. חֳדָשִׁים, חָדְשֵׁי)—I. new moon: hence,— II. certain feasts regulated by the moon.— III. month which began with the new moon; חֹדֶשׁ יָמִים a whole month. — IV. p. n. of a

woman; חָדְשִׁי the son of Ho-dash.

חֲדַת m. Ch., new.

חוֹב. Pi. חִיֵּב render due, forfeit, Dan. 1:10.

חוֹב m., debt, Eze. 18:7.

חוֹבָה p. n.; see חָבָה.

חוּג circumscribe, Job 26:10.

חוּג m., sphere, globe.

מְחוּגָה f., compasses, Isa. 44:13.

חוּד propose a riddle, problem.

חִידָה f., parable, riddle.

אֲחִידָה f. Ch., the same, Dan. 5:12.

חָוָה. Pi. חִוָּה shew, declare.

חַוִּי, חַוָּה, חַוָּא. Pa. Ch., shew, de-clare. Aph. the same.

אַחֲוָה f., shewing, argument, Job 13:17.

אַחֲוָיָה f. Ch., the same, Dan. 5:12.

חַוָּה f., pl. חַוּוֹת villages of huts; see also under חוי.

חַיָּה f., crowd of men, 2 Sa. 23:11, 13; Ps. 68:11; see also under חוי.

חוֹז root not used; (Arab. shore, coast).

מָחוֹז m., haven, harbour, Ps. 107:30.

חוֹזַי p. n. of a man.

חוֹחַ m. (pl. חֲוָחִים, חוֹחִים).—I. thorn or bramble generally.—II. fish hook, Job 40:26.—III. a ring with spikes put round the necks of captives, 2 Ch. 33:11.

חָח m.—I. hook or ring put into the nose of animals, e.g. the camel. —II. a nose jewel, worn as an or-nament.

חוּט Ch. Aph., join in one thread, Ezr. 4:12.

חוּט m., thread; מֵחוּט וְעַד שְׂרוֹךְ־נַעַל from a thread to a shoe-latchet, Gen. 14:23, i. e. nothing whatever.

חִוִּי p. n., the Hivites, a people of Canaan.

חֲוִילָה p. n. of an unknown district where there was gold.

חוּל and חִיל (fut. יָחִיל, יָחוּל; apoc. וַתָּחֶל, וַיָּחֶל; imp. f. חוּלִי; pl. חִילוּ).—I. feel, be in pain.—II. tremble as a woman in labour.—III. bring forth, Isa. 54:1.—IV. precipitate, fall upon.—V. be strong, durable.—VI. waited; see יָחַל Hiph. fut. יָחִיל.—I. shake, Ps. 29:8.—II. exult, Job 20:21. Hoph. fut. יוּחַל shall be brought forth, Isa. 66:8. Pil. חוֹלֵל.—I. dance in a circle, Jud. 21:23.—II. humble, Job 26:5.—III. bring forth.—IV. wait, Job 35:14. Pul. חוֹלָל was born. Hithpo. הִתְחוֹלֵל.—I. was tormented.—II. fell upon.—III. waited, Ps. 37:7. Hithpal. הִתְחַלְחַל was pained, Est. 4:4.

חוֹל m.—I. sand.—II. measure, number, Job 29:18.—III. weight.—IV. abundance.

חוּל p. n. of a son of Aram, Gen. 10:23.

חַיִל m. (const. חֵיל; with suff. חֵילוֹ; pl. חֵילִים).—I. strength, power; עָשָׂה חַיִל did valiantly.—II. an army; אַנְשֵׁי חַיִל or בְּנֵי חַיִל soldiers; שַׂר הַחַיִל general.—III. riches, wealth; עָשָׂה חַיִל acquired wealth.—IV. virtue, integrity.—V. חֵיל הָעֵץ strength (i. e. fruit) of the tree, Joel 2:22.

חַיִל m. Ch.—I. strength.—II. army.

חֵיל and חֵל m.—I. army.—II. outwork, space before a fortification.

חִיל m. } —I. pain.—II. trembling,
חִילָה f. } fear, Ex. 15:14.

חֵילָה Ps. 48:14, same as חֵיל fortification; others read חֵילָה.

חַלְחָלָה f., great, grievous pain.

מָחוֹל m.—I. dance, dancing.—II. p. n. of a man.

מְחֹלָה f., dance.

חוּם root not used; (Arab. was black).

חוּם m., black.

חוֹמָה f., a wall; const. חוֹמַת; pl. חוֹמוֹת; dual חֹמָתַיִם.

חוּם (fut. יָחֹם, יָחוּם; 1. pers. אָחוּם) spare, pity, grieve for; often with עַיִן the eye.

חוֹף shore; see חפף.

חֻפִּים, חֻפָּם p. n. of a son of Benjamin; חוּפָמִי a Chuphamite.

חוּץ root not used; (Arab. surrounded).

חוּץ m. (pl. חֻצּוֹת, חוּצוֹת).—I. open place, court, garden.—II. out-fields, lands (without a city).—Adv. I. without, opposed to within, חוּצָה, הַחוּצָה without; בַּחוּץ the same; לַחוּצָה, לַחוּץ the same; מְחוּץ the same; with לְ besides; מֵהַחוּץ without, Eze. 41:25; מִן הַחוּץ without; מְחוּצָה the same, Eze. 40:40, 44; אֶל־הַחוּץ, the same, Eze. 41:9; אֶל הַחוּצָה the same, Eze. 34:21; אֶל מָחוּץ לְ the same; חוּץ מִן more than, Ecc. 2:25.

חַיִץ m., a wall, Eze. 13:10.

חִיצוֹן m., חִיצוֹנָה f., outer, exterior; הַמְּלָאכָה הַחִיצֹנָה לַחִיצוֹן without; outward business, i. e. civil, opposed to sacred, 1 Ch. 26:29.

חוֹג, חוֹק same as חֵיק.

חָוַר, fut. pl. יֶחֱוָרוּ shall be white, pale, Isa. 29:22.

חֹר, חוּר, חֻר m.—I. white linen.—II. nobles.—III. cavern, aperture, hole; pl. חֹרִי, חֹרִים, חוֹרֵי; see also חרר.

חִוָּר m. Ch., white, Dan. 7:9.

חֹרִי m., white bread, Gen. 40:16.

חֹרִי (τρωγλοδύτης) p.n., a Horite, i.e. dweller in a cave, a Canaanitish nation.—II. p.n. of a man.

חוּרִי p.n. of a man.

חוּרַי same as הַדַּי p.n. of a man.

חִירָם חוּרָם p.n.—I. of a king of Tyre.—II. of a man.

חַוְרָן p.n. of a country beyond Jordan, Eze. 47:16, 18.

חֹרֹנַיִם p.n. of a city of the Moabites; חֹרֹנִי a Horonite.

חוֹרִים white, &c.; see חֹר in חרר.

חוּשׁ and חִישׁ (fut. יָחִישׁ; apoc. וַתָּחַשׁ; imp. חוּשָׁה).—I. hasten (part. חָשִׁים hasting).—II. felt, enjoyed, Ecc. 2:25, with לְ. Hiph. הֵחִישׁ—I. hasten, accelerate.—II. stumble, fail.

חוּשָׁה p.n. of a man; חוּשָׁתִי a Cushathite.

חוּשַׁי p.n. of one of David's companions.

חוּשִׁים p.n. of a man.

חִישׁ adv., hastily, Ps. 90:10.

חוֹתָם seal; see חתם.

חָזָה (inf. חֲזוֹת; imp. חֲזֵה; fut. יֶחֱזֶה; apoc. אֶחַז, תַּחַז).—I. saw visions.—II. saw with pleasure.—III. look at, regard, with בְּ; look for, search out, choose, with מִן; part. חֹזֶה;

subst. const. חֹזֶה, חוֹזֶה; pl. חֹזִים.—I. prophet, seer.—II. agreement, Isa. 28:15.

חֲזָא, חֲזָה Ch., he saw.

חָזֶה m., breast of an animal cut up; const. חֲזֵה; pl. חָזוֹת.

חֶזֵו m. Ch., vision.

חָזוֹ p.n. of a man.

חָזוֹן m., vision, revelation.

חָזוּת f.—I. vision, revelation.—II. matter of vision.—III. agreement, Isa. 28:18.

חָזוֹת f., vision, 2 Ch. 9:29.

חֱזוֹת f. Ch., appearance, Dan. 4:8, 17; חִזָּיוֹן m. const. חֶזְיוֹן; pl. חֶזְיֹנוֹת dream, vision.

חֶזְיוֹן p.n. of a man, 1 Ki. 15:18.

מַחֲזֶה m., vision.

מֶחֱזָה f., window, 1 Ki. 7:4, 5.

מַחֲזִיאוֹת p.n. of a man.

חֲזָאֵל p.n. of a king of Syria.

חֲזִיאֵל p.n. of a man.

חֲזָיָה p.n. of a man.

יַחְזִיאֵל p.n. of a man.

יַחְזְיָה p.n. of a man.

חָזַז root not used; (Arab. pierced).

חָזִיז or חֲזִין m., thunder-bolt, Zec. 10:1.

חֲזִיר m., hog, swine.

חֶזִיר p.n. of a man.

חָזַק (fut. יֶחֱזַק) was strong, firm, powerful, unyielding, applied to persons, mind, or things: const. with בְּ in; עַל, אֶל on, to; מִן more than; לְ to, for. Pi. חִזַּק made strong, firm.—I. with יָד 1. strengthened the hand.—2. supported.—II. with לֵב 1. hardened the heart.—2. restored, healed Hiph. הֶחֱזִיק I. take fast *hold of, obtain, retain,* with בְּ, לְ, עַל.—II. *applying strength to, repairing, confirming, prevailing.* Hith. הִתְחַזֵּק *became, waxed strong, received strength,* &c.; with לִפְנֵי *oppose, resist;* with בְּ or עִם *assist, aid.*

חָזֵק m., *becoming strong;* הוֹלֵךְ וְחָ׳ *waxing strong.*

חָזָק m., *strong, mighty, unyielding, prevailing,* used either in a good or bad sense.

חֹזֶק m., *strength;* with suff. חִזְקִי Ps. 18:2.

חֹזֶק m., the same; with suff. חָזְקִי.

חֶזְקָה f. (same as חָזָק inf., see חָזַק), בְּחֶזְקָתוֹ *when he gained strength,* with בְּ; בְּחֶזְקַת־יָדֶיךָ *when the hand of God impelled.*

חָזְקָה f.—I. *force, vehemence;* בְּחָזְקָה *with power, vehemently.*—II. *repairing an edifice,* 2 Ki. 12:13.

חֶזְקִי p.n. of a man.

חִזְקִיָּה, חִזְקִיָּהוּ, יְחִזְקִיָּה, יְחִזְקִיָּהוּ p.n., *Hezekiah,* king of Judah, and others; LXX. Ἐζεχίας.

יְחֶזְקֵאל (*the Lord strengthens*), p. n., *Ezekiel* the prophet; LXX. Ἰεζεκιήλ.

חָח, חַחִים *hook;* see חוֹחַ.

חָטָא (inf. חֲטוֹא, חֲטֹא; fut. יֶחֱטָא).—I. *err, wander from.*—II. *sin;* with בְּ, לְ, or עַל *by, against.*—III. *miss the mark, fall short of,* with מִן; part. m. חוֹטֵא, חוֹטֶא; pl. חֹטְאִים; f. חֹטֵאת. Pi. חִטֵּא *expiate, cleanse, free from sin.* Hiph. הֶחֱטִיא I. *miss the mark.*—II. *cause to sin.* Hith. I. *be, become erring,* Job 41:17.—II. *be cleansed from sin.*

חֵטְא m. (with suff. חֶטְאִי; pl. חֲטָאִים, חֲטָאֵי), *sin, wickedness.*

חֲטִי or חֲטָי m. Ch., *sin,* Dan. 4:24.

חֲטָאָה f., *sin.*

חַטָּא m., *sinner;* חַטָּאָה f., Am. 9:8.

חֲטָאָה f., *sin,* Gen. 20:9.

חַטָּאָה f., *sin,* Ex. 34:7; Isa. 5:18.

חֲטָאָה f., *sin,* Nu. 15:28.

חַטָּאת f. (const. חַטַּאת; pl. חַטָּאוֹת; const. חַטֹּאאת).—I. *sin.*—II. *sin-offering.*—III. *idol.*—IV. *punishment of sin,* Zec. 14:19; Pro. 10:16.

חַטָּאָה Ch. (Kri), חַטָּיָא (Ketib), *sin-offering,* Ezr. 6:17.

חָטָא, חָטוֹר Kal inf. const., from חָטָא.

חָטַב (fut. יַחְטֹב) *cutting wood.* Pu. part. f. מְחֻטָּבוֹת *hewn stones,* Ps. 144:12.

חֲטֻבוֹת f. pl., *striped, variegated,* Pro. 7:16.

חִטָּה f., *wheat;* pl. חִטִּים; Ch. חִטִּין and חַנְטִין *grains of wheat.*

חָטוּשׁ p. n. of a man.

חֲטִיטָא p. n. of a man.

חַטִּיל p. n. of a man.

חָטַם (lit. *ring a camel through the nose,* which is the mode of bitting that animal); fut. אֶחֱטָם־לָךְ *I will restrain my anger against thee,* Isa. 48:9.

חָטַף (fut. יַחְטֹף) *rob, take by violence.* חֲטִיפָא p. n. of a man.

חֹטֶר m., *stick, rod,* Pro. 14:3; Isa. 11:1.

חִיאֵל, חַי see חיי.

חִידָה *riddle;* see חוד.

חָיָה (inf. חָיֹה, חָיוֹ; const. חֲיוֹת; imp. חֲיֵה; fut. יִחְיֶה; apoc. יְחִי) *he lived in health, safety, vigour,* &c.; with

מֵן *recovered after sickness.* Pi.
חִיָה—I. *giving, preserving, restor-*
ing life.—II. *strengthen, make ef-*
fectual; חִיָה זֶרַע *preserve seed,*
Gen. 7:3. Hiph. הֶחֱיָה *give, pre-*
serve life.

חָיָה or חָיָא Ch., *he lived;* imp. חֱיִי·
Aph. part. מַחֵא *giving life.*

חָיֶה m., not used; f. חָיָה; pl. חָיוֹת
lively, strong, Ex. 1:19.

יְחַוְאֵל p.n. of a man.

מִחְיָה f.—I. *means of living, food.*—
II. *crude, raw,* i.e. *unsound, diseased,*
Lev. 13:10, 24; *see also in* חוה·

חָיַי *lived;* pret. m. חַי, וָחַי; f. חָיְתָה,
Ex. 1:16.

חַי m. (const. חֵי; pl. חַיִּים; with
suff. חַיֶּיךָ), s. *living, alive,* חַי יְהוָה
וְחֵי נַפְשֶׁךָ *as the Lord liveth and*
thy soul liveth; adj. (f. חַיָּה; pl.
חָיוֹת) *living, alive, safe, reviving;*
כָּעֵת חַיָּה *according to the time of*
life; metaphorically, *living* (i. e.
springing) *water; living* (i.e. *fresh*)
meat.

חַי m. Ch., *living;* pl. חַיִּין, חַיֵּי, s. *life.*

חַיָּה f. (const. חַיַּת; חַיְתוֹ; with suff.
חַיָּתוֹ; pl. חָיוֹת).—I. *life.*—II. *ani-*
mal, wild beast; see also in חוה·

חַוָּה (same as חָיָה *life*), p.n. *Eve* the
first woman; LXX. Ἔυα, Vulg.
Heva; *see also in* חוה·

חַיָּא f. Ch., *living creature.*

חַיּוּת f., *life.*

חַיְתוֹ const. state with ו parag. for
חַיַּת; from חָיָה; *see in* חַיָי·

יְחִיאֵל p.n. of a man; יְחִיאֵלִי one of
the family of Jehoel.

חִיאֵל p.n. of a man.

חִילָה, חֵיל, חַיִל, חֵיל; *see* חול·

חֵילָם, חֵלָם p. n. of a city not far
from the Euphrates.

חִילֵן same as חֹלֹן·

חִין; *see* חנן·

חִיצוֹנָה, חַיָן; חִיצוֹן; *see* חוץ·

חֵיק and חֵק, חֹק m., *the bosom.*—I. in a
conjugal sense.—II. in a dishonest
sense, Pro. 5:20.—III. in a moral
sense, *the feelings, affections.*—IV.
bosom, lappet of a *garment.*—V.
hollow place in a chariot, 1 Ki. 22:
35; *in the altar,* Eze. 43:13, &c.

חִירָה p. n. of a man.

חִישׁ *hastily;* *see* חוש·

חַךְ, חֵךְ *palate;* *see* חנך·

חָכָה *waiting,* with לְ, Isa. 30:18. Pi.
חִכָּה the same.

חַכֵּי for חַכֵּה Pi. inf. of חָכָה·

חַכְלִילִי m., *brightened with wine* (of
the eyes), Gen. 49:12.

חַכְלִלוּת f., *fierceness of eyes,* Pro. 23:
29.

חֲכִילָה p. n. of a hill in the wilderness of Ziph.

חֲכַלְיָה p. n. of a man.

חָכַם (fut. יֶחְכַּם) *was wise, intelligent,*
taught. Pi. *made wise, taught.*
Pu. part. מְחֻכָּם *made wise.* Hiph.
part. f. מַחְכִּימָה *making wise,* Ps.
19:8. Hithp. *account oneself wise,*
cunning.

חָכָם m. (f. חֲכָמָה).—I. *wise.*—II.
teacher of wisdom.—III. *intelli-*
gent, clever; חֲכָמִים *wise men* (of
soothsayers, &c.); חַכְמוֹת (i.e. קִינָה)
women skilled in lamenting at fu-
nerals, Jer. 9:16.

חַכִּים m. Ch., *wise man, magician.*

חָכְמָה f., *wisdom.*

חָכְמָה f. Ch., *wisdom.*

חָכְמוֹת, חַכְמוֹת f., *the same.*

חַכְמֹנִי p.n. of a man.

חָל same as חִיל *pain;* see חול.

חֹל *profane;* see חלל.

חֵלָא same as חָלָה *sick, weak, afflicted.*

חֶלְאָה f.—I. *refuse, filth, scum,* Eze. 24:6.—II. p.n. of a woman.

חֲלָאִים *diseases;* see חֲלִי in חלה.

חָלָב m. (const. חֲלֵב; with suff. חֲלָבִי), *new milk* or *cream.*

חֵלֶב and חֶלֶב m. (with suff. חֶלְבּוֹ; pl. חֶלְבֵּי חֲלָבִים).—I. *fat, fatness, the best of any thing;* ח' הָאָרֶץ *the fatness of the earth;* ח' חִטָּה *the best of the wheat.*—II. *hardness, impenitency,* Ps. 17:10, &c.—III. p.n. of a man.

חֶלְבָּה p. n. of a town in the tribe of Asher.

חֶלְבּוֹן p.n. of a city in Syria, Χαλυβών.

חֶלְבְּנָה f., *galbanum,* an odoriferous gum, Ex. 30:34.

חֶלֶד root not used; (Arab. *duration*).

חֶלֶד m. (with suff. חֶלְדִּי), *time, duration;* מְתִים מֵחֶלֶד *men of time,* i.e. of this world, Ps. 17:14.

חֹלֶד m., *a mole.*

חֻלְדָּה p.n. of a prophetess; LXX. Ὀλδά.

חֶלְדַּי p.n. of a man.

I. חָלָה (fut. apoc. וַיִּחַל), *was sick, weak, afflicted,* with עַל. Niph. נֶחְלָה *became sick, weak, afflicted;* part. נַחְלָה (f. נַחְלָה), *diseased, infirm.* Pi. חִלָּה *afflicted;* with suff. חִלּוֹתִי *my sickness.* Pu. חֻלָּה *afflicted, infirm,* Isa. 14:10. Hiph. הֶחֱלִי (for הֶחֱלָה) *afflicted, made sick, infirm.* Hoph. הָחֳלָה *wounded.* Hith. *feigned sickness;* imper. apoc. הִתְחַל, fut. apoc. וַיִּתְחַל. חַלּוֹתִי Ps. 77:11. Pi. inf. with suff., from I. חלה.

חֳלִי with pause חֹלִי m. (with suff. חָלְיוֹ; pl. חֳלָיִים). *disease, sickness, evil, inconvenience.*

חֲלִי m., *ornament, necklace;* pl. חֲלָאִים.

חֶלְיָה f., *the same.*

אַחֲלַי, אַחֲלֵי m., *prayer;* אָחֲל *would that!*

מַחֲלֶה m., מַחֲלָה f., } *sickness, disease.*

מַחֲלָה p. n. of a woman.

מַחְלוֹן p. n. of a man.

מַחְלִי p. n. of a man.

מַחֲלוּי m., pl. מַחֲלָיִים *circumstances of disease,* 2 Chron. 24:25.

מַחֲלַת m., a title of Ps. 53 and 88; meaning uncertain.

מַחֲלַת p. n. of a woman.

תַּחֲלֻאִים m., pl. תַּחֲלוּאִים *diseases.*

II. חָלָה Kal not used; (Arab. *was sweet*). Pi. חִלָּה, with פְּנֵי *make propitious, conciliate favour, satisfy;* imp. apoc. חַל, fut. apoc. וַיְחַל.

חַלּוֹן, חַלָּה; see חלל.

חֲלוֹם *dream;* see חלם.

חֹלוֹן p. n. of a town in the land of Moab.

חֲלוֹף *passing away;* see חלף.

חֲלוּשָׁה *defeat;* see חלש.

חֲלַח p. n. of a province in the kingdom of Assyria (Καλαχηνη).

חַלְחָלָה *pain;* see חול.

חָלַט. Hiph. fut. וַיַּחְלְטוּ 1 Ki.20:33, "did hastily catch," Eng. Ver.; "hasted greatly" (Lee).

חֶלְיָה, חֲלִי, חֲלִי see חלה.

חָלִיל pipe; see חלל.

חֲלִיפָה change; see חלף.

חֲלִיצָה spoil; see חלץ.

חָלַךְ root not used; (Arab. intense blackness).

חֵלְכָה with pause חֵלְכָה m., very miserable, Ps.10:8,14; pl. חֵלְכָּאִים, v.10.

חָלַל pierced, wounded, Ps. 109:22. Niph. נָחַל profaned, became common, prostituted; inf. הֵחַל; fut. תֵּחַל, יֵחַל. Pi. חִלֵּל—I. wounded, Eze. 28:9. — II. profaned, made common, violated (a covenant).— III. played upon the flute, 1 Ki.1:40, from חָלִיל. Pu. part. מְחֻלָּל profaned. Po. חוֹלֵל wounding. Poal. part. מְחוֹלָל wounded. Hiph. הֵחַל—I. make profane, violate, loose, set free.—II. begin; pret. 1. pers. הַחִלּוֹתִי; inf. with suff. הָחִלָּם their beginning; fut. יָחֵל shall begin; יָחֵל shall loose. Hoph. הוּחַל was begun, Gen. 4:26.

חֲלִילָה m., pipe; pl. חֲלִילִים; חֲלִילָה int. profane! fie! with לְ of the pers. and inf. with מִן ח' לְךָ מֵעֲשׂוֹת that be far from thee to do so.

חָלָל (const. חֲלַל m.).—I.pierced, wounded, slain.—II. profane, common; f. חֲלָלָה prostitute, Lev. 21:7, 14.

חֹל m., profane, common.

חַלָּה const. חַלַּת f., cake (pierced with holes).

חַלּוֹן com., window, (i. e. opening); pl. חַלּוֹנִים.

מְחִלָּה f., pl. מְחִלּוֹת caves, holes of the earth, Isa. 2:19.

תְּחִלָּה f., beginning; בַּתְּחִלָּה at first, formerly.

חָלַם (fut. יַחֲלֹם).—I. dream.—II. be fat, Job 39:4. Hiph.— I. make stout, strong, Isa. 38:16.—II. part. מַחֲלִמִים causing to see visions, Jer. 29:8.

חֲלוֹם m., a dream; pl. חֲלֹמוֹת.

חֵלֶם m. Ch.—I. dream.—II. p. n. of a man.

חֲלֻמוֹת f., Job 6:6, "egg," Eng. Ver.; cheese, (Lee).

חַלָּמִישׁ m., flint, stone striking fire.

אַחְלָמָה f., a precious stone; LXX. ἀμέθυστος.

חֹלֹן p. n.—I. of a town in the tribe of Judah; same as חִילֵן.—II. in the land of Moab; same as חֹרוֹן.

חָלַף (יַחֲלֹף).—I. pass by, away.—II. put away. Pi. חִלֵּף change (as clothes). Hiph. הֶחֱלִיף—I. change (as clothes).—II. renew.

חֲלַף Ch., pass by or away.

חֵלֶף prep. for, instead of, Nu. 18:21, 31.

חֲלוֹף m.; בְּנֵי ח' children of those passed away, orphans, Pro. 31:8.

חֲלִיפָה f., change, renewal (of clothes, troops, &c.).

מַחֲלָף m., knife for sacrifice, Ezr. 1:9.

מַחְלְפוֹת pl f., locks of hair, Jud. 16:13, 19.

חָלַץ (fut. יַחֲלַץ).—I. deliver, free.—II. give the breast, Lam. 4:3.—III. gird, arm for battle, with מִן; חֲלוּץ הַנַּעַל without sandals. Niph.—I. was delivered.—II. was armed.

Pi. *deliver, set free*; חָלוּץ *girt, armed, ready*; חֲלוּץ צָבָא *host armed*; חֲלֻצֵי־מוֹאָב *warriors of Moab*. Hiph. יַחֲלִיץ *make strong*, Isa. 58: 11.

חֲלִיצָה f., *spoil*, Jud. 14: 19; 2 Sa. 2: 21.

חָלָץ m., dual חֲלָצִים *loins*.

חֵלֶץ p. n. of a man.

מַחֲלָצוֹת f. pl., *dress of honour, mantle.*

חָלַק (fut. יַחֲלֹק).—I. *apportioned, divided land, wealth, spoil.*—II. *was smooth, fallacious*, with עִם. Niph. *was divided, distributed.* Pi.—I. *divided, distributed*, with אֶת—II. *dispersed*, with לְ. Pu. *was divided.* Hiph. הֶחֱלִיק. — I. *make smooth, flattering.*—II. *taking portion*, Jer. 37: 12. Hithp. *dividing, apportioning*, Jos. 18: 5.

חָלָק m., *smooth, slippery, fallacious, flattering.*

חֵלֶק m. (with suff. חֶלְקִי; pl. חֲלָקִים). —I. *part, portion, lot of land, field.* —II. *portion of the sacrifice.*—III. *prey*; חֶלְקֵי נַחַל Isa. 57: 6, "*smooth stones*;" Eng. Ver. *river gods* (Lee); חֵלֶק לִי with אֶת, עִם, בְּ *my portion is with*, &c.—IV. *smoothness.*—V. p. n. of a son of Gilead; חֶלְקִי *son of Chelek.*

חֲלָק m. Ch., *part, portion.*

חַלָּק m., pl. חַלֻּקִים *smooth stones*, 1 Sa. 17: 40.

חֶלְקָה f.—I. *slipperiness.*—II. *flattery.* —III. *portion*; pl. חֲלָקוֹת *slippery ways*, Ps. 73: 18.

חֲלֻקָּה f., *division, divided part*, 2 Chron. 35: 5.

חֲלָקוֹת f. pl. Ch., *blandishments*, Dan. 11: 32.

חֶלְקֵי pl. const. with dag. euphon., from חֵלֶק.

חֶלְקִי p. n. of a man.

חִלְקִיָּה, חִלְקִיָּהוּ p. n.—I. of a man.— II. the high priest in Josiah's reign. —III. the father of Jeremiah the prophet.— IV. the father of Eliakim.

חֲלַקְלַקּוֹת *very slippery ways, devices.*

מַחֲלֹקֶת f. (with suff. מַחֲלֻקְתּוֹ; pl. מַחְלְקוֹת).—I. *appointment, distribution, order, course.*—II. p. n. of a place; סֶלַע הַמַּחְלְקוֹת.

מַחְלְקָה f. Ch., *distribution, order*, Ezr. 6: 18.

חָלַשׁ (fut. יֶחֱלַשׁ) *grow feeble*, Job 14: 10; (fut. יַחֲלֹשׁ) *discomfit, reduce*, with עַל, Ex. 17: 13.

חַלָּשׁ m., *weak person*, Joel 4: 10.

חֲלוּשָׁה f., *discomfiture*, Ex. 32: 18.

חָם m. (with suff. חָמִיהָ, חָמִיךְ) *father-in-law*; see also in חמם.

חָמוֹת f., *mother-in-law.*

חֹם *hot*; see חמם.

חָמָא root not used; (Arab. *curdled, of milk*).

חֶמְאָה (Syr. חֵמָה) *cheese, curd.*

חֵמָה f., *the same*; see also in יחם.

מֵחֶמָאֹת f. pl., Ps. 55: 22; read מֵחֶמ׳ *than butter.*

חָמַד (fut. יַחְמֹד) *desired, coveted*; part. (חֲמֻדוֹת f. חֲמוּדִים pl. m.) חָמוּד *desirable thing.* Niph. part. נֶחְמָד *desirable.* Pi. *greatly desired*, Cant. 2: 3.

חֶמֶד m., חֶמְדָּה f., *desire, that which is desirable*; חֶמְדַּת כָּל גּוֹיִם *the desire of all nations*, i. e. Messiah, Hag. 2: 7.

חֲמוּדוֹת, חֲמֻדוֹת f. pl., *desirable things.*

חֶמְדָּן p.n. of a man.

מַחְמָד m. (pl. מַחְמַדִּים) *desirable, desirable things.*

מַחְמַדִּים m. pl., the same, Lam. 1:7, 11.

חַמּוֹן, חַמּוּאֵל, חַמָּה; see חמם.

חֶמְאָה same as חֶמְאָה *butter;* see also in יחם.

חֲמוּטַל p. n. of the wife of Josiah.

חָמוּץ *sour;* see חמץ.

חָמוּק *surround;* see חמק.

חֲמוֹר *ass;* see חמר.

חָמוֹת *mother-in-law;* see חם.

חֹמֶט m., kind of *lizard,* Lev. 11:30; LXX. σαύρα.

חֲמִישִׁי *fifth;* see חָמֵשׁ.

חָמַל (fut. יַחְמֹל; inf. חֶמְלָה) *bear with, forbear with,* with עַל; *spare,* with אֶל.

חֶמְלָה f., *clemency.*

מַחְמָל *support, comfort,* Eze. 24:21.

חָמַם (fut. וַיָּחָם, יֵחַם; inf. חֹם, with suff. חֻמּוֹ).—I. *be, grow hot;* כְּחֹם הַיּוֹם *in the heat of the day;* חַם לוֹ *he becomes warm.*—II. *hot with lust.* Niph. *became hot, inflamed;* fut. יֵחַם, יֵחָם; part. pl. נֵחָמִים. Pi. *warms, hatches,* Job 39:14. Hithp. *becomes warm,* Job 31:20.

חָם m.—I. *warm, growing hot;* pl. חַמִּים.—II. p. n. of a son of Noah.—III. perhaps Egypt (Copt. χημι), Ps. 78:51, &c.; see also חָם in its place.

חֹם m., *heat;* לֶחֶם חֹם *hot bread,* i.e. new.

חַמָּה f., const. חֲמַת *heat;* see in יחם.

חַמָּה f.—I. *heat, glow,* Ps. 19:7.—II. *the sun.*

חַמּוּאֵל p.n. of a man.

חַמּוֹן p. n.—I. of a town in the tribe of Asher.—II. of a town in the tribe of Naphtali.

חַמָּן m., pl. חַמָּנִים *sun-images;* probably the *Amoun* of Egypt; Greek ἀμουν.

חָמַס (fut. יַחְמֹס), *doing violence, injury, wrong,* with עַל. Niph. *violated,* Jer. 13:22.

חָמָס m. (const. חֲמַס; with suff. חֲמָסִי; pl. חֲמָסִים), *violence, injury, that which is obtained by violence.*

תַּחְמָס m., *ostrich;* LXX. γλαύξ; Vulg. noctua.

חָמֵץ (fut. יֶחְמַץ; with pause יֶחְמָץ; inf. חֲמֹצָה), *fermented, leavened;* part. חָמוּץ *scarlet;* part. חֹמֵץ. Hiph. part. f. מַחְמֶצֶת *fermented.* Hith. *was excited, perturbed,* Ps. 73:21.

חָמֵץ m., *leavened, fermented.*

חֹמֶץ m., *vinegar.*

חָמוּץ m., *injured, oppressed,* Isa. 1:17.

חָמִיץ m., "clean provender," Isa. 30:24, Eng. Ver.; "a salt, sour plant of the desert, much relished by the camel" (Lee).

חָמַק *withdrew, disappeared,* Cant. 5:6. Hith. *loiter, act undecidedly,* Jer. 31:22.

חַמּוּק m., חִ' יְרֵכַיִךְ Cant. 7:2; probably *large beads,* strung together and worn as a girdle; such girdles are often represented in the tombs of Egypt.

חָמַר (fut. pl. יֶחְמָרוּ), *fermented, was excited.* Poal. חֳמַרְמָר *excited, become inflamed.* (From חֵמָר) Hiph. fut. with suff. וַתַּחְמְרָה *she cemented it with pitch,* Ex. 2:3.

חֵמָר m., *mineral pitch,* ἄσφαλτος.

חֶמֶר m., *wine.*

חֲמַר m., *the same.*

חֹמֶר m. (pl. חֳמָרִים).—I. *clay, earth, mire.*—II. *heap, mound of earth.*—III. *measure of capacity,* containing ten baths.

חֲמֹר ,חֲמוֹר m.—I. *an ass.*—II. *a heap,* Jud. 15:16, same as חֹמֶר; dual חֲמֹרָתָיִם.—III. p.n. of a man.

חֶמְדָּן ,חַמְרָן p. n. of a man.

יַחְמוּר m., *goat* or *gazelle of a brown colour.*

חֹמֶשׁ m., *the abdomen;* see also in חָמֵשׁ.

חָמֵשׁ const. חֲמֵשׁ f., חֲמִשָּׁה ,חֲמֵשֶׁת m., *five;* pl. חֲמִשִּׁים *fifty;* with suff. חֲמִשֶׁיךָ ,חֲמִשָׁיו; שַׂר חֲמִשִּׁים *captain of fifty.*

חִמֵּשׁ Pi. *divided into fifth part,* Gen. 41:34.

חֹמֶשׁ m., *fifth part,* Gen. 47:26.

חֲמִישִׁי ,חֲמִשִּׁי m., *fifth;* f. חֲמִישִׁית; pl. with suff. חֲמִשִׁיתָיו *the fifth part of it.*

חֲמֻשִׁים m. pl., *compact in battle array;* Aquila ἐνωπλισμένοι; Vulg. armati.

חֵמֶת m., *bottle, skin for holding liquids;* const. חֵמַת חֲמַת.

חֲמָת p. n., *Hamath in Syria,* north of Palestine; חֲמָתִי *a Hamathite.*

חַמֹּת דֹּאר p. n. of a town in the tribe of Naphtali.

חֵן ,חֲנָדָד; see חנן.

חָנָה (fut. יֶחֱנֶה; apoc. וַיִּחַן).—I. *declined* (of the day), Jud. 19:9.—II. *pitch a tent, encamp;* with עַל *encamp against;* with לְ *defended.*—III. *dwell, reside,* Isa. 29:1.

חָנֻת f., pl. חֲנֻיּוֹת *wells* used as dungeons, Jer. 37:16.

חֲנִית f., *spear, lance;* pl. חֲנִיתִים, חֲנִיתוֹת.

מַחֲנֶה m. (f. Gen. 32:9).—I. *camp.*—II. *army, body of people.*—III. *flock of cattle, locusts,* &c.; const. מַחֲנֵה; pl. מַחֲנִים (מַחֲנַיִם), מַחֲנוֹת; מַחֲנֵה־דָן (*camp of the Danites*), p. n. of a place in the tribe of Judah.

מַחֲנַיִם (*two troops*), p. n. of a town in the tribe of Gad.

תַּחֲנוֹת f. pl., *camp,* 2 Ki. 6:8.

תַּחַן p. n. of a man; תַּחֲנִי *son of Tachan.*

חֲנֻרָה ,חָנוּן ,חַנִּיאֵל ,חֲנִינָה; see חנן.

חָנוּף ,חָנִיךְ; see חנך.

חָנַט I. *ripened,* Cant. 2:13.—II. *embalmed, mummified,* Gen. 50:2, 2, 26.

חֲנָטִים m. pl., *mummy, embalmed body.*

חִטָּה ,חִטִּים ,חִטִּין *wheat;* see חִטָּה.

חָנַךְ *adapt, fit to certain ends.*—I. *teach a child,* Pro. 22:6.—II. *dedicate a temple.*

חֵךְ m. (with suff. חִכִּי).—I. *palate, taste.*—II. *moral perception,* Pro. 8:7.

חַכָּה f., *fish-hook.*

חָנִיךְ m., *trained men,* Gen. 14:14.

חֲנוֹךְ p. n. of a man; חֲנֹכִי *the son of Chanoch.*

חֲנֻכָּה f., dedication.

חֲנֻכָּה Ch., the same.

חִנָּם in vain; see חנן.

חֲנַמְאֵל p. n. of a man.

חֲנָמָל m., frost.

חָנַן (fut. יָחֹן יֶחֱנַן וַיָּחָן; with suff. יְחָנְךָ יְחָנְנוּ תְּחָנֵּם; with נ epenth. יְחֻנֶּךָּ; inf. abs. חָנוֹן; const. חֲנֹן; with suff. חֲנֻכֶם חָנְנָה; imper. with suff. חָנֵּנִי חָנְנֵנִי חָנֵּנִי; pl. חָנֵּנוּ חָנְנֵנִי (חָנֵּנִי חָנֵּנוּ), being, acting favourably, graciously, kindly. Niph. נֵחַן was pitiable, Jer. 22:23. Pi. fut. יְחַנֵּן be favourable, gracious to. Po. חוֹנֵן the same, Pro. 14:21. Hoph. fut. יֻחַן be favoured, find favour. Hith. הִתְחַנֵּן implore, supplicate favour, with לְ, אֶל, לִפְנֵי; inf. with suff. הִתְחַנְּנוּ.

חֲנַן Ch., show favour. Hith. implore favour.

חֲנַנְאֵל p. n. of a fortress of Jerusalem.

חֲנָנִי p. n. of a man.

חֲנַנְיָה ('Avavías), p. n. of a man.

חֵן m. (with suff. חִנּוֹ).—I. grace, favour; מָצָא חֵן בְּעֵינֵי פ׳ found favour in his sight; נָתַן חֵן בְּעֵינֵי פ׳ gave favour in the sight of him.—II. elegance, grace of deportment.—III. worth, value.—IV. prayer for grace, Zec. 12:10.—V. p.n. of a man.

חֵנָדָד p. n. of a man.

חִין m., destructiveness, Job 41:4.

חַנָּה f. (pl. חַנּוֹת).—I. entreaty for favour, showing favour.—II. p.n. of a woman, "Avva.

חָנוּן p. n. of a man.

חַנּוּן m., very gracious.

חֲנִיאֵל p. n. of a man.

חֲנִינָה f., grace, favour, Jer. 16:13.

חִנָּם adv.—I. freely, for nothing.—II. in vain.—III. for nothing, undeservedly.

תְּחִנָּה f.—I. favour, mercy.—II. prayer for favour, prayer.

תַּחֲנוּנִים m. pl., prayers for mercy, supplications.

תַּחֲנוּנוֹת f. pl., the same.

חָנֵס p. n. of a city in Egypt ('Ηρακλέους πόλις).

חָנֵף (fut. יֶחֱנַף), was heathenish, profane, ungodly. Hiph. הֶחֱנִיף the same.

חָנֵף m., profane, ungodly; חֲנֵפִים, חַנְפֵי.

חֹנֶף m., heathenism, Isa. 32:6.

חֲנֻפָּה f., the same, Jer. 23:15.

חָנַק. Niph. fut. וַיֵּחָנַק hanged himself, 2 Sa. 17:23. Pi. part. מְחַנֵּק suffocating, Nah. 2:13.

מַחֲנַק m., suffocation, Job 7:15.

חָסַד. Pi. חִסֵּד accuse of baseness, impiety, Pro. 25:10. Hith. (fut. תִּתְחַסָּד) show thyself merciful, 2 Sa. 22:26; Ps. 18:26.

חֶסֶד m. (with suff. חַסְדּוֹ; pl. חֲסָדִים, חֲסָדַי).—I. favour, kindness, mercy; עָשָׂה חֶסֶד with אֶת, עַל, לְ, עִם he showed mercy to him.—II. goodness, benevolence.—III. shame, disgrace, incest, Lev. 20:17.—IV. p. n. of a man.

חֲסַדְיָה p. n. of the son of Zerubbabel.

חָסִיד m., gracious, confident; חֲסִידֵי יְהֹוָה they that trust in the Lord.

חֲסִידָה f., stork, supposed by the ancients to be pious to its parents.

חָסָה (fut. אֶחֱסֶה, אֶחְסֶה), *trust, confide in*, with בְּ.

חֹסֶה p. n. of a man.

חָסוּת f., *confidence*, Isa. 30:3.

חָסְיָה for חָסְתָה Kal pret. f.; pl. חָסָיוּ for חָסוּ, from חסה.

(מַחֲסִי) **מַחֲסֶה, מַחְסֶה** m. (with suff.), *refuge*.

מַחְסֵיָה p. n. of a man.

חָסַל *crop off, devour*, Deu. 28:38.

חָסִיל m., *kind of locust*, LXX. βροῦχος.

חָסַם (fut. יַחְסֹם), *bind, tie up, stop* (the mouth).

מַחְסֹם m., *bridle, curb*, Ps. 39:2.

חָסַן. Niph. fut. יֵחָסֵן *was strong, powerful*, Isa. 23:18.

חֲסַן Ch. Aph. *confirm, make strong*.

חֵסֶן m. Ch., *might, power*.

חֹסֶן m., *strength, power, wealth*.

חָסוֹן m., *strong, powerful*.

חָסִין m., *mighty*, Ps. 89:9.

חֶסֶף m., *potter's clay*.

מְחֻסְפָּס m., *scaly, having scales*, Ex. 16:14.

חָסֵר (נֶחְסְרוּ; inf. חֲסוֹר; fut. יֶחְסַר), *want, lack, be in need.* Pi. *diminish, make to want.* Hiph. הֶחְסִיר *cause to fall short*.

חָסֵר m., *wanting, destitute of*, with מִן; חֲסַר־לֵב *without heart* (i. e. sense), *foolish*.

חֶסֶר m., *deficiency, want.*

חֹסֶר m., *the same.*

(תַּרְחַם) **חֶסְרָה** p. n. of a man.

חֶסְרוֹן m., *much want*, Ecc. 1:15.

חַסִּיר m. Ch., *deficient*, Dan. 5:27.

מַחְסוֹר m. (with suff. מַחְסֹרוֹ; pl. מַחְסֹרִים) *want, lack, need.*

חָפָא same as חָפָה. Pi. *acted secretly, clandestinely*, 2 Ki. 17:9.

חָפָה *covered, veiled*. Pi. חִפָּה *overlaid, cased* (with gold). Pu. חֻפָּה " *defence;*" Eng. Ver., Isa. 4:5; see חָפַף. Niph. נֶחְפָּה *covered. overlaid*, with בְּ, Ps. 68:14.

חָפַז (יַחְפֹּז).—I. *affright, alarm.*— II. *hurry.* Niph. נֶחְפַּז *was hurried.*

חִפָּזוֹן m., *haste, hurry.*

חָפַן root not used; (Arab. a measure containing two hands full).

חֹפֶן m., dual חָפְנַיִם חָפְנֵי *both hands* closed so as to contain something.

חָפְנִי p. n. of the son of Eli.

חָפַף *cover, protect*, Deu. 33:12, with עַל.

חוֹף, חֹף m., *shore of the sea.*

חַף m., *pure, faultless*, Job 33:9 (lit. *protected*).

חֻפָּה f.—I. *defence;* see חפף.—II. *bridal chamber.*—III. p. n. of a man.

חֻפִּים p. n. of a man.

חָפֵץ (יַחְפֹּץ, יֶחְפַּץ).—I. *delight, be pleased with*, with לְ and בְּ.— II. *bend, move.*

חָפֵץ m., *willing, delighting, acquiescing;* אִם חֹ' אַתָּה *if thou wilt;* חֹ' רֶשַׁע *delighting in wickedness.*

חֵפֶץ m. (with suff. חֶפְצִי).—I. *pleasure, delight.*—II. *wish, desire, will.*— III. *costly, precious.*—IV. *business, concern, affair;* pl. חֲפָצִים *precious things.*

חֶפְצִי־בָהּ *my delight* (is) *in her.*—I. a mystic title of Christ's true church, Isa. 62:4.—II. p. n. of the mother of Manasseh, 2 Ki. 21:1.

חָפַר (fut. יַחְפֹּר).—I. *dig* (as a well, &c). —II. *search out, investigate;* חָפֵר (fut. יֶחְפַּר) *blush, be ashamed, confounded.* Hiph. הֶחְפִּיר—I. *blush.* —II. *cause to blush, put to shame.*

חֵפֶר p. n.—I. of a city of Canaan.— II. of a man; חֶפְרִי *a Hepherite.*

חֲכָרִים p. n. of a town in the tribe of Issachar.

חֲפַר־פֵּרוֹת (digger), *a mole,* Isa. 2: 20; probably wrong reading for חֲפַרְפֵּרוֹת *moles.*

חָפְרַע p. n., *Pharaoh Hophra* king of Egypt; LXX. Ουαφρη.

חָפַשׂ *search, investigate.* Niph. *shall be sought out,* Obad. v. 6. Pi. חִפֵּשׂ *search diligently.* Pu. חֻפַּשׂ *is searched.* Hithp. הִתְחַפֵּשׂ (from another root), *was clothed, bound, equipped, accoutred.*

חֵפֶשׂ m., *search, enquiry,* Ps. 64:7.

חָפַשׁ. Pu. חֻפְּשָׁה *she was freed,* Lev. 19:20.

חֹפֶשׁ m. בִּגְדֵי ח׳ *clothes of liberation,* i. e. *spread out to exhibit for sale,* Eze. 27:20.

חֻפְשָׁה f., *freedom,* Lev. 19:20.

חָפְשִׁי m. (pl. חָפְשִׁים), *free from servitude, evil, &c.;* בַּמֵּתִים ח׳ *free from the dead,* Ps. 88:6, i. e. *free from the evils of life.*

חָפְשׁוּת חָפְשִׁית f., *freedom from business, servitude, &c.;* בֵּית ח׳ *retreat, place of retirement,* 2 Ki. 15:5.

חֵץ *arrow;* see חצץ.

חָצַב and חָצֵב (fut. יַחְצֹב) *cut, hew out wood, stone, metal, &c.;* part.

חֹצֵב s., *hewer;* applied to lightning, 1 Chron. 22:2, 15. Niph. *was engraven,* Job 19:24. Pu. *hewn,* Isa. 51:1. Hiph. *cause to cut to pieces.*

מַחְצֵב m., *hewing* (of stones).

חָצָה (fut. יֶחְצֶה; apoc. וַיַּחַץ) *divide, apportion,* Ps. 55:24; לֹא־יֶחֱצוּ יְמֵיהֶם *shall not live out half their days.* Niph. *was divided.*

חָצוֹת const. חֲצוֹת f., *middle.*

חֲצִי with pause חֵצִי m. (with suff. חֶצְיוֹ) *half, part, portion of any thing;* see also in חצץ.

חֲצִי הַמְּנֻחוֹת p. n. of a man; patron. חֲצִי הַמְּנַחְתִּי.

מֶחֱצָה f., *half,* Nu. 31:36, 43.

מַחֲצִית f., *the same.*

חָצִיר, חֲצוֹצְרָה, חָצוֹר; see חצר.

חָצַן root not used; (Arab. *bosom*).

חֹצֶן m.—I. *bosom, chest.*—II. *bosom of garment,* perhaps, *girdle,* Neh. 5: 13; with suff. חָצְנוֹ.

חֵצֶן m., *the same;* with suff. חָצְנִי.

חֲצַף Ch. Aph. *was urgent, pressing,* Dan. 2:15; 3:22.

חָצַץ part. חֹצֵץ *rushing on,* Pro. 30: 27. Pi. part. pl. מְחַצְצִים *persons taking part* (in conversation), Jud. 5:11. Pu. *are cut, decided,* Job 21:21.

חָצָץ m.—I. *gravel.*—II. *arrow,* i. e. *lightning,* Ps. 77:18.

חֵץ m. (with suff. חִצִּי; pl. חִצִּים, בַּעֲלֵי־חִצִּים).—I. *arrow;* *bowmen.*—II. metaph. *lightning.*

חַצְצֹן־תָּמָר and חַצְצוֹן p. n. of a place in the tribe of Judah.

חֲצֹצְרָה *trumpet;* see חצר.

חָצֵר root not used.—I. (Arab. *sur-rounding*).—II. (Arab. *field*).

חָצֵר com. (pl. חֲצֵרִים, חֲצֵרוֹת).—I. enclosure, area, court.—II. village; חֲצַר־אַדָּר (*threshing-floor of Addar*), p. n. of a town in the tribe of Judah; חֲ׳ סוּסִים, חֲ׳ סוּסָה p. n. of a town in the tribe of Simeon; חֲ׳ עֵינָן, חֲ׳ עֵינָן a town in the north of Palestine; חֲ׳ שׁוּעָל a town in the tribe of Simeon; חָצֵר הַתִּיכוֹן a town on the borders of Syria; חֲצֵרוֹת p. n. of a station in the desert.

חָצוֹר p.n.—I. of a town in the tribe of Naphtali.—II. of a town in the tribe of Benjamin.—III. of a region of Arabia.

חֶצְרוֹן p.n.—I. of a son of Reuben.—II. of a son of Perez; patron. חֶצְרוֹנִי.

חֶצְרַי p.n. of a man.

חֲצַרְמָוֶת (*court of death*), p. n. of a district in Arabia.

חָצִיר m.—I. enclosure (habitable place).—II. grass; see root II.

חֲצוֹצְרָה, חֲצֹצְרָה f., trumpet; from this word comes Pi. מְחַצְּרִים or Hiph. מַחְצְרִים (ketib מַחַצְצְרִים, מְחַצְרְרִים) persons blowing with trumpets.

חֵק bosom; see חֵיק.

חֹק־ חָק, חָקָה; see חקק.

חָקָה. Pu. part. מְחֻקֶּה engraven, carved. Hith. with עַל impressed, furrowed, Job 13:27.

חֲקוּפָא p. n. of a man.

חָקַק carve, engrave, inscribe; part. חֹקֵק legislator, Jud. 5:9. Pu. part. מְחֻקָּק statute, Pro. 31:5. Po.

decide, decree, Pro. 8:15; part. מְחֹקֵק lawgiver. Hoph. fut. יֻחְקוּ engraven, inscribed, Job 19:23.

חֵקֶק m., pl. const. חִקְקֵי.—I. impressions, imaginations, Jud. 5:15.—II. decrees, Isa. 10:1.

חֹק, חָק m. (with suff. חָקְּךָ, חֻקּוֹ; pl. חֻקִּים, חֻקֵּי, חוּקֵּי).—I. statute, law.—II. custom, privilege.

חֻקָּה f.—I. statute.—II. custom.

חָקַר (fut. יַחְקֹר; inf. חֲקֹר), search, investigate, try. Niph. נֶחְקַר that may be searched. Pi. חִקֵּר like Kal, Ecc. 12:9.

חֵקֶר m., investigation, search, enquiry. מֶחְקָר m., pl. const. מֶחְקְרֵי depths (of the earth), Ps. 95:4.

חָתוּר חָרַר; see חֹר, חָר.

חָרָא root not used; (Arab. *dung*).

חָרָא or חֲרָא m., pl. חֲרָאִים dung, Isa. 36:12.

חַר or חֹר m., the same; pl. const. חֲרֵי.

מַחֲרָאָה f., draught-house, 2 Ki. 10:27.

חָרֵב (fut. יֶחֱרַב, יֶחְרַב).—I. dry, be dry.—II. desolate, ruin. Niph. נֶחֱרַב was ruined. Pu. חֹרַב been dried. Hiph. הֶחֱרִיב I. dry up.—II. ruin. Hoph. הָחֳרַב was wasted, destroyed.

חֲרַב Ch. Hoph. f., הָחֳרְבַת is wasted, Ezr. 4:15.

חָרֵב m.—I. dry.—II. desolate, devastated; f. חֲרֵבָה; pl. חֲרֵבוֹת.

חֶרֶב f. (with suff. חַרְבִּי; pl. חֲרָבוֹת).—I. sword.—II. sharp weapon or cutting instrument.—III. drought, Deut. 28:22.

חֹרֶב m.—I. drought.—II. heat.—III. desolation.

חֹרֵב ,חָרֵב (dry, desolate), p. n. of one of the summits of Sinai.

חָרְבָּה f., pl. חָרְבוֹת (const. חָרְבוֹת) desolations.

חָרָבָה f., drought.

חֲרָבוֹן m., pl. const. חַרְבֹנֵי great droughts, Ps. 32:4.

חַרְבוֹנָא p.n. of a Persian eunuch.

חָרַג suffer pressure, trouble, Ps.18:46.

חַרְגֹּל m., the larva of the locust, Lev. 11:22.

חָרַד or חָרֵד (fut. יֶחֱרַד), was timid, fearful, trembling, with אֶל, לְ or מִן. Hiph. affrighted.

חָרֵד m.—I. fearful, anxious, with בְּ, אֶל, עַל.—II. trembling.

חֲרָדָה const. חֶרְדַּת f.—I. fear.—II. trembling.—III. p. n. of a station of the Israelites, Nu. 33:24.

חָרֹד p.n. of a place in the mountain of Gilboa, Ju. 7:1; חֲרֹדִי a Harodite, 2 Sa. 23:25.

חָרָה (inf. abs. חָרֹה; fut. יֶחֱרֶה; apoc. יִחַר), was, became hot, angry; חָרָה אַפּוֹ with עַל, אֶל, בְּ his anger was kindled against; חָרָה לוֹ he was angry; חָרָה בְּעֵינָיו it grieved him. Niph. נֶחֱרוּ were enraged, angry; part. נֶחֱרִים angry. Hiph. הֶחֱרָה.—I. made angry.—II. became warm, zealous, Neh. 3:20. Hithp. fut. apoc. תִּתְחַר be thou vexed.

חָרוֹן m.—I. ח' אַף heat of anger.—II. angry person, Ps. 58:10.

חֲרִי m.; ח' אַף heat, burning.

תַּחְרָא m., "habergeon," Eng. Ver., Ex. 28:32, &c.; meaning uncertain.

תַּחֲרָה contend with, emulate, Jer. 12:5; 22:15.

חָרוּז m., pl. חֲרוּזִים necklace of precious stones, Cant. 1:10.

חָרוּל m., a thorny shrub; pl. חֲרֻלִּים.
חָרוּץ fine gold; see חרץ.
חַרְחֻר heat; see חרר.

חָרֵט (Arab. engraver).

חָרִיט m., pl. חֲרִיטִים pockets, purses.

חֶרֶט m.—I. graving tool, Ex. 32:4. —II. writing style, Isa. 8:1.

חַרְטֹם m., pl. חַרְטֻמִּים.—I. the sacred scribes of Egypt who engraved hieroglyphics, ἱερογραμματεῖς.— II. the wise men of Babylon, Dan. 1:20; 2:2.

חַרְטֻמִּין m. pl. Ch., same as חַרְטֻמִּים wise men, magicians.

חֳרִי heat; see חָרָה.
חֹרִי bread; see חוּר.
חֲרִי pl. const. from חַר dung; see חרא.
חָרִיץ cutting; see חרץ.
חֲרִישִׁי ; see חרש.

חָרַךְ (fut. יַחֲרֹךְ), roasts, Pro. 12:27.
חֲרַךְ Ch. Hith. was burnt, Dan. 3:27.
חֲרַכִּים m. pl., latticed windows, LXX. δίκτυα, Cant. 2:9.

חָרַם Kal not used; (Arab. forbidden, sacred). Hiph. הֶחֱרִים.—I. devote to destruction.— II. apply to sacred uses. Hoph. הָחֳרַם.—I. was devoted to destruction, slain. —II. was consecrated.

חֵרֶם m. (with suff. חֶרְמִי).—I. devotion to destruction.—II. the thing so devoted.

חָרְמָה p.n. of a town in the tribe of Naphtali.

חֵרֶם m. with suff. חֶרְמִי; (pl. חֲרָמִים).
I. *a net.*— II. *allurements,* Ecc. 7:
26.

חָרֻם m. (Arab. *cut off, tear*), *flat-
nosed,* Lev. 21:18.

חָרִם p. n. of a man.

חָרְמָה p. n. of a town of the Canaanites.

חֶרְמוֹן p. n. of a range of hills in
Anti-Libanus; חֶרְמוֹנִים *Hermonites.*

חֶרְמֵשׁ m. (from חָרַשׁ and חֶרֶם),
sickle, reaping hook.

חָרָן p. n.—I. of a city of Mesopotamia,
Χαῤῥάν.—II. of a city of Arabia.
—III. of a man.

חֹרֹנַיִם p. n. of a place; see חוֹר.

חַרְנֶפֶר p. n. of a man.

חָרַשׁ, חָרַם root not used; (Arab.
scratching).

חֶרֶם m., *the itch,* Deu. 28:27.

חֶרֶם m. (with ה parag. חַרְסָה), *the
sun,* Ju. 8:13; 14:18; עִיר הַחֶרֶם
prophetic name of a city in Egypt,
Isa. 19:18; see חֶרֶם.

חֶרֶשׂ m., *earthenware, potsherd;* כְּלִי
חֶרֶשׂ *earthen vase.*

חַרְסוּת f., *pottery;* שַׁעַר הַחַרְסוּת *the
potter's gate,* one of the gates of
Jerusalem.

חָרַף (fut. יֶחֱרַף).—I. *pluck* (the fruit
of), *eat up,* Isa. 18:6.—II. *strip of
honour, value; reproach.* Pi. חֵרֵף
I. *reproach, blaspheme.*—II. *expose
to reproach,* Ju. 5:18. Niph. part.
f. נֶחֱרֶפֶת *deprived of all right, espoused,* Lev. 19:20.

חֹרֶף m.—I. *autumn.*—II. *youth,* Job
29:4, (the year was supposed to
begin in autumn).

חֶרְפָּה f. (pl. חֲרָפוֹת; const. חֶרְפוֹת).
—I. *reproach, contempt.*—II. *person* or *thing reproached.*

חָרִיף p. n. of a man; patron. חֲרִיפִי.

חָרֵף p. n. of a man.

חָרַץ (fut. יֶחֱרַץ).—I. *was sharp, active,
courageous.*—II. *was decided, determined;* part. חָרוּץ.—I. *maimed,
rent,* Lev. 22:22.—II. *decided, determined.*—III. *punishment.* Niph.
part. f. נֶחֱרֶצֶת, נֶחֱרָצָה *decided, determined, decreed.*

חָרוּץ m.—I. *ditch, foss.*—II. *the sharp
spikes of a thrashing dray;* pl.
const. חֲרֻצוֹת.—III. *sharpened, in-
structed.*—IV. *gold.*—V. *decree;*
pl. חָרוּצִים; see חרץ.—VI. p. n. of
a man.

חָרִיץ m. (pl. const. חֲרִיצֵי).—I. *cut-
tings of cheese,* LXX. τρυφαλίς,
1 Sa. 17:18.—II. same as חָרוּץ
spikes, sharp points.

חַרְצָן m., pl. חַרְצַנִּים *sour grapes,*
Nu. 6:4.

חֲרַץ Ch., same as Heb. חָלָץ *loins,*
Dan. 5:6.

חַרְצֻבּוֹת f. pl.—I. *bonds, bandages,*
Ps. 73:4.—II. *grievous pains,* Isa.
58:6.

חָרַק (fut. יַחֲרֹק), *ground, gnashed the
teeth;* (with בְּשִׁנַּיִם and עַל שִׁנַּיִם
against).

חָרַר.—I. *was hot.*—II. *was dry.* Niph.
נָחַר, נִחַר (fut. יֵחַר), *was hot, dry;*
נָחַר *became dry.* Pilp. inf. חַרְחַר
make hot, kindle, as fire, Pro.
26:21.

חֲרֵרִים m. pl., *dry, parched places,*
Jer. 17:6.

חֹר m., pl. חוֹרִים ,חֹרִים *nobles, great men;* see also חָוֻר.

חַרְחֻר m.—I. *inflammation, fever,* Deu. 28:22.—II. p.n. of a man.

חֶרֶשׂ *potsherd;* see חרם.

חָרַשׁ (fut. יַחֲרשׁ).—I. *cut, plough the land.*—II. *engrave, sculpture,* with חֹרֵשׁ עַל *ploughman).*—III. (fut. יֶחֱרַשׁ) *was dumb, silent, was deaf,* with מָן. Niph. *was ploughed.* Hiph.—I. *engrave, carve.*—II. *fabricate, devise evil,* 1 Sa. 23:9.—III. *be still, quiet.* Hith. fut. pl. יִתְחָרְשׁוּ *were silent,* Ju. 16:2.

חָרִישׁ m., *ploughing, tilling the land;* חֲרִישׁוֹ *his field.*

חֲרִישִׁי m., חֲרִישִׁית f., *very drying,* Jon. 4:8.

חָרָשׁ m. (const. חָרַשׁ; pl. חָרָשִׁים, חָרָשֵׁי), *worker, artificer, in wood, stone, metal, &c.;* חָרָשֵׁי מַשְׁחִית *forgers of destruction,* Eze. 21:36.

חֲרָשִׁים m.—I.*cunning work;* גֵּי חֲרָשִׁים *valley of the mechanics, near Jerusalem).* — II. *silence, silently.*—III. p. n. of a man.

חֹרֶשׁ m. *wood, forest;* pl. חֳרָשִׁים; בַּחֹרְשָׁה *into the wood;* חֹרְשָׁה *in the wood.*

חֶרֶשׁ m., *artificer; cutting instrument* (Gesen.), Gen. 4:22.

חֵרֵשׁ m., *deaf;* pl. חֵרְשִׁים.

חַרְשָׁא p. n. of a man.

חֲרשֶׁת f.—I. *sculpture.*—II. p. n. of a place in North Palestine.

מַחֲרֵשָׁה f., *coulter,* 1 Sa. 13:21; pl. מַחֲרֵשׁוֹת.

מַחֲרֶשֶׁת f. (with suff. מַחֲרַשְׁתּוֹ), *ploughshare,* 1 Sa. 13:20.

חָרַת same as חָרַשׁ; part. חָרוּת *cut, engraven,* Ex. 32:16.

חֶרֶת (same as חֹרֵשׁ), p. n. of a wood in the tribe of Judah.

חָשִׂיף ,חֲשׂוּפָא see חשׂף.

חָשַׂךְ (fut. אֶחְשׂךְ ,תַּחְשׂךְ ,וְאַחְשׂךְ).—I. *withhold, keep back.*—II. *save,* with מִן.—III. *refuse.*—IV. *spare.* חשׂךְ *sparing,* Pro. 13:24. Niph. fut. יֵחָשֵׂךְ *is restrained,* Job 16:6; יֶחְשַׂךְ id. 21:30.

חָשַׂף (fut. יֶחְשׂף), *make bare, denudate, expose.*—II. *draw (as water)*

חֲשׂוּפָא p.n. of a man.

חָשִׂיף m., *flock,* 1 Ki. 20:27.

מַחְשׂף m., *laying bare,* Gen. 30:37.

חָשַׁב (fut. יַחְשׁב- יַחֲשׁב).—I. *think, devise, meditate.*— II. *consider, esteem, reckon, impute,* with inf. and חשֵׁב לְ *artificer, deviser;* with לֹא *of no esteem.* Niph. נֶחְשַׁב (fut. יֵחָשֵׁב) *was thought, esteemed, computed, reckoned,* with בְּ, עִם, כְּ, לְ, עַל. Pi. חִשֵּׁב *think, compute, esteem, reckon,* with אֶל. Hithp. *was accounted,* Nu. 23:9.

חֲשַׁב Ch., *considered, esteemed,* Dan. 4:32.

חֵשֶׁב m., *the belt, girdle of the ephod.*

חֶשְׁבּוֹן m.—I. *device, discovery.* — II. p.n. of a city of the Amorites, Ἐσβοῦς.

חִשָּׁבוֹן m. pl., חִשְּׁבֹנוֹת *warlike machines,* 2 Chron. 26:15.

חֲשַׁבְּדָּנָה p.n. of a man.

חָשׁוּב p.n. of a man.

חֲשֻׁבָה p.n. of a man.

חֲשַׁבְיָהוּ ,חֲשַׁבְיָה p.n. of a man.

חֲשַׁבְנְיָה ,חֲשַׁבְנָה p.n. of a man.

מַחֲשָׁבוֹת .f (pl. ;מַחֲשָׁבָה, מַחֲשֶׁבֶת
const. מַחְשְׁבוֹת).—I. *thought, design, project.*—II. *work of art, in-
genuity.*

חָשָׁה *was silent.* Hiph. הֶחֱשָׁה, part.
מַחְשֶׁה *was or made silent.*

חֲשַׁח Ch., *persons, things wanting.*
חַשְׁחוּת f. Ch., *want, necessity,* Ezr.
7:20.

חֲשֵׁיכָה *same as* חֲשֵׁכָה *dark;* see חֹשֶׁךְ.

חָשַׁךְ (fut. יֶחְשַׁךְ) *be, become obscure,
dark.* Hiph. הֶחְשִׁיךְ *made dark,
obscure;* fut. יַחְשִׁיךְ.

חָשֹׁךְ m., pl. חֲשֻׁכִים *obscure persons,*
Pro. 22:29.

חֹשֶׁךְ m. (with suff. חָשְׁכִּי).—I. *darkness.*—II. *ignorance.*—III. *calamity,
misery, destruction.*

חֲשׁוֹךְ m. Ch., *darkness.*

חָשֹׁךְ m., pl. חֲשֻׁכִים *obscured, darkened.*

חֲשֵׁכָה, חֲשֵׁיכָה f., *obscurity, darkness.*
חֶשְׁכָּה, חָשְׁכָּה f., *the same.*

מַחְשָׁךְ m., I. *darkness.*—II. *adversity,
trouble;* pl. מַחֲשַׁכֵּי, מַחֲשַׁכִּים.

חָשַׁל. Niph. part. נֶחֱשָׁלִים *debili-
tated, infirm persons,* Deu. 25:18.

חֲשַׁל Ch., *pounded to powder,* Dan.
2:40.

חַשְׁמַל *some brilliant white or pale
yellow metal;* LXX. ἤλεκτρον.

חֻשָׁם p.n. of a man.

חֶשְׁמוֹן p.n. of a town in the tribe of
Judah.

חַשְׁמוֹנָה p.n. of a station of the
Israelites in the desert.

חַשְׁמָן m., pl. חַשְׁמַנִּים *rich, powerful
men,* Ps. 68:32

חָשַׁן (Arab. *to adorn*).

חֹשֶׁן m., *breast-plate* of the high priest,
called also חֹ׳ הַמִּשְׁפָּט.

חָשַׁק.—I. *desire, delight in,* with בְּ.
—II. *it pleased, seemed good,* with לְ
and inf. Pi. חִשַּׁק *attached to,* Ex.
38:28. Pu. *was joined to,* Ex. 27:17.

חֵשֶׁק m. (with suff. חִשְׁקִי), *desire,
delight.*

חֲשֻׁקִים, חֲשׁוּקִים m. pl.—the *tie-rods*
or *poles* which passed through the
upright pillars of the forecourt of
the tabernacle.

חִשֻּׁקִים m. pl., *spokes of a wheel,*
1 Ki. 7:33.

חָשַׁר root not used; (Arab. *collected*).

חַשְׁרָה f., *collection of waters,* 2
Sam. 22:12.

חִשֻּׁרִים m. pl., *naves of wheels,* 1 Ki.
7:33.

חָשַׁשׁ m., *dry grass, hay.*

חֵת, pl. חִתִּים p. n. of a people of
Canaan.

חָתָה (fut. יַחְתֶּה), *take up and remove*
(as fire, coals, &c.), *lay hold of;*
fut. with suff. יַחְתְּךָ *he will lay
hold on thee,* Ps. 52:7.

מַחְתָּה f.—I. *shovel* or *pan* for removing hot coals.—II. *censer.*—
III. *dishes* for receiving the snuffs
of the lamps; LXX. ὑπόθεμα.

חֲתִית, חַתְחַת, חִתָּה, חַת; see חתת.

חָתַךְ. Niph. נֶחְתַּךְ *has been determined,* Dan. 9:24.

חָתַל. Pu. and Hoph. הָחְתֵּל לֹא חֻתָּלְתְּ,
thou wast not bandaged, Eze. 16:4.

חִתּוּל m., *bandage for a wound,* Eze.
30:21.

חֲתֻלָּה f., *swaddling, bandage,* Job 38:9.

חֶתְלֹן p. n. of a place in Syria.

חָתַם (fut. יַחְתֹּם).—I. *seal, seal up.*—II. *conclude, finish,* with בְּ, בְּעַד. Niph. *was, became sealed.* Pi. *sealed, determined upon,* Job 24:16. Hiph. הֶחְתִּים *seal, shut up,* Lev. 15:3.

חֲתַם Ch., *sealed.*

חוֹתָם m. (with suff. חֹתָמְךָ).—I. *seal-ring.*—II. *seal.*—III. p. n. of a man.

חֹתֶמֶת f., *seal,* Gen. 38:25.

חָתַן, part. m. חֹתֵן *father-in-law, wife's father;* f. חֹתֶנֶת *mother-in-law, wife's mother;* with suff. חֹתְנוֹ. Hith. הִתְחַתֵּן *became related by marriage,* specially with a daughter, with לְ, בְּ, אֵת.

חָתָן m. (const. חֲתַן; with suff. חֲתָנוֹ; pl. חֲתָנִים).—I. *relative.*—II. *son-in-law.*—III. *bridegroom.*—IV. *relative by blood,* i. e. circumcision, חֲתַן־דָּמִים Ex. 4:25, 26.

חֲתֻנָּה f., *marriage,* Cant. 3:11.

חָתַף same as חָטַף; (Arab. *destruction;*) fut. יַחְתֹּף *snatch away,* Job 9:12.

חֶתֶף m., אִישׁ ח' *man of rapine,* Pro. 23:28.

חָתַר (fut. יַחְתֹּר).—I. *dig, delve,* with בְּ *into.*—II. *row* (dig into water), Jon. 1:13.

מַחְתֶּרֶת f., *digging through,* i. e. breaking in.

חָתַת *be, become broken with shame, fear, &c.* Niph. נָחַת (fut. יֵחַת;

pl. יֵחַתּוּ), *same as* Kal, with מִן, מִפְּנֵי. Pi. חִתַּת I. *broken to pieces, shivered.*—II. *affrighted,* Job 7:14. Hiph. הֵחַת (pret. הַחְתַּתְ, הַחְתַּתִּי), *break to pieces, ruin.*

חַתַת m.—I. *ruin,* Job 6:21.—II. p. n. of a man.

חַת m. (with suff. חִתְּכֶם; pl. חַתִּים) *broken, spoiled,* applied to persons or things.

חִתָּה f.—I. *the same.*—II. *fear,* Gen. 35:5.

חֲתִית f., *fear, terror, dread.*

חַתְחַת m., pl. חַתְחַתִּים *broken down with fear,* Ecc. 12:5.

מְחִתָּה f.—I. *stroke, injury, ruin.*—II. *fear, terror.*

ט

טְאֵב Ch., *was glad,* Dan. 6:24.

טָאמָא *debase;* see טוא.

טָבָאֵל, טָב; see טוב.

טְבוּלִים m. pl. (Ethiop. טבלל *folded*) *turbans,* Eze. 23:15.

טַבּוּר m., *mountain, high place.*

טָבַח (inf. const. טְבֹחַ; imp. טְבַח) *slaughter,* specially animals for eating, also of men.

טַבָּח m.—I. *cook, butcher.*—II. *officer of state,* probably, executioner; שַׂר (רַב) טַבָּחִים *chief officer.*

טַבָּח m. Ch., *officer of state.*

טַבָּחָה f., *female cook.*

טֶבַח m. (with suff. טִבְחָהּ).—I. *slaughter of animals.* — II. *animals slaughtered.*—III. p. n. of a man.

טִבְחָה f., *the same.*

אֲבַטִּיחִים (trans.) m. pl., *melons,* Nu. 11:5.

מַטְבֵּחַ m., *slaughter*, Isa. 14:21.

טִבְחַת (elsewhere בֶּטַח), p. n. of a city of Syria.

טָבַל I. *dip, plunge.* — II. *stain, dye.* Niph. *were dipped*, Jos. 3:15.

טְבוּלִים ; see in its place.

טְבַלְיָהוּ p.n. of a man.

טָבַע *sank down* (as into mud). Pu. טֻבַּע *sank in, were immerged*, Ex. 15:4. Hoph. הָטְבַּע *were let in* (as pillars in their bases, &c.).

טַבַּעַת f. (pl. טַבָּעוֹת ; const. טַבְּעוֹת). —I. *seal ring.*—II. any *ring.*

טַבְּעוֹת p.n. of a man.

טַבְרִמּוֹן ; see טוֹב.

טֵבֵץ p.n. of a town in the tribe of Ephraim.

טֵבֵת m., the tenth month of the Hebrew year, Est. 2:16.

טָהַר (fut. יִטְהַר) *was, became, clean, pure*, from disease, from legal uncleanness, from moral impurity. Pi. טִהַר.—I. *cleanse, purify.*—II. *declare clean.* Pu. *was purified.* Hithp. הִטַּהֵר (pl. הִטֶּהֲרוּ) ; imp. pl. (הִטַּהֲרוּ) *was, became clean, purified.* טָהוֹר (const. טְהָר־, טְהָר־ ; f. טְהָרָה ; pl. טְהֹרוֹת) *clean, pure.*

טֹהַר m.—I. *brightness, glory.* — II. *purification.*

טָהֳר m., } the same.
טָהֳרָה f., }

טְוָא Ch., root not used; (Syr. *fasted*). טְוָת f. Ch., *fasting*, Dan. 6:19.

טוּא or טוֹא Pil. מָאטְמָא *humble, debase*; part. מַטְאֲטֵא *humbling, debasing*, Isa. 14:23.

טוֹב (pret. pl. טֹבוּ ; fut. יִיטַב from

טוֹב לִי (יָטַב) *was good, agreeable; it pleases me*, Nu. 24:1; with בְּעֵינַי the same. Hiph. הֵטִיב *do well, liberally, make good*, Hos. 10:1; *make happy*, Ecc. 11:9.

טוֹב m. טוֹבָה f.—I. *good.*—II. *happy, prosperous.* — III. *valuable.* — IV. *handsome* (goodlike).—V. *kind.*— VI. used adverbially, *well, rightly*; s. m. and f. טוֹבָה.—I. *goodness.* —II. *wealth.*—III. *prosperity, happiness*; לְטוֹבָה, לְטוֹב, with לְ *that it may be well with thee.*—IV. *beauty.* —V. p.n. of a country on the other side Jordan.

טָב m. Ch., *good, excellent.*

טָבְאֵל with pause טָבְאָל p.n. of a man, Syrian or Persian.

טַבְרִמּוֹן p. n., the father of Benhadad, king of Syria.

טוּב m.—I. *goodness.*— II. *wealth.*— III. *prosperity.*— IV. *beauty.*—V. *goodness* (of discernment). — VI. *God*, as the source of all good. טוּב אֶרֶץ *the best part of the land*, Gen. 45:18.

טוֹב אֲדֹנִיָּהוּ p.n. of a man.

טוֹבִיָּה, טוֹבִיָּהוּ p. n. of a man.

טָוָה *spin* (lit. *twine*), Ex. 35:25, 26.

מַטְוֶה m., *yarn*, Ex. 35:25.

טוּחַ I. *plaister, paint.* — II. *overlay.* Niph.inf. הִטּוֹחַ *was covered, plastered*, Lev. 14:43, 48.

טִיחַ m., *plastering*, Eze. 13:12.

טֻחוֹת f. pl.—I. *inward parts, viscera*, Ps. 51:8.—II. *the motive power of the heavenly bodies*, Job 38:36.

טוֹטָפוֹת *bandages*; see טוּף.

טוּל. Hiph. הֵטִיל *cast forth, out, into.*

Hoph. הוּטַל *was, became cast out, forth, &c.* Pil. טִלְטֵל *cast out,* Isa. 22:17.

טַלְטֵלָה f., *entire casting out,* Isa. 22:17.

טוּף (Arab. *surrounded*).

טוֹטָפוֹת f. pl., φυλακτήρια, *frontlets;* probably jewels worn on the forehead.

טוּר see דּוּר and תּוּר.

טוּר m. (pl. טוּרִים, טָרִים), *series, order, range.*

טִירָה f.—I. *any series of buildings.*—II. *palace.*—III. *certain chambers in the Temple.*

טוּר m. Ch., same as צוּר *mountain,* Dan. 2:35, 45.

טוּשׂ *fly swiftly,* Job 9:26.

טְוָת *fasting;* see צוּא.

טָחָה (Arab. *expand*). Pil. part. מְטַחֲוֵי־ קֶשֶׁת *archers,* Gen. 21:16.

טְחוֹת *viscera;* see טוּחַ.

טְחוֹרִים *hæmorrhoids;* see טחר.

טָחַן (fut. יִטְחַן).—I. *grind with a hand-mill.*—II. *oppress.*

טְחוֹן m., *hand-mill,* Lam. 5:13.

טַחֲנָה f., *the same,* Ecc. 12:4.

טְחָר (Syr. *arms*).

טְחוֹרִים m. pl., *emerods* (hæmorrhoids).

טִיחַ *plaster;* see טוּחַ.

טִיט m., *mud, mire.*

טִין m. Ch., *clay, potter's clay.*

טִירָה *row;* see טוּר.

טַל *dew;* see טלל.

טָלָא, part. טָלוּא *patched, having patches of various colours;* pl. f. טְלָאֹות, טְלָאִים. Pu. part. f. pl.

מְטֻלָּאֹות *patched* (of shoes), Jos. 9:5.

טָלֶם; see טְלִי, טְלָאִים.

טָלֶה (Syr. *an infant*).

טָלֶה const. טְלֵה m., *young lamb.*

טְלִי m.—I. *the same;* pl. טְלָאִים.—II. p. n. of a town; see טָלֶם.

טַלְטֵלָה, טִלְטֵל; see טוּל.

טָלַל Pi. טִלֵּל *covered, roofed,* Neh. 3:15.

טְלַל Ch. Aph. אַטְלֵל *takes shade,* Dan. 4:9.

טַל m. (with pause טָל, with suff. טַלָּם), *dew.*

טַל m. Ch., *dew.*

טָלֶם p. n. of a town in the tribe of Judah; also טְלָאִים.

טַלְמוֹן p. n. of a man.

טָמֵא (fut. יִטְמָא; inf. with ה parag. טָמְאָה), *was unclean, polluted,* with בְּ. Niph. נִטְמָא *was polluted,* with בְּ. Pi. טִמֵּא.—I. *polluted, defiled.*—II. *pronounced unclean.* Pu. part. f. מְטֻמָּאָה *polluted.* Hith. הִטַּמֵּא *polluted,* with לְ. Hothp. pret. f. הִטַּמָּאָה *the same,* Deu. 24:4.

טָמֵא m., *unclean, polluted;* f. טְמֵאָה.

טֻמְאָה f. (pl. const. טֻמְאֹת), *polluted, defiled.*

טָמָה same as טָמֵא. Niph. pl. נִטְמִינוּ *we are unclean, despised.*

טָמַן *conceal, hide in the earth.* Niph. *was hidden.* Hiph. *hide,* 2 Ki. 7:8.

מַטְמוֹן m. (pl. מַטְמֹנִים), *treasure, that which is laid up, hidden.*

טֶנֶא (with suff. טַנְאֲךָ) m., *basket.*

טָנַף. Pi. *soil*, Cant. 5:3.

טָעָה same as **תָּעָה**. Hiph. **הִטְעָה** *made to err*, Eze. 13:10.

טָעַם (fut. **יִטְעַם**).—I. *taste.*—II. *discriminate, judge.*

טְעַם Ch. Pa. *make to eat.*

טַעַם m.—I. *reason, -judgment.*—II. *taste.*

טְעֵם m. Ch., *edict.*

טְעֵם m. Ch.—I. *taste.*—II. *judgment.* —III. *edict.*

מַטְעַמִּים m., **מַטְעַמּוֹת** f. pl., *dainty meats.*

טָעַן.—I. *load* (of beasts of burden), Gen. 45:17.–II. Pu. **טֹעַן** *pierced through*, Isa. 14:19.

טַעַת Kal. inf.; see **נטע**.

טַף *infant*; see **טפף**.

טָפַח. Pi. **טִפַּח** *spread out, extend* (from **טָפַח**), spec. with the hand.

טֶפַח m.—I. *palm, hand-breadth*, a measure of about three and-a-half inches; pl. **טְפָחוֹת** Ps. 39:6.—II. *coping stones of a building.*

טֹפַח m., *hand-breadth, measure.*

טִפֻּחִים m. pl., Lam. 2:20, *that which is stroked with the hand.*

מִטְפַּחַת f. (pl. **מִטְפָּחוֹת**), *upper garment, mantle.*

טָפַל.—I. *lay on or over.*—II. *cover, conceal.*

טִפְסָר m., *prince, general.*

טַפְסָר m., the same; pl. **טַפְסָרִים**.

טָפַף *tripping, mincing*, Isa. 3:16.

טַף m. (with pause **טָף**; with suff. **טַפֵּנוּ**), *child, infant.*

טְפַר m. Ch., *nails, claws.*

טָפֵשׁ *fat, stupid*, Ps. 119:70.

טָפַת p. n. of a daughter of Solomon.

טָרַד *driving out*; part. **טֹרֵד** *perpetual, successive* (i. e. one driving out the other), Pro. 19:13; 27:15.

טְרַד Ch., *driving out, driven out.*

טָרָה root not used; (Arab. *was fresh*).

טָרִי m., **טְרִיָּה** f., *fresh, moist*, Jud. 15:15; Isa. 1:6.

טְרוֹם ketib, same as **טֶרֶם**.

טָרַח. Hiph. *stretches out*, Job 37:11.

טֹרַח m. (with suff. **טָרְחֲכֶם**), *pressure, wearying.*

טָרַם root not used; (Arab. *cut off*).

טֶרֶם adv., *not yet*; **בְּטֶרֶם** and *before that*; **מִטֶּרֶם** the same.

טָרַף (fut. **יִטְרֹף**, **יִטְרַף**), *tear in pieces, wound, injure.* Niph. *be torn in pieces.* Pu. **טֹרַף** the same. Hiph. *feed, provide for.*

טֶרֶף m., *prey, provision, food.*

טָרָף m., *leaf* (that which is plucked), Gen. 8:11.

טְרֵפָה f.—I. *any thing torn.*—II. *animal torn by a wild beast.*

טַרְפְּלָיֵא Ch., p. n., a people so called, Ezr. 4:9; LXX. Ταρφαλαῖοι.

י

יָאַב *desired, longed for*, with **לְ**.

יָאָה with **לְ** *it becometh*, Jer. 10:7.

יְאֹר same as **יְאֹר**.

יֵאוֹתוּ Niph. fut. pl., from **אֹת**.

יַאֲזַנְיָה (*whom the Lord hears*), p. n. of a man.

יַאֲזַנְיָהוּ (contr. **יְזַנְיָה**, **יְזַנְיָהוּ**), p. n. of a man.

יָאִיר (the Lord enlightens, 'Ιάειρος), p. n. of a man; patron. יָאִירִי.

יָאַל I. same as אָוַל. Niph. נוֹאַל was foolish.—II. same as אול. Hiph. הוֹאִיל (fut. וַיּוֹאֶל.—1. undertook, began, with inf.—2. was willing, contented.

וַיָּאֶל, יָאֶל Hiph. fut. apoc., from אלה.

וְיָאֶל, יָאֶל Hiph.fut.apoc., from יאל II.

יָאֶר Hiph. fut. apoc., יָאֵר Niph. fut., from אור.

יָאֹר Kal fut., from ארר.

יְאוֹר, יְאֹר m., a river, specially the Nile; pl. יְאֹרִים rivers.

יָאַשׁ. Niph. נוֹאַשׁ was hopeless, desperate, with מִן; part. נוֹאָשׁ desperate, in vain. Pi. inf. יָאֵשׁ rendered hopeless, Ecc. 2:20.

יֹאשִׁיָּה p. n. of a man.

יֹאשִׁיָּהוּ ('Ιωσίας) p. n. of a man.

וַיֵּאת; יָאת Kal fut. apoc., יֶאֱתָיוּ fut. pl., יֶאֱתָיְנִי fut. with suff.; see אתה.

יֶאֱתְרַי p.n. of a man (same as אֶתְנִי).

יָבֵא Hiph. fut. apoc.; see בוא.

יְבָאֵנִי for יְבָאוּנִי Kal fut. pl. with suff.; see בוא.

יָבַב. Pi. יְבֵב cried out, Jud. 5:28.

יוֹבָב p. n.—I. of a people in Arabia Felix.—II. of a king of Edom.—III. of a man.

יָבוּ וַיְבוּ 2 Ki. 12:12, for וַיָּבֵא Kal fut.; see בוא.

יְבוּס p. n. of the Canaanitish inhabitants of Jerusalem; יְבוּסִי Jebusite.

יְבוּל produce; see יבל.

יָבוֹשׁ Kal fut., from בושׁ.

יִבְחַר (chosen of the Lord), p. n. of a man.

יָבִין p. n. of two Canaanitish kings.

יַבְךְ, וַיֵּבְךְ Kal fut. apoc.; see בכה.

יָבַל. Hiph. הוֹבִיל bare, carried, led. Hoph. הוּבַל was borne, carried, led. Ch. Aph. הֵיבַל bring, Ez. 5:14; 6:5.

יְבוּל m. (with suff. יְבוּלֹה, יְבוּלָהּ).—I. produce (of the earth, &c.)—II. provision, wealth.

בּוּל m.—I. produce, increase.—II. name of a month 1 Ki. 6:38, the eighth of the calendar, answering to our October.

מַבּוּל m. flood of Noah, deluge.

יֻבַל m.—I. stream of water.—II. p. n of a son of Lamech.

יוֹבֵל com. (lit. a protracted note or sound), the Jubilee, a feast of the Jews announced by the sounding of horns; שְׁנַת הַיּוֹבֵל and יֹבֵל the year of Jubilee.

יוּבַל m.—I. canal, Jer. 17:8.—II. p. n. of a son of Lamech.

אֲבֵל, אוּבָל m., a river, canal, Dan. 8:2, 3, 6.

יַבֶּלֶת f., issue, running disease, Lev. 22:22; Vulg. papulas habens.

תֵּבֵל f., same as אֶרֶץ.—I. the world, the earth, specially the inhabited part of it.—II. the world's inhabitants, mankind.

יִבְלְעָם p. n. of a town in the tribe of Manasseh.

יָבָם m. husband's brother; יִבֵּם. Pi. marry the brother's wife; see Deu. 25:5, 7.

יְבָמֶת f. (with suff. יְבִמְתּוֹ) brother's wife; one married to her husband's brother.

יַבְנְאֵל p. n., two towns in the tribes of Judah and Naphtali.

יַבְנֶה p. n. of a town of the Philistines, Ἰαμνία, Ἰάμνεια.

יִבְנְיָה p. n. of a man.

יַבֹּק p. n. of a brook which runs into the river Jordan.

יְבֶרֶכְיָהוּ (blessed of the Lord), p. n. of a man.

יִבְשָׂם p. n. of a man.

יָבֵשׁ (inf. const. יְבֹשׁ; fut. יִיבַשׁ; pl. יִיבְשׁוּ) was or became dry, arid. Pi. יִבֵּשׁ dry up. Hiph. הוֹבִישׁ. —I. dry up, make to wither.—II. was ashamed, confounded; see בּוּשׁ.

יָבֵשׁ m., יְבֵשָׁה f.—I. dry.—II. p. n. of a town in Gilead; called also יָבֵישׁ. —III. p. n. of a man.

יַבָּשָׁה, יַבֶּשֶׁת f., dry land.

יַבֶּשֶׁת f. Ch., the same.

יַבֶּשֶׁת f., dried, Gen. 8:7.

וַיַּבְשֵׁהוּ, וַיַּבִּשֵׁהוּ for וַיְיַבְּשֵׁהוּ Pi. fut. with suff.; see יבשׁ.

יַבֶּשֶׁת Kal inf. const.; see יבשׁ.

יִגְאָל (the Lord redeemeth), p. n. of a man.

יָגֵב same as גּוּב ploughed; part. יוֹגְבִים ploughmen.

יְגֵב m. pl., יְגֵבִים ploughed lands, Jer. 39:10.

יָנְבָּה with ה parag. יָנְבָּה p. n. of a town in the tribe of Gad.

יִגְדַּלְיָהוּ (let the Lord be magnified), p. n. of a man.

יָגָה. Niph. part. נוּגָה pained (perhaps cast out). Pi. יִגָּה afflict, pain, Lam. 3:33. Hiph. הוֹנָה.—I. afflicted.— II. removed, 2 Sa. 20:13.

וַיִּגַּה, יַגֶּה for וַיִּיגֶּה Pi. fut., from יגה.

יָגוֹן m., affliction, grief.

תּוּגָה f., sorrow, grief.

יָגוּר (the Lord dwelleth there), p. n. of a town in the tribe of Judah.

יַגְלִי p. n. of a man.

וַיָּגֶל יֶגֶל Hiph. fut. apoc.; see גלה.

יָגַע (fut. יִיגַע; pl. יִיגְעוּ), labour to weariness; with בְּ and לְ, be wearied. Pi. יִגַּע fatigue, cause to labour to weariness. Hiph. הוֹגִיעַ same as Pi. with בְּ.

יָגֵעַ m., wearying, wearied.

יְגִיעַ const. יְגִיעַ m.—I. wearied, fatigued.—II. labour.—III. the fruit of labour, wealth.

יֶגַע m., wealth, Job 20:18.

יְגִיעָה f., hard labour, exertion, Ecc. 12:12.

יְגַר m. Ch., heap of stones, Gen 31:47.

יִגַּר Niph. fut., from נגר.

יָגֹר (pret. יָגֹרְתִּי, יָגֹרְתָּ), fear, be afraid of, with מִפְּנֵי.

יָגוֹר m., fearing, afraid of.

יָד com., generally f. (const. יַד; with suff. יָדִי, יֶדְכֶם; dual יָדַיִם, יָדַיִ const. יְדֵי, with suff. יָדָיו (יְדֵיכֶם. —I. hand; with עִם, אֶת assist, aid; with בְּ, אֶל hand against, afflicting, troubling; with עַל upon him, inspiring, strengthening.—II. power, spirit or word of God, 1 Sa. 5:11, &c.—III. with prep. עַל יַד, לְיַד, בְּיַד same as בְּ; בְּעַד יַד, אֶל יַד, עַל יְדֵי at hand, near.—IV. space, place; אִישׁ עַל יָדוֹ every man in his place.—V. memorial, monument, 1 Sa. 15:12;

2 Sa. 18:18. — VI. *by means of.*
Pl. יָדוֹת; const. יְדוֹת.—I. *tenons
of planks.*—II. *axletrees of wheels,*
1 Ki. 7:32, 33.—III. *arms of a
throne,* 1 Ki. 10:19. Used with
pref. בְּיַד with בְּיָדוֹ) *with him), by,
before, against;* מִיַּד, מִידֵי *from,
out of;* יָד לְיָד *hand in hand,* as
striking a bargain, Pro. 11:21.

יַד com. Ch., *hand.*

יְדָא *put forth;* see ידה.

יְדָא וַיְדֵא fut. apoc.; see דאה.

יְדַאֲלָה p. n. of a place in the tribe of
Zebulun.

יִדְבָּשׁ p. n. of a man.

יָדַד, same as דוד *loved.*

יָדִיד m., *beloved,* specially of God's
children; pl. f., יְדִידוֹת.

יִדּוֹ p. n. of a man.

יְדִידָה p. n. of the mother of king
Josiah.

יְדִידוּת f., *love,* Jer. 12:7.

יְדִידְיָה *beloved of the Lord,* a title of
Solomon.

יָדָה.—I. *put forth* (as casting stones).
—II. *uttering praise;* imp. pl. יְדוּ
they cast at her, Jer. 50:14. Pi. *cast
stones or lots;* fut. וַיַּדּוּ; inf. יַדּוֹת.
Hiph. הוֹדָה (fut. יוֹדֶה, יְהוֹדֶה;
with suff. אוֹדְךָ, אֲהוֹדֶנּוּ), *recount,
commemorate* (God's mercies, with
עַל); *praise, celebrate,* with לְ.—Hith.
הִתְוַדָּה *become known,* with עַל
and לְ.

יְדָא Ch. Aph. *praise, celebrate.*

תּוֹדָה f.—I. *confession.*—II. *praise,
thanksgiving.*—III. *company of persons giving thanks.*

וַיַּדּוּ יָדוּ for וַיִּדּוּ. Pi. fut.; see ידה.

יִדּוֹן יָרְכָם; see יָד with suff.

יָדֹם Kal fut.; pl. יִדְּמוּ; see דמם.

יְהוּדָה p. n.—I. the patriarch *Judah*
—II. Afterwards applied to the
kingdom of the house of David.
—III. Ultimately to the whole of
Palestine.—IV. p. n. of a man.

יְהוּד Ch., *the Jews,* the kingdom of
Judah.

יְהוּדִי (pl. יְהוּדִים, יְהוּדִיִּים).—I. *a
Jew;* f. יְהוּדִיָּה *Jewess;* יְהוּדִית adv.
Hebrew, the Hebrew tongue.—II.
p. n. of a man.

הִתְיַהֵד. Hith. *became a Jew.*

יְהוּדִי Ch., *a Jew.*

יְהוּדִית; see יְהוּדִי p. n. of a wife of
Esau.

יְהֻד p. n. of a town in the tribe of
Dan.

הוֹדַוְיָה p. n. of a man.

הוֹדַוְיָהוּ p. n. of a man.

יָדוֹן p. n. of a man.

יַדּוּעַ p. n. of a man.

יְדִיתוּן, יְדֻתוּן, יְדֻתּוּן p. n. of a Levite
skilled in music; probably also a
musical instrument invented by
him.

יַדַּי p. n. of a man.

יְדִידְיָה, יְדִידוּת, יְדִידָה, יָדִיד; see ידד.

יִדְיָה p. n. of a man.

יְדִיעֲאֵל p. n. of a son of Benjamin.

יִדְלָף p. n. of a son of Nahor.

יָדַע (fut. יֵדַע, וַיֵּדַע; inf. abs. יָדֹעַ;
const. דַּעַת; with suff. דְּעֹתָּה; imp.
דַּע, דְּעֶה; part. יֹדֵעַ, יוֹדֵעַ; f.
לָדַעַת.—I. *perceive, become informed, aware of, feel.*—II. *know
carnally.*—III. *recognise, acknow-
ledge.*—IV. *regard;* part. יֹרֵעַ *wise;*
יָדוּעַ *noted, illustrious.* Niph. נוֹדַע
known, apparent, recognised. Pi

יָדַע *made to know.* Pu. part. מְיֻדָּע *known, familiar.* Po. יוֹדֵעַ *declared, indicated.* Hiph. הוֹדִיעַ (imp. הוֹדַע; fut. יוֹדִיעַ; apoc. יוֹדַע), *make known, show, confess, inform, teach.* Hoph. הוֹדַע *was, made known.* Hith. הִתְוַדַּע *made himself known;* with אֶל.

יְדַע Ch., *know, understand, perceive;* fut. יִנְדַּע. Hoph. הוֹדַע *made known, taught.*

דֵּעַ m., pl. דֵּעִים } *knowledge, science,*
דֵּעָה f., pl. דֵּעוֹת } *opinion.*

דַּעַת f., *knowledge, science, opinion.*

יָדָע p.n. of a man.

יְדַעְיָה p.n. of a man.

יִדְּעֹנִי m. (pl. יִדְּעֹנִים), *false prophet, soothsayer.*

מַדָּע ,מַדַּע m.—I. *knowledge, experience.*—II. *mind.*

מַדּוּעַ adv. interrog., *why then? why indeed?*

מַנְדַּע m. Ch.—I. *knowledge.*—II. *intelligence.*

מוֹדַע m., *familiar, friend.*

מוֹדַעַת f., *the same.*

יַדְשְׁנָה Pi. fut. with ה parag.; see דשׁן.

יָהּ *one of the names of God;* probably an abbreviation of יְהֹוָה.

יָהַב I. *give, allow.*—II. *appoint, place;* imper. הַב; with ה parag. הָבָה; f. הָבִי. pl. הָבוּ.

יְהַב Ch., *give, place.* Ith. *was given.*

יְהָב m., *burden;* with suff. יְהָבְךָ Ps. 55:23.

הַבְהָבִים m. pl., *gifts,* Hos. 8:13.

יֶהְדַּי p.n. of a man.

יְהוּא for יְהוּ fut. apoc. pl., from הוה.

יֵהוּא p.n.; see הוה.

יְהוֹבֵד Ch. Aph. fut.; see אבד.

יְהוֹדֶה for יוֹדֶה Hiph. fut.; see ידה.

יְהוּדִית, יְהוּדִי, יְהוּדָה, יְהוּד; see ידה; יְהֹוָה *the most sacred and unalienable name of God;* see הוה.

יְהוֹשִׁיעַ for יוֹשִׁיעַ Hiph. fut.; see ישע.

וַיְהִי, יְהִי fut. apoc.; see היה.

יְהֵלִילוּ for יְיֵלִילוּ Hiph. fut.; see ילל.

יְהָךְ Ch. fut.; see הוך.

יַהֵל for יַאֲהֵל Pi. fut.; see אהל.

יָהִיר m., *haughty, vain.*

יַהֲלֹם see הלם.

יַהֲמִיּוּן fut. pl. with ן parag.; see המה.

יַהַץ ,יָהְצָה p.n. of a city of Moab.

יַהְתֵלּוּ Pi. fut. pl. with dag. euphon. see התל.

יוֹב p.n. of a son of Issachar.

יוֹבָב; see יבב.

יוֹבֵל ,יוּבַל; see יבל.

יוּכְלוּ Eze. 42:5, for יָאְכְלוּ, Hoph. fut.; see אכל.

יוֹלֶדֶת for יוֹלֶדֶת part. f.; see ילד.

יוֹם m.—I. *day;* הַיּוֹם *this day, to-day, now;* בַּיּוֹם *this very day, immediately;* בְּיוֹם with inf. *on the day, when;* כַּיּוֹם *now, at present;* כַּיּוֹם הַזֶּה *as it is at this day;* מִיּוֹם *from the day since;* יוֹם יוֹם ,בְּיוֹם בְּיוֹם ,כְּיוֹם בְּיוֹם *daily;* dual יוֹמַיִם *two days;* pl. יָמִים, const. יְמֵי, sometimes יְמוֹת *days, many days;* מִקֵּץ יָמִים ,מִיָּמִים *after many days, some days, some time after;* יֶרַח יָמִים i. e. *an entire month;* יְ שְׁנָתַיִם *two whole years.*—II. *duration, time;* יָמֶיךָ *so long as thou livest;* כָּל־הַיָּמִים פ' *all his days;* בָּא בַּיָּמִים *advanced in years.*—III. *anniversary;* מִיָּמִים

יְמָימָה annually; לְיָמִים the same, Jud. 17:10; זֶבַח יָמִים annual sacrifice.

יוֹם m. Ch., day, period.

יוֹמָם adv., by day.

יָוָן p.n. Javan the founder of the Greeks, Ionians; בְּנֵי הַיְּוָנִים Ionians, Greeks.

יָוֵן mire, clay.

יַיִן m. (const. יֵין; with suff. יֵינִי).—I. wine.—II. intoxication.

יוֹנָה f. (pl. יוֹנִים).—I. dove.—II. p.n. of a prophet; see also in ינה.

יוֹנֶקֶת ,יוֹנֵק; see ינק.

יוֹסֵף ,יְהוֹסֵף (from אָסַף or יָסַף).—I. p.n. Joseph, the son of Israel, Ἰωσήφ.—II. given afterwards specially to the tribes of his sons, and generally to the kingdom of Israel.—III. p. n. of a man.

יוֹסִפְיָה p.n. of a man.

יוֹעֵאלָה p.n. of a man.

יוֹצֵאת for יֹצֵאת part. f.; see יצא.

יוֹר ,וַיּוֹר Hiph. fut. apoc; see ירה.

יוֹרֶא Pro. 11:25 (shall be watered), for יְרֻוֶּה Hoph. fut., see רוה; or for יוֹרֶה Hoph. fut., see ירה.

יוֹרֶה ,יוֹרִי teach; see ירה.

יוֹשֵׁב חֶסֶד (confirming mercy), p.n. of a man.

יוֹשַׁבְיָה (the Lord confirmeth), p.n. of a man.

יוֹשָׁה p.n. of a man.

יוֹשַׁוְיָה p.n. of a man.

יוֹתֵר ,יוֹתֶרֶת; see יתר.

יוֹשַׁבְתִּי Jer. 22:23, for יֹשֶׁבֶת, part. f. with ' parag.; see ישב.

יֵז ,וַיֵּז ,יֵן ,יֵז Kal fut. apoc; see נזה.

יֵז ,וַיֵּז Hiph. fut. apoc.; see נזה.

יְזִיאֵל p. n. of a man.

יֻזַּח Niph. fut.; see זחה.

יְזִיָּה p. n. of a man.

יְזְלִיאָה p. n. of a man.

יָזְמוּ for יָזֹמּוּ Kal fut. pl.; see זמם.

יָזַן (Arab. weighed, was heavy). Pu. part. מְיֻזָּנִים appointed, accoutred for war (of horses), Jer. 5:8, Kri.

יְזַנְיָהוּ ,יְזַנְיָה; see אֲזַנְיָה.

יִזְרָחְיָה ,יִזְרָח; see זרח.

יֵזַע m., sweat, Eze. 44:18.

יָזַר ,וַיָּזַר Kal fut. apoc; see זור.

יִזְרְעֶאל p.n.; see זרע.

יָחַד (fut. יֵחַד) unite, be as one, with בְּ ,אֵת. Pi. יִחֵד unite, make as one, Ps. 86:11.

יָחִיד m., solitary one, only one; f. יְחִידָה.

יַחַד m., union, 1 Chron. 12:17; adv.—I. as one.—II. singly, at once.—III. wholly, entirely, together; יַחְדָּו ,יַחְדָּיו the same; the pron. is a pleonasm.

יִחַד ,וַיִּחַד Kal fut. apoc.; see חדה.

יַחֵד for יָחֵד Hiph. fut.; see חדד.

יַחְדּוֹ (united), p.n. of a man.

יַחְדִּיאֵל (united with God), p.n. of a man.

יֶחְדְּיָהוּ (united to the Lord), p.n. of a man.

יַחֲזָיָה ,יַחֲזִיאֵל p.n.; see חזה.

יְחִזְקִיָּהוּ ,יְחִזְקִיָּה ,יְחֶזְקֵאל p. n.; see חזק.

יֶחֱזָיוּן fut. pl. with נ parag.; see חזה.

יַחְזֵרָה p. n. of a man.

יְחִיאֵל ,יְחַוְאֵל p.n.; see חיה ,חיי.

וַיְחִי ,יְחִי fut. apoc.; see חיה.

יְחִיתַן Hiph. fut. with suff. ן— for ן— because of the pause; see חתת.

יָחִיד; see יחד.

יָחַל Pi.—יִחֵל.—I. *hope for, expect, wait.*—II. *cause to hope,* with לְ, אֶל. Hiph. הוֹחִיל same as Pi., with לְ, לִפְנֵי. Niph. נוֹחַל (fut. יִיָּחֵל) same as Pi.

יָחֵל *he will begin;* יָחֵל *he will play,* Hiph. fut.; see חלל.

יָחִיל n., *one waiting,* Lam. 3 : 26.

יַחְלְאֵל p. n. of one of the sons of Zebulon ; patron. יַחְלְאֵלִי.

יַחֲלוּ Pi. pret. pl. with dag. euphon., from יחל.

תּוֹחֶלֶת f., *expectation, hope.*

יָחַם (fut. יֵחַם, יֶחֱמוּ; pl. וַיֶּחֱמוּ; f. וַיֵּחַמְנָה).—I. *be in heat* (for sexual intercourse): hence,—II. *conceive.*—III. *be hot with anger.* Niph. part. pl. m. נֵחָמִים *heated with idol worship,* Isa. 57:5. Pi. (inf. יַחֵם; pret. f. with suff. יְחֵמַתְנִי) *conceived.*

יֶחֱמוּ for יֶחֱמוּ Pi. pret. pl., from יחם.

יֵחַמְנָה, Gen. 30:38. for תֵּחַמְנָה Kal fut. pl. f., from יחם.

חֵמָה, const. חֲמַת f.—I. *heat.*—II. *anger, fury.*—III. *venom of noxious creatures,* Deut. 32:33.

חֲמָא f. Ch., *heat, anger.*

יַחְמַי p. n. of a man.

יַחְמוּר *gazelle;* see חמר.

יְחֵמַתְנִי for יְחֵמַתְנִי Pi. pret. f. with suff.; see יחם.

וַיִּחַן, יִחַן Kal fut. apoc.; see חנה.

יָחְנְךָ for יְחָנְךָ Kal fut. with suff.; see חנן.

יֶחֱסָיוּן fut. pl. with נ parag.; see חסה.

יָחֵף m., *barefooted.*

יַחֲצְאֵל, יַחְצִיאֵל p. n. of a man.; see

יָחַר same as אָחַר *tarrying,* 2 Sa. 20: 5; fut. וַיִּיחַר; וַיּוֹחֶר Kri Hiph. fut. Ch.; see אָחַר.

וַיִּחַר, יִחַר Kal fut. apoc.; see חרה.

יַחַשׂ m., *generation, family;* סֵפֶר הַיַּחַשׂ *register of descent,* Neh. 7 : 5.

הִתְיַחֵשׂ Hiph. *being, becoming registered* (as to pedigree); ἀπο-γράφεσθαι; inf. s., *registration.*

יָחַת Kal fut. pl. יֶחְתּוּ with dag. euphon., see נחת. Niph. fut.; see חתת.

וַיֵּט, יֵט Kal fut. apoc.; see נטה.

וַיֵּט, יֵט Hiph. fut. apoc.; see נטה.

יָטַב same as טוֹב (fut. יִיטַב, תֵּיטְבִי) *be* or *seem, good, happy;* with לְ *it was well with him;* with לִפְנֵי, בְּעֵינֵי *it seemed good to him;* with לֵב *was glad* (did the heart good). Hiph. הֵיטִיב (fut. יֵיטִיב, יֵטִיב, יֵטֵב) *do good, well to;* הֵיטַבְתָּ לִרְאוֹת *thou hast rightly seen,* Jer. 2:12; מֵיטִיב לְנַגֵּן *skilled in music;* with עִם, לְ, אֶל; inf. הֵיטֵב adv. *well, rightly.*

יְטַב Ch., *was good, happy;* with עַל *it pleased him.*

מֵיטָב m., *good, choice, best.*

יָטְבָה p.n. of a place.

יָטְבָתָה p. n. of a station of the Israelites in the desert.

יוּטָה, יֻטָּה p. n. of a city in the tribe of Judah.

יְטוּר p.n. of a son of Ishmael and of the people descended from him, *the Itureans.*

יֵדַע for יֵדַע Kal fut.; see ידע.

יֵיטִיב for יֵיטִיב Hiph. fut.; see יטב.

יְיֵלִיל for יְיֵלִיל Hiph. fut.; see ילל.

יַיִן; see ין.

יָיף Kal fut. apoc.; see יפה.

יַּד 1 Sa. 4:13. for יַד hand.

יַּךְ Hiph. fut. apoc.; see נכה.

יְכַבְּדָנְנִי Pi. fut. with suff. and נ epenth; see כבד.

יְכוֹנְנֶנּוּ for יְכוֹנְנֶנּוּ Pil. fut. with suff.; see כון.

יָכַח Hiph. הוֹכִיחַ.—I. show, evince.—II. convince, chastise, punish, with אֶת, אֶל, עִם. Hoph. הוּכַח was reproved, Job 33:19. Niph. נוֹכַח be contending. Hith. הִתְוַכַּח same as Niph., with עִם Mic. 6:2.

תּוֹכֵחָה f., reproof, punishment.

תּוֹכַחַת f. (with suff. תּוֹכַחְתִּי; pl. תּוֹכָחוֹת).—I. argument.—II. reproof, punishment.

יָכִין p. n.; see כון.

יָכֹל (fut. יוּכַל; inf. abs. יָכוֹל; const. יְכֹלֶת) capable of, equal to, any action, so as to succeed, prevail, overcome, with לְ.

יְכֵל Ch. (part. יָכִיל, יָכֵל; fut. יוּכַל, תֻּכַל) was able, prevailed, overcame.

יְכָלְיָהוּ, יְכָלְיָה (the Lord who prevaileth), p. n., the mother of king Uzziah.

יְהוּכַל p. n. of a man.

יֵכֵל Kal fut. apoc.; see כלה.

יְכֵל Ch. fut.; see יכל.

יְכֹלֶת inf. const.; see יכל.

יָכָנְיָה p. n.; see יְהוֹיָכִין in הוה.

יְכַסְיֻמוּ Ex. 15:5, for יְכַסְיֻמוּ, Pi. fut. with suff.; see כסה.

יֻבַּתּוּ, יֻבַכַת for יֻבַּתּוּ, יֻבַת Hoph. fut.; see כתת.

יֻבַתּוּ for יֻבַּתּוּ, יַכַתּוּ Hiph. fut. pl.; see כתת.

יָלַד, יֶלֶד, יָלַד (fut. יֵלֵד, יֵלֶד; inf. abs. יָלֹד; const. לֶדֶת, לֶת; with suff. לְדְתָּה).—I. bring forth.—II. beget (part. יוֹלֶדֶת mother). Niph. נוֹלַד (fut. יִוָּלֵד), was born. Pi. יִלֵּד aiding to bring forth, Ex. 1:16; part. מְיַלֶּדֶת midwife; pl. מְיַלְּדוֹת. Pu. יֻלַּד, יֻלַּד was born. Hiph. הוֹלִיד cause to bring forth, produce, beget. Hoph. inf. הֻלֶּדֶת be born; יוֹם הֻלֶּדֶת אֶת פַּרְעֹה Pharaoh's birthday, Gen. 40:20. Hith. הִתְיַלֵּד recorded in the genealogies as begotten, Nu. 1:18.

וָלָד m., son, progeny.

וֶלֶד m., the same.

יֶלֶד m.—I. lad, youth, child.—II. young of beasts, Isa. 11:7.

יְלִיד m., offspring, son; יְלִיד בַּיִת household slave.

יִלּוֹד m., offspring, son.

יַלְדָּה f., girl, female child.

יַלְדוּת f.—I. birth, Ps. 110:3.—II. youth, Ecc. 11:9, 10.

מוֹלָדָה p. n. of a town in the tribe of Judah.

מוֹלֶדֶת f. (pl. מוֹלָדוֹת).—I. nativity, birth.—II. birth-place.—III. person born.—IV. relatives, members of the same family.

מוֹלִיד p. n. of a man.

תּוֹלָד p. n. of a town in the tribe of Simeon; same as אֶלְתּוֹלַד.

תּוֹלֵדוֹת f. pl.—I. birth, Ex. 28:10.—II. posterity.—III. history; סֵפֶר תּוֹלֵדוֹת genealogy, Gen. 2:4; 6:9.

יָלוֹן p. n. of a man.

יַלִּינוּ Rabbinical, for יָלִינוּ, Hiph. fut. pl.; see לון.

יַלִּינוּ Hiph. fut. pl.; see II. לוּן.

יֵלֵךְ walk; see הָלַךְ.

יָלַל Hiph. הֵילִיל, יְיֵלִיל (fut. וַיְהֵילִיל), wail, howl, cry, mourn.

יְלֵל m., howling, Deu. 32:10.

יְלָלָה const., יִלְלַת f., wailing, lamenting.

תּוֹלֵלִים m. pl., those who cause to lament, Ps. 137:3.

יָלַן Kal fut. apoc. in pause for יָלֶן; see לוּן.

יָלַע retain, hold, Pro. 20:25.

יַלֶּפֶת f., itching scurvy, Lev. 21:20; 22:22.

יֶלֶק m., a hairy, winged locust.

יַלְקוּט bag; see לקט.

יָם const. יַם, יָם־ m.—I. the sea.—II. any great lake.—III. any large river; pl. יַמִּים; הַיָּם הַגָּדוֹל or הָאַחֲרוֹן the Mediterranean, i.e. Western Sea: hence יָם the west; רוּחַ יָם the west wind; יָמָּה westward; מִיָּם from the west; מִיָּם לְ from the west of a district; פְּאַת־ יָם sea (that is western) quarter; יָם הַנְּחֹשֶׁת brazen sea, a large vessel for ablution in the temple of Solomon.

יְמוּאֵל p.n. of a son of Simeon.

יָמִים, יְמוֹת days; see יוֹם.

יִמַּח, וַיִּמַּח Kal fut. apoc.; see מחה.

יֵמִים m. pl., Gen. 36:24, perhaps hot springs; Vulg. aquæ calidæ.

יְמִימָה p.n. of one of Job's daughters.

יְמִינִי, יָמִין right hand; see ימן.

יִמְלָה, יִמְלָא p.n. of the father of Micaiah the prophet.

יִמְלָה for יִמְלָא Pi. fut.; see מלא.

יַמְלֵךְ p.n. of a prince of the Simeonites.

יָמַן Hiph. הֵימִין take the right hand or southward.

יָמִין m.—I. the right side, hand, leg, eye; יַד יְמִינוֹ his right hand; מִימִין, מִימִין עַל with לְ and suff., יְמִין at the right hand; יָמִין, אֶל הַיָּמִין, לַיָּמִין to, towards the right.—II. south; מִימִין southward of any where.—III. p. n. of a man.

יִמְנָה p.n. of a son of Asher.

יְמָנִי m., יְמָנִית f., right hand, side, &c. יְמִינִי a Benjamin; see בֶּנְיָמִין in בָּנָה.

תֵּימָן lit. right (because a man facing the rising of the sun would have his hand to the south).—I. the south. —II. the south wind; תֵּימָרָה towards the south.—III. p. n. of a city and district of the Edomites; תֵּימָנִי a Temanite.

יִמְנָע p. n. of a man.

יִמְצֻא for יִמְצְאוּ Niph. fut. pl.; see מצא.

יָמַר same as מוּר. Hiph. הֵימִיר change, exchange, Jer. 2:11. Hith. הִתְיַמֵּר ye shall obtain rule, Isa. 61:6 (like Arab. word for commanded; whence "Emir"—Lee).

יֵמַר for יִמְרַר (was bitter) fut.; see מרר.

יִמְרָה p. n. of a man.

יִמְרוּךְ for יֹאמְרוּךְ Kal fut. pl. with suff.; see אמר.

יָמֵשׁ same as מָשַׁשׁ. Hiph. imp. הֲמִישֵׁנִי Kri, הַיְמִשֵׁנִי Ketib, let me grope, feel, Jud. 16:26.

יָנַאץ Syr. for יִנְאַץ Hiph. fut.; see נאץ.

יִנְדַּע for יֵדַע Ch. Pe. fut.; see יָדַע.

יָנָה oppress, ruin; (part. f. יוֹנָה).
Hiph. הוֹנָה (fut. יוֹנֶה) same as
Kal; with מִן drove away.

יָנוֹהַ p. n., a town in the confines of
Ephraim and Manasseh.

יָנוּם p. n. of a place in the tribe of
Judah.

יָנַח, see נוּחַ. Hiph. הֵנִיחַ (fut. יָנִיחַ,
וַיָּנַח).—I. gave rest to.—II. gave
comfort to.—III. allowed to fall
down.—IV. caused to rest upon,
with לְ. Hoph. הֻנִּיחַ I. was placed,
Zec. 5 : 11.—II. left, remaining,
Eze. 41 : 9, 11.

יָנִי for יָנִיא Hiph. fut.; see נוּא.

יָנִיחַ Hiph. fut. וַיָּנַח fut. apoc.; see
יָנַח.

יָנַק (fut. יִינַק) suck in; trop. enjoy;
part. יוֹנֵק sucking infant. Hiph.
הֵנִיק suckle, give suck; part. f.
מֵנֶקֶת, מֵינֶקֶת nurse; with suff.
מֵנִקְתָּהּ, מֵנִקְתּוֹ; pl. מֵנִיקוֹת.

יוֹנֵק m.—I. suckling.—II. sucker
(young shoot).

יוֹנֶקֶת f., the same.

יְנִיקָה f., the same; pl. יְנִיקוֹת.

יִנָּשֵׂוּא Niph. fut. with א parag.; see
נָשָׂא.

יַנְשׁוּף owl; see נָשַׁף.

יָסֹב for יָסֹב Kal fut.; see סָבַב.

יָסֵב for יָסֵב Hiph. fut.; see סָבַב.

יָסַד I. founded, established, placed.—
II. fixed, laid up. Niph. נוֹסַד was
plotting, laying the ground-work
of, Ps. 2 : 2; was founded, Isa. 44 :
28. Pi. יִסַּד cause to found, fix,
establish. Pu. יֻסַּד was founded,
Hoph. inf. הוּסַד was founded;

part. מוּסָד founded, secure, Isa
28 : 16, &c.

יְסוֹד m., foundation; pl. יְסוֹדִים
יְסוֹדוֹת.

סוֹד m.—I. setting a fence about.—
II. decree, counsel.—III. delibera-
tion.—IV. consideration, prudence.
—V. assembly for deliberation.—
VI. secret.

סוֹדִי p. n. of a man.

יְסֻד m., beginning, i. e. foundation of
a building, Ezr. 7 : 9.

יְסֻדָה f., foundation, Ps. 87 : 1.

מוּסָד m., foundation, support, prop.

מוּסָדָה f., the same.

מוֹסָד m., foundation, support; pl.
מוֹסָדוֹת and מוֹסָדִים.

מַסָּד m., foundation, 1 Ki. 7 : 9.

יֻסָּךְ was poured out, Ex. 30 : 32; see
נָסַךְ.

יִסְכָּה p. n. of Lot's sister.

יִסְמַכְיָהוּ p. n. of a man.

יָסַף (part. יוֹסֵף; pl. יוֹסְפִים and Hiph.
יָאסִיף וַיֹּסֶף, יוֹסֵף, יוֹסִיף; fut. הוֹסִיף
וַיֹּאסֶף; part. מוֹסִיף).—I. added,
repeated, with עַל, אֶל, לְ.—II. used
as an auxiliary, with לְ, אֶל, עַל
before the inf. when it may mostly
be translated by again. Niph.
נוֹסַף was added, repeated; part.
f. pl. נוֹסָפוֹת additions of calamity.

יָסַף Ch., Hoph. הוּסַף was added.

יָסַר (fut. with suff. אֶסָּרֵם; part. יֹסֵר).
Pi. יִסַּר (fut. יְיַסֵּר; inf. יַסֵּר, יַסְּרָה,
יִסְּרָה) chastised, corrected (as parents their
children), with מִן. Niph. נוֹסַר
was chastised; pl. נִוָּסְרוּ. Hiph.
fut. אִיסִירֵם I will chastise them,
Hos. 7 : 12.

יְפוּר will chastise, Job 40:2.

מוֹסֵר chains; see אָסַר.

מוּסָר m. — I. chastisement, discipline. — II. learning, doctrine.

מֹסָר m., the same, Job 33:16.

יָע shovel; see יָעָה.

יַעְבֵּץ p.n. — I. of a man. — II. of a town in the tribe of Judah.

יָעַד (fut. וַיִּיעַד) appoint, determine. Niph. נוֹעַד. — I. brought together, assembled, met. — II. agreed, with עַל, אֶל, לְ. Hiph. הוֹעִיד appoint. Hoph. הוֹעַד appointed, fixed, Jer. 24:1.

עֵדָה const. עֲדַת f. — I. an assembly. — II. party, persons united for a purpose. — III. a family. — IV. the congregation of Israel. — V. עֵ דְּבוֹרִים swarm of bees, Jud. 14:8.

מוֹעֵד m. (pl. מוֹעֲדִים, מוֹעֲדֵי). — I. coming together, congregation; אֹהֶל מוֹעֵד the tabernacle of the congregation. — II. time, season. — III. place appointed; see also מֵעַד.

מוֹעֵד m., assembly, host, Isa. 14:31.

מוֹעָדָה f., pl. מוֹעָדוֹת solemn feasts, 2 Chron. 8:13.

מוּעָדָה f., appointment; עָרֵי הַמֻּעָדָה appointed cities of refuge.

וַיֹּעַד Hiph. fut.; see עוּד.

יָעָה carry off, destroy, Isa. 28:17.

יָע m., pl. יָעִים shovels or fire-pans.

יְעִיאֵל יְעוּאֵל p.n. of a man.

יְעוּץ p.n. of a man.

יְעוֹרִים m. pl., woods, Eze. 34:25; see יַעַר.

יְעוּשׁ p.n. of a man.

יָעַז Niph. part. נוֹעָז, Isa. 33:19; Vulg. impudens, powerful, formidable.

יַעֲזִיאֵל p.n. of a man.

יַעֲזִיָּה p.n. of a man.

יַעְזֵר, יַעְזוֹר (the Lord helpeth) p.n. of a town beyond Jordan of the tribe of Gad.

יָעַט clothe, cover, Isa. 61:10.

יְעַט Ch. same as Heb., יָעַץ advise, counsel. Ith. consulted together, Dan. 6:8.

יָעֲטִין m. pl., councillors.

עֵטָא f., counsel, wisdom, Dan. 2:14.

וַיָּעַט יָעַט Kal fut.; see עוּט.

יָעִיר, יָעוּר p.n. of a man.

יַעְכָּן p.n. of a man.

יָעַל. Hiph. הוֹעִיל be profitable, advantageous, with לְ.

יָעֵל m. — I. ibex, mountain goat; pl. יְעֵלִי, יְעֵלִים. — II. p.n. of a judge of Israel. — III. p.n. of a woman. — IV. צוּרֵי הַיְּעֵלִים p.n. of a rock in the desert of Engaddi.

יַעֲלָה f. — I. female ibex. — II. p.n. of a man.

יַעְלָם p.n. of the son of Esau.

יַעֲמֹדְנָה Dan. 8:22. Kal fut. pl. f. for תַּעֲמֹדְנָה; see עָמַד.

יַעֲנִי יַעַן; see עָנה.

יַעַן perhaps from עָנָה cried.

יְעֵנִים pl. יַעֲנָה f., ostriches, Lam. 4:3.

בְּנוֹת יַעֲנָה (pl. בַּת הַיַּעֲנָה f. יַעֲנָה female ostriches.

יָעַף (fut. יִיעַף) lit. ran swiftly, was fatigued, wearied. Hoph. part. מֻעָף swift, Dan. 9:21.

יָעֵף m., weary, fatigued, Isa. 40:29; 50:4.

יָעַף m., flight, Dan. 9:21.

תּוֹעָפוֹת f. pl. — I. swiftness. — II

wealth, treasure (acquired by fatigue).

יָעַץ (fut. יִיעַץ) *advise, admonish, counsel self* or *others*, with עַל, אֶל; part. יוֹעֵץ *counsellor.* Niph. נוֹעַץ *be advised, counselling, consulting,* with עִם, אֶל, אֶת. Hithp. יִתְיָעֲצוּ same as Niph.

עֵצָה const. עֲצַת f., *counsel;* בְּעֵצָה *deliberately;* see also עצה

מוֹעֵצָה f., pl. מוֹעֵצוֹת *counsels, devices.*

יַעֲקֹבָה p. n.; see עקב.

בְּנֵי־יַעֲקָן; see יַעֲקָן.

יַעַר m.—I. *honey-comb* (const. יַעְרַת). —II. *wood, forest;* יַעְרָה *to the wood;* pl. יְעָרִים, יְעוֹרִים, יְעָרוֹת.—III. p. n.: יַעַר אֶפְרָיִם *grove of Ephraim;* קִרְיַת יְעָרִים *a city in the tribe of Judah;* יַעַר חָרֶת *the wood of Hereth* in the tribe of Judah.

וַיַּעַר Hiph. fut.; see עור.

יַעְרָה same as יְהוֹעַדָּה p. n. of a man.

יַעֲרֵי אֹרְגִים (*thickets*, perhaps abbreviated יַעֲרוֹ) p. n. of a man.

יַעֲרֵשִׁיָה p. n. of a man.

יַעְשַׁי p. n. of a man.

יַעֲשִׂיאֵל p. n. of a man.

יִפְדְּיָה (*the Lord redeemeth*), p. n. of a man.

יָפָה (fut. וַיִּיף, יִיפֶה) *was fair, beautiful.* Pi. *beautified,* Jer. 10:4. Pul. יֻפְיָפָה *was very beautiful.* Hith. *beautify oneself.*

יָפֶה const. יְפֵה m.; יָפָה const. יְפַת f., *beautiful, excellent.*

יָפוֹ, יָפוֹא p. n., *Joppa,* a celebrated port on the Mediterranean, Ἰόππη.

יְפִי m. (with pause יֳפִי; with suff. יָפְיוֹ), *beauty, excellence.*

יְפֵה־פִיָה f., *very beautiful,* Jer. 46:20

יְפֵיפִית Pul., Ps. 45:3, from יפה.

יָפַח same as פוּח. Hith. *was panting in agony,* Jer. 4:31.

יָפֵחַ m.—I. *breathing out.*—II. *panting after, longing for.*

יַפְלֵט p. n. of a man; patron. יַפְלֵטִי.

יְפֻנֶּה p. n. of the father of Caleb and others.

יָפַע. Hiph. הוֹפִיעַ *exhibit brilliancy, shine forth.*

יִפְעָה f., *beauty, brilliancy,* Eze. 28: 7, 17.

יָפִיעַ p. n.—I. of a town in the tribe of Zebulun.—II. of a man.

יֶפֶר Hiph. fut. apoc.; see פרה.

יַפְתְּ Hiph. fut. apoc.; see פתה.

יָפַת *root not used.*

מוֹפֵת m.—I. *sign, wonder.*—II. *intimation, portent* (τύπος).

יֶפֶת p. n., *Japheth,* son of Noah; LXX. Ἰάφεθ.

יִפְתָּח p. n.—I. a town in the tribe of Judah.—II. a judge of Israel (Ἰεφθά).

יִפְתַּח־אֵל p. n., a valley in the tribes of Zebulun and Asher.

יָצָא (fut. יֵצֵא; inf. abs. יָצֹא; const. צֵאת; imp. צֵא; with ה parag צֵאָה; part. m. יוֹצֵא, f. יֹצֵאת, יֹצֵאת, יֹצֵת).—I. *go out, go forth;* with מִן of the place whence; with בְּ of the place whither.—II. *issue* (from the womb), *be born.*—III. *descended.*—IV. *go forth* (from captivity or into captivity).—V. *shooting of a tree,* Isa. 11:1, also *grew, came forth* (of plants and flowers).—VI. *arose* (of the sun

and stars).—VII. *issue a decree.*
There are many similar usages, all
modifications of the primary meaning *go forth.* Hiph. הוֹצִיא *cause
to come out, bring out;* with דִּבָּה
brought up an evil report, Nu. 14:
36. Hoph. הוּצָא *was brought
forth, out.*

יְצָא Ch., Shaph. שֵׁיצִיא *wrought out,
finished,* Ezr. 6:15.

יָצִיא m., *issue, child,* 2 Chron. 32:21.

מוֹצָא m.—I. *outgoing.*—II. *time of
outgoing.*—III. *place of outgoing.*
—IV. *the east.*—V. *that which
goeth out,* production, speech, &c.
—VI. p. n. of a man.

מוֹצָאָה f.—I. *going forth,* Mic. 5:1.—
II. *draught-house,* 2 Ki. 10:27.

תּוֹצָאוֹת f. pl.—I. *termination.*—II.
escape, Ps. 68:21.—III. *result,*
Pro. 4:23.

צֶאֱצָאִים m. pl.—I. *productions of the
earth.*—II. *offspring.*

יָצַב same as נָצַב. Hith. הִתְיַצֵּב I.
was set up, stood fast, with עַל,
לְפָנַי.—II. *stood up against,* with
עַל.—III. *stood before, in presence
of,* with עִם, בִּפְנֵי, לִפְנֵי.

יְצַב Ch. Pa. *certify.*

יַצִּיב m. Ch., *firm, fixed, settled;*
מִן יַצִּיב adv., *surely.*

יָצַג, הִצִּיג, יָצַג; see נצג.

יִצְהָר p.n.; see צהר.

יִצְחָק p.n.; see צחק.

יִצְטַבַּע Ch. Ithp. fut.; see צבע.

יְצְטַיָּרוּ Hith. fut. pl.; see ציר.

יָצַע, part. יָצוּעַ *laid, placed,* s. *bed.*
Hiph. הִצִּיעַ *place, strew.* Hoph.
הֻצַּע *spread* (as a couch), Isa. 14:11.

יָצִיעַ same as יָצוּעַ.

מַצָּע m., *bed* or *couch,* Isa. 28:20.

יָצַק (fut. יִצַּק, וַיִּצֶק; inf. const. צֶקֶת;
imp. יְצֹק, צַק).—I. *pour out.*—II.
fuse (as metal), with בְּ, עַל; part.
יָצוּק *hard* (like a cast of metal).
Hiph. הִצִּיק *put down, place, lay
out,* Jos. 7:23; 2 Sa. 15:24. Hoph.
הוּצַק *be, become poured out;* part.
מֻצָּק *firm,* Job 11:15.

יִצֶק, וַיִּצֶק Kal fut., from יצק.

יִצֹק Kal fut., from יצק.

יְצֻקָה f., *casting, cast,* 1 Ki. 7:24.

מוּצָק, const. מֻצַק m., *cast of brass;*
see also in צוק.

מוּצָקָה f., pl. מוּצָקוֹת *funnels* for
pouring the metal into moulds or
casts, Zec. 4:2.

מוּצֶקֶת f., with suff. מֻצַקְתוֹ *its being
fused,* 2 Chron. 4:3.

I. יָצַר (fut. יָצֹר, וַיָּצֶר, וַיִּיצֶר), *form,
fashion, make;* part. יוֹצֵר *moulder,
potter;* כְּלֵי יוֹצֵר *fictile vases;
creator.* Niph. נוֹצַר and Hoph.
הוּצַר *was formed, made.* Pu. יֻצַּר
the same.

יֵצֶר m. (with suff. יִצְרֵנוּ).—I. *figment,
any thing formed.*—II. *thought,
imagination.*—III. p. n. of a son
of Naphtali; patron. יִצְרִי.

וַיָּצֶר, יֵצֶר Kal fut., Gen. 2:19, from I. יצר.

יְצֻרִים m. pl., *things formed, members,*
Job 17:7.

II. יָצַר same as צור but intrans., *was
straitened, distressed, anxious;*
וַיֵּצֶר לוֹ *and he was in anxiety,*
Gen. 32:8.

יְצָרֵהוּ, יֵצֶר Kal fut. with suff., from
II. יצר.

וַיֵּצֶר, יֵצֶר Kal fut., from II. יָצַר.

וַיָּצַר, יָצַר Kal fut. apoc.; see צוּר.

יָצַת (fut. יִצַּת, יַצַתּוּ).—I. burn, Isa. 9:17, with בְּ.—II. was on fire. Niph. נִצַּת I. was on fire, burnt.— II. burnt with anger, with בְּ, 2 Ki. 22:13,17. Hiph. הִצִּית, הוֹצִית kindle, set fire to.

יַצַתּוּ Kal fut. pl. with dag. euphon., from יָצַת.

יָצָתִי for יָצָאתִי; see יצא.

יָקֶב root not used; (Arab. a tank).

יֶקֶב m. (with suff. יִקְבְךָ).—I. wine or oil vat.—II. the trough in which grapes are trodden, Job 24:11.

יַקַבְצְאֵל p.n., same as קַבְצְאֵל.

יָקַד (fut. יִקַּד, יִיקַד burnt (as fire). Hoph. הוּקַד became, was, burning.

יְקַד Ch., burning, Dan. 3:6, &c.

יָקוֹד m., the same, fire-brand, Isa. 10:16.

יְקֵדָה f. Ch., the same. Dan. 7:11.

מוֹקֵד m.— I. burning, Isa. 33:14.— II. fire-brand, Ps. 102:4.

מוֹקְדָה f., hearth where the burnt-offerings were consumed, Lev. 6:2.

יָקְדְעָם p.n. of a city in the tribe of Judah.

יָקָה root not used; (Arab. he obeyed).

יִקְּהָה or יְקָהָה, const. יְקָהַת f. obedience.

יָקֶה p.n. of a man.

יְקוּם whatever has been called into existence, Gen. 7:4, 23; Deut. 11:6; see קוּם.

יָקוֹשׁ יְקוּשׁ; see יקשׁ.

יְקוּתִיאֵל p.n. of a man.

יִקַּח Kal fut.; יֻקַּח Hoph. fut.; see לקח.

יָקְטָן p.n., a descendant of Shem, the son of Eber, Gen. 10:25, 26.

יָקִים p.n. of a man.

יָקַמְיָה p.n. of a man.

יָקַמְעָם p.n. of a man.

יָקְמְעָם p.n., a city of the Levites in the tribe of Ephraim; see also קִבְצַיִם.

יָקְנְעָם p.n. of a city in the tribe of Zebulun.

יָקַע (fut. יִיקַע; pret. נָקַע which see).— I. fell, became dislocated, Gen. 32: 26.—II. fell away (in mind, affection). Hiph. הוֹקִיעַ suspend, hang, ἀνασκολοπίζειν. Hoph. part. מוּקָעִים hanged, 2 Sa. 21:13.

יָקַץ (fut. וַיִּיקַץ, יָקַץ, יִיקַץ) awake out of sleep; see קוּץ.

יְקַץ Kal fut.; see יקץ.

יָקַר (fut. וַיִּיקַר, יֵקַר, יִיקַר) became precious, prized, valued, with בְּעֵינֵי, לְ. Hiph. הוֹקִיר (lit. make precious), rare, scarce.

יָקָר m. יְקָרָה f.—I. precious, dear.— II. rare, scarce. — III. honorable, glorious.

יְקָר m., weight, value, honour, glory.

יְקָר m. Ch.— I. costly things, Dan 2:6.—II. honor, glory.

יַקִּיר m., precious, honored, Jer. 31:20.

יַקִּיר m. Ch., honored, grave.

יִקְּרֶךָ Kal. fut. with suff. and dag. euphon.; see קרה.

יָקֹשׁ, יָקַשׁ (see קוֹשׁ נָקַשׁ) snaring, taking by means of snares; part. יוֹקֵשׁ a fowler. Niph. נוֹקַשׁ was ensnared as a bird.

יָקוֹשׁ, יָקֻשׁ m., fowler.

יֻקְשׁ m., pl. יֻקְשִׁים snared, Ecc. 9:12.

יָקְשָׁן p. n. of a son of Abraham.

מוֹקֵשׁ m. (pl. מוֹקְשִׁים, מוֹקְשׁוֹת) *snares* or *traps* for birds or beasts; mostly used metaphorically, as מוֹקְשֵׁי מָוֶת *snares of death*, &c.

וַיָּקֹשׁ יָקֹשׁ Kal fut. apoc.; see קשה.

יֵקֹשׁ Hiph. fut. apoc.; see קשה.

יָקְתְאֵל p. n.—I. a town in the tribe of Judah.—II. a city in Arabia.

יָרֵא (fut. אִירָא, יִירָא; imp. יְרָא; inf. const. יְרֹא; with pref. לִרֹא; with ה parag. (יִרְאָה)), *feared* God, man, anything; with מִן, לְ, בְּ, אֶת. Niph. fut. תִּוָּרֵא *thou art to be feared*, Ps. 130:4; part. נוֹרָא *fearful, terrible, marvellous thing*; pl. נוֹרָאוֹת. Pi. יֵרֵא *alarm, cause to fear.*

יָרֵא, const. יְרֵא m. (יְרֵאָה, const. יִרְאַת f.), *fearing* God or man, with מִפְּנֵי.

יִרְאָה, const. יִרְאַת f., *the same.*

יִרְאוֹן p. n. of a city in the tribe of Naphtali.

מוֹרָא m.—I. *fear.*—II. *reverence*, Mal. 1:6.—III. *object of fear, reverence.*—IV. *fearful, stupendous act.*

מוֹרָה same as מוֹרָא; see also in מרה.

וַיִּרָא יָרֵא Kal fut. apoc.; see ראה.

יִרְאוּ for יִירְאוּ Ps. 34:10, imp. pl.; see ירא.

יִרְאוּ Kal fut. pl., see ירא; יִרְאוּ Kal fut. pl., see ראה.

וַיִּרְאוּ 2 Sa. 11:24, for יִירוּ Hiph. fut. pl. apoc.; see ירה.

יְרָאִיָּה p. n. of a man.

יָרֵב; יְרֻבַּעַל יְרֻבֶּשֶׁת see ריב.

וַיָּרֶב יָרֵב, for יָאֵרֶב, Hiph. fut.; see ארב.

יְרִבְּיוּן Kal fut. pl. with נ parag.; see רבה.

יָרָבְעָם p. n., *Jeroboam*, the name of two of the kings of Israel.

יָרַד (fut. יֵרֵד, וַיֵּרֶד; imp. רֵד, וַיֵּרֶד רְדָה; inf. abs. יָרֹד, const. רֶדֶת, יָרֵד; רְדָה). — *descended, went down*, κατέβη (used both of men and things in a great variety of acceptations). Hiph. הוֹרִיד *make descend, bring down, cast down* (of men and things); *subdued*, with תַּחַת. Hoph. הוּרַד *brought down, lowered.*

יֶרֶד p. n. of a man, Ἰαρέδ.

יַרְדֵּן p. n. of the river *Jordan.*

מוֹרָד m., *descent, declivity;* מַעֲשֵׂה מוֹרָד *sloping*, perhaps *arched work*, 1 Ki. 7:29.

יַרְדֹּף Ps. 7:6, apparently a corruption, from יִרְדֹּף Kal fut. and יְרַדֵּף Pi. fut.; or possibly from two readings יְרַדֵּף and יִרְדֹּף.

יָרָה (fut. יִירֶה; inf. יָרֹה, const. יְרוֹת; יָרוֹא; imp. יְרֵה).—I. *cast out, shoot*, as arrows, &c.; part. יוֹרִים *archers*, Pro. 26:18.—II. *cast, lay a foundation*; see יוֹרָה. Niph. fut. יִיָּרֶה *shall be shot*, Ex. 19:13. Hiph. הוֹרָה (fut. יוֹרֶה, וַיּוֹר).—I. *cast forth, shoot*, as arrows, rain, &c. (מוֹרִים *archers*); see מוֹרָה.—II. *put forth*, as instruction, *teach*, with מִן, אֶל, בְּ, לְ.

יוֹרָה m. (part. Kal).—I. *the former rain*, i. e. of the autumn.—II. p. n. of a man; same as חָרִיף.

יוֹרִי p. n. of a man.

מוֹרֶה m. (part. Hiph.).—I. *teacher, doctor.*—II. *arrow, archer.*—III. *former rain.*— IV. p. n. אֵלוֹן or

אֵלֹנֵי מוֹרֶה the oaks of Moreh, near Sichem; גִּבְעַת־הַמּוֹרֶה hill of Moreh in the valley of Jezreel.

תּוֹרָה f.—I. instruction, direction.— II. law, enactment.—III. the law, as revealed to Moses and recorded in the Pentateuch.

יָרֵה (fut. תִּרְהוּ), was astounded with fear, Isa. 44:8.

וַיֹּרוּ, יֹרוּ Hiph. fut. pl.; see ירה.

יְרוֹא for יְרוֹ לִירוֹא Kal inf.; see ירה.

יְרוּאֵל p. n. of a desert.

יָרוֹחַ (same as יֶרַח, p. n. of a man.

יָרוּן Kal fut. pl. with נ parag.; see רוח.

יָרֹן Pro. 29:6, Kal fut.; see רנן. Others refer it to רון.

יָרוּץ for יָרֹץ Kal fut.; see רצץ.

יְרוּשָׁא p. n. of the mother of king Jotham.

יְרוּשָׁלַם, יְרוּשָׁלַיִם for יְרוּשָׁלַם (the habitation of peace), p. n. of the principal city of Palestine, Ἱερου-σαλήμ, Ἱεροσόλυμα.

יְרוּשָׁלֵם Ch., the same.

יָרֵחַ m., the moon.

יֶרַח m., (pl. יְרָחִים, יַרְחֵי).—I. month, one revolution of the moon round the earth.—II. p. n. of a people and country, Gen. 10:6.

יְרַח m. Ch., month.

יְרִיחֹה, יְרֵחוֹ, יְרִיחוֹ p.n., Jericho, a city in Palestine.

יָרְחָם p. n. of a man.

יְרַחְמְאֵל p. n. of a man; patron. —ִי.

יְרַחַע p. n. of a woman.

יָרַט cast down to ruin, ruin.

מוֹרַט m., "peeled" Eng. Ver.; "ruined" (Gesenius), Isa. 18:2, 7.

יְרִיאֵל p. n. of a man.

יָרִיב, יְרִיבַי; see ריב.

יִרְיָּה, יִרְיָהוּ p. n. of a man.

יְרִיחֹה, יְרֵחוֹ p.n.; see יְרֵחוֹ.

יְרִיעָה, יְרִיעוֹת shouting; see ירע.

יָרֵךְ m. (const. יֶרֶךְ; with suff. יְרֵכוֹ).—I. thigh; שׁוֹק עַל־יָרֵךְ hip and thigh, i. e. wholly, Ju. 15:8; יֹצְאֵי יֶרֶךְ offspring, Ex. 1:5.—II. stem of the candlestick in the tabernacle; dual יְרֵכַיִם both thighs.

יַרְכָה f., side, part, quarter; dual יַרְכָתַיִם, const. יַרְכְּתֵי, the two sides.

יַרְכָּה f. Ch., thigh.

יֻרַךְ Niph. fut., from רכך.

יַרְמוּת p. n. — I. a town in the tribe of Judah.—II. a town of Israel.

יְרֵמוֹת, יְרִימוֹת p.n. of a man.

יְרְמַי p. n. of a man.

יִרְמְיָהוּ, יִרְמְיָה (exalted of the Lord), p. n. Jeremiah, the prophet.

יָרַע same as רוע.—I. was in evil con-dition; fut. יֵרַע with לִי I am in affliction; with בְּעֵינֵי it was evil in the eyes of.—II. was grieved, pained.

I. יֵרַע Kal fut., from II. ירע Job 20:26; fut. apoc., from רעה.

יְרִיעָה f., veil, curtain of a tent.

יְרִיעוֹת (veiled), p. n. of a woman.

יִרְפְּאֵל p. n. of a place in the tribe of Benjamin.

יָרַק same as רָקַק spit.

יָרוֹק m., green herb, shoot, Job 39:8.

יָרָק m., green herb.

יֶרֶק m., freshness, green herbage.

יֵרָקוֹן m.—I. *withering, wasting*; LXX. ὤχρα.—II. *the smut in corn.*

יְרַקְרַק m.—I. *gold colour,* Ps. 68:14. —II. *greenish or yellowish*; pl. f. יְרַקְרַקּוֹת.

יָרַשׁ, יֵרֵשׁ (fut. יִירַשׁ, יִרַשׁ); inf. const. רֶשֶׁת; imp. (יֵרַשׁ, רֵשׁ, רַשׁ).—I. *possess, inherit.*—II. *dispossess others.* —III. *be, become poor*; יוֹרֵשׁ *heir.* Niph. *be, become poor.* Pi. יֵרַשׁ *take into possession,* Deu. 28:42. Hiph. הוֹרִישׁ.—I. *cause to possess.* —II. *dispossess.*—III. *make poor, desolate.*

יְרֵשָׁה f., *possession,* Nu. 24:18.

יְרֻשָּׁה f., *the same.*

רֶשֶׁת f. (inf. *to take*; with suff. רִשְׁתּוֹ) —I. *net.* — II. *snare.* — III. *network.*

מוֹרָשׁ m. } *possession.*
מוֹרָשָׁה f. }

מוֹרֶשֶׁת גַּת p. n. of a district near Gath; מוֹרַשְׁתִּי *a Moreshethite.*

תִּירוֹשׁ, תִּירֹשׁ m., *new wine, must.*

יִשְׂחָק same as יִצְחָק p. n.; see צחק.

יִשְׂמָעֵאל p. n. of a man.

יָשַׂם same as שׂוּם intrans. *was set, laid*; fut. וָאִישְׁמָה, וַיִּישֶׂם.

יִשְׂרָאֵל (*a prince with God*), p. n., *Israel,* the new name given by God to Jacob, afterwards applied to his descendants; m. יִשְׂרְאֵלִי, f. יִשְׂרְאֵלִית *an Israelite.*

יִשָּׂשכָר p. n. *Issachar,* the son of Jacob, and the tribe that descended from him.

יֵשׁ־, יֶשׁ (τὸ εἶναι), *is, are, was, were*; with suff. יֶשְׁךָ *thou art*; יֶשְׁנוֹ *he is*; יֶשְׁכֶם *ye are*; יֶשׁ לִי *I have*;

יֵשׁ וָיֵשׁ *it is, because that*; יֵשׁ אֲשֶׁר *it is, yea it is,* 2 Ki. 10:15.

יָשַׁב, יֵשֵׁב (fut. יֵשֵׁב; inf. יְשֹׁב; const. שֶׁבֶת; with suff. שִׁבְתִּי; imp. שֵׁב, שְׁבָה).—I. *sit, sit down,* with בְּ, עַל.— II. *lie in wait for.*—III. *have intercourse with,* with עִם.—IV. *remain.*—V. *dwell in.*—VI. *was inhabited,* with בְּ, עַל. Niph. נוֹשַׁב *was inhabited.* Pi. יֵשֵׁב *cause to remain,* Eze. 26:4. Hiph. הוֹשִׁיב *cause to sit, dwell, reside in* or *with, inhabit.* Hoph. הוּשַׁב *made, caused to dwell.*

יוֹשַׁבְתִּי; see יָשַׁבְתִּי.

שִׁיבָה f., *residing,* 2 Sa. 19:33; see in שׁוּב.

יֹשֵׁב בַּשֶּׁבֶת p. n. of one of David's generals.

יֶשְׁבְּאָב p. n. of a man.

יֶשְׁבּוֹ בְּנֹב p. n. of a man.

יָשָׁבְקָשָׁה p. n. of a man.

מוֹשָׁב m. (pl. f. מוֹשָׁבוֹת; const. מוֹשְׁבֵי m.).—I. *residence.*—II. *seat.* —III. *time of residing,* Ex. 12: 40.—IV. *act of sitting.*—V. *inhabitants.*

תּוֹשָׁב m., *settler, sojourner.*

יִשְׁבַּח p. n. of a man.

יָשֳׁבִי לֶחֶם p. n. of a man.

יָשָׁבְעָם p. n. of a man.

יִשְׁבָּק p. n. of a son of Abraham.

יָשׁוּב p. n. of a man; patron. יָשֻׁבִי.

יְשׁוּד for יָשֹׁד Kal fut.; see שׁרד.

יִשְׁוִי, יִשְׁוָה p. n. of a man.

יְשׁוֹחָיָה p. n. of a man.

יְשׁוּעָה, יֵשַׁע *salvation*; see ישׁע.

יֶשַׁח m., *baseness, hypocrisy,* Mic. 6: 14.

יִשָּׁחוּ Niph. fut.; see שׁחה.

יָשַׁט. Hiph. הוֹשִׁיט *extend, stretch out.*

יִשַׁי p. n., *Jesse,* the father of David; LLX. Ἰεσσαί.

יִשָּׂא for יַשִּׂיא Hiph. fut.; see נשׂא.

יִשִׁיָּה, יְשִׁיָּהוּ p. n. of a man.

יָשֵׂם for יָשִׂים Hiph. fut.; see שׂים.

יִשָּׁל Kal. fut. apoc., from III. שׁלה.

יָשַׁם *was desolate, laid waste;* fut. תִּישַׁמְנָה, תֵּשַׁם; see שׁמם.

יְשִׁימוֹן m.— I. any *great desert.*—II. specially, *the Desert of Sinai.*

יְשִׁימוֹת f., *desolations,* Ps. 55:16.

בֵּית-הַיְשִׁמוֹת p. n. of a place near the Dead Sea.

יֹשֵׁם for יָשֹׁם Kal. fut.; see שׁמם.

יַשְׁמֵם Hiph. fut.; see שׁמם.

יִשְׁמָא p. n. of a man.

יִשְׁמָעֵאל p. n.—I. *Ishmael,* the son of Abraham and Hagar. — II. of a man; יִשְׁמְעֵאלִים *Ishmaelites.*

יִשְׁמַעְיָה, יִשְׁמַעְיָהוּ p. n. of a man.

יִשְׁמְרַי p. n. of a man.

יָשֵׁן, יָשַׁן (fut. יִישַׁן) *slept, slumbered, dozed.* Niph. נוֹשַׁן *grew old, dry.* Pi. יִשֵּׁן *made to sleep,* Jud. 16:19.

יָשֵׁן m., *old.*

יְשֵׁנָה f.—I. the same.—II. p. n. of a town in the tribe of Judah.

יָשֵׁן m. יְשֵׁנָה f.—I. *sleepy.*—II. p. n. of a man.

שֵׁנָה f. — I. *sleep.* — II. *dream,* Ps. 90:5.

שְׁנָא f., *sleep,* Ps. 127:2.

שְׁנָא or שְׁנָה f. Ch., the same.

שְׁנַת f., *sleep,* Ps. 132:4.

יֶשְׁנוּ compounded of יֵשׁ and suff. וֹ with נ epenth.

יָשַׁע. Hiph. הוֹשִׁיעַ (fut. יוֹשִׁיעַ, יְהוֹשִׁיעַ; apoc. יוֹשַׁע) *deliver, set free, save,* with לְ, מִיַד, מִן. Niph. נוֹשַׁע *was delivered,* with מִן; part. נוֹשָׁע *one saved,* Zec. 9:9.

יֵשַׁע, יֶשַׁע m. (with suff. יִשְׁעִי, יִשְׁעֲךָ), *deliverance, freedom, safety, salvation.*

וַיֹּשַׁע, יֵשַׁע Kal fut. apoc., from שׁעה.

יֹשַׁע Hiph. fut. apoc. יִשַׁעֲכֶם fut. with suff., from ישׁע.

יִשְׁעִי p. n. of a man.

יְשַׁעְיָהוּ p. n., *Isaiah* the prophet; LXX. Ἡσαίας; Vulg. Isaias.

יְשַׁעְיָה p. n. of a man.

יֵשׁוּעַ (same as יְהוֹשֻׁעַ, Ἰησοῦς), p. n. of a man.

יְשׁוּעָה f., *freedom, safety, salvation.*

מוֹשָׁעוֹת f. pl., *great salvation,* Ps. 68: 21.

יָשְׁפֵה, יָשְׁפֶה *the jasper,* a variegated gem.

יִשְׁפָּה p. n. of a man.

יִשְׁפָּן p. n. of a man.

יָשַׁר (fut. יִישַׁר, יִישָׁר).—I. *proceed, go right,* i. e. directly onwards; יָשַׁר בַּדֶּרֶךְ *he went straight on his way.* —II. with בְּ, בְּעֵינֵי *he was right, upright, good.* Pi. יִשֵּׁר *make right, direct.* Pu. part. *made direct, plain, laid smooth,* 1 Ki. 6:35. Hiph. *made direct, straight forward,* Pro. 4:25.; (imp. הַיְשַׁר) *make direct,* Ps. 5:9.

יָשָׁר m., יְשָׁרָה f., *right, upright, righteous, true;* יֹשֶׁר s., *the book of right,* i. e. right things, Deu. 6:18.

יֶשֶׁר p. n. of a man.

יֹשֶׁר m., *rectitude, integrity.*

יִשְׁרָה f., the same.

יִשְׂרְאֵלָה p.n. of a man.

יְשֻׁרוּן m., a periphrastic title of Israel, applied to the whole people generally, lit. *entirely righteous.*

תִּשַׁרְנָה 1 Sa. 6:12, for תִּשַׁרְנָה Kal fut. f. pl. 3. pers., from יָשַׁר.

מֵישׁוֹר m.—I. *a plain.*—II. *truth, righteousness;* adv. *righteously, truly.*

מֵישָׁרִים, מֵשָׁרִים m. pl.—I. *true men.* —II. *truth, righteousness.*—III. לְמֵישָׁרִים, בְּמֵישָׁרִים *truly, righteously.*

יָשֵׁשׁ m., 2 Chron. 36:17, *aged, elderly person.*

יָשִׁישׁ m., the same.

יְשִׁישַׁי p.n. of a man.

וַיִּשְׁתַּחוּ, יִשְׁתַּחוּ Hith. fut. apoc. sing. for יִשְׁתַּחֲוֶה; see שׁחה.

יִשְׁתָּיוּן Kal fut. pl. with נ parag., from שׁתה.

יִשְׁתַּקְשְׁקוּן Hith. fut. pl:, from שׁקק.

יָת Ch., same as Heb. אֶת.

וַיֵּתֶא, יֵתֵא Kal fut. apoc. for יֶאְתֶּה, יֶאְתֶּה; see אתה.

יִתְאָו Hith. fut. apoc., from אוה.

יְתִב Ch., same as יָשַׁב *sit.* Aph. *reside,* Ezr. 4:17.

וַיִּתְגַּל, יִתְגַּל Hith. fut. apoc., from גלה.

יָתֵד root not used; (Arab. *pin, nail*).

יָתֵד, const. יְתַד f. (pl. יְתֵדוֹת).—I. *pin, peg.*—II. *tent-pin;* hence *wise* (i. e. firmly fixed) *rulers,* Isa. 22: 23, 25.—III. *dibble, to bore holes in the earth,* Deu. 23:14.

וַיִּתָו, יִתָו Pi. fut. apoc., from תוה.

יִתּוֹכַּח Hith. fut., from יכח.

יָתוּר *abundance;* see תוּר.

יִתְזִין Ch. Ithp. fut., from זון.

יָתַח root not used; (Arab. *smote with a club*).

תּוֹתָח m., *club;* LXX. σφύρα, Job 41:21.

יִתְכַּס Hith. fut. apoc., from כסה.

יִתְלָה p.n. of a city of the Danites.

יָתַם root not used; (Arab. *was an orphan*).

יָתוֹם m., *orphan.*

יִתַּם, in pause יִתַּמּוּ Kal fut., from תמם.

יִתַּמּוּ Niph. fut. pl., from תמם.

יִתְמָה p.n. of a man.

יָתַן root not used; (Arab. *was enduring*).

אֵתָן, אֵיתָן m.—I. *mighty, irresistible, violent;* יֶרַח הָאֵיתָנִים *the month of the powerful,* i. e. Tisri, 1 Ki. 8:2.—II. *might, irresistibleness.*— III. p. n., perhaps the author of Ps. 89.

יַתְנִיאֵל p.n. of a man.

יִתְנָן p.n. of a city in the tribe of Judah.

יָתַר, part. יוֹתֵר *exceeding, redundant.* Hiph. הוֹתִיר I. *cause to remain, leave.*—II. *abound, be wealthy.* Niph. נוֹתַר *be left, remain;* part. m. נוֹתָר, f. נוֹתֶרֶת *that which is left.*

יֶתֶר m.—I. *excellence, abundance,* עַל־יֶתֶר *unto abundance,* Ps. 31: 24; adv., *abundantly, exceedingly.* — II. *residue, the rest of.* — III. *string* or *cord.*—IV. p. n. of a man; patron. יִתְרִי.

יִתְרָה f., *abundance, excess.*

יֹתֵר, יָתַר (part. Kal).—I. *abundance, profit.*—II. adv., *more, further, moreover, excessively.*

יֹתֶרֶת f.—I. *exceeding, redundant.*—II. *lobe*, i. e. excess of the liver.

יַתִּיר m. Ch.—I. *excellent, extraordinary;* יַתִּירָה adv., *very, exceedingly.*—II. Heb. p. n., a tówn in the tribe of Judah.

יִתְרוֹ p. n., the father-in-law of Moses, who was also called יֶתֶר and חוֹבָב.

יִתְרוֹן m., *gain, profit, good.*

יִתְרְעָם p. n. of a man.

מוֹתָר m.—I. *increase.*—II. *excellence,* Ecc. 3:19.

מֵיתָר m.—I. *bow-string,* Ps. 21:13.—II. *tent-cord.*

יִתְשָׂם Ch. Ithp. fut., from שׂום.

יְתֵת p. n. of a prince of Edom.

כ

כְּ, כ pa. pref. signifying comparison, resemblance.—I. *as, as if, like;* כְּ...כֵּן, כְּ...וּכְ, כְּ...כְּ *as...so;* with suff. כָּהֶם, כָּכֶם; see כְּמוֹ.—II. *according to* (κατά).—III. *nearly, almost;* כַּיּוֹם הַזֶּה *as on this day;* כַּחֲצֹת הַלַּיְלָה *about midnight.*—IV. with inf. (sometimes with part.) *when,* ὡς.

כָּאַב (fut. יִכְאַב) *be pained.* Hiph. I. *cause pain,* Eze. 13:22.—II. *mar, ruin,* 2 Ki. 3:19.

כְּאֵב m., *pain.*

מַכְאוֹב m. (pl. ־ים, ־וֹת).—I. *pain.*—II. *cause of pain.*—III. *sorrow.*

כָּאָה. Niph. *pained, enfeebled,* Dan. 11:30. Hiph. *pain, enfeeble the heart,* Eze. 13:22.

כָּאֶה m., *afflicted, helpless,* Ps. 10:10

כָּאֹר Am. 8:8, for כִּיאֹר.

כָּאֲרִי Ps. 22:17; see כּוּר.

כָּבֵד and כָּבַד (fut. יִכְבַּד).—I. *be heavy, grievous.*—II. *be grave, respectable, honorable,* with עַל, אֶל. Niph. *became honorable, glorious;* part. נִכְבָּדִים *nobles,* נִכְבָּדוֹת *made glorious,* with בְּ. Pi. כִּבֵּד I. *make heavy, sullen, unrelenting.*—II. *make honourable, honour,* with לְ, לְשֵׁם. Pu. כֻּבַּד *was honoured.* Hiph. I. *made heavy, grievous, sullen.*—II. *made honorable, glorious.*—Hith. מִתְכַּבֵּד *fancying himself honorable,* Pro. 12:9.

כָּבֵד const. כְּבַד, כָּבֵד m.—I. *heavy.*—II. *rich.*—III. *numerous.*—IV. *stupid, sullen.*—V. *grievous.*—VI. *dense.*—VII. *slow of utterance.*—VIII. *hard to be understood.*—IX. *the liver.*

כָּבוֹד m., lit. *heaviness:* hence,—I. *glory, splendour, majesty.*—II. *abundance, wealth.*—III. *multitude.*—IV. *mind, soul.*—V. *honour;* כְּבוֹד יְהֹוָה *the glory of God;* LXX. δόξα Κυρίου.

כָּבֹד, f. כְּבוּדָּה *glorious, precious.*

כֹּבֶד m.—I. *weight.*—II. *abundance.*

כְּבֵדֻת f., *heavily,* Ex. 14:25.

כָּבָה *was extinguished.* Pi. *extinguished.*

כָּבוּל p. n.—I. *a district of Galilee.*—II. *a town in the tribe of Asher.*

כַּבּוֹן p. n., *a town in the tribe of Judah.*

כַּבִּיר, כְּבִיר see כבר.

כָּבַל root not used; (Arab. *iron fetter*)

כֶּבֶל m., *footlock of iron.*

כָּבַס part. כּוֹבֵס *fuller.* Pi. כִּבֵּם,
כִּבֵּם *wash, cleanse* clothes and the
like, not the body. Pu. כֻּבַּם *was
washed.* Hothp. inf. הֻכַּבֵּם *to be
washed,* Lev. 13:55, 56.

כָּבַע root not used; see נבע, קבע.
כּוֹבַע כּוֹבַע m., *helmet.*

כָּבַר. Hiph. *multiplied,* Job 35:16;
part. *abundance,* Job 36:31.
כְּבָר p. n. of a river in Mesopotamia,
the Chaboras.
כְּבָר adv., *already, now.*
כַּבִּיר m., *mighty, powerful, great.*
כְּבִיר m., *cushion* or *pillow* cased with
goat skin, 1 Sa. 19:13, 16.
כְּבָרָה f., *sieve,* Am. 9:9.
כִּבְרָה f., an unknown measure of
length; LXX. ἱππόδρομος.
מִכְבָּר m., *brazen lattice-work.*
מַכְבֵּר m., *carpet, coarse cloth,* 2 Ki.
8:15.

כָּבַשׁ root not used; same as כָּבַשׁ
subdue.
כֶּבֶשׂ m., *a lamb.*
כַּבְשָׂה, כִּבְשָׂה f. (pl. כְּבָשׂת const.
כִּבְשׂת) *a she-lamb.*

כָּבַשׁ I. *trample, tread under foot;* metaph. *shall trample on sling stones,*
i.e. not be harmed by them, Zec. 9:
15.—II. *subdue, humble.*—III. *force,*
Est. 7:8. Niph. *be subdued, humbled.* Pi. *subdued,* 2 Sa. 8:11.
כֶּבֶשׁ m., *footstool,* 2 Chron. 9:18.
כִּבְשָׁן m., *smelting furnace.*
כַּד *jar;* see כדד.
כָּרָב m., כִּדְבָה f. Ch., *lying, false,*
Dan. 2:9.

כָּדַד root not used; (perhaps from
Arab. *straitness*).
כַּד f. (with suff. כַּדֵּךְ; pl. m. כַּדִּים)
earthen jar, water vessel.
כִּידוֹד m., *spark of fire,* Job 41:11.
כַּדְכֹּד m., *a precious stone,* perhaps
the ruby.
כִּדְנָה, see דֵּי; כְּדִי, see דִּי; כְּדִי, see
דֵּן.
כִּידוֹר m., *attack, onset,* Job 15:24.
כְּדָרְלָעֹמֶר p. n. of a king of Elam.

כֹּה pa.—I. *so, thus, in this form,
manner, &c.;* בְּכֹה…כֹּה *on this
manner and on that manner,* 1 Ki.
22:20.—II. *here, hither;* וָכֹה…כֹּה
hither and thither, Ex. 2:12; עַד
כֹּה *yonder,* Gen. 22:5.—III. *now;*
עַד כֹּה *until now,* Ex. 7:16;
עַד כֹּה וְעַד כֹּה *so and so long,* i.e.
a very short time, 1 Ki. 18:45.
כָּה Ch., עַד כָּה *thus far,* Dan. 7:28.

כָּהָה (fut. יִכְהֶה; apoc. וַתֵּכַהּ).—I.
become weak, languid (of the eyes).
—II. of the mind or person, Isa.
42:4. Pi. כֵּהָה, כִּהָה *made weak,
disheartened.*
כֵּהֶה f. כֵּהָה.—I. *expiring, fading* (of
a lamp), Isa. 42:3.—II. of the eyes.
—III. of a disease or eruption.—
IV. אֵין כֵּהָה *not weak,* i.e. vigorous, Nah. 3:19.
כֵּהוֹת Pi. inf., from כהה.
כְּהַל Ch., *able, adequate.*
כָּהַן. Pi. כִּהֵן *act, officiate as priest.*
כֹּהֵן m. (pl. כֹּהֲנִים, כֹּהֲנֵי) *priest;* with
הַמָּשִׁיחַ or הָרֹאשׁ or הַגָּדוֹל *the
high priest.*
כָּהֵן m. Ch., *priest.*

כְּהֻנָּה f., priesthood, office of the priest.

כּוּב p. n., a country in the south, Eze. 30:5.

כּוֹבַע helmet; see כבע.

כָּוָה. Niph. תִּכָּוֶה was, became burnt.

כַּו m. Ch., pl. כַּוִּין windows, casements, Dan. 6:11

כְּוִיָּה f., burning, branding, Ex. 21:25.

כִּי m. (for כְּוִי) branding, Isa. 3:24.

כִּי pa.; see further.

מִכְוָה f., inflamed part (of body), Lev. 13:24, 25, 28.

כּוּחַ root not used; (Arab. conquer in battle).

כֹּחַ, כּוֹחַ m.—I. strength, vigour, power, ability.—II. wealth; כֹּחַ הָאָרֶץ fruit of the earth, Gen. 4:12.—III. a kind of lizard (from its strength), Lev. 11:30.

כּוֹכָב m., star, constellation.

כּוּל measured, Isa. 40:12. Hiph. הֵכִיל I. contain.—II. sustain. Pil. כִּלְכֵּל I. contain (as a vessel).—II. sustain (with food).—III. bear (with firmness). Pu. כָּלְכַּל were sustained.

כִּימָה the constellation of the pleiades.

כּוּמָז bracelet of gold beads.

כּוּן fashioned, set in order, Job 31:15. Pil. כּוֹנֵן dispose, prepare, fix, establish, with עַל, בְּ, אֶת. Pul. כּוֹנַן established, confirmed. Hiph. הֵכִין dispose, prepare, fix, establish. Hoph. הוּכַן was disposed, prepared. Niph. be, become disposed, set in order, fixed, established (of person or thing); part. נָכוֹן (f. נְכֹנָה) firm, established, sure;

שַׁחַר נָכוֹן the true dawn, as opposed to the false, or premature twilight in the East, Hos. 6:3; אֶל־נָכוֹן certainly, for certain. Hith. הִכּוֹנֵן, הִתְכּוֹנֵן same as Niph.

כֵּן adj.—I. substantial, true; pl. כֵּנִים.—II. part. really, truly: whence,—III. as, so, thus; אַחֲרֵי־כֵן, אַחַר כֵּן afterwards; בְּכֵן thus; לָכֵן therefore; עַל־כֵּן because; לָכֵן אֲשֶׁר because; עַד־כֵּן hitherto; see also in כנן.

כֵּן Ch., thus.

אָכֵן pa. (for הָכֵן inf. abs. Hiph. confirmed), surely, certainly, truly.

כּוּן p. n., a Phenician city, 1 Chron. 18:8, called in 2 Sa. 8:8, בֵּרֹתַי Berytus.

כַּוָּן m., small round cake, Jer. 7:18; 44:19.

כִּיּוּן p.n. of an idol, Am. 5:26, called Ρεμφαν, Acts 7:43, the planet Saturn.

יָכִין I. p. n. of a son of Simeon; patron. יָכִינִי.—II. one of the columns in the temple of Solomon.

מָכוֹן m.—I. place, establishment.—II. foundation.

מְכוֹנָה f.—I. basis.—II. p. n. of a town in the tribe of Judah.

מְכֻנָה f., place, Zec. 5:11.

תְּכוּנָה f.—I. presence.—II. arrangement.—III. furniture, stores.

כּוֹס f.—I. drinking cup; pl. כֹּסוֹת.—II. rough-billed pelican, Lev. 11:17; Deu. 14:16; Ps. 102:7.

כּוּר root not used; (Arab. digging, piercing); כָּאֲרִי piercing, Ps. 22:17.

כַּר m., *camel's pack-saddle,* Gen. 31: 34 ; see also כרר.

כְּרִי an officer of a certain rank, 2 Ki. 11:4,19; כְּרֵתִי Kri, 2 Sa. 20:23.

כּוּר m., *furnace for melting metals.*

כּוּר עָשָׁן (*smoking furnace*), p. n. of a city in the tribe of Simeon.

כֹּר m., a measure of capacity, containing 10 baths.

כִּיּוֹר m. (pl. כִּירוֹת, כִּיֹּרִים).—I. *a pot* or *brazier* for fire, Zec. 12:6.— II. *laver of brass.*—III. *chafing dish,* 1 Sa. 2:14. — IV. *pulpit,* 2 Chron. 6:13.

כִּירַיִם m. dual, *pots* or *jars,* Lev.11:35; LXX. χυτρόποδες.

כִּכָּר f. (for כִּרְכָּר).—I. *tract of country.* — II. כִּכַּר לֶחֶם *cake of bread;* pl. m. כִּכָּרוֹת *talent* (of gold or silver); dual כִּכָּרַיִם; const. כִּכְּרֵי; pl. f. כִּכְּרֵי, כִּכָּרִים.

כִּכָּר f. Ch., pl. כִּכְּרִין the same.

מְכוֹרָה, מְכֻרָה f., *place of origin, birth,* lit. *digging;* see Isa. 51:1.

מְכֵרָה f., *sword,* Gen.49:5.

כּוּשׁ p. n.—I. *Ethiopia.*—II. name of a man, Ps. 7:1.

כּוּשִׁי m. (pl. כּוּשִׁיִּים; f. כּוּשִׁית).—I. *an Ethiopian.*—II. p. n. of a man.

כּוּשָׁן f., Hab. 3:7, same as כּוּשׁ *Ethiopia.*

כּוּשַׁן רִשְׁעָתַיִם p. n. of a king of Mesopotamia.

כּוּשָׁרָה f., *wealth;* see כשר.

כּוּת, כּוּתָה p. n. of a region whence the kingdom of Israel was colonised after its depopulation.

כָּזָב, part. כֹּזֵב *deficient, falling short,* Ps. 116:11. Pi. כִּזֵּב.—I. *lie, deceive.*

—II. *fail,* with לְ or בְּ. Hiph. *convict of falsehood,* Job 24:25. Niph. *was fallacious, false.*

כָּזָב m., *falling short of truth, lying, falsehood.*

כֹּזְבָא p. n., same as כְּזִיב.

כָּזְבִּי p. n. of a Midianitish woman.

כְּזִיב p. n. of a town in the tribe of Judah.

אַכְזָב m., *deficient, deception, unstable.*

אַכְזִיב p.n.—I. a town in the tribe of Judah.—II. a town in the tribe of Asher, on the Mediterranean. Ἔκδιππα.

כָּזַר root not used; (Arab. *mudd turbid*).

אַכְזָר m., *untractable, cruel, fierce.*

אַכְזָרִי *very cruel.*

אַכְזְרִיּוּת f., *great cruelty,* Pro. 27:4. כֹּחַ *strength;* see כּוֹחַ.

כָּחַד. Pi. כִּחֵד *keep back, conceal,* with מִן or לְ. Niph. I. *was concealed.*—II. *made useless, destroyed.* Hiph. I. *hold back.*—II. *bring* a *nought.*

כָּחַל *black* (the eyes) *with antimony,* Eze. 23:40.

כָּחַשׁ *fail, be deficient.* Pi. כִּחֵשׁ I. *withhold.*—II. *fail, deceive, deny, lie,* with בְּ and לְ. Niph. and Hith. *were, became liars,* with לְ.

כַּחַשׁ m.—I. *deficiency.*—II. *failure, falsehood.*

כֶּחָשׁ m., *lying,* Isa. 30:9.

כִּי pa.—I. *if, for,* at the beginning of a speech.—II. *because, therefore,* in the second member of a sentence: also,— III. *surely, without doubt.*

It connects the hypothesis and condition of an entire sentence, and may be translated by almost any particle that is so used; הֲכִי whether? is not? עַל כִּי יַעַן כִּי because; עַד כִּי until; כִּי עַל־כֵּן therefore; see also כֵּנָה.

כִּי אִם I. that.—II. if not, with oaths. —III. except, after a negative.— IV. but, only.

כִּיד m., ruin, destruction, Job 21:20.

כִּידוֹן m.—I. spear.—II. גֹּרֶן כִּידוֹן (the plain of spears), p. n. of a district; see נָכוֹן.

כִּידוֹד sparks; see כדד.

כִּידוֹר attack; see כדר.

כִּיּוּן an idol; see כון.

כִּיוֹר pot; see כור.

כְּלִי, כֵּלַי vessel; see נבל.

כִּלַפּוֹת axes; see כלף.

כִּימָה Pleiades; see כום.

כִּים bag; see נכם.

כִּיר pot; see כּוּר.

כִּיתְרוֹן Syr. for כִּיתָרוֹן.

כָּכָה same as כֹּה thus; אֵיכָכָה how? see אֵי in אֵיךְ.

בְּכֹר ; see כּוּר.

כָּל־ כֹּל all; see כלל.

כָּלָא restrain, confine, withhold (part. כֹּלֵא כָּלוּא shut up), with מִן; fut. יִכְלָה. Niph. restrained, withholden.

כֶּלֶא m. (with suff. כִּלְאוֹ), prison; בֵּית הַכֶּלֶא בֵּית כֶּלֶא the same; pl. בָּתֵּי כְלָאִים

כְּלָה כִּלָּה f., all that, from כֹּל; see כלל.

כִּלְאַיִם dual, of two sorts or kinds, ἑτερογενῆ.

כֶּלוּא (כְּלִיא) m., prison.

מִכְלָה f. (pl. מִכְלָאוֹת), fold or pen for flocks.

כִּלְאָב p. n. of a son of David.

כְּלוּב m.—I. fruit-basket, Am. 8:1,2. —II. bird-cage, Jer. 5:27.—III. p. n. of a man.

כֶּלֶב m.—I. a dog.—II. bad, cruel man.

כָּלֵב p. n. of a man, Caleb; patron. כָּלִבִּי.

כָּלָה (fut. תִּכְלֶה, יִכְלֶה; apoc. יִכֶל וַתֵּכֶל).—I. was completed, finished. —II. was wasted, ruined, decayed. Pi. כִּלָּה I. complete, determine.— II. waste, ruin, destroy, with לְ. Pu. כֻּלָּה (fut. יְכֻלֶּה), were completed.

כָּלֶה f. כָּלָה consuming, Deu. 28:32.

כָּלָה f., completion, destruction; עָשָׂה כָלָה hath done even to destruction, altogether, with בְּ; אֶת; adv. כָּלָה לְכָלָה completely, entirely.

כְּלִי m. (with pause כֶּלִי; pl. כֵּלִים, כְּלֵי).—I. vessel.—II. boat, Isa. 18: 2.—III. musical instrument.—IV. arms, weapon.—V. implement of husbandry.—VI. clothing.

כְּלָיוֹת const., כִּלְיוֹת f. pl., the reins, kidneys, metaph. as the seat of sense, the feeling.

כִּלָּיוֹן const. כִּלְיוֹן m.—I. consumption, Isa. 10:22.—II. wasting of the eyes, Deu. 28:65.

כִּלְיוֹן p. n. of a man.

מִכְלוֹת f. pl., with זָהָב, 2 Chron. 4: 21. pure gold.

תִּכְלָה f., perfection; LXX. συντέλεια.

תַּכְלִית f.—I. extremity, Neh. 3:21.— II. boundary. — III. completeness, perfection.

כְּלִלוֹת ,כַּלֵּה; see כלל.

כְּלוּהִי p.n. of a man.

כִּלְהֶם for כֻּלָּם, from כֹּל; see כלל.

כִּלְהֵנָה for כֻּלָּנָה, from כֹּל; see כלל.

כֵּלוּ 1 Sa. 6:10, Kal pret. pl., from כלא.

כֶּלַח m.—I. wealth.—II. insolence, Job 30:2.

כֶּלַח p.n. of a city, Gen. 10:11.

כְּלִי ,כִּלְיוֹת ,כִּלָיוֹן; see כלה.

כַּלְכֹּל p.n. of a man.

כָּלַל perfected, Eze. 27:4, 11.

כְּלַל Ch., finished, completed; Shaph. שַׁכְלֵל the same; passive אִשְׁתַּכְלֵל was completed.

כָּלִיל m.—I. whole, entire; adv. wholly, entirely; כְּלִיל הָעִיר the whole city.—II. whole burnt-offering, i.e. offering entirely consumed, Deu. 33:10; Ps. 51:21.

כַּלָּה f.—I. daughter-in-law.—II. spouse.

כְּלוּלֹת f. pl., espousals, Jer. 2:2.

כֹּל (כּוֹל Jer. 33:8) כָּל—I. the whole, all.—II. complete, entire.—III. all, every.—IV. many, most of; לֹא כֹל none: with suff. כֻּלָּנוּ all we; כֻּלְּכֶם ,כֻּלְּכֶם all ye; כֻּלָּהֶם all they; כֻּלְהֵנָה ,כֻּלָּנָה all they, f.; כֻּלּוֹ all of it, m.; כֻּלָּה the same, f.; with adv. כָּל־עֻמַּת שֶׁ as long as, כָּל־עוֹד just as, Ecc. 5:15.

כֹּל ,כָּל Ch., the same; כְּלָא adv., altogether, entirely.

מִכְלַל m., perfection, Ps. 50:2.

מִכְלוֹל m., the same (of clothing), Eze. 23:12, &c.

מַכְלֻלִים m. pl., splendid garments, Eze. 27:24.

כָּלַם Hiph. הִכְלִים ,הַכְלִים put to

shame, make ashamed, injure. Hoph. was ashamed, confounded. Niph. was ashamed, confounded.

כְּלִמָּה f., shame, ignominy.

כְּלִמּוּת state of shame, Jer. 23:40.

כִּלְמָד p.n. of a region or city.

כַּלְנֶה ,כַּלְנֵה ,כַּלְנוֹ p. n. of a city on the river Tigris (Ctesiphon?).

כָּלַף root not used; (Arab. drove).

כֵּילַפּוֹת f. pl., axes or hammer, Ps. 74:6; LXX. λαξευτήρια.

כִּלְּתִי Pi. pret. 3. pers. f. with suff., from כלה.

כְּלָתַנִי 1 Sa. 25:33, Kal pret. 2. pers. f. with suff., from כלא.

כָּמַהּ desired intensely even to fainting.

כִּמְהָם p. n. of a man.

מָה; see כָּמָה ,כַּמָּה ,כַּמֶּה.

כְּמוֹ ,כְּמוֹ pa., same as כְּ thus, as, whether; with suff. כָּמוֹנִי as I am, כָּמוֹךָ ,כָּמֹכָה as thou art; כָּמֹהוּ as he is; כָּמוֹהָ as she is; כָּמוֹנוּ as we are, sometimes for כָּכֶם, כָּהֶם ,כְּמוֹכֶם ,כְּמוֹהֶם as ye, they, are; כְּמוֹ...כְּמוֹ as...so.

כְּמוֹשׁ p. n., an idol of the children of Moab and Ammon; עַם כְּמוֹשׁ the Moabites.

כַּמֹּן m., the herb cummin, Isa. 28: 25, 27.

מִכְמַנִּים m. pl., treasures, Dan. 11:43.

כָּמֻס laid, treasured, up, Deu. 32:34.

כָּמַר Niph. נִכְמַר I. was affected (warmed with intense feeling, love, compassion).—II. was black with burning, Lam. 5:10.

כֹּמֶר m., pl. כְּמָרִים idolatrous priests.

כִּמְרִיר blackest, gloomiest thing, Job 3:5.

מַכְמֹר, מִכְמָר m., pl. מַכְמֹרִים *net* used by fishermen.

מִכְמֶרֶת, מִכְמֹרֶת f., *net* used by fisher-men.

כֵּן; see כּוּן and כָּנָה.

כָּנָה Kal not used; (Syr. *named*). Pi. כִּנָּה I. *call by name.*—II. *flatter.*

כְּנָת m. (man of the same name), *companion, associate*; pl. כְּנָוֹת (σύνδουλοι).

כְּנָת Ch., the same; pl. כְּנָוָן; with suff. כְּנָוָתֵהּ, כְּנָוָתְהוֹן.

כַּנָּה; see כֵּן.

כַּנֵּה p. n. of a city (perhaps for כַּלְנֵה).

כִּנּוֹר m. (with suff. כִּנֹּרִי; pl. כִּנֹּרִים, כִּנֹּרוֹת), *harp* (κινύρα).

כִּנּוֹת, כִּנָּוָן from כָּנָה; see כנה.

כָּנְיָהוּ p. n. of a king of Judah; same as יְהוֹיָכִין.

בַּנֹּלְתְךָ Hiph. inf. with pref. and suff. for כְּהַנְלֹתְךָ; see נלה.

כַּנָּם; see כֵּן.

כִּנְאֵמָא Ch., "as it is said" (for Lee).

כַּנָּה f., *stock, root*, Ps. 80:16.

כְּנָנִי p. n. of a man.

כְּנַנְיָה, כְּנַנְיָהוּ p.n. of a man.

כְּנַנְיָהוּ p. n. of a man.

כֵּן m. (with suff. כַּנּוֹ, כַּנֶּךָ.—I. *place, station.*—II. *base*, foot of the laver; see also כּוּן.

כֵּן m.; *lice*; pl. כִּנִּים LXX. σκνίφες.

כַּנָּם for כַּנָּם same as כִּנִּים; see preceding word, Ex. 8:12.

כָּנַס *collect, gather together.* Pi. like Kal. Hith. *being collecting, comprehending*, Isa. 28:20.

מִכְנָס m., dual const. מִכְנְסֵי *drawers, breeches of linen* (for the priests).

כָּנַע. Hiph. הִכְנִיעַ *humble, debase, bring down.* Niph. נִכְנַע *was humbled, debased.*

כְּנָעָה f., *package, bale of merchandise*, Jer. 10:17.

כְּנַעַן I. p. n. of a son of Ham.—II. of the land inhabited by his posterity.—III. m., *a merchant.*

כְּנַעֲנִי (f. כְּנַעֲנִית; pl. כְּנַעֲנִים).—I. *a Canaanite.*—II. *a merchant.*

כְּנַעֲנָה p. n. of a man.

כְּנַעֲנֶיהָ pl. with suff., from כְּנַעַן.

כָּנַף root not used; (Arab. *put away*). Niph. יִכָּנֵף *put away, remove*, Isa. 30:20.

כָּנָף f. (dual כְּנָפַיִם, כְּנָפֵי f.; pl. const. כַּנְפוֹת m. and f.).—I. *wing* (of a bird, &c.).—II. *wing* (of an army).—III. *skirt* (of a garment).—IV. *extreme part* (of the earth or land).—V. by meton. *person protected,* i. e. *wife* &c.

כִּנֶּרֶת, כִּנְּרוֹת, כִּנָּרוֹת p. n., a city in the tribe of Naphtali, near the sea of Galilee (Γεννησαρέτ); יָם כִּנֶּרֶת *the sea of Galilee.*

כְּנַשׁ Ch., *collect*, Dan. 3:2. Hith. *being assembled*, Dan. 3:3, 27.

כַּסְדָּי Ch., same as כַּשְׂדָּי *a Chaldean.*

כָּסָה, part. כֹּסֶה *covering, concealing*, Pro. 12:16, 23; כָּסוּי *covered*, Nu. 4:6, 14. Niph. נִכְסָה *being covered, concealed.* Pi. כִּסָּה *cover, conceal*, with אֶל, אֵת, בְּ, לְ, עַל. Pu. כֻּסָּה, כָּסָה *covered, was covered*, with בְּ. Hith. same as Niph. Pu. with בְּ.

כֵּם m., כִּסֵּא יָהּ the throne of Jehovah, Ex. 17:16.

כֵּסֶה, כֶּסֶה m., the new moon, Ps. 81:4; Pro. 7:20.

כִּסֵּא, כִּסֵּא m. (with suff. כִּסְאִי; pl. כִּסְאוֹת), regal chair, throne.

כְּסוּת f.—I. covering.—II. clothing.

סוּת f., a false reading for כְּסוּת garments, Gen. 49:11.

כְּסָתוֹת f. pl., Eze. 13:18, 20, LXX. προσκεφάλαια, cushions, probably ornaments.

מִכְסֶה m., covering.

מְכַסֶּה m., covering, Isa. 14:11.

כָּסָה, part. כָּסוּחַ cut off.

כַּסּוּחָה like filth, Isa. 5:25; see סוּחַ.

כָּסַל was a fool; fut. יִכְסְלוּ Jer. 10:8.

כְּסִיל m.—I. a fool.—II. the constellation Orion.—III. p. n. of a city in the tribe of Judah.

כְּסִילוּת f., foolish woman, Pro. 9:13.

כֶּסֶל m.—I. the loins.—II. the viscera; pl. כְּסָלִים.—III. expectation, confidence.—IV. foolishness.

כִּסְלָה f.—I. confidence.—II. folly.

כִּסְלֵו m., the ninth month of the Hebrew year, answering to our November and December.

כִּסָלוֹן p. n. of a town on the borders of the tribe of Judah.

כִּסְלוֹן p. n. of a man.

כִּסְלוֹת p. n. of a town in the tribe of Issachar.

כִּסְלוֹת־תָּבוֹר p. n. of a town at the foot of Mount Tabor.

כַּסְלֻחִים m. pl., p. n. a people so called.

כָּסַם adorn, Eze. 44:20.

כֻּסֶּמֶת f., a kind of corn, spelt, ζέα; pl. כֻּסְּמִים.

כָּסַס apportion, divide out, Ex. 12:4.

מֶכֶס m., fractional part, number.

מִכְסָה f., number.

כָּסַף desired intensely (lit. grew pale with desire), with לְ. Niph. become desirous, earnestly longing for, with לְ.

כֶּסֶף m. (with suff. כַּסְפִּי; pl. כְּסָפִים).—I. silver.—II. money; with numerals, the shekel of silver; אֶלֶף כ' 1,000 shekels.

כְּסַף m. Ch., silver.

כָּסְפִיָא p. n. of a country.

כְּסָתוֹת ornaments; see כסה.

כִּסְּתַנִי Pi. pret. 3 pers. f. with suff., from כסה.

כְּעַן adv. Ch.—I. so, therefore.—II. but.—III. now; כְּעֶנֶת so on; see עתת.

כָּעַס (fut. יִכְעַס).—I. was angry.—II. irritated. Pi. כִּעֵס irritate. Hiph הִכְעִים.—I. was angry.—II. made angry, irritated.

כַּעַס m.—I. vexation, sadness.—II. anger; pl. כְּעָסִים excitements to anger.

כַּעַשׂ m., the same, in Job only.

כַּף, כִּפָּה, כַּפּוֹת; see כפף.

כֵּף rock, Job 30:6; Jer. 4:29.

כָּפָה avert, appease, Pro. 21:14; see כבה.

כְּפִירָה, כְּפִיר; see כפר.

כָּפַל doubled; part. כָּפוּל. Niph. be repeated, Eze. 21:19.

כֶּפֶל m., doubling, twofold; dual כִּפְלַיִם Job 11:6; Isa. 40:2.

כָּפֵן became languid, Eze. 17:7.

כָּפָן m., hunger, Job 5:22; 30:3.

כָּפַם (Syr. *tie, join*).

כָּפִים m., *tie-beam*; *"tenon"* (Lee); LXX. κάνθαρος.

כָּפַף *bend, bow down*, with distress. Niph. *bow myself down*, with לְ *before*, Mic. 6:6.

כַּף f.—I. *palm of the hand*.—II. *hand* (with suff. כַּפִּי; dual כַּפַּיִם *both hands*; pl. כַּפּוֹת).—III. *sole of the foot*.—IV. *foot of a beast*.—V. *bason or phial*.—VI. *receptacle for the stone in a sling*; כַּף־הַקֶּלַע *cup of the sling*, 1 Sa. 25:29.—VII. *bent palm branches*; כַּפּוֹת תְּמָרִים *bent palm branches*, Lev. 23:40.—VIII. כַּף־הַיָּרֵךְ *cup of the thigh joint*, Gen. 32:26, &c.

כִּפָּה f., *curved branch, branch*.

כָּפַר.—I. generally *cover*.—II. specially, *pitch, smear with pitch*, Gen. 6:14, with בְּ. Pi. כִּפֶּר (fut. יְכַפֵּר) I. *cover, expiate for sin*, used of the sinner and the sin.—II. *appease anger*.—III. *avert calamity*, with אֶת, בְּעַד, לְ, עַל. Pu. כֻּפַּר—I. *was expiated*.—II. *was abolished*. Hith. *was expiated*; נִתְכַּפֵּר for נְכַפֵּר Deu. 21:8.

כְּפוֹר m.—I. *vessel, covered cup*.—II. *hoar frost*, Ex. 16:14; Ps. 147:16.

כְּפִיר m.—I. *a young lion*.—II. metaph. *fierce, bold man*.—III. *village*, Neh. 6:2.

כָּפָר m., *village*.

כְּפִירָה p. n. of a city of the Hivites.

כְּפַר הָעַמֹּנִי p. n., a town in the tribe of Benjamin.

כֹּפֶר m.—I. *pitch*, Gen. 6:14.—II. *a village*, 1 Sa. 6:18.—III. *expiation*,

lit. *covering for sin*, λύτρον.—IV the *cypress tree*, Cant. 1:14.

כִּפֻּרִים m. pl., *expiation*.

כַּפֹּרֶת f., *the covering of the ark*; *mercy-seat*; בֵּית הַכַּפֹּרֶת *the holy of holies*.

כָּפַשׁ. Hiph. *overwhelmed, covered*, Lam. 3:16.

כְּפַת Ch., *bound, tied*.

כַּפְתּוֹר p. n., a country of the Philistines; כַּפְתֹּרִים its inhabitants, Gen. 10:14.

כַּפְתֹּרִים m. pl.—I. *twisted capitals or columns*.—II. *ornamented bowls* of the golden candlestick, Ex. 25:36.

כַּר, see כּוּר; כָּר, see כּוּר and כָּרַר.

כְּרָה or כְּרָא Ch. Ithp. *was pained, afflicted*.

כַּרְבֵּל. Pu. part. מְכָרְבָּל *equipped clothed*, 1 Chron. 15:27.

כַּרְבְּלָא Ch., *a cloak*, Dan. 3:21.

כָּרָה *dig* (as a well, pit); with אָזְנַיִם *mine ears hast thou digged, opened*, Ps. 40:7. Niph. I. *was dug*.—II. *buy, purchase*, Deu. 2:6; Hos. 3:2.—III. *feast*, 2 Ki. 6:23.

כֵּרָה f.—I. *digging*, Zep. 2:6; pl. const. כְּרֹת.—II. *feast*, 2 Ki. 6:23. מִכְרֶה m., *pit*, Zep. 2:9.

כְּרוּב m., pl. כְּרֻבִים, כְּרוּבִים—I. *cherub*; a symbolical figure over the mercy-seat; described Eze. 4:6.—II. p. n. of a man, Ezr. c. 2; Neh. c. 7.

כְּרַז Ch. Aph. *proclaim*, κηρύσσειν, Dan. 5:29.

כָּרוֹז m. Ch., *herald*, Dan. 3:4.

כְּרִי; see כּוּר.

כְּרִיתוּת, כְּרִית; see כרת.

כַּרְכֹּב m. (with suff. כַּרְכֻּבּוֹ) *brazier* (on the grating of the altar for containing the fire).

תַּכְרִיךְ m., *robe*, Est. 8:15.

כַּרְכְּמִישׁ p. n. of a city on the Euphrates, *Carchemish* (Κιρκήσιον).

כַּרְכֹּם m., *saffron*, Cant. 4:14.

כַּרְכַּס p. n. a Persian eunuch.

כִּרְכָּרוֹת; see כרר.

כֶּרֶם m. (f. Isa. 27:2, 3).—I. *vineyard.* —II. *olive yard.*—III. *orchard.*

כֹּרֵם m., *vine-dresser.*

כַּרְמִי p. n. of a man.

כַּרְמֶל m. (quasi כֶּרֶם־אֵל; with suff. כַּרְמִלּוֹ).—I. *well-cultivated plain, or-chard, field.*—II. *Carmel,* a very fruit-ful hill south of Asher, near the Me-diterranean; כַּרְמְלִי m.; כַּרְמְלִית f., *a Carmelite.*—III. גֶּרֶשׁ כַּרְמֶל and כַּרְמֶל *first fruits* (of the most fertile land), Lev. 2:14; 23:14.

כַּרְמִיל m., *crimson.*

כְּרָן p. n. of a man.

כָּרְסֵא m. Ch., same as כִּסֵּא *throne.*

כִּרְסֵם quadrilit. *devoured*, Ps. 80:14.

כָּרַע.—I. *bent his legs* (as an animal to lie down).—II. *bowed, lay down, crouched* (with לְ or לִפְנֵי before any one).—III. *was weak.* Hiph. *cause to bow down, depress, afflict.*

כְּרָעַיִם f. dual, *both the legs* or *leg bones.*

כַּרְפַּס m., *cotton cloth, calico*, Est. 1: 6; (Arab. the same).

כָּרַר. Pil. כִּרְכֵּר *leap about, dance*, 2 Sa. 6:14, 16.

כַּר m. (p. .כָּרִים).—I. *fatted lamb.*— II. *the pasture where lambs feed.* —III. *battering ram.*

כִּרְכָּרוֹת f. pl., *dromedaries*, Isa. 66:20.

כָּרֵשׂ m., *belly*, Jer. 51:34.

כֹּרֶשׁ p. n., *Cyrus* king of Persia.

כַּרְשְׁנָא p. n., a Persian prince.

כָּרַת (imp. כְּרָת־; with ה parag. כָּרְתָה; fut. יִכְרֹת).—I. *cut off, down;* כָּרוּת and שָׁפְכָה כָרוּת *eunuch.* — II. with or without בְּרִית *make a covenant* (ὅρκια τέμνειν), (lit. strike a bargain), with אֶת, עִם, לְ.—III. *kill men*, Jer. 11:19. Niph. *was cut down, cut off.* Pu. כֹּרַת, כֹּרָת *cut off.* Hiph. הִכְרִית *cut off, destroy.* Hoph. הָכְרַת *was cut off,* Jo. 1:9.

כְּרֻתוֹת f. pl., *beams* (things cut).

כְּרִית p. n. of the brook *Cherith*, which falls into the Jordan not far from Samaria.

כְּרִיתֻת, כְּרִיתֻת f., *divorce*; with סֵפֶר *bill of divorce.*

כְּרֵתִי p. n.—I. a tribe of the Phi-listines of the south west coast of Judea, derived from the Island of *Crete.*—II. title of certain brave soldiers in David's army.

כֶּשֶׂב m., same as כֶּבֶשׂ *lamb.*

כִּשְׂבָּה *female-lamb.*

כֶּשֶׂד p. n., a son of Nahor; the pro-genitor of the Chaldees.

כַּשְׂדִּים pl.—I. *Chaldees*, inhabitants of Babylon.—II. *astrologer.*

כַּשְׂדַּי m. Ch., *a Chaldee.*

כָּשָׂה *covered with fat*, Deu. 32:15

כָּשַׁל (fut. יִכְשׁוֹל).—I. *totter, stagger.*
—II. *stumble.*—III. *stumble to fall*
(part. כּוֹשֵׁל *weak, weary*), with בְּ.
Niph. נִכְשַׁל *be tottering from*
weakness. Pi. and Hiph. I. *cause*
to stumble.—II. *fail, become weak.*
Hoph. part. מֻכְשָׁלִים *made to*
stumble, Jer. 18:23.

כַּשִּׁיל m., *an axe,* Ps. 74:6.

כִּשָּׁלוֹן m., *ruin,* Pro. 16:18.

מִכְשׁוֹל m.—I. *offence, delusion.*—II.
σκάνδαλον, *cause of offence, place,*
instrument or *cause of sin.*

מַכְשֵׁלָה f., *fall, ruin,* Isa. 3:6; Zep.
1:3.

כָּשַׁף. Pi. כִּשֵּׁף *used witchcraft,* 2 Ch.
33:6; part. מְכַשֵּׁף *magician, wi-*
zard; מְכַשֵּׁפָה *witch.*

כַּשָּׁף m., *magician,* Jer. 27:9.

כְּשָׁפִים m. pl., *magical rites, incan-*
tations.

כָּשֵׁר *do well, be acceptable,* Est. 8:5;
Ecc. 11:6. Hiph. *give prosperity,*
Ecc. 10:10.

כּוֹשָׁרָה f., pl. כּוֹשָׁרוֹת *great prosperity,*
wealth, Ps. 68:7.

כִּשְׁרוֹן *prosperity, profit,* Ecc. 5:10.

כִּישׁוֹר m., *distaff,* Pro. 31:19.

כָּתַב I. *write, engrave,* with עַל, בְּ,
אֶל before the material written
upon; with עַל, אֶל, לְ before the
person to whom the writing was
addressed. Niph. *was written.* Pi.
wrote, Isa. 10:1.

כְּתַב Ch., *he wrote.*

כְּתָב m.—I. *writing.*—II. *epistle.*—
III. *record.*—IV. *Scripture.*

כְּתָב m. Ch., *writing, edict.*

כְּתֹבֶת f., *writing,* Lev. 19:28.

מִכְתָּב m.—I. *writing.*—II. *epistle*
ordinance (thing written).

כִּתִּים, כִּתִּיִּים p.n. the *Chittim,* probably the inhabitants of Cyprus
and of some part of Asia Minor.

כָּתִית *beaten small;* see כתה.

כֹּתֶל m., *wall,* Cant. 2:9.

כְּתַל m. Ch., *wall;* pl. emph. כָּתְלַיָּא
Dan. 5:5.

כִּתְלִישׁ p.n. of a town in the tribe of
Judah.

כָּתַם Kal not used; (Arab. *treasure*
up). Niph. נִכְתָּם *treasured up,* or
as some interpret, *embroidered with*
gold; see the next word, Jer.
2:22.

כֶּתֶם m., *the purest gold.*

מִכְתָּם m., *Michtam,* a word of uncertain meaning, occurring in the
titles of Psalms 16, 56—60, probably the name of the tune or air
to which they were sung.

כֻּתֹּנֶת, כְּתֹנֶת (with suff. כֻּתָּנְתִּי;
pl. כֻּתָּנוֹת; const. כָּתְנוֹת), *garment,*
shirt, χιτών.

כָּתֵף f. const. כֶּתֶף.—I. *shoulder* (with
suff. כְּתֵפִי; pl. כְּתֵפִים).—II. *side*
(of a building, the sea, a town);
pl. כְּתֵפוֹת; const. כִּתְפוֹת; with
suff. כְּתֵפָיו *sides, jambs of doors,*
Eze. 41:2, 26.—III. *shoulders of*
axles, pivots, 1 Ki. 7:30, 34.

כָּתַר. Pi. כִּתֵּר *surround, encompass*
Hiph. I. *surround, come about.*—
II. *comprehend.*

כֶּתֶר m., *diadem, crown.*

כּוֹתֶרֶת f. (pl. כֹּתָרוֹת), *cincture,*
capital of a column.

כָּתַשׁ *break, bruise.*

מַכְתֵּשׁ m.—I. *mortar,* Pro. 27:22.—
II. p. n. of a place, Jud. 15:19;
Zep. 1:11.

כָּתַת (fut. יִכֹּת; imp. pl. כֹּתּוּ).—I.
break to pieces (as a vessel, &c.).
—II. *beat out* (as iron).—III. *beat
down* (as enemies); part. כָּתוּת
θλαδίας, *eunuch.* Pi. כִּתֵּת *same
as Kal.* Pu. *was broken.* Hiph.
(fut. יַכַּתּוּ) *defeat.* Hoph. (fut.
יֻכַּתּוּ) *pounded to dust.*

כָּתִית m., *fine, pure oil.*

מְכִתָּה f., *breaking,* Isa. 30:14.

ל

לְ insep. pa.—I. *to, towards.*—II. *at,
in.*—III. *till, until.*—IV. *in order
to, for the purpose of.*—V. *for,
belonging to, with respect to:*
לָהֵן *therefore;* לָכֵן *so, thus, therefore;* לָמָּה *why?* When joined
with subs. and adjs. it sometimes
admits of being translated adverbially: לְשֶׁקֶר *falsely;* לְצֶדֶק *justly.*
It is also used in a sense allied
to that of the Arab. ل, and very
foreign to the idiom of any European language: e. g. וַיִּקַּח לְיִרְמְיָהוּ
he took hold on Jeremiah, Jer. 40:
2, where it is equivalent to אֵת;
probably it corroborates the meaning like the Arabic. With suff. לִי;
לָנוּ, לוֹ (לְכִי) לָךְ (לְכָה) לָךְ
(לָהֶן) לָהֶם; לְמוֹ, see מָן; לְכֶם, לָכֶם
לָנָה, לָהֶנָּה. Ch., *to, in order to, &c.,* like
the Hebrew.

לֹא sometimes לוֹא *not, no;* כֹּל לֹא

no one, none; אִישׁ לֹא *no one;* לֹא
דָבָר *nothing,* used for בְּלֹא *without,* and הֲלֹא *is it?* with pref. בְּלֹא
without, there is none; הֲלֹא *is it
not? ἰδού;* לְלֹא *without;* לֹא...גַּם
not even.

לָה, לָא Ch., *not, nothing.*

לָהֵן Ch., *therefore, on that account*
(see לְ), for לָא הֵן *unless.*

לָכֵן *therefore* (see לְ), for לָא כֵן *but if.*

לוֹ דָבָר, לֹא דְבָר p. n., a town in Gilead.

לֹא עַמִּי (*not my people*) mystic name
given to the prophet Hosea, Hos.
1:9.

לָאַב (Arab. *thirsted*).

תַּלְאֻבוֹת, תַּלְאָבוֹת *thirst, drought,*
Hos. 13:5.

לְהַאֲדִיב for לְהַאֲדִיב Hiph. inf. with
pref., from אדב.

לָאָה I. *be weary, faint,* Job 4:2, 5.—
II. *be vexed,* Gen. 19:11. Niph.
נִלְאָה I. *become weary, faint.*—II.
was vexed.—III. *dislike.* Hiph.
הֶלְאָה I. *make weary.*—II. *vex.*—
III. *ruin.*

לֵאָה p. n., *Leah,* one of Jacob's wives.

תְּלָאָה f., *weariness, trouble, vexation.*

לְהָאוֹר for לְהֵאוֹר Niph. inf. with pref.,
from אוֹר.

לָאַט *same as* לוּט *vail, cover the
face,* 2 Sa. 19:5; see also לָאַט,
אַט in לָאַט.

לָאַט *same as* לָט, בַּלָּאַט *secretly,*
Jud. 4:21.

לָאַךְ *root not used;* (Ethiop. *he sent,
ministered*).

מַלְאָךְ m.—I. *messenger.*—II. *angel*
(messenger of God).—III. *the Word*

of God, Jesus Christ, Ex. 23:20, seq., &c.—IV. prophet.—V. priest.

מַלְאַךְ m. Ch., angel.

מְלָאכָה f. (const. מְלֶאכֶת; with suff. מְלַאכְתּוֹ; pl. const. מַלְאֲכוֹת).—I. ministry.—II. work.—III. making, acquisition, wealth.—IV. flocks.

מַלְאֲכוּת f., message, embassy, Hag. 1:13.

מַלְאָכִי p. n., Malachi, the prophet, Μαλαχίας.

לָאֵל p. n. of a man.

לְאֹם (Arab. assemblage).

לְאֹם m. (with suff. לְאֻמִּי; pl. לְאֻמִּים).—I. family, tribe, nation.—II. לְאֻמִּים p. n. of a people, Αλλου- μαίωται, Gen. 25:3.

לֵב, לֵב־ (with suff. לִבִּי; pl. לִבּוֹת).

לֵבָב (const. לְבַב; with suff. לְבָבִי; pl. לְבָבוֹת; לִבַּבְכֶם) m.—I. the heart of man or beast.—II. the seat of thought, affection, &c., in man; בְּלֵב וָלֵב with a double heart, i.e. deceitful, Ps. 12:3.—III. the middle or interior of any thing.

לֵב, לְבַב m. Ch., heart, mind, as Heb.

לָבַב Niph. take heart, be bold, daring, Job 11:12. Pi. לִבֵּב give heart, encourage, Cant. 4:9; see also in לְבִיבָה.

לִבָּה f., heart, mind, as לֵב.

לְבִיבָה f., pl. לְבִיבוֹת pancakes made of fine wheaten flour. Pi. לִבֵּב he made such pancakes, 2 Sa. 13: 6—10, only.

לַבָּה for לַהֲבָה flame, Ex. 3:2.

לָבִיא; לְבָאוֹת, לְבָאִים see לָבִיא.

לְבַד alone; see בַּד, בָּדָד.

לָבַט Niph. נִלְבַּט stumbled, fell, Pro. 10:8, 10; Hos. 4:14.

לָבִיא lioness; perhaps also lion. לָבִי m., pl. m. לְבָאִים.— I. lions; f. לְבָאוֹת lionesses.— II. p. n. of a town in the tribe of Simeon.

לְבִיָּא f., lioness.

לִבִּבוֹת; see in לֵב.

לָבַן (from לְבֵנָה) make bricks, Gen. 11:3. Hiph.—I. was white, pure. —II. made white, clean, Dan. 11: 35. Hithp. shall become white, clean, Dan. 12:10.

לָבָן m.—I. white.—II. p. n., Laban, the father-in-law of Jacob.— III. a place in the desert.

לְבָנָה f.—I. the moon (from her white- ness).—II. p. n. of a man.

לָבָן, לְבֶן m., white.

לִבְנֶה m., the white poplar.

לְבָנָה f.—I. whiteness, clearness, Ex. 24:10.— II. p. n., a city in the tribe of Judah.— III. a station of Israel in the desert.

לְבֵנָה f. (pl. לְבֵנִים) brick or tile.

לְבֹנָה, לְבוֹנָה f.—I. pure frankincense, λίβανος.—II. p. n. of a town near Shiloh.

הַלְּבָנוֹן, לְבָנוֹן p. n., Mount Lebanon; so called from the whiteness of the snow on its eastern peak.

לִבְנִי p. n. of a man.

מַלְבֵּן m., brick kiln.

לָבַשׁ, לָבֵשׁ (fut. יִלְבַּשׁ).—I. put on clothing, cloak; part. לָבוּשׁ clothed. —II. used metaphorically for the possession of certain qualities, as clothed with, glory, justice, &c.,

covered with flocks (as a pasture); with many others. Pu. מְלֻבָּשִׁים clothed.—Hiph. I. clothe, invest, with עַל.—II. cover (as the sky with clouds).

לְבַשׁ Ch., clothe. Aph. the same.

לְבֻשׁ, לְבוּשׁ m., upper or outer garment, cloak.

מַלְבּוּשׁ m., the same.

תִּלְבֹּשֶׁת f., the same.

לַבַּת, Ex. 3:2, for לֶהָבַת const., from לֶהָבָה.

לֹג m., the log, a liquid measure containing 24.3 solid inches.

לֹד p.n., a town in the tribe of Benjamin, Lydda.

לֵדָה Kal inf., from ילד.

לֶדֶת Kal inf., from ילד.

לְדִתְּנָה Kal inf. with suff. and ה parag., from ילד.

לָהַב root not used; (Arab. tongue of fire, flame).

לַהַב m.—I. flame.—II. glitter of a sword or other weapon.—III. the weapon itself.

לֶהָבָה f., flame; pl. לֶהָבוֹת; const. לַהֲבוֹת; s. const. לַבַּת, Ex. 3:2.

לַהֶבֶת f., the same.

שַׁלְהֶבֶת flame, destruction, fire.

לְהָבִים same as לוּבִים the Lybians, Gen. 10:13.

לָהַג root not used; (Arab. intense occupation).

לַהַג m., much study, Ecc. 12:12.

לַהַד p.n. of a man.

לָהָה (fut. וַתֵּלַהּ) same as לָאָה was faint, feeble, Gen. 47:13.

לָהַהּ. Hithp. part. מִתְלַהְלֵהַּ insane, mad person, Pro. 26:18.

לָהַט flaming, Ps. 104:4; part. לֹהֲטִים inflamed (i.e. furious) men, Ps. 57:5. Pi. לִהַט set on fire, inflame.

לַהַט m., flame, Gen. 3:24.

לְהָטִים lit. flames: hence, dazzlings, delusions, Ex. 7:11.

לָהַם. Hith. part. מִתְלַהֲמִים enchanting, fascinating things, dainties, Pro. 18:8; 26:22.

לֶהֱוֵן, f. לֶהֱוְיָן (that they may be) Ch. fut., the preformant dropped with the pref. ל, from הוה, הוא; see ל and לא.

לְהָקָה (const. לַהֲקַת) trans. for קְהָלָה congregation, 1 Sa. 19:20.

לוּא, לוּ, לֹא I. if, εἰ, ἐάν.—II. would that! לוּלֵי, לוּלֵא (compound of לוּ, לֹא for לֹא) unless.

לְבִים, לוּבִים p.n., the Lybians, inhabitants of the deserts west of Egypt.

לוּד p.n. of a people descended from Shem, Gen. 10:22; pl. לוּדִים; they inhabited some part of Africa, and probably Asia Minor.

לָוָה I. borrow at usury.—II. get, obtain. Niph. נִלְוָה become turned, attached, joined, with עַל, אֶל, עַם. Hiph. הִלְוָה.—I. cause to borrow.—II. lend.

לֵוִי p.n.—I. Levi, one of the sons of Jacob and Leah.—II. and לֵוִי a Levite; pl. בְּנֵי לֵוִי and לְוִיִּם Levites.

לֵוִי Ch., a Levite.

לִוְיָה const. לִוְיַת chaplet, garland, Pro. 1:9, &c.

לִוְיָה for לֹוְיָה, לֹוְיָה f., pl. לִוְיֹת perhaps

architectural ornaments like *garlands*, 1 Ki. 7:29, 30, 36.

לִוְיָתָן m.—I. any *sea monster*.—II. *the sea serpent*, Isa. 27:1.—III. one of the carnivorous whales, Job 3:8, &c.

לְוָת Ch., *with*, Ezr. 4:12.

לוּז *escape, depart from*, Pro. 3:21. Niph. part. נָלוֹז *perverse, incorrigible.* Hiph. fut. יַלִּיזוּ *escape, flee from.*

לוּז m.—I. *almond tree*, Gen. 30:37.—II. p.n. of the town afterwards called בֵּית־אֵל, in the tribe of Benjamin.

לְזוּת f., *perverseness*, Pro. 4:24.

לוּחַ m.—I. *tablet of stone* or *wood*.—II. metaphorically, *of the heart*.—III. *leaf of a folding-door*, Cant. 8:9; לֻחֹת הָעֵדוּת, לוּחֹת הַבְּרִית *tables of the covenant, testimony*; dual לֻחֹתַיִם *benches* for the rowers of a ship, Eze. 27:5.

לוּחִית p.n. of a town in Moab.

לוֹחֵשׁ, הַלּוֹחֵשׁ p.n. of a man.

לוּט *cover, conceal*; part. לוֹט *covering*; לוּטָה f., *concealed.* Hiph. hid.

לָט m., *covert*; בַּלָּט *secretly*; pl. לָטִים *secret parts.*

לוֹט m.—I. *veil, covering*, Isa. 25:7.—II. p.n., *Lot*, the nephew of Abraham.

לֹט m., *gum-ladanum.*

לוֹטָן p.n. of a man.

לֵוִי, לִוְיָה, לִוְיָתָן; see לוה.

לוּלִים m.pl., *winding-stairs*, 1 Ki. 6:8.

לֻלָאֹת, const. לֻלְאֹת f. pl., *loops* or *eyes* for hooks.

לוּלֵי, לוּלֵא; see לוּ.

I. לוּן and לִין (fut. יָלִין; apoc. יָלֶן; with pause יָלִין, יָלַן; imper. לִין).—I. *lodge, remain, pass the night*, with אֶת, בְּ. Hiph. הֵלִין *cause to remain*, Jer. 4:14. Hith. הִתְלוֹנֵן *lodge, remain*, Ps. 91:1; Job 39:28.

מָלוֹן m.—I. *lodging-house, inn.*—II. *quarters* (as of soldiers).—III. *tent, cot, hut*; f. מְלוּנָה.

II. לוּן Niph. נָלוֹן *complain, murmur*; with עַל *against*; fut. pl. יִלֹנוּ. Hiph. הֵלִין the same; fut. apoc. יָלֵן, וַיִּלֶן; part. מַלִּינִים.

תְּלֻנּוֹת f. pl. (with suff. תְּלֻנֹתֵיכֶם), *murmurings.*

לוּעַ *swallow*, Obad. v. 16.

לֹעַ m., *throat*, Pro. 23:2.

לוּץ *deride, scorn*, Pro. 9:12; part. לֵץ *scorner.* Hiph. הֵלִיץ *derided*; part. מֵלִיץ *interpreter, orator, ambassador.* Hith. הִתְלוֹצֵץ *was mocking*, Isa. 28:22.

לָצוֹן m., *derision*, Pro. 1:22.

מְלִיצָה f.—I. *interpretation.*—II. *saying, parable, enigma*, Pro. 1:6; Hab. 2:6.

לוּשׁ *knead dough.*

לַיִשׁ p.n. of a man, same as לָיִשׁ.

לְוָת; see לוה.

לְזוּת; see לוּן.

לחה root not used; (Arab. *cheek-bone*).

לְחִי, with pause לֶחִי f. (dual לְחָיַיִם; const. לְחָיֵי).—I. *cheek, jaw.*—II. לֶחִי and רָמַת לֶחִי p.n., a place on the borders of Philistia.

לחח root not used; (Arab. *eyes wet with tears*).

לָח m., *moist, green, fresh, new.*

לֵחַ m. (with suff. לֵחֹה Deu. 34:7), *vigour of youth.*

לָחַךְ (inf. לְחֹךְ) and Pi. לִחֵךְ *licked*, Nu. 22:4, *lapped up* (as a dog); with עָפָר *lick the dust.*

לָחַם (fut. יִלְחַם; inf. לְחֹם; imp. לְחַם).—I. *eat, feast upon, devour;* with בְּ *of;* לַחְמֵי רֶשֶׁף *consumed of fever.*—II. *make, wage war,* with לְ, אֶת. Niph. נִלְחַם (inf. abs. לְחֹם; fut. pl. תִּלָּחֲמוּ).—I. *make war;* with בְּ, עַל, עִם, אֶל *against;* with לְ *for.*—II. with בְּ, עַל *besiege.*

לָחֻם m.—I. *eating, feasting* (with suff. לְחֻמוֹ).—II. *flesh* (with suff. לְחֻמָם Zep. 1:17).

לֶחֶם com.—I. *provision;* עֵץ בְּלַחְמוֹ *tree with its provision,* i. e. *fruit,* Jer. 11:19.—II. *feast.*—III. *bread.*—IV. *bread-corn,* Isa. 28:28; לֶחֶם הַפָּנִים (ἄρτος τοῦ προσώπου) *shew-bread,* lit. bread of the presence.

לְחֵם m. Ch., *a feast,* Dan. 5:1.

לָחֶם m. (inf. Pi.), const. לְחֶם *war,* Jud. 5:8.

לַחְמִי p. n. of a man, 1 Chron. 20:5.

מִלְחָמָה f.—I. *battle, war.*—II. *instruments of war,* Ps. 76:4; עָשָׂה מִלְחָמָה with אֶת, עִם *made war;* אִישׁ מִ׳ *warrior, soldier;* עִם מִ׳ the same.—III. *event of war, victory,* Ecc. 9:11.

מִלְחֶמֶת f., *the same;* with suff. מִלְחַמְתּוֹ.

לַחְמָס p. n. of a place in the tribe of Judah.

לְחֵנָה f. Ch., *concubine,* Dan. 5:2, 3, 23.

לָחַץ (יִלְחַץ) *oppress, afflict;* part. לֹחֲצִים *oppressors.* Niph. *was pressed, injured,* Nu. 22:25.

לַחַץ m. *oppression, affliction.*

לָחַשׁ. Pi. לִחֵשׁ; part. pl. מְלַחֲשִׁים *whisperers, pronouncers of charms.* Hith. *muse of, secretly consider, discuss.*

לַחַשׁ m.—I. *whisper.*—II. *incantation, charm.*—III. pl. לְחָשִׁים *amulets,* Isa. 3:20.

לָט, לֵט; see לוט.

לָטָא (Arab. *cleave to the ground*). לְטָאָה f., *a kind of lizard.*

לָטַשׁ *sharpen.* Pu. part. מְלֻטָּשׁ *sharpened,* Ps. 52:4.

לִיוֹת; see לוט.

לַיְל (const. לֵיל) לַיְלָה (pl. לֵילוֹת) m.—I. *night.*—II. *time of adversity;* adv. בְּלֵילוֹת, בַּלַּיְלָה, לֵילוֹת *by night;* יוֹמָם וָלַיְלָה *day and night.*

לֵיל m., *night,* Isa. 21:11.

לֵילְיָא m. Ch., *night.*

לִילִית f., *screech owl,* Isa. 34:14.

לִין; see לון.

לִיסוֹד Kal inf. with pref. and dag. euphon., from יסד.

לִיקֳחַת for לִיקַחַת; see יקח.

לַיִשׁ m.—I. *strong lion.*—II. p. n. of a man.—III. of a town in the north of Palestine.

יֵלֵךְ imp., from הלך, לֵךְ, לְכָה, לֵךְ.

לָכַד I. *take,* (as a beast in toils, captives in war, &c.)—II. *intercept.*

Niph. *was taken.* Hith. *was, be-came adhering,* Job 41:9.

לֶכֶד m., *capture,* Pro. 3:26.

מַלְכֹּדֶת f., *snare, trap,* Job 18:10.

לְכָה imp. of יָלַךְ; לְכָה for לֵךְ; see לְ.

לָכְדָ p. n. of a town in the tribe of Judah.

לָכִישׁ p. n. of a city in the tribe of Judah.

לָכֵן; see לֹא, לְ, כֵּן.

לֶכֶת Kal inf., from הָלַךְ, יָלַךְ.

לְלָאוֹת; see לוּל.

לָמַד (fut. יִלְמַד).— I. *accustom to,* with אֶל.—II. *learn,* with acc. inf. Pi. לִמַּד.—I. *accustom to.*—II. *teach,* with לְ of the person, and בְּ of the thing taught. Pu. לֻמַּד.—I. *was accustomed.*—II. *was taught.*

לָמֵד, לִמּוּד m.—I. *accustomed.*—II. *trained, taught.*—III. *disciple.*

מַלְמָד m., *ox-goad,* Jud. 3:31.

תַּלְמִיד m., *learner,* 1 Ch. 25:8.

לָמָה, לָמֶה *why;* see מָה.

לָמוֹ; see לְ.

לְמוּאֵל, לְמוֹאֵל p. n. or title of king Solomon, Pro. c. 31.

לֶמֶךְ p. n. of a man, *Lamech.*

לְמַעַן; see ענה.

לָנָה Zec. 5:4, for לָנָה Kal pret. f., from לוּן.

לַנּוּ for לַנְנוּ Kal pret. pl., from לוּן.

לָנִים Kal part. pl., from לוּן.

לֹעַ *throat;* see לוּעַ.

לָעֵב. Hiph. *ridiculing, deriding,* with בְּ, 2 Chron. 36:16.

לָעַג (fut. יִלְעַג) *mock, deride, scorn.* Niph. *stammer,* Isa. 33:19. Hiph. *mock,* with בְּ, לְ, עַל.

לַעַג m.—I. *derision, ridicule.*—II. *cause of derision.*

לָעֵג m., *mocker,* Ps. 35:16.

לַעְדָּה p. n. of a man.

לַעְדָּן p. n. of a man.

לָעָה *was rash,* Job 6:3.

לָעַז *spoke barbarously,* Ps. 114:1.

לָעַט. Hiph. *feed, give to eat.*

לָעַן (Arab. *drove away*).

לַעֲנָה f.—I. *wormwood.*—II. metaph. *distress.*

לַפִּיד m., *lamp or torch.*

לַפִּידוֹת p. n., *Lapidoth* the husband of Deborah.

לִפְנֵי; see פָּנִים or פנה.

לָפַת *turned to, towards,* Jud. 16:29. Niph. *turned about.*

לַצְבוֹת for לְהַצְבוֹת Hiph. inf. with pref., from צבה.

לָצוֹן *scorn;* see לוּץ.

לֵץ, part. לֵצִים *scorners,* Hos. 7:5.

לַקּוּם p. n., a town in the tribe of Naphtali.

לָקַח (fut. יִקַּח; inf. abs. לָקוֹחַ; const. קַחַת; imp. קַח, לְקַח; with pause קָח; with ה parag. קְחָה).—I. *take,* with בְּ.—II. idiom, like the English *take* and *do.*—III. *take away.*—IV. *take possession of.*—V. *receive.* Niph. נִלְקַח *was taken.* Pu. לֻקַּח same as Niph. Hoph. (fut. יֻקַּח the same). Hith. part. f. מִתְלַקַּחַת *being taken with,* i. e. mixed, mingled with (of fire), Ex. 9:24; Eze. 1:4.

לֶקַח m., *taking, receiving,* specially instruction in religion.

לָקְחִי p. n. of a man.

מַלְקוֹחַ m., *capture, spoil*; dual מַלְקֹחַיִם *the jaws.*

מֶלְקָחַיִם m. dual.—I. *tongs.*—II. *snuffers.*

מַלְקָחַיִם m. dual, the same.

מִקָּח m., *accepting* (of gifts), 2 Chron. 19:7.

מַקָּחוֹת f. pl., *merchandise*, Neh. 10:32.

לָקַט and Pi. לִקֵּט *collect, gather, glean.* Pu. and Hith. *was gathered.*

לֶקֶט m., *collecting, gleaning.*

יַלְקוּט m., *bag* or *purse*, 1 Sa. 17:40.

לָקַק *lick* (as dogs); fut. יָלֹק; pl. יָלֹקּוּ. Pi. part. מְלַקְקִים *licking.*

לָקַשׁ (Syr. *late*). Pi. *cut, crop*, Job 24:6.

לֶקֶשׁ m., *latter grass, aftermath*, Am. 7:1.

מַלְקוֹשׁ m., *the latter rain* (in March and April).

לְרֹא for לִירֹא Kal inf. with pref., from ירא.

לָשַׁד (Arab. *sucking*).

לֶשֶׁד m. (with suff. לְשַׁדִּי) *moisture*, Ps. 32:4; לְשַׁד הַשָּׁמֶן perhaps *fluid oil*, Nu. 11:8.

לָשׁוֹן com.—I. *tongue*; אִישׁ לָשׁוֹן *calumniator.*—II. *language.*—III. *nation, community* (having one language).—IV. *tongue of flame*, Is. 5:24.—V. *tongue* (wedge) *of gold*, Jos. 7:21, 24.

לָשַׁן Po. part. with ' parag. מְלוֹשְׁנִי *calumniator*, Ps. 101:5. Hiph. the same, Pro. 30:10.

לִשָּׁן com. Ch., *tongue, language.*

לִשְׁכָּה f., *chamber*, specially those attached to the temple; with ה parag. לִשְׁכָּתָה *to the chamber*; pl. לְשָׁכוֹת.

לֶשֶׁם m.—I. *ligure*, a precious stone; LXX. λιγύριον.—II. p. n. of a city called also לַיִשׁ and דָּן.

לֶשַׁע p. n. of a city not far from Sodom

לָרֶדֶת for לָרֶדֶת with pref. לָלֶת Kal inf., from ילד.

לֶתֶךְ m., *measure* (of capacity), *the half-homer*, Hos. 3:2.

לָתַע (Arab. *he bites*).

מַלְתָּעוֹת f. pl., *teeth*, Ps. 58:7.

מְתַלְּעוֹת f. pl. (trans.), *teeth.*

מ

מ pref. prep.; see מן.

מָא Ch., same as מה.

מַאֲבוּס m., *granary*, see אבס.

מְאֹד; see אוד.

מֵאָה const. f.—I. *a hundred*; dual מָאתַיִם *two hundred*; pl. מֵאוֹת *hundreds*; שֵׁשׁ מֵאוֹת *six hundred*; שְׁמֹנֶה מֵאוֹת *eight hundred.*—II. *a hundred-fold.*—III. *a hundredth part*, Neh. 5:11.—IV. p. n. of one of the towers of Jerusalem, Neh. 3:1.

מְאָה f. Ch., *a hundred*; dual מָאתַיִן *two hundred.*

מַאֲוַיִים *desires*; see אוה.

מְאוּם; see מום.

מְאוּמָה; see מה.

מְאֵרָה, מָאוֹר *curse*; see אור.

מֹאזְנַיִן, מֹאזְנַיִם *balances*; see אזן.

מַאֲכֶלֶת, מַאֲכֹלֶת, מַאֲכָל; see אכל.

מָאן m. Ch., *vessel.*

מָאֵן or מָאַן. Pi. מֵאֵן (inf. מָאֵן; fut. יְמָאֵן) refuse, be unwilling.

מָאֵן m., refusing.

מֵאֵן m., pl. מְאָנִים recusants.

מָאַס (inf. מָאוֹס; const. with suff. מָאָסְם; fut. יִמְאַס).—I. despise, reject.—II. set at nought, lightly esteem, with בְּ. Niph. I. was despised, rejected. — II. same as מָסַס. Niph. dissolve, waste, Ps. 58:8; Job 7:5.

מַאֲפֶה baked; see אפה.

מַאְפֵּלְיָה, מַאֲפֵל; see אפל.

מָאַר (Arab. irritate a wound). Hiph. הִמְאִיר irritated, pained; צָרַעַת מַמְאֶרֶת the inflamed leprosy.

מַאֲרָב ambush; see ארב.

מְאֵרָה curse, see ארר.

מֵאֵת from the; see אֵת.

מִבְדָּלוֹת separations; see בדל.

מָבוֹא entry; see בוא.

מְבוּכָה confusion; see בוך.

מַבּוּל deluge; see יבל.

מְבוּסָה treading down; see בוס.

מְבוֹנִים understanding; see בון.

מַבּוּעַ spring; see נבע.

מְבוּקָה void; see בוק.

מְבֻשִׁים, מְבֻשִׁים prudence; see בוש.

מִבְחָר, מִבְחוֹר choice; see בחר.

מִבָּט, מַבָּט hope; see נבט.

מִבְטָא rashness; see בטא.

מִבְטָח confidence; see בטח.

מֵבִי for מֵבִיא Hiph. part., from בוא.

מַבְלִיגִית exhilaration; see בלג.

מִבַּלְעֲדֵי besides; see בַּלְעֲדֵי in בלה.

מִבְנֶה building; see בנה.

מִבְּנֵי for סָבְכַי, 2 Sa. 23:27.

מִבַּעְתָּךְ for מְבַעֲתָתָךְ Pi. part. f. with suff., from בעת.

מִבְצָר fortress; see בצר.

מִבָּרֹאשָׁנָה and מֵרִאשֹׁנָה comp. of מָה, בְּ and רִאשֹׁנָה

מָג m., fire worshipper, magian, Jer 39:3.

מַנְבִּישׁ p. n. of a place or person.

מִנְבָּלוֹת devices; see גבל.

מִצְנֶפֶת mitre; see נבע.

מָגַד (Arab. glory).

מֶגֶד m., excellence, glory.

מְגִדּוֹן, מְגִדּוֹ p. n., a city of the Manassites in the tribe of Issachar; LXX. Μαγεδδώ; בְּקַעַת־מְגִדּוֹ valley of Megiddo; מֵי מְגִדּוֹ brook Kishon.

מִגְדָּנוֹת f. pl., choice, precious things.

מַגְדִּיאֵל p. n. of a prince of the Edomites.

מִגְדּוֹל, מִגְדָּל p. n.; see גדל.

מָגוֹג p. n. of a people and country, Magog.

מְנוֹרָה, מָגוֹר, מָגוֹר, מָנוֹד; see גור.

מַגְזֵרָה axes; see גזר.

מַגָּל sickle; see נגל.

מִגְלָה mound; see גלל.

מְגַמָּה desire; see גמם.

מָגַן. Pi. מִגֵּן give, give freely.

מִגְנָה, מָגֵן; see גנן.

מִגְעֶרֶת rebuke; see גער.

מַגֵּפָה plague; see נגף.

מַגְפִּיעָשׁ p. n. of a man.

מָגַר, part. pl. const. מֻגְרֵי fallen, delivered up, Eze. 21:17. Pi. מִגֵּר cast down.

מַגַּר Ch. Pa. מַגַּר cast down, Ezr 6:12.

מִגְרוֹן p. n., a town in the tribe of Benjamin.

מְגֵרָה saw; see גרר.

מְגָרֵפָה *furrow;* see נגרף.

מִגְרָשׁ ; see נרש.

מִדְבָּר *wilderness;* see דבר.

מָדַד (יָמָד ; fut. מַדֹּתִי ,מָדַדְתִּי .pret).
—I. *extend a line.*—II. *measure.*
—III. *apportion,* Isa. 65:7. Niph.
(fut. יִמַּד) *be, can be, measured.*
Pi. מִדַּד *measure* (see also in נדד).
Po. מוֹדֵד *the same,* Hab. 3:6;
"viewed" (Lee); see מוג. Hith.
הִתְמֹדֵד *extended, stretched out.*

מַד m.—I. *measure, extent;* with suff.
מִדָּה; pl. מַדִּים.—II. *upper garment, tunic,* with suff. מַדּוֹ ,מַדּוֹ
pl. מַדִּים.—III. *hammer-
cloth, covering for a throne,* Jud.
5:10.—IV. מָדִין p.n., *a city in the
desert of Judah.*

מִדָּה f. (m. Neh. 3:30).—I. *extent,
measure;* אִישׁ מִדָּה *tall man,*
1 Chron. 11:23; בֵּית מִדּוֹת *spacious house,* Jer. 22:14; מִדַּת יָמַי
measure of my days.—II. *tribute.*
—III. *vesture,* Ps. 133:2.

מִנְדָּה ,מִדָּה f. Ch., *tribute.*

מְמַדִּים m. pl., *extents, measure,* Job
38:5.

מַדְוֶה m. (pl. with suff. מַדְוֵיהֶם), *garment.*

מָדוֹן m., *height, tallness,* 2 Sa. 21:20;
see also in דין.

מַדְוֶה *disease;* see דָּוָה.

מַדּוּחִים *drivings out;* see נדח.

מַדּוּעַ *why;* see ידע.

מַדְחֵפוֹת ; see דחף.

מָדַי f., *Media, the Medes;* מָדַי Ch. *a
Median,* const. emph. מָדָאָה *the
same.*

מָדַי ; see מָה. מָדַי ; see דַּי.

מִדְיָן p.n., *the son of Abraham and*

מִדְיָנִית f., *a* מִדְיָנִי m., מִדְיָנִי Keturah;
Midianite.

מַדִּים ; see מַד in מדד pl. for מִדְיָן.

מְדִינָה ; see דִּין.

מַדְלֵכָה *mortar;* see דוך.

מַדְמַנָּה ,מַדְמֵנָה ,מַדְמֵן ; see רמן.

מְדָן ,מְדָנִים ; see דִּין.

מַדָּע ,מַדַּע ; see ידע.

מְדָר Ch., *same as* מָדוֹר *habitation;*
see דור.

מַדְרֵךְ ; see דרך.

מְדָתָא with art. הַמְּדָתָא p.n. *the father
of Haman.*

מָה ,מֶה ,מַה ,מָה inter. pron.—I. *what?*
מַה־לָּךְ *what wilt thou?* מַה־לִּי
וָלָךְ *what have I to do with thee?*
—II. *how? how much?*—III. *for
what? why?*—IV. *what? what
sort?* — V. *something, anything,
anything whatever;* מָה שֶׁ... *that
which, the thing which* (in the
book of Ecclesiastes only); מַה־
מַה־זֶּה *how terrible;* מַזֶּה *for* נוֹרָא
what is this? מַלְּכֶם *what mean
ye?* Isa. 3:15; לַמָּה־דִּי *for* לְמַדִּי
sufficiently, 2 Chron. 30:3. Compounds: בַּמֶּה ,בַּמָּה *why? how?
wherefore?* כַּמָּה ,כַּמֶּה *how many?
how long? how much?* לָמֶה ,לָמָה
why? לָמָה זֶּה *why? wherefore?*
(for 'למה ב) לְמַבְּרִאשֹׁנָה *because
at first,* 1 Chron. 15:13; עַד־מָה
how long? עַל־מָה ,עַל־מֶה *wherefore?*

מָה (מָא) Ch., *why, wherefore?*
לְמָה *that which,* Dan. 2:28, 29;
עַלְמָה *wherefore?* כְּמָה *how?
how much? so much?* Dan. 3:33;
מָה דִי *that which.*

מְאוּמָה (comp. of מָה וּמָה or מָה אוֹ

אֵל ,אֵין ,לֹא with ;any thing (מָה)
nothing.

מָהַהּ. Hith. הִתְמַהְמֵהַּ delay, tarry,
wait.

מְהוּמָה tumult; see הום·

מְהוּמָן p.n. of a Persian eunuch.

מְהֵיטַבְאֵל p. n.—I. of a man, Neh. 6:
10.—II. of a woman, Gen. 36:39.

מְהֵימָן Ch., Aph. part. pass.; see אמן·

מְהַחֲתִין Ch. Aph. part.; see נחת·

מְהָךְ Ch. Pe. inf., from הוך·

מָהַל ,part. מָהוּל debased, adulterated,
Isa. 1:22.

מְהֻמָהֶם Eze. 7:11, from הֵם; see
הֵמָּה·

מְהִקְצָעוֹת for מָקְצָעוֹת Hoph. part. f.
pl., from קצע·

I. מָהַר hasten, hurry, Ps. 16:4. Pi.
מִהַר hasten, hurry; used as an
auxiliary, e. g. מִהֲרוּ שָׁכְחוּ they
soon forgot, Ps. 106:13, &c. Niph.
נִמְהַר was hasty, hurried, rash.

מָהִיר m., ready, quick, skilful, hasty,
speedy.

מַהֵר m., מְהֵרָה f., quick, ready, hasty,
speedy, speed; עַד־מְהֵרָה ,בִּמְהֵרָה
מְהֵרָה adv., quickly, readily,
speedily.

II. מָהַר endow (a wife with a dowry),
Ex. 22:15; or buy (a wife with a
dowry)·

מֹהַר m., gift or dower (present made
by a suitor to the parents of a
damsel).

מַהֲרַי p. n., one of David's generals.

מוֹאָב p.n.—I. of a man, Moab, the
descendant of Lot.—II. f., the
land of Moab, situated between

the Dead Sea and the river Arnon;
מוֹאָבִי m. מוֹאָבִית ,מוֹאָבִיָּה f. a
Moabite.

מוֹאֵל same as מוּל over against, Neh.
12:38.

מוֹבָא entrance; see בוא·

מוּג (fut. יָמוּג).—I. flow.—II. dissolve,
melt (indicating weakness). Niph.
נָמוֹג were dissolved, undone. Pil.
מוֹגֵג I. dissolve, Ps. 65:11.—II.
waste away, Job 30:22. Hith.
was dissolved, undone.

מוּד Kal not used; see מוט· Po.
מוֹדֵד moved, Hab. 3:6.

תָּמִיד m.—I. perpetuity.—II. perpetual.—III. continually;
עוֹלַת הַתָּמִיד the continual, i. e. daily
offering; לֶחֶם הַתָּמִיד the bread
constantly placed in the temple.

מוֹדַעַת ,מֹדַע ,מָדָע; see ידע·

מוֹט (fut. יָמוֹט) totter (to a fall), fail.
Niph. נָמוֹט be moved, tottering.
Hiph. fut. יָמִיטוּ cause to fall, come
down. Hithpo. be moved, Isa.
24:19.

מוֹט m.—I. tottering, vacillating:—
II. pole, staff.—III. yoke (for burdens), Nah. 1:12.

מוֹטָה f., pole or staff.

מוּךְ same as מָכַךְ become indigent.

מוּל circumcise. Niph. I. was circumcised.—II. circumcise one's self. Pil
מוֹלֵל cut off, Ps. 90:6. Hiph. cu
off, down, Ps. 118:10-12. Hithpo
הִתְמוֹלֵל is cut off, down, Ps. 58:8.

מוּל מוֹאֵל Deu. 1:1, מוֹאֵל Neh. 12:
38).—I. near, with.—II. opposite,
over against, ἀντικρύ: compounds

אֶל־מוּל before, over against; אֶל־
מוּל פְּנֵי in front of, before; מְמוּל
from before, opposite.

מוּלָה f. (pl. מוּלֹת), circumcisions, Ex. 4:26.

מוֹלִיד, מוֹלֶדֶת, מוֹלָדָה; see ילד.

מוּם (מאוּם) m., spot, blemish from disease.

מוּמַת Hoph. part., from מות.

מוּן; see מִין.

מוּסָב Hoph. part.; see סבב.

מוֹסָד, מוּסָדָה, מוֹסָדוֹת; see יסד.

מוּסָךְ porch; see סכך.

מוֹסֵר (from אסר), pl. מוֹסְרִים and מוֹסְרוֹת chains.

מוֹסֵר and –וֹת p.n. of a place in the wilderness.

מוּסָר bonds; see יסר.

מוֹעֵד, מוֹעָדָה, מוֹעֵדָה, מוֹעֵד; see יעד.

מוֹעֵד, מוֹעֶדֶת for מוֹעֶדֶת Kal part. f., from מעד.

מוּעָף darkness; see עוף.

מוֹעֵצָה counsel; see יעץ.

מוּעָקָה pain; see עוק.

מוֹפֵת sign; see יפת.

מוּץ, part. מֵץ oppressor, Isa. 16:4. מוֹץ, מֹץ m., chaff.

מִיץ m., pressing, squeezing (cream to make butter), Pro. 30:33.

מוֹצָא, מוֹצָאָה; see יצא.

מוּצָא Hoph. part., from יצא.

מוּצָק, מוּצָקָה fused, cast; see יצק.

מוּצָק, מוּצָק; see צוק.

מוּק Hiph. הֵמִיק mock, insult, Ps. 73:8.

מוֹקֵד, מוֹקְדָה burning; see יקד.

מוֹקֵשׁ snare; see יקשׁ.

מוּר Hiph. הֵמִיר —I. change, alter,

with בְּ. — II. exchange. Niph. נָמַר was changed, Jer. 48:11.

תְּמוּרָה f.—I. equivalent, recompense. —II. restitution, Job 20:18. — III. exchange, Ru. 4:7.

מוֹרָא; see ירא.

מוֹרִים for מוֹרָאִים Hiph. part. pl., from ירה.

(מוֹרִינִים, מֹרִגִּים .מוֹרַג or מוֹרָג m. (pl threshing wain.

מוֹרָד descent, declivity; see ירד.

מוֹרָה, Ps. 9:21, same as מוֹרָא fear; see also in מָרָה; מוֹרֶה teacher; see ירה.

מוֹרָט ruin; see ירט.

מוֹרִיָּה p.n., same as מוֹרִיָּה.

מוֹרִינִים for מוֹרִגִּים pl., from מוֹרַג.

מוֹרָשָׁה, מוֹרָשׁ possession, inheritance; see ירשׁ.

I. מוּשׁ I. move. — II. remove, Zec. 3:9. Hiph. הֵמִישׁ. I. move, depart.—II. remove, put away.—III. cease, desist, Jer. 17:8, with מִן.

II. מוּשׁ same as מָשַׁשׁ feel, Gen. 27:21, &c. Hiph. the same, Ps. 115:7, &c.

מוּשִׁי, מוּשִׁי p.n. of a man.

מוֹשָׁב dwelling, &c.; see ישׁב.

מוֹשָׁכוֹת; see משׁך.

מוֹשָׁעוֹת salvation; see ישׁע.

מוּת (pret. מֵת; 1. pers. מַתִּי; pl. מֵתוּ; part. מֵת; f. מֵתָה; inf. abs. מוֹת; const. מוּת; imp. מֵת; fut. יָמוּת; apoc. (וַיָּמָת, יָמֹת) die (of man or beast). Pil. מוֹתֵת put to death, caused to die. Hiph. הֵמִית the same. Hoph. הוּמַת was caused to die.

מָוֶת m. (with ה parag. מָוְתָה; const.

מוֹת; with suff. מוֹתוֹ; pl. מוֹתִים (מוֹתִים).
—I. *death;* מִשְׁפַּט מָוֶת *sentence
of death,* Deut. 19:6; בֶּן־מָוֶת or
אִישׁ־מָ׳ *one guilty of a capital
crime.*—II. *the grave;* שַׁעֲרֵי מָוֶת
gates of death.—III. *person dead,*
Isa. 38:18.— IV. *pestilence.*— V.
destruction, ruin.

מוֹת m. Ch., *death.*

מָמוֹת m., pl. מְמוֹתִים *deaths,* Jer. 16:
4; Eze. 28:8.

תְּמוּתָה f., *death;* בֶּן־תְּמוּתָה *condemned to death.*

מוֹתָר *abundance;* see יתר.

מְזָא, with suff. מְזֵיהּ Ch. Pe. inf., from
אזא.

מִזְבֵּחַ *altar;* see זבה.

מֶזֶג (Arab. *mixture*); see מָסָךְ.
מֶזֶג m., *mixed wine,* Cant. 7:3.

מָזֶה *exhausted, reduced* (by famine),
Deut. 32:24.

מִזֶּה for מַה־זֶּה, from מָה.
מִזָּה p. n. of a man.
מְזָוִים *cellar;* see זוה.
מְזוּזָה *door-post;* see זוז.
מָזוֹן *food;* see זון.
מָזוֹר *bandage;* see זור.

מֵזִיחַ, מֵזַח m.— I. *a girdle.* — II.
pride, Job 12:21.

מֵזִין for מַאֲזִין Hiph. part., from אזן.
מַזָּלוֹת; see נזל.
מִזְלָגָה *fork;* see זלג.
מְזִמָּה *invention;* see זמם.
מַזְמֵרוֹת, מִזְמֹרוֹת, מִזְמוֹר see זמר.
מִזְרֶה, מְזָרִים; see זרה.
מַזָּרוֹת; see נזל.
מִזְרָח *east;* see זרח.
מִזְרָק *cup;* see זרק.
מֹחַ, מֵחַ: see מחח.

מָחָא *smite, clap;* with יַד, כַּף *hands.*
Pi. the same, Eze. 25:6.

מְחָא Ch., *struck, smote.* Pa. *exult,*
Dan. 4:32. Ithp. *was smitten,*
Ezr. 6:11.

מָחָא Ch. Aph. part., from חיא;see חיה

מַחֲבֹאִים, מַחֲבֵא *hiding-place;* see
חבא.

מַחְבְּרֹת, מַחְבֶּרֶת; see חבר.

מַחֲבַת *frying-pan;* see חבת.

מָחָה I. *wipe away.*— II. *arrive at,*
Nu. 34:11, with עַל. Niph. (fut.
apoc. יִמַּח) *was blotted out.* Hiph.
(fut. apoc. תֶּמַח) *blot out.*

מְחִי m., *striking,* Eze. 26:9.

מְחוּגָה *compasses;* see חוג.

מָחוֹז *harbour;* see חוז.

מְחִיָּאֵל, מְחוּיָאֵל p. n., a descendant of
Cain.

מַחֲיִם p. n. of a place unknown.

מָחוֹל, מְחֹלָה *dance;* see חול.

מַחֲזָיאוֹת, מֶחֱזֶה, מַחֲזֶה; see חזה.

מֹחַח (Arab. *marrow*).
מֵחַ m., *fat, rich.*
מֹחַ m., *marrow,* Job 21:24.

מְחִידָא p. n. of a man.

מִחְיָה; see חיה, חוה.

מְחִיר *price;* see מחר.

מַחְלִי, מַחְלוֹן, מַחֲלָה, מַחֲלָה, מַחֲלֶה,
מַחֲלַיִים; see חלה.

מְחִלָּה *hole;* see חלל.

מַחֲלָפוֹת, מַחֲלָף; see חלף.
מַחְלְקוֹת, מַחֲלֹקֶת; see חלק.
מַחֲלַת, מָחֲלַת; see חלה.
מְחֹלָתִי *Meholathite;* see אבל.
מַחֲמָאוֹת; see חמא.
מַחֲמֶצֶת; see חמץ.

מֵחַן Ch. Pe. inf., from חנן.

מַחֲנַיִם, מַחֲנֶה camp; see חנה.

מַחְסְיָה, מַחֲסֶה, מַחְסֶה; see חסה.

מַחְסוֹם curb; see חסם.

מְחַסְפַּס part. of the quadriliteral verb חַסְפַּס; see חסף.

מָחַץ (fut. יִמְחַץ).—I. *dash violently* (the head to pieces)—(the foot into blood), Ps. 68:22.—II. *shoot arrows,* Nu. 24:8.

מַחַץ m., *contusion, bruise,* Isa. 30:26.

מַחֲצִית, מֶחֱצָה; see חצה.

מַחְצְצְרִים; see in חצר.

מָחַק *destroyed,* Jud. 5:26.

מֶחְקָר; see חקר.

מָחָר same as מכר.

מְחִיר m.—I. *price;* בִּמְחִיר *with a price.*—II. *p.n. of a man.*

מָחָר m. — I. *morrow,* some *future day;* לְמָחָר *to-morrow;* בְּיוֹם מָחָר *for the morrow;* כָּעֵת מָחָר and מָחָר כָּעֵת הַזֹּאת *about this time to-morrow;* כָּעֵת מָחָר הַשְּׁלִישִׁית *this time the day after to-morrow.*—II. adv. *hereafter, henceforward.*

מָחֳרָת f., *to-morrow;* לְמָחֳרָת *the day after;* מִמָּחֳרַת הַשַּׁבָּת *the day after the sabbath;* עַד־מִמָּחֳרַת *until the next day;* לְמָחֳרָתָם adv. *the day after.*

מַחֲרֶשֶׁת, מַחֲרֵשָׁה; see חרש.

מַחְשֹׂף; see חשף.

מַחֲשֶׁבֶת, מַחֲשָׁבָה; see חשב.

מַחְשָׁךְ *darkness;* see חשך.

מַחַת p.n. of a man.

מַחְתָּה *shovel, &c.;* see חתה.

מְחִתָּה *breaking, &c.;* see חתת.

מַחְתֶּרֶת *digging;* see חתר.

מְטָא Ch., *come on, to, arrive at,* with עַל.

מַטְאֲטֵא; see טוא.

מִטַּהֵר for מִתְטַהֵר Hith. part.; see טהר.

מָטוֹת, מַטֶּה, מִטָּה, מַטָּה, מֻטֶּה; see נטה.

מַטְוֶה *yarn;* see טוה.

מְטַל (Arab. *forged iron*): hence, the English word *metal.*

מְטִיל m., *iron bar,* Job 40:18.

מַטְמוֹן *treasure;* see טמן.

מַטָּע *plant;* see נטע.

מַטְעַמִּים *dainties;* see טעם.

מִטְפַּחַת *mantle;* see טפח.

מָטַר. Hiph. הִמְטִיר *rain, cause, give rain;* used also of *lightning, hail, fire and brimstone, manna, bread.* Niph. *was rained on,* Am. 4:7.

מָטָר m. (pl. מְטָרוֹת; const. מַטְרוֹת) *rain, shower.*

מַטְרִי p.n. of a man.

מַטְרֵד p.n. of a woman.

מַטָּרָא, מַטָּרָה; see נטר.

מִי interrog. pron.—I. *who?* בַּת־מִי *whose daughter?* לְמִי *to whom?* בְּמִי *whom?* אֶת־מִי *by whom?* מִי מָנָה *who can number?* מִי יִתֵּן *would that it were!* מִי יִתֵּן וְהָיָה עֶרֶב *would that it were evening!*—II. without interrog., *who, every one;* מִי אֲשֶׁר *whoever.*

מֵידְבָא p.n. of a city in the tribe of Reuben.

מֵידָד p.n. of a man.

מֵיטַב *good;* see יטב.

מִיכָא p.n. of a man, same as מִיכָיָא.

מִיכָאֵל (*who is like unto God?*) p.n

—I. *Michael* the archangel.—II. of a man.

מִיכָה,מִיכָיָה p. n.—I. *Micah* the prophet.—II. also of other men.

מִיכָיְהוּ p. n.—I. of a man.—II. of a woman.

מִיכָה,מִיכָיְהוּ p. n. of a man.

מִיכָל p. n; see מכל.

מַיִם m. pl. (const. מֵימֵי ,מֵי; with suff. מֵימֶיךָ; with ה loc. הַמַּיְמָה).—I. *water, waters,* used with pl. adj., with verb either pl. or sing.—II. *seed;* 'פ מְמֵי יָצָא *whose son, descendant he is,* Isa. 48:1.

מֵי־הַיַּרְקוֹן p. n., a city in the tribe of Dan.

מֵי־נִפְתּוֹחַ p. n., a fountain near Jerusalem.

מוּן ,מִין (Syr. *family*).

מִין m., *kind, species,* always with לְ pref.; לְמִינוֹ פְּרִי *fruit after his kind.*

תְּמוּנָה f., *resemblance, likeness.*

מֵינִיקוֹת ,מֵינֶקֶת; see ינק.

מֵיפַעַת ,מֵיפָעַת p. n., a town of the Levites in the tribe of Reuben.

מִיץ *chaff*; see מוץ.

מֵישָׁא p. n. of a man.

מִישָׁאֵל p. n. of a man.

מֵישׁוֹר; see ישר.

מֵישַׁךְ p. n., *Meshach,* one of the captivity, called also מִישָׁאֵל.

מֵישַׁע p. n., a king of Moab.

מֵישָׁע p.n., a son of Caleb.

מֵישָׁרִים; see ישר.

מֵיתָר *cord*; see יתר.

מַכְאוֹב *pain*; see כאב.

מַכְבְּנָא same as כַּבּוֹן.

מַכְבַּנַּי p. n. of a man.

מַכְבָּר ,מִכְבָּר *carpet*; see כבר.

מַכָּה *stroke*; see נכה.

מִכְוָה *burning*; see כוה.

מָכוֹן ,מְכוֹנָה ,מְכוּנָה; see כון.

מְכוּרָה; see כור.

מָכִיר p. n., *Machir* the son of Manasseh, Gen. 50:23; perhaps for a *Manassite,* Jud. 5:14; patronymic מָכִירִי.

מָכַךְ. Niph. fut. יִמַּךְ *become weak,* Ecc. 10:18. Hoph. pl. הֻמְּכוּ for הֻמַּכּוּ *they perish,* Job 24:24.

מָכַל root not used; (Arab. *empty of water*).

מִיכַל m.; מִיכַל הַמַּיִם *brooks of water,* 2 Sa. 17:20.—II. p. n., *Michal,* the daughter of Saul and wife of David.

מִכְלוֹת ,מִכְלָאוֹת, see כלא; מִכְלָה, see כלה.

מַכְלֻלִים ,מִכְלֻל ,מִכְלוֹל; see כלל; מַאֲכֶלֶת for מַאֲכַלְת *food;* see אכל.

מִכְמָס (see כָּמַס) ,מִכְמָשׁ ,מִכְמַשׁ p. n. a town in the tribe of Benjamin, Μαχμάς.

מִכְמֶרֶת ,מַכְבֹּר ,מִכְמָר *net;* see כמר.

מִכְמְתָת p. n., a town on the borders of Ephraim and Manasseh.

מַכְנַדְבַי p. n. of a man.

מִכְנָס *breeches*; see כנס.

מִכְסָה ,מֶכֶס *price;* see כסס.

מִכַסֶּה ,מִכְסֶה; see כסה.

מַכְפֵּלָה p. n. of a district near Hebron.

מָכַר (fut. יִמְכֹּר; inf. with suff. מָכְרָה, מִכְרָם; imp. with ה parag. מִכְרָה).—I. *he sold,* with בְּ of the price.—II. *he gave a daughter in marriage* (in consideration of a gift).—III. *he gave up men* into the power of others. Niph. נִמְכַּר *was sold*. Hith. הִתְמַכֵּר I. *was sold.*—II. *was surrendered.*

מֶכֶר m. (with suff. מִכְרָם).—I. *value, price.*—II. *valuable article*, Neh. 13:16.

מִכְרִי p. n. of a man.

מִמְכָּר m., מִמְכֶּרֶת f.—I. *sale.*—II. *thing sold.*

מַכָּר *relative*; see נכר.

מִכְרֶה *pit of salt*; see כרה.

מְכֵרָה *sword*; see כּוּר.

מְכֵרָתִי *Macherathite*, patron. 1 Chron. 11:36.

מַכְשֵׁלָה, מִכְשׁוֹל; see כשל.

מִכְתָּב *writing*; see כתב.

מְכִתָּה *breaking*; see כתת.

מִכְתָּם; see כתם.

מַכְתֵּשׁ *mortar*; see כתש.

מָלֵא, מָלָא (fut. יִמְלָא; inf. מְלֹאת).—I. *fill*; מָלְאוּ הַשְּׁלָטִים *fill the shields*, i. e. enlarge them so as to cover you, Jer. 51:11; מָלֵא יָד *filled the hand*, i. e. conferred an office.—II. *fulfil, execute fully, thoroughly*; מָלְאָה צְבָאָהּ *her warfare is accomplished*; מָלְאָה נַפְשִׁי *my soul is full*, Ex. 15:9. Niph. נִמְלָא (fut. יִמָּלֵא) *is full, filled*, with מִן, לְ, מִן. Pi. מִלֵּא, מִלָּא (inf. מַלֹּאת, מַלֵּא; fut. יְמַלֵּא).—I. *fulfil* (of time, promise, &c.).—II. *fill the hand*, i. e. consecrate to the priest's office.—III. *fill as a vessel* (with accus. מִן), *insert*, i. e. *fill in*, of the stones in the breast-plate, Ex. 28:17.—IV. used with other verbs, &c., implying the completion of their action; מִי יָדוֹ בַקֶּשֶׁת *he fully drew the bow*, lit. filled his

hand with, 2 Ki. 9:24; קָרְאוּ מָלֵאוּ *cry out strongly*; מָלֵא אַחֲרֵי *fulfilled the followings*, i. e. followed fully. Pu. part. מְמֻלָּאִים *filled with gems*, Cant. 5:14. Hith. fut. יִתְמַלָּאוּן *they are fully set against me*, Job 16:10.

מְלָא Ch., *filled*, Dan. 2:35. Hith. *was filled*, Dan. 3:19.

מָלֵא m., מְלֵאָה f., *full* (used as מָלָא, see above Pi. IV.); כֶּסֶף מָלֵא *full* (i. e. just), *money*; מֵי מָלֵא *waters of fulness* (i. e. ample), *abundant*; מְלֵא יָמִים *full of days*, Jer. 6:11.

מְלֹא, מְלוֹא, מְלוֹ m.—I. *filling, fulness*; מְלֹא כַף *the filling of the palm, palm full*; מִ׳ חָפְנֵיכֶם פִּיחַ *both your closed hands full of ashes*, Ex. 9:8; מִ׳ קוֹמָתוֹ *his full stature*, 1 Sam. 28:20.—II. *multitude*, Gen. 48:19.

מְלֵאָה f., *overplus*, excess of corn and wine which was to be offered to the Lord, Ex. 22:28; Nu. 18:27.

מְלֹאות for מְלֹאת Kal inf., from מלא.

מְלָכִים for מ׳ בּ pl., from מֶלֶךְ.

מִלּוֹא m., p. n.—I. a certain part of the citadel of Jerusalem, called also בֵּית מִלּוֹא 2 Ki. 12:21.—II. a castle of the Sichemites, Jud. 9:6, 20.

מִלוּאָה, מִלֻּאָה f., *insertion of gems* (see above מלא Pi. III.).

מִלֻּאִים m. pl.—I. *inauguration, consecration* (of priests).—II. אַבְנֵי מִלֻּאִים *set* (inserted jewels); see מִלֻּאָה.

מִלֵּאת f., Cant. 5:12, *fulness*, perhaps *prominency*, some peculiar mode of setting jewels.

see ; מַלְאָכִי ,מַלְאָכוֹת ,מְלָאכָה ,מַלְאָן לאך.

מַלְבּוּשׁ same as לְבוּשׁ clothing ; see לבש.

מַלְבֵּן brick kiln ; see לבן.

מִלָּה saying ; see מלל.

מָלוּ for מָלְאוּ Kal pret. pl., from מלא.

מַלּוּךְ ,מְלוּכָה rule ; see מלך.

מָלוֹן ,מְלוּנָה inn ; see לון.

I. מָלַח. Niph. נִמְלַח pass away, vanish, Isa. 51:6.

מְלָחִים m. pl., rolling, passing away, Jer. 38:11, 12.

II. מָלַח (from מֶלַח), salted, Ex. 30:35. Pu. part. מְמֻלָּח. Hoph. salted, Eze.16:4.

מֶלַח m., salt; יָם־הַמֶּלַח the salt sea, i. e. the Dead Sea; בְּרִית מֶלַח covenant of salt, i. e. perpetual, Nu. 18:19.

מְלַח m. Ch., salt.

מְלַח Ch., eat salt, Ezr. 4:14.

מַלּוּחַ m., ἅλιμος, salt plant, (halimus atriplex—Linn.).

מַלָּח m., pl. מַלָּחִים sailors.

מְלֵחָה f., salt land, waste.

מִלְחָמָה war ; see לחם.

מָלַט. Pi. מִלֵּט ,מָלַט.—I. cause to escape, slip.—II. deliver, save.—III. hatch (of eggs), Isa. 34:15. Hiph. same as Pi. Niph. was delivered, set at liberty, saved. Hith. same as Niph.

מֶלֶט m., clay.

מְלַטְיָה p. n. of a man.

מְלִילוֹת ears of corn ; see מלל.

מַלִּינִים Hiph. part. pl., from לון.

מְלִיצָה saying ; see ליץ.

מָלַךְ reigned; with בְּ, עַל was made a king. Hiph. make any one a king, with לְ. Hoph. was made king, Dan. 9:1. Niph. took, sought, counsel.

מֶלֶךְ m. (with suff. מַלְכִּי; pl. מְלָכִים, מַלְכֵי) king, applied to God and also to idols; דֶּרֶךְ הַמֶּלֶךְ royal way.—II. p. n. of a man.—III. עֵמֶק הַמֶּלֶךְ p. n., a valley not far from the Dead Sea.

מֶלֶךְ m. Ch., king.

מְלַךְ m. Ch., counsel, Dan. 4:24.

מֹלֶךְ, with art. הַמֹּלֶךְ Μολόχ, Moloch, an idol of the Ammonites.

מַלְכָּה f., queen. Ch. the same.

מִלְכָּה p. n. of a daughter of Haran.

מְלֶכֶת f., מ׳ הַשָּׁמַיִם the queen of Heaven, Ashtoreth, Astarte, an idol of Canaan.

מֹלֶכֶת p. n. of a woman.

מַלּוּךְ (מְלִיכוּ, מַלּוּבִי) p. n. of a man.

מְלוּכָה f., rule, government, royalty.

מַלְכוּת f., rule, kingdom, royal dignity.

מַלְכוּ, מַלְכוּת f. Ch., the same.

מַלְכִּיאֵל p. n. of a man; י׳— patron.

מַלְכִּיָּה, מַלְכִּיָּהוּ p. n. of a man.

מַלְכִּי־צֶדֶק p. n., Melchizedek, king of Salem.

מַלְכִּירָם p. n. of a man.

מַלְכִּי־שׁוּעַ p. n. of one of Saul's sons.

מַלְכֹּם, מִלְכֹּם same as מֶלֶךְ.

מַה־לָכֶם for מֶה־לָכֶם ; see מָה.

מַמְלָכָה f.(const. מַמְלֶכֶת; with suff. מַמְלַכְתּוֹ; pl. מַמְלָכוֹת rule, regal government; בֵּית מ׳ seat of government; עִיר מ׳ capital city; זֶרַע מ׳ royal family.

מַמְלָכוּת const. מַמְלְכוּת f., the same.

מַלְכֹּדֶת trap; see לכד.

מָלַל speaking. Pi. מִלֵּל announce, tell.

מְלַל Ch. Pa. מַלֵּל speak, announce.

מִלָּה f. (pl. מִלִּים, מִלִּין).—I. saying, argument.—II. thing spoken of.

מִלָּה f. Ch. (pl. מִלִּין) saying, decree.

מְלָלַי p.n. of a man.

מַלֻּתִּי p.n. of a man.

מְלִילָה f., pl. מְלִילוֹת ears of corn, Deu. 23:26.

מַלְמָד goad; see למד.

מָלַץ Niph. נִמְלְצוּ are become smooth, agreeable, Ps. 119:103.

מֶלְצַר a certain office in the king of Babylon's palace; nature of the office unknown, Dan. 1:11, 16.

מָלַק break, bruise, Lev. 1:15; 5:8; LXX. ἀποκνίζειν.

מַלְקָחַיִם, מֶלְקָחַיִם, מַלְקוֹחַ; see לקח.

מַלְקוֹשׁ latter rain; see לקש.

מֶלְתָּחָה f., wardrobe, 2 Ki. 10:22.

מַלְתָּעוֹת jaws; see לתע.

מַמְּגֻרוֹת granary; see גור.

מְמַדִּים measures; see מדד.

מְמוּכָן p.n. of a prince of Persia.

מְמוֹת, מְמוֹתִים; see מות.

מַמְזֵר m.—I. foreigner.—II. bastard.

מִמְכָּר, מִמְכֶּרֶת sale; see מכר.

מַמְלָכָה, מַמְלָכוּת kingdom; see מלך.

מַמְרֹרִים, מְמֹרִים see מרר.

מַמְרֵא p.n.; see מרא.

מֶמְשָׁלֶת, מֶמְשָׁלָה, מִמְשָׁל see משל.

מָן manna; see מן; מִמַּיִם; see מן.

מַן, מֵן Ch. pron.—I. who?—II. what? מַן־דִּי whoever.

מְנִי, מִנִּי, מֶ, מַד, מִן (with suff. מִמֶּם; מֶנְהוּ, מִגֶּהוּ; מֶנִּי, מִנִּי; מֶהֶן, מִנְהֶם or מֵהֶם; see מִן in (מן) prep.—I. from.—II. from out of.—III. of.—IV. by.—V. because of.—VI. besides.—VII. among; תִּשָּׁכֵל מֵאֲנָשִׁים she shall be barren among women.—VIII. some of, part of.—IX. more than; used also with inf.; הִשְׁחִיתוּ מֵאֲבוֹתָם they are worse than the fathers; מָתוֹק מִדְּבַשׁ sweeter than honey; אֶגְדַּל מִמְּךָ I shall be greater than thee; מִן...וְעַד from ...unto; לְמִן from thence.

מִן Ch., the same.

מִנָּה; see מְנָת in מנה.

מִנְדָּה same as מִדָּה; see מדד.

מַנְדַּע knowledge, &c.; see ידע.

מָנָה I. number.—II. appoint, constitute, with ל. Niph. נִמְנָה was numbered, with אֶת. Pi. מִנָּה appoint, constitute, with עַל, ל. Pu. part. מְמֻנִּים persons appointed, 1 Chron. 9:29.

מְנָא, מְנָה Ch., numbered, tried. Pa. constituted, appointed.

מָנֶה m., a certain weight, perhaps of one hundred shekels.

מָנָה f. (pl. מָנוֹת) part, portion.

מְנָת f. (pl. מְנִיוֹת, מְנָאוֹת) part, portion.

מֹנִים m. pl., times; עֲשֶׂרֶת מֹ' ten times, Gen. 31:7, 41.

מְנִי m., an idol, Isa. 65:11.

מִנְיָן m. Ch., number, Ezr. 6:17.

מְנֹרוֹת; see נהר.

מָנוֹד refuge; see נוד.

מְנוּחָה, מָנוֹחַ; see נוח.

מָנוֹן; see נון.

מָנוֹס, מְנוּסָה; see נוס.

מָנוֹר; see ניר.

מְנוֹרָה see נור.

מְנֹרִים same as נְזוּרִים.

מָנַח (Arab. *he gave*).

מִנְחָה f. (pl. מְנָחוֹת; with suff. מִנְחֹתֵיכֶם).—I. *gift to men.*—II. *to God, meat-offering.*

מִנְחָה f. Ch., *gift.*

מְנַחֵם p. n. of a man.

מְנַחַת p.n.—I. of a man.—II. of a place.

מִנִּי p.n. of a place, perhaps *Armenia*, Jer. 51:27; see also in מֶן, מִן, מנן.

מִנִּי, מְנָיוֹת, מִנְיָן; see מנה.

מִנְיָמִין, מִנְיָמִין p. n. of a man.

מָן m., *manna*, the food miraculously supplied to the Israelites in the wilderness.

מָן m. with suff. מִנֵּהוּ *part of him*, with prep. מִן and suff.; מִמֶּנִּי *from me*; מִמְּךָ, מִמֵּךְ f.; מִמֶּנּוּ *from him*; מִמֶּנָּה *from her*; see מִן.

מִנִּי, מִנִּים pl., *strings of an instrument*, Ps. 150:4; 45:9.

מִנִּית p.n., a place in Ammon.

מָנַע (fut. יִמְנַע) *keep back, withhold*, with מִן and לְ. Niph. נִמְנַע *was withholden, kept back.*

מִנְעָל, מַנְעוּל; see נעל.

מַנְעַמִּים *delicacies*; see נעם.

מְנַעְנְעִים *cymbals*; see נוע.

מְנַקִּיּוֹת *bowls*; see מְנַקִּית in נקה.

מֶנֶקֶת; see ינק.

מְנַשֶּׁה (*that which is forgotten*), p. n.

— I. *Manasseh* the son of Joseph, Μανασσῆς; patron. מְנַשִּׁי, הַמְנַשֶּׁל.—II. given also to other men.

מְנָת *part*; see מנה.

מָס, מַס, מִסִּים; see מסס.

מְסִבּוֹת, מְסִבֵּי, מְסִבָּה; see סבב.

מִסְגֶּרֶת, מַסְגֵּר; see סגר.

מַסָּד *foundation*; see יסד.

מִסְדְּרוֹן *portico*; see סדר.

הִמְסָה same as מָסַס. Hiph. I. *dissolved, melted.*—II. *fainted.*

מַסָּה, see מסס; מַסָּה, see נסה.

מַסְוֶה m., *veil of Moses*, Ex. 34:33-35.

מְסוּכָה same as מְשׂוּכָה *hedge*; see שׂוך.

מַסָּח see נסח.

מִסְחָר *traffic*; see סחר.

מָסָך *mixed.*

מֶסֶךְ m., *mixture*, Ps. 75:9.

מִמְסָךְ *mixed wine.*

מְסֻכָּה, מָסָךְ; see סכך.

מַסֶּכֶת, מַסֵּכָה; see נסך.

מִסְכְּנוֹת, מִסְכְּנֻת; see סכן.

מַסְלוּל, מְסִלָּה; see סלל.

מַסְמְרוֹת, מַסְמְרִים, מַסְמְרִים; see סמר.

מָסַס I. *dissolve, melt.*—II. *faint.* Niph. נָמֵס, with pause נָמָס (fut. יִמַּס; inf. הִמֵּס).—I. *was dissolved, melted.*—II. *enervated* by fear, grief, pain. Hiph. pl. הִמְסִי *cause to faint*, Deu. 1:28; see מאס.

מָם m., *wasting, miserable*, Job 6:14.

מַם m., *tribute, tax*; הָיָה לָמַס and הָיָה לְמַס עֹבֵד *became tributary*; שׂוֹם לָמַס or נָתַן the same; אֲשֶׁר עַל הַמַּם *who was over the tribute*; pl. שָׂרֵי מִסִּים *chief collectors* (of tribute), Ex. 1:11.

מִסָּה f., const. מִסַּת *tribute, offering*, Deu. 16:10.

תֶמֶם m., *melting, wasting away*, Ps. 58:9.

מַסָּע ,מַסַּע ; see נסע.

מִסְעָד *prop*; see סעד.

מִסְפֵּד *grief*; see ספד.

מִסְפּוֹא *provender*; see ספא.

מִסְפָּחוֹת ,מִסְפַּחַת ; see ספח.

מִסְפָּר ,מִסְפֶּרֶת *number*; see ספר.

מָסַר, inf. לִמְסֹר to *stir up, wring out rebellion*, Nu. 31:16. Niph. fut. וַיִּמָּסְרוּ *were extracted, selected*, Nu. 31:5.

מָסֹרֶת f., *fetters, bonds*, Eze. 20:37, from אסר.

מֹסָר *discipline*; see יסר.

מִסְתּוֹר ,מִסְתָּר ; see סתר.

מַעֲבָד *work*, see עבד; מַעֲבֶה *deep*, see עבה.

מַעֲבָר ,מַעֲבָרָה *passage*; see עבר.

מַעְגָּל ,מַעְגָּלָה ,מַעְגָּל ; see עגל.

מָעַד *vacillate*. Hiph. *cause to vacillate*. Hoph. *made to vacillate*, Pro. 25:19.

מַעֲדִי p.n. of a man.

מוֹעַדְיָה ,מַעַדְיָה p.n. of a man.

מַעֲדַנּוֹת ,מַעֲדַנִּים *delicacies*; see עדן.

מֵעָה (Arab. *bowels*).

מֵעִים const. מְעֵי m. pl. (with suff. מֵעַי ,מֵעֶיךָ).—I. *intestines.*—II. *belly.*—III. *womb.* — IV. *heart, mind.*

מְעִין m. pl. Ch., *belly.*

מֵעָה f., מְעוֹתָיו " *its extent*" (Lee), Isa. 48:19.

מָעוֹג *cake*; see עוג.

מָעוֹז ,מָעֹז ; see מעוז.

מָעוֹן p.n. of a man, 1 Sa. 27:2.

מְעוֹנֹתֵי ,מְעוֹנָה ,מְעוֹנִים ,מָעוֹן ; see עון.

מָעוּף ; see עוף.

מָעוֹר *nakedness*; see עור.

מַעֲזְיָה ,מַעַזְיָהוּ p.n. of a man.

מָעַט *was, became, few, small.* Pi. מֵעַט the same, Ecc. 12:3. Hiph. הִמְעִיט I. *make few.*—II. *give little.*

מְעַט (מְעַט) *a little, few*; pl. מְעַטִּים *few*; מְעַט מַיִם *a little water*, Gen. 18:4; מְתֵי מְעַט *few men*, Deu. 26:5; מְעַט מְעַט *by little and little*, Ex. 23:23; בִּמְעַט I. *within a little.*—II. *shortly, soon.*—III. *as a few, as nothing.*

מָעָט, f. מְעֻטָּה *drawn, naked* (lit. *bald*), of a sword, Eze. 21:20.

מַעֲטֶה *garment*; see עטה.

מַעֲטָפָה ; see עטף.

מְעִי ; see עוה.

מְעִי p.n. of a man.

מְעִיל *cloak*; see מעל.

מֵעִים *bowels, &c.*; see מעה.

מַעְיָן *well*; see עין.

מָעֵךְ, part. מָעוּךְ I. *pressed*, 1 Sa. 26:7.—II. *bruised, injured* (θλα-δίας), Lev. 22:24. with בְּ. Pu. מֹעַךְ *pressed*, Eze. 23:3.

מַעֲכָה ,מַעֲכָת p.n.—I. *of a region and city near Mount Hermon.*—II. *a name applied both to men and women*; מַעֲכָתִי *a Maachathite.*

מָעַל (inf. מַעַל; fut. יִמְעַל ,יִמְעָל), *do perversely, wickedly, rebel*, with בְּ.

מַעַל m., *perverseness, sin*, Job 21:34; see also in עלה.

מְעִיל m., *long upper garment* worn by persons of rank.

עלה see ;מַעַל, מַעַל, מַעֲלֶה, מַעֲלָה
עלל see ;מַעֲלִיל, מַעֲלָל, מַעֲלִין
עמד see ;מָעֳמָד, מַעֲמָד
עמם see ;מַעֲמָסָה
עמק see ;מַעֲמַקִּים depths
מַעֲנִית, מַעֲנָה, מַעֲנֶה, (לְמַעַן) מַעַן; see
ענה.
מְעֹנָה same as מְעוֹנָה habitation; see
עון.
מַעַץ p. n. of a man.
עצב see ;מַעֲצֵבָה labour
עצד see ;מַעֲצָד axe
עצר see ;מַעְצוֹר, מַעֲצָר
עקה see ;מַעֲקֶה
עקש see ;מַעֲקַשִּׁים
;מַעֲרָת, מְעָרָה, מְעָרֹת, מְעָרָה, מַעַר
see ערה.
ערב see ;מַעֲרָבָה, מַעֲרָב
ערך see ;מַעֲרֶכֶת, מַעֲרָכָה, מַעֲרָךְ
ערם see ;מַעֲרֵמִּים
ערץ see ;מַעֲרָצָה terror
עשה see ;מַעֲשֶׂה, מַעֲשִׂיָּה, מַעֲשַׂי
עשר see ;מַעֲשֵׂר, מַעַשְׂרוֹת, מַעֲשֵׂר
עשק see ;מַעֲשַׁקּוֹת
מֹף and נֹף p. n., a city of Egypt.
נפח see ;מַפֵּחַ, מַפָּח
מְפִיבֹשֶׁת p. n.—I. a son of
Saul.—II. a son of Jonathan.
פוץ see ;מֵפִיץ
נפל see ;מַפֶּלֶת, מַפָּלָה, מַפָּל
פלא see ;מִפְלָאָה
פלג see ;מִפְלַגָּה classes
פלט see ;מִפְלָט escape
פלץ see ;מִפְלֶצֶת idol
פלס see ;מִפְלָשׂ poising
פעל see ;מִפְעָלָה, מִפְעָל
מֵיפַעַת same as מִפַעַת.
נפץ see ;מַפֵּץ, מַפָּץ

פקד see; מִפְקָד
פרץ see; מִפְרָץ
מַפְרֶקֶת vertebra; see פרק.
פרש see; מִפְרָש
מִפְשָׂעָה buttocks; see פשע.
פתח see ;מִפְתָּח, מַפְתֵּחַ
מִפְתָּן threshold; see פתן.
מֹץ chaff, same as מוֹץ.

מָצָא (fut. יִמְצָא; imp. מְצָא; pl. f.
מְצֶאןָ; inf. מְצֹא; with suff. מֹצַאֲכֶם;
part. מֹצֵא, מוֹצֵא; f. מֹצֵאת
(מֹצָאת).—I. come to, arrive at.—
II. obtain, acquire.—III. find, discover.—IV. find, i. e. meet with,
discover.—V. be enough, with ל
עַד. Niph. נִמְצָא (fut. יִמָּצֵא).—
I. was obtained, acquired.—II. was
found, arrived at.—III. was present, at hand, with ל. Hiph. הִמְצִיא
I. cause to come, deliver up, with
בְּיַד into the power of any one.—II.
recompense, repay.—III. present,
offer up.

מַצָּב, מַצָּבָה, מִצָּב, מַצֵּבָה, מַצֵּבָה,
מַצֶּבֶת; see נצב.
מִצְבָּיָה p. n. of an unknown place.
מְצָד, מְצוּד, מְצוּדָה, מְצוֹדָה;
see צוד.
מָצָה suck, drain, wring out, with
מִן. Niph. נִמְצָה become sucked,
drained, wrung out.
מָצָה see in מצץ and נצה.
מֹצָה p. n., a town in the tribe of Benjamin.
מִצְהָלָה neighing; see צהל.
צוה see ;מִצְוָה
מְצוּלָה, מְצוֹלָה depth; see צול.
מְצוּקָה, מָצוֹק, מָצוּק restraint; see
צוק.

מָצוֹר p. n., *Egypt*; יְאֹרֵי מ׳ *the river of Egypt, the Nile*; see also מָצוֹר, צור in מְצוּרָה.

מִצְרַיִם p. n.—I. *a son of Ham*.—II. *Egypt*.—III. *an Egyptian*.

מִצְרִי m.; pl. מִצְרִים; f. מִצְרִית; pl. מִצְרִיּוֹת *an Egyptian*.

מַצּוּת *contention*; see נצה.

מֵצַח m. (with suff. מִצְחוֹ; pl. const. מִצְחוֹת), *forehead*.

מִצְחָה f., *greaves* (guards for the legs), 1 Sa. 17:6.

מְצִלָּה, מְצִלּוֹת, מְצִלְתַּיִם see צלל.

מִצְנֶפֶת *turban*; see צנף.

מַצָּע *bed*; see יצע.

מִצְעָד see צעד.

מִצְעָרָה, מִצְעָר *little*; see צער.

מִצְפֶּה, מִצְפָּה; see צפה.

מַצְפֻּנִים *hidden places*; see צפן.

מָצַץ *suck* (as an infant), Isa. 66:11.

מַצָּה f., ἄζυμον, pl. מַצּוֹת *pure, unleavened bread*, τὰ ἄζυμα, חַג הַמַּצּוֹת ἡ ἑορτὴ τῶν ἀζύμων, *the feast of unleavened bread*; see also in נצה.

מֵצַר, מְצָרִים *trouble*; see צרר.

מָצוֹר מִצְרַיִם *Egypt*, &c.; see מצור.

מַק *rottenness*; see מקק.

מַקֶּבֶת, מַקָּבָה; see נקב.

מַקֵּדָה p. n., a town in the tribe of Judah.

מִקְדָּשׁ see קדש.

מַקְהֵלוֹת, מַקְהֵלִים *assemblies*; see קהל.

מִקְוֶה, מִקְנָה *hope*; see קוה.

מָקוֹם *place*; see קום.

מָקוֹר *fountain*; see קור.

מַקָּחוֹת, מֶקַח; see לקח.

מִקְטֶרֶת, מִקְטָר; see קטר.

מַקֵּל m. (const. מַקֵּל, מַקֶּל; with suff. מַקְלִי, מַקֶּלְכֶם; pl. מַקְלוֹת), *stick*.

מְקֹלוֹת p. n. of a man.

מִקְלָט *safety*; see קלט.

מִקְלַעַת *sculpture*; see קלע.

מִקְנֶה, מִקְנָה, מִקְנֵיָהוּ see קנה.

מָקֵץ p. n. of a place.

מַקְצֹעַ, מִקְצֹעוֹת, מַקְצֻעוֹת; see קצע.

מָקַק Niph. נָמַק *waste away, consume, fail*. Hiph. הֵמֵק *cause to waste*, Zec. 14:12.

מַק m., *rottenness*, Isa. 3:24.

מִקְרָא see קרא.

מִקְרֶה, מְקֹרֶה see קרה.

מְקֵרָה *coolness*; see קרר.

מְקַרְקַר Pi. part., from קור.

מִקְשֶׁה, מִקְשָׁה; see קשה.

מַר, מֹר, מוֹר, מָר; see מרר.

מָרָא part. מוֹרָאָה *rebellious*, Zep. 3:1. Hiph. *put forth courage*, Job 39:19; see מרה.

מְרִיא m.—I. *fattened*.—II. specially *a fatted calf*.

מָרֵא m. Ch., *Lord*.

מֻרְאָה f., *crop* (of birds), Lev. 1:16.

מַמְרֵא p. n.—I. of a man, *Mamre*.—II. אֵלוֹנֵי מַמְרֵא (*oaks of Mamre*), and מַמְרָא p. n. of a place near Hebron.

מָרָא p. n. of a woman.

מְראֹדַךְ בַּלְאֲדָן, בּ׳ מְרֹאדַךְ p. n., one of the kings of Babylon.

מַרְאֶה, מַרְאָה see ראה.

מַרְאֲשֹׁת, מְרַאֲשֹׁות, מַרְאֲשָׁה; see ראש.

מֵרָב p. n., *Merab*, a daughter of Saul.

מַרְבַדִּים *coverlets*; see רבד.

מַרְבָּה, מַרְבִּית see רבה.

מַרְבֵּץ, מִרְבָּץ; see רבץ.

מַרְבֵּק *stall*; see רבק.

מַרְגֵּעָה, מַרְגּוֹעַ see רגע.

מַרְגְּלוֹת at the feet; see רגל.

מַרְגֵּמָה heap of stones; see רגם.

מָרַד rebelled, with בְּ, עַל.

מֶרֶד Ch., rebellion, Ezr. 4:19.

מֶרֶד m.—I. the same, Jos. 22:22.—II. p. n. of a man.

מָרָד Ch., f. מָרָדָא rebellious, Ezr. 4:12,15.

מַרְדּוּת f., rebellion, 1 Sa. 20:30.

מְרֹדָךְ m., perhaps the name of an idol of Babylon, Jer. 50:2.

מָרְדְּכַי p. n., Mordechai, a Jew in Persia, Μαρδοχαῖος.

מָרָה rebelled, rebelled against, disobeyed, with בְּ; מ' אֶת־פִּי יְהוָֹה; they rebelled against the mouth (i. e. words) of the Lord. Hiph. הִמְרָה fought against, embittered, angered, with בְּ, עִם.

מוֹרָה m., razor.

מְרִי m. (with pause מֶרִי; with suff. מֶרְיְךָ, מֶרְיָם).—I. bitterness.—II. rebellion.—III. rebellious.

(מְרִיב בַּעַל מְרִי בַעַל) p. n., the son of Jonathan, called also מְפִיבֹשֶׁת.

מְרָיָה p.n. of a man.

מְרָיוֹת p. n. of a man.

מִרְיָם p. n., Miriam the sister of Moses, Μαρία.

מְרָתַיִם dual f. (double rebellion), a prophetic title of Babylon, Jer. 50:21.

מָרָה, מֹרָה, מָרוֹת; see מרר.

מֹרַד persecuted; see רוד.

מֵרוֹן p. n., a town in the north of Palestine.

מָרוֹחַ; see מרח.

מֵרוֹם, מָרוֹם see רום.

מְרוּצָה מֵרוֹץ see רוץ.

מָרְזַח, מַרְזֵחַ; see רזח.

מָרַח apply (as a plaster). Isa. 38:21, with עַל.

מְרוֹחַ אֶשֶׁךְ m., מְרוֹחַ with crushed testicles, Lev. 21:20.

מֶרְחָב wide; see רחב.

מַרְחַקִּים, מֶרְחָק; see רחק.

מַרְחֶשֶׁת pot; see רחש.

מָרַט I. pluck out hair: hence,—II. made smooth, polished. Niph. became bald. Pu. polished, 1 Ki. 7:45.

מְרַט Ch., plucked, Dan. 7:4.

מָרְיָם, מֵרָיוֹת, מְרִי; see מרה.

מְרִיא fat; see מרא.

מְרִיבָה strife; see ריב.

מוֹרִיָּה, מֹרִיָּה f. p. n., Moriah, a hill in Jerusalem.

מְרִירִי מְרִירוּת; see מרר.

מֹרֶךְ m., softness, cowardice, Lev. 26:36; LXX. δειλία.

מֶרְכָּבֶת, מֶרְכָּבָה, מֶרְכָּב; see רכב.

מַרְכֹּלֶת merchandise; see רכל.

מִרְמָה deceit; see רמה.

מְרֵמוֹת p. n. of a man.

מֶרֶס p. n. of a Persian prince.

מַרְסְנָא p. n. of a Persian prince.

מַרְעִית, מַרְעֶה, מֶרַע; see רעה.

מְרֹנֹתִי m., a Maronothite.

מַרְעֲלָה p. n., a town in the tribe of Zebulun.

מַרְפֵּה, מַרְפֵּא; see רפא, רפה.

מָרַץ Niph. was, became, unsound, weak, diseased. Hiph. urge to folly, Job 16:3.

מַרְצֵעַ awl; see רצע.

מַרְצֶפֶת; see רצף.

מָרַק rubbed bright, polished. Pu. was polished, Lev. 6:21.

מְרוּקִים m. pl., *purifications*, Est. 2: 12.

מָרָק m., *broth*, Jud. 6:19, 20.

תַּמְרוּק m., *purification, cleansing*.

מֶרְקָח, מֶרְקָחָה, מִרְקַחַת; see רקח.

מָרַר ; מַר לִי *it is bitter to me*, with מִן. Niph. נָמַר *was offensive* (an odour), Jer. 48:11. Pi. מֵרַר (fut. יְמָרֵר) *makes bitter, grieves*; מ' בַּבְּכִי *was bitter in weeping, wept bitter tears*. Hiph. הֵמַר (inf. הָמֵר) *make bitter*. Hithpalp. הִתְמַרְמֵר *was angry*, Dan. 8:7; 11:11.

מַר m.—I. *a drop*, Isa. 40:15.—II. *bitterness*; adj. מַר (pl. מָרִים; f. מָרָה) *bitter, bitterly*.

מֹר, מוֹר, מָר m., *myrrh*.

מָרָה f.—I. *bitterness, sorrow*, 2 Sa. 2: 26.—II. p. n. *a well in the desert of Sinai.*— III. *title which Naomi gave herself*, Ru. 1:20.

מָרָה f., *sorrow*, Pro. 14:10.

מֹרָה f., *the same.*, Gen. 26:35.

מָרוֹת p. n, *a town of Judah*.

מְרִירִי m., *bitter*, Deu. 32:24.

מְרִירוּת f., *bitter sorrow*, Eze. 21:11.

מְרֹרָה f.—I. *gall.*—II. *bitterness*.

מְרֵרָה f., *gall bladder*, Job 16:13.

מְרֹרִים m. pl., *bitter herbs*.

מְרָרִי p. n., *a son of Levi*.

מֶמֶר m., *bitterness*, Pro. 17:25.

מְמֹרֹרָה f., *gall bladder*, Job 20:25.

מַמְרֹרִים m. pl., *bitter things*, Job 9: 18.

תַּמְרוּרִים m. pl., *bitterness, bitter sorrow*; see also תמר.

מַשֵּׂאת, מַשֹּׁא, מַשָּׂא, מַשָּׂאָה, מַשֵּׂאת; see נשא.

מִשְׂנָב; see שֹגב.

מְשׁוּבָה, see שׁוּב; מְשׁוּכָּה, see שֹבך.

מַשּׂוֹר *saw*; see נשר.

מְשׂוּרָה; see משר.

מָשֹׁושׁ; see שׂושׂ.

מִשְׂחָק *object of laughter*; see שֹחק.

מַשְׂטֵמָה *hatred*; see שֹטם.

מַשְׂכִּית, מַשְׂכִּיּוֹת; see שׂכה.

מַשְׂכֹּרֶת *wages*; see שֹכר.

מַשְׂמְרוֹת *nails*; see סמר.

מִשְׁפָּת; see שפת.

מָשַׂר (Arab. *divided*).

מְשׂוּרָה f., *measure for liquids*.

מִשְׂרָה *government*; see שֹרה.

מִשְׂרָפוֹת *burning*; see שֹרף.

מַשְׂרֵקָה p. n., *a place in Edom*.

מַשְׂרֵת m., *frying-pan*, 2 Sa. 13:9.

מַשׁ p. n., *Mash*, Gen. 10:23, probably the district called Mount Masius, which separates Armenia from Mesopotamia.

מְשָׁא p. n., *Mesha*, one of the boundaries of the district of the Joktanites, Gen. 10:30, not exactly known.

מַשְׁאָה, מַשָּׁאָה, מַשָּׁא, see נשה; מַשָּׁאוֹן, see נשא.

מַשְׁאַבִּים *watering places*; see שֹאב.

מִשְׁאָלָה, מִשְׁאָל; see שֹאל.

מִשְׁאֶרֶת *kneading trough*; see שֹאר.

מִשְׁבְּצוֹת; see שֹבץ.

מִשְׁבָּר, מַשְׁבֵּר *pain*; see שֹבר.

מִשְׁבַּתִּים; see שֹבת.

מִשְׁנֶה *mistake*; see שֹנה.

מָשָׁה *drew* (out of the water), Ex. 2: 10. Hiph. the same.

מֹשֶׁה (*drawn out of water*, Ex. 2:10), p. n., *Moses*, the lawgiver, Μωϋσῆς (Josephus).

מְשִׁי m. *figured silk,* Eze. 16:10,13.

מַשֶּׁה *debt; see* נשה.

מְשׁוֹאָה *desolation; see* שׁוא.

מַשֻּׁאוֹת ,מְשׁוּאוֹת; *see* שׁאה.

מְשׁוּבָה ,מְשׁוּבָה *apostasy; see* שׁוב.

מְשׁוּגָה *error; see* שׁוּג.

מָשׁוֹט ,מְשׁוֹט *oar; see* שׁוט.

מָשַׁח (inf. מְשֹׁחַ, with ה parag. מָשְׁחָה; imp. מְשַׁח; fut. יִמְשַׁח). —I. *anointed.*—II. *anointed to an office.*—III. *set apart to an office,* Isa. 61:1.—IV. *dedicate by anointing.*—V. *anoint oneself for a banquet,* Am. 6:6, const. with בְּ. Niph. נִמְשַׁח *was anointed.*

מָשִׁיחַ m.—I. *anointed.*—II. *the anointed One,* Christ.

מְשַׁח m. Ch., *oil.*

מִשְׁחָה f.—I. *unction.*— II. *portion,* Lev. 7:35.

מָשְׁחָה inf., see מָשַׁח, Nu. 18:8; לְמ' *for a dedication,* i.e. thing set apart for them.

מִמְשָׁח m., *extension, stretching out,* Eze. 28:14.

מִשְׁחָת ,מָשְׁחָת ,מָשְׁחַת ,מַשְׁחִית; *see* שׁחת.

מִשְׁחָר *dawn; see* שׁחר.

מְשִׁי; *see above* משׁה.

מְשֵׁיזַבְאֵל p. n. of a man.

מָשַׁךְ I. *stretched out the hand,* Hos. 7:5.—II. *took hold of,* Ex. 12:21. —III. *seized as spoil.*—IV. *drew, a bow, yoke, net.* &c., with בְּ.—V. מָשַׁךְ הַיּוֹבֵל *lengthened the sound of the trumpet,* Ex. 19:13.—VI. *scattered seed,* Am. 9:13.—VII. *continued in a thing.*—VIII. *reckon with* (עם), Ps. 28:3.—IX. *cheered,*

Ecc. 2:3. Niph. *was protracted, delayed.* Pu. I. *spoiled,* Isa. 18:2, 7.—II. *obtained,* Pro. 13:12.

מֶשֶׁךְ m.—I. *acquiring,* Job 28:18. —II. מֶשֶׁךְ הַזֶּרַע *scattering of seed,* Ps. 126:6.

מֹשְׁכוֹת f. pl., *attractions, influences,* Job 38:31.

מֶשֶׁךְ p.n.—I. one of the sons of Japhet. —II. the people descended from him, Gen. 10:2. They were probably the Muscovites; LXX. Μοσόχ; Vulg. *Mosoch.*

מִשְׁכָּב ,מִשְׁכַּב *bed; see* שׁכב.

מִשְׁכָּן *dwelling; see* שׁכן.

מָשַׁל I. *ruled.*—II. *had power over,* with בְּ.—III. *had power to do,* with לְ.—IV. *assimilated, compared to,* with בְּ, עַל. Niph. *became like,* with בְּ, עִם, אֶל. Pi. *speaking parables,* Eze. 21:5. Hiph. I. *give authority* (inf. הַמְשֵׁל)Dan. 11:39. —II. *made like,* Isa. 46:5. Hith. *become like,* Job 30:19.

מֹשֵׁל m.—I. *authority,* Zec. 9:10.— II. *anything like,* Job 41:25.

מָשָׁל m.—I. *solemn declaration.*—II. *decision, rule, proverb,* γνώμη.— III. *bye word, subject of taunt.*

מְשֹׁל m., *taunting proverb,* Job 17:6.

מֶמְשָׁל m., *dominion;* pl. *rulers,* 1 Ch. 26:6.

מֶמְשָׁלָה f., *dominion, rule.*

מֶמְשֶׁלֶת f. (pl. מֶמְשָׁלוֹת ,מַמְשְׁלוֹת), the same.

מִשְׁלַחַת ,מִשְׁלוֹחַ ,מִשְׁלָח ,מִשְׁלַחַת; *see* שׁלח.

מְשֻׁלָּשׁ; *see* שׁלשׁ.

מְשֻׁלָּם p. n. of a man.

שְׁלֶמְיָה, מְשֶׁלֶמְיָה p. n. of a man.

מְשִׁלֵמוֹת מְשִׁלֵמִית p. n. of a man.

מְשֻׁלֶּמֶת p. n., **Meshullemeth**, the wife of Manasseh.

מְשַׁמָּה desolation, &c.; see שמם.

מִשְׁמָן, מִשְׁמַנָּה, מִשְׁמַנִּים; see שמן.

מִשְׁמָע, מִשְׁמַעַת; see שמע.

מִשְׁמָר, מִשְׁמֶרֶת, מִשְׁמָרוֹת; see שמר.

מִשְׁנֶה; see שנה.

מִשְׁסָּה prey; see שסם.

מִשְׁעוֹל narrow way; see שעל.

מָשַׁע (Arab. *take pains*).

לְמִי מִשְׁעִי carefully, Eze. 16:4.

מִשְׁעָם p. n. of a man.

מִשְׁעָן, מַשְׁעֵנָה, מַשְׁעֵן, מִשְׁעֶנֶת; see שען.

מִשְׁפַּחַת, מִשְׁפָּחָה family; see שפח.

מִשְׁפָּט judgment; see שפט.

מִשְׁפְּתַיִם; see שפה.

מֶשֶׁק m., בֶּן־מֶשֶׁק, LXX. υἱὸς Μέσεκ, Gen. 15:2, probably the name of a tribe or district in Syria, whence דַּרְמֶשֶׂק *Damascus*.

מִמְשָׁק m., overspreading, Zep. 2:9; but LXX. read Damascus.

מָשָׁק running about; see שקק.

מַשְׁקֶה drink; see שקה.

מִשְׁקֹל, מִשְׁקָל, מִשְׁקֶלֶת, מִשְׁקֶלֶת; see שקל.

מַשְׁקוֹף see שקף.

מִשְׁרָה juice; see שרה.

מַשְׁרוֹקִיתָא flute; see שרק.

מִשְׁרָעִי p. n. of a man.

מָשַׁשׁ same as מוש touch, feel, Gen. 27:12. Pi. מִשֵּׁשׁ I. examine by feeling.—II. felt his way, groped. Hiph. (fut. יָמֵשׁ) that may be felt, Ex. 10:21; see in מוש.

מִשְׁתַּחֲוִיתֶם Eze. 8:16. Hith. part. pl. with pers. pron., from שחה.

מֵת or מַת m., pl. מְתִים, מְתֹם, const. מְתֵי men.

מֵת, מֵתָה, מַת, מַתָּה, מַתִּי, מֵתוּ, מֵתִים, from מות Kal.

מֵתָא Ch. Pe. inf., from אתה.

מַתְבֵּן heap of straw; see תֶּבֶן.

מֶתֶג m. (with suff. מִתְגִּי), bridle.

מָתוֹק, מְתוּקָה; see מתק.

מְתוּשָׁאֵל p. n., **Methusael**, one of Cain's descendants.

מְתוּשֶׁלַח p. n., **Methuselah**, the patriarch, the son of Enoch.

מָתַח stretched out (as a curtain), Isa. 40:22.

אַמְתַּחַת f. (pl. const. אַמְתְּחוֹת), sack or bag.

מָתַי pa.—I. when?—II. when; אַחֲרֵי מָתַי after how long? Jer. 13:27; עַד מָתַי how long?

מַתְכֹּנֶת; see תכן.

מַתְלָאָה for מַה־תְּלָאָה what trouble. see לאה.

מִתְלַהְלֵהַּ Hith. part., from לההּ.

מְתַלְּעוֹת teeth; see לתע.

מְתֹם soundness; see תמם.

מָתַן root not used; (Arab. was firm).

מָתְנַיִם m. dual, loins.

אֲמַתְנִי Ch. f., powerful, mighty, Dan. 7:7.

מַתְּנָה, מַתְּנָא, מַתְּנַי, מַתָּן, מַתַּנְיָה, מַתַּנְיָהוּ; see נתן.

מִתְנִי p. n. of a man.

מָתַק (fut. יִמְתַּק), were, became sweet. Hiph. הִמְתִּיק I. was sweet, Job 20:12.—II. made sweet, Ps. 55:15.

מָתוֹק m. (pl. מְתוּקִים; f. מְתוּקָה).
—I. sweet.—II. sweetness.—III.
pleasant.

מֶתֶק m., sweetness.

מֹתֶק m., the same, Jud. 9:11.

מִתְקָה p. n., a station of the Israelites
in the desert.

מַמְתַּק m., pl. מַמְתַקִּים sweetness,
Neh. 8:10; Cant. 5:16.

מִתְרְדָת p. n., Mithridates the Persian
(Μιθριδάτης).

מַתְּתָיָהוּ ,מַתַּתְיָה ,מַתָּת; see
נתן.

מַתֹּתִי Pil. pret. 1. pers., from מות.

נ

נָא interj., I pray! used,—I. in supplication.—II. in exhortation.—
III. in irony or blame; בָּא־נָא
go I pray! אִמְרִי־נָא speak I pray!
אֵלְכָה נָא let me go, I pray!
אַל־נָא תַּעֲבֹר pass not over, I
pray! יֻאֻמַּר־נָא let it be told, I
pray! אַל־נָא do not I pray! with
particles: אִם־נָא if indeed; אַל־נָא
not so, I pray! הִנֵּה־נָא behold!
אוֹי־נָא alas! see also in נִיא.

נֹא־אָמוֹן ,נֹא p. n.; Διόσπολις, μέ-
ρις Ἀμμών, perhaps the city of
Thebes in Egypt.

נָאד root not used; (Arab. poured out
water).

נֹאד (נֹאוד) m. skin bottle; pl. נֹאדוֹת
bottles.

נָאוָה (pl. const. נָאוּ), became, was
fair, Ps. 93:5; see אָוָה.

נָאָה f., pl. const. נְאוֹת the best, choice,
parts of any thing; נְ' דֶּשֶׁא plea-

sant herbage, Ps. 23:2; generally
translated habitation, Ps. 74:20,
and elsewhere; but the former
appears to give a better sense.

נָאוֶה ,נָאֶה m.,—I. becoming, seemly.
—II. fair.

נָאוּ for נָאוָה, from נאה.

נָאוֹת Niph. fut. pl. 1. pers., from אות.

נָאַם make a solemn declaration, Jer.
23:31; part. נְאֻם; נ' יְיָ saith the
Lord, passim: used of Agur, Pro.
30:1.

נָאַף (fut. יִנְאַף).—I. committed adultery.—II. worshipped false gods,
Jer. 3:9; part. נֹאֵף adulterer,
נֹאָפֶת adulteress. Pi. נִאֵף the
same.

נִאֻפִים m. pl.—I. adulteries.—II. acts
of idolatry.

נַאֲפוּפִים m. pl., repeated acts of
adultery, Hos. 2:4.

נָאַץ (fut. יִנְאַץ turned away from,
despised, rejected. Pi. נִאֵץ (fut.
יְנָאֵץ) the same. Hiph. fut. יִנְאַץ
it is despised, Ecc. 12:5. Hith.
part. מִנֹּאָץ contemned, Isa. 52:5.

נְאָצָה f., reproach, insult, 2 Ki. 19:
3; Isa. 37:3.

נֶאָצָה f., pl. נֶאָצוֹת (נֶאָצוֹתֶיךָ), the
same.

נָאַק same as אָנַק cry out, Job 24:12.

נְאָקָה const. נַאֲקַת f., cry of sorrow.

נָאַר Pi. נִאֵר (pret. 2. pers. נֵאַרְתָּה)
rejected as worthless, Ps. 89:40;
Lam. 2:7.

נֶאְשָׁר Eze. 9:8, perhaps comp. of
נִשְׁאַר and אֶשָׁאֵר; see שאר.

נֹב p. n., a city of the Levites in the

tribe of Benjamin; with ה, נֹבָה *towards Nob.*

נָבָא Niph. נִבָּא *announced as the will of God, prophesied.* Hith.—I.—(הִתְנַבּוֹת (inf. הַנִּבֵּא, הִתְנַבֵּא *prophecy.*—II. *be mad.*

נְבָא Ch. Ithp. הִתְנַבִּי *prophesied,* Ezr. 5:1.

נָבִיא m. (with suff. נְבִיאֲכֶם).—I. *a prophet, one who declares future events.*—II. *probably one devoted to the study of the revealed will of God;* whence בְּנֵי הַנְּבִיאִים *the sons,* i.e. *disciples of the prophets who studied under them.*

נָבִיא m. Ch., the same.

נְבִיאָה f.—I. *prophetess.*—II. *prophet's wife.*

נְבוּאָה f.—I. *prediction,* Neh. 6:12. —II. *prophetical book.*

נְבוּאָה f. Ch., the same.

נְבוֹ p. n., *Nebo.*—I. *one of the idols of Babylon,* Isa. 46:1.—II. *a mountain and city in the land of Moab.* —III. *a town in the tribe of Judah.*

נְבוּזַרְאֲדָן p. n., *one of Nebuchadnezzar's generals.*

נְבוּכַדְרֶאצַּר, נְבוּכַדְנֶצַּר, נְבוּכַדְרֶאצַּר p. n., *Nebuchadnezzar, the king of Babylon;* LXX. Ναβουχοδονόσορ.

נְבוּשַׁזְבָּן p. n., *a prince of Assyria.*

נָבוּב *proud;* see בּוּב.

נָבוֹת p. n. of a man.

נְבִזְבָּה, נְבִזְבָּה f. Ch., *gift, reward.*

נִבְּחָה, 1 Sa. 14:36, Kal fut. pl. 1. pers. with ה parag. and dag. f. dropped; see בזז.

נָבַח *bark* (as a dog), Isa. 56:10.

נָבָח p. n. of a man; also of a town in Gilead, Nu. 32:42; Jud. 8:11

נִבְחַז p.n., *an idol of the Avites,* 2 Ki. 17:31.

נָבַט. Pi. נִבֵּט and Hiph. הִבִּיט.—I. *looked.*—II. *look at, towards,* with אֶל, לְ; *looked after,* with אַחֲרֵי— III. *looked favourably at,* with בְּ; same as רָאָה *perceived.* — IV. *attended to.*—V. *noticed,* Ps. 10: 14.

נְבָט p. n., *Nebat, the father of Jeroboam.*

מַבָּט m., *expectation, hope,* Isa. 20: 5:6.

מֶבָּט m., the same, Zec. 9:5.

נְבִיאָה, נָבִיא; see נבא.

נְבָיוֹת p. n., *Nebaioth, a people of the race of Ishmael,* Gen. 25:13, &c.

נִבֵּאתִי for נָבָאתִי, נְבֵיתִי Niph. pret., from נבא.

נֵבֶךְ "*mazes of the sea*" (Lee), Job 38:16.

נָבֵל (fut. יִבֹּל).— I. *became shrivelled and fell* (as flowers, &c.). — II. *wasted away.* — III. *crumbled to dust.*—IV. *acted foolishly,* Pro. 30: 32. Pi. נִבֵּל *treated as worthless, set at nought.*

נָבָל m., נְבָלָה f.—I. *foolish.*—II. *impious.*—III. p. n. of a man, 1 Sa. c. 25.

נַבְּל, וַנְּבֵל, Isa. 64:5, Hiph. fut. pl. 1. pers. from בלל; or for וַנְּבֵל Kal fut., from נבל.

נִבְלָה for נָבְלָה Kal fut. pl. 1. pers., with ה parag.; see בלל.

נְבָלָה f.—I. *disgraceful action.*—II. *punishment of such an action,* Jos

7:15.— III. *impiety*, Isa. 32:6.—
IV. *folly*, 1 Sa. 25:25.

נְבֵלָה f. (const. נִבְלַת; with suff.
נִבְלָתִי, נִבְלָתוֹ).—I. *carcase of an
animal*.— II. *dead body of a man*.
—III. *idols*, Jer. 16:18; collect.
carcases.

נַבְלוּת f., *shame, nakedness*, Hos. 2:
12.

נֵבֶל, נֶבֶל m. (pl. נְבָלִים).—I. *bottle*
(of skin).— II. *earthen jar*.— III.
lute, νάβλιον.

נְבַלָּט p. n., a town in the tribe of Benjamin.

נוֹבֵע, נָבַע *springing* (as a fountain),
Pro. 18:4. Hiph. הִבִּיעַ.— I. *ut-
ters, declares*.—II. *prepares*.

מַבּוּעַ m., *spring, fountain of water*.

נִבְקָה for נָבְקָה Niph. pret. f., from
בקק.

נָבַר Niph., from ברר.

נֶבְרַשְׁתָּא f. Ch., *lamp*, Dan. 5:5.

נִבְשָׁן p. n. of a town in the tribe of
Judah.

נִגְאֲלוּ for נִגְאֲלוּ Niph. pret. pl., from
גאל II.

נָגַב (Ch. נְגֵב *was dry*.)

נֶגֶב m. — I. the arid desert to the
south of Judea. — II. the south;
נֶגְבָּה towards, on, the south;
לַנֶּגְבָּה, בַּנֶּגְבָּה towards the south;
מִנֶּגֶב from the south.

נָגַד. Hiph. הִגִּיד *brought before, told,
made known*; with לְ of the per-
son to whom. Hoph. הֻגַּד *was
told*.

נְגַד Ch., *proceeding, flowing*, Dan.
7:10.

נֶגֶד subst. *fore part of the body*; prep
before, in front of, opposite to;
adv. *straightforwards*; כְּנֶגֶד, כְּנֶגְדּוֹ
opposite to him; לְנֶגֶד *before, opposite to*; מִנֶּגֶד *in presence of, in
sight, out of sight, over against,
opposite to, against*.

נָגִיד m.—I. *leader*.—II. *prince*.—III.
chief.—IV. *one appointed to any
charge*.

נָגַהּ *shined*. Hiph. הִגִּיהַּ *caused to
shine*, Isa. 13:10, *made light*.

נֹגַהּ f. (with suff. נָגְהָם).—I. *the dawn*.
— II. *light*. — III. p. n. a son of
David.

נֹגַהּ f. Ch., *dawn*, Dan. 6:20.

נְגֹהָה f., *light*, Isa. 59:9.

נָגַח (fut. יִגַּח), *push with the horn*.
Pi. נִגַּח the same. Hith. הִתְנַגַּח
entered into conflict, Dan. 11:40.

נַגָּח m., *addicted to pushing with the
horn*, Ex. 21:29, 36.

נָגַל root not used; (Arab. *sickle*).

מַגָּל m., *sickle*, Jer. 50:16; Joel 4:13.

נָגַן and Pi. נִגֵּן *performed music*.

נְגִינָה f.—I. *music*.—II. *a song*.—III.
subject of a song.

מַנְגִּינָה f., *song of ridicule*, Lam.
3:63.

נָגַע (inf. נְגֹעַ, נַּעַת; with suff. נָגְעוֹ;
imp. גַּע; fut. יִגַּע; part. f. נֹגַעַת).
—I. *touched*, with בְּ, אֶל, עַל.—II
touched gently, awakened, with בְּ.
—III. *touched the heart*, with בְּ,
1 Sa. 10:26.—IV. *touched so as to
injure*, with בְּ.—V. *struck*, with
בְּ, Job 1:19. — VI. *arrived*. —
VII. *arrived at, reached*, with
עַל, אֶל, בְּ.—VIII. *reached the*

ear of, with אֶל, Jon. 3:6. Niph. *were beaten in battle*, Jos. 8:15. Pi. נִגַּע *struck with disease*. Pu. *are afflicted*, Ps. 73:5. Hiph. הִגִּיעַ I. *made to touch*, with אֶל, לְ, עַד.—II. *reached*, with אֶל, לְ, עַד, עַל.—III. *reached the ears of*, with אֶל, Est. 9:26.—IV. *reached its proper time*, with לְ, Est. 9:1.—V. *came near*, with לְ, Ps. 88:4.—VI. *arrived* (of time).—VII. *arrived at*, with עַד, לְ, אֶל.

נֶגַע m. (with suff. נִגְעִי; pl. נְגָעִים, נִגְעֵי).—I. *stroke, blow.*—II. *infliction of evil.*—III. *affliction.*—IV. *mark of a blow, spot.*

נָגַף (fut. יִגֹּף).—I. *struck.*—II. *wounded.*—III. *killed.* — IV. *defeated.* — V. *struck with disease.*—VI. *stumbled.* Niph. נִגַּף (inf. abs. נָגוֹף), *was defeated, routed* (of an army), with לִפְנֵי *of the enemy.* Hith. *stumble*, Jer. 13:16.

נֶגֶף m.—I. *infliction of disease.*—II. *act of stumbling*, Isa. 8:14.

מַגֵּפָה, const. מַגֵּפַת f.—I. *plague, pestilence.*—II. *defeat.*

נָגַר. Niph. נִגַּר I. *was put forth* (the hand), Ps. 77:3.—II. *overflowed, was spilt.*—III. *was scattered*, as wealth, Job 20:28. Hiph. הִגִּיר I. *dragged away.*—II. *poured out*, Ps. 75:9.—III. *scattered*, Mic. 1:6. Hoph. *poured out*, Mic. 1:4.

נָגַשׂ (fut. יִגֹּשׂ, תִּנְגְּשׂוּ), *exacted a task, debt* or *tax* ; part. נוֹגֵשׂ *exactor, taskmaster, slave-driver.* Niph. נִגַּשׂ *was pressed, vexed, fatigued.*

נָגַשׁ (fut. יִגַּשׁ ; inf. גֶּשֶׁת ; with suff.

גִּשְׁתּוֹ ; imp. גַּשׁ, גְּשָׁה־ and (גְּשָׁה) Niph. נִגַּשׁ I. *came near to, up to, touched*, with אֶל, בְּ, לְ, עַד, עַל.—II. perhaps *depart, go away*, Gen. 19:9. Hiph. הִגִּישׁ I. *brought near.*—II. *offered*, i. e. brought near (an offering). Hoph. הֻגַּשׁ *was brought, placed.* Hith. *approach*, Isa. 45:20.

נֵד *heap* ; see נדד.

נָדָא, fut. וַיַּדֵּא *drave away*, 2 Ki. 17:21.

נָדַב I. *rendered willing*, with לֵב and רוּחַ.—II. *impelled.* Hith. הִתְנַדֵּב *offered* or *performed willingly.*

נְדַב Ch. Hith. *was willing, gave willingly.*

נָדָב p. n., *Nadab.* —I. the son of Aaron.—II. given also to other men.

נְדָבָה, const. נִדְבַת f.—I. *voluntary offering.* — II. *free-will* (בִּנְדָבָה, נְדָבָה *of his own accord, willingly*), —III. pl. *abundance*; גֶּשֶׁם נְדָבוֹת *plenteous rain*, Ps. 68:10.

נְדַבְיָה p. n. of a man.

נָדִיב m.—I. *willing, liberal.*—II. *noble, distinguished.* — III. Job 21:28 ; perhaps " *a libertine*" (Lee).

נְדִיבָה f., *liberality.*

הִתְנַדְּבוּת (inf. Hith.) f. Ch., *free-will offerings*, Ezr. 7:16.

נִדְבָּךְ m. Ch., *layer, course of stones*, Ezr. 6:4.

נָדַד (inf. נְדֹד ; fut. יִדֹּד, יִדַּד).—I. *fled.*—II. *wandered, walked to and fro.*—III. *flapped the wings*, Isa. 10:14 ; part. נוֹדֵד. Po. נוֹדַד *was driven away*, Nah. 3:17. Hiph. הֵנִד *cause to wander*, Job 18:18. Hoph. הֻנַּד *made to wander*, Job

20:8; *driven about*, 2 Sa. 23:6.
Hith. *was agitated.*

נְדַד Ch., *fled*, Dan. 6:19.

נְדֻדִים m. pl., *restlessness* (of body or mind), Job 7:4.

נֵד m.—I. *a heap*, Isa. 17:11.—II. *a mound.*

נִדָּה f.—I. *legal impurity.*—II. *a woman in that state.*—III. *moral impurity.*—IV. *that which is impure, worthless*, Eze. 7:19, 20; מֵי הַנִּדָּה *water of impurity*, i. e. for the cleansing of legal impurity.

נִידָה f., *impurity*, Lam. 1:8.

מְנֻדָּד m., *flight*, Job 7:4.

נָדָה same as נוּד. Pi. נִדָּה *put aside, desired to avoid*, with לְ, Isa. 66:5; Am. 6:3.

נֵדֶה m., *present, gift*, Eze. 16:33.

נֵדֶן m., the same; see also below.

נָדַח (fut. יִדַּח).—I. *drove an axe*, Deu. 20:19.—II. *drove away*, 2 Sa. 14:14. Hiph. הִדִּיחַ 1. *brought with violence*, with עַל.—II. *drove away.*—III. *induced to any thing*, Pro. 7:21. Niph. נִדַּח I. *was impelled.*—II. *was driven away.*—III. *was induced to an action*; part. נִדָּח (with suff. נִדְחוֹ, נִדַּחֲךָ; f. נִדָּחָה). Pu. part. מְנֻדָּח *driven*, Isa. 8:22. Hoph. part. מֻדָּח *driven astray*, Isa. 13:14.

מַדּוּחִים m. pl., *expulsions, drivings out*, Lam. 2:14.

נְדִיבָה, נָדִיב; see נדב.

נִדְמָה for נִדְמָה Niph. fut. pl. 1. pers. with ה parag., from דמם.

נֵדֶן m., *sheath* (of a sword), 1 Chron. 21:27; see also in נָדָה.

נִדְנֶה m. Ch., "midst," Eng. Ver.; "sheath," Marg., Dan. 7:15.

נָדַף (fut. יִדֹּף, יִנְדֹּף).—I. *scattered, drove about.*—II. *routed, conquered* (an enemy), Job 32:13. Niph. נִדַּף (inf. הִנָּדֵף) *driven away.*

I. נָדַר (fut. יִדֹּר, יִדַּר) *made a vow.*

נֶדֶר, נֵדֶר m. (with suff. נִדְרִי; pl. נְדָרִים, נִדְרֵי).—I. *vow.*—II. *thing vowed.*

II. נָדַר root not used; (Arab. *thresh corn*).

אִדַּר Ch., *threshing-floor*, Dan. 2:35; (Arab. the same).

נֹהַּ *lamentation*, Eze. 7:11; see נָהָה.

נָהַג (imp. נְהַג; fut. יִנְהַג).—I. *led, conducted.*—II. *drave cattle, &c.*—III. *guided.*—IV. *commanded an army.* Pi. נֵהַג (fut. יְנַהֵג) I. *brought on a wind*: hence—II. *נְהַג breathed*, Nah. 2:8.—III. *led.*—IV. *drave.*

מִנְהָג m., *driving of horses*, 2 Ki. 9:20.

נָהַד root not used; (Arab. *swelled, grew vigorous*).

הוֹד m.—I. *vigour*, Pro. 5:9.—II. *glory, majesty.*—III. p. n. of a man.

הוֹדַוְיָהוּ, הוֹדַוְיָה p.n.; see ידה.

הוֹדִיָּה p.n. of a man.

הוֹדִיָּה p. n. of a man.

נָהָה *lamented*, Mic. 2:4. Niph. fut. וַיִּנָּהוּ *mourn after the Lord*, 1 Sa. 7:2.

נְהִי, with pause נֶהִי m., *lamentation.*

נָהִי, וַנַּהִי fut. apoc. pl. 1. pers., from היה Mic. 2:4; see הָוָה.

נָהַל. Pi. נִהֵל (fut. יְנַהֵל).—I. *led.*—

II. *tended, fed.*—III. *gave rest to,* 2 Chron. 32:22. Hith. *proceed with a flock,* Gen. 33:14.

נַהֲלָל m. — I. *pasture,* Isa. 7:19.—II. p. n., a town in the tribe of Zebulun, called also נַהֲלֹל.

נָהַם (fut. יִנְהֹם).—I. *roared,* Isa. 5:29,30.—II. *groaned.*

נַהַם m., *roaring of a lion.*

נְהָמָה, const. נַהֲמַת f., *roaring of the sea,* Isa. 5:30.—II. *groaning,* Ps. 38:9.

נָהַק (fut. יִנְהַק) *brayed* (as an ass), Job 6:5; 30:7.

נָהַר I. *brighten* (of the face), Isa. 60:5; Ps. 34:6.—II. (fut. יִנְהַר) *flow unto, assemble in.*

נָהָר m. (pl. נְהָרִים, נְהָרוֹת, נַהֲרוֹת).—I. *river, stream.*—II. *current of the sea,* Jonah; הַנָּהָר, הַנָּהָר הַגָּדוֹל same as נְהַר פְּרָת *Euphrates;* אֲרַם נַהֲרַיִם *Aram* (Syria) *of the rivers,* Mesopotamia.

נְהַר m. Ch., *river.*

נְהוֹר (נְהִיר) m. Ch., *light,* Dan. 2:22.

נַהִירוּ f. Ch., *light, wisdom,* Dan. 5:11,14.

נְהָרָה f., *light of day,* Job 3:4.

מִנְהָרוֹת f. pl., *clefts* in mountains, serving as channels for the rain, Jud. 6:2.

נוּא or נוֹא. Hiph. הֵנִיא.—I. *discouraged,* Nu. 32:7.—II. *prohibited.*—III. *frustrated.*

תְּנוּאָה f.—I. *aversion,* Nu. 14:34.—II. *heavy things,* Job 33:10.

נוּב (fut. יָנוּב).—I. *threw out shoots,* Ps. 92:15.—II. *produced fruit,* Pro.

10:31.—III. *increased,* Ps. 62:11. Pi. נוֹבֵב *makes fruitful,* Zec. 9:17.

נִיב m., *produce, fruit.*

נֵיבִי p. n. of a man.

תְּנוּבָה f., *produce, fruit.*

נוֹגוֹת Niph. part. pl. f. for נוֹגְגוֹת, from ינה.

נוֹגִי Niph. part. pl. for נוֹגֵי, from ינה. נוֹגִים; see ינה.

נוּד (fut. יָנוּד).—I. *move to and fro.*—II. *wandered as a fugitive;* part. נָד *a fugitive.*— III. *departed.*—IV. *shook the head,* expressing pity, condoled. Hiph. הֵנִיד.—I. *moved to and fro.*—II. *drove out.*—III. *disturbed.*—IV. *shake the head* in pity, Jer. 18:16. Hoph. part. מֻנָּד *expelled,* 2 Sa. 23:6. Hithpol. הִתְנוֹדֵד *bemoan himself,* Jer. 31:18.

נוּד Ch., *departs,* Dan. 4:11.

נוֹד m.—I. *wandering,* Ps. 56:9.—II. p. n. (*exile*), the country to which Cain was banished.

נִיד m., *moving of the lips,* Job 16:5.

מָנוֹד m., *shaking the head,* Ps. 44:15.

נוֹדָב p. n., a son of Ishmael.

נָוָה (fut. יִנְוֶה) *dwelt,* Hab. 2:5. Hiph. *prepare a dwelling;* fut. with suff. אַנְוֵהוּ, Ex. 15:2.

נָוֶה m. (const. נְוֵה; with suff. נָוֵךְ, נָוֵהוּ, נְוֵהֶם).—I. *fold for cattle.*—II. *dwelling of men.*—III. *habitation of God.*

נָוָה f., *habitation,* Job 8:6; נְוַת בַּיִת *she that remaineth at home;* οἰκουρός, Ps. 68:13.

נָוָה *dwelt quietly,* Jer. 6:2.

נִיֹת, Ketib נָוֹית (*habitations*), p.n., a place near Ramah.

נוּחַ (fut. יָנוּחַ, וַיָּנַח).— I. *lay down, rested.*— II. *halted, ceased.*— III. *abode in,* with בְּ.—IV. *alighted on.* — V. *came down and possessed,* with עַל.— VI. *settled on* (as on a shoal, of the ark), Gen. 8:4. Hiph. I. הֵנִיחַ:— 1. *gave rest to.* — 2. *comforted.*— 3. *let fall,* Ex. 17:11.— 4. *caused to rest upon.*— II. הִנִּיחַ and הַנַּח:—1. *placed.*— 2. *left, forsook, quitted.*—3. *let rest, remain.*— 4. *permitted, gave into the power of.*— 5. *left untouched,* 2 Ki. 23:18, with לְ. Hoph. הוּנַח I. *rest was given,* Lam. 5:5.—II. *was placed, left, remaining.*

נוֹחַ, נַח m. (with suff. נוּחֶךָ).—I. *rest,* Est. 9:16-18.— II. p. n., *Noah;* LXX. Νῶε.

נַחַת f., *being placed,* Job 36:16; see also נחת.

הֲנָחָה (verb. Hiph.) f., *rest, peace,* Est. 2:18.

מָנוֹחַ m. (pl. with suff. מְנוּחָיְכִי).—I. *place of rest.*—II. p. n., *Manoah,* the father of Samson.

מְנוּחָה, מְנֻחָה f.— I. *rest, quiet.*— II. *place of rest.*—III. metaphorically, the land of Canaan.

נִיחֹחַ, נִיחוֹחַ m., *satisfaction, approbation;* רֵיחַ הַנִּיחֹחַ *a sweet* (pleasant) *savour.*

נִיחוֹחַ m. Ch., *offerings to God or man.*

נוּט same as מוֹט *agitate, shake,* Ps. 99:1.

נול root not used; Ch. Pa., *polluted.*

נְוָלִי, נְוָלִי Ch. f., *dunghill.*

נוּלְדוּ Niph. pret. pl. with dag. euphon. for נוֹלְדוּ, from ילד.

נוּם *slept.*

נוּמָה f., *sluggishness,* Pro. 23:21.

תְּנוּמָה f., *sleep, slumber.*

נוּן. Niph. fut. יִנּוֹן (Ketib יָנִין Hiph. fut.) *drawn out, perpetuated,* Ps. 72:17.

נוּן p. n., *Nun,* the father of Joshua.

נִין m., *posterity.*

מָנוֹן m., *despiser,* Pro. 29:21.

נוּס I. *fled.*—II. *escaped.*—III. *passed away.* Pol. נוֹסֵס *drive away,* Isa. 59:19. Hiph. הֵנִיס *caused to flee, put to flight;* see נסס.

נִיס m., *fugitive,* Jer. 48:44; Kri. נָס.

מָנוֹס m. (with suff. מְנוּסִי).—I. *flight.* —II. *refuge.*

מְנוּסָה, const. מְנֻסַת f., *flight.*

נָתְוַסְרוּ, Eze. 23:48 for נִתְוַסְּרוּ Nith., from יסר.

נוּעַ (fut. יָנוּעַ).—I. *was shaken.*— II. *was disturbed.* — III. *wandered about.*—IV. *varied,* Pro. 5:6.—V. *staggered* (as one drunken).—VI. *moved* (as the lips), 1 Sa. 1:13. Niph. *was shaken;* fut. יִנּוֹעַ. Hiph. הֵנִיעַ.— I. *shook.*— II. *caused to wander,* πλάζειν.— III. *dispersed* (as fugitives), Ps. 59:12.

מְנַעְנְעִים m. pl., *a musical instrument,* allied to the tambourine; Vulg. "sistra."

נוֹעַדְיָה p. n. of men and women.

נוּף *have sprinkled,* Pro. 7:17. Hiph. הֵנִיף I. *cause to sprinkle,* Ps. 68: 10.—II. *shake to and fro.*—III.

lifted up the hand, over, and against, with אֶל.—IV. lifted up an instrument, with עַל.—V. presented an offering. Hoph. הוּנַף was offered, Ex. 29:27. Pil. נוֹפֵף beckons with his hand, Isa. 10:32.

נוֹף m., elevated situation; יְפֵה נ׳ beautiful for situation, Ps. 48:3; see also נֹף in מֹף.

נָפָה f.—I. a sieve, Isa. 30:28.—II. נָפַת דּוֹר p. n. of a city.

נֶפֶת f., elevated district, Jos. 17:11.

נֹפֶת f., dropping liquid, honey.

תְּנוּפָה f.—I. lifting up the hand, Isa. 19:16.—II. agitation, tumult, Isa. 30:32.—III. an offering.

נוּץ Hiph. הֵנֵץ blossomed; see נצץ.

נִיצוֹץ m., a spark, Isa. 1:31.

נוֹצָה crest; see נצה.

נוּק same as יָנַק. Hiph. fut. with suff. תֵּנִיקֵהוּ gave him suck, Ex. 2:9.

נוּר f. Ch., fire.

נֵר m.—I. a light.—II. prosperity.—III. p.n. of a man.

נִיר same as נֵר.

נִיר m., a light, metaph. prosperity, rank; see also in נִיר.

נֵרִיָּה p. n. of a man.

מְנוֹרָה f., the candlestick used in the Jewish ritual.

נוּשׁ be diseased, Ps. 69:21, same as אָנַשׁ.

נָזָה (fut. יִזֶּה יַזֶּה, וַיִּז), was sprinkled, with עַל and מִן. Hiph. הִזָּה (fut. יַזֶּה וַיַּז), sprinkled, specially with blood, with עַל.

נָזִיד; see זוד.

נָזִיר; see נזר.

נָזַל (fut. יִזַּל).—I. sank down, Jud. 5: 5.—II. dropped, dropped down; part. נוֹזְלִים flowing streams. Hiph. הִזִּיל caused to flow, Isa. 48:21.

מַזָּלוֹת f. pl., the planets, 2 Ki. 23:5.

מַזָּרוֹת a constellation; according to some from נָזַר the northern crown. Others read מַאְזָרוֹת a belt, the belt of Orion.

נֶזֶם m.—I. a nose-jewel.—II. an ear-ring, Gen. 35:4.

נְזַק Ch., suffered loss. Aph. caused loss.

נֵזֶק m., injury, loss, Est. 7:4.

נָזַר. Niph. נִזַּר I. restricted himself.—II. devoted him to, with לְ.—III. withdrew from.—IV. abstained from, with מִן. Hiph. הִזִּיר I. set apart to, with אֶת, אֶל.—II. restrained from, with מִן, אֵת.—III. devoted himself to.

נָזִיר m.—I. a Nazarite, one precluded by a vow from certain things lawful to others.—II. Gen. 49:26, applied to Joseph as separate from his brethren.—III. Lev. 25:5, 11, vines not pruned.

נֵזֶר m. (with suff. נְזְרֶךָ, נִזְרוֹ).—I. state of separation and dedication.—II. mark of such separation, specially the plate of gold in the high priest's mitre.—III. diadem.—IV. sovereignty, Pro. 27:24.—V. hair of the head, as shorn by the Nazarites, Jer. 7:29.

מִנְזָרִים m. pl., nobles, princes, Nah. 3:17.

נַחְבִּי; see חבה.

נָחָה (pret. with suff. נָחָם; imp. נְחֵה; with suff. נְחֵנִי). Hiph. הִנְחָה (fut. with suff. יַנְחֵנִי), *led, conducted, guided.*

נָחוּם same as רָחוּם p. n. of a man.

נָחוּם, נְחוּמִים see נחם.

נָחוֹר, נְחִירִים; see נחר.

נְחוּשָׁה, נָחוּשׁ; see נחשׁ.

נָחַל (inf. נְחֹל; fut. יִנְחַל).—I. *took possession of.*—II. *possessed.*—III. *took, received, as his portion.*—IV. *apportioned,* Nu. 34:17. Pi. נִחַל *gave settlement to.* Hiph. הִנְחִיל I. *caused to possess.*—II. *left as an inheritance to,* 1 Chron. 28:8. —III. *gave an inheritance,* Eze. 46:18. Hoph. הָנְחַל *was made to possess,* Job 7:3. Hith. הִתְנַחַל I. *took for himself.*—II. *left as an inheritance,* Lev. 25:46.

נַחֲלָה f.—I. *settlement, dwelling.*—II. *possession.*—III. *assigned portion, share;* נַחֲלַת יְהֹוָה *the Lord's portion,* i. e. Israel, his chosen people. —IV. *inheritance.*

נַחֲלָת f., *portion,* Ps. 16:6.

נְחִילוֹת f. pl. nom., *flutes* (root חָלַל), Ps. 5:1.

נָחַל Niph. pret., from חלל; also Pi. pret., from נחל.

נַחַל m. (dual נְחָלִים; pl. נְחָלִים, נַחֲלֵי; with ה loc. נַחְלָה).—I. *stream;* נַחַל מִצְרַיִם *the stream that divides* Egypt *and Palestine.*—II. *torrent.*—III. *valley.*

נַחֲלָה same as נַחַל *stream,* Ps. 124:4.

נַחֲלִיאֵל p. n., one of the stations of Israel in the wilderness.

נֶחֱלָמִי p. n., *Nehelamite,* a title.

נָחַם. Niph. נִחַם I. *was grieved, repented,* with עַל.—II. *pitied, felt pity,* with מִן, לְ, אֶל, עַל.—III. *pitied and withdrew an infliction,* with עַל.—אֶל—IV. *recovered from his grief,* with עַל.—V. אַחֲרֵי, עַל. *avenged, freed himself from one displeasing,* with מִן.—VI. *mourned over,* with אֶל or לְ, אֶל—VII. *changed his purpose,* with עַל. Pi. נִחַם *sympathised with, comforted,* with עַל, מִן. Pu. נֻחַם *comforted, appeased.* Hith. הִתְנֶחָם, הִנָּחֵם I. *comforted himself.*—II. *changed his purpose,* with עַל, Nu. 23:19. —III. *gratified his anger,* with לְ.

נַחַם p. n. of a man.

נֹחַם m., *pity, change of purpose,* Hos. 13:14.

נִחֻמִים, נְחֻמִים m. pl.—I. *consolations.*—II. *pity,* Hos. 11:8.

נַחוּם p. n., *Nahum* the prophet, Ναούμ.

נֶחָמָה f., *consolation.*

נְחֶמְיָה p. n. of a man, *Nehemiah,* Νεεμία.

נַחֲמָנִי p. n. of a man.

תַּנְחוּמִים m. pl., *consolations, comforts.*

תַּנְחוּמוֹת f. pl., the same, Job 15:11; 21:2.

תַּנְחֶמֶת p.n. of a man.

נִחַם pret. Niph. and Pi., from חמם.

נֶחָמִים Niph. part. pl., from חמם.

נַחְנוּ *we;* see אֲנִי.

נְחַנְתִּי Niph. pret. f. 2. pers. with parag., from חנן.

נָחוּץ part. נָחוּץ *urgent,* 1 Sa. 21:9.

נָחַר (Arab. *snorted*).

נַחַר m., *snorting,* Job 39:20.

נַחֲרָה f., the same, Jer. 8:16.

נַחֲרִי ,נַחֲרַי p. n. of a man.

נָחוֹר p. n., *Nahor*, the brother of Abraham.

נְחִירִים m. pl., *nostrils*, Job 41:12.

נִחַר Niph. pret., from חרר.

נָחָשׁ m.—I. *serpent*.—II. p. n. of a man.—III. עִיר נָחָשׁ p. n., a city in the tribe of Judah.

נִחֵשׁ Pi. (denom. from ὀφιομαντεία, *divination by serpents*).—I. *used divination*.—II. *watched, observed*.

נַחַשׁ m., *divination*.

נַחְשׁוֹן p. n., *Naashon*, the son of Amminadab.

נְחָשׁ m. Ch., *brass or copper*.

נְחֹשֶׁת com. (with suff. נְחֻשְׁתֶּךָ).—I. *brass*.—II. *chain*, Lam. 3:7; dual נְחֻשְׁתַּיִם *fetters, shackles*.—III. *money*, Eze. 16:36.

נְחֻשְׁתָּא p. n. of a woman.

נְחֻשְׁתָּן m., *the brazen serpent idolized*, 2 Ki. 18:4.

נָחוּשׁ m., *copper or brass*, Job 6:12.

נְחֻשָׁה ,נְחוּשָׁה f., the same.

נָחַת (fut. יִנְחַת ,יֵחַת) same as ירד.—I. *came down*, Job 17:16.—II. *came down violently*, with עַל.—III. *penetrated the mind*, with בְּ. Niph. נִחַת *penetrated* (of arrows), with בְּ, Ps. 38:3. Pi. נִחַת *brought down, levelled* (the bow), Ps. 65:11. Hiph. imp. הַנְחַת *depress*, Joel 4:11.

נְחַת Ch., *came down*. Aph. *placed*. Hoph. *made to descend*, Dan. 5:20.

נַחַת m.—I. *descent, lighting down*, Isa. 30:30.—II. *being placed*, Job 36:16; see also in נוּחַ.

נָחֵת m., pl. נְחָתִים *coming down* (of an army), 2 Ki. 6:9.

נַחַת p. n. of a man; same as חתת.

נְחַת Niph. pret., from חתת.

נָטָה (inf. const. נְטוֹת; fut. יִטֶּה; apoc. יֵט ,וַיֵּט ,(וַיֵּ.)—I. *stretch out, extend* (the hand, &c.).—II. *spread out, stretch, pitch a tent*.—III. *bowed, inclined*.—IV. *turn, lead to*, with אֶל ,אַחֲרֵי ,לְ; or *from*, with מִן.—V. *go, depart*, 1 Sa. 14:7. Niph. נִטָּה *stretched out*. Hiph. הִטָּה (fut. יַטֶּה; apoc. יֵט ,יַט; imp. הַטֵּה; apoc. הַט).—I. *stretch out*.—II. *spread out*.—III. *incline, bend down, lower*.—IV. *turn away, put away*.—V. *wrest, pervert*. Hoph. part. מֻטֶּה s., *wresting, perversion*.

מַטֶּה ,מַטָּה const. m. (f., Mic. 6:9).—I. *branch of a tree*.—II. *staff*; שָׁבַר מַטֵּה־לֶחֶם *he brake the staff of bread*, i.e. support, that on which life leans.—III. *rod*.—IV. *sceptre*.—V. *tribe, government*, of which the sceptre was a symbol; pl. מַטּוֹת. מַטָּה *downwards*; לְמַטָּה ,מִלְמַטָּה the same.

מִטָּה f.—I. *couch, bed*.—II. *bier* (for the dead), 2 Sa. 3:31.

נְטִיפוֹת *earrings*; see נטף.

נָטַל (fut. יִטּוֹל).—I. *lifted up*, Isa. 40:15.—II. *laid a burden on*, with עַל, Lam. 3:28. Hiph. *took up and removed*.

נְטַל Ch., *lifted up*.

נֵטֶל m., *burden*, Pro. 27:3.

נָטִיל m., *loaded*, Zep. 1:11.

נִטְמְתֶם for נִטְמְאתֶם Niph. pl., from טמא.

נָטַע (טַעַת).—I. (fut. יִטַּע; inf. נְטוֹעַ, נְטַעַת)
planted.—II. pitched a tent.—III.
set up an idol temple, Deut. 16:
21.— IV. drove a nail. Niph.
planted, Isa. 40:24.

נָטִיעַ m., pl. נְטִעִים planted, Ps. 144:
12.

נֶטַע m. (with suff נִטְעֶךָ; pl. נְטָעִים,
נִטְעֵי).—I. plant.—II. plantation.

נֶטַע const. נֶטַע m., plant, Isa. 5:7.

מַטָּע m., planting.

נָטַף (fut. יִטֹּף).—I. drop, Job 29:22.—
II. let drop. Hiph. הִטִּיף.—I. let drop
(water), Am. 9:13.—II. let fall (sen-
timents, prophetic declarations).

נָטָף m.— I. drop, Job 36:27. — II.
στακτή, myrrh, Ex. 30:34.

נְטֹפָה p.n., a town near Bethlehem;
נְטֹפָתִי a Netophathite.

נְטִיפוֹת f. pl., earrings or drops, Jud.
8:26; Isa. 3:19.

נָטַר (fut. יִנְטוֹר, יִטֹּר) watched,—1. for
good.—2. for evil, with לְ, אֶת.

נְטַר Ch., kept, Dan. 7:28.

מַטָּרָה (מַטָּרָא, Lam. 3:12) f.—I. cus-
tody, prison.—II. mark, object, butt.

נָטַשׁ (fut. יִטֹּשׁ).—I. left.—II. forsook,
God, a law, &c.—III. left.—IV.
ceased to think of, 1 Sa. 10:2.—
V. spread, scattered.— VI. drew a
sword, Isa. 21:15.—VII. allowed.
Niph. I. was forsaken.—II. spread
itself.—III. became loose. Pu. was
forsaken, Isa. 32:14.

נְטִישׁוֹת f. pl.—I. shoots of the vine.
—II. small towns, shoots of the capital, Jer. 5:10.

נִי בְּנִיהֶם an error for בְּנֵיהֶם, Eze. 27:
32.

נִיא (Arab raw).

נָא m., raw (uncooked), Ex. 12:9.

נִיבַי, נִיב; see נוב.

נִידָה, נִיד; see נוד.

נָיוֹת; see נוה.

נִיחֹחַ; see נוח.

נִין posterity; see נון.

נִינְוֵה p.n., Nineveh, a city of Assyria;
LXX. Νινευί.

נִינָם Kal fut. pl. 1. pers. with suff., from
ינה.

נִים; see נום.

נִיסָן m., the first month of the Hebrew year, called also אָבִיב, which
see.

נִיצוֹץ sparks; see נוץ.

נִיר light; see נור.

נִיר I. clear ground for cultivation.—
II. cultivate ground.

נִיר m., field newly cultivated; see
also in נור.

מָנוֹר m.; מְנוֹר אֹרְגִים weaver's beam,
1 Sa. 17:7; 2 Sa. 21:19.

וַנִּירָם Kal fut. pl. 1. pers. with
suff., from ירה.

וַנַּךְ, נַךְ Hiph. fut. apoc. pl. 1. pers.,
from נכה.

נִבְאוּ, see כאה.נִכָּא, נֵכָא, see נכה; נִבְאוּ.

נְכֹאת f., storax, Gen. 37:25; 43:11;
LXX. θυμίαμα; Aquila στύραξ.

נֶכֶד m. (with suff. נֶכְדִּי), posterity;
always with נִין, which see.

נָכָה Hiph. הִכָּה (imp. הַךְ, הַכֵּה; fut.
יַךְ, יַכֶּה; with ה parag. הַכָּה).—I.
struck.—II. wounded.—III. killed.
—IV. conquered. — V. taunted
(struck with the tongue).—VI.
struck the hands together.—VII

וַיַּךְ לֵב his heart smote him, 1 Sa. 24:6. Hoph. הֻכָּה, הוּכַּד was smitten, &c., pass. of Hiph. Niph. נִכָּה was wounded, 2 Sa. 11:15. Pi. inf. נַכֵּה ,נַכֵּה־ smiting. Pu. נֻכָּה smitten.

נָכֶה m.—I. נְכֵה רַגְלָיִם lame (smitten in the feet), 2 Sa. 4:4; 9:3.— II. רוּחַ נ' afflicted in spirit, Isa. 66:2.

נָכֶה m., pl. נֵכִים smiting (with the tongue), calumniators, Ps. 35:15.

נָכֵא m., f. רוּחַ נְכֵאָה afflicted, broken spirit, Pro. 15:13, &c.

נָכָא m., pl. נְכָאִים smitten, Isa. 16:7.

מַכָּה f. (pl. מַכּוֹת, מַכִּים).—I. stroke, blow.—II. wound.—III. slaughter. —IV. calamity.

נְכֹה, נְכוֹ p. n., Pharaoh Necho, king of Egypt; LXX. Νεχαώ.

נָכוֹן (same as כִּידוֹן), p. n. of a place.

נֹכַח I. straight forwards.—II. op- posite, over against.—III. in sight of; אֶל־נֹכַח towards; לְנֹכַח in front of, in behalf of, straight forwards; עַד־נֹכַח as far as.

נֶכַח (with suff. נִכְחוֹ) opposite to, against.

נָכֹחַ m. (f. נְכֹחָה; pl. נְכֹחוֹת).—I. straight forward, upright.—II. up- rightness, Isa. 57:2.

נֹכַחַת Niph. part. f., from יכח.

נָכַל withholding, Mal. 1:14. Pi. used artifice, with לְ, Nu. 25:18. Hith. the same, with בְּ.

נֵכֶל m., pl. נְכָלִים, נִכְלֵי artifices, Nu. 25:18.

כִּילַי, כֵּלַי m., avaricious, oppressive, Isa. 32:5, 7.

נְכַס root not used; same as כָּנַס.

נֶכֶס m., pl. נְכָסִים treasures, wealth.

נְכַס m. Ch., pl. נִכְסִין treasures, wealth.

כִּיס m., purse, bag.

נִכַּפֵּר Nith., from כפר.

נָכַר. Pi. נִכֵּר I. recognised.—II. con- sidered.—III. acknowledged.—IV. alienated, Deu. 32:27.—V. rejected, with בְּ, 1 Sa. 23:7. Niph. נִכַּר I. feigned himself unknown, Pro. 26: 24.—II. was recognised, Lam. 4:8. 11.—Hiph. הִכִּיר I. recognised, knew, acknowledged.—II. was par- tial in judgment, with פָּנִים.—III. beheld. — IV. regarded. — V. es- teemed, accounted.—VI. took judi- cial cognizance of. Hith. הִתְנַכֵּר make one's self strange, Gen. 42:7.

נֵכָר, const. נֵכַר m., strange, foreign, a foreigner; בֶּן־נֵכָר son of the stranger, foreigner; אֱלֹהֵי נֵכָר strange gods.

נָכְרִי m. (pl. נָכְרִים; f. נָכְרִיָּה, pl. נָכְרִיּוֹת).—I. foreign.—II. a stran- ger.—III. strange, singular.

נֵכֶר m., treating as a stranger, punishment.

הַכָּרָה (verb Hiph.) f., astonishment, consciousness of guilt, Isa. 3:9.

מַכָּר m., relative, neighbour, 2 Ki. 12:6, 8.

נְכֹת בֵּית נְכֹתֹה 2 Ki. 20:13; Isa. 39:2, treasury, γαζοφυλάκιον.

נָלָה root not used; (Arab. succeeded). Hiph. inf. with pref. and suff. כְּהַנְלוֹתְךָ for כַּנְלֹתְךָ when thou hast accomplished, Isa. 33:1.

מִנְלֹה possession, wealth, Job 15:29.

נִמְבְּזֶה despised; see בזה.

נְמוּאֵל p. n. of a man.

נָמַל (fut. יִמָּל; pl. יִמֹּלוּ).—I. circumcise, Gen. 17:11.— II. withered, Ps. 37:2; Job 14:2. (some derive it from מָלַל same as מוּל). Niph. נִמּוֹל was circumcised; part. נְמוֹלִים (some derive it from מוּל).

נְמָלָה f., ant, Pro.6:6; pl. נְמָלִים, Pro. 30:25.

נָמֵר root not used; (Arab. was spotted).

נָמֵר m., a panther, Jer. 5:6; Hab. 1:8.

נְמַר m. Ch., the same, Dan. 7:6.

נָמֵר Niph. pret., from מרר.

נִמְרֹד p. n., Nimrod, the builder of Babylon, Νεβρώδης; אֶרֶץ נִמְרֹד Babylon.

נְמָרִים p. n., same as בֵּית נִמְרָה, see בַּיִת.

נִמְשִׁי p.n., father of Jehu.

נֵס, נְסִי; see נסס.

נָסַבָּה for נָסַבָּה Niph. pret. fem., from סבב.

נָסַבָּה; see סבב.

נָסַג recoil shrink back; inf. נָסוֹג, Isa. 59:13; fut. יִסַּג, Mic. 2:6. Hiph. וְהִסִּיג I. remove a boundary.—II. carry away property, Mic. 6:14. Hoph. הֻסַּג was perverted, Isa. 59:14.

נָסָה imp. נַסֵּה; (see נשא). Pi. נִסָּה I. tried.—II. proved, made a trial.—III. found on trial, experienced.

מַסָּה f.—I. trial.—II. temptation by trial.

נָסָה Ps. 4:7, for נְשָׂא imp., from נשא

נָסַח (fut. יִסַּח) dispersed, scattered. Niph. was dispersed.

נְסַח Ch. Ith. was pulled down, Ezr 6:11.

מַסָּח m., disperser, driver away, 2 Ki. 11:6.

I. נָסַךְ I. poured out, Isa. 29:10.—II. melted.— III. anointed, Ps. 2:6.— IV. poured out a libation. Niph נִסַּךְ was anointed, Pro. 8:23. Pi. נִסֵּךְ and Hiph. הִסִּיךְ poured a libation.—Hoph. was poured out.

נְסַךְ Ch., Pa. made an offering, Dan. 2:46.

נָסִיךְ m.— I. libation. — II. molten image, Dan. 11:8.— III. anointed one, prince.

נֶסֶךְ, נֵסֶךְ m. (with suff. נִסְכּוֹ, נִסְכֹּה; pl. נְסָכִים).— I. drink-offering.— II. molten image.

נְסַךְ m. Ch., drink-offering, Ezr. 7:17.

מַסֵּכָה I. fusing; אֱלֹהֵי מ' molten images.—II. libation, Isa. 30:1.

II. נָסַךְ same as סָכַךְ covered, Isa.25:7.

מַסֵּכָה covering, Isa. 25:7; 28:20.

מַסֶּכֶת f. (Arab. he wove), web, Jud. 16:13, 14.

נָסַס raised, bore a standard, Isa. 10:18; 59:19. Hithpo. הִתְנוֹסֵם I. rally round a standard, Ps. 60:6.—II. raise oneself as a standard, Zec. 9:16.

נֵס m. (with suff. נִסִּי).—I. banner.—II. flag-staff.—III. sail.— IV. example, warning.—V. the leader to whom the banner belongs, Isa. 11:10.

נָסַע (fut. יִסַּע; inf. נְסֹעַ; imp.pl. סְעוּ)—I. departed.—II. travelled.—III. arose (a wind), Nu. 11:31.—IV. removed.— V. pulled up or out.

Niph. נִסַּע was pulled up. Hiph. הִסִּיעַ 1. caused to depart, &c.—II. made to blow, Ps. 78:26. — III. quarried stone, 1 Ki. 5:31.

מַסָּע m.—I. missile weapon, Job 41:18. — II. march, journey; pl. מַסָּעִים.

נָסַק go up, Ps. 139:8.

נְסַק Ch., go up. Aph. lifted up, Dan. 3:22. Hoph. was lifted up, Dan. 6:24.

נִסְרֹךְ p. n., Nisroch, an idol of the Ninevites.

נֵעָה p.n., a town in the tribe of Zebulon.

נֹעָה p. n. of a woman.

נֵעוֹר for נָעוֹר Niph. pret., from עוּר.

נְעוּרִים youth; see נַעַר.

נְעִיאֵל p. n., a town in the tribe of Naphtali.

נָעִים pleasant; see נעם.

נָעַל I. put on sandals, Eze. 16:10, lit. latch them.—II. bolted, latched the door. Hiph. fut. with suff. וַיַּנְעִלוּם shod them, 2 Chron. 28:15.

נַעַל f., shoe, sandal; dual נַעֲלַיִם pair of sandals; pl. נְעָלוֹת, נְעָלִים.

מַנְעוּל m., bolt, lock of a gate.

מִנְעָל m., defence, Deu. 33:25.

נָעֵם (fut. וּנְעַם) was pleasant, agreeable, with לְ.

נָעִים m.—I. pleasant.—II. sweet music.—III. amiable.—IV. becoming.—V. prosperous; pl. נְעִימִים.

נַעַם p. n. of a man.

נֹעַם m.— I. pleasantness.— II. kindness, grace.

נַעֲמָה p.n.—I. a town in the tribe of Judah.—II. the daughter of La-

mech.—III. the mother of Rehoboam.

נָעֳמִי p. n., Naomi, the mother-in-law of Ruth.

נַעֲמִי patron.; see נַעֲמָן.

נַעֲמָן m.—I. pleasantness, Isa. 17:10.—II. p.n. of a man.

נַעֲמָתִי p. n., Naamathite, a title.

מַנְעַמִּים m. pl., delicacies, Ps. 141:4.

נַעַץ (Arab. a thorny bush in the Hedjaz).

נַעֲצוּץ m., a species of thorn bush, Isa. 7:19; 55:13.

נָעַר I. roar as a lion, Jer. 51:38.—II. shook off, out. Niph. was shaken out. Pi. נִעֵר threw out. Hithp. Isa. 52:2, shake thyself, with מִן.

נַעַר m., straying, strayed (cattle), Zec. 11:16; see also below.

נְעֹרֶת f., tow, Jud. 16:9; Isa. 1:31.

נַעַר m. (with suff. נַעֲרֶךָ, נַעֲרוֹ; pl. נְעָרִים, נְעָרֵי).—I. infant.—II. boy.—III. youth.—IV. servant.

נַעֲרָה f.—I. girl.—II. young woman.—III. female servant.—IV. p. n. of a woman.—V. p. n., a town in the tribe of Ephraim, also נַעֲרָן.

נֹעַר m., childhood, youth.

נְעוּרִים m. pl., youth, early life.

נְעֻרוֹת f. pl., the same.

נְעַרְיָה p. n. of a man.

נַעֲרָן p.n., same as נַעֲרָה.

נֹף same as מֹף.

נֶפֶג p. n. of a man.

נֹפָה; see נוּף.

נְפוּשְׁסִים, נְפִיסִים, נְפוּסִים p.n. of a m.

נָפַח I. blew, blew upon, with בְּ.—II. blew a fire.—III. with נֶפֶשׁ expired; יֹגֵד נָפוּחַ seething pot, Jer.

15:9. Pu. נֻפַּח *was blown* (of a fire), Job 20:26. Hiph. *puffed at, despised.*

נֹפַח p. n., a town in Moab.

מַפֻּחַ m., *bellows,* Jer. 6:29.

מַפַּח m. מַפַּח נֶפֶשׁ מ', Job 11:20, *expiring,* "giving up the ghost," Eng. Ver.

נְפִילִים; see נפל.

נָפִישׁ p. n., *Naphish,* a son of Ishmael.

נֹפֶךְ m., an unknown precious stone; LXX. ἄνθραξ.

נָפַל (fut. יִפֹּל; inf. נְפֹל; with suff. נָפְלוֹ, נָפְלוּ).—I. *fell, fell down, was killed,* &c.; (נֹפֵל *one prostrate*).—II. *fell upon,* with עַל.—III. *fell to* (of an inheritance), with לְ.—IV. *fell on his face,* with or without עַל פָּנָיו, אֶל פָּנָיו.—V. *fell on* (was confined to) *his bed,* Ex. 21:18.—VI. *deserted to, joined,* with עַל or אֶל.—VII. *fell into the hand of,* with בְּיַד.—VIII. *perished,* Pro. 11:5, &c.—IX. *fell into a pit, mischief,* with בְּ, לְ.—X. נ' בְּעֵינָיו *sank in his own esteem,* Neh.6:16.—XI. נ' בְּנַחֲלָה *obtained an inheritance,* Eze. 47:22.—XII. *sank* (of the heart), 1 Sa. 17:32.—XIII. נ' אַרְצָה *perished.* Hiph. הִפִּיל I. *caused to fall.*—II. *killed.*—III. *annihilated.*—IV. *threw down.*—V. *divide* (by lot), Jos.23:4. with לְ.—VI. *knock out a tooth,* Ex. 21:27.—VII. *overcame.*—VIII. *cause to settle,* Ps. 78:55.—IX. *cast out, forsook.*—X. *threw into the fire,* with עַל or בְּ. Hith. I. *prostrate myself.*—II. *fell upon violently,* with עַל.

נְפַל Ch.—I. *fall, fell down.*—II. *prostrated.*—III. *was thrown down.*—IV. *descended,* Dan. 7:20.—V. *fell* (became needful) to one, Ezr. 7:20.

נֵפֶל, נֶפֶל m., *abortion.*

נְפִילִים m. pl., a tribe of the first inhabitants of Canaan, who were of gigantic stature.

נִפְלְאָתָה Niph. pret. f. with ה parag., from פלא.

נִפְלַל Eze. 28:23, probably an error for נָפַל.

מַפָּל m.—I. *that which falls out of the ear, the worst,* of the corn, Am. 8:6.—II. *pendulous, flaccid parts* (of the flesh), Job 41:15.

מַפֵּלָה, מַפָּלָה f., *ruins* of an edifice, Jeremiah only.

מַפֶּלֶת f.—I. *fall, ruin.*—II. *that which falls, leaf,* Eze. 31:13.—III. *carcase,* Jud. 14:8.

נָפַץ same as פּוּץ.—I. *broke, dashed down.*—II. *dispersed,* Isa. 11:12.—III. *dispersed itself.* Pi. same as Kal I., II. Pu. *was broken down,* Isa. 27:9.

נֶפֶץ m., *breaking forth, bursting.*

מַפֵּץ m., "*battle axe,*" Eng. Ver., Jer. 51:20.

מַפָּץ m., *bruising,* Eze. 9:2.

נְפַק Ch., *came forth.* Aph. *brought out.*

נִפְקָא Ch. f., *outgoings, expence,* Ezr. 6:4,8.

נָפַשׁ. Niph. I. *had breathing time, rest,* Ex. 23:12.—II. *rested.*

נֶפֶשׁ f., seldom m. (with suff. נַפְשִׁי; pl. נְפָשִׁים: const. נַפְשׁוֹת).

—1. *breath.*—II. *an animal* (that which breathes).—III. *a person;* שִׁבְעִים נֶפֶשׁ *seventy souls,* i. e. persons; כָּל נֶפֶשׁ *every one, whosoever.*—IV. *self;* נַפְשִׁי *myself;* נַפְשְׁךָ *thyself.* — V. נֶפֶשׁ מֵת *dead body, carcase;* טָמֵא לָנֶפֶשׁ טָמֵא נֶפֶשׁ *polluted by a dead body.*—VI. *livelihood,* Deu. 24:6.—VII. *the feelings, desire, inclination.*

נֹפֶת, נֹפֶת, see נוּף.

נַפְתּוּלִים; see פתל.

נַפְתֻּחִים p.n. of a people.

נַפְתָּלִי (*my wrestlings,* Gen. 30:8), p.n., *Naphtali,* the son of Jacob and Bilhah.

נֵץ *hawk;* see נצץ.

נָצָא, **נָצָה** *flew away,* Jer. 48:9; Lam. 4:15.

נָצַב. Niph. נִצַּב I. *stood.*—II. *was placed, appointed,* with עַל; part. נִצָּב *one set over, officer.* Hiph. הִצִּיב I. *placed.*—II. *set up.*—III. *fixed, appointed.*—IV. *set a trap,* Jer. 5:26.—V. *uphold,* Ps. 41:13. Hoph. הֻצַּב *set up,* Gen. 28:12.

נְצִיב m.—I. *pillar,* Gen. 19:26.—II. *garrison.*—III. *chief commander,* 1 Ki. 4:19.—IV. p. n., a town in the tribe of Judah.

נָצָב m. (part. Niph.), *handle of a knife,* Jud. 3:22.

נִצְבָּא f. Ch., *firmness, strength,* Dan. 2:41.

מַצָּב, const. מַצַּב m.—I. *standing place.*—II. *station, dignity,* Isa. 22:19.—III. *station, column of soldiers.*

מֻצָּב m. (part. Hoph.), *the same.*

מַצָּבָה, מַצֵּבָה f., *the same.*

מַצֵּבָה, const. מַצֶּבֶת f.—I. *pillar set up as a memorial.*—II. *image, statue of an idol.*

מַצֶּבֶת f.—I. *pillar.*—II. *monument.*—III. *stem, root,* Isa. 6:13.

נָצַג. Hiph. הִצִּיג *set up, make stand up.* Hoph. הֻצַּג *was stayed,* Ex. 10:24.

נָצָה. Kal *was laid waste;* fut. תִּצֶּינָה, Jer. 4:7. Niph. נִצָּה I. *excited to quarrel.*—II. *was stripped;* (part. pl. נִצִּים). Hiphil הִצָּה *was desolate;* see also נָצָא.

נֹצָה, f. affix נֹצָתָהּ *contents of a bird's crop, entrails,* Lev. 1:16.

נוֹצָה *a feather,* Eze. 17:3.

מַצָּה f., *quarrel, strife,* Pro. 13:10; 17:19; see also in מצץ.

מַצּוּת f., *the same,* Isa. 41:12.

נִצָּה *blossom;* see נצץ.

נָצַח Kal not used; (Arab. *was innocent*). Pi. נִצַּח *superintend, preside over;* part. מְנַצֵּחַ I. *leader, chief.* — II. *choragus, leader of music.*

נְצַח Ch. Ith. *superior,* with עַל.

נֶצַח, נֵצַח m.—I. *a title of God;* נ' יִשְׂרָאֵל *strength of Israel,* 1 Sa. 15:29.—II. *perpetuity.*—III. *success;* לָנֶצַח and נֶצַח I. *according to truth.* — II. *entirely, wholly;* לָנֶצַח, נֶצַח *continually, for ever.*

נֵצַח m., *juice of grapes,* Isa. 63:3, 6; (Arab. *sprinkled*).

נִצָּה (part. Niph.) f. נִצַּחַת *was perfected, finished.*

נִצְטַדָּק Hith. fut. pl. 1. pers., from צדק.

נְצִיב; see נצב.

נָצַל. Pi. נִצֵּל I. delivered, Eze. 14:14.
—II. plundered.—III. gained spoil,
2 Chron. 20:25. Hiph. הִצִּיל I.
delivered, rescued.— II. took away,
with מִן.—III. parted, with בֵּין—
IV. deliver himself. Hoph. part.
מֻצָּל rescued. Niph. נִצַּל I. was
delivered, escaped.— II. ran away
to, with אֶל. Hith. strip themselves, Ex. 33:6.

נְצַל Ch. Aph. rescued.

הַצָּלָה (verb Hiph.) f., deliverance,
Est. 4:14.

נָצַץ I. glittering, Eze. 1:7.—II. fled.

נֵץ m. (with suff. נִצּוֹ).—I. flower,
Gen. 40:10.—II. hawk.

נִצָּה f., blossom.

נִצָּן m., pl. נִצָּנִים flowers, Cant. 2:12.

נָצַר (fut. יִנְצֹר, יִצֹּר; inf. abs. נָצוֹר,
const. נְצֹר; imp. נְצֹר; with ה
parag. נִצְרָה; with suff. נִצְרָהָ—
I. guarded. — II. preserved from
evil.—III. watched.—IV. besieged,
shut up.— V. observed; נֹצְרִים
keepers.

נֵצֶר m., shoot, branch; (Arab. shone).

נָצִיר m., pl. const. נְצִירֵי (נְצוּרֵי) preserved, liberated.

נִצְרָה Kal imp. with ה parag. and dag.
euphon., from נצר.

נְקֵא white; see נקה.

נָקַב (fut. יִנְקֹב, יִקֹּב).— I. pierced.—
II. bored through.— III. bored a
hole.— IV. broke the head with a
staff, Hab. 3:14.— V. marked.—
VI. named.—VII. pronounced un-
fortunate.— VIII. cursed. Niph.
were marked by name.

נֶקֶב m.— I. holes bored in precious
stones, Eze. 28:13.—II. הַנֶּקֶב p.n.,
a city in the tribe of Naphtali.

נְקֵבָה f., female.

מַקֶּבֶת f., hammer

מַקֶּבֶת f.—I. hammer.—II. hole, shaft
of a well, Isa. 51:1.

נָקֹד root not used; (Ch. נְקַד mark
with spots).

נָקֹד m. (pl. נְקֻדִּים; f. נְקֻדָּה) spotted
sheep or goats, Gen. 30:32, 33.

נְקֻדָּה f., studs of silver, Cant. 1:11.

נֹקֵד m., shepherd, 2 Ki. 3:4; Am.
1:1.

נִקֻּדִים m. pl.—I. bread, Jos. 9:5, 12.
—II. cakes (probably pricked like
Passover cakes), 1 Ki. 14:3.

נְקוֹדָא p. n. of a man.

נָקָה inf. נָקֹה was pure, Jer. 49:12.
Niph. נִקָּה.—I. was innocent, clear.
—II. was made innocent, cleared,
with מִן.— III. was swept away,
devastated. Pi. נִקָּה I. cleansed.
— II. treated as innocent, freed
from punishment, with מִן.

נְקֵא Ch., Pe. part. נְקֵא pure, white,
Dan. 7:9.

נָקִי m. (pl. נְקִיִּים).—I. innocent.—II.
clear from guilt, an oath, &c., with
מִן.—III. exempt, 1 Ki. 15:22.

נָקִיא the same, Joel 4:19; Jonah 1:
14.

נִקָּיוֹן m.—I. innocency.—II. cleanness
of teeth, i. e. hunger, Am. 4:6.

מְנַקִּית f., pl. מְנַקִּיּוֹת bowls for drink-
offerings.

נָקַט same as קוט loathe, Job 10:1.

נָקַל Niph. pret., from קלל.

נָקַם (fut. יִקֹּם).—I. avenged, took re-

venge on, with מִיַּד, מֵאֵת, מִן, עַל,
לְ.— II. punished.—Niph. נִקַּם I.
revenged himself on.—II. was punished, with מִן, בְּ. Pi. נִקַּם I.
revenged, with מִן and בְּ. Hoph.
fut. יֻקַּם shall be avenged. Hith.
I. revenged himself. — II. part.
מִתְנַקֵּם desired vengeance.

נָקָם m., נְקָמָה f. (with suff. נִקְמָתִי;
pl. נְקָמוֹת).—I. vengeance taken
or inflicted; עָשָׂה לָקַח הֵשִׁיבנ'
took vengeance; נָתַן נְקָמוֹת let
vengeance come upon any one.—II.
punishment.—III. thirst for revenge, Lam. 3:60.

נָקַע (fut. יָקַע; see יָקַע) fell away,
was estranged from, Eze. 23:18,
22, 28.

נָקַף "חַגִּים יִנְקֹפוּ let them kill sa-
crifices," Eng. Ver., Isa. 29:1.
Pi. נִקֵּף I. cut down, Isa. 10:34.—
II. pierced, Job 19:26. Hiph.
הִקִּיף I. fixed, placed around, with
עַל—II. surrounded. — III. went
round a place, Isa. 15:8.—IV. came
round (of time), Job 1:5. — V.
shaved the head in a circle, Lev.
19:27; inf. הַקֵּף הַקִּיף.

נֹקֶף m., shaking of an olive tree to
make the fruit fall, Isa. 17:6; 24:13.

נִקְפָּה f., "a rent" (in a garment),
Eng. Ver., Isa. 3:24.

נָקַק same as נָקַב.

נָקִיק m., fissure in a rock.

נָקַר (fut. יִקֹּר) and Pi. נִקֵּר.—I. pierced
through.—II. pecked out (as a bird).
—III. put out an eye. Pu. dug out,
Isa. 51:1.

נִקְרָה f., cleft (of a rock).

נָקֹשׁ snared (as a fowler). Niph. is
ensnared, Deu. 12:30. Pi. spread
a snare for, with לְ. Hith. the
same, with בְּ.

נְקַשׁ Ch., struck each other (of knees),
Dan. 5:6.

נֵר, נֵר, נֵרִיָּה; see נוּר.

נֵרְגַל m., name of an idol, 2 Ki. 17:30.

נֵרְגַל שַׁרְאֶצֶר p. n. of an Assyrian
prince, Jer. 39:3, 13.

נִרְגָּן m., babbler, calumniator.

נֵרְדְּ m. (with suff. נִרְדִּי; pl. נְרָדִים),
spikenard, Cant. 1:12; 4:13, 14.

נָשָׂא (fut. יִשָּׂאוּ, יִשָּׂא, יִשָּׂא; inf. abs.
נָשׂוֹא; const. שְׂאֵת, שְׂאֵת, נָשֹׂא,
שׂוֹא; imp. שָׂא, נְשָׂא, נָסָא, שְׂא).—I.
lifted up: (a) his hand; (b) with
בְּ against; (c) beckoned; (d) lifted
up his voice; (e) lifted up his feet;
(f) lifted up his face, looked towards,
with אֶל; (g) lifted up his eyes;
(h) lifted up his soul (set his
heart on, paid regard, with נֶפֶשׁ);
(i) raised the head, elevated, with
רֹאשׁ; (k) took the sum of, examined
the case of, with רֹאשׁ.—II. took,
took up: (a) took into hand; (b)
took into the mouth; (c) uttered,
offered a prayer; (d) received a
precept; (e) took away, took hold
of, obtained.—III. נ' פָנִים accepted
the person, acted with partiality.
—IV. (a) נ' עָוֹן took away iniquity; (b) forgave (without עָוֹן,
with לְ of the person).—V. (a) carried, brought; (b) carried away;
(c) endured; (d) bore punishment;
(e) supported dignity; (f) assisted;

(g) *bore fruit, &c.;* (h) *supported,* with בְּ; (i) *laid upon,* with עַל; (k) *imposed an oath upon,* 1 Ki. 8:31; (l) *removed itself* (of the earth), Nah. 1:5. Niph. נִשָּׂא I. *was lifted up;* part. נִשָּׂא *lifted up.*—II. *raised himself.*—III. *was carried.*—IV. *was carried away.* Pi. נִשָּׂא, נִשָּׂא I. *took away.*—II. *presented a gift.*—III. *carried.*—IV. *assisted.*—V. *raised in rank,* Est. 3:1.—VI. נ' נֶפֶשׁ *set his heart.* Hiph. הִשִּׂיא I. *caused to bear.*—II. *brought,* 2 Sa. 17:13. Hith. הַנַּשֵּׂא, הִתְנַשֵּׂא I. *arose.*—II. *exalted himself.*—III. *was exalted.*

נְשָׂא Ch.—I. *carried away,* Dan. 2: 35.—II. *took,* Ezr. 5:15. Ithpa. *exalted himself,* Ezr. 4:19.

נָשִׂיא m.—I. *chief.*—II. *chief of a tribe* among the Israelites.—III. *chief of a subdivision of a tribe.*—IV. *prince.* — V. pl. נְשִׂיאִים *vapours.*

נְשׂוּאָה f., *burden,* Isa. 46:1.

נִשֵּׂאת (Niph. part.) *a gift,* 2 Sa. 19:43.

שִׂיא m., *elevation, dignity,* Job 20:6.

שְׂאֵת inf.—I. *lifting up, elevation,* Gen. 4:7.—II. *swelling in the skin.*—III. *exaltation, dignity.*—IV. *judgment, sentence,* Hab. 1:7.

שֵׂת same as שְׂאֵת *rising,* Job 41:17.

מַשָּׂא m., מַשָּׂא פָנִים *preference of persons,* 2 Chron. 19:7.

מַשָּׂא m.—I. *carrying.*—II. *a burden.*—III. *a load.*—IV. *that which is burdensome.*—V. *a tribute.*—VI. *calamity.*—VII. *lifting up the*

voice to sing.—VIII. *solemn declaration.*—IX. *prophecy.*

מַשָּׂאָה f., *rising of flame, burning,* Isa. 30:27.

מַשְׂאֵת f. (const. מַשְׂאַת; pl. מַשְׂאֹת). —I. *the act of lifting up.*—II. *a signal.*—III. *prophecy.*—IV. *gift.*—V. *tribute.*

I. נָשַׂג. Hiph. הִשִּׂיג I. *reached.*—II. *was able to reach.*—III. *attained, obtained, overtook.*—IV. *befel.*

II. נָשַׂג same as סוג. Hiph. הִשִּׂיג *removed* (land marks), Job 24:2.

נָשַׂק. Hiph. הִשִּׂיק *kindled a fire.* Niph. *was kindled.*

נָשַׂר root not used; (Arab. *saw*). מַשּׂוֹר m., *a saw,* Isa. 10:15.

I. נָשָׁא. Hiph. הִשִּׁיא I. *caused to err, led astray.*—II. *deceived,* with אֶת, בְּ, לְ.—III. *laid a burden on,* with בְּ. Niph. *was deceived.*

מַשָּׁאוֹן m., *deceit,* Pro. 26:26.

II. נָשָׁא same as נָשָׁה which see.

נָשַׁב *blew,* Isa. 40:7. Hiph. הִשִּׁיב I. *caused to blow.*—II. *dispersed,* as dust.

I. נָשָׁה I. *forgot.*—II. *neglected,* Jer. 23:39. Niph. the same, Isa. 44: 21. Pi. *cause to forget.* Gen. 41: 51. Hiph. הִשָּׁה *cause to forget,* Job 11:6; 39:17.

II. נָשָׁה, נָשָׁא *lent money,* Jer. 15: 10, with בְּ; נֹשָׁה, נֹשָׁא *creditor;* נֹשֶׁה *money lender.* Hiph. the same, with בְּ; fut. יַשִּׁיא.

נָשֶׁה m., *the ischiatic nerve,* Gen. 32: 33; (Arab. the same).

נְשִׁי m., *a debt,* 2 Ki. 4:7.

נְשִׁיָּה f., *forgetfulness,* Ps. 88:13.

מַשֶּׁה m., *debt,* Deu. 15:2.

מַשָּׁא m., *interest,* Neh. 5:7.

מַשָּׁאָה const. מַשַּׁאת f., *debt.*

נָשׂוּ for נָשְׂאוּ from נשׂא.

נְשׂוּי Ps. 32:1. for נָשׂוּא Kal part. pass., from נשׂא.

נָשִׁים *woman;* see אֶשָּׁה in אנשׁ.

נַשֶּׁה for נָשִׁים or נָשִׁם Hiph. fut. pl. 1. pers., from שׁמם.

נָשַׁךְ (fut. יִשַּׁךְ, יִשֹּׁךְ) I. *bit.*—II. *annoyed.*—III. *was lent on interest,* Deu. 23:20. Pi. *bit* (of a serpent). Hiph. *lent on interest,* with לְ, Deu. 23:20, 21.

נֶשֶׁךְ m., *interest.*

נִשְׁכָּה f., (pl. נִשְׁכוֹת for לִשְׁכָּה) *chamber of the temple* (book of Nehemiah only).

נָשַׁל (fut. יִשַּׁל; imp. שַׁל.)—I. *fell off.*—II. *pulled off a shoe.*—III. *drove out.* Pi. *drove out,* 2 Ki. 16:6.

נָשַׁם *snort;* fut. אֶשֹּׁם, Isa. 42:14; see שׁמם.

נְשָׁמָה f.—I. *breath.*—II. *life.*—III. *a human being.*—IV. *breath of God:* (a) *his anger;* (b) *the life he gives.* —V. *the wind.*

נִשְׁמָא f. Ch., *breath, life,* Dan. 5:23.

תִּנְשֶׁמֶת f.—I. *an unclean bird* (species uncertain), Lev. 11:18; Deu. 14:16.—II. *an unclean beast,* Lev. 11:30. (species unknown).

נָשַׁף I. *blew.*—II. *blew on,* with בְּ.

נֶשֶׁף m. (with suff. נִשְׁפּוֹ.)—I. *dawn.* —II. *evening, twilight.*—III. *darkness.*

יַנְשׁוּף, יַנְשׁוֹף m., *bittern;* LXX. ἴβιϛ.

נָשַׁק (fut. יִשַּׁק, יִשֹּׁק; imp. שַׁק, שָׁקָה.) —I. *kissed;* with לְ and אֶל *kissed each other.*—II. *adored,* with לְ.— III. *rule, order,* Gen. 41:40.—IV. *draw up in battle array,* with עַל. Pi. *kissed.* Hiph. *joined, touched,* Eze. 3:13.

נֶשֶׁק, נֵשֶׁק m.—I. *battle,* Ps. 140:8. —II. *battle array,* Job 39:21.—III. *arms.*—IV. *an armoury.*

נְשִׁיקָה f., *kiss.*

נֶשֶׁר (Arab. *eagle*).

נֶשֶׁר m., *an eagle.*

נְשַׁר m. Ch., *an eagle.*

נָשַׁת I. *was parched,* Isa. 41:17.—II. *wasted away,* Jer. 51:30. Niph. *dried up,* Isa. 19:5.

נִשְׁתַּוָּה Nith., from שׁוה.

נִשְׁתְּוָן m., *a letter.* Ch. the same (book of Ezra only).

נָתַב (Arab. *was lofty, raised up*).

נָתִיב m., נְתִיבָה f.—I. *path.*—II. *drift of a vein of metal,* Job 28:7. —III. *course of life.*

נָתַח. Pi. נִתַּח *divided, cut in pieces* (a slaughtered animal).

נֵתַח m., *joint, piece of flesh;* pl. נְתָחִים.

נָתַךְ (fut. יִתַּךְ) *poured out.* Niph. I. *was poured out.*—II. *was melted.* Hiph. הִתִּיךְ I. *poured out.* — II. *melted.* Hoph. הֻתַּךְ *be melted,* Eze. 22:22.

הִתּוּךְ (verb Hiph.) m., *melting* (metal), Eze. 22:22.

נָתַן (fut. יִתֵּן, יִתַּן; pl. נִתַּן, נָתַן; inf. abs. נָתוֹן; const. תֵּת, נְתֹן; with

ff. תְּתִּי ;imp. תֵּן, (תְּנָה).—I. *gave*
(as a present, in marriage, &c.).—
II. *gave forth* (produced fruit,
emitted odour, &c.).—III. *ascribed.*
—IV. *sold.*—V. *offered*, Lev. 20:2,
3, with אֶת.—VI. *placed*, with אֶל,
בְּ, לְ, עַל.—VII. *appointed.*—VIII.
imposed tribute, with עַל.—IX. *inflicted.*—X. *wrought miracles.*—
XI. *rendered like, considered as,*
with כְּ.—XII. *made, rendered,*
with לְ; מִי יִתֵּן; see מִי. Niph.
נִתַּן pass. of Kal.—Hoph. fut. יֻתַּן
shall be given, &c.

נְתַן Ch., *gave.*

נָתָן p. n.—I. *Nathan*, the prophet.
—II. the name also of a son of
David and of other men.

נְתַנְאֵל (*gift of God*), p. n. of a man,
Ναθαναήλ.

נְתַנְיָהוּ, נְתַנְיָה (*gift of the Lord*), p. n.
of a man.

נְתַן־מֶלֶךְ p. n. of king Josiah's cham-
berlain, 2 Ki. 23:11.

נְתִינִים m. pl., (*devoted*), *Nethinim,*
servants of the Temple, waiting
upon the Levites; Ch. נְתִינִין.

מַתָּן m.—I. *gift.*—II. p. n. of a
man.

מַתָּנָה f.—I. the same.—II. p.n. of
a place between Moab and the
desert.

מַתְּנָא f. Ch., the same.

מַתְּנִי (for מַתַּנְיָה), p. n. of a man.

מַתַּנְיָה, מַתַּנְיָהוּ p.n. of a man.

מַתָּת f., *a gift.*

מַתִּתְיָה, מַתִּתְיָהוּ p. n. of a man,
Ματθαθίας.

מַתִּתָּה p. n. of a man.

נָתַם *break down, cut off*, Job 30:13.

נָתַע. Niph. *broken down, cut off*, Job
4:10, for נָתַץ.

נָתַץ (fut. יִתֹּץ).—I. *broke down, destroyed.*—II. *ruined a person.*—III.
struck out teeth, Ps. 58:7. Pi.
נִתֵּץ *destroyed.* Niph. נִתַּץ, Pu.
נֻתַּץ and Hoph. הֻתַּץ *was destroyed.*

נָתַק I. *drew one away from* (a place),
Jud. 20:32.—II. *drew off* (a ring),
Jer. 22:24.—III. part. נָתוּק *cas-
trated*, Lev. 22:24. Niph. נִתַּק
I. *drawn away.*—II. *purged away,*
Jer. 6:29.—III. *broken* (of a shoe-
string, cord). Pi. נִתֵּק I. *removed,
took off*, Isa. 58:6.—II. *pulled up,
uprooted.* — III. *broke a cord.*—
IV. *broke off, frustrated*, Job 17:
11, &c. Hiph. הִתִּיק *drew away.*
Hoph. הָנְתַּק pass. of Hiph., Jud.
20:31.

נֶתֶק m., *scalled head*; lit. plucking
off of hair, Lev. 13:30 — 37;
14:54.

נְתַקְנוּהוּ Jud. 20:32, Kal pl. 1. pers.
with suff. and dag. euphon., from
נתק.

נָתַר (fut. יִתַּר), *beat violently* (the
heart), Job 37:1. Pi. *leap* (as
locusts), Lev. 11:21. Hiph. הִתִּיר
I. *loosened*, Ps. 105:20, &c.—II.
stretched out the hand, Job 6:9.—
III. *straightened*, 2 Sa. 22:33.—
IV. *made vibrate, caused to tremble*, Hab. 3:6.

נְתַר Ch., *fell off.* Aph. *shake off,*
Dan. 4:11.

נֶתֶר m.—I. *nitre, natron*, Pro. 25:20.
—II. *soap made of natron and oil,*
Jer. 2:22.

נָתַשׁ (fut. יִתּשׁ), with אֶת.—I. *ex-pelled.*—II. *destroyed.* Niph. I. *was expelled, destroyed.*—II. *failed* (of waters). Hoph. הֻתַּשׁ *plucked up* (of trees), Eze. 19:12.

נָתַתָּ, נָתַתְּ, נָתַתִּי, נָתַתָּה Kal pret., from נתן.

ס

סְאָה f., *a dry measure,* containing one third of an ephah, σάτον; dual סָאתַיִם; pl. סְאִים.

סַאסְּאָה f., *the same,* Isa. 27:8.

סְאָן, part. סֹאֵן *having greaves,* Isa. 9:4.

סְאוֹן m., *greaves* (armour for the legs), Isa. 9:4.

סָבָא *drank wine, became drunk;* part. סוֹבֵא *drinker* (pl. סוֹבְאִים Ketib, סָבְאִים Kri, Eze. 23:42).

סֹבֶא m. (with suff. סָבְאֵךְ).—I. *wine.*—II. *the act of drinking wine,* Nah. 1:10.

סְבָא p. n.—I. *the son of Cush,* Gen. 10:7.—II. *the people descended from him;* סְבָאִים *the Sabeans.*

סָבַב (pret. סַבּוֹתִי, סָבְבוּ, סָבֹּתִי; fut. יָסֹב; pl. יָסֹבּוּ; inf. סְבֹב, סֹב; imp. סֹב; part. סוֹבֵב, סֹבֵב).—I. *turned about.*—II. *made a circuit,* with אֶת, בְּ.—III. *reached round.*—IV. *surrounded,* with אֶת, עַל.—V. *ended a circuit at,* with אֶל or לְ.—VI. *an act overtaken in its consequences,* with אֶת.—VII. *circumvented, entrapped.* — VIII. *went round, examined in succession,* Ecc. 7:25.—IX. *arrived at a conclusion* (after going round), Ecc. 2:20. Niph. נָסֵב (fut. יִסֹּב; pl. יִסַּבּוּ).—I. *turn about, make a circle, surround.*—II. *returned.*—III. *came round in turn.*—IV. *was changed, changed, changed his conduct.* Pi. סִבֵּב *brought to pass,* 2 Sa. 14:20. Poel סוֹבֵב I. *made a circuit,* with עַל.—II. *surrounded,* with עַל. Hiph. הֵסֵב (fut. יָסֵב, יָסֵבּוּ).—I. *caused to turn about, make a circuit, surround.* — II. *changed his name to.* Hoph. הוּסַב *was turned round, enclosed.*

סָבִיב m.—I. *a circuit;* adv. מִסָּבִיב *around, from around;* סָבִיב סָבִיב *around.*—II. pl. סְבִיבִים *around.*—II. pl. סְבִיבוֹת *surrounding places, sub-urbs,* Jer. 17:26; 33:13; with suff. סְבִיבוֹתַי *around me.*

סֹבֵב for סֹבֵב Kal part., from סבב.

סִבָּה f., *change, turn in affairs,* 1 Ki. 12:15.

נְסִבָּה f., *the same,* 2 Chron. 10:15.

מוּסָב m., *the wall that surrounds a house,* Eze. 41:7.

מֵסַב m. (pl. const. מְסִבֵּי, מְסִבּוֹת).—I. *sofas for reclining on* (ranged round), Cant. 1:12.—II. *places surrounding.* — III. adv. *round about,* 1 Ki. 6:29.

סָבַךְ *wrapped, folded, coiled, entan-gled,* Pu. סֻבַּךְ.

סְבָךְ m., *thicket, tangled place.*

סֹבֶךְ m., pl. const. סִבְכֵי; *the same.*

סֹבֶךְ m., *the same;* with suff. סֻבְּכוֹ.

סֻבְּכוֹ with dag. euphon. for סֻבְכוֹ, from סֹבֶךְ.

סִבְּכַי p. n., *Sibbechai,* one of Da-vid's generals, 2 Sa. 21:18, &c.

שַׂבְּכָא, שַׂבְּכָא f. Ch., a certain musical instrument, σαμβύκη, of what kind is unknown, Dan. 3:5, 7, 10.

סָבַל I. carried (a load), Isa. 46:4.—II. carried (as a child).—III. bore consequences of. Pu. laden, Ps. 144:14. Hith. הִסְתַּבֵּל become a burden.

סְבַל Ch., the same. Po. brought, Ezr. 6:3.

סֵבֶל m., burden, task.

סַבָּל m., porter.

סֹבֶל m. (with suff. סָבְּלוֹ), burden, Isaiah only.

סַבְּלוֹ; see above.

סִבְלָה f., pl. const. סִבְלוֹת burdens, labours, tasks, Exodus only.

סִבֹּלֶת f. (in the dialect of the tribe of Ephraim, for שִׁבֹּלֶת), ear of corn, Jud. 12:6.

סְבַר Ch., hope, propose, Dan. 7:25.

סִבְרַיִם p.n., a city between Damascus and Hamath.

סַבְתָּה, סַבְתָּא p.n., Sabtah, one of the sons of Cush, Gen. 10:7, and the people descended from him.

סַבְתְּכָא, סַבְתְּכָה p.n., Sabtechah, one of the sons of Cush, Gen. 10:7.

סָגִים same as סִינִים; see סוּג.

סָגַד worshipped, with לְ.

סְגַד Ch., the same.

סָגַל root not used; סְגַל bought, acquired.

סְגֻלָּה f.—I. collection of valuables.—II. an object of special regard.

סָגָן m., pl. סְגָנִים.—I. chiefs among the Babylonians and Persians.—

II. chiefs among the Jews after the second captivity.

סְגַן m. Ch., pl. סִגְנִין the same.

סָגַר (fut. יִסְגֹּר).—I. shut a door, shut in.—II. closed a breach, 1 Ki. 11: 27, with בְּעַד, עַל; part. סָגוּר shut up; זָהָב סָגוּר pure gold, lit. such gold as is shut, hoarded up. Niph. נִסְגַּר was shut. Pi. סִגַּר, with בְּיַד delivered up, surrendered. Pu. סֻגַּר was shut up. Hiph. הִסְגִּיר I. shut up, with בְּיַד, אֶל, לְ.—II. delivered up; part. מַסְגִּיר.

סְגַר Ch., shut. Dan. 6:23.

סָגוּר m.—I. enclosure, Hos. 13:8.—II. refined gold, Job 28:15.

סוּגַר m., prison, Eze. 19:9.

סַגְרִיר m., rain, Pro. 27:15.

מַסְגֵּר (part. Hiph.) m.—I. confinement, prison.—II. joiner, i.e. closer.

מִסְגֶּרֶת f. (pl. מִסְגְּרוֹת).—I. inclosure.—II. border, moulding.

סָדַד root not used; (Arab. shut up).

סַד m., fetters.

סְדֹם p.n., Sodom, one of the cities of the plain, Σόδομα.

סָדַן root not used; (Arab. wool, covering).

סָדִין m.—I. fine cloth of Syrian manufacture.—II. a dress made of it, Isa. 3:23.—III. a piece of it used as a sheet, Jud. 14:12, 13.

סָדַר root not used; (Syr. set in order).

סֵדֶר m., pl. סְדָרִים ranks, orderly arrangement, Job 10:22.

שְׂדֵרָה f., pl. שְׂדֵרוֹת the same.

מִסְדְּרוֹן m., portico, Jud. 3:23.

סָהַר root not used (Samar. סהר), encompassed about, was round.

סַהַר m., roundness (like the full moon), Cant. 7:3.

סֹהַר m., בֵּית הַסֹּהַר prison, Gen. 39 & 40, only.

שַׁהֲרֹנִים m. pl., small moons (ornaments).

סוֹא p. n., Sevechus king of Egypt, 2 Ki. 17:4.

I. סוּג slid back from God. Niph. נָסוֹג (fut. יִסוֹג).—I. driven back.—II. induced to go back.

II. סוּג fenced, Cant. 7:3.

סוּג m. (pl. סְגִים, סִיגִים), סִיג, dross (of metals).

סוֹד, סוֹדִי; see יסד.

סוּחָה root not used; same as סחה cleanse.

סוּחַ p. n. of a man.

סוּחָה f., filth, Isa. 5:25.

סוֹטַי (see שׁוֹט) p. n. of a man.

סוּךְ same as נָסַךְ.—I. anoint himself.—II. anoint another, with בְּ. Hiph. anointed himself; fut. וַיָּסֶךְ.

אָסוּךְ m., vessel for anointing oil, 2 Ki. 4:2.

סוּמְפֹּנְיָה f. Ch., συμφωνία, a musical instrument, the hautboy, Ital. zampogna, Dan. 3:5, 15.

סְוֵנֵה p. n., Syene, a city of Egypt; (hierog. Soun).

סוּס m.—I. a horse.—II. a swallow, Isa. 38:14; Jer. 8:7.

סוּסָה f., horses, Cant. 1:9.

סוּסִי p.n. of a man.

סוּף come to an end, perish. Hiph. cause to perish.

סוּף Ch., came to an end, was completed. Aph. destroyed.

סוּף m.—I. end, termination, comple-tion, result.—II. rear of an army, Joel 2:20.

סוֹף m. Ch., the same.

סוּפָה f., whirlwind, tornado, with ה parag. סוּפָתָה.

סוּף m.—I. sea weed; יַם־סוּף the Red Sea.—II. p. n. of a man.

סוּר (fut. יָסוּר, וַיָּסַר).—I. went, turned aside, with מֵאַחֲרֵי, מֵעַל, מִן, אֶל.—II. went away, with מִן.—III. was removed.—IV. ceased.—V. rebelled against, with בְּ. Pil. סוֹרֵר turned away, Lam. 3:11. Hiph. הֵסִיר (fut. יָסִיר, וַיָּסַר).—I. removed, Lev. 1:16.—II. laid aside, gave up.—III. drew off (a ring).—IV. set aside.—V. destroyed. ה' רֹאשׁ מֵעַל cut off his head; ה' מֵאַחֲרֵי יְהֹוָה 'פ estranged him from following the Lord. Hoph. הוּסַר was removed, taken away.

סוּר m.—I. degenerate branch, Jer. 2:21.—II. p. n., one of the gates of the temple, 2 Ki. 11:6, called יְסוֹד in the parall. pass., 2 Chron. 23:5.

סִיר com.—I. a thorn; pl. סִירִים.—II. pl. סִירוֹת hooks, Am. 4:2.—III. pot, vessel; pl. סִירוֹת.

סָרָה f.—I. turning from God, rebellion.—II. ... from the truth, falsehood, Deu. 19:16; see סָרַר.

סִרָה p.n. of a well or tank, 2 Sa. 3:26.

סוּת. Hiph. הֵסִית, הִסִּית (fut. יָסִית, וַיָּסֶת, יַסִּית; part. מֵסִית) urged, excited, induced, with אֶת and בְּ.

סֻת, Gen. 49:11, wrong reading for כְּסוּת covering; see כסה.

סָחַב I. *drew along the ground*, 2 Sa. 17:13, &c.—II. *tore in pieces and devoured*, Jer. 49:20, &c.

סְחָבָה f., *tearing to pieces*; בְּלוֹי הַסְּחָבוֹת "old cast clouts;" Eng. Ver., Jer. 38:11, 12.

סָחָה. Pi. סִחָה *swept away*, Eze. 26:4.

סְחִי m., *offscouring*, Lam. 3:45.

שָׂחִים, סָחִישׁ m., *spontaneous produce*, that which comes without sowing, 2 Ki. 19:29; Isa. 37:30; LXX. αὐτόματα; Aquila αὐτοφυῆ.

סָחַף *beat down, crush*, Pro. 28:3. Niph. *beaten down*, Jer. 46:15.

סָחַר *travelled to a place*, with אֶל; *over a country*, with אֵת; part. סֹחֵר (pl. סֹחֲרִים) *traveller, merchant*; f. סֹחֶרֶת. Pil. סְחַרְחַר *was agitated* (the heart), Ps. 38:11.

סַחַר m.—I. *commerce*.—II. *wealth acquired by commerce*.—III. *seat of commerce*, Isa. 23:3.

סָחַר m., the same.

סְחֹרָה f., *seat of commerce*, Eze. 27:15.

סֹחֵרָה f., *tower*, Ps. 91:4; (Syr. *tower*).

סֹחֶרֶת f., *black marble* or *tortoise-shell* (uncertain which), Est. 1:6; LXX. πάρινος λίθος.

מִסְחָר m., *traffic*, 1 Ki. 10:15.

סֵטִים *sinners*; same as שֵׂטִים; see שׂוּט.

סִין *dross*; see סוּג.

סִין m., *name of the third month of the Jewish year*, Est. 8:9.

סִיחוֹן p. n.—I. *Sihon, king of the Amorites*.—II. *the district over which he ruled*.

סִין p. n., *a city of Egypt*, "Pelusium," (Jerome); probably Syene; Eze. 30:15, 16; see סְוֵנָה.

מִדְבַּר־סִין p. n., *the wilderness of Sin*.

סִינִי p. n.—I. *a people of Canaan*, Gen. 10:17; 1 Ch. 1:15.—II. אֶרֶץ סִינִים *the land of Sin*.

סִינַי p. n., *a mountain on the promontory between Egypt and Canaan*; its two summits are called *Sinai* and *Horeb*.

סִים Jer. 8:7, same as סוּס *a swallow*.

סִיסְרָא p. n., *Sisera, a Canaanitish leader, and other men*.

סִיעָא סִיעֲהָא p. n. of a man.

סִיר; see סוּר.

סָכַךְ I. *covered*.—II. *protected by covering*.—III. *placed as a covering*, with עַל.—IV. *compacted, put together*, Ps. 139:13; part. סוֹכֵךְ *defence*. Hiph. הֵסֵךְ I. *covered*, with עַל.—II. *protected*, with לְ.—III. *dressed himself*, 2 Sa. 12:20.—IV. *confined*, with בְּעַד. Hoph. הֻסַּךְ *was covered*, with בְּ. Pilp. סִכְסֵךְ *armed*, Isa. 9:10; 19:2.

סָךְ m., *multitude, crowd*, Ps. 42:5.

סֹךְ m. (with suff. סֻכּוֹ, סֻכֹּה), *thicket, hiding-place, dwelling*.

סֻכָּה f.—I. *thicket*, Job 38:40.—II. *hiding-place*, Ps. 31:21.—III. *hut* (of branches or wattles).—IV *dwelling*; pl. סֻכּוֹת I. *tabernacles*; חַג הַסֻּכּוֹת *feast of tabernacles*.—II. סֻכּוֹת בְּנוֹת, 2 Ki. 17:30, probably a proper name.—III. p. n., a station of the Israelites.— IV. a town of the Gadites.

סֻכּוֹת f., *shrine*, Am. 5:26.

סֻכִּיִּים p. n., *Sukkiims*, 2 Ch. 12:3, some part of the invading army of Shishak; meaning unknown.

סְכָכָה p. n., *a town in the tribe of Judah.*

מָסָךְ const. מֵסַךְ m.—I. *covering* (of tabernacle).— II. (with פָּרֹכֶת) *a veil.*—III. *curtain of a fortress*, Isa. 22:8.

מְסֻכָּה f., *covering*, Eze. 28:13.

מֵיסָךְ (מוּסָךְ) m., *covering, porch*, 2 Ki. 16:18.

סָכַל. Niph. *became foolish, acted foolishly.* Pi. *made foolish.* Hiph. *acted the fool.*

סָכָל m., *a fool, foolish.*

סֶכֶל m., *folly*, Ecc. 10:6.

שִׂכְלוּת סִכְלוּת f., *folly, book of Eccles. only.*

סָכַן, with עַל, לְ,—I. *was prosperous*, Job 34:9.—II. *was beneficial*, Job 15:3.—III. part. סֹכֵן *a companion, counsellor*; f. סֹכֶנֶת. Hiph. *was familiar with, accustomed to*, with עִם. Pu. part. מְסֻכָּן *poor, needy* (Arab. *was poor*), Isa. 40:20. Niph. נִסְכַּן *exposed himself to danger* (Ch. סְכַן *was in danger*), Ecc. 10:9.

מִסְכֵּן m., *poor.*

מִסְכְּנֻת f., *poverty*, Deu. 8:9.

מִסְכְּנוֹת f. pl. (same as מְכְנְסוֹת; see כְּנָס), *magazines, treasuries.*

I. סָכַר. Niph. *was shut.* Pi. (see סָגַר), *delivered up*, Isa. 19:4.

II. סָכַר same as שָׂכַר *hired*, Ezr. 4:5.

סָכַת. Hiph. הִסְכִּית *was silent*, Deu. 27:9.

סַל, סָלִים; סְלָא; see סלל.

סָלָא. Pu. *valued*, Lam. 4:2.

סָלַד. Pi. *harden oneself*, Job 6:10.

סֶלֶד p. n. of a man.

סָלָה *trampled on*, Ps. 119:118. Pi. the same, Lam. 1:15. Pu. *valued, estimated*, Job 28:16, 19.

סֶלָה a musical note, in the Psalms and the prayer of Habakkuk.

סָלַח (fut. יִסְלַח), *forgave.* Niph. *was forgiven.*

סַלָּח m., *one who forgives, is placable*, Ps. 86:5.

סְלִיחָה f., *forgiveness.*

סַלְכָה p. n., a town in the land of Bashan.

סָלַל *threw up an embankment, levelled, made a road.* Pilp. סִלְסֵל *exalt*, Pro. 4:8. Hithpo. הִסְתּוֹלֵל *opposing, exalting himself*, with בְּ, Ex. 9:17.

סַל m. (pl. סַלִּים) *basket.*

סִלָּא p. n. of a place.

סַלּוּ p. n. of a man.

סַלָּא, סַלּוּא p. n. of a man.

סַלּוּא p. n. of a man.

סַלַּי p. n. of a man.

סִלּוֹן a thorn, Eze. 28:24.

סַלּוֹן m., the same; metaph. *wicked man*, Eze. 2:6.

סֹלְלָה f., *a mound.*

סֻלָּם m., *a ladder*, Gen. 28:12.

סַלְסִלּוֹת f. pl., *baskets*, Jer. 6:9.

מְסִלָּה f.—I. *raised highway.*—II. *road, path.*—III. *terraces* (Lee).

"*steps*" (Gesenius), 2 Chron. 9:
11.

מַסְלוּל m., *highway*, Isa. 35:8.

סֶלַע m.—I. *cleft in a rock, cavern.*
—II. *rock.*—III. p. n. of a city,
perhaps *Petra* in Edom.

סָלְעָם m., a kind of *locust*, Lev. 11:22.

סָלַף. Pi. סִלֵּף I. *perverts.*—II. *over-
throws.*

סֶלֶף m., *capriciousness, perverseness.*

סְלִק Ch., *came up, grew up.*

סָלַת root not used; (Arab. *shelled
grain*).

סֹלֶת com., *shelled grain, fine flour.*

סַמִּים ,סַם; see סמם.

סַמְגַּר־נְבוּ p.n., a prince of Babylon.

סְמָדַר m., *flower* (of the grape).

סָמַךְ I. (with אֶת יָדָיו, עַל) *laid his
hands on.*— II. *supported.* — III.
pressed, weighed upon, with עַל, Ps.
88:8.—IV. *advanced towards,* with
אֶל, Eze. 24:2. Niph. I. *leaned
on.*— II. *trusted in.*— Pi. *support,*
Cant. 2:5,

שְׂמִיכָה f., *coverlet,* Jud. 4:18.

סְמַכְיָהוּ p. n. of a man.

סֵמֶל ,סֶמֶל m., *figure, form.*

סָמַם (Arab. *exhaled perfume*).

סַם m., pl. סַמִּים *perfumes.*

סָמַן. Niph. part. נִסְמָן "appointed"
Eng. Ver. (of barley), Isa. 28:25.

סָמַר *grew hard, rigid,* Ps. 119:120.
Pi. the same, Job 4:15.

סָמָר m., *rough, bristly* (of a locust),
ὀρθόθριξ, Jer. 51:27.

מַסְמְרִים ,מִסְמְרִים m. pl., *nails.*

מַשְׂמְרוֹת ,מַסְמְרוֹת ,מַסְמְרֹת f. pl.,
the same.

סְנָאָה p.n., a town of Judah.

סְנוּאָה p.n., probably of a woman,
Neh. 11:9.

סַנְבַלַּט p. n. of a Persian governor of
Samaria.

סְנֶה m., *the bush of Sinai,* Ex. 3:
2—4; Deu. 33:16.

סֶנֶּה p.n., a rock near Michmash, 1 Sa.
14:4.

סַנְוֵרִים m. pl., *blindness,* Gen. 19:11;
2 Ki. 6:18.

סַנְחֵרִיב p. n., *Sennacherib,* king of
Assyria.

סַנְסִנִּים m. pl., *the plume of the palm-
tree,* Cant. 7:9.

סַנְסַנָּה p. n. of a city of the tribe of
Judah.

סְנַפִּיר m., *fin of a fish,* Lev. 11:9;
Deu. 14:9.

סָס m., *clothes-moth,* Isa. 51:8.

סִסְמַי p. n. of a man.

סָעַד (fut. יִסְעַד; imp. סְעָד ,סַעַד,
סְעָד־; with ה parag. סָעֲדָה).—I.
was prosperous, Pro. 20:28.— II.
made prosperous, Ps. 20:3.— III.
supported.—IV. *cheered, refreshed,*
with לֵב.

סְעַד Ch., *assisting,* Ezr. 5:2.

מִסְעָד m., *prop, support,* 1 Ki. 10:12.

סְעָה ,סֹעָה רוּחַ סֹעָה *rapid wind,* Ps. 55:9.

סָעַף Kal not used; (Arab. *palm
branch*). Pi. סִעֵף (perhaps from
סְעִיף) *cut off branches,* Isa. 10:33.

סְעִיף m.—I. *cleft, cavern.*— II. *sect,
party,* 1 Ki. 18:21.—III. *a branch.*

סְעַפּוֹת f. pl., *branches,* Eze. 31:6, 8.

סַרְעַפּוֹת f. pl., the same, Eze. 31:5.

סָעֵף m., pl. סְעַפִּים persons of divided minds, Ps. 119:113.

שְׂעִפִּים thoughts of the mind (lit. branches).

שַׂרְעַפִּים m. pl., thoughts, Ps. 94:19; 139:23.

סָעַר I. was tempestuous, Jon. 1:11, 13, &c.—II. tossed by calamity, Isa. 54:11. Niph. was agitated (the heart), 2 Ki. 6:11. Pi. סֵעַר scattered, Zec. 7:14. Po. scattered, Hos. 13:3; see שָׂעַר.

סַעַר m., pestilential, violent wind, whirlwind.

סְעָרָה, const. סַעֲרַת f., the same.

סַף with pause. סָף m. (pl. סִפִּים, סִפּוֹת).—I. dish, bason, goblet, bowl.—II. threshold.—III. p. n. of a man.

הִסְתּוֹפֵף Hith. inf., remain at the threshold, Ps. 84:11.

סָפָא (Arab. filled).

מִסְפּוֹא m., provender, fodder.

סָפַד lamented, bewailed, with עַל, ל, לִפְנֵי. Niph. was lamented.

מִסְפֵּד, const. מִסְפַּד m., lamentation.

סָפָה I. came to an end, perished.—II. brought to an end, destroyed; inf. סְפוֹת increase, Nu. 32:14. Niph. נִסְפָּה was perished. Hiph. הִסְפָּה heap, accumulate (trouble), Deu. 23:23.

סִפֻּן; see ספן.

סְפוֹרָה; see ספר.

סָפַח admitted, 1 Sa. 2:36. Niph. was admitted, Isa. 14:1. Pi. poured out, Hab. 2:15. Pu. scattered, Job

30:7. Hith. הִסְתַּפֵּחַ obtained admission, 1 Sa. 26:19.

סָפִיחַ m.—I. pouring out of water, Job 14:19.— II. spilt, self-sown, grain; pl. סְפִיחִים.

סַפַּחַת f., a scar, scald, Lev. 13:2; 14:56.

מִסְפַּחַת f., scurf, scab, Lev. 13:6—8.

מִסְפָּחוֹת f. pl., cushions, pillows, Eze. 13:18, 21.

סִפִּי p. n., same as סַף.

סַפִּיר m., a sapphire.

סֵפֶל m., a bowl, Jud. 5.25; 6:38.

סָפַן I. covered.—II. secured, Deu. 33:21.

סִפֻּן m., ceiling, 1 Ki. 6:15.

סְפִינָה f., ship, Jon. 1:5.

סָפַף, הִסְתּוֹפֵף; see סַף.

סָפַק I. clapped the hands together.—II. smote upon the thigh.—III. expressed contempt for.

סֵפֶק m., abundance, sufficiency, with suff. סִפְקוֹ, Job 20:22.

סָפַר (fut. יִסְפֹּר) numbered, reckoned; part. סֹפֵר (pl. סֹפְרִים) writer, scribe, γραμματεύς. Niph. was numbered. Pi. סִפֵּר I. counted.—II. recounted.—III. talked. Pu. סֻפַּר was related, &c.

סָפַר m. Ch., scribe.

סְפָר m., enumeration, 2 Chron. 2:16.

סֵפֶר m. (with suff. סִפְרְךָ; pl. סְפָרִים, סִפְרֵי).—I. enumeration, Gen. 5:1.—II. register.—III. book.—IV. letter.—V. writing.

סְפַר m. Ch., book.

סִפְרָה f., book, Ps. 56:9.

סִפְרַת p. n. of a man.

סְפוֹרָה f., number, Ps. 71:15.

מִסְפָּר m.—I. number; אַנְשֵׁי מ' or
מְתֵי מ' few men.—II. narrative,
Jud. 7:15.—III. p. n. of a man;
מִסְפֶּרֶת the same.

סְפָר p. n. of a city, Gen. 10:30.

סְפָרַד p. n., a country into which
the Jews were carried, Obad. v. 20.

סְפַרְוַיִם p. n., Sepharvaim, a city of
Assyria; סְפַרְוִים Sepharvites.

סָקַל stoned. Pi.—I. as Kal.—II.
cleared of stones. Niph. and Pu.
was stoned.

סָרָב rebellious, Eze. 2:6.

סַרְבָּלִין m. pl. Ch., drawers, trousers,
Dan. 3:21, 27.

סַרְגּוֹן p. n., Sargon, king of Assyria.

סֶרֶד p. n. of a man; patron. סַרְדִּי.

סָרָה, סֶרֶה see סרר, סור.

סָרַח I. unconfined, loose, Ex. 26:12,
13, &c.—II. luxuriant (of a vine),
Eze. 17:6.—III. loose, dissolute,
Am. 6:4, 7. Niph. scattered, va-
nished (of wisdom), Jer. 49:7.

סֶרַח m., portion of a thing left loose,
Ex. 26:12.

סִרְיוֹן corslet, same as שִׁרְיוֹן; see שרה.

סָרִיס m. (const. סָרִיס; pl. סָרִיסִים,
const. סָרִיסֵי).—I. eunuch.—II. any
chief officer.

סָרְכִין m. pl. Ch., superintendants of
the whole empire, Dan. 6:3.

סְרָנִים, const. סַרְנֵי m. pl.—I. axles,
1 Ki. 7:30.—II. the name of the
five princes of the Philistines.

סַרְעַפּוֹת branches; see סעף.

שָׂרַף same as שָׂרַף. Pi. part. מְסָרֵף
burning, he who burns, Am. 6:10.

סַרְפָּד m., the name of an unknown
shrub; LXX. κόνυζα; Vulg. urtica.

סָרַר was perverse, refractory, Hos. 4:
16; part. סֹרֵר (pl. סוֹרְרִים; f.
סוֹרֶרֶת, סוֹרְרָה) perverse, rebellious
סַר m., סָרָה f., averse, disinclined, sad;
see also another סָרָה in סור.

סְתָה root not used; (Arab. winter).
סְתָו (סְתִיו) m., winter, Cant. 2:11.

סָתַם I. filled, blocked up.—II. repaired.—III. shut up, concealed.
Niph. was repaired, Neh. 4:1. Pi.
blocked up, Gen. 26:15, 18.

סָתַר concealed, Pro. 22:3. Niph.
נִסְתַּר I. concealed himself.—II.
was concealed, unknown.—III. was
sheltered.—IV. was distant.—V.
was excluded; part. נִסְתָּר hidden,
hidden thing; pl. נִסְתָּרוֹת hidden
things. Pi. hide, shelter, Isa. 16:3.
Pu. concealed, Pro. 27:5. Hiph.
הִסְתִּיר I. concealed.—II. sheltered
—III. placed for security, Isa.
49:2.—IV. turned his face from.
Hith. הִסְתַּתֵּר I. concealed, lost.—
II. hid himself.

סְתַר Ch. Pa. סַתַּר put out of sight,
destroyed.

סְתוּר p. n., a prince of Assher.

סֵתֶר m. (with suff. סִתְרִי).—I. secresy.
—II. secret place.—III. בַּסֵּתֶר
secretly.—IV. place of conceal-
ment.—V. place of security.

סִתְרָה f., shelter, protection, Deu.
32:38.

סִתְרִי p. n. of a man.

מִסְתָּר m.—I. ambush.—II. secret
place.

מִסְתּוֹר hiding place, Isa. 4:6.

ע

עֹב m., *epistyle, frieze* (in architecture), 1 Ki. 7:6; Eze. 41:25, 26; pl. עָבִים; see also עוּב.

עָבַד (inf. and imp. עֲבֹד; fut. יַעֲבֹד).
—I. *served* (God or man).—II. *worked, laboured.*—III. *tilled the ground.*—IV. *assented to,* 1 Ki. 12:7.—V. *performed a religious service.*—VI. *made to serve,* with בְּ of the person. Niph. נֶעְבַּד I. *became, was, served,* Ecc. 5:8.—II. *was tilled.* Pu. עֻבַּד *labour was imposed upon,* with בְּ. Hiph. הֶעֱבִיד I. *caused to labour.*—II. *caused to serve.*—III. *wearied,* Isa. 43:23, 24. Hoph. הָעֳבַד *was induced to worship.*

עֲבַד Ch.—I. *made.*—II. *performed, did,* with בְּ, עִם. Ith. *was made.*

עֶבֶד m. (with suff. עַבְדּוֹ; pl. עֲבָדִים).
—I. *slave, servant.*—II. *vassal.*—III. עֶבֶד יְהוָֹה *servant of the Lord,* i. e. one who worships and serves him, or executes some special commission for him.—IV. *a submissive epithet.*—V. p. n. of a man.

עֲבֵד m. Ch., the same.

עֹבֵד p.n. of a man.

עַבְדָּא p. n. of a man.

עַבְדְּאֵל p. n. of a man.

עַבְדּוֹן p. n., a city of the Levites in the tribe of Asher.

עַבְדִּי p.n. of a man.

עַבְדִּיאֵל p. n. of a man.

עֹבַדְיָה, עֹבַדְיָהוּ (*servant of the Lord,* 'Αβδίας), p.n., *Obadiah* the prophet and others.

עֶבֶד מֶלֶךְ p.n., an Ethiopian in the service of king Zedekiah, Jer. 38:7, &c.

עֲבֵד נְגוֹ (נְגוֹא) p.n., *Abednego,* one of the three holy children, Dan. chaps. I. II. III.

עֹבֵד m., *work,* Ecc. 9:1.

עֲבֹדָה f.—I. *servitude.*—II. *employment.*—III. *tillage.*—IV. *religious service, worship.*—V. *service required by the king.*—VI. לַעֲבֹדַת הָאָדָם *for the service* (use) *of man,* Ps. 104:14.

עֲבֻדָּה f., *slaves, gang of slaves,* Gen. 26:14; Job 1:3.

עֲבִידָא f. Ch.—I. *work, building.*—II. *worship, service,* Ezr. 6:18.—III. *business,* Dan. 2: 49 ; 3 : 12.

עַבְדוּת f., *slavery,* Ezr. 9:8,9; Neh. 9:17.

מַעֲבָּד m. (Heb. and Ch.), pl. מַעֲבָד *works, doings,* Job 34:25; Dan. 4: 34.

עָבָה *became large, thick, heavy.*

עֳבִי m., *thickness.*

עֲבִי m., the same.

מַעֲבֶה m., *thickness,* 1 Ki. 7:46.

עָבַט *gave a pledge;* fut. יַעֲבֹט. Pi. יַעֲבֹטוּן *break ranks,* Joel 2:7. Hiph. הַעֲבִיט *lent on security,* Deu. 15:6,8.

עֲבוֹט m., *pledge,* Deu. 24:10-13.

עַבְטִיט m., *accumulation of pledges* in the hands of an unfeeling usurer; "thick clay," Eng. Ver., Hab. 2:6.

עָבַר (inf. and imp. עֲבֹר; fut. יַעֲבֹר).
—I. *passed on.*—II. *passed away, ceased.*—III. *passed* a person, place, river, &c.—IV. *passed* a limit.—V. *trespassed, transgressed;* עָבַר

בְּרִית transgressed a covenant.—
VI. exceeded, went beyond.—VII.
overflowed, overwhelmed, with עַל.
—VIII. passed through, with עַל,
מֵעַל, עַל פְּנֵי, לִפְנֵי.—IX. passed
away, disappeared. — X. passed
through, with בְּ.—XI. entered into,
with בְּ; עִ' בִּבְרִית made a covenant.—XII. dropped (as liquid).—
XIII. כֶּסֶף עֹבֵר current money,
Gen. 23:16. Niph. can be passed,
Eze. 47:5. Pi. עִבֵּר I. conceived,
Job 21:10.—II. caused to pass,
1 Ki. 6:21. Hiph. הֶעֱבִיר I. caused,
allowed to pass.—II. removed, took,
or put away.—III. removed guilt,
&c.—IV. destroyed.—V. trans-
ferred.—VI. offered presents to
God or idols; ה' לַמֹּלֶךְ caused to
pass through fire to Moloch.—VII.
שׁוֹפָר ה' blew a trumpet, lit. caused
the breath to pass through it.
Hith. הִתְעַבֵּר allowed himself beyond proper limits, was angry,
with עִם, בְּ, עַל.

עֲבוּר (only with pref.), בַּעֲבוּר I. prep.
because of, in return for; with suff.
בַּעֲבוּרִי on my account; בַּעֲבוּרְךָ
because of thee.— II. conj. 1. for
the purpose that (בַּ' אֲשֶׁר לְבַעֲבוּר
the same).—2. because, while.

עֲבוּר m., produce of the ground, Jos.
5:11, 12.

עֵבֶר m.—I. ford.—II. mountain pass.
—III. passage over.—IV. banks of
a river.—V. side; אֶל־עֵבֶר towards,
on the other side; אֶל־עֶבְרוֹ sepa-
rately, alone; מֵעֵבֶר beyond, opposite to, across; מִכָּל־עֲבָרִים from
every side; עֵבֶר אֶחָד עֵבֶר אֶחָד

on this and on that side; עַל־עֵבֶר
אֶל־ פְּנֵי in front of it, Ex. 25:37;
עֵבֶר פָּנָיו forwards, Eze. 1:9, 12.
—VI. p. n., Eber, the grandson of
Shem, Gen. 10:24, 25, and pro-
genitor of Abraham, whose descendants were called from him;
עֵבֶר, בְּנֵי עֵבֶר Hebrews; הָרֵי or הַר
הָעֲבָרִים a range of hills beyond
Jordan.

עֲבַר Ch., beyond.

עִבְרִי m., a Hebrew; pl. עִבְרִים,
עִבְרִיִּים; f. עִבְרִיָּה; pl. עִבְרִיּוֹת.

עֲבָרָה f., raft, passage boat, 2 Sa. 19:
19.

עֶבְרָה f., any unrestrained feeling,
specially, anger.

מַעֲבָר m.—I. ford. — II. mountain
pass.

מַעֲבָרָה f., pl. מַעְבְּרוֹת the same.

עַבְרֹנָה p. n., a station of the Israelites.

עָבֵשׁ became shrivelled, worthless, Joel
1:17.

עָבַת Pi. confirm, establish, Mic. 7:3.

עָבֹת m., עֲבֻתָּה f., thick, entangled.

עֲבֹת m. (pl. עֲבֹתִים, עֲבֹתוֹת).— I.
thick branches, Eze. 31:3, 10, 14.
—II. cord, rope.—III. twisted chain.
—IV. obligation, restraint.

עָגַב (fut. יֶעְגַּב) loved, fell in love with,
with עַל, אֶל, Eze. c. 23.

עֲגָבָה f., love; with suff. עֲגָבָתָהּ, Eze.
23:11.

עֲגָבִים m. pl., the same, Eze. 33:31, 32.

עֻגָב, עוּגָב m., a musical instrument,
probably, the pipe, Gen. 4:21, &c.

עָנָה, עֲנָה; see עוּג.

עָגוּר m., crane.

עָגֹל (Syr. *turned round*).

עָגֹל m., עֲגֻלָה f., *round, circular*.

עָגִיל m., *ear-ring*.

עֵגֶל m. (with suff. עֶגְלְךָ).—I. *calf.*—
—II. *image of one.*—III. עֶגְלֵי
עַמִּים *princes, leaders, of the people*,
Ps. 68:31.

עֶגְלָה f.—I. *she-calf, heifer.*—II. p. n.,
one of the wives of David.

עֲגָלָה f. (with suff. עֶגְלָתוֹ, pl. עֲגָלוֹת
עֶגְלוֹת).—I. *waggon drawn by two
bullocks.*—II. *war chariot*, Ps. 46:10.

עֶגְלוֹן p. n.—I. *a city in the tribe of
Judah.*—II. *a king of Moab.*

מַעְגָּל or מַעְגָּל m. (pl. מַעְגָּלִים,
מַעְגְּלוֹת).—I. *wheel.*—II. *track of
a wheel.*—III. *way, path.*—IV.
way, manner.—V. *waggon.*—VI.
barricade of waggons.

מַעְגָּלָה f., *the same.*

עָגַם *despise.* Job. 30:25.

עָגַן. Niph. *prevented from marrying*,
Ru. 1:13.

עַד, see עֵדָה; עֵד, עֹד, see עוּד.

עָדַד (Arab. *numbered, computed*).

עִדִּים *menstruous*, Isa. 64:5; (Arab. the
same).

עִדָּן m. Ch.—I. *time.*—II. *a prophetic
period of time.*

עֵדָה; see יָעַד, עוּד.

עָדָה (fut. יַעֲדֶה).—I. *passed through*,
with עַל, Job 28:8.—II. *adorned.*
—III. *put on as an ornament.*
Hiph. *stripped off a garment*, Pro.
25:20.

עֲדָה עֲדָא Ch.—I. *passed upon*, with
בְּ.—II. *passed away*, with מִן—III.
was altered. Aph. *removed.*

עַד m.—I. *spoil*, Gen. 49:27; Isa.
33:23; Zep. 3:8.—II. *perpetuity,
eternity.*—III. *antiquity ;* לָעַד,
for ever; עַד (pl. עֲדֵי) pa. *unto, as far
as, until, before, while, during,
still;* עַד־אֲשֶׁר *while;* עַד־אָם
(שׁ־) *while;* עַד־אֲשֶׁר אִם *until;*
עַד־לֹא, עַד־אֲשֶׁר לֹא *before;* with
suff. עָדַי *to me;* עָדֶיךָ; עָדָיו,
עֲדֵיכֶם, עָדֶיהָ.

עַד Ch., *to, as far as, until;* עַד־דִּי
while.

עַד־הֵנָּה, Ecc. 4:3, same as עֲדֶנָה
hitherto, as yet.

עֲדֶנָּה Ecc. 4:2, the same.

עָדָה p. n., *Adah.*—I. *the wife of Lamech.*—II. *the wife of Esau.*

עֲדִי m. (with pause עֶדְי; with suff.
עֶדְיוֹ, עֶדְיֵךְ, pl. עֲדָיִים).—I. *ornaments.*—II. *trappings of a horse.*
—III. *lot, appointment*, Ps. 103:5.

עֲדִיאֵל p. n. of a man.

עֲדָיָהוּ, עֲדָיָה p. n. of a man.

עֲדִיתַיִם p. n., *a town in the tribe of
Judah.*

עִדּוֹ, עִדּוֹא p. n. of a man.

עֶדְנָת; see עוּד.

עַדְלַי p. n. of a man.

עֲדֻלָּם p. n., *a cave and city of the
tribe of Judah;* עֲדֻלָּמִי *an Adul-
lamite.*

עָדַן. Hith. *live luxuriously*, Neh. 9:25.

עָדִין, f. עֲדִינָה *luxurious, delicate*,
Isa. 47:8; (s. *smiting*, perhaps),
2 Sa. 23:8; a very difficult place,
see Ges. Thes.

עֲדִינָא p. n. of a man.

עֵדֶן m.—I. *pleasure.*—II. *Eden*, the
abode of our first parents.

עֵדֶן p. n., a district of Mesopotamia; בֵּית ע׳, see בַּיִת.

עֶדְנָה f., *pleasure*, Gen. 18:12.

עַדְנָא p. n. of a man.

עַדְנָה p. n. of a man.

מַעֲדַנִּים, מַעֲדַנִים, מַעֲדַנּוֹת pl., *delicacies, delights*; adv. *willingly*; מַעֲדַנּוֹת trans. for מַעֲדֹרוֹת *bands*, i.e. *influences*, Job 38:31; see עָנַד.

עִדָּן *time*; see with עַד.

עֲדְעָדָה p. n., a town in the tribe of Judah.

עָדַף I. *was superfluous*.—II. *exceeded*, with עַל. Hiph. הֶעְדִּיף *allowed to exceed*.

עָדַר *arranged, set in order*. Niph. נֶעְדַּר I. *was missing, left behind*.—II. *was dilatory, delayed*, Zep. 3:5.—III. *was cleared out*. Pi. עִדֵּר *omitted, neglected*, 1 Ki. 5:7.

עֵדֶר m. (with suff. עֶדְרוֹ; pl. עֲדָרִים, עֶדְרֵי).—I. *flock or herd*.—II. p.n., a town in the tribe of Judah.— III. p. n. of a man.

עֶדֶר p. n. of a man.

עַדְרִיאֵל p. n., *Adriel*, son-in-law of Saul, 1 Sa. 18:19, &c.

מַעְדֵּר m., *rake*, Isa. 7:25.

עֲדָשִׁים m. pl., *lentiles*.

עַוָּא, עַוָּה p. n. of an ancient unknown city; עַוִּים *the Avims*, either the inhabitants of this city, or the early settlers in Canaan.

עוּב. Hiph. הֵעִיב *treated as worthless, rejected*, Lam. 2:1.

עָב com. (pl. עֲבוֹת, עָבֵי עָבִים).—I.

cloud.— II. *covering*, Ex. 19:9; see also עֹב in its place.

עֵיבָל, עוֹבָל p. n. of a people descended from Shem.

עוּג *bake cakes*, Eze. 4:12.

עֻגָה, עֻגָּה, f., *cakes*, ἐγκρυφίας.

מָעוֹג m., *round cake of bread*.

עוֹג p. n., *Og*, king of Bashan.

עוּד *testified*, Lam. 2:13, Ketib. Pi. עוֹדֵד *surrounded*, Ps. 119:61. Hiph. הֵעִיד I. *called witnesses, to, for*, or *against*.— II. *called as a witness*, with אֵת and בְּ.—III. *made a declaration*. — IV. *enjoined, commanded, reproved*, with בְּ, עַל; הֵעִיד עֵדוּת בְּ *gave commandment to*, &c. Hoph. הוּעַד *information was given*, Ex. 21:29, with בְּ. Pil. עוֹדֵד *raised up, confirmed*, Ps. 146:9; 147:6. Hithpo. הִתְעֹדָד *stood upright*, Ps. 20:9, &c.

עֵד m.—I. *witness*.— II. *testimony*.— III. *proof*, עָנָה עֵד בְּ *gave testimony against*. — IV. *commander*, Isa. 55:4.

עֵדָה f.—I. *eye or ear witness*.—II. *proof*; see also in יָעַד.

עֵדוּת f. (pl. עֵדֹת, עֵדְוֹת).—I. *covenant*. —II. *the law*.—III. *the book of the law*. — IV. *the decalogue*. — V. *religious ordinance*, Ps. 122:4; אֹהֶל, אֲרוֹן הָעֵדוּת, לֻחֹת הָעֵדוּת *the tables, the ark, the tabernacle of the covenant*.—VI. Ps. 60:1; 80:1, the name of some unknown musical instrument.

עֹד, עוֹד I. *again*.— II. *besides*.—III. *still*.—IV. *any longer*; with suff. עוֹדֶנִּי I (am) *still*; עוֹדְךָ *thou (art)* still; עוֹדֶנָּה, עוֹדֶנּוּ he, she (is) still; עוֹדָם they (are) still, &c.; בְּעוֹד as yet, while, within; מֵעוֹד since; מֵעוֹדִי since I (am)).

עוֹדֵד p.n., Oded.—I. the father of Azariah the prophet, 2 Chron. 15:1, 8.—II. another prophet, 2 Chron. 28:9.

תְּעוּדָה f.—I. institution, custom, Ru. 4:7.—II. law, oracle, Isa. 8:16, 20.

עַוָּה עֲוִים p.n.; see עַוָּא.

עָוָה was crooked, perverse, did wrong, Est. 1:16; Dan. 9:5. Niph. נַעֲוָה I. bent with pain, Isa. 21:3.—II. bowed with sorrow, Ps. 38:7.—III. perverse in mind, Pro. 12:8. Pi. עִוָּה I. made crooked, Lam. 3:9.—II. overturned, Isa. 24:1. Hiph. הֶעֱוָה I. made crooked, Jer. 3:21.—II. perverted, Job 33:27.—III. walked perversely.

עַוָּה f., being overturned, Eze. 21:32.

עֲוָיָא f. Ch., iniquities, Dan. 4:24.

עוּגָּה for עֲוָה Kal imp. with ה parag., from עוז.

עָוֹן, עָווֹן m. (const. עֲוֹן; with suff. עֲוֹנָה; pl. עֲוֹנִים, עֲוֹנוֹת).—I. sin, iniquity.—II. guilt.—III. punishment.

עֲוִית p. n., a town of Edom.

עִי m. (pl. עִיִּים).—I. ruin, heap of ruins, heap.—II. עִיִּים p. n.—1. a part of Mount Abarim.—2. a town in the tribe of Judah.

עַי, עַיָּא, עַיָּת, עַיָּה p.n., a city of the Canaanites in the tribe of Benjamin.

עִיּוֹן p.n., a strong city in the tribe of Naphtali.

עִוְעִים m. pl., giddiness; Vulg. vertigo, Isa. 19:14.

מְעִי m., heap of ruins, Isa. 17:1.

עוז took refuge with, Isa. 30:2. Hiph. הֵעִיז I. took refuge, Isa. 10:31.—II. caused to take refuge, collected in a place of safety.

עֹז see עזז.

עוּט (Arab. dug into any thing).

עֵט m.—I. graver.—II. pen.

עוּל part. f. pl. עָלוֹת.—I. being with young.—II. suckling.

עוּל m., infant at the breast.

עֲוִיל m., suckling, Job 21:11; see also עוֹלֵל

עוּל. Pi. עִוֵּל acts unjustly.

עֲוִיל wicked.

עַוָּל m., one habitually unfair, unjust wicked.

עָוֶל עֶוֶל m.—I. unfairness.—II. injustice.—III. iniquity.

עַוְלָה f., the same; with ה parag. עַוְלָתָה.

עוֹלָה f., the same; with ה parag. עֹלָתָה; pl. עוֹלוֹת; see also in עֹלָה.

עוֹלֵל, עוֹלָל, עוֹלְלוֹת; see עלל.

עוֹלָם; see עלם.

עוּן (Arab. to live with).

עֹנָה f., conjugal rites, Ex. 21:10.

מָעוֹן m.—I. habitation.—II. refuge.—III. den of wild beasts.—IV. p.n.: (a) of a town in the tribe of Judah; (b) of a strange people, Jud. 10:12, &c.; (c) of a man.

מְעֹנָה, מְעוֹנָה f., the same.

מְעוּנִים p.n., the inhabitants of the city of Meon.

מְעוֹנֹתַי p.n. of a man.

עֲוֹעִים, עָוֹן; see עוה.

עוּף I. (fut. יָעוּף).—I. flew.—II. flew

away.—III. *flew upon* (as a bird of prey). Pil. עוֹפֵף I. *flew.* — II. *brandished* (a sword), Eze. 32:10. Hiph. *turned the eyes on*, Pro. 23: 5. Hithpo. same as Kal II., Hos. 9:11.

עוֹף m. collect., *birds.* Ch. the same.

II. עוּף (fut. וַיָּעַף) *fainted.*

עֵיפָה f.—I. *darkness*, Am. 4:13. (with ה parag. עֵיפָתָה *great darkness*, Job 10:22.—II. p. n.: (a) of a son of Midian and the people descended from him; (b) of a man; (c) of a woman.

עַפְעַפַּיִם const. עַפְעַפֵּי m. dual.—I. *eyelids.*—II. synec. *eyes.*

מָעוּף m., *darkness*, Isa. 8:22.

מוּעָף m., the same, Isa. 8:23.

עוּץ (imp. pl. עֻצוּ) *consult ye,* Jud. 19: 30; Isa. 8:10.

עוּץ p. n., a district of Arabia, Αυσῖτις.

עוּק. Hiph. הֵעִיק *presses, rushes*, Am. 2:13.

עָקָה f., *pressure, oppression*, Ps. 55:4.

מוּעָקָה f., *pressure, pain*, Ps. 66:11.

עוּר *aroused, awoke, arose* (imp. עוּרָה, עוּרִי *arise!*) Niph. נֵעוֹר I. *was awakened.* — II. *was raised to strike* (shoot), Hab. 3:9. Pil. עוֹרֵר. —I. *roused.*—II. *excited, stirred up.* —III. *raised a spear, scourge, cry.* Hiph. הֵעִיר I. *roused, excited.*—II. *awoke*, Ps. 57:9; 108:3. Hith. הִתְעוֹרֵר *awoke.*

עִיר m. Ch., *watcher*, probably an angel, Dan. 4:10, 14, 20.

עוֹר m. (pl. עוֹרוֹת) *the skin of man or animals*; עוֹר שַׁנַּיִם *skin of his teeth*, Job 19:20, i.e. *gum.*

מְעָרָה f., *cave;* (Arab. *went under ground*).

מְעוֹרִים m. pl., *nakedness*, Hab. 2:15

עֵוֵר. Pi. עִוֵּר *blinded.*

עוּר m. Ch., *chaff*, Dan. 2:35.

עִוֵּר m., עִוְרָה f.—I. *blind.*—II. *mentally blind.*

עִוָּרוֹן m., *blindness.*

עַוֶּרֶת f., the same, Lev. 22:22.

עוּשׁ *assemble yourselves*, Joel 4:11.

עוּת *aid, help*, Isa. 50:4.

עָוַת. Pi. עִוֵּת I. *made crooked.*—II. *perverted.*—III. *treated unfairly, unjustly.* Pu. part. מְעֻוָּת *bowed down.* Hith. *bowed himself*, Ecc. 12:3.

עַוְתָה f., *oppression*, Lam. 3:59.

עוּתַי p. n. of a man.

עֵז f. (pl. עִזִּים).—I. *goat.*—II. *she goat.* —III. pl. *goats' hair.*

עֵז f. Ch., the same, Ezr. 6:17.

עֵז, עָז, עָזָא, עַז; see עזז.

עֲזָאזֵל m. (lit. *goat of departure;* see אֵל) *the scape-goat*, Lev. 16:8, 10, 26; LXX. ἀποπομπαῖος.

עָזַב (fut. יַעֲזֹב). — I. *left behind.*—II. *allowed to remain.*—III. *went away from.*—IV. *forsook, neglected.*—V. *failed, allowed to fail.*— VI. *took away.*—VII. *gave loose to.*—VIII. with אֶל, לְ, *entrusted to, left with*; also with עַל. Niph. נֶעֱזַב *was forsaken, entrusted*, &c., with לְ. Pu. עֻזַּב *was forsaken.*

עֲזוּבָה f.—I. *ruins*, Is. 17:9.—II. p. n. of a woman.

עִזְבוֹנִים I. *merchandise.*—II. *a market*, Eze. c. 27.

עַזְבּוּק p. n. of a man.

עַזְגָּד p.n. of a man.

עָזַז (fut. יָעֹז ,וַיָּעָז; inf. עָזוֹז).—I. *was
strong*.— II. *prevailed.*— III. *considered himself strong*, Ps. 52:9.—
IV. *showed himself strong*, Ps. 68:
29. Hiph. הֵעֵז *made bold;* פָּנָיו ה'
or בְּפָנָיו *put on a bold face*, Pro.
7:13; 21:29.

עַז, with pause עָז m. (pl. עַזִּים; f.עַזָּה,
pl. עֻזּוֹת).—I. *strong.*—II. *harsh.*—
III. *strength.*—IV. עַז־פָּנִים *bold.*

עַזָּה p.n., *Gaza*, a city of the Philistines; עַזָּתִי *a Gazathite.*

עֹז, עוֹז עֻזִּי עָזִּי m. (with suff. עָזִּי ,עֻזִּי,
עֻזֵּנוּ).—I. *strength, power, might.*
—II. *ascription of power, praise*,
Ps. 8:3.— III. *source of strength,
refuge.*—IV. עֹז פָּנִים *impudence.*

עָנָה עֶנָא p.n. of a man.

עִזּוּז m.—I. *might of God.*—II. *might
in war,* Isa. 42:25.

עִזּוּז m.— I. *mighty,* Ps. 24:8.— II.
mighty men, Isa. 43:17.

עֶזֶן p. n. of a man.

עֲזַזְיָהוּ p.n. of a man.

עֻזִּי p.n. of a man.

עֲזִיאֵל p. n..of a man.

עֲזִיאֵל same as יַעֲזִיאֵל.

עֻזִּיָּה ,עֻזִּיָּהוּ (*the strength of the Lord*),
p.n., *Uzziah*, king of Judah; LXX.
'Οζίας; elsewhere עֲזַרְיָה; applied
also to other men.

עֻזָּיָּא p.n. of a man.

עַזְמָוֶת p. n. of a man; בֵּית ע' a
place in Judah or Benjamin.

מָעוֹז מָעוּז m. (with suff. מָעֻזִּי ,מָעֻנִּי;
pl. מָעֻזִּים) *place of strength, mu-
nition;* often applied to persons.

עָזְנִיָּה f., *the sea-eagle,* Lev. 11:13
Deu. 14:12.

עָזַק. Pi. עִזֵּק *digged,* Isa. 5:2.

עִזְקָא f. Ch., *engraved ring, seal,* **Dan.**
6:18.

עֲזֵקָה p.n., *Azekah,* a city in the tribe
of Judah.

עָזַר (fut. יַעֲזֹר; pl. יַעֲזֹרוּ; imp. with
suff. עָזְרֵנִי; pl. עָזְרוּנִי) *helped, assisted,* with אַחֲרֵי ,עִם ,לְ; part.
עֹזֵר *helper, patron, companion*
Niph. נֶעֱזַר *was holpen.* Hiph.
helped, 2 Ch. 28:23.

עֵזֶר m. (with suff. עֶזְרוֹ).—I. *help.*—
II. *helper.*—III. p. n. of a man.

עֵזֶר p.n. of a man.

עֶזְרָה ,עֶזְרָת f. (with ה parag. עֶזְרָתָה).
— I. *help.*— II. p. n. of a man;
same as עֵזֶר.

עֶזְרָא p.n., *Ezra;* LXX. Ἔσδρας.

עַזּוּר ,עַזּוּר p. n. of a man.

עֲזַזְאֵל p.n. of a man.

עֲזָרָה f.—I. *court of the temple.*—II.
border, moulding.

עֶזְרִי p.n. of a man.

עַזְרִיאֵל p.n. of a man.

עֲזַרְיָהוּ ,עֲזַרְיָה p.n., *Azariah.*—I. king
of Judah; called also עֻזִּיָּה.—II.
used also for other men.

עַזְרִיקָם p.n. of a man.

עָט, see עוּט; עָטָא, see יעט.

עָטָה I. *put on, wore.* — II. *covered,*
with עַל.—III. *invested.*—IV. *took
possession of, invested with,* Jer.
43:12. with אֶת. Hiph. הֶעֱטָה
placed as a covering, Ps. 89:46,
with עַל.

מַעֲטֶה m., *garment* (of praise), Isa
61:3.

עֲטַלֵּף m., bat. Lev. 11 : 19; Isa. 2 : 20.

עֲטַן (Arab. prepared skin).

עֲטִין m., pl. עֲטִינִים water or milk skin, Job 21 : 24.

עָטַף (fut. יַעֲטֹף).—I. covered, with לְ.—II. covered himself.—III. covered his face, was exhausted; párt. עָטוּף worn out, weak. Niph. was exhausted, Lam. 2 : 11. Hiph. הֶעֱטִיף the same, Gen. 30 : 42. Hith. הִתְעַטֵּף the same.

מַעֲטָפָה f., mantle, Isa. 3 : 22.

עָטַר I. surrounded.—II. covered, Ps. 5 : 13. Pi. עִטֵּר I. crowned, Cant. 3 : 11.—II. adorned, blessed, with לְ. Hiph. part. f. מַעֲטִירָה giving crowns, Isa. 23 : 8.

עֲטָרָה (const. עֲטֶרֶת; pl. עֲטָרוֹת) f.—I. crown, royal diadem.—II. p. n. of a woman.

עֲטָרוֹת p. n., a city in the tribe of Gad; עֲטָרוֹת אַדָּר and עֲטָרוֹת a city in the tribe of Ephraim; ע׳ בֵּית יוֹאָב a place in Judah; ע׳ שׁוֹפָן a place in Gad.

עָטַשׁ (Arab. sneezed).

עֲטִישָׁה f., sneezing, Job 41 : 10.

עִיּוּת, עִיּוֹן, עַיָּא, עַיָּה, עַיִּים, עִי, עַי; see עוה.

עֵיבָל p. n.—I. same as עוֹבָל.—II. a rock in the northern range of Mount Ephraim; LXX. Γαιβάλ.

עִיט I. was angry with, with בְּ.—II. rushed on with anger, pounced on, with אֶל; fut. וַיַּעַט.

עַיִט, const. עֵיט m., rapacious bird or beast.

עֵיטָם p. n., a town and hill in the tribe of Judah.

עֵילוֹם same as עוֹלָם; see עלם.

עִילַי p. n., one of David's generals.

עֵילָם p. n., a people and district, situation uncertain; עֵלְמָיֵא pl. Ch., the Elamites.

עַיִם m., drought, Isa. 11 : 15.

עַיִן f. (const. עֵין; with suff. עֵינוֹ; dual עֵינַיִם).—I. an eye.—II. the sight.—III. the judgment.—IV. appearance in the eye.—V. עֵינַיִם outward appearance, 1 Sa. 16 : 7; בְּעֵינֵי in the sight of; לְעֵינֵי פ׳ in the judgment of; מֵעֵינֵי without the knowledge of; בֵּין עֵינַיִם between the eyes, on the forehead; עַיִן בְּעַיִן eye to eye.—VI. fountain, spring; with ה parag. עֵינָה to the fountain; pl. עֵינוֹת, const. עֵינוֹת hence many p. n.:—I. עַיִן a town of the Levites in the tribe of Simeon.—II. a town in the north of Canaan.—III. עֵינַיִם a town of Judah.—IV. עֵין גֶּדִי a town of Judah.—V. עֵין גַּנִּים a town of Judah.—VI. a town of Issachar.—VII. עֵין דּוֹר, עֵין דֹּאר a town of the Manassites.—VIII. עֵין חַדָּה a town of Issachar.—IX. עֵין חָצוֹר a town of Naphtali.—X. עֵין חֲרֹד a well near the town of Charod.—XI. עֵין מִשְׁפָּט a well in Kadesh.—XII. עֵין עֶגְלַיִם a town of Moab.—XIII. עֵין רֹגֵל a well on the confines of Judah and Benjamin.—XIV. עֵין רִמּוֹן a town in the tribe of Judah.—XV. עֵין שֶׁמֶשׁ a town on the confines of Judah and

Benjamin.—XVI. עֵין תַּנִּים a well near Jerusalem.—XVII. עֵין תַּפּוּחַ a town of Manasseh.

עַיִן com. Ch., *eye.*

עֵין m., *watching with an evil eye,* 1 Sa. 18:9.

עֵינָן p. n. of a man.

מַעְיָן m. (with ו parag. מַעְיָנוֹ; with suff. מַעְיָנוֹ; pl. מַעְיָנִים, מַעְיְנֵי, מַעְיָנוֹת, מַעְיְנוֹת) *fountain, well of water.*

עָיֵף *is weary,* Jer. 4:31; וַיַּעַף, see עוף.

עָיֵף m., עֲיֵפָה f. — I. *weary.* — II. *parched.*

עֵיפִי p. n. of a man.

עֵיפָה *darkness;* see עוף.

עַיִר m. (with suff. עִירֹה; pl. עֲיָרִים). —I. *ass.*—II. *young ass.*

עִיר m.—I. *heat, anger, fear,* Ps. 73: 20; Jer. 15:8; Hos. 7:4; 11:9; (Ges.)—II. *a city, town, settlement;* עִירָה *towards the city;* pl. עֲיָרִים; see next word.

עָר m.—I. *an enemy.*—II. *city;* pl. עָרִים; עָר־מוֹאָב *Ar of Moab,* otherwise *Rabbah,* the chief city of Moab.

עָר m. Ch., *an enemy.*

עִיר Ch.; see עוּר.

עִירָא p. n. of a man.

עִירוּ p. n. of a man.

עִירָם p. n., a prince of Edom.

עִירָד p. n. of a man.

עֵירֹם, עֵירֻמִּים; see ערם.

עַיִשׁ; see עָשׁ.

עַיִת same as עִי; see עוה.

עַכָּבִישׁ m., *a spider.*

עַכְבָּר *the jerboa;* "dipus jaculus" (Linn.)

עַכְבּוֹר p. n. of a man.

עַכּוֹ p. n., a city in the tribe of Asher, Ακη, "Ptolemais."

עָכָן (עָכָר) p. n. of a man.

עֶכֶס m.—I. *fetter,* Pro. 7:22.—II. pl. עֲכָסִים *anklets, rings for the feet,* Isa. 3:18.

עָכַס, Pi. *wear anklets,* Isa. 3:16.

עַכְסָה p. n., the daughter of Caleb.

עָכַר (fut. with suff. יַעְכָּרֶךָ) *caused sorrow, vexation, disgrace.* Niph. נֶעְכָּר *was irritated, excited.*

עָכוֹר p. n., a valley near Jericho.

עַכְרָן p. n. of a man.

עַכְשׁוּב m., *an asp,* Ps. 140:4.

עַלָּא, עַל, עַל, see עלה.

עֶלָּא, עֶלָּא, עַל; see עלל.

עִלֵּג m., *foreigner, stammerer,* Isa. 32:4.

עָלָה (fut. יַעֲלֶה; apoc. יַעַל) const. with בְּ, לְ, אֶל, עַל.—I. *went up, came up.*—II. *arose* (of the dawn).—III. *grew up, grew.*—IV. *increased.*—V. *produced,* Pro. 24:31.—VI. *was put upon.* Niph. נַעֲלָה I. *is exalted* (God).—II. *was lifted up,* Eze. 9:3.—III. *was led away,* 2 Sa. 2:27.—IV. *was taken up,* Eze. 36: 3. Hiph. הֶעֱלָה, הֶעֱלָה (pret. הַעֲלִיתָ, הֶעֱלִיתָ; imp. apoc. הַעַל; fut. יַעֲלֶה; apoc. יַעַל).—I. *caused to go up.* — II. *offered a burnt-offering.*—III. *placed a thing on another.*—IV. *placed, set up,* Nu. 8:2. Hoph. הֹעֲלָה I. *was offered,* Jud. 6:28.—II. *was brought up,*

Nah. 2:8.— III. *was placed upon,
inscribed,* 2 Chron. 20:34. Hith.
fut. apoc. יִתְעָל *lifts up himself,*
Jer. 51:3.

עַל m., *the Lofty One, the Most High;*
adv. *on high,* 2 Sa. 23:1; מֵעַל I.
from above, Gen. 27:39; 49:25.
—II. *above,* Ps. 50:4, &c.

עַל, עֲלֵי; (with suff. עָלַי, עָלֶיךָ, עָלָיו;
(עֲלֵיהֶם, עֲלֵיכֶם, עֲלֵיהֶם, עָלֵימוֹ)
prep. (ὑπὲρ, ἐπί).—I. *upon, on.*—II.
above, over.—III. *beside, near, before.*—IV. *besides, over and above.*
— V. *in reference to, towards,
against.*— VI. *for, on account of,
in behalf of;* עָלַי לָתֵת *it is mine
to give* (the kingdom); חָיָה עַל,
ζῆν ἐπὶ, *live by* (bread), Deu. 8:3.
מֵעַל (with suff. מֵעָלֶיךָ, מֵעָלָיו,
מֵעֲלֵיכֶם, &c.).—I. *from upon.*—II.
from above.—III. *above.*

עַל Ch. same as Heb., *upon, above,
besides, for.*

עֵלָּא Ch., with מִן *above,* Dan. 6:3.

עָלֶה, const. עֲלֵה m. (with suff. עָלֵהוּ;
pl. const. עֲלֵי).— I. *leaf.*— II. *foliage.*

עוֹלָה, עֹלָה f.—I. *a step.*—II. *a burnt-
offering.*

עֲלָתָא f. Ch., *burnt-offering.*

עִלִּי, f. עִלִּית *upper,* Jos. 15:19; Jud.
1:15; pl. עִלִּיֹת.

עִלִּי m. Ch.— I. *high, supreme* (of
God).—II. *the Most High.*

עִלִּית f. Ch., *upper room, chamber,*
Dan. 6:11.

עֵלִי p.n., *Eli,* Ἡλὶ, the priest.

עֱלִי m., *pestle,* Pro. 27:22.

עֲלִיָּה f.— I. *upper room, chamber.*—
II. *ascent, staircase,* 2 Chron. 9:4.

עֶלְיוֹן m., עֶלְיוֹנָה f.— I. *lofty.*— II.
higher, upper (in place).—III. *high*
(in rank).— IV. *the Supreme, the
Most High* (of God).

עֶלְיוֹן m. Ch., *the Most High.*

מַעֲלֶה m.—I. *ascent.*—II. *mount.*

מַעַל m., with מַעֲלָה ה — I. *over
against, near,* Isa. 6:2, &c.— II.
above; לְמַעֲלָה *upwards, onwards,
over, above;* מִלְמַעֲלָה *from above,
upward;* מִמַּעַל *from above,* with
לְ *over, above.*

מֹעַל m., *elevating, lifting up of,* Neh.
8:6.

מַעֲלָה f.—I. *ascent.*—II. *step of stairs.*
—III. *graduated face of a sun-
dial.*—IV. *mental suggestions,* Ezr.
7:9.—V. an unknown title of some
of the Psalms.

תְּעָלָה f.— I. *channel for water.*— II.
recovery from illness, Jer. 30:13;
46:11.

עַלְוָה f.—I. same as עוֹלָה.—II. p.n., a
tribe of the Edomites.

עֲלוּמִים *youth;* see עֶלֶם.

עַלְיָן, עַלְוָן p.n. of an Edomite.

עֲלוּקָה f., *a leech,* Pro. 30:15.

עָלַז (fut. יַעֲלֹז, pl. יַעַלְזוּ) *rejoiced, exulted,* with עַל or בְּ (of the sub-
ject of joy).

עָלֵז m., *rejoicing,* Isa. 5:14.

עָלִיז m., *rejoicing, expressing joy.*

עָלַט (Arab. *was covered with clouds*).

עֲלָטָה f., *darkness.*

עֶלְיוֹן, עֲלִיָּה, עֲלִית, עֲלִי; see עלה.

עֲלִיצֻת; see עלץ.

עָלַל (Syr. *entered*). Po. עוֹלֵל I. *made
to enter,* Job 16:15.— II. *treated,*

acted towards, with לְ. — III. affected. — IV. gleaned. — V. part. מְעוֹלֵל babyish boy, Isa. 3:12. Poa. was done, caused, Lam.1:12. Hith. I. exerted himself against. —II. insulted. Hithpo. practised, Ps. 141:4

עֲלַל Ch., entered. Aph. הַנְעֵל brought in. Hoph. הֵעַל was brought in.

עֹל עוֹל m. (with suff. עֻלּוֹ).—I. yoke, —II. servitude.

עִלָּא p.n. of a man.

עִלָּה f. Ch., pretext, ground for complaint, Dan. 6:5, 6.

עָלִיל m., crucible, Ps. 12:7.

עוֹלֵל עוֹלָל m. (pl. עוֹלָלִים, עוֹלֲלִים) infant, young child, child.

עוֹלֵלוֹת עֹלֵלוֹת f. pl., gleanings.

עֲלִילָה f.— I. action.— II. an action (good or bad).

עֲלִילִיָּה f., action, Jer. 32:19.

מֵעַל m. Ch., setting (of the sun), Dan. 6:15.

מַעֲלָל m., pl. מַעֲלָלִים habitual doings (good or bad).

תַּעֲלוּל m., pl. תַּעֲלוּלִים.— I. children, Isa. 3:4.—II. vexations, calamities, Isa. 66:4.

עָלַם, part. עֹלְמִים hidden things, sins, Ps. 90:8. Niph. נֶעְלַם was hidden; part. נַעֲלָמִים hidden (crafty) men. Hiph. הֶעְלִים hide, conceal; הֶעְלִים עֵינָיו מִן ה' turned his eyes away from, Pro. 28:27. Hith. הִתְעַלָּם was hidden, with מִן.

עֹלָם עוֹלָם m.— I. antiquity.— II. eternity.—III. duration of the earth. — IV. whole life.— V. unlimited, future time; מֵעוֹלָם from of old;

יְמוֹת עוֹלָם the ancient days; עַד־עוֹלָם, לְעוֹלָם, עוֹלָמִים for ever; future duration, unlimited, but not endless.

עֵילוֹם m., eternity, 2 Chron. 33:7.

עָלַם m. Ch., eternity.

עֶלֶם m., a young man.

עַלְמָה f., damsel, virgin, ἡ παρθένος.

עֲלוּמִים m. pl., youth.

עַלְמוֹן p. n. of a town in the tribe of Benjamin; ע' דִּבְלָתַיְמָה p.n., a station of Israel.

עֲלָמוֹת f. pl., an unknown title of Psalm 46.

עַלְמוּת f., the same, Ps. 9:1; 48:15.

עֲלֶמֶת p. n. of a man.

עַלְמֶת p.n., same as עַלְמוֹן.

תַּעֲלֻמָה f., any thing hidden, secret; pl. תַּעֲלֻמוֹת.

עֵלְמָיֵא Elamites; see עֵילָם.

עָלַס exult, rejoice, Job 20:18. Niph. is exulting, Job 39:13. Hith. be exulting, Pro. 7:18.

עָלַע gulped, swallowed down, Job 39:30.

עֲלַע com. Ch., rib, Dan. 7:5.

עָלַף. Pu. I. fainted, Isa. 51:20.— II. covered, overlaid, Cant. 5:14. Hith. was clothed, Gen. 38:14, fainted.

עֻלְפֶּה m., languor, fainting, Eze. 31:15.

עָלַץ (fut. יַעֲלֹץ) exult, rejoice; with בְּ in, לְ against, לִפְנֵי before.

עֲלִיצוּת f., rejoicing, Hab. 3:14.

עַם, עִם, עֵם; see עמם.

עָמַד (fut. יַעֲמֹד).—I. stood fast, stu.. — II. stood over, overlooked, with

לִפְנֵי.— III. *stood over, presided,*
with עַל.—IV. *stood before,* with
אֵת, עַל.—V. *cease.,* with מִן.—VI.
stood before, with בִּפְנֵי, לִפְנֵי, מִן,
נֶגֶד—VII. *persevere, remain in any
occupation,* with בְּ.— VIII. *stood
against, opposed,* with עַל. Hiph.
הֶעֱמִיד I. *cause to stand.*—II. *set
up, raise.*—III. *establish.*—IV. *appoint.* — V. *confirm, accomplish.*
(הַעֲמָדְתָּ, Eze. 29:7, a wrong reading for הַמְעַדְתָּ *thou madest to
tremble.*) Hoph. הָעֳמַד *made to
stand.*

עֹמֶד m., *standing-place, station.*

עַמּוּד m., *pillar.*

עֻמְדָּה f., *station, standing.* Mic. 1:11.

מַעֲמָד m.—I. *standing, order.*—II.
station.

עָמָד, see עַם; עָמָּה see עמם; עַמּוֹן, see
עַמּוֹם, see עמם; עָמוֹק, see עמק;
עָמִיר; see עמר.

עֲמִית *society, company.*

עָמַל *wrought, laboured.*

עָמֵל m.—I. *working, labouring;* pl.
עֲמֵלִים *labourers.* — II. *weary,
wretched.*

עָמָל m.—I. *labour.*—II. *sorrow, vexation.*—III. *sorrow brought on by
sin.*— IV. *weariness.*—V. *fruit of
labour.*—VI. p. n. of a man.

עֲמָלֵק p.n., *Amalek,* a people inhabiting the south of Palestine and
the borders of the desert of Sinai;
עֲמָלֵקִי *Amalekite;* הַר הָעֲמָלֵקִי *hill
of the Amalekites* in the tribe of
Ephraim.

עָמַם *concealed,* Eze. 28:3; 31:8.

Hoph. הוּעַם *was obscured,* Lam.
4:1.

עַם, עָם com. (with suff. עַמִּי), *people,
nation;* בְּנֵי עַמִּי *the children of
my people;* pl. עֲמָמִים, עַמִּים.

עַם m. Ch., *people;* pl. עַמְמִין.

עִם prep. (with suff. עִמָּדִי, עִמִּי,
עִמָּם; עִמָּכֶם; עִמָּנוּ, עִמּוֹ; עִמָּךְ,
(עִמָּהֶם) with, *along with;* מֵעִם
from with, (like the French *de
par*).

עִם Ch., *the same.*

עֻמָּה f.—I. כָּל-עֻמַּת שֶׁ... *in the same
way as;* לְעֻמַּת *near, towards, like,
opposite to;* pl. לְעֻמּוֹת *like :*
מִלְעֻמַּת *near.*—II. p.n., a town of
Asher.

עַמּוֹן p.n., *Ammon,* the son of Lot's
daughter, and his descendants,
בְּנֵי עַמּוֹן; pl. עַמּוֹנִים, עַמּוֹנִי; f.
עַמּוֹנִית; pl. עַמּוֹנִיּוֹת *Ammonites.*

עַמִּיאֵל p.n. of a man.

עַמִּיהוּד p.n. of a man.

עַמִּינָדָב p.n. of a man.

עַמִּיחוּר p.n. of a man.

עַמִּינָדָב p.n. of a man.

עַמִּישַׁדָּי p.n. of a man.

עַמְעָד p.n., a town in the tribe of
Asher.

עַמְרָם p.n. of a man; patron. עַמְרָמִי.

עִמָּנוּאֵל (*God with us*), *Immanuel,*
one of our Lord's prophetic titles,
'Εμμανουηλ, Isa. 7:14.

עָמַשׂ, עָמַס (fut. יַעֲמֹס) *load, lay a
burden upon.* Hiph. הֶעֱמִיס *caused
to be laden,* 1 Ki. 12:11; 2 Chron.
10:11.

עָמוֹם p.n., *Amos,* the prophet.

עֲמַסְיָה p.n. of a man.

מַעֲמָסָה f., *burden,* Zec. 12:3.

עָמַה *was very deep*, Ps. 92:6. Hiph. הֶעֱמִיק *make deep*, Isa. 30:33.

עֹמֶק m.—עֲמֻקָּה f.—I. *deep.*—II. *subtle, unsearchable.*

עָמֵק or עָמֹק m., *the same;* pl. const. עִמְקֵי.

עָמוֹק p. n. of a man.

עֵמֶק m. (with suff. עִמְקֶךָ; pl. עֲמָקִים).—I. *deep place.*—II. *unintelligible.*

עֹמֶק m., *depth*, Pro. 25:3.

עַמִּיק m. Ch., *deep, profound thing*, Dan. 2:22.

מַעֲמַקִּים m. pl., *depths.*

עָמַר. Pi. עִמֵּר *binding-sheaves*, Ps. 129:7. Hith. הִתְעַמֵּר *treat as a slave*, with בְּ.

עָמִיר m., *sheaf of corn.*

עֹמֶר m.—I. *sheaf;* pl. עֳמָרִים.—II. *omer*, a dry measure, the tenth part of an ephah.

עֲמֹרָה p. n., *Gomorrah*, one of the cities of the plain; LXX. Γομόρρα.

עָמְרִי p. n.—I. *Omri*, king of Israel.—II. of other men.

עֲמַר m. Ch., *wool*, Dan. 7:9.

עַמְרָם p. n.; see עמם.

עָמַשׂ same as עָמַס *carried.*

עֲמָשָׂא p. n. of a man.

עֲמָשַׂי p. n. of a man.

עֲמַשְׂסַי p. n. of a man.

עֵנָב (Arab. *grapes*).

עֵנָב p. n., a town in the tribe of Judah.

עֵנָב m. (pl. עֲנָבִים, עִנְּבֵי), *grapes.*

עָנוּב p. n. of a man.

עִנְּבֵי pl. const. with dag. euphon., from עֵנָב.

עָנַג Pu. *delicately brought up*, Jer.

6:2. Hith. *delighted himself in*, with עַל, מִן.

עָנֹג m.—עֲנֻגָּה f., *delicate, tender.*

עֹנֶג m., *delight, pleasure.*

תַּעֲנוּג m., *delight, pleasure, enjoyment, luxury.*

עָנַד *bound*, Job 31:36; Pro. 6:21.

I. עָנָה (fut. אֶעֱנֶה, יַעֲנֶה, וַיַּעַן).—I. *spoke.*—II. *celebrated.*—III. *shout.*—IV. *bellow, bleat.*—V. *answer.* Niph. נַעֲנָה *was answering, answered.* Pi. עִנָּה *answered, sang in response.* Hiph. *answer favorably*, Ecc. 5:19.

עֲנָה Ch.—I. *answered, spoke, began to speak.*—II. *was afflicted;* see below.

II. עָנָה I. *was humbled.*—II. *was afflicted.* Niph. *was humbled, afflicted*, with מִפְּנֵי. Pi. I. *humbled, subdued.*—II. *afflicted;* with אִשָּׁה *had connexion with a woman;* with נֶפֶשׁ *fasted.* Pu. *was afflicted, humbled;* inf. עֻנֹּתוֹ *his suffering affliction*, Ps. 132:1. Hiph. *oppressed.* Hith. הִתְעַנָּה I. *was afflicted*, 1 Ki. 2:26.—II. *was humbled*, with לִפְנֵי.

עֲנָה p. n.—I. the son of Seir, and his descendants.—II. the son of Zibeon.

עָנִי m. (pl. עֲנָיִים, עֲנָוִי), *humble, meek, poor, afflicted.*

עֲנָוָה f., *meekness, humility.*

עֲנָוָה f., *the same.*

עֱנוּת f., *affliction of the humble* (Lee), Ps. 22:25.

עָנִי adj. m. (pl. עֲנִיִּים; f. עֲנִיָּה), *afflicted miserable, poor.*

עֳנִי, with pause עֳנִי m., *misery*

עֻנִּי p. n. of a man.

עֲנָיָה p. n. of a man.

עִנְיָן m., thing, matter.

עֲנָת p. n. of a man; see בֵּית.

עֲנָתוֹת p.n.—I. a city of the Levites in Benjamin; עֲנְתֹתִי inhabitant of Anathoth.—II. of a man.

עֲנְתֹתִיָּה p. n. of a man.

יַעַן pa., because; יַעַן כִּי, יַעַן אֲשֶׁר because, because of; יַעַן וּבְיַעַן, יַעַן בְּיַעַן the same.

יַעֲנִי p. n. of a man.

מַעֲנֶה m.—I. answer.—II. answer to prayer, Pro. 16:1.

לְמַעַן, מַעַן intent, purpose.—I. because.—II. thence, so, accordingly; לְמַעַן אֲשֶׁר in order that, because that.

מַעֲנָה f., furrow, Ps. 129:3.

מַעֲנִית Kri, the same.

תַּעֲנִית f., self-humiliation, Ezr. 9:5.

עָנִים p.n., a town of Judah.

עֲנֵם p.n., a town of Issachar; elsewhere עֵין־גַּנִּים.

עֲנָמִים p.n., a foreign people unknown.

עֲנַמֶּלֶךְ p.n., an idol of the Sepharvites.

עָנַן (part. עֹנֵן f. עֹנְנָה) and Po. עוֹנֵן (fut. יְעוֹנֵן; part. מְעוֹנֵן) divined, used auguries, Isa. 2:6, &c. Pi. (inf. with suff. עַנְנִי) my bringing on a cloud, Gen. 9:14; see עָנָן.

עָנָן, const. עֲנַן m.—I. a cloud.—II. p. n. of a man.

עֲנָנָה f., cloud, Job 3:5.

עֲנָן m. Ch., cloud, Dan. 7:13.

עֲנָנִי p.n. of a man.

עֲנָנְיָה ('Avaviaç) p.n.—I. of a man.—II. of a place in Benjamin.

עָנָף, const. עֲנַף m. (pl. with suff. עַנְפֵיכֶם, עֲנָפֶיהָ) a branch.

עֲנַף m. Ch., a branch.

עֲנָפָה f. עֲנֵפָה branching out, Eze. 19. 10.

עֲנָק m. (pl. עֲנָקִים, עֲנָקוֹת).—I. a chain (collar for the neck).—II. p.n.. הָעֲנָק, יְלִידֵי עֲנָק (הָעֲנָק), בְּנֵי עֲנָק, עֲנָקִים בְּנֵי עֲנָקִים the Anakims, the first inhabitants of Canaan, who were giants.

עָנַק put on a collar, i.e. exalted, lifted up, Ps. 73:6. Hiph. הַעֲנִיק place on the neck like a collar, Deu. 15:14.

עָנֵר p.n.—I. a man of Canaan, Gen. 14: 13, 24.—II. p. n., 1 Chron. 6:55, probably a wrong reading for תַּעְנַךְ.

עָנַשׁ (fut. יַעֲנֹשׁ).—I. taxed.—II. fined in money, with לְ. Niph. was fined, mulcted.

עֹנֶשׁ m., mulct, fine, tax.

עֲנַשׁ m. Ch., tax.

עֲנָתֹתִיָּה, עֲנָתוֹת, עֲנָת; see עָנָה.

כְּעֶנֶת, עֲנָת; see עֵתָת.

עָסַס tread (as grapes), Mal. 3:21.

עָסִיס m.—I. new wine-juice.—II. juice of the pomegranate, Cant. 8:2.

יַעְרְעוּר for יְעַרְעֲרוּ, עָעַר raised a cry, Isa. 15:5; see עוּר Pil.

עֲפָתָה, עָפָה; see עֵיפָה in עוּף.

עָפָה root not used; (Syr. flourished.)

עֳפִי m., pl. עֳפָאִים leaves, Ps. 104:12.

עֳפִי m. Ch., leaves.

עָפַל. Pu. swollen, inflated, Hab. 2: 4. Hiph. raised themselves, Nu. 14:44.

עֹפֶל m.—I. swelling tumour.—II mount, hill.

הָעֹפֶל p.n. of a peak of Mount Zion, to the east.

עֳפָלִים, pl. const. עׇפְלֵי hæmorrhoids, emerods; see also מְחוֹרִים.

עׇפְנִי p.n., a city of Benjamin, Jos. 18:24.

עׇפְעַפֵּי, עַפְעַפִּים; see עוּף.

עׇפַר Pi. עִפֵּר dashed with dust, 2 Sa. 16:13.with בֶּעׇפָר.

עֹפֶרֶת f., lead.

עׇפָר, const. עֲפַר m.—I. earth, mould, clay.— II. dust.—III. the earth.— IV. depth of the earth; pl. const. עׇפְרוֹת dusts, i.e. small dust, molecules.

עֹפֶר m., kid, young goat.

עֵפֶר p. n. of a man.

עׇפְרָה p.n.—I. a city of Benjamin. —II. a city of Manasseh.—III. of a man.

עֶפְרוֹן (עֶפְרַיִן) p.n.—I. a town on the borders of Ephraim.—II. a mountain between Judah and Benjamin. —III. the name of a Hittite, Gen. 23:8, &c.

עֵץ, עֲצִים, עֲצֵי; see עצה.

עׇצַב pained, grieved, thwarted. Niph. was pained, grieved, with עַל, בְּ, אֶל. Pi. I. bound together, Job 10: 8.—II. pained, thwarted. Hiph. I.grieved, thwarted, Ps.78:40.—II. worship, Jer. 44:19; (see Lee). Hith. was grieved.

עֲצַב Ch., grieved.

עׇצָב m., pl. עֲצַבִּים idols.

עֶצֶב, עֹצֶב m.— I. tendon, sinew, Jer. 22:28.—II. labour.—III. pain.

עׇצָב m.—I. idol.—II. pain, grief.

עֹצֶב m. (pl. with suff. עֶצְבֵיכֶם) your labours, Isa. 58:3.

עֲצֶבֶת, עַצֶּבֶת f. (const. עַצֶּבֶת; pl. with suff.עַצְּבוֹתָם).—I. pain,grief. —II. "sorrows," Eng. Ver.; perhaps idols, Ps. 16:4.

עׇצָּבוֹן m., painful, great, labour, Gen. 3:16, 17.

מַעֲצֵבָה f., labour, affliction, Isa. 50: 11.

עׇצַד (Arab. axe).

מַעֲצָד m., axe.

עׇצָה close the eyes,Pro. 16:30.

עֵץ m. (pl. עֲצִים, עֲצֵי).— I. a tree, עֵץ פְּרִי fruit-tree.—II. wood.—III. gallows.

עֵצָה f., wood, Jer. 6:6; see also in יעץ.

עׇצֶה m., spine of the back, Lev. 3:9.

עֶצְיוֹן גֶּבֶר p.n., a sea-port, probably on the eastern coast of the Red Sea.

עׇצַל. Niph. be sluggish, Jud. 18:9.

עׇצֵל m., sluggard; book of Proverbs only.

עַצְלָה sloth, Pro. 19:15, עַצְלוּת f., Pro. 31:27; dual עַצְלָתַיִם great sloth, Ecc. 10:18.

עׇצַם, עׇצֵם I. was numerous.—II. was strong.—III. was great. Pi. עִצֵּם I. bind the eyes, Isa. 29:10.—II. break the bones, Jer. 50:17, from עֶצֶם. Hiph. strengthens, Ps. 105:24.

עׇצוּם m.—I. numerous.— II. strong. —III. great; pl. עֲצוּמִים great ones, Ps. 10:10.

עֶצֶם f. (pl. עֲצָמִים).—I. bone —II. body.—III. self-same (never of persons); בְּעֶצֶם הַיּוֹם הַזֶּה or this very day —IV. p.n., a city o Judah.

עֹצֶם m., עָצְמָה f.—I. *strength.*—II. *power.*—III. *multitude*, Nah. 3:9.

עַצְמוֹן p. n., a town in the southern borders of Canaan.

עֲצֻמוֹת f. pl., *defence in argument*, Isa. 41:21.

תַּעֲצֻמוֹת f. pl., *strength*, Ps. 68:36.

עֵצֶן m., p. n. of a place, 2 Sa. 23:8.

עָצַר (fut. יַעְצֹר).—I. *shut up, restrain, detain*, with לְ.—II. with כֹּחַ *retain power, reign.* Niph. נֶעְצַר *was shut up, detained.*—II. *was assembled.*

עֵצֶר m., *rule, supreme power*, Jud. 18:7.

עֹצֶר m.—I. *shutting up the womb from child-bearing*, Pro. 30:16.—II. *in prison*, Isa. 53:8.

עֲצָרָה עֲצֶרֶת f.—I. *day of assembly.*—II. *restraint.*

מַעְצָר m., *restraint, hindrance*, Pro. 25:28.

מַעְצוֹר m., the same, 1 Sa. 14:6.

עָקַב (fut. יַעְקֹב).—I. *take by the heel*, Hos. 12:4; see עָקֵב.—II. *circumvent, defraud*; part. עֲקֻבָּה *traced, marked*, Hos. 6:8. Pi. *trace*, Job 37:4.

עָקֵב m.—I. *heel.*—II. *impression of the heel, track*; pl. עֲקֵבִים *heels*; עִקְּבוֹת *footsteps.*—III. *rear of an army*, Gen. 49:19, &c.—IV. עֲוֹן עֲקֵבַי *iniquity of my tracks*, i. e. *ways*, Ps. 49:6.

עָקֹב m., *steep place*, Isa. 40:4; see above.

עֵקֶב m.—I. *in consequence that, for the sake of.*—II. *consequence, fruit*; עֵ׳ רַב, Ps. 19:12, "great reward,"

Eng. Ver.; עַל עֵקֶב, עֵקֶב *in consequence, because, for that reason*, with כִּי אֲשֶׁר the same.

עָקְבָה f., *fraud, deceit*, 2 Ki. 10:19.

עָקוּב p.n. of men.

יַעֲקֹב (*took by the heel*), p. n., *Jacob*, the son of Isaac, afterwards Israel; קְהִלַּת יַ׳, בֵּית יַ׳, בְּנֵי יַעֲקֹב, זֶרַע יַ׳ I. his descendants, the Israelites.—II. the name also of their land and national polity.

יַעֲקֹבָה p. n. of a man.

עָקַד (fut. יַעְקֹד) *he binds, ties*, Gen. 22:9.

עָקֹד m. (pl. עֲקֻדִּים) *stripe, streak on cattle.*

עָקָה s., *oppression*; see עוּק.

מַעֲקֶה m., *parapet, battlement*; LXX. στεφάνη, Deut. 22:8.

עָקַל. Pu. part. מְעֻקָּל *became perverted*, Hab. 1:4.

עֲקַלָּתוֹן m., *very crooked*, Isa. 27:1.

עֲקַלְקַל m., עֲקַלְקַלּוֹת f. pl., *very crooked, perverted.*

עָקַר *eradicate*, Ecc. 3:2. Niph. *was rooted up, destroyed*, Zep. 2:4. Pi. עִקַּר *hough, cut the hamstring.*

עֲקַר Ch. Ith. *was rooted*, Dan. 7:8.

עָקָר m., עֲקָרָה, עֲקֶרֶת f., *barren, sterile.*

עֵקֶר m.—I. *root*, i. e. head of a strange family, Lev. 25:47.—II. p. n. of a man.

עִקַּר m. Ch., *nerve, stump*, Dan. 4:12.

עֶקְרוֹן p. n., one of the five principal cities of the Philistines, Ἀκαρών; עֶקְרֹנִי *an Ekronite.*

עַקְרָב m.—I. *a scorpion.*—II. *some implement of torture.*—III. *a war-*

like engine.—IV. מַעֲלֵה עַקְרַבִּים p. n., a place in the south of Palestine, Ἀκραβίν.

עָקַשׁ convict of perverseness, Job 9:20. Niph. is perverse, Pro. 28:18. Pi. made crooked.

עִקֵּשׁ m.—I. perverse, tortuous.—II. p. n. of a man.

עִקְּשׁוּת m., perverseness.

מַעֲקָשׁ m., pl. מַעֲקַשִּׁים unlevel, abrupt places, Isa. 42:16.

עָר, עָרִים; see עִיר.

עֵר p. n., Er, the son of Judah, and other men.

עָרַב I. was agreeable, sweet.—II. agreed, made compact.—III. became surety, pledged, with לְ.—IV. became dark; imp. עֲרֹב; fut. יֶעֱרַב. Hith. הִתְעָרַב I. intermixed with, with בְּ, לְ, עִם.—II. agreed, made compact with, with אֶת. Hiph. inf. הַעֲרִיב growing late (of the day), 1 Sa. 17:16.

עֲרַב Ch., mixed. Ith. was mixed, associated.

עֲרָב, עֲרָבִי Arabia; עַרְבִי an Arab; pl. עַרְבִיאִים, עַרְבִים Arabs.

עֹרֵב m.—I. a raven.—II. p. n., a prince of Midian.—III. Oreb, a rock beyond Jordan.

עָרֵב m., agreeable, sweet, Pro. 20:17, &c.

עָרֹב m., gad-fly; LXX. κυνόμυια.

עֵרֶב m. (with art. הָעֵרֶב).—I. foreigner, stranger, mixed multitude.—II. woof in weaving.

עֶרֶב m. (f. 1 Sa. 20:5).—I. evening, לָעֶרֶב, עֶרֶב, בָּעֶרֶב in the evening; pl. עֲרָבוֹת; dual הָעַרְבַּיִם בֵּין from

evening to evening, i.e. a whole day.—II. pl. עֲרָבִים, עַרְבֵי oziers, willows.—III. נַחַל הָע' a stream in Moab, Isa. 15:7.

עֲרָבָה f.—I. plain, open country.—II. desert.—III. הָעֲרָבָה the country between Jericho and the gulf of Akabah, called by the Arabs El Arabah; יָם הָע' Sea of Arabah, Dead Sea; נַחַל הָע' brook Kedron.—IV. p. n., a town in Benjamin; עַרְבָתִי an Arbite.

עֲרֻבָּה f., pledge, surety.

עֵרָבוֹן m. (ἀῤῥαβών), security, pledge, Gen. 38:17, &c.

מַעֲרָב m.—I. the west.—II. merchandise, Eze. c. 27; מַעֲרָבָה towards the west.

מַעֲרָבָה f., the west.

תַּעֲרוּבָה f., security, hostages.

עָרַג bleat, cry as an animal from desire, with עַל, אֶל; fut. יַעֲרֹג.

עֲרוּגָה f., raised bed in a garden, parterre.

עָרַד root not used; (Arab. fled away).

עָרוֹד m., wild ass, Job 39:5.

עֲרָד m. Ch.—I. wild ass, Dan. 5:21.—II. p. n., a place in the wilderness of Judah.—III. p. n. of a man.

עָרָה Pi. עֵרָה (inf. עָרוֹת; fut. apoc. תְּעַר).—I. make naked.—II. empty, pour out. Hiph. הֶעֱרָה I. make bare, expose, Lev. 20:18, 19.—II. pour out, Isa. 53:12. Niph. נֶעֱרָה was poured out, Isa. 32:15. Hith. הִתְעָרָה I. was stripped, exposed, Lam. 4:21.—II. was spread abroad, Ps. 37:35.

עֲרָה f., pl. עָרוֹת *bare places, pastures,* Isa. 19:7.

עֶרְוָה f.— I. *unfortified country,* Gen. 42:9, 12.—II. *nudity.*—III. *shame, disgrace.*

עֶרְוָה f. Ch., *loss,* Ezr. 4:14.

עֶרְיָה f., *nakedness.*

מַעֲרֶה m., *bare place, moor,* Jud. 20: 33.

מַעַר m., *nudity.*

מַעֲרוֹת f. pl., *plains, suburbs,* 1 Sa. 17:23.

מַעֲרָת p. n., a town in Judah.

תַּעַר m. (with suff. תַּעֲרָהּ).—I. *razor* — II. *penknife,* Jer. 36:23. — III. *scabbard of a sword.*

עָרֵם ,עֲרוּמִים ,עָרוֹם; see עֲרֹם.

עֲרוֹעֵר p. n.; see יָרַע.

עֵרִי p. n., one of the sons of Gad.

עֲרִיסוֹת *dough;* see עֲרֹם.

עֲרִיפִים *nobles;* see עֲרֹף.

עָרִיץ; see עֲרֹץ.

עֲרִירִי ,עֲרִירִים; see עֲרַר.

עָרַךְ (fut. יַעֲרֹךְ).—I. *set in order, arrange, dispose;* with or without מִלְחָמָה *set in battle array;* with or without מִלִּים *prepared an address, speech;* with לְ *to any one;* with אֶל *against any one;* with or without מִשְׁפָּט *prepared a cause for judgment;* עֲ בְּרִית *prepare a covenant.*—II. *compared together, valued, estimated,* with לְ. Hiph. הֶעֱרִיךְ *valued, set a tax on.*

עֵרֶךְ m.—I. *order, arrangement, system.*—II. *value, estimation.*

מַעֲרָךְ m., *disposings* (of the heart), Pro. 16:1.

מַעֲרָכָה f., *disposition, arrangement.*

מַעֲרֶכֶת f., the same.

עָרֵל *esteem profane,* Lev. 19.23. Niph. *appeared uncircumcised,* Hab. 2:16.

עָרֵל, const. עֲרַל ,עָרֵל m., *uncircumcised person;* עֲ שְׂפָתַיִם *hesitating of speech;* עֲרַל לֵב *uncircumcised of heart;* לְבָבָם הֶעָרֵל *their heart uncircumcised;* עֲרֵלָה אֹזֶן *uncircumcised of ears.*

עׇרְלָה f., *foreskin;* עֲ לֵב *uncircumcised of heart;* עָרְלָתוֹ פִּרְיוֹ *uncircumcision of its fruits,* i.e. first fruits of a tree, Lev. 19:23; pl. עֲרָלוֹת, const. עׇרְלוֹת I. *foreskins.* — II. p. n., a hill not far from Gilgal.

עָרַם *was cunning, subtle.* Hiph. הֶעֱרִים I. *act cunningly.*—II. *act prudently, wisely.* Niph. נֶעְרְמוּ *became swollen, heaped,* Ex. 15:8.

עָרוּם m.— I. *cunning.* — II. *prudent, cautious.*

עָרֹם m. (pl. עֲרוּמִּים; f. עֲרֻמָּה), עֵרֹם —I. *naked.*—II. *exposed, spoiled.*

עֵירֹם ,עֵרֹם m. — I. *nakedness.* — II. *naked;* adj. pl. עֵירֻמִּים.

עָרְמָה m., *craftiness, cunning,* Job 5: 13.

עׇרְמָה f.—I. *cunning.*—II. *prudence.*

עֲרֵמָה f., pl. ־ים ־וֹת *heap* (of ruins, of corn, &c.).

עַרְמוֹן m., *the plane tree.*

מַעֲרֹם m., pl. מַעֲרֻמִּים *nudities,* 2 Chron. 28:15.

עֵרָן p. n. of a man.; patron. עֵרָנִי.

עָרַס *root not used;* (Ch. עֲרַס *mixed*).

עֲרִיסָה f., pl. עֲרִיסוֹת *dough;* LXX φύραμα.

עַרְעֹר, עַרְעָר, עַרְעוּר; see עָרַר.

עָרַף (fut. יַעֲרֹף).—I. *behead*, Ex. 13:13, &c.— II. *destroy, ruin*, Hos. 10:2. —III. *drop* (as blood from a decapitated bird); applied to speaking.

עֹרֶף m., *neck*; פָּנָה ע' or נָתַן עֹרֶף *he turned the back, turned from any one*, with אֶל; פָּנָה ע', הָפַךְ ע' *turned the back, fled*; נָתַן אוֹיְבִים עֹרֶף *gave him the back of his enemies*, i.e. made them flee before him, Ps. 18:41, with לְ or אֶל.

עָרְפָּה p. n., *Orpah*, a woman of Moab.

עֲרִיפִים m. pl., *clouds*; metaph. nobles, Gen. 37:9.

עֲרָפֶל m., *thick darkness*.

עָרַץ (fut. יַעֲרֹץ).—I. *feared, trembled.* — II. *affrighted, alarmed.* — III. *shook*, with acc. מִפְּנֵי. Niph. part. נַעֲרָץ *terrible*, Ps. 89:8. Hiph. הֶעֱרִיץ *causing to fear*, Isa. 8:13.

עָרוּץ m., *abrupt, fearful place*, Job 30:6.

עָרִיץ m.—I. *strong, mighty.*—II. *violent, cruel.*

מַעֲרִיץ m., *terrible, fearful one*, Isa. 8:13.

מַעֲרָצָה f., *fearfulness, terror*, Isa. 10: 33.

עָרַק *fled, escaped*, Job 30:3.

עֹרְקִי *my nerves*, Job 30:17.

עַרְקִי p. n., *the Arkites*, a people of Canaan.

עָרַר (imp. עֹרָה) *was naked*, Isa. 32: 11. Po. עוֹרֵר I. *stir up.*—II. *make*

naked. Pil. עִרְעֵר and Hithpal הִתְעַרְעֵר *was, became, exposed.*

עֲרִירִי m. (pl. עֲרִירִים) *childless.*

עַרְעָר m., *naked, destitute, poor.*

עַרְעֵר, עֲרוֹעֵר I. perhaps *stump, dead tree*, Jer. 48:6.—II. p. n., *Aroer*, a town on the river Arnon, called also עֲרוֹעוֹר.— III. a town near Rabbath Ammon. — IV. p. n., a town in Judah; עַרְעֵרִי *an inhabitant of Aroer*.

עֶרֶשׂ f. (pl. עֲרָשׂוֹת) *couch, bed.*

עֵשֶׂב m. (with suff. עֶשְׂבָּם; pl. const. עֶשְׂבוֹת) *green herb* (considered as food).

עֲשַׂב m. Ch., the same.

עָשָׂה (fut. יַעֲשֶׂה, וַיַּעַשׂ; inf. abs. עָשׂה; const. עֲשׂוֹת, עֲשׂוֹ).— I. *wrought, laboured in*, with בְּ.— II. *made, fabricated, produced, constituted, appointed*, with לְ.— III. *did, performed, made, exercised.*— IV. *passed time*, Ecc. 6:12. Niph. נַעֲשָׂה (pret. f. נֶעֶשְׂתָה; fut. f. תֵּעָשֶׂה; apoc. תֵּעַשׂ).—I. *was made.* —II. *was done*; יֵעָשֶׂה *to be done.* Pu. עֻשֵּׂיתִי *I was made*, Ps. 139:15. Pi. עִשָּׂה *pressed, injured*, Eze. 23: 3, 8.

עֲשָׂהאֵל p. n. of a man.

עֲשִׂיאֵל p. n. of a man.

עֲשָׂיָה p. n. of a man.

מַעֲשֶׂה m. (pl. מַעֲשִׂים).— I. *work* (of an artificer).—II. *labour, business, occupation.*

מַעֲשַׂי p. n. of a man.

מַעֲשֵׂיָהוּ, מַעֲשֵׂיָה p. n. of a man.

עֵשָׂו (*hairy*), p. n., *Esau*, the son of Isaac; עֵשָׂו, בֵּית ע', בְּנֵי עֵשָׂו *the*

sons of Esau, Edomites; see אֱדֹם;
הַר עֵשָׂו *mountains of Edom*.

עֲשׂוֹר, עֲשִׂירִי; see עֶשֶׂר.

עָשַׁק. Hithp. *contend with*, Gen. 26:
20.

עֵשֶׂק (*strife*), p.n. of a fountain.

עֶשֶׂר f., עֲשָׂרֶת, עֲשָׂרָה m., *ten*; pl.
עֲשָׂרוֹת *tithes*.

עֶשֶׂר m., עֶשְׂרֵה f. (used only in com-
position with the other numbers),
ten; אַחַד עָשָׂר *eleven, the eleventh*;
f. אַחַת עֶשְׂרֵה; שִׁשָּׁה עָשָׂר m.,
שֵׁשׁ עֶשְׂרֵה f., *sixteen*; pl. עֶשְׂרִים
twenty.

עָשַׂר v. (fut. יַעֲשֹׂר) *decimate, tithe*, 1 Sa.
8:15, 17. Pi. עִשֵּׂר *take or pay
tithe*. Hiph. inf. with pref. לַעְשֵׂר
to pay tithe.

עָשׂוֹר m., *ten*; בֶּעָשׂוֹר לַחֹדֶשׁ *the
tenth (day) of the month*; נֵבֶל
עָשׂוֹר *a lute of ten strings*.

עֶשֶׂר f., עֶשְׂרָה m. Ch., *ten*; עֶשְׂרִין
twenty.

עֲשִׂירִי m., *tenth*; f. עֲשִׂירִית, עֲשִׂירִיָּה.

עִשָּׂרוֹן m. (pl. עִשְׂרֹנִים) *a dry measure*,
the tenth part of an ephah.

מַעֲשֵׂר m. (const. מַעֲשַׂר; with suff.
מַעַשְׂרוֹ; pl. מַעַשְׂרוֹת) *tithe*.

עָשְׁתָ for עָשְׂתָה Kal pret. f., from עָשָׂה

עַשׁ m., name of a constellation, probably the great bear, Job 9:9; (38:
32;) see also עַיִשׁ.

עַיִשׁ m.; בְּנֵי עַיִשׁ *the three stars in
the tail of the bear*, Job. 38:32.

עָשׁוֹת p.n. of a man.

עָשַׁן (fut. יֶעְשַׁן).—I. *smoked*.—II. metaphorically, *of the divine wrath*.

עָשָׁן m., *smoking*, Ex. 20:18.

עָשָׁן m. (const. עֲשַׁן; with suff. עֲשָׁנוֹ).

—I. *smoke*.—II. *fierce anger.*—III.
cloud.— IV. p. n. of a town, same
as כּוֹר עָשָׁן.

עָשֵׁן m., the same, Ex. 19:18.

עָשַׁק (fut. יַעְשֹׁק).—I. *oppressed, injured, wronged, defrauded.*—II.
press upon. Pu. part. f. מֶעֻשָּׁקָה
one oppressed, Isa. 23:12.

עָשׁוֹק m., *fraudulent, oppressive person*,
Jer. 22:3.

עֲשׁוּקִים m. pl., *frauds, oppressions*.

עֵשֶׁק p. n. of a man.

עֹשֶׁק m.—I. *oppression, injury.*—II.
that which is obtained thereby.

עָשְׁקָה f., *oppresses, ruins me*, Isa.
38:14.

מַעֲשַׁקּוֹת f. pl., *oppressions*.

עָשַׁר (fut. יַעְשַׁר) *was rich.* Hiph.
הֶעֱשִׁיר I. *made rich.*—II. *was, became, rich.* Hith. part. מִתְעַשֵּׁר
becomes rich, Pro. 13:7.

עָשִׁיר m.—I. *rich.*—II. *proud.*—III.
rich (in grace), Ecc. 10:6.

עֹשֶׁר m., *riches*.

עָשֵׁשׁ *became old, wasted.*

עָשׁ m., *moth (that which wastes, eats).*

עָשַׁת *was made smooth, shone*, Jer.
5:28. Hith. *remember*, Jon. 1:6.

עֲשִׁית, עֲשֵׁת Ch., *thought, designed*,
Dan. 6:4.

עֶשֶׁת m.—I. *net-work of ivory*, Cant.
5:14.—II. עֶשֶׂר, עֶשְׂרֵה with עַשְׁתֵּי
(perhaps *excess beyond ten*) *eleven.*

עַשְׁתּוּת f., *taunting*, Job 12:5.

עֶשְׁתֹּנוֹת f. pl., *devices, machinations*,
Ps. 146:4.

עַשְׁתֹּרֶת f., 'Ἀστάρτη, perhaps the
deified planet Venus. It is probably the feminine of אֲשֵׁרָה;

pl. עַשְׁתָּרוֹת *statues of Ashtoreth.* —II. p. n. of a city of Bashan, called also עַשְׁתָּרוֹת קַרְנַיִם *Ashtoreth with horns;* עַשְׁתָּרָתִי *an inhabitant of Ashtoreth;* עַשְׁתְּרוֹת צֹאן *produce of the flock;* LXX. ποιμνία τῶν προβάτων, Deu. 7: 13, &c.

עֵת, עֵת־ com. (with suff. עִתִּי), *time, season,* ὁ καιρός; כָּעֵת הַזֹּאת *about this time;* כָּעֵת מָחָר *about this time to-morrow;* כָּעֵת חַיָּה *this time next year, or, as in the times of a vigorous woman* (Lee), Gen. 18:10, 14; כָּעֵת *as at this time;* בָּעֵת הַהוּא *in that time;* בְּעִתּוֹ *in his time;* לְעֵת עֶרֶב *in the evening;* מֵעֵת עַד עֵת *from time to time, always;* עֵת adv. *now, sometimes;* pl. עִתִּים, עִתּוֹת *times, vicissitudes;* רַבּוֹת עִתִּים *many times, on many occasions,* Neh. 9:28.

עַתָּה (with pause עָתָּה adv. νῦν, νύν). —I. *now, shortly, speedily.*—II. *then;* מֵעַתָּה *from this time;* עַד עַתָּה *until this time.*

עִתִּי m., *seasonable,* Lev. 16:21.

עִתִּי p. n. of a man.

עֵת קָצִין p. n. of a man; with ה loc. עִתָּה קָצִין p. n., *a city of Zebulon.*

עָתַד Pi. *prepare,* Pro. 24:27. Hith. *have become prepared,* Job 15:28.

עָתִיד m., *prepared, ready.* Pl. עֲתִידוֹת I. *things ready to take place.*—II. *wealth.*

עַתִּיד m. Ch., *ready,* Dan. 3:15.

עַתּוּד m.—I. *he-goat.*—II. *leader, governor.*

עֲתָיָה p. n. of a man.

עָתָךְ p. n., a town of Judah.

עַתְלַי p. n. of a man.

עֲתַלְיָהוּ עֲתַלְיָה p. n.—I. *Athaliah,* the wife of Joram.—II. used also for men.

עָתַם. Niph. נֶעְתַּם *is burnt, consumed,* Isa. 9:18.

עָתְנִי p. n. of a man.

עָתְנִיאֵל p. n., *Othniel,* a judge of Israel; LXX. Γοθονιήλ.

עָתַק (fut. יֶעְתַּק).—I. *remove quickly, hurry from,* with מִן.—II. *grow old.* Hiph. הֶעְתִּיק I. *cause to remove.*—II. *transcribe,* Pro. 25:1.— III. *put away, silenced,* Job 32:15.

עָתָק m., *insolent, biting word.*

עֵתֶק m., *freedom, liberty,* Pro. 8:18.

עָתִיק m., *freely,* Isa. 23:18.

עַתִּיק m.—I. *ancient,* 1 Chron. 4:22. —II. *removed,* with מִן, Isa. 28:9.

עַתִּיק m. Ch., *ancient,* Dan. 7:9, 13, 22.

עָתַר (fut. יֶעְתַּר), *prayed, supplicated,* with לְ, אֶל. Niph. נֶעְתַּר (inf. נַעְתּוֹר) I. *was prevailed upon by prayer, was made propitious.*—II. נַעְתָּרוֹת *seemingly propitious* (false), Pro. 27:6, with לְ. Hiph. הֶעְתִּיר I. *prayed,* with לְ, בְּעַד.—II. *multiplied,* Eze. 35:13.

עָתָר m.—I. *suppliant,* Zep. 3:10.— II. *abundance,* Eze. 8:1.

עֶתֶר p. n., *a town of Simeon.*

עֲתֶרֶת f., *riches, abundance,* Jer. 33:6.

פ

פֹּא *here,* Job 38:11, for פֹּה.

פָּאָה. Hiph. fut. with suff. אַפְאֵיהֶם *I will scatter them far and wide.* Deu. 32:26.

פֵּאָה, const. פְּאַת f.—I. *corner, angle*
(of a field, table, &c.).—II.
קְצוּצֵי פֵאָה *having the hair clipped* or
shaven in angles; a Canaanitish
custom forbidden to the Israelites;
פַּאֲתֵי מוֹאָב, Nu. 24:17, *the clipped cornered ones of Moab,* i. e. who
trim their hair thus.

פֶּה m. (const. פִּי; with suff. פִּיךָ,
פִּיהֶם ;פִּיהוּ ,פִּיהָ; pl. פִּים, פִּיּוֹת).
—I. *mouth;* פֶּה אֶל פֶּה *mouth to
mouth, without intervention,* Nu.
12:8; פֶּה אֶחָד *unanimously.—*
II. *mouth of a sack, aperture in
anything.—* III. *edge of a sword,
&c.—* IV. *border of the sea,* Pro.
8:29.—V. פֶּה לָפֶה *from end to
end.—*VI. *share, portion;* פִּי שְׁנַיִם
two parts.— VII. *word, command.
—* VIII. *expression, tenor;* with
pref. כְּפִי *as, according to;* כְּפִיךָ
as thou (art); כְּפִי אֲשֶׁר *so as;* לְפִי
according to; עַל פִּי *according to.*

פִּיָּה f., *edge of a sword;* pl. פִּיּוֹת,
Jud. 3:16.

פִּיפִיּוֹת f. pl., *edges, two-edged,* Ps.
149:6; Isa. 41:15.

פִּי־בֶסֶת p.n., a city of Egypt, *Bu-
bastis.*

פִּי־הַחִירוֹת, הַחִירוֹת p.n., a place on
the Red Sea.

פִּיבֶל p.n. of a man.

פִּינְחָס p. n. of a man.

פָּאַר. Pi. פֵּאַר I. *adorned, made beautiful.—* II. *went over the branches
accurately,* Deu. 24:20. Hith.
הִתְפָּאֵר I. *felt complacency,* with
בְּ.—II. *boasted himself,* with עַל.

פְּאֵר m. (pl. פְּאֵרִים, פַּאֲרֵי) *ornamental
head-dress.*

פֹּארָה, פֻּארָה f., *a branch.*

פָּארוּר m., *blackness, paleness* (of face),
Joel 2:6; Nah. 2:11.

תִּפְאֶרֶת, תִּפְאָרָה f.—I. *beauty, ornament.—* II. *glory.—* III. *boast, subject of glorying.*

פָּארָן p. n., *Paran,* the wilderness between Egypt and Palestine.

פָּגַג (Arab. *unripe fig*).

פַּג m., pl. פַּגִּים *unripe figs,* Cant. 2:
13.

פִּגּוּל m., pl. פִּגֻּלִים *impure, disgusting*
(thing).

פָּגַע I. *came to a place, reached,* with
בְּ.—II. *met, fell in with,* with אֶל,
בְּ.— III. *met hostilely, fell upon,*
with בְּ.—IV. *waited on in prayer,
entreated.* — V. *admitted favourably.* Hiph. הִפְגִּיעַ I. *cause to
come, fall in with, wait upon.—II.
fell upon.—*III. *entreated.*

פֶּגַע m., *occurrence, accident.*

פַּגְעִיאֵל p. n., a prince of Asher.

מִפְגָּע m., *object of attack, butt,* Job
7:20.

פָּגַר. Pi. פִּגַּר *became languid, unable
to proceed,* 1 Sa. 30:10, 21, with
מִן.

פֶּגֶר m. (pl. פְּגָרִים, פִּגְרֵי) *dead body of
man or beast.*

פָּגַשׁ I. *met,* with בְּ.—II. *met hostilely,*
Hos. 13:8, &c. Niph. נִפְגַּשׁ *met
each other.* Pi. *stumble against,*
Job 5:14.

פָּדָה I. *redeemed,* with בְּ (of the price).
—II. *delivered.* Niph. נִפְדָּה *was
redeemed, delivered.* Hiph. הָפְדָּה
allowed to be redeemed, Ex. 21:8.

Hoph. inf. הָפְדֵּה same as Niph., Lev. 19:20.

פְּדָהאֵל p. n. of a man.

פְּדָהצוּר p.n. of a man.

פְּדוּיִים m. pl., λύτρον.—I. redemption price, ransom. — II. redeemed, delivered persons.

פְּדוֹן p. n. of a man.

פְּדוּת f.— I. redemption.— II. separation, Ex. 8:19.

פְּדָיָה פְּדָיָהוּ p. n. c. a man.

פִּדְיוֹן, פִּדְיוֹם m., ransom.

פַּדָּן m., plain, Gen. 48:7; פַּדַּן אֲרָם Padan-Aram; with ה, פַּדֶּנָה אֲרָם towards Padan-Aram.

אַפֶּדֶן Ch., palace, camp, Dan. 11:45.

פָּדַע redeem, deliver, Job 33:24.

פֶּדֶר m. (with suff. פִּדְרוֹ) fat.

פֵּה; see פאה.

פֹּה (פֹּא, פּוֹ).— I. here.— II. hither; מִפֹּה hence; עַד פֹּה thus far; אֵיפֹה where?

פּוּאָה (פֻּוָּה) p. n. of a man.

פּוּג (fut. יָפוּג, וַיָּפָג) became chilled, languid, ceased to act. Niph. the same, Ps. 38:9.

פּוּגָה f., intermission, Lam. 2:18.

הַפוּגָה f., intermission, Lam. 3:49.

פּוּחַ I. blew.— II. became cool by a breeze. Hiph. הֵפִיחַ I. inflamed, Pro. 29:8.—II. blew, blew a fire, with בְּ.—III. puffed at (scornfully), with בְּ.—IV. uttered.—V. (from פַּח) ensnared, Ps. 12:6.

פִּיחַ m., ashes, Ex. 9:8, 10.

פּוּט p. n., one of the sons of Ham, and his descendants.

פּוּטִיאֵל p. n. of a man.

פּוֹטִיפַר p. n. (πετεφρη, he who is devoted to the sun), an officer in Pharaoh's household.

פּוֹטִי פֶרַע (the same); p. n., Joseph's father-in-law.

פּוּךְ m.— I. stibium, powdered antimony.—II. אַבְנֵי פוּךְ; LXX. λίθοι πολυτελεῖς, a precious stone; קֶרֶן הַפּוּךְ p. n. of a woman.

פוֹל m., beans.

פּוּל p.n.—I. a people and nation of Africa.—II. a king of Assyria.

פֻּם, פּוּם m. Ch., mouth, aperture.

פּוּן, fut. אָפוּנָה; LXX. ἐξηπορήθην; Vulg. conturbatus sum, I pine away, Ps. 88:16.

פּוּנָה p.n., a gate of Jerusalem.

פּוּנִי p.n. of a man.

פּוּנֹן p.n., a town on the borders of the desert.

פּוּעָה p.n. of a woman.

פּוּץ I. dispersed themselves, were scattered.—II. overflowed. Niph. were scattered. Pil. פֹּצֵץ and Pilp. פְּצְפֵּץ shatter, shake to pieces. Hiph. הֵפִיץ I. scattered, confused. —II. poured out.— III. was scattered. Hithpo. are shattered, Hab. 3:6. Tiphel תְּפוֹצֹתִיכֶם I will scatter you, Jer. 25:34.

מֵפִיץ m.—I. disperser.—II. club, Pro. 25:18.

I. פּוּק stagger, stumble, Isa. 28:7. Hiph. stagger, stumble, Jer. 10:4.

II. פּוּק Hiph. הֵפִיק 1. supplied, Isa. 58:10.—2. obtained.—3. prospered, Ps. 140:9.

פּוּקָה f., *cause of stumbling*, 1 Sa. 25:31.

פִּיק m., *staggering*, Nah. 2:11.

I. פּוּר (Arab. *bubbled*); see פָּרַר.

פּוּרָה f., *wine-press*.

פָּרוּר m., *pot for boiling*.

II. פּוּר m., a Persian word.—I. *lot*; pl. פּוּרִים.—II. *the feast of Purim*.

פּוֹרָתָא p.n., a son of Haman.

פּוּשׁ (pret. פָּשְׁתֶּם).—I. *became numerous, flourished.* — II. *spread themselves*, Hab. 1:8. Niph. *were scattered*, Nah. 3:18.

פָּשׁ m., *extent*, Job 35:15.

פִּישׁוֹן p.n., one of the rivers of Paradise.

פּוּת (Arab. *interstice*).

פֹּת m., Isa. 3:17; pl. פֹּתוֹת *hinges*, 1 Ki. 7:50.

פּוּתִי p. n. of a man.

פָּזַז (fut. pl. יָפֹזּוּ) *are strong and active*, Gen. 49:24. Pi. פִּזֵּז *dancing*, 2 Sa. 6:16. Hoph. part. מוּפָז *purified*, 1 Ki. 10:18.

פָּז m.—I. *refined gold.* — II. *refined*, Cant. 5:11.

פָּזַר *dispersed*, Jer. 50:17. Pi. פִּזַּר I. *dispersed.*—II. *distributed liberally*. Niph. and Pu. *was scattered*.

פַּח m. (pl. פַּחִים).—I. *snare, gin.*—II. *any concealed danger.*—III. *plate of metal*, Ex. 39:3; Nu. 17:3.

פָּחַד (fut. יִפְחַד).—I. *feared*, with מִן, מִפְּנֵי.—II. *was agitated.*—III. *hastened*. Pi. *feared greatly, continually.* Hiph. *caused to shake, tremble*, Job 4:14.

פַּחַד m. (with suff. פַּחְדְּכֶם; pl. פְּחָדִים).—I. *fear, dread, reverence.* —II. *object of fear.*— III. *thigh*, Job 40:17; פּ' אֱלֹהִים *fear of God*.

פַּחְדָּה f., *fear*, Jer. 2:19.

פֶּחָה m. (const. פַּחַת; with suff. פֶּחָם, פֶּחָתֶךָ; pl. פַּחוֹת; const. פַּחֲווֹת).—I. *governor of a province.* — II. *captain;* Ch. the same; hence the modern word *Pacha*.

פָּחַז (*swelling like boiling water*).—I. *was dissolute*, Jud. 9:4.— II. *was proud*, Zep. 3:4.

פַּחַז m., *wantonness, pride*, Gen. 49:4.

פַּחֲזוּת f., *pride*, Jer. 23:32.

פָּחַם root not used; (Arab. *charcoal*).

פֶּחָם m., *charcoal*.

פָּחַר root not used; (Syr. *he founded*).

פֶּחָר m. Ch., *potter*, Dan. 2:41.

פַּחַת m. (pl. פְּחָתִים).—I. *a pit, well.* —II. *destruction.*

פְּחֶתֶת f., *corrosion, fretting into a garment*, Lev. 13:55.

פַּחַת־מוֹאָב p. n. of a man.

פַּחַת Kal inf., from נפח.

פִּטְדָה f., a precious stone, *topaz* or *emerald*.

פָּטַר (fut. יִפְטַר).—I. *slipped out*, or *away.*—II. *let out* (of water).— III. *expand* (of flowers), 1 Ki. c. 6. —IV. *exempt from duty*, 1 Chron. 9:33. Hiph. *open wide* (the mouth), Ps. 22:8.

פָּטִיר Ketib, same as פָּטוּר (part. see פָּטַר), *exempt from duty*, 1 Chron. 9:33.

פֶּטֶר m., *opening, beginning;* פֶּטֶר רֶחֶם *first-born.*

פִּטְרָה f., the same, Nu. 8:16.

פָּטַשׁ root not used; (Arab. *beat out iron with a hammer, spread out*).

פַּטִּישׁ m., *a hammer.*

פַּטִּישׁ m. Ch., *a tunic,* Dan. 3:21.

פִּי with comp. פִּיָה; see פֶּה in פָּאָה.

פִּיד root not used; (Arab. *disappeared, died*).

פִּיד m., *destruction.*

פִּיחַ פּיח; see פּוּחַ.

פִּילֶגֶשׁ; see פִּלֶגֶשׁ.

פִּים root not used; (Arab. *was fat*).

פִּימָה f., *fatness, food, strength,* Job 15:27.

פִּינֹן p. n., a prince of Edom.

פִּיפִיּוֹת; see פאה.

פִּיק; see פּוּק.

פִּישׁוֹן; see פּוּשׁ.

פִּיתֹן p. n. of a man.

פָּכָה. Pi. *flowing out,* Eze. 47:2

פַּךְ m., *flask, cruse.*

פֹּכֶרֶת הַצְּבָיִים p. n. of a man.

פָּלָא. Niph. נִפְלָא I. *was marvellous.* —II. *appeared marvellous,* with בְּעֵינֵי—III. *was concealed,* with מִן—IV. *was struck with wonder;* part. pl. נִפְלָאִים, נִפְלָאוֹת *wonderful things, wonderfully.* Pi. פִּלֵּא *set apart;* פִּלֵּא נֶדֶר *set apart by vow, devoted.* Hiph. הִפְלִיא I. *set apart.*—II. *made wonderful.* —III. *acted wonderfully.* Hith. *show one's self wonderful,* with בְּ, Job 10:16.

פֶּלֶא m. (with suff. פִּלְאֲךָ).—I. *sepa-*

ration, peculiarity.—II. *marvellous-ness.*—III. *a miracle;* pl. פְּלָאִים adv. *wonderfully;* פְּלָאוֹת *wonder-ful things.*

פִּלְאִי or פֶּלִי m., *wonderful,* Jud. 13:18; Ps. 139:6.

פְּלִיאָה f., or פְּלָאִיָה the same.

פְּלָאִיָה p. n. of a man.

פְּלָיָה p. n. of a man.

פַּלּוּא p. n., a son of Reuben; patron. פַּלֻּאִי.

מִפְלָאָה f., *miracle,* Job 37:16.

פָּלַג. Niph. *was divided.* Pi. I. *cut out, formed,* Job 38:25.—II. *divided,* Ps. 55:10.

פְּלַג Ch., *divided,* Dan. 2:41.

פְּלַג m. Ch., *half,* Dan. 7:25.

פֶּלֶג m.—I. *channel, stream.*—II. p. n., a son of Eber.

פְּלָגוֹת f. pl., *brooks.*

פְּלַגָּה f., pl. פְּלַגּוֹת *divisions,* 2 Chron. 35:5.

מִפְלַגָּה f., pl. מִפְלַגּוֹת the same, 2 Chron. 35:12.

פִּילֶגֶשׁ, פִּלֶגֶשׁ f. (pl. פִּילַגְשִׁים, פִּלַגְשֵׁי), *concubine,* παλλακή.

פְּלָדָה f., pl. פְּלָדוֹת *iron of chariots,* perhaps *scythes,* Nah. 2:4.

פִּלְדָּשׁ p. n. of a man.

פָּלָה same as פָּלָא. Niph. *are sepa-rated,* Ex. 33:16. Hiph. הִפְלָה I. *separated.*—II. *set apart,* Ps. 4:4.

פְּלֹנִי m.—I. with אַלְמֹנִי ὁ δεῖνα, *a certain one.*—II. p. n. of a man.

פַּלְמֹנִי m., *this particular one,* Dan. 8:13.

פָּלַח *cut,* Ps. 141:7. Pi. פִּלַּח I. *cut to*

pieces, 2 Ki. 4:39.—II. *disentangle,* Job 39:3. — III. *pierce through,* Pro. 7:23.—IV. *harrow,* Job 16:13.

פֶּלַח m.—I. *piece, part.*—II. *mill-stone;* פֶּלַח רֶכֶב *upper mill-stone;* פ׳ תַּחְתִּית *nether mill-stone.*

פִּלְחָא p. n. of a man.

פְּלַח Ch., *served, worshipped.*

פָּלְחָן m. Ch., *service, worship,* Ezr. 7:19.

פָּלַט *escaped,* Eze. 7:16. Pi. I. *delivered.*—II. *bring forth safely,* Job 21:10. Hiph. *delivered.*

פָּלֵיט, פָּלִיט m., *fugitive, one escaped.*

פְּלֵיטָה, פְּלֵטָה f., *the escaped, remnant.*

פֶּלֶט m., *deliverance.*

פֶּלֶט p. n. of a man.

פַּלְטִי p. n. of a man.

פִּלְטִי p. n. of a man.

פְּלַטְיָה p. n. of a man.

פְּלַטְיָהוּ p. n. of a man.

מִפְלָט m., *escape, safety,* Ps. 55:9.

פְּלָיָה, פְּלִיאָה, פְּלָיָה, פְּלִי; see פלא.

פְּלִילִי, פְּלִילָה, פְּלִיל; see פלל.

פֶּלֶךְ root not used; (Arab. *was round*).

פֶּלֶךְ m.—I. *spinning distaff.*—II. *circuit, district.*

פָּלַל Pi. פִּלֵּל I. *judged,* 1 Sa. 2:25.—II. *adjudged punishment,* with לְ, Eze. 16:52.—III. *inflicted punishment,* Ps. 106:30.—IV. *expected,* Gen. 48:11. Hith. *prayed* (lit. appealed to a judge), with בְּעַד, לִפְנֵי, אֶל, לְ, עַל.

פָּלִיל m., *a judge;* pl. פְּלִילִים.

פְּלִילָה f., *justice,* Isa. 16:3.

פְּלִילִי m., *judicial,* Job 31:28.

פְּלִילִיָּה f., *judgment,* Isa. 28:7.

פָּלָל p. n. of a man.

פְּלַלְיָה p. n. of a man.

תְּפִלָּה f.—I. *prayer.*—II. *intercession.*—III. *hymn,* Ps. 72:20.

פְּלֹנִי, פַּלְמֹנִי; see פלה.

פָּלַס Pi.—I. *pondered,* Isa. 26:7.—II. *approved.*—III. *planned.*

פֶּלֶס m., *balance, steel-yard.*

מִפְלָשׂ m., *poising, balancing,* Job 37:16.

פָּלַץ Hith. *shook, trembled,* Job 9:6.

פַּלָּצוּת f., *trembling, fear.*

מִפְלֶצֶת f., *idol, image.*

תִּפְלֶצֶת f., *terror,* Jer. 49:16.

פָּלַשׁ Hith. *rolled themselves in dust.*

פְּלֶשֶׁת p. n., *Philistia,* the sea-coast of the south of Palestine; it was divided into five provinces. פְּלִשְׁתִּי *a Philistine,* pl. פְּלִשְׁתִּים *Philistines;* LXX. Ἀλλόφυλοι.

פֶּלֶת p. n. of a man.

פְּלֵתִי m., *mercenary soldier,* Pelethite.

פֵּן, פֶּנָּה, פֶּן, see פנן; פֵּן, see פנה.

פַּנַּג, perhaps *millet,* in English, *panic,* Eze. 27:17.

פָּנָה (fut. יִפְנֶה, תֵּפֶן, וַיִּפֶן, עֹרֶף).—I. *turn himself to go away.*—II. *turned towards.*—III. *changed, declined, began;* לִפְנוֹת בֹּקֶר *at the turn of the morning,* i. e. in the morning; לִפְנוֹת עֶרֶב *in the evening.* Pi. פִּנָּה I. *removed.*—II. *cleared a road or house.* Hiph. הִפְנָה (fut. apoc. וַיִּפֶן).—I. *turned.*—II. *turned himself.* Hoph. *were made to turn themselves,* Jer. 49:8.

פִּנָּה m., pl. פָּנִים; const. פְּנֵי I. *face*

פָּנִים בְּפָנִים, פָּנִים אֶל־פָּנִים *face to face.*—II. *person, presence;* שׂוֹם פָּנִים, with אֶל or עַל *he set his face toward;* נָתַן שׂוּם פ׳, with לְ and inf. *he designed to do;* פָּנַי *my person,* i.e. I; פָּנֶיךָ *thy person,* i.e. thou, &c.— III. *surface.*—IV. *front;* פָּנִים *in front;* לְפָנִים *before, formerly;* מִפָּנִים *in, from the presence of;* מִלְּפָנִים *from ancient time;* with prefixes אֶל־פְּנֵי *before, in presence of;* אֶת־פְּנֵי *before;* מֵאֵת פְּנֵי *from before;* בִּפְנֵי *before;* לִפְנֵי *in the sight of, before, preceding, against, in time;* with suff. לְפָנָיו, לְפָנֶיךָ, לְפָנַי, מִלְּפְנֵי, לִפְנֵיהֶם, לִפְנֵיכֶם *from, because of;* מִפְּנֵי אֲשֶׁר *because of;* עַל־פְּנֵי *in presence of, in preference to, towards;* מֵעַל־פְּנֵי *from before.* פֶּן, part. μή, *lest.*

פְּנוּאֵל, פְּנִיאֵל p.n.—I. a place beyond Jordan.—II. of a man.

פְּנִים m., *within;* פְּנִימָה *to, on, the inside;* לִפְנִימָה *within, on the inside;* מִלְּפָנִים, מִפְּנִימָה *within.*

פְּנִימִי m., פְּנִימִית f., *inner.*

פְּנִינִים m. pl., *pearls.*

פֵּן m. (with suff. פִּנָּהּ; pl. פִּנִּים) *corner.*

פִּנָּה f.—I. *corner;* אֶבֶן פ׳, רֹאשׁ פ׳ *chief corner-stone.*—II. *battlement, parapet.*—III. *dignitary, prince.*

פְּנֻנָּה p.n. of a woman.

פָּנַק. Pi. *brought up delicately,* Pro. 29:21.

פְּנִי, פָּסִים, פָּסָה; see פסס.

פָּסַג. Pi. *count, observe,* Ps. 48:14.

פִּסְגָּה p.n., a peak on the mountains of Moab.

פָּסַח *passed over for defence, defended, protected.* Niph. *was lamed,* 2 Sa. 4:4. Pi. *leaped about,* 1 Ki. 18:26.

פֶּסַח p.n. of a man.

פֶּסַח m.—I. *feast of the Passover.*—II. *the paschal lamb;* עָשָׂה פ׳ *keep the Passover.*

פִּסֵּחַ m. (pl. פִּסְחִים) *lame.*

תִּפְסַח p.n., a city on the Euphrates, *Thapsacus.*

פָּסַךְ p.n. of a man.

פָּסַל *hewed, carved.*

פָּסִיל m., pl. פְּסִילִים *carved images, idols.*

פֶּסֶל m. (with suff. פִּסְלִי) *an idol.*

פְּסַנְתֵּרִין, פְּסַנְטֵרִין m. Ch., ψαλτήριον, *a musical instrument.*

פָּסַס *ceased to exist, disappeared,* Ps. 12:2.

פַּס m. כְּתֹנֶת פַּסִּים *coat of many colours,* Gen. 37:3; *long cloak,* covering the hands and feet (Ges. and Lee); but Jacob knew Joseph's coat when torn and dipped in blood; it was the quality or colour of the cloth, therefore, not the shape that distinguished it; LXX. χιτὼν ποικίλος.

פַּס m., *palm of the hand.*

פִּסָּה f., *abundance,* Ps. 72:16.

אֶפֶס דַּמִּים פַּס דַּמִּים p. n., same as

פִּסְפָּה p.n. of a man.

פָּעָה *cry out,* Isa. 42:14.

אֶפְעֶה com., *adder, viper.*

אָפַע the same.

פְּעִי, פְּעוּ p.n., a city of Edom.

פְּעוֹר see פֵּעֹר.

פָּעַל v. (fut. יִפְעַל יִפְעָל)—I worked.—II. made, formed.—III. did, performed.—IV. practised, with לְ or בְּ of the person for whom the action is performed.

פֹּעַל m. (with suff. פָּעֳלֶךָ, פָּעֳלוֹ, פָּעֳלוֹ; pl. פְּעָלִים).—I. work, action, practice.—II. wages.—III. acquisition, Pro. 21:6.

פְּעֻלָּה f.—I. work, employment.—II. wages, Lev. 19:13.—III. reward or punishment.

פֹּעֲלוֹ for פָּעֳלוֹ, from פֹּעַל.

פְּעֻלְּתַי p.n. of a man.

מִפְעָל m., מִפְעָלָה f., } work, doings.

פָּעַם moved, excited to action, Jud. 13:25. Niph. was moved, disturbed. Hith. same as Niph., Dan. 2:1.

פַּעַם f. (m. Jud. 16:28).—I. pl. פְּעָמִים footsteps, feet.—II. progress.—III. an anvil, Isa. 41:7.—IV. pl. פַּעֲמוֹת feet of the ark (Lee).—V. an act, and the time of its performance, a time, once; dual פַּעֲמַיִם twice; שֶׁבַע פְּעָמִים seven times; פַּעַם וּשְׁתַּיִם once or twice, Neh. 13:20; בְּפַעַם הַזֹּאת, הַפַּעַם, בַּפַּעַם הַהִיא now, at the present time; כְּפַעַם בְּפַעַם even so as before; פַּעַם...פַּעַם sometimes.

פַּעֲמֹן m., bell, Ex. chapters 38 and 39 only.

פַּעֲנֵחַ; see צָפְנַת פ׳.

פָּעַר open the mouth, gape, with פֶּה, בְּפֶה.

פְּעוֹר p.n. of a mountain of Moab;

בַּעַל־פְּעוֹר and פְּעוֹר an idol of Moab.

פַּעֲרַי p.n., one of David's generals; elsewhere נַעֲרַי.

פָּצָה I. opened the mouth.—II. rescued.

פָּצַח broke forth into singing, with רִנָּה. Pi. broke to pieces, Mic. 3:3.

פְּצִירָה; see פצר.

פָּצַל Pi. פִּצֵּל peeled, Gen. 30:37,38.

פְּצָלוֹת f. pl., the parts peeled, stripped of bark, Gen. 30:37.

פָּצַם broke the earth, Ps. 60:4.

פָּצַע wounded; פְּצוּעַ דַּכָּה eunuch.

פֶּצַע m. (with suff. פִּצְעִי; pl. פְּצָעִים), a wound.

פָּצַץ Hithpo.; see פוץ.

פָּצֵץ p. n. of a man.

פָּצַר (fut. יִפְצַר).—I. pressed upon to injure, Gen. 19:9.—II. urged to consent, with בְּ. Hiph. inf. הַפְצֵר was too urgent, obstinate, 1 Sam. 15:23.

פְּצִירָה f., a file, 1 Sam. 13:21.

פָּקַד I. visited, enquired for.—II. enquired for without finding, missed.—III. enquired into or after, cared for.—IV. punished, with אֶל of the crime, or עַל of the person, and בְּ of the punishment.—V. examined and arranged—VI. numbered, took account of.—VII. placed, appointed, set over, with אֶת, עַל, (פְּקוּדִים officers).—VIII. laid a charge upon any one, with עַל. Niph. I. was missed.—II. was punished.—III. was numbered.—IV. punishment was inflicted.—V. was visited with evil. Pi. ex-

amined, numbered. Pu. I. *was taken account of,* Ex. 38:21,—II. *was deprived of,* Isa. 38:10. Hiph. I. *placed, appointed,* with עַל or לְ.—II. *committed to some one,* with אֶת ,עַל־יְדֵי ,בְּיַד. Hoph. I. *was punished,* Jer. 6:6.—II. *placed, appointed;* part. מֻפְקָדִים *officers.* Hith. *was examined, numbered.* Hoth. pl. הָתְפָּקְדוּ *the same.*

פְּקֻדָּה f.—I. *providence,* Job 10:12.—II. *office.*—III. *government.*—IV. *class,* 1 Chron. 23:11.—V. *treasure,* Isa. 15:7.—VI. *punishment;* בֵּית הַפְּקֻדוֹת *prison.*

פִּקָּדוֹן m., *deposit.*

פְּקִדֻת f., *captain of the guard,* Jer. 37:13.

פְּקוּד m.—I. *punishment,* an allegorical name of Babylon, Jer. 50:21.—II. *dominion,* Eze. 23:23.

פִּקּוּדִים m. pl., *precepts of God.*

פָּקִיד m., *officer, chief, superintendent.*

מִפְקָד m.—I. *arrangement,* 2 Chron. 31:13.—II. *census publicly appointed,* 2 Sa. 24:9.—III. שַׁעַר הַמִּפְקָד *one of the gates of Jerusalem,* Neh. 3:31.

פָּקַח (fut. יִפְקַח) *opened the eyes or ears.* Niph. *was opened.*

פֶּקַח p.n., *Pekah, king of Israel.*

פְּקַחְיָה p.n., *Pekahiah, king of Israel.*

פִּקֵּחַ m., *having the eyes opened, able to see.*

פְּקַח־קוֹחַ m., *complete opening, opening of the prison,* Isa. 61:1.

פָּקִיד *officer;* see פקד.

פַּקֻּעוֹת f. pl., *the fox-grape,* 2 Ki. 4:39.

פְּקָעִים m. pl., *architectural ornaments of a globular form,* 1 Ki. 6:18; 7:24.

פַּר ,פָּר m., *young bull.*

פָּרָה f.—I. *young cow, heifer.*—II. הַפָּרָה p.n., a town in the tribe of Benjamin.

פָּרָא same as פָּרָה Hiph., *propagate,* Hos. 13:15.

פֶּרֶא ,פָּרָא com. (pl. פְּרָאִים), *wild ass.*

פִּרְאָם p.n., a king of Canaan.

פֹּרֹאת same as פֹּארֹת; see פֹּארָה.

פַּרְבָּר ,פַּרְוָר m., *suburb.*

פָּרַד *separated, spread* (of wings). Niph. *separated himself,* with מִן ,מֵעַל. Pi. *go aside,* Hos. 4:14. Pu. part. מְפֹרָד *separate,* Est. 3:8. Hiph. same as Kal. Hith. same as Niph.

פֶּרֶד m. (with suff. פִּרְדּוֹ; pl. פְּרָדִים), *a mule.*

פִּרְדָּה f., *she-mule.*

פְּרֻדוֹת f. pl., *seeds scattered, corn sown,* Joel 1:17.

פַּרְדֵּס m., παράδεισος, *enclosure, park,* Neh. 2:8; Cant. 4:13; Ecc. 2:5.

פָּרָה *heifer;* see פָּר; פֶּרֶה same as פֶּרֶא *wild ass.*

פָּרָה *bore fruit, was fruitful* (of trees, plants, men, animals, &c.); part. f. פֹּרִיָּה ,פֹּרַת *fruit tree.* Hiph. הִפְרָה (fut. apoc. וַיֶּפֶר) *made fruitful.*

פְּרִי m. (with pause פֶּרִי; with suff. פִּרְיִי ,פֶּרְיְךָ ,פִּרְיָם ,פְּרִיכֶם ,פְּרִיהֶם). I. *fruit of a tree;* עֵץ פְּרִי *fruit tree.*—II. *produce of the ground;* אֶרֶץ פְּרִי *a fruitful land.*—III. *fruit of the womb, offspring.*—IV.

result of actions, reward or punishment.

פֻּרָה p. n. of a man.

פְּרִידָא, פְּרוּדָא p.n. of a man.

פַּרְוָיִם p. n. of a country, same as
סְפַרְוַיִם, which see.

פַּרְוָר suburb; see פַּרְבָּר.

פָּרוּר pot; see פּוּר.

פָּרַז (Arab. separated). see פָּרַז.

פֶּרֶז m., ruler, Hab. 3:14.

פְּרָזוֹן m., justice; with suff. פִּרְזוֹנוֹ
Jud. 5:7, 11.

פְּרָזוֹת f. pl., unwalled towns, villages.

פְּרָזִי m., one living in a village;
pl. פְּרָזִים; Ketib פְּרוֹזִים.

פְּרִזִּי p. n., the Perizzite, a people of
Canaan.

פַּרְזֶל m.Ch., iron; Heb. בַּרְזֶל.

פָּרַח (fut. יִפְרַח).—I. budded.—II. shot
up, flourished.—III. spread, extended
itself. Hiph. caused to bud, budded.

פֶּרַח m. (with suff. פִּרְחָם; pl. פְּרָחִים).
—I. young shoot.—II. bud.—III.
the artificial representation of a
bud.

פָּרוּחַ p.n. of a man.

פִּרְחָח m., insolent, with insult, Job
30:12.

אֶפְרֹחַ m., pl. אֶפְרֹחִים young of birds.

פָּרַט abounded or sang; LXX. ἐπικρο-
τοῦντες, Am. 6:5.

פֶּרֶט m., omission, what is omitted,
Lev. 19:10.

פְּרִי fruit; see פרה.

פְּרִיץ wild beast; see פרץ.

פֶּרֶךְ m., harshness, oppression.

פָּרֹכֶת f., the veil which separates the
holy place from the holy of holies.

פָּרַם (fut. יִפְרֹם) rent, torn (of garments), Leviticus only.

פַּרְמַשְׁתָּא p.n., a son of Haman.

פַּרְנָךְ p. n. of a man.

פָּרַס broke, distributed, bread. Hiph.
dividing the hoof; see פַּרְסָה.

פְּרַס Ch., divide.

פֶּרֶס m., the osprey, Lev. 11:13; Deu.
14:12.

פַּרְסָה f., a hoof; pl. const. פַּרְסוֹת,
פַּרְסֵי.

פָּרַס Persia; פַּרְסִי a Persian, Parsee.

פָּרַע I. uncovered the head.—II. placed
in a state of disorder, Ex. 32:25.
III. was disregarded.—IV. left a
road, Pro. 4:15. — V. exempted,
Eze. 24:14.—VI. avenged, Jud. 5:
2. Niph. became lawless, Pro. 29:
18. Hiph. I. made idle, Ex. 5:4.—
II. brought vengeance on, 2 Chron.
28:19.

פֶּרַע m., head of hair; pl. פְּרָעוֹת,
פְּרָעוֹת, vengeance, Deu. 32:42;
Jud. 5:2.

פִּרְעָתוֹן p.n., a town of Ephraim;
פִּרְעָתֹנִי a Pirathonite.

פַּרְעֹה title of all monarchs of Egypt
(lit. φρη the sun); Φαραώ.

פַּרְעֹשׁ m.—I. a flea.—II. p. n. of a
man.

פַּרְפַּר p. n., a small river which joins
the Amana near Damascus, 2 Ki.
5:12.

פָּרַץ (fut. יִפְרֹץ).—I. broke down, made
a breach in, a wall.—II. burst
forth, overflowed (of water).—III.
broke in pieces, afflicted.—IV. urged
(a person).—V. dispersed an enemy.

VI. *distributed* persons, 2 Chron. 11:23. Niph. part. נִפְרָץ *much, frequent* (Lee), 1 Sa. 3:1. Pu. *broken down*, Neh. 1:3. Hith. *breaking loose*, 1 Sa. 25:10.

פָּרִיץ m.—I. *violent, lawless, person.* —II. *wild beast*, Isa. 35:9.

פֶּרֶץ m. (pl. פְּרָצִים, פְּרָצוֹת).—I. *breach in a wall.*—II. *overflowing of water.*—III. *sudden calamity.*— IV. p. n. of a man; patron. פַּרְצִי.

מִפְרָץ m., probably, *creek*, marg. (*breach*, Eng. Ver.), Jud. 5:17.

פָּרַק I. *pulled off*, with מֵעַל, Gen. 27: 40.—II. *tore in pieces*, Ps. 7:3.— III. *rescued.* Pi. פֵּרֵק I. *tore in pieces.* — II. *pulled off*, Ex. 32:2. Hith. הִתְפָּרֵק I. *was broken off*, Eze. 19:12.—II. *pulled off from himself.*

פְּרַק Ch., *break off*, Dan. 4:24.

פֶּרֶק m. (Kri מָרֶק *without authority*), *fragments*, Isa. 65:4.

פֶּרֶק m.—I. *tearing in pieces, prey*, Nah. 3:1.—II. *cross way*, Obad. v. 14.

מַפְרֶקֶת f., *vertebræ of the neck*, 1 Sa. 4:18.

פָּרַר *cleft, divided*; inf. abs. פּוֹר. Pil. פּוֹרֵר *cleft*, Ps. 74:13. Hithpo. *was cloven*, Isa. 24:19. Pilp. פִּרְפֵּר *shattered, agitated, the mind*, Job 16:12. Hiph. הֵפִיר, הָפֵר; with pause הָפַר I. *broke a covenant* or *command.*—II. *frustrated.* — III. *annulled.* — IV. *withdrew, broke off.* Hoph. הֻפַר *was disannulled.*

פָּרַשׂ (fut. יִפְרֹשׂ).—I. *spread.*—II. *stretched out the hands.*—III. *gave, assisted*, Pro. 31:19.—IV. *seized*, Lam. 1:10.—V. *broke*, like פָּרַם. Niph. *was scattered*, Eze. 17:21. Pi. פֵּרֵשׂ, with pause פֵּרֵשׂ I. *spread out the hands.*—II. *scattered.*

מִפְרָשׂ m.—I. *expansions of*, Job 36: 29.—II. *sail of a ship*, Eze. 27:7.

פָּרַשׁ *mark distinctly*, Lev. 24:12. Niph. *scattered*, Eze. 34:12; see פָּרַשׂ. Pu. פֹּרַשׁ I. *was marked out distinctly*, Num. 15:34.—II. *made clear*, Neh. 8:8. Hiph. *stung*, Pro. 23:32.

פְּרַשׁ Ch., the same. Pa. part. מְפָרַשׁ *made clear.*

פֶּרֶשׁ m. (with suff. פִּרְשׁוֹ) *dung.*

פָּרָשָׁה f., *distinct account*, Est. 4:7; 10:2.

פָּרָשׁ m., pl. פָּרָשִׁים *horses*; בַּעֲלֵי הַפָּרָשִׁים *horsemen.*

פָּרָשׁ, const. פָּרַשׁ m., *horseman*; pl. פָּרָשִׁים.

(פַּתְשֶׁגֶן),פַּרְשֶׁגֶן)m. Heb. and Ch., *copy of a writing*, Ezra only.

פַּרְשְׁדוֹנָה or פַּרְשְׁדֹן *dung*, as some render, *podex*, as others, Jud. 3:22.

פַּרְשֵׁז *spreading*, Job 26:9.

פַּרְשַׁנְדָתָא p.n., a son of Haman.

פְּרָת p. n., the river *Euphrates*, Εὐ- φράτης.

פְּרָת; see פָּרָה.

פַּרְתְּמִים m. pl., *chiefs, nobles.*

פָּשָׂה *spread itself* (an eruption), Le- viticus only.

פָּשַׂע *stepped, t. od*, with בְּ, Isa. 27:4.

פֶּשַׁע m., *a step*, 1 Sa. 20:3.

מִפְשָׂעָה f., *buttocks*, 1 Chron. 19:4.

פָּשַׂק *opened, expanded*, Pro. 13:3. Pi. the same, Eze. 16:25.

פָּשׁ *spreading;* see פּוּשׁ.

פִּשַּׁח. Pi. *tore to pieces*, Lam. 3:11.

פַּשְׁחוּר p.n. of a man.

פָּשַׁט (fut. יִפְשֹׁט).—I. *stripped off his dress.*— II. *spread, extended itself,* with אֶל, עַל, בְּ, Pi. *stripped another.* Hiph. I. *stripped another.* II. *skinned*, with מֵעַל. Hith. *stripped himself*, 1 Sa. 18:4.

פָּשַׁע I. *rebelled, rebelled against,* with מִתַּחַת and בְּ. — II. *transgressed.* Niph. *transgressed against*, Pro. 18:19.

פֶּשַׁע m. (with suff. פִּשְׁעִי; pl. פְּשָׁעִים). —I. *rebellion.* — II. *transgression, sin.* — III. *injury* (by loss), Ex. 22:8.

פְּשַׁר Ch., *interpreted, explained.* Pa. the same.

פְּשַׁר m. Ch., *interpretation.*

פֵּשֶׁר m. Heb., the same, Ecc. 8:1.

פִּשְׁתָּה m.—I. *flax.*—II. *linen.*

פִּשְׁתָּה f., *a lamp-wick of flax*, Isa. 42:3; 43:17; (pl. פִּשְׁתִּים) *linen*, Ex. 9:31.

פַּת, פָּתִים, see פָּתַת; פֹּת, see פּוּת.
פְּתָאִים see פֶּתִי.
פִּתְאֹם *suddenly;* see פֶּתַע.

פַּתְבַּג m. Heb. and Ch., *portion of food, mess.*

פִּתְגָּם m. Ch.— I. *decree.* — II. *royal letter.*—III. *epistle;* Heb. *decree, sentence.*

פָּתָה *was silly*, Deu. 11:16, Job 31. 27. Niph. *was persuaded, enticed.* Pi. I. *led to folly, persuaded, enticed.*—II. *deceived.*—III. *used fair words to.* Pu. pass. of Pi. Hiph. (fut. apoc. יַפְתְּ) *declared foolish, idolatrous*, with לְ, Gen. 9:27.

פְּתוּאֵל p.n. of a man.

פֶּתִי, with pause פֶּתִי m. (pl. פְּתָיִים, פְּתָאִים).—I. *ignorant.*—II. *foolish.* —III. *folly*, Pro. 1:22.

פְּתַי m. Ch., *breadth.*

פְּתַיּוּת f., *folly*, Pro. 9:13.

פָּתוֹר, see פתר; פָּתוֹת, see פתת.

פָּתַח (fut. יִפְתַּח).— I. *opened.*—II. *uttered, opened his mouth.*—III. *opened the ears*, Isa. 50:5.—IV. *cleft a rock*, Ps. 105:41.— V. *loosened, untied*, Isa. 14:17.—VI. *brought out for sale.*—VII. *drew a sword*, Ps. 37:14. Niph. *was opened, unloosed.* Pi. I. *opened, &c.,* as Kal. — II. *carved, engraved.* Pu. *engraven.* Hith. *loose thyself*, Isa. 52:2.

פְּתַח Ch., *opened.*

פֶּתַח m. (with suff. פִּתְחוֹ; pl. פְּתָחִים, פִּתְחֵי). — I. *opening, gateway, entrance.*—II. *door or gate;* בְּפֶתַח הַפֶּתְחָה פֶּתַח *to the gate.*

פֵּתַח m., *opening, laying open*, Ps. 119:130.

פְּתִיחוֹת f. pl., *drawn swords*, Ps. 55:22.

פִּתּוּחַ m., *engraving, carving.*

פִּתְחוֹן, const. פִּתְחוֹן m., *opening of the mouth.*

פְּתַחְיָה p.n. of a man.

מַפְתֵּחַ m., *key.*

מִפְתָּח m., *opening the lips*, Pro. 8:6.

פְּתִיגִיל m., "stomacher," Eng. Ver., Isa. 3:24, meaning uncertain.

פָּתַל. Niph. *was twisted with, struggled together*, Gen. 30:8. Hith. *struggled against*, Ps. 18:27; תִּתְפַּל for תִּתְפַּתָּל the same, 2 Sa. 22:27.

פָּתִיל m.—I. *lace, thread, cord.*—II. *string* for a signet-ring.—III. *plate of gold.*—IV. *cloth for a cover*, Nu. 19:15.

פְּתַלְתֹּל m., *perverse*, Deu. 32:5.

נַפְתּוּל m., *struggles*, Gen. 30:8.

פָּתֹם p. n., *a city of Egypt in the vicinity of Goshen, probably Damietta.*

פֶּתֶן m., *an asp.*

מִפְתָּן m., *threshold of a door, gate, &c.*

פֶּתַע m.—I. *suddenness.*—II. adv. *suddenly*; בְּפֶתַע the same.

פִּתְאֹם adv., *suddenly, immediately*; בְּפֶתַע פִּתְאֹם the same; לְפֶתַע פּ׳ and פֶתַע פּ׳ the same; פַּחַד פּ׳ *sudden fear.*

פָּתַר (fut. יִפְתֹּר) *interpreted, explained*, Gen. chaps. 40 and 41 only.

פִּתְרוֹן m., *interpretation*, Gen. chaps. 40 and 41 only.

פְּתוֹר p. n., *the country of the prophet Balaam, probably Petra.*

פַּתְרוֹס p. n., *some nation bordering upon Egypt*; פַּתְרֻסִים *its inhabitants.*

פַּתְשֶׁגֶן same as פַּרְשֶׁגֶן.

פָּתַת *broke to pieces*, Lev. 2:6.

פַּת f. (with suff. פִּתִּי; pl. פִּתִּים), *a piece, piece of bread.*

פְּתוֹת m., the same, Eze. 13:19.

צ

צֵא, with ה parag. צֵאָה Kal imp, from יָצָא.

צֵאָה *excrement*; see צֹוא.

צֶאֱלִים m. pl., *trees in dry places, shady bushes*, Job 40:21, 22.

צֹאן (צְאֹון) com.—I. coll. *sheep or goats.*—II. *a flock of sheep or goats.*—III. *a people* (the flock of God).

צַעֲנָן p. n., *a city in the tribe of Judah; called also* צֵנָן.

צֶאֱצָאִים; see יָצָא.

צֵאת Kal inf., from יָצָא.

צַבִּים, צָב; see צָבַב.

צָבָא I. *assembled for war, fought.*—II. *assembled for a service, performed it.* Hiph. *marshalled an army.*

צָבָא m. (pl. צְבָאִים, צְבָאוֹת Ps. 103: 21).—I. *an army.*—II. *any multitude*; אַנְשֵׁי הַצָּבָא *soldiers*; שַׂר הַצָּבָא *commander in chief.*—III *warfare, military service.*—IV. *any appointed service* or *trial* צְבָא הַשָּׁמַיִם *the host of heaven*, i. e.—1. *the stars.*—2. *the angels*; יְהוָֹה צ׳, אֱלֹהֵי צְבָאוֹת *the Lord of Hosts*, one of the titles of God; see also צְבָאוֹת, צְבָאִים in צְבִי under צְבָה.

צְבֹאִים, צְבוֹיִם p. n., *one of the cities of the plain destroyed with Sodom.*

צְבָא Ch., *wished, was willing.*

צְבוּ f. Ch., *determination, resolution*, Dan. 6:18.

צָבַב (Arab. *hid, concealed*).

צָב m.—I. *a covered waggon*; pl. צַבִּים.—II. *a kind of lizard*, Lev. 11:29.

צֹבֶבָה p. n. of a woman.

צָבָה I. same as צָבָא; part. צֹבֶה
waging war.—II. burst, Nu. 5:27.
Hiph. caused to burst, Nu. 5:22.

צָבֶה m., צָבָה f., swelling, Nu. 5:21.

צְבִי m.—I. beauty, ornament, honour.
— II. an antelope; pl. צְבָיִים,
צְבָאוֹת .f ;צְבָאִים.

צְבִיָּה f., she antelope.

צִבְיָה p. n. of a woman.

צְבִיָּא p. n. of a man.

צָבַט took up in his hand, Ru. 2:14.

צָבַע (Arab. dyed).
צְבַע Ch. Pa. dyed, made wet. Hith.
was dyed.

צֶבַע m., a dyed dress, Jud. 5:30.

צָבוּעַ m., hyæna, Jer. 12:9 (Arab.
hyæna).

צְבֹעִים p. n., a valley and town of
Benjamin.

צִבְעוֹן p. n., a son of Seir.

אֶצְבַּע f. (with suff. אֶצְבָּעוֹ; pl.
אֶצְבָּעוֹת).—I. a finger.—II. a toe.
—III. the hand.—IV. a digit. Ch.
the same.

צָבַר (fut. יִצְבֹּר).—I. heaped up.—II.
laid up, treasured up.

צִבֻּרִים m. pl., heaps, 2 Ki. 10:8.

צָבַת (Arab. took in his hand).
צֶבֶת m., pl. צְבָתִים handfuls, Ru.
2:16.

צָדַד (Arab. turned the face away).
צַד m. (with suff. צִדּה; pl. צִדִּים).
—I. side, with ה parag. צִדָּה to
the side; מִצַּד at the side; עַל צַד
the same.—II. adversary, Jud. 2:3.

צַד m. Ch. side; מִצַּד at the side;
לְצַד against.

צָדָד p. n., a town in the north of
Palestine.

צָדִים p. n., a town of Naphtali.

צָדָה laid wait for, Ex. 21:13. Niph.
was destroyed, Zep. 3:6.

צְדָא m. Ch., perverseness, Dan. 3:14.

צְדִיָּה f., lying in wait, Nu. 35:20, 22.

צָדַק (fut. יִצְדַּק).—I. was righteous,
equitable.—II. acted justly.—III.
was in the right.—IV. was acknowledged to be just, in the right.
Niph. was purified, exculpated,
Dan. 8:14. Pi. justified, cleared,
himself or another. Hiph. — I.
did justice.—II. gave judgment in
favour of, acquitted.—III justified
before God, Ex. 23:7. Hith. fut.
pl. נִצְטַדָּק cleared himself, Gen
44: 16.

צֶדֶק m. (with suff. צִדְקוֹ).—I. truth.
—II. fairness, equity.—III. a just
cause.—IV. acquittal, justification.
V. righteousness.

צְדָקָה f.—I. truth, equity.—II. a just
cause or claim.—III. righteousness.—IV. favor, approbation.

צִדְקָה f. Ch., equity, righteousness.

צַדִּיק m.—I. righteous.—II. having a
just cause.—III. innocent.—IV.
true, Isa. 41:26.

צָדוֹק p. n. of a man.

צִדְקִיָּה, צִדְקִיָּהוּ p. n.—I. Zedekiah
king of Judah.—II. also of other
men.

צַדְקָתֵךְ Eze. 16:52. Pi. inf., with
suff. and f. termination, from צדק.

צָהַב. Hoph. part. מֻצְהָב of a gold
colour, Ezr. 8:27.

צָהֹב m., red.

I. צָהַל 1. *neighed.* — 2. *shouted for joy.* Pi. *shouted for joy or sorrow,* with קוֹל.—II. same as זָהַר. Hiph. הִצְהִיל *caused to shine,* Ps. 104: 15.

מִצְהָלָה f., *neighing.*

צָהַר same as זָהַר. Hiph. *made the fine oil called* יִצְהָר, Job 24:11.

צֹהַר m.—I. *a light, window, &c.*—II. *noon.*

יִצְהָר m.—I. *fine olive oil.*—II. p.n. of a man; *patron.* יִצְהָרִי

צַו, צֻו; see צוה.

צוֹא m., *filthy,* Zec. 3:3, 4.

צוֹאָה f., *filth, dung.*

צֵאָה f., *excrement.*

צַוָּר, צַוָּאר, const. צַוַּאר m. (pl. צַוָּארִי, צַוָּארֵי, צַוָּארֹת) *neck, shoulder, back;* Ch. the same.

צַוְּרֹנִים m. pl., *the neck,* Cant. 4:9.

צוֹבָא, צוֹבָה or אֲרַם צ' p. n., a city and district of Syria.

צוּד *hunted, pursued, watched for,* men or animals. Pil. צוֹדֵד *ensnare, beguile.* Hith. הִצְטַיָּד (see צַיִד) *furnished with provisions,* Jos. 9: 12.

צַיִד, const. צֵיד m.—I. *hunting.*—II. *game, prey.*—III. *provisions* (of any kind).

צֵדָה, צֵידָה f., *provisions.*

צַיָּד m., *hunter,* Jer. 16:16.

צִידוֹן p.n., *Zidon,* a city of Phenicia; צִידֹנִי m., צִידֹנִית f., *a Zidonian.*

מָצֵד m. (pl. מְצָדוֹת) *fortress, strong place.*

מָצוֹד m. } —I. *prey.*—II. *net.*—III.
מְצוֹדָה f. } *fortress.*

מָצוּד m., *hunter's net,* Job 19:6.

מְצָדָה, מְצוּדָה f.—I. *prey.*—II. *net.* —III. *fortress.*

צָוָה. Pi. צִוָּה (fut. יְצַוֶּה; apoc. יְצַו imp. צַוֵּה; apoc. צַו).—I. *commanded, gave orders,* with אֶל, עַל, לְ.—II. *appointed.*—III. *caused,* i.e. appointed a thing; צִוָּה אֶל בֵּיתוֹ *he gave his last orders to his house,* 2 Sa. 17:23. Pu. צֻוָּה *was commanded.*

צַו, צֻו m., *precept, command.*

צִיּוּן m.—I. *sepulchral monument.*— II. *waymark,* Jer. 31:21.

מִצְוָה f. (pl. מִצְוֹת) *command, precept.*

צָוַח *shouted for joy,* Isa. 42:11.

צְוָחָה f., *cry of sorrow.*

צוּל (Arab. *lay hid*); see צָלַל *sank.*

צוּלָה f., *the deep,* Isa. 44:27.

מְצוֹלָה, מְצוּלָה f., *depth* (of the sea, &c.)

צוּם *fasted.*

צוֹם m. (pl. צוֹמוֹת) *fasting.*

צוּעַ (Arab. *formed, designed*).

מַעֲשֵׂה צ' m. pl., צַעֲצֻעִים *carvings,* 2 Chron. 3:10.

צוֹעֵר, צֹעֵר; see צער.

צוּף *flowed,* Lam. 3:54. Hiph. הֵצִיף I. *caused to flow.* — II. *caused to float.*

צוּף m. — I. *honey-comb.* — II. צוּף, צִיף, צוֹפַי p.n., *the son of Elkanah.*

צָפָה f., *overflowing,* Eze. 32:6.

צַפְצָפָה f., *a willow,* Eze. 17:5.

צוּץ; see ציץ.

I. צוּק same as יָצַק *pour,* Job 28:2; 29:6.

II. צוּק ‎ *was in difficulty*, Dan. 9:25.
Hiph. הֵצִיק ‎ I. *urged, constrained.*
—II. *distressed.*

צוּקָה ‎ f., *distress.*

מָצוֹק ‎ m., *restraint, difficulty, trouble.*

מָצוּק ‎ m.—I. *pillars, supports.*— II.
peaks, projections of rocks, 1 Sa.14:5.

מוּצָק ‎ with pause מוּצָק ‎ m., *constraint;*
see also in יָצַק.

מְצוּקָה ‎ f., *restraint, difficulty, trouble.*

צוּר ‎ I. *formed, fashioned.*—II. *tied up
money.* — III. *surrounded.* — IV.
overlaid.—V. *acted hostilely.*—VI.
besieged, with עַל, אֶל.

צוּר ‎ m. (pl. צוּרִים, צוּרוֹת).—I. *a rock.*
—II. *a refuge* (applied to God).—
III. *a stone,* Isa. 8:14. — IV. *a
sharp stone used as a knife,* Jos.
5:2, 3.—V. *edge of a sword,* Ps.
89:44.— VI. *form, figure,* Ps. 49:
15.—VII. p. n. *of a man.*

צֹר ‎ m.—I. *a rock,* Eze. 3:9. — II. *a
knife,* Ex. 4:25.

צֹר, צוּר ‎ p. n., *Tyre,* the capital of
Phenicia, Τύρος; צֹרִי ‎ *a Tyrian.*

צוּרָה ‎ f., *form, figure,* Eze. 43:11.

צוּרִיאֵל ‎ p. n. of a man.

צוּרִישַׁדָּי ‎ (*my rock is the Almighty*),
p. n. of a man.

צִיר ‎ m.—I. *figure, image,* Isa. 45:16.
—II. *hinge,* Pro. 26:14. — III.
pangs of a woman in labour; see
also in loc.

צַר ‎ m., צָרָה ‎ f., *narrow, small, close;*
see also in צרר.

צֵר ‎ p.n., a town in the tribe of Naphtali.

מָצוֹר ‎ m.—I. *restraint.*—II. *siege.*—
III. *mound of besiegers.*—IV. *mu-
nition, citadel.* — V. p. n., *Egypt,*
same as מִצְרַיִם, which see.

מְצוּרָה ‎ f., *fortress, citadel, mound.*

צַוְּרֹנִים, צַוָּר ‎; see צַוָּאר.

צוּת ‎. Hiph. הֵצִית ‎ *set on fire,* Isa. 27:
4; same as יָצַת.

צָחָה ‎ root not used; Ch. *thirsted.*

צָחֶה ‎ m., *parched,* Isa. 5:13.

צָחָא ‎ p. n. of a man.

צָחַח ‎ *was white,* Lam. 4:7.

צַח ‎ m., צָחָה ‎ f.—I. *hot, burning.*—
II. *bright, white.*— III. *distinctly,
plainly,* Isa. 32:4.

צָחִיחַ ‎ m.—I. *dry, bare.*—II. *open, exposed,* Neh. 4:7.

צְחִיחִי ‎ m., pl. צְחִיחִים ‎ *dry places,*
Neh. 4:7.

צְחִיחָה ‎ f., *a parched land,* Ps. 68:7.

צְחָצָחוֹת ‎ f. pl., *dry places,* Isa. 58:
11.

צָחַן ‎ (Arab. *was hot*).

צַחֲנָה ‎ f., *the heat of putrefaction
stench,* Joel 2:20.

צָחַק ‎ *laughed,* with לְ. Pi. צִחֵק ‎ I.
made laughter, joked.—II. *laughed
at, insulted,* with בְּ.

צְחֹק ‎ m., *laughter, ridicule.*

יִצְחָק, יִשְׂחָק ‎ p. n., *Isaac,* the son of
Abraham and Sarah; LXX.
Ἰσαάκ.

צַחַר ‎ m., *whiteness,* Eze. 27:18.

צָחֹר ‎ m., *white,* Jud. 10:5.

צֹחַר ‎ p. n. of a man.

צִיבָא ‎ p. n. of a man.

צֵיד, צֵידָה, צַיָּד, צָיַד, צִידוֹן ‎; see צוד.

צִיָּה ‎ root not used; (Arab. *drought*).

צִי ‎ m. (see צִיָּה), *a ship;* pl. צִיִּים,
צִים.

צִיָּה ‎ f.—I. *drought,* Job 24:19.—II
parched land, wilderness.

צִיִּים m. pl., *inhabitants of the desert, men or beasts.*

צִיּוֹן m., *parched land.*

צִיּוּן; see צִוָּה.

צִיּוֹן f. (*citadel*), p. n., *Zion*, the well known hill on and around which Jerusalem was built.

צִין, צִן p.n., *the desert between Canaan and the land of Edom.*

צִינֹק *fetters;* see צָנַק.

צִיעֹר p. n., *a town of Judah.*

צִיץ (pret. צָץ; fut. יָצִיץ).—I. *flowered.* — II. *flourished.* Hiph. *looked cheerfully,* Cant. 2:9.

צִיץ m.—I. *a flower;* pl. צִצִּים.—II. *anything shining, plate of metal.*— III. *plumage, wings.*—IV. p. n. of a place.

צִיצָה f., *flower,* Isa. 28:4.

צִיצִת f.—I. *lock of hair,* Eze. 8:3.— II. *fringe,* Nu. 15:38,39.

צִקְלַג, צִיקְלַג, צִיקְלָג p. n., *a city of the Philistines in the land of Simeon.*

צִיר Kal not used; (Arab. *went*). Hith. הִצְטַיַּר *prepared for a journey,* Jos. 9:4.

צִיר m., *person sent on a journey, messenger;* see also in צֹר.

צֵל, צָלָה, צָלוּל; see צָלַל.

צְלָא Ch. Pa. *prayed.*

צָלָה *roasted,* Isa. 44:16,19.

צָלִי m., *roasted.*

צָלַח, צָלֵחַ (fut. יִצְלַח).—I. *crossed a river.*—II. *fell upon, descended,* with עַל.—אֶל III. *advanced, flourished.*—IV. *was useful, fit,* with לְ. Hiph. הִצְלִיחַ I. *made to pros-*

per, with לְ.—II. *accomplished.*— III. *was prosperous.*

צְלַח Ch. Aph. הַצְלַח I. *made prosperous.*—II. *was prosperous.*

צְלָחוֹת f. pl., *dishes.*

צְלוֹחִית f., *a dish,* 2 Ki. 2:20.

צַלַּחַת f., *the same.*

I. צָלַל I. *sank in the water,* Ex. 15:10.—II. *became shaded,* Neh. 13:19. Hiph. part. מֵצֵל *giving shade,* Eze. 31:3.

צְלִיל (צָלוּל) m., *a barley cake,* Jud. 7:13.

צֶלֶל m. (with suff. צִלֲלוֹ; pl. צְלָלִים, צְלָלֵי), *a shadow.*

צֵל m. (with suff. צִלָּה).—I. *a shadow.* —II. *dusk.*—III. *shelter, protection.*

צִלָּה p.n., *Zillah*, the wife of Lamech.

צַלְמָוֶת m., *shadow of death,* applied to any thick darkness.

צַלְמֻנָּע p.n., *a king of the Midianites.*

צַלְפֹנִי (with art.), p. n. of a man.

מְצִלָּה f., *shady place.*

II. צָלַל I. *tingled (of the ears).*—II. *quivered (of the lips),* Hab. 3:16.

צְלָצַל, const. צִלְצַל m.—I. *a cymbal.*— II. *a species of locust,* Deu. 28:42. — III. *tumult of an army* or *shadowing;* see I. צָלַל Isa. 18:1. —IV. *harpoon,* Job 40:31.

צֶלְצְלִים, pl. const. צִלְצְלֵי *cymbals.*

מְצִלָּה f., pl. מְצִלּוֹת.—I. *cymbals.*— II. *bells.*

מְצִלֶּת f., dual מְצִלְתַּיִם *pair of cymbals.*

צָלַם root not used; (Arab. *was dark*).

צֶלֶם m.—I. *a shadow,* Ps. 39:7.—II. *an imagination,* Ps. 73:20.—III.

representation, picture, image.—IV. *resemblance.*

צֶלֶם ,צְלֵם m. Ch., *an image.*

צַלְמוֹן (*shady ?*) p. n., a mountain of Ephraim.

צַלְמֹנָה p. n., one of the stations in the wilderness.

צַלְמָוֶת; see in I. צלל.

צָלַע part. צֹלֵעַ; f. צֹלְעָה *halting, lame.*

צֶלַע m., *limping, falling.*

צֵלָע f. (const. צֶלַע ,צְלַע; with suff. צַלְעוֹ).—I. *a rib.*—II. *a plank for wainscoting.*—III. *a side.*—IV. *side chamber;* pl. צְלָעוֹת; const. צַלְעוֹת *side planks, side chambers;* צְלָעִים *folding doors.*—V. p. n., the town of Benjamin where Saul was buried.

צֶלֶף p. n. of a man.

צְלָפְחָד p. n. of a man.

צֶלְצַח p. n., a piace in Benjamin.

צְלָצַל ,צַלְצַל ,צְלְצְלִים; see II. צלל.

צֶלֶק p. n., one of David's captains.

צִלְתַי p. n. of a man.

צָמֵא, fut. יִצְמָא.—I. *thirsted.*—II. *earnestly desired.*

צָמֵא m., צְמֵאָה f., *thirsty.*

צָמָא m., *thirst.*

צִמְאָה f., *thirst,* Jer. 2:25.

צִמָּאוֹן m., *thirsty land.*

צָמַד. Niph. *was bound, yoked* (to idolatry). Pu. *tied, fastened,* 2 Sa. 20:8. Hiph. *contrived,* Ps. 50:19.

צָמִיד m.—I. *tied, fastened,* Nu. 19:15.—II. *a band, bracelet.*

צֶמֶד m. (with suff. צִמְדּוֹ; pl. צְמָדִים,

צִמְדֵי).—I. *a pair, yoke* (of oxen, &c.).—II. *the quantity of land ploughed in a day by a yoke of oxen.*

צָמוּק; see צמק.

צָמַח (fut. יִצְמַח).—I. *shot, grew up.*—II. *flourished.*—III. *sprang up, arose, began.*—IV. *produced.* Pi. *grew* (of hair). Hiph. (fut. יַצְמִיחַ וַיְצַמַּח) *caused to grow, produced.*

צֶמַח m. (with suff. צִמְחָהּ).—I. *shooting.*—II. *a shoot.*—III. *plants.*—IV. *the Branch* (a title of Christ).

צְמִיתַת; see צמת.

צָמַם root not used; (Arab. *tied*); Ch. *covered.*

צַמָּה f., *a woman's veil.*

צַמִּים m.—I. *noose, snare.*—II. *destruction.*

צָמַק *dry* (of the breasts), Hos. 9:14.

צִמּוּק m., *dry grapes;* Ital. *simmuki.*

צֶמֶר m. (with suff. צַמְרִי), *wool.*

צַמֶּרֶת f., *foliage.*

צְמָרִי p. n., an unknown people, Gen. 10:18.

צְמָרַיִם p. n., a town of Benjamin.

צָמַת *silenced, destroyed,* Lam. 3:53. Niph. *was put to silence.* Pi. and Hiph. *put to silence, destroyed.* Pilp. צִמְתֵת the same.

צְמִיתֻת f., *perfect silence;* לִצְמִתֻת, לַצְמִיתֻת *completely* (without power of redemption), Lev. 25:23, 30.

צִמְּתֻתֻנִי Ps. 88:17. Pil. pret. pl., with suff., from צמת.

צֵן; see צין.

צִנָּה ,צֹנָא ,צֹנֶה; see צאן.

צְנֶה ,צְנִים ,צְנִינִים; see צנן.

צִנּוֹר m., watercourse, cataract.

צָנַח I. dismounted.—II. went down, Jud. 4:21.

צָנֵם part., f. pl. צְנֻמוֹת " withered," Eng. Ver.; Gen. 41:23 (meaning not very certain).

צְנִים m. pl., fence of thorns, thorns.
צְנִינִים m. pl., thorns.
צִנָּה f.—I. barb of hook, Am. 4:2.—II. a shield.—III. a shield-shaped vessel used for snow, Pro. 25:13.
צִנְצֶנֶת f., a basket, Ex. 16:33.
צֹנֵן same as צָאנָן.

צָנַע ready, prepared, Pro.11:2. Hiph. being ready, Mic. 6:8.

צָנַף I. bound, wrapped round, Isa. 22:18. — II. wrapped round the head, Lev. 16:4.
(צָנוֹף) צָנִיף m., turban.
צְנֵפָה f., wrapping, Isa. 22:18.
מִצְנֶפֶת f., turban worn by the high priest.

צָנַק root not used; (Arab. fetters).
צִינֹק m., fetters, Jer. 29:26.

צַנְתָּרוֹת f. pl., pipes, tubes, Zec. 4:12.

צָעַד (fut. יִצְעַד; inf., with suff. צֶעְדְּךָ). —I. walked, advanced.—II. went over a country.—III. shot up, Gen. 49:22. Hiph. caused to walk, brought over, Job 18:14.
צַעַד m.—I. stepping, Pro. 30:29.—II. a step, 2 Sa. 6:13.—III. progress, action, conduct.
צְעָדָה f., marching; pl. צְעָדוֹת anklets, Isa. 3:20.
אֶצְעָדָה f., bracelet.

מִצְעָד m., step, proceeding.

צָעָה wandering for plunder, losing one's way, perishing. Pi. צִעָה plundered, Jer. 48:12.

צָעִיף m., woman's veil.
צְעִירָה ,צְעִיר little; see צער.

צָעַן removed, Isa. 33:20.
צַעֲנַנִּים p. n., a city of the Kenites in Naphtali.
צֹעַן p. n., Zoan, a city of Lower Egypt; possibly Tanis.
צַעֲצֻעִים; see צוע.

צָעַק (fut. יִצְעַק) cried out for help, with לְ, אֶל. Pi. cried vehemently, 2 Ki. 2:12. Hiph. cause to be summoned, 1 Sa. 10:17. Niph. I. were called, summoned.— II. assembled themselves.
צְעָקָה const. צַעֲקַת f., a cry for help.

צָעַר was small, of little importance.
צֹעַר ,צֹעַר p. n., one of the cities of the plain, formerly בֶּלַע.
צָעִיר m., צְעִירָה f.—I. small.—II. young.—III. p. n. of a place, 2 Ki. 8:21.
צָעוֹר Ketib, same as צָעִיר, Jer. 14:3; 48:4.
צְעִירָה f., smallness, inferiority in age.
מִצְעָר m., little, small; לְמִצְעָר for a little time.
מִצְעָרָה f., of a small kind, Dan. 8:9.

צָפַד adhered, cleaved to, Lam. 4:8.

I. צָפָה I. kept watch.—II. looked for, expected; צוֹפֶה observer, watchman.—III. watched, observed, with בְּ.—IV. plotted against, with

ל. Pi. צָפָה I. kept watch.—II. looked, expected help.

צִפִּיָּה f., watch-tower, Lam. 4:17.

צָפִית f., watch-tower, Isa. 21:5.

צָפַת p.n., a town of Canaan, afterwards called חָרְמָה.

צִפְקָתָה p.n., a valley near Maresha in Judah.

מִצְפֶּה m.—I. watch-tower.—II. p.n., a town in Judah.—III. in Moab.—IV. in Gad.—V. in Benjamin.—VI. a valley in the north of Palestine.

מִצְפָּה p.n.—I. a town in Gilead, same as מִצְפֵּה-גִלְעָד.—II. a town in Benjamin, same as מִצְפֶּה.

II. צָפָה covered, overlaid with wood or metal, with בְּ, אֶל. Pu. was overlaid.

צָפָה s. f.; see צוּף.

צְפוֹ, צְפִי p.n., a son of Eliphaz.

צִפּוּי m., covering, coat.

צָפוֹן, צִפְיוֹן p.n. of a man; patron. צְפוֹנִי.

צָפוֹן, צְפוֹנִי; see צפן.

צְפוֹר, צִפֳּרִים; see צפר.

צָפַח (Arab. made broad).

צוֹפַח, צֶפַח p.n. of a man.

צַלַּחַת f., a dish, vessel.

צַפִּיחִית f., flat cake, cake.

צְפִיעַ, צְפִיעוֹת; see צפע.

צָפִיר, צְפִירָה; see צפר.

צְפִית; see צפה.

צָפַן I. hid, concealed.—II. excluded, Job 17:4.—III. laid up, treasured up.—IV. lay hid, lay in wait, with ל; part. צָפוּן a secret, treasure, one hidden (of God). Niph. I. was hidden, with מִן.—II. was laid up, destined for, with ל. Hiph. hid.

צָפוֹן com. (hidden, dark quarter).—I. the north.—II. the north wind; מִצָּפוֹן, לְצָפוֹן northward of any where; צָפוֹנָה towards the north; לַצָּפוֹנָה the same; מִצָּפוֹנָה from the north; with ל from the north of any where.—II. p.n., a town of Gad; see also צָפוֹן same as צָפִיוֹן in II.; צָפָה; see also in בַּעַל.

צְפוֹנִי m., northern, Joel 2:20.

צָפִין (צָפֻן) m., treasure.

צְפַנְיָה, צְפַנְיָהוּ (whom the Lord hath hidden), p.n.—I. Zephaniah, the prophet; LXX. Σοφονίας.—II. other men.

מַצְפוּן m., hidden place, Obad. v. 6.

צָפְנַת פַּעְנֵחַ the Egyptian title of Joseph; its meaning altogether unknown, Gen. 41:45.

צֶפַע m., basilisk, Isa. 14:29.

צִפְעוֹנִי m. (pl. צִפְעֹנִים) the same.

צָפִיעַ m., pl. צְפִיעִים dung, Eze. 4:15.

צְפִיעָה f., pl. צְפִיעוֹת, "issue," Eng. Ver., Isa. 22:24.

צָפַף Pil. צִפְצֵף I. chirped (as a bird), Isa. 10:14, &c.—II. spoke in a low voice.

צַמְצָפָה; see צוּף.

צָפַר hastened (fut. וַיִּצְפֹּר), Jud. 7:3.

צָפִיר m., goat, he-goat.

צְפִיר m. Ch., the same.

צְפִירָה f.—I. a crown, Isa. 28:5.—II. "morning," Eng. Ver., Eze. 7:7, 10; sense uncertain.

צִפּוֹר com. (pl. צִפֳּרִים).—I. a bird.—II. specially, a sparrow.—III. p.n. the father of Balaam the prophet

צִפֹּר com. Ch., *a bird.*

צִפֹּרָה p. n., the wife of Moses.

צְפַרְדֵּעַ com., *a frog.*

צִפֹּרֶן m.—I. *nail of the finger.*—II. *point of the graver.*

צְפָת, צְפָתָה; see צפה.

צֶפֶת f., *capital of a pillar,* 2 Chron. 3:15.

צִיִּים; see צִיּץ.

צַק Kal. imp., from יצק.

צִיקְלָן same as צִקְלָן.

צִקְלוֹן m., *husk,* 2 Ki. 4:42.

צֶקֶת Kal inf., from יצק.

צַר, צֵר, צֹר; see צוּר; צָרִי, צָר, see צרר.

צָרַב Niph. *was scorched,* Eze. 21:3.

צָרֶבֶת f.—I. *burning,* Pro. 16:27.—II. *inflammation,* Lev. 13:23, 28.

צְרֵדָה p. n., a town of Manasseh; צָרְתָן, צְרֵרָה the same.

צָרָה s. f.; see צרר.

צְרִי, צֳרִי, with pause צֳרִי m., *mastich,* the gum from the pistachia lentiscus.

צְרִי p. n., same as יְצְרִי; see יֵצֶר.

צְרוּיָה, צְרִידָה p.n., the mother of Joab.

צְרוֹר same as צְרֹר.

צָרַח *shouted,* Zep. 1:14. Hiph. the same, Isa. 42:13.

צְרִיחַ m., *a high tower.*

צֹרֶךְ m., *need, necessity,* 2 Chron. 2:15.

צָרַע, part. צָרוּעַ and Pu. part. מְצֹרָע m., מְצֹרַעַת f., *struck with leprosy.*

צְרוּעָה p.n., the mother of Jeroboam.

צָרְעָה p.n., a town of the Danites in Judah; צָרְעָתִי, צָרְעִי *a Zarathite.*

צִרְעָה f., coll. *wasps, hornets.*

צָרַעַת f. (with suff. צָרַעְתּוֹ) *the leprosy.*

צָרַף (fut. יִצְרֹף).—I. *refined metals.*—II. *purified a person's character.*—III. *tried a person's character;* part. צֹרֵף *refiner, goldsmith, silversmith;* צָרוּף *purified, pure.* Niph. *shall be purified,* Dan. 12:10. Pi. part. מְצָרֵף *goldsmith,* Mal. 3: 2, 3.

צָרְפִי (with art.), p. n. of a man.

צָרְפַת p. n., a town between Tyre and Zidon; Σάρεπτα, with ה loc. צָרְפַתָה.

מַצְרֵף m., *crucible.*

צָרַר I. *tied* or *bound up.*—II. *acted hostilely to.*—III. *was straitened;* part. צֹרֵר *an adversary;* impers. צַר לִי *I am distressed, grieved, concerned for some one,* with עַל. Niph. הֵצַר (inf. הָצֵר) *distressed.* Pu. part. מְצֹרָר.

צַר, with pause צָר m.—I. *difficulty, adversity, distress;* f. צָרָה; בַּצַּר לִי *when I am in distress.*—II. *enemy, besieger.*—III. *rival;* with art. הַצָּר; with suff. צָרִי; pl. צָרִים.—IV. *rock;* see צוּר.

צָרָה f., *enemy, adversary;* with ה parag. בְּצָרָתָה לִי *when I am in trouble.*

צְרוֹר, צְרֹר m. (pl. צְרֹרוֹת).—I. *a bundle.*—II. *a bag of money.*—III. *a small stone, a particle, grain.*—IV. p. n. of a man.

מֵצַר m., *restraint, trouble.*

צְרֵרָה; see צְרֵדָה.

צֶרֶת p.n. of a man.

צֶרֶת הַשַּׁחַר p. n., a town of Reuben.
צְרֵדָה ; see צָרְתָן.

ק

קֵא vomit; see קוֹא.

קָאם for קָם Kal pret., from קוּם.

קָאם Ch. Pe. part., from קוּם.

קָאַת (f.) (with art. הַקָּאַת; const. קָאַת),
a pelican or heron, not certain
which.

קָבַב cursed; imp. with suff. and נ
epenth. קָבְנוּ; with ה parag. קָבָה.
קַב m., a measure, the sixth part of
סְאָה, 2 Ki. 6:25.
קֻבָּה f., alcove, tent, Nu. 25:8, again
in the same verse אֶל קֻבָּתָהּ " in
her alcove" (Lee), generally interpreted of the person of the
woman.
קֻבָתָהּ,קֻבָה ; see נקב.

קָבָה root not used; (Arab. stomach).
קֵבָה f., the stomach, Deut. 18:3.
קֻבָּה (pronounced kŏbāh), Kal imp. with
ה parag., from קבב.

קָבַל. Pi. קִבֵּל I. accepted.—II. took.
—III. undertook, Est. 9:23, 27.
Hiph. taking hold of.
קַבֵּל Ch. Pa., received, took.
קְבָל prep., before, the front, 2 Ki.
15:10.
קֳבָל m. (with suff. קְבָלוֹ or קָבְלוֹ),
opposing, Eze. 26:9.
לָקֳבֵל,קֳבֵל m. Ch., the front;
1. in front of.—2. in consideration
of; with דִּי in consequence of;
כָּל קֳבֵל דְּנָה all before that, i. e.
for this reason, therefore; כָּל קֳבֵל
דִּי because.

קָבְנוּ Kal imp. with suff. and נ epenth.,
from קבב.

קָבַע forsook, neglected.
קוֹבַע m., a helmet.
קֻבַּעַת f., a drinking cup, Isa. 51:
17, 22.

קָבַץ collected, gathered together. Niph.
were assembled, assembled themselves. Pi. I. collected.—II. acquired. Pu. was gathered together,
Eze. 38:8. Hith. assembled themselves.
קְבֻצָה f., collection, heap, Eze. 22:20.
קִבּוּץ m., company, troop, Isa. 57:13.
קִבְצַיִם (two heaps), p. n., a town in
Ephraim.
יָקְבְצְאֵל,קַבְצְאֵל p. n., a town of
Judah.

קָבַר (fut. יִקְבֹּר) and Pi. קִבֵּר buried.
Niph. and Pu. was buried.
קֶבֶר m., burial place, sepulchre,
with suff. קִבְרוֹ; pl. קְבָרִים,קִבְרֵי;
קְבָרוֹת,קְבָרוֹת.
קִבְרוֹת הַתַּאֲוָה (the graves of lust);
p. n., a place in the wilderness of
Sinai, Nu. 11:34.
קְבוּרָה const. קְבֻרַת,קְבֻרַת f.—I.
burial.—II. burial place.

קָדַד bowed his head; fut. יִקֹּד.
קִדָּה f., cassia.
קָדְקֹד m. (with suff. קָדְקֳדוֹ), crown
of the head.
קָדוֹשׁ; see קדש.

קָדַח I. struck, kindled a fire.—II.
a fire was kindled.
קַדַּחַת f., a fever.
אֶקְדָּח m., a precious stone, the carbuncle, Isa. 54:12.

קָדַם Pi. קִדֵּם I. *preceded, came before.* — II. *came upon, against.* — III. *hastened, was early,* Ps. 119: 147. Hiph. I. *anticipate,* Job 41:3. — II. *come upon any one of misfortune,* Am. 9:10.

קֶדֶם m. (*that which precedes*). — I. adv., *before, in place.* — II. s., *the east;* אֶרֶץ קֶדֶם and קֶדֶם *the east,* i. e. *eastern country;* קֵדְמָה *towards the east;* מִקֶּדֶם *from the east;* with לְ *from the eastward of any place;* בְּנֵי קֶדֶם *those to the east of Palestine.* — III. *antiquity;* מִקֶּדֶם *from of old;* adv. *formerly;* קַדְמֵי אֶרֶץ *the ancient ones of the earth.*

קָדִים m. — I. *the east.* — II. *the east wind;* קָדִימָה *eastward.*

קְדוּמִים m. pl., *the ancients,* Jud. 5:21.

קֳדָם,קֳדָם Ch. — I. *before.* — II. מִן קֳדָם *from the presence, power of, by order of.*

קַדְמָה f. — I. *former condition.* — II. *origin,* Isa. 23:7. — III. const. קַדְמַת *before* (in time), Ps. 129:6.

קַדְמָה f. Ch., *former state or time;* מִן קַדְמַת דְּנָה *before.*

קֵדְמָה f., const. קֵדְמַת *eastward of any place.*

קֵדְמָה p. n., *a son of Ishmael.*

קְדֵמוֹת p. n., *a town of the Reubenites.*

קַדְמָי m. Ch., *first, former.*

קַדְמִיאֵל p. n. of a man.

קַדְמוֹן m., קַדְמוֹנָה f., *eastern,* Eze. 47:8.

קַדְמֹנִי m. — I. *eastern.* — II. *former, ancient;* pl. קַדְמֹנִים *ancestors;* f.

קַדְמֹנִיּוֹת *former things.* — III. p. n. of a man.

קָדְקֹד *crown of head;* see קדר.

קָדַר I. *was dark, black, darkened.* — II. *was gloomy, distressed;* קֹדֵר *darkening, mourning.* Hiph. *made dark,* Eze. 31:15; 32:7, 8. Hith. *became dark,* 1 Ki. 18:45.

קֵדָר (*blackness*), p. n., *Kedar,* the son of Ishmael and his descendants; בְּנֵי קֵדָר *the sons of Kedar.*

קִדְרוֹן p. n., *Kedron,* a brook which flows by Jerusalem.

קַדְרוּת f., *darkness,* Isa. 50:3.

קְדֹרַנִּית adv., *mournfully,* Mal. 3:14.

קָדַשׁ,קָדֵשׁ (fut. יִקְדַּשׁ). — I. *hallowed, consecrated.* — II. *rendered sacred, set apart from,* Isa. 65:5. Niph. I. *was made holy,* Ex. 29:43. — II. *was reverenced,* with בְּ. Pi. קִדֵּשׁ I. *hallowed, set apart.* — II. *reverenced,* Deu. 32:51. — III. *kept holy.* — IV. *rendered sacred by contact,* Eze. 44: 19. — V. *purified by rites.* — VI. *appointed a religious service.* — VII. *prepared,* Mic. 3:5. Pu. *was consecrated, &c.* pass. of Pi. Hiph. I. *hallowed.* — II. *reverenced.* — III. *purified.* — IV. *prepared.* Hith. I. *made himself to be reverenced.* — II. *was celebrated* (a festival). — III. *purified himself.* — IV. *kept himself pure.*

קָדֵשׁ, קָדוֹשׁ m. — I. *holy, pure* (of God, angels, and men). — II. *sacred, set apart to God;* pl. קְדוֹשִׁים.

קַדִּישׁ m. Ch., *holy.*

קֹדֶשׁ, קֹדֶשׁ m. (with suff. קָדְשִׁי; pl. קְדָשִׁים or קֳדָשִׁים, const. קָדְשֵׁי). — I. *holiness.* — II. *that which is*

consecrated to God, holy; קֹדֶשׁ קָן; see קוה.
קָדָשִׁים Holy of Holies (the place within the vail of the tabernacle and temple).

קָדֵשׁ m. (one devoted to an idol).—I. Sodomite or, perhaps, priest of Baal-peor.—II. f. קְדֵשָׁה a harlot. III. קָדֵשׁ בַּרְנֵעַ, קָדֵשׁ p. n., a city of the wilderness, between Edom and Egypt.

קֶדֶשׁ p. n.—I. a town of Judah.—II. of Naphtali.—III. of Issachar, called also קִשְׁיוֹן.

מִקְדָּשׁ (מִקְדָּשׁ) m.—I. sanctuary (the tabernacle or temple).—II. sacred thing, part, Nu. 18:29.—III. asylum (place of safety).

קָהָה were set on edge (of teeth). Pi. קֵהָה became blunt (of an instrument), Ecc. 10:10.

קְהָת p. n., Kohath, the son of Levi; patron. קְהָתִי.

קָהַל. Hiph. הִקְהִיל called together, summoned. Niph. assembled themselves.

קָהָל m.—I. a meeting.—II. assemblage, multitude.—III. הַקָּ׳ the congregation of Israel.

קְהֵלָה p. n., a station of Israel in the wilderness.

קְהִלָּה f., assembly.

קֹהֶלֶת m. (f., Ecc. 7:27), p. n. (preacher), applied to Solomon in the book of Ecclesiastes; LXX. ἐκκλησιαστής.

מַקְהֵלִים m. pl., congregations, assemblies.

מַקְהֵלוֹת f. pl.—I. the same.—II. p. n., a station in the wilderness.

קוֹא I. vomited.—II. expelled with disgust. Hiph. הֵקִיא the same.

קֵא m., a vomit, Pro. 26:11.

קִיא m., the same.

קִיקָלוֹן m., "shameful spewing," Eng. Ver.; Hab. 2:16.

קוֹבַע; see קבע.

קָוָה hoped in, waited for; part. קֹוֶה. Pi. קִוָּה (inf. קַוֵּה, קַוֹּה; fut. יְקַוֶּה, יְקַו).—I. trusted in, expected, with ל, אֶל.—II. watched for evil, plotted against. Niph. assembled themselves.

קָו, קַו m.—I. a measuring line.—II. a boundary line.—III. a limit, rule, direction, Ps. 19:5; with suff. קַוָּם.

קָוֶה m., 1 Ki. 7:23, Ketib for קַו.

מִקְוֶה m.—I. expectation, confidence, hope.—II. one confided in.—III. collection, assemblage.

מִקְוָה f., collection, repository, Isa. 22:11.

תִּקְוָה f.—I. hope, expectation.—II. a cord, thread.—III. p. n. of a man.

קוֹחַ; see פקח.

I. קוּט (fut. יָקוּט), was wearied, loathed, scorned, with בְּ. Niph. were loathed. Hith. הִתְקוֹטֵט same as Kal, with בְּ.

II. קוּט (Arab. was broken); fut. יָקוֹט will be broken, Job 8:14.

קוּל (Arab. he said).

קוֹל m. (with suff. קוֹלוֹ, קֹלְךָ; pl. קֹלוֹת).—I. voice.—II. cry of animals.—III. any sound; קוֹל יְהֹוָה the voice of the Lord, thunder.

קוֹלָיָה p. n. of a man.

קָל m. Ch., voice, sound.

קוּם (fut. יָקוּם, יָקֹם, וַיָּקָם).—I. rose up.—II. arose from bed.—III. arose from an ambush.—IV. with עַל, אֶל, בְּ, arose against in anger (abs. קָמַי they that rise up against me).—V. stood up.—VI. began anything.—VII. came into being, appeared.—VIII. took place.—IX. stood, stood firm.—X. was permanent (an office).—XI. was fixed (of the eyes). Pi. קִיֵּם I. strengthened, supported.—II. kept a resolution.—III. fixed a time. Pil. קוֹמֵם I. set up, restore.—II. set himself up, Mic. 2:8. Hiph. הֵקִים (fut. וַיָּקֶם, יָקֶם, יָקִים).—I. caused to rise up.—II. raised up.—III. strengthened.—IV. set up, fixed.—V. raised up, appointed.—VI. made or confirmed a covenant, or other engagement.—VII. put in force. Hoph. הוּקַם I. was set up.—II. was appointed.—III. was confirmed. Hith. הִתְקוֹמֵם arose against, with לְ.

קוּם Ch. I. arise.—II. stand up.—III. stand. Pa. קַיֵּם confirmed an engagement. Aph. אָקִים, הָקִים (fut. יְהָקִים, יְקִים).—I. set up.—II. established.—III. appointed.—IV. confirmed. Hoph. הֲקִים was set up, Dan. 7:4.

קוֹמָה f., height, stature.

קִים an adversary, Job 22:20.

קִימָה f., the act of rising up, Lam. 3:63.

קְיָם m. Ch., a decree, Dan. 6:8, 16.

קַיָּם m., קַיָּמָה f. Ch., enduring, steadfast.

קָמָה f. (pl. קָמוֹת), standing corn, specially in the ear.

קָמוֹן p. n., a town of Gilead.

קוֹמְמִיּוּת adv., at full height, erect, Lev. 26:13.

יְקוּם m., all that lives, i.e. has been raised up, Gen. 7:4, 23; Deu. 11:6.

מָקוֹם com. (pl. מְקוֹמוֹת).—I. place.—II. habitation, residence.—III. room, space.—IV. place, country, neighbourhood; בִּמְקוֹם אֲשֶׁר in the place where.

תְּקוּמָה f., power of resisting, Lev. 26:37.

תְּקוֹמֵם m., an adversary, Ps. 139:21.

קוּן. Pil. קוֹנֵן uttered a lamentation, lamented, with אֶל, עַל.

קִינָה f.—I. lamentation; pl. קִינִים, קִינוֹת—II. p. n., a city of Judah.

קוּם or קָסַם. Pil. קוֹסֵם cut off, Eze. 17:9, same as קָצַץ.

קוֹץ m., prince, Eze. 23:23; etymon unknown.

קוֹף ape, 1 Ki. 10:22; 2 Chron. 9:21.

קוּף go round, like נָקַף; not used.

תְּקוּפָה f.—I. orbit of the sun, Ps. 19:7.—II. circle of the year.

קוּץ I. loathed, with בְּ.—II. feared, with מִפְּנֵי.—I. Hiph. הֵקִיץ besieged, Isa. 7:6.—II. Hiph.—1. awoke.—2. arose from the dead, came to life.—3. was vigilant, active; קוּץ from קַיִץ pass the summer, Isa. 18:6.

קוֹץ m.—I. a thorn bush; pl. קֹצִים, קוֹצֵי—II. p. n. of a man.

קַיִץ m.—I. summer.—II. summer fruits.

קֻוְּצוֹת f. pl., *locks of hair*, Cant. 5:2.

קוּר *dig a well*. Pil. קִרְקֵר I. *dug down*, Num. 24:17.—II. *destroyed a people*, Isa. 22:5. Hiph. הֵקִיר *threw up water* (a well), Jer. 6:7.

קוּר m., *thread*, Isa. 59:5, 6.

קוֹרַת; see קרה.

מָקוֹר I. *spring*.—II. *origin*.—III. *wife*.

קוֹשׁ (fut. pl. יְקוֹשׁוּן) *ensnared*, Isa. 29:21. קִישׁ p.n. of a man.

קוּשָׁיָהוּ קִישִׁי p.n. of a man.

קִישׁוֹן p.n., *Kishon*.—I. a river of Palestine.—II. a town in Issachar.

קֶשֶׁת com. (pl. קְשָׁתוֹת, קְשָׁתוֹת).—I. *a bow*.—II. *the rainbow*.

קַשָּׁת m., *an archer*, Gen. 21:20.

קַח, in pause קָח, with ה parag. קְחָה Kal imp., from לקח.

קְחָ for לָקַח, Eze. 17:5; with suff. קָחָם for לְקָחָם, Hos. 11:3.

קַחַת, קֶחַת Kal inf., from לקח.

קֶטֶב קֶטֶב m. (with suff. קָטְבְךָ) *cutting down, destruction*.

קָטַט same as קוט.

קָטַל *slew*.

קְטַל Ch., *slew*. Pa. קַטֵּל the same. Ithpe. and Ithpa. *was slain*.

קֶטֶל m., *slaughter*, Obad. v. 9.

קָטֹן (fut. יִקְטַן) *was small, of little importance*. Hiph. *made small*, Am. 8:5.

קָטֹן, קָטָן m. (pl. קְטַנִּים; f. קְטַנָּה).— I. *small, in size, quantity* or *importance*.— II. *young*.— III. s. *the little finger*; with suff. קָטְנִי or קָטְנִי.—IV. הַקָּטָן p.n. of a man.

קָטַף *plucked off*. Niph. *was cut off, withered*, Job 8:12.

קָטַר. Pi. קִטֵּר I. *burnt incense*.—II. *fumigated*.—III. *burnt fat*; part. f. pl. מְקַטְּרוֹת *altars of incense*. Pu. part. f. מְקֻטֶּרֶת *was perfumed*, Cant. 3:6. Hiph. הִקְטִיר I. *burnt incense*.—II. *burnt sacrifice*. Hoph. הָקְטַר *was burnt in sacrifice*; part. מֻקְטָר *offering of incense*, Mal. 1:11.

קְטוֹרָה f., *incense*, Deu. 33:10.

קְטוּרָה p.n., *Keturah*, one of Abraham's wives.

קִטֹּר, pl. חֲצֵרוֹת קְטֻרוֹת "courts joined," Eng. Ver.; "with chimneys," marg.; *covered* (Ges.), Eze. 46:22.

קְטֹרֶת f., *incense*.

קִיטוֹר m.—I. *smoke*.—II. *vapour*, Ps. 148:8.

מֻקְטָר m., *incense*, Ex. 30:1.

מִקְטֶרֶת f., *a censer*.

קְטַר (Syr. *bound*).

קְטַר m. Ch., pl. קִטְרִין.—I. *joints, ligatures*.—II. *difficulties*.

קִטְרוֹן p.n. of a place in Zebulun, called also קַטָּת.

קִיא; see קוא.

קִיָה *vomited*; imp. pl. קִיוּ, Jer. 25:27.

קַיִט m. Ch., *summer*, Dan. 2:35.

קִיטוֹר; see קטר.

קִימָה, קַיִם, קָים, קִים; see קום.

קִימוֹשׁ same as קִמּוֹשׁ; see קמשׁ.

קִין root not used; (Arab. *cane, a spear*).

קַיִן m.—I. *a spear made of cane*, 2 Sa. 21:16.—II. p.n., *Cain*, the son of Adam.—III. p.n., the *Kenites*, a tribe of Canaan.—IV. הַקֵּין a town of Judah.

קִינִי, קֵנִי, קֵינִי the *Kenites*, one of the tribes inhabiting Canaan.

קֵינָה; see קוּן.

קֵינָן p. n. of a man.

קַיִץ *summer*, &c.; see קוּץ.

קִיצוֹן, קֵיצוֹנָה, קִיצוֹן; see קצץ.

קִיקָיוֹן m., the shrub *palma Christi, ricinus comm.,* κίκι.

קִיקָלוֹן; see קוֹא.

קִיר, קֹר com. (pl. קִירוֹת).—I. *a wall.* —II. *side of the altar.*—III. *sides of the heart,* Jer. 4:19.—IV. *city,* Isa. 15:1; 16:7.—V. קִיר מוֹאָב, קִיר חֲרֶשֶׁת, קִיר חֶרֶשׁ p. n., a city of Moab.—VI. p. n., a part of Assyria.

קֵרֹס, קֵירֹס p. n. of a man.

קֵישׁוֹן, קֵישׁ; see קוּשׁ.

קִיתָרֹס m. Ch., κιθαρις, *a harp.*

קַל, קָלָה; see קלל.

קָל Ch., קֹל *voice*; see קוֹל.

I. קָלָה I. *roasted.* — II. *burnt alive,* Jer. 29:22. Niph. part. נִקְלָה *burning disease,* Ps. 38:8.

קָלִי, קָלִיא m., *corn roasted in the ear.*

II. קָלָה *same as* קלל. Niph. *was despised;* part. *despised, mean.* Hiph. *despised,* Deu. 27:16.

קָלוֹן m.—I. *worthlessness.*—II. *shame.* —III. *contempt.*—IV. *pudenda.*

קַלַחַת f., *a caldron.*

קָלַט (Arab. *deformity*); part. קָלוּט *dwarfish.*

מִקְלָט *asylum, place of refuge.*

קְלִיטָה, קְלָיָה p. n. of a Levite.

קָלַל (fut. יֵקַל, יִקַּל).—I. *was diminished, became shallow.*—II. *was swift.*—III. *was worthless, unworthy.* Niph. נָקַל, נָקֹל (fut. יִקַּל, יִקָּלוּ).—I. *was thought a small, easy thing;* impers. מִן נָקַל *it is a small thing that;* עַל־נְקַלָּה *lightly, easily.*—II. *was despised.* —III. *lowered himself,* 2 Sa. 6:22. — IV. *became easy,* Pro. 14:6. Pi. קִלֵּל *revile, wished ill to,* with בְּ. Pil. קִלְקַל I. *shook arrow in divination,* Eze. 21:26 (like the Arab. *removed, shook*). Hiph. הֵקַל I. *slighted.*—II. *lightened, removed a load,* with מֵעַל, מִן. Hithpal. *was shaken,* Jer. 4:24.

קַל m. (pl. קַלִּים). f. קַלָּה).—I. *swift.* —II. *swiftly.*—III. *swift-footed.*

קָלַי p. n. of a man.

קָלָל m., *polished, shining.*

קְלָלָה, const. קִלְלַת f.—I *reviling.*— —II. *a curse.*—III. *object of reviling.*

קִלְקֵל m., *worthless food,* Nu. 21:5.

קָלַס Pi. and Hith. *mocked, scorned.*

קֶלֶס m., *scorn, contempt.*

קַלָּסָה f., *the same,* Eze. 22:4.

קָלַע I. *cut out, carved.*—II. *slung,* Jud. 20:16.—III. *expelled,* Jer. 10: 18; קֹלֵעַ *a slinger.* Pi. *slung a stone.*

קֶלַע m. (with suff. קַלְעוֹ; pl. קְלָעִים) —I. *a sling.*—II. *a curtain,* from its tremulous motion.

קַלָּע m., pl. קַלָּעִים *slingers,* 2 Ki. 3:25.

מִקְלַעַת f., *carving, sculpture,* 1 Ki only.

קַלְקֵל; see קלל.

קִלְּשׁוֹן m., ק׳ שְׁלֹשׁ *three pronged pitch-fork*, 1 Sa. 13:21.

קְמוּאֵל p.n. of a man.

קָמוֹן, see קום; קָמוֹשׁ, see קמש.

קֶמַח m., *flour*.

קָמַט (Arab. *bound with a rope*), *bound as a captive*, Job 16:8. Pu. *was seized and carried off*, Job 22:16.

קָמֵל, קָמַל *withered*.

קָמַץ *grasped, took up in the hand.*

קֹמֶץ m. (with suff. קֻמְצוֹ).—I. *the hand, fist.*—II. *abundance.*—III. pl. קְמָצִים *handfuls.*

קמשׁ *root not used.*

קִמּוֹשׁ, קִימוֹשׁ, pl. קִמְּשׁוֹנִים m., *nettles.*

קֵן, קֵן, קְנִים; see קנן.

קָנָא. Pi. קִנֵּא I. *was jealous for,* with לְ (ζηλοῦν).—II. *emulated,* with בְּ; *envied,* with בְּ, לְ.—III. *was jealous of,* with בְּ. Hiph. הִקְנִיא *made jealous, angry.*

קַנָּא m., *jealous* (of God against idols only).

קַנּוֹא m., the same.

קִנְאָה f.—I. *jealousy.*—II. *envy.*—III. *anger.*—IV. *zeal.*

קָנָה (fut. apoc. וַיִּקֶן).—I. *make.*—II. *acquire, appropriate to oneself.* Niph. *was acquired, purchased,* Jer. 32:15, 43. Hiph. I. *appropriated as a slave,* Zec. 13:5.—II. *provoked to jealousy,* Eze. 8:3.

קְנָא Ch., *acquired, procured,* Ezr. 7:17.

קְנָת p.n., a town of Manasseh.

קִנְיָן m., *possession, wealth.*

מִקְנֶה m. (with suff. מִקְנֵהוּ; pl. מִקְנִים) *possession, wealth of land, flocks, cattle;* אַנְשֵׁי מ׳ *possession of cattle;* אֶרֶץ מ׳ *land full of cattle.*

מִקְנָה f., *acquirement, purchase, possession.*

מִקְנֵיָהוּ p. n. of a man.

קָנֶה m. (const. קְנֵה; with suff. קָנֵהּ; pl. קָנִים (קְנוֹת.)—I. *reed, cane.*—II. *sweet cane.*—III. *measuring reed of six cubits.*—IV. *beam of the balance.*—V. *stalk of wheat.*—VI. *branch of candlestick.*—VII. *arm-bone above the elbow,* Job 31:22.—VIII. *a staff to lean upon.*

קָנֶה p.n.—I. *a place on the borders of Ephraim and Manasseh.*—II. *a town in Asher.*

קַנּוֹא same as קַנָּא; see קנא.

קְנַז p.n.—I. *of a man;* קְנִזִּי *patron.*—II. *of a people of Canaan.*

קְנִי same as קֵינִי.

קִנָּמוֹן, const. קִנְּמָן m., *cinnamon.*

קָנַן. Pi. קִנֵּן *built a nest.* Pu. part. מְקֻנֶּנֶת(ב׳) *was built* (of a nest).

קֵן, const. קַן m. (with suff. קִנִּי; pl. קִנִּים).—I. *a nest.*—II. *a dwelling.*—III. *a family.*—IV. *cells, chambers.*

קִנְצֵי for קִצֵּי, Job 18:2; see קֵץ in קצץ.

קָסַם *divine with arrows, &c.;* part. קֹסֵם *diviner.*

קֶסֶם m.—I. *divination, enchantment.*—II. *the reward of divination.*

מִקְסָם m., divination, Eze. 12:24; 13:7.

קֶסֶם; see קַּוּם.

קֶשֶׂת; see קשׂה.

קְעִילָה p.n., a city of Judah.

קַעְקַע m., mark, impression, Lev. 19:28.

קָעַר root not used; (Arab. being deep).

קְעָרָה f. (const. קַעֲרַת, pl. קְעָרוֹת, קְעָרֹת; with suff. קְעָרוֹתָיו) deep saucer, dish.

קָפָא I. congealed (of waters).—II. hardened (of men), Zep. 1:12. Hiph. condense, Job 10:10.

קִפָּאוֹן m., congealing, denseness, Zec. 14:6.

קָפַד (Arab. finished his work). Pi. finished, cut short, Isa. 38:12.

קִפָּדָה with ה parag. m., destruction, Eze. 7:25.

קִפֹּד m., a hedge-hog; (Arab. the same).

קִפָּז (Arab. springing serpent).

קִפּוֹז m., one of the springing snakes, Isa. 34:15.

קָפַץ shut up, close, constrict (the hand, &c.)—Niph. are shut up, Job 24:24. Pi. leaping, Cant. 2:8.

קֵץ end; see קצץ.

קָצַב I. cut wood, 2 Ki. 6:6.—II. shear sheep, Cant. 4:2.

קֶצֶב m., clefts of the mountains.—II. form, character, Jon. 2:7.

קָצָה I. cut off, destroy.—II. cut down. Pi. cutting off, down, 2 Ki. 10:32; Pro. 26:6. Hiph. cut, scraped, off; inf. הַקְצוֹת.

קָצֶה m. (const. קְצֵה; with suff. קָצֵהוּ; pl. קָצִים, קְצֵי) end, extremity, limit; מִקְצֵה הָעָם men from all parts; מִקְצֵה שְׁלֹשֶׁת יָמִים at the end of three days.

קָצֶה m., the same.

קָצָה f., extremity, border, limit; מִקָּצֶה from the extreme parts; pl. קָצוֹת, with הָעָם the extremities of the people, i. e. any of them.

קָצָה f. Ch., end.

קָצֶו m., pl. const. קַצְוֵי extremities, borders.

קְצָווֹת f. pl., the same.

מִקְצָת f.—I. end, limit; מִקְצָת יָמִים at the end of ten days.—II. Ch. a part.

קָצִין m.—I. judge.—II. governor.—III. prince.

מִקְצָת f., part, limit.

קֶצַח m., black pepper, Isa. 28:25, 27.

קָצִיר harvest; see קצר.

קָצַע. Hiph. הִקְצִיעַ scrapes off, Lev. 14:41. Pu. part. מְקֻצְעוֹת and Hoph. part. מְהֻקְצָעוֹת small courts, Eze. 46:22.

קְצִיעָה f., κασσία.—I. cassia, Ps. 45:9.—II. p. n., a daughter of Job, Keziah.

מִקְצוֹעַ m., corner, angle; pl. מִקְצֹעִים, מִקְצֹעוֹת.

מַקְצֻעָה f., "planes," Eng. Ver., Isa. 44:13.

קָצַף was angry, wroth, enraged, with אֶל, עַל. Hiph. made angry, with אֶת. Hithp. became wroth, Isa. 8:21.

קְצַף Ch., was angry.

קֶצֶף m.—I. a broken branch, stick,

Hos. 10:7. — II. *anger, wrath of God*, with suff. קִצְפְּךָ, קִצְפִּי.

קְצַף m. Ch., *anger*.

קְצָפָה f., *fracture, wasting*, Joel 1:7.

קָצַץ *cut off*. Pi. קִצֵּץ *cut off*. Pu. part. מְקֻצָּצִים, Jud. 1:7.

קְצַץ Ch. Pa. *cut off*.

קֵץ m. (with suff. קִצּוֹ; pl. קְצִים, קְצֵי).—I. *end, limit.*—II. *end, cessation.*—III. *end, ruin;* מִקֵּץ *from the end* (of the earth), *at the end* (of a time);* the same; עֵת קֵץ, לְקֵץ *the time of* קֵץ הַיָּמִים, מוֹעֵד קֵץ *the end*, i.e. *of our Lord's first and second advent.*

קִיצוֹן m., קִיצוֹנָה f., *the last*, Exodus only.

I. קָצַר (fut. יִקְצֹר), *cut down, reap; part. reaper.* Hiph. *reaped*, Job. 24:6.

קָצִיר I. *crop.* — II. *harvest.* — III. *branches.*

II. קָצַר (fut. יִקְצַר).—1. *short, deficient, unable for.*—2. with רוּחַ or נֶפֶשׁ *unable to bear up, discouraged.* Pi. קִצֵּר *made short*, Ps. 102:24. Hiph. *made short*, Ps. 89:46.

קָצֵר m., *short, cut off;* קְצַר אַפַּיִם, ק' רוּחַ *angry.*

קֹצֶר m., with רוּחַ *impatience*, Ex. 6:9.

קַר, קָרִים, קֹר; see קרר.
קֹר same as קִיר.

I. קָרָא (inf. קְרֹא, קְרֹאות with suff. קָרְאִי; imp. קְרָא; fut. יִקְרָא).—1. *cried, called, shouted.*—2. *called to or for*, with אֶל.—3. *called after*, with אַחֲרֵי.—4. *call upon in prayer.*—5. *celebrate.*—6. *call*

by name, name, with לְ.—7. *call together, assemble, invite,* with אֶל, אֵת.—8. *called into question litigation.*—9. *appointed to an office.*—10. *called forth soldiers*, Isa. 13:3. — 11. *proclaim, publish, preach.*—12. *read from a book, read aloud.* Niph. נִקְרָא 1. *called for, summoned.*—2. *called together, assembled*, with בְּ or בְּשֵׁם פּ' *in the name of some one.*—3. *named*, with שֵׁם פּ' עַל *the name of some. one is upon thee*, with שֵׁם יְהֹוָה עַל *the name of the Lord is named upon thee*, Deu. 28:10. Pu. קֹרָא *called, named*, with לְ.

קְרָא Ch., *read, recited, proclaimed.* Ithp. *was called*, Dan. 5:12.

קֹרֵא m.—I. *partridge.*—II. p. n. of a man.

קָרִיא m., *called, sent*, Numbers only.

קְרִיאָה f., *cry, proclamation*, Jon. 3:2.

מִקְרָא m.—I. *act of assembly.*—II. *convocation.*—III. *reading, reciting*, Neh. 8:8.

II. קָרָא *same as* קָרָה 1. *approached, met hostilely.*—2. *met.*—3. *happened;* inf. קְרָאָה, לִקְרַאת *to meet, meeting with;* with suff. לִקְרָאתְךָ *over, against thee;* לִקְרָאתְכֶם *over, against you.* Niph. 1. *met, happened to meet*, with עַל.—2. *happened;* fut. יִקָּרֵא; inf. נִקְרָא. Hiph. *cause to happen to*, Jer. 32:23.

קְרָאנָה for קְרֶאןָ Kal imp. pl. f., Ex. 2:20, from I. קרא

קְרֹאות Kal inf., with ו quiescent, Jud. 8:1, from I. קרא

קָרֵב, קָרַב (fut. יִקְרַב); inf. קְרֹב, קָרְבָה; imp. קְרַב).—I. *approached,*

drew near, with לִפְנֵי, לְ, בְּ, אֶל.
—II. attacked, with עַל, אֶל.—III.
keep by thyself, with אֶל, Isa. 65:5.
Niph. should, ought to draw near.
Pi. קֵרֵב made, caused to draw near.
Hiph. I. made approach.— II. pre-
sented.—III. removed, with מִן, בְּ.

קְרֵב Ch., came to. Pa. offered. Aph.
brought to, offered.

קָרֵב m., approaching, drawing near.

קָרוֹב m., קְרוֹבָה f., near, at hand,
with אֶל, לְ (of time, place, things,
&c.); מִקָּרוֹב adv., short, shortly,
soon.

קְרָב m., contest, battle, war; pl.
קְרָבוֹת.

קְרָב m. Ch., the same.

קֶרֶב m. (with suff. קִרְבִּי; pl. with
suff. קְרָבַי).—I. inward part, entrails.—II. amidst, among, often
בְּקֶרֶב מִקֶּרֶב the same.

קִרְבָה const. קִרְבַת f., approach, access.

קָרְבָּן const. קָרְבַּן m., offering.

קֻרְבָּן m., the same.

קָרְבָתָם Kal inf., with ה parag. and
suff., from קרב.

קַרְדֹּם (with suff. קַרְדֻּמּוֹ; pl. קַרְדֻּמִּים,
קַרְדֻּמּוֹת), an axe.

קָרָה s. f.; see קרר.

קָרָה (וַיִּקֶר, יִקְרֶה; see קָרָא II. (fut.
met, happened, with לְ. Niph. met
with persons only, with לִפְנֵי, אֶל,
עַל met accidentally, dropped in
with. Pi. קֵרָה framed together,
made to join. Hiph. I. made,
caused to meet with him, Gen.
27:20.—II. הִקְרָה לוֹ made con-
venient for him, Nu. 35:11.

קְרֵה־לַיְלָה m., accidental pollution during sleep, Deu. 23:11.

קוֹרָה f.—I. a beam.—II. a roof, Gen.
19:8.

קְרִי in pause קֶרִי m., meeting, opposing; בְּקֶרִי or הָלַךְ קֶרִי עִם he
opposed, resisted.

קִרְיָה f., a town or city, combined in
the names of many cities.—I. קִרְיַת
in the tribe of Benjamin.—II.
קִרְיַת אַרְבַּע in the tribe of Judah,
afterwards Hebron.—III. קִ' בַּעַל
same as קִ' יְעָרִים.—IV. קִ' חָצוֹת
in Moab.—V. קִ' עָרִים, קִ' יְעָרִים
in Judah.—VI. קִ' סֵפֶר, קִ' סַנָּה in
Judah, called also דְּבִיר.— VII.
קִרְיָתַיִם 1. in Reuben.—2. in Naphtali, called also קַרְתָּן.—VIII. קְרִיּוֹת
in Moab. קִרְיָה, קִרְיָא Ch.

קֶרֶת f.—I. a city.—II. a pulpit, Job
29:7.

קַרְתָּה p. n., a town of Zebulun.

מִקְרֶה m.—I. accident.—II. event,
result.

מְקָרֶה m., building, edifice, Ecc.10:18.

קָרַח and Hiph. הִקְרִיחַ shaved, made
bald. Niph. and Hoph. have made
themselves, become, bald.

קָרֵחַ p. n. of a man.

קֵרֵחַ m., bald (on the crown of the
head).

קֶרַח m.—I. cold.—II. frost, ice.—III.
crystal, Eze. 1:22.

קֹרַח m.—I. frost, ice, Ps. 147:17.—
II. p. n., Korah, a son of Esau.—
III. a son of 'Eliphaz.—IV. the
Levite who conspired against Moses,
patron. קָרְחִי.—V. applied to other
men.

קָרְחָה, קָרְחָא f., baldness.

קָרַחַת f., thread bare (of cloth), Lev.
c. 13 only.

קְרָיוֹת‎, קְרִיַת‎, קְרָיָה‎; see קרה.‎
קְרִיָּא‎, קְרִיאָה‎; see קרא.‎

קָרַם‎ overlaid, cased, with עַל‎; fut. יִקְרָם‎ Eze. 37:6, 8.

קֶרֶן‎ f. (dual. קְרָנַיִם‎, קַרְנַיִם‎; pl. קְרָנוֹת‎, קַרְנוֹת‎).—I. the horn of an animal.—II. used as a vessel for oil.—III. used as a trumpet, Jos. 6:5.—IV. Isa. 5:1, " a very fruitful hill," Eng. Ver.; " a horn, the son of oil ;" marg. perhaps Mount Tabor.—V. metaphorically, power, strength, in men or states.—VI. probably the name of a weapon, 2 Sa. 22:3.—VII. the ornaments at each corner of the altar.—VIII. rays of light, Hab. 3:4.

קֶרֶן‎ com. Ch., horn.

קָרַן‎ v. denom., emitted rays, shone (the face of Moses), Exodus c. 34 only. Hiph. produced horns, Ps. 69:32.

קָרַס‎ became bent, bowed down, Isa. 46:2.

קֶרֶס‎ m., hook, link, loop.

קֶרֶס‎ same as קִירָס‎.

קַרְסֻלַּיִם‎ m. dual, ankles.

קָרַע‎ tore, rent (as a garment, &c.); once, of the eyes, Jer. 4:30, "thou rendest thine eyes with stibium," i. e. givest them an enlarged appearance as if they were torn open; this is the effect of it. Niph. was torn, rent.

קְרָעִים‎ m. pl., rendings, pieces, rags.

קָרַץ‎ closed, pressed together (the lips or eyes, denoting fraud or cunning). Pu. was cut, hewn out, Job 33:6.

קֶרֶץ‎ m., destruction, Jer. 46:20.

קְרָץ‎ m. Ch., rending.

קַרְקַע‎ m.—I. basis, foundation of the Tabernacle.—II. p.n., a town of Judah.

קַרְקֹר‎ p. n. of a place.

קָרַר‎ (Arab. was cold, quiet).

קַר‎ or קָר‎ m., cold water; pl. קָרִים‎ cool, quiet, Pro. 17:27.

קֹר‎ m., cold (season), Gen. 8:22.

קָרָה‎ f., cold, chilliness.

מְקֵרָה‎ f., coolness, refreshing, Jud. 3:20.

קָרַשׁ‎ (Arab. he cut).

קֶרֶשׁ‎ m.—I. plank or board.—II. bench of a ship, Eze. 27:6.

קַרְתָּן‎, מְרֵתָה‎, קֶרֶת‎; see קרה.‎

קָשָׂה‎ (Arab. wicker basket).

קָשׂוֹת‎, קְשָׂוֹת‎ f. pl., small vessel, patten, phial, or the like.

קֶסֶת‎ f., inkhorn carried in the girdle, Eze. 9:2, 3, 11.

קַשְׂקֶשׂ‎ m., pl. קַשְׂקַשִּׂים‎.—I. scales of a fish.—II. scale armour, 1 Sa. 17:5.

קַשְׂקֶשֶׂת‎ f., the same.

קָשַׂט‎ (Arab. pair of scales).

קְשִׂיטָה‎ f., a piece of silver, weighed out to pass for a given value as money.

קַשׁ‎; see קשׁשׁ‎.

קִשֻּׁאִים‎; see קשׁה‎.

קָשַׁב‎ (fut. יִקְשַׁב‎) attend, listen, Isa. 32:3. Hiph. attended to, regarded with בְּ‎, לְ‎, עַל‎, אֶל‎.

קֶשֶׁב‎ m., attention, hearkening.

קַשָּׁב‎, f. קַשֶּׁבֶת‎ attentive, Neh. 1:6, 11.

קָשֻׁב, f. pl. קַשֻּׁבוֹת attentive.

קָשָׁה I. was hard, grievous.—II. was difficult, Deu. 1:17. Niph. part. נִקְשֶׁה subject to difficulty, Isa. 8: 21. Pi. hardened (fut. apoc. וַתְּקַשׁ). Hiph. הִקְשָׁה (fut. apoc. וַיֶּקֶשׁ).— I. hardened.—II. made grievous, difficult.—III. made refractory, Pro. 28:14; Job 9:4.

קָשֶׁה m., קָשָׁה f.—I. obdurate, unyielding, cruel.—II. with עֹרֶף stiff-necked, obstinate.—III. with פָּנִים impudent, Eze. 2:4.—IV. hard, grievous (of servitude).—V. with רוּחַ overwhelmed, depressed, 1 Sa. 1:15.

קְשִׁי m., obstinacy, Deu. 9:27.

קִשְׁיוֹן p.n., a place in Issachar; קֶדֶשׁ the same.

קִשֻּׁאִים m. pl., cucumbers, Nu. 11:5.

מִקְשֶׁה m., wreathed work.

מִקְשָׁה f.—I. wreathed work.—II. place, garden, of cucumbers, Isa. 1:8.

קָשַׁח. Hiph.—I. made obdurate, Isa. 63:17.—II. treated hardly, Job 39: 16.

קֹשֶׁט, קְשֹׁט m., religious truth. קְשׁוֹט m. Ch., truth.

קָשַׁר (fut. יִקְשֹׁר).—I. tied, bound; part. קָשׁוּר bound, firm.—II. conspired against. Niph. bound, made firm, sure, Neh. 3:38; metaph., 1 Sa. 18:1. Pi. I. bind on (as ornaments), Isa. 49:18.—II. secure to thyself, Job 38:31. Pu. part. f. מְקֻשָּׁרוֹת compact, Gen. 30:41. Hith. conspired.

קֶשֶׁר m. (with suff. קִשְׁרוֹ) conspiracy, treason.

קִשֻּׁרִים m. pl., bandages, belts.

קָשַׁשׁ collect, assemble together, Zep. 2:1. Po. קֹשֵׁשׁ collect, gather. Hithpo. assemble yourselves, Zep. 2:1.

קַשׁ m.—I. stubble.—II. chaff.

קֶשֶׁת, קָשַׁת; see קוּשׁ.

קִתָרֹם same as קִיתָרֹם.

ר

רָאָה (inf. abs. רָאֹה, רָאוֹ; const. רְאוֹת, רָאֹה; imp. רְאֵה; fut. יִרְאֶה; apoc. יֵרֶא, וַיֵּרָא, וַתֵּרֶא).— I. saw, viewed, observed, with לְ.— II. looked out, provided, chose, cared for, with עַל, אֶל, בְּ.—III. visited (a sick person, &c.).—IV. saw the sun, lived, Ecc. 7:11.—V. perceived, found, felt, with בְּ.— VI. discern, discriminate (as a soothsayer). Niph. נִרְאָה (inf. הֵרָאֹת, הֵרָאֹה; imp. הֵרָאֶה; fut. יֵרָאֶה; apoc. וַיֵּרָא).—I. was seen, apparent, appearing, with אֶל, לְ, אֶת־פְּנֵי.—II. was provided. Pu. רֹאוּ were seen, Job 33:21. Hiph. הֶרְאָה (fut. וַיַּרְא, יַרְאֶה).—I. showed.—II. see, experience, evil, with בְּ. Hoph. הָרְאָה.—I. was seen.—II. was shown. Hith. הִתְרָאָה looked at each other.

רָאָה Deu. 14:13, an incorrect reading for דָּאָה, a vulture or kite.

רֹאֶה m., seer, prophet.

רַאֲוָה Eze. 28:17, Kal inf., from רָאָה.

רְאִית, רְאוּת seeing, viewing, Ecc. 5: 10.

רְאוּבֵן (behold a son!), p.n., Reuben, Jacob's eldest son; patron. רְאוּבֵנִי a Reubenite.

רְאִי m., mirror, Job 37:18.

רְאִי with pause רֹאִי m.—I. vision, revelation.—II. appearance, sight.—III. monstrosity, Nah. 3:6.

רְאָיָה p.n. of a man.

רֵו m. Ch., aspect, appearance.

מַרְאֶה m.—I. vision, appearance.—II. view, sight.

מַרְאָה f.—I. vision (seen by a seer).—II. mirror, Ex. 38:8.

רָאַם was raised, elevated, Zec. 14:10.

רְאֵם m.(pl. רְאֵמִים ,רְאֵים ,רֵים, רָמִים) buffalo, wild ox; LXX. unicorn, μονόκερως.

רָאמוֹת f. pl.—I. things high, sublime, Pro. 24:7.—II. most precious.—III. p.n.: (a) a town of Issachar; (b) of Gilead.

רְאוּמָה p. n. of a woman.

רָאמַת נֶגֶב p.n., same as רָמוֹת נֶגֶב

רֵאשׁ ,רֹאשׁ; see רוּשׁ.

רֹאשׁ m. (pl. רָאשִׁים; with suff. רָאשֵׁיהֶם ,רָאשָׁיו).—I. head of man or beast.—II. chief, leader.—III. metropolis, chief city.—IV. top of a mountain, &c.—V. first, chief, principal of any thing; רֹאשׁ שִׂמְחָה chief joy.—VI. capital, amount, sum (of numbers, money, &c.).—VII. source, commencement (of a river).—VIII. an unknown poisonous plant, poison. Phrases: נָשָׂה רֹאשׁ appointed a chief; מֵרֹאשׁ from the beginning; רֹאשׁ חֳדָשִׁים the first month (of the year); רֹאשׁ

רֹ' פִּנָּה head stone of the corner; רֹ' דֶּרֶךְ a cross way, Eze. 16:25; חוּצוֹת the head of the streets; רָאשִׁים sources of rivers, Gen. 2:10.

רֵאשׁ .(רָאשִׁין ,רֵאשִׁין pl.) Ch. m.—I. head.—II. chapter, summary, Dan. 7:1.

אֶבֶן הָרֹאשָׁה f., רֹאשָׁה head stone, Zec. 4:7.

רֵאשָׁה f., beginning, Eze. 36:11.

רַאֲשׁוֹת pl. const. רַאֲשֹׁתָי the part about the head (of Saul), 1 Sa. 26:12.

רִאשׁוֹן (for רִאישׁוֹן), m.—I. first, former, foremost (in time, place, dignity, &c.); pl. רִאשֹׁנִים ancestors; מֵרִאשׁוֹן from the beginning; f. רִאשֹׁנָה the same.—II. adv. formerly; בָּרִאשֹׁנָה in front; כְּבָרִאשֹׁנָה as formerly, Isa. 1:26; לָרִאשֹׁנָה formerly; pl. רִאשֹׁנוֹת former things.

רִאשֹׁנִי, f. רִאשֹׁנִית first, Jer. 25:1.

רֵאשִׁית f.—I. first, former, in state or time.—II. firstfruits, firstborn.—III. first of way, beginning.

מַרַאֲשׁוֹת f.pl., places or things where the head is.

מְרַאֲשׁוֹת f. pl., the same; with suff. מְרַאֲשֹׁתָיו at his head.

מָרֵשָׁה ,מַרְאֵשָׁה p.n.: (a) a fortress of Judah, Μαρισά; (b) of a man.

רוֹשׁ ,רֹאשׁ m., poison; see רֹאשׁ.

רֹאשׁ p.n., a northern nation: probably the Ῥῶς of the Byzantine authors; now Russia.

רָב same as רִיב.

רָבַב (pret. רָב, inf. רֹב).—I. became many, numerous. Pu. see רְבָבָה.

רַב m. (in pause רָב, pl. רַבִּים; f. רַבָּה, pl. רַבּוֹת).—I. *much, many.* — II. *abundant, enough.* — III. *great, vast,* in extent, station, dignity, &c.

רַבָּה (*metropolis*) p. n. — I. the chief city of Ammon.—II. a city of Judah.

רַב m. Ch. (pl. רַבְרְבִין).— I. *great, large.*—II. s., *great men, nobles.*

רֹב, רוֹב, רָב־ m. (with suff. רֻבְּכֶם) *multitude, abundance.* לָרֹב *abundantly.*

רְבָבָה f., *ten thousand, myriad;* pl. רְבָבוֹת, רְבָבֹת *myriads.* Pu. denom. part. מְרֻבָּבוֹת *increased to myriads,* Ps. 144:13.

רִבּוֹ, רְבוֹא f., *the same;* dual רִבּוֹתַיִם *two myriads;* pl. רִבֹּאוֹת, רִבְּאוֹת, רִבּוֹת *myriads.*

רִבּוֹ Ch., *the same;* pl. רִבְוָן (רִבְּבָן).

רְבִיבִים m. pl., *showers.*

רַבִּית p. n., a city of Issachar.

רַבְרְבָן m. Ch., *a prince.*

רַבְשָׁקֵה p. n., *Rabshakeh,* leader of the Assyrians.

II. רָבַב *shot,* as arrows, &c. Pret. pl. רַבּוּ.

רָבַד *spread, strewed, made up,* Pro. 7:16; (Arab. *tied, bound*).

רָבִיד m., *collar, neck-chain;* (Arab. the same.)

מַרְבַדִּים m. pl., *coverlets.*

רָבָה (רָבַב).— (fut. יִרְבֶּה, apoc. יֵרֶב, יִרְב).— I. *became many, multiplied.* — II. *grew.* — III. *was great, powerful.* Pi. רִבָּה *made much,* Ps. 44:13. Hiph. הִרְבָּה (fut. יַרְבֶּה, apoc. יֶרֶב; imp. הֶרֶב; inf. abs. הַרְבֵּה, הַרְבֶּה,

const. הַרְבּוֹת).—I. *multiplied, increased.*—II. *extended, made large.* — III. *made great.* Inf. הַרְבֵּה, sometimes הַרְבּוֹת adv. *much, very much;* לְהַרְבֵּה *plentifully.*

רְבָה Ch., *grew great,* Dan. 4:8, 19. Pa. *became great,* Dan. 2:48.

רְבִיבִים, רְבֻבוֹת, רִבּוֹ, רִבּוֹא, רַבָּה, רַבִּית; see רבב.

רְבוּ f. Ch., *greatness.*

אַרְבֶּה m., a species of *locust,* so called from the multitudes of them.

מַרְבֶּה m., *greatness, abundance.*

מִרְבָּה f., *much, too much,* Eze. 23:32.

מַרְבִּית f. — I. *abundance.* — II. *increase, interest.*—III. *offspring.*

תַּרְבּוּת f., *progeny,* Nu. 32:14.

תַּרְבִּית f., *usury.*

רָבִיד; see רבד.

רְבִיעִית, רְבִיעִי; see רבע.

רָבַךְ (Arab. *mixed*). Hoph. part. מֻרְבֶּכֶת *mixed, saturated.*

רִבְלָה p.n., *Riblah,* a city to the north of Palestine.

I. רָבַע *lying with* (carnally). Hiph. *cause to lie with.*

רִבְעִי m., *lying down,* with suff. Ps. 139:3; see also below.

II. רָבַע from אַרְבַּע, רֶבַע; part. רָבוּעַ *four-sided;* pl. רְבֻעִים. Pu. part. מְרֻבָּע m., מְרֻבַּעַת f., *made four-sided.*

רֶבַע I. *fourth part of anything, side of anything square.*—II. p.n., a king of Midian.

רֹבַע m., *fourth part.*

רְבִיעִי m., *the fourth,* רְבִיעִית f., *fourth part;* בְּנֵי רִבֵּעִים *children of the fourth generation.*

רְבִיעִי m. Ch., *fourth.*

רִבֵּעִים m. pl., *posterity in the fourth degree.*

אַרְבַּע, אַרְבָּעָה f., אַרְבַּעַת m. — I. *four;* with suff. אַרְבַּעְתָּם *they four;* dual אַרְבַּעְתַּיִם *fourfold;* pl. אַרְבָּעִים *forty.* — II. p. n. of a giant.

אַרְבַּע f., אַרְבָּעָה m. Ch., *the same.*

רָבַץ (fut. יִרְבַּץ). — I. *lie down* (of beasts, &c.) — II. *lie upon the conscience, soul,* of sin, Gen. 4:7, &c. Hiph. I. *cause to lie down.* — II. *set* (of precious stones), Isa. 54:11.

רֶבֶץ m. — I. *crib, lying place of cattle.* — II. *resting place* (for man), Pro. 24:15.

מַרְבֵּץ m., *a resting place, for cattle or wild beasts,* Zep. 2:15.

מִרְבָּץ m., the same, Eze. 25:5.

רָבַק (Arab. *tied up to fatten.*)

רִבְקָה p. n., *Rebecca,* the wife of Isaac, Ῥεβέκκα.

מַרְבֵּק m., *stall for feeding cattle.*

רַבְשָׁקֵה ; see I. רבב.רַבְרְבָן, רַבְרְבִין

רֶגֶב m., pl. רְגָבִים, רִגְבֵי. — I. *clods of earth,* Job 38:38. — II. *stones set up as monuments,* Job 21:33.

רָגַז (imper. רְגַז, רָגְזָה, pl. רִגְזוּ ; fut. יִרְגַּז). — I. *shook, trembled.* — II. *became disturbed, agitated.* Hiph. I. *move.* — II. *agitate, disturb,* with לְ. Hith. *thy commotion, excitement,* with אֶל.

רְגַז Ch. Aph., *provoked, excited to anger.*

רֹגֶז m. — I. *vexation, trouble.* — II. *neighing,* Job 39:24. — III. *fury,*

anger, Hab. 3:2. — IV. *roar of thunder,* Job 37:2.

רְגַז m. Ch., *anger,* Dan. 3:13.

רַגָּז m., *trembling,* Deu. 28:65.

רָגְזָה f., *perturbation,* Eze. 12:18.

אַרְגָּז m., "*coffer,*" Eng. Ver., 1 Sa. 6:8, 11, 15 ; (Arab. *a panier,* on one side of a camel's pack saddle: also, the sack of stones hung on the other side when but one panier is used.)

רָגַל *go about speaking evil, backbite,* Ps. 15:3. Pi. I. *goes about calumniating,* with בְּ, 2 Sa. 19:28. — II. *explore as a spy;* part. מְרַגְּלִים *spies,* Gen. 42:9. Tiphel תִּרְגַּל *was near* (at foot, i. e., at hand), Hos. 11:3.

רֶגֶל com. (dual רַגְלֵי, רַגְלַיִם) *the foot;* בְּרַגְלֵי פּ׳ *at the feet of any one;* לְרַגְלֵי פּ׳ *on account of any one.* (For many other idiomatic usages of רֶגֶל see Fürst's Concordance.) Pl. רְגָלִים *strokes of the feet, times, repetitions.*

רְגַל com. Ch., *foot.*

רַגְלִי m., *foot soldier;* pl. רַגְלִים *infantry,* Jer. 12:5.

רֹגְלִים p. n. — I. see עֵין. — II. pl. רֹגְלִים a place in Gilead.

מַרְגְּלוֹת f. pl., *at the feet, anything at the feet.*

רָגַם *stone to death,* with בְּ, עַל.

רִגְמָה f., *stone of defence,* Ps. 68:28.

מַרְגֵּמָה f., *heap of stones,* Pro. 26:8.

רֶגֶם p. n. of a man.

רֶגֶם מֶלֶךְ p. n. of a man.

רָגַן and Niph. נִרְגַּן *murmuring;* with בְּ *against.*

רָגַע. I. *hastens to decay* (the skin), Job 7:5.—II. *calms* (the sea), Job 26:12. Niph. *rested*, Jer. 47:6. Hiph. I. *rested, found rest.* — II. *give, restore to, make to, rest.*

רָגַע m., *quiet, peaceable*, Ps. 35:20.

רֶגַע m., *instant, moment of time;* בְּרֶגַע, כְּרֶגַע, רֶגַע adv., *in a moment, suddenly;* לִרְגָעִים *moment after moment, incessantly.*

מַרְגּוֹעַ m., *rest, quiet*, Jer. 6:16.

מַרְגֵּעָה f., *the same*, Isa. 28:12.

רָגַשׁ *are tumultuous, in uproar*, Ps. 2:1.

רְגַשׁ Ch., *the same.* Aph. *assembled tumultuously.*

רֶגֶשׁ m., *tumult, multitude shouting*, Ps. 55:15.

רִגְשָׁה f., *the same*, Ps. 64:3.

רַד, Isa. 45:1, Kal inf., from רדד; Jud. 19:11, for יָרַד.

רֵד Kal imp., from יָרַד.

רָדַד *brings down, subdues*, Ps. 144:2; Isa. 45:1. Hiph. *lays down on*, 1 Ki. 6:32.

רַדַּי p.n. of a man.

רָדִיד m., *loose mantle, veil*, Cant. 5:7; Isa. 3:23.

רָדָה (fut. apoc. יֵרְדְּ; pl. יִרְדּוּ).— I. *subdue, rule, govern*, with בְּ; of fire, Lam. 1:13. — II. *took down*, Jud. 14:9. Hiph. *cause to rule, govern;* fut. apoc. יַרְדְּ, Isa. 41:2.

רְדָה I. in pause רֵדָה Kal imp. with ה parag.—II. Gen. 46:3, inf. with ה parag., from יָרַד.

רָדַם. Niph. נִרְדָּם *be insensible, as in deep sleep, fast asleep.*

תַּרְדֵּמָה f., *deep sleep, stupor, trance.*

רֻדָם Kal part. with suff., from רדה.

רוֹדָנִים p.n., 1 Chron. 1:7, an unknown people to the west of Canaan.

רָדַף I. *followed after.*—II. *pursued as an enemy*, with אַחֲרֵי, לְ, אֶל. Pi. *followed, pursued.* Hiph. *chased*, Jud. 20:43. Niph. and Pu. I. *was pursued.* — II. *succeeded*, Ecc. 3:15.

מֻרְדָּף m. (Hoph. part.) *pursued, chased*, Isa. 14:6.

רֶדֶת Kal inf., from יָרַד.

רָהַב I. *deal with as fearing*, Pro. 6:3.—II. *insult*, with בְּ. Hiph. *embolden*, Cant. 6:5.

רַהַב m.—I. *insolence*, Job 9:13; 26:12. — II. *a prophetic name for Egypt.*

רְהָב m., *insolent*, Ps. 40:5.

רֹהַב m., *pride, insolence*, Ps. 90:10.

רְהַגָּה p. n. of a man.

רָהָה, תִּרְהוּ; see יָרָה.

רַהַט (Syr. *stream;* Arab. *strap, thong, household goods*).

רַהַט m., pl. רְהָטִים.— I. *watering trough.* — II. *thongs*, Cant. 7:6; " *like a king bound in thongs*" (Lee).

רָהִיט m., pl. רָהִיטִים *furniture, furnishing* (of a house), φατνώματα, Cant. 1:17.

רֵו *aspect;* see ראה.

רוּב *strife;* see ריב.

רוֹב *same as* רֹב *many;* see רבב.

רוּד *walked with* (God), Hos. 12:1. Hiph. I. *wander* (mentally), Ps. 55:3.—II. *wander, be a nomade people*, Gen. 27:40.

מָרוּד m., one persecuted, Lam. 3:19; מְרוּדִים persecuted ones, Lam. 1:7.

רָוָה was satiated (with anything), with מִן. Pi. רִוָּה I. was satiated, filled. — II. fill, delight, satisfy. Hiph. הִרְוָה satiate, fill.

רָוֶה m., רָוָה f.—I. soaked, satiated.— II. drunken, Deu. 29:18.

רִי m., irrigation, Job 37:11.

רְוָיָה f., abundance, plenty of water.

רָז m. Ch., a secret.

רִיחַ ,רוּחַ. Hiph. הֵרִיחַ I. smell (sweet odour).—II. was satisfied, appeased. —III. was inspired with, with בְּ, Isa. 11:3.—IV. feel the fire, Jud. 16:9. —V. perceive, Job 39:25.

רוּחַ com. (pl. רוּחוֹת ,רְחוֹת).—I. air, breeze, cool breeze.— II. breath.— III. spirit, soul of man.—IV. mind, spirit, disposition. — V. spirit of God.—VI. the wind.—VII. anger, wrath.— VIII. vanity, folly (used idiomatically in many ways; see Concordance).

רוּחַ com. Ch.—I. the wind.—II. spirit, mind.

רַחַת f., winnowing fan, Isa. 30:24.

רֵיחַ m., odour, smell; Ch. the same.

רָוַח (fut. יִרְוַח) there was relief, with לְ 1 Sa.16:23; Job 32:20. Pu. part. מְרֻוָּחִים spacious, ample, Jer.22:14.

רֶוַח m.— I. space, distance.—II. deliverance, quiet.

רְוָחָה ,רַוְחָה f., the same.

רוּם (fut. יָרוּם ,יָרֹם ,וַיָּרָם).— I. was high, lofty. — II. raised himself, was raised.—III. was high in rank or power. — IV. was lifted up, haughty (fut. וַיָּרֶם); part. רָם m.,

רָמָה f. — I. high.—II. loud, Deu. 27:14.— III. high in rank. — IV. haughty; pl. רָמִים the heights of heaven.—V. p.n. of a man.. Pil. רוֹמֵם I. lifted up, raised.—II. made to grow. — III. brought up (children).—IV. exalted with praise.— V. raised a building. Pul. רוֹמַם was lifted up, raised, high. Hiph. הֵרִים I. lifted up.—II. took up.— III. took out for an offering.—IV. offered.—V. removed.—VI. set up. Hoph. הוּרַם I. was offered. — II. was removed. Hithpal. raised, exalted himself, Dan. 11:36.

רוּם Ch., was lifted up, Dan. 5:20. Pil. exalting with praise, Dan. 4:34. Aph. exalting in power, Dan. 5:19. Ithpal. exaltest thyself, Dan. 5:23.

רָמָה f.—I. high place for idolatry, Eze. c. 16.—II. p.n., Ramah: (a) a town of Benjamin; (b) a town of Ephraim, called also רָמָתַיִם צֹפִים; (c) a town of Naphtali; (d) רָמַת הַמִּצְפֶּה a town in Gilead, called also רָמוֹת ,רָאמוֹת Ramoth Gilead; (e) רָמַת לֶחִי same as לֶחִי; רָמָתִי a Ramathite.

רָמוּת f., pile, heap of dead bodies, Eze. 32:5.

רוּם m. — I. height, Pro. 25:3.— II. haughtiness.

רוּם m. Ch., height.

רוֹם m., רוֹמָה f.—I. height, Hab. 3:10.— II. on high, haughtily, Mic. 2:3.

רוּמָה p.n. of a place.

רוֹמֵם m., extolling praise; pl. const. רוֹמְמוֹת, Ps. 149:6.

רוֹמֵמוּת f., *exaltation, majesty,* with suff. רֹמְמֻתֶךָ, Isa. 33:3.

רְמַמְתִּי־עֶזֶר p. n. of a man.

רֶמֶת p.n., a town of Issachar.

מָרוֹם m.—I. *high, on high, height.*—II. *a high place.*—III. *haughtiness; adv. haughtily.*

מֵי מָרוֹם p.n., a lake in the north of Canaan, Σαμοχωνίτις.

תְּרוּמָה f.—I. *contribution, gift.*—II. *offering to God.* — III. *sacrificial gift, heave-offering.*

תְּרוּמִיָּה f., *offering,* Eze. 48:12.

רֹן (Arab. *conquer*). Hithpa. part. מִתְרוֹנֵן *overcome* (of wine), Ps. 78:65.

I. רוּעַ (pret. רַע; inf. רֹעַ) *was evil,* with בְּעֵינֵי *displeased.* Niph. (fut. יֵרוֹעַ).—I. *got worse,* Pro. 13:20.—II. *suffer evil, injury,* Pro. 11:15. Hiph. הֵרֵעַ, הָרַע I. *did evil.* — II. *did evil to, afflicted;* part. מֵרַע, מְרֵעַ *evil doer,* with בְּ, עַל, לְ, עִם. Hith. הִתְרוֹעֵעַ *suffered injury,* Pro. 18:24.

רַע in pause רָע m., רָעָה f.—I. *wicked.* II. *fatal, deadly.*—III. *calamitous.* IV. *sad.*—V. *ill-favoured.*—VI. s.: (a) *wickedness;* (b) *harm, injury, calamity.*

רוֹעַ, רֹעַ m.—I. *badness, evil condition.* —II. *sadness of countenance,* Ecc. 7:3.

II. רוּעַ *shout, call together,* רֹעוּ, Isa. 8:9. Hiph. הֵרִיעַ (pl. הָרִיעוּ).—I. *shouted.*—II. *sounded a trumpet.* Pil. fut. יָרֹעַ *there shall be shouting,* Isa. 16:10. Hithpal. *shouted.*

רֵעַ m., *shouting, crying out;* see also רָעָה.

תְּרוּעָה f.—I. *shout of joy.*—II. *shout of battle.*—III. *sound of a trumpet.*

רוּץ I. *ran, ran to, after.* — II. *rushed upon,* with עַל, אֶל.—III. *ran into for a refuge,* with בְּ.—IV. *hastened.* —V. *did a thing readily,* Hab. 2: 2. Part. pl. רָצִים *runners, couriers.* Pil. רוֹצֵץ *ran swiftly,* Nah. 2:5. Hiph. I. *caused to run.*—II. *brought quickly.*—III. *stretched out his hands quickly,* Ps. 68:32.

מֵרוֹץ m., *a race,* Ecc. 9:11.

מְרוּצָה f.—I. *mode of running.*—II. *course of life.* See also רָצַץ.

רוּק; see רִיק.

רוּר *spat,* Lev. 15:3.

רִיר m.—I. *spittle,* 1 Sa. 21:14.—II. *whey,* Job 6:6.

רוֹשׁ; see רֹאשׁ.

רוּשׁ *was poor, in want,* Ps. 34:11; part. רָשׁ, רָאשׁ *poor, a poor man.* Hith. הִתְרוֹשֵׁשׁ *feigned himself poor,* Pro. 13:7.

רֵאשׁ, רִישׁ, רֵישׁ m., *poverty.*

רוּת p. n. of a woman, *Ruth.*

רָזָה *diminished, brought low,* Zep. 2:11. Niph. *was wasted away,* Isa. 17:4.

רָזֶה m.—I. *lean* (of cattle), Eze. 34:20.—II. *barren* (of land), Nu. 13:20.

רָזִי m., *destruction;* רָזִי לִי *woe is me!*

רָזוֹן m., *wasting, destruction.* See also in רָזַן.

רָזַח root not used ; (Arab. *cried out*).

מַרְזֵחַ m., *lamentation,* Jer. 16:5.

מִרְזַח *cry of merriment,* Am. 6:7.

רָזַם *laid hold on,* Job 15:12.

רָזַן (Arab. *weighty*); part. רוֹזְנִים *chiefs, princes.*

רָזוֹן m., *prince;* see also רָזָה.

רְזוֹן p.n., *Rezon,* king of Damascus.

רָחַב *was widened, enlarged, opened.* Niph. part. *enlarged, extended,* Isa. 30:23. Hiph. הִרְחִיב I. *made broad.*—II. with נֶפֶשׁ *extended his desires, enlarged itself.*—III. *opened the heart, mouth, &c.*—IV. with לְ, *liberated, made room for, gave way.*

I. רָחָב m., רְחָבָה f., *broad, large, extensive, capacious;* with יָדַיִם *broad on both hands, very broad;* with לֵב *of unlimited desires.*

II. רָחָב p.n., *Rahab,* the woman of Jericho.

רַחַב m., *plenty,* Job 36:16; 38:18.

רֹחַב m. (with suff. רָחְבָּהּ).—I. *breadth, width.*—II. *extent, expanse,* Job 37:10.—III. with לֵב *extent of understanding,* 1 K. 5:9.

רְחֹב, רָחוֹב f. (pl. רְחֹבוֹת).—I. *broad, open place in a town, square, street, market-place.*—II. בֵּית רְחֹב and רְחֹב p.n., *a town in the north of the tribe of Asher; a Syrian city near it was called אֲרַם בֵּית רְחוֹב* and אֲרַם רְחֹב.—III. רְחֹבוֹת p.n., (a) the name of a well; (b) עִיר ר׳ *a town in Assyria;* (c) ר׳ הַנָּהָר *a town on the Euphrates.*

רְחַבְיָהוּ p.n. of a man.

רְחַבְעָם p.n., *Rehoboam,* the son of Solomon, king of Judah. LXX. Ῥοβοάμ.

מֶרְחָב m.—I. *wide places.*—II *prosperity,* considered as freedom.

רָחִיק, רָחוֹק; see רחק.

רָחִימִים Ketib for רָחֳמִים; see רהט.

רֵחַיִם m. dual, *pair of millstones.*

רָחֵל f.—I. *a ewe.*—II. *any sheep.* —III. p.n., *Rachel,* the wife of Jacob; LXX. Ῥαχήλ.

רָחַם or רָחֵם *loved,* Ps. 18:2. Pi. רִחַם *loved, pitied, had mercy on,* with accus. עַל. Pu. רֻחַם *obtained mercy.*

רָחָמָה, רָחָם m., *the aquiline vulture;* vultur percnopterus (Linn.), Lev. 11:18; Deu. 14:17.

רַחוּם m., *merciful* (of God only).

רְחוּם p.n. of a man.

רֶחֶם, רַחַם m. (f. Jer. 20:17).—I. *the womb.*—II. *a girl;* dual רַחֲמָתָיִם. —III. רַחַם p.n. of a man.

רַחֲמִים m. pl.—I. *the viscera.*—II. *pity, mercy.*

רַחֲמִין m. pl. Ch., *mercy.*

רַחֲמָנִי m., f. pl. רַחֲמָנִיּוֹת *tender, merciful,* Lam. 4:10.

רָחַף *shook, trembled,* Jer. 23:9. Pi. רִחֵף *fluttered, hovered,* Deu. 32:11; part. מְרַחֶפֶת *hovering, brooding* (of the Spirit of God), Gen. 1:2.

רָחַץ (fut. יִרְחַץ; imp. רְחַץ, pl. רַחֲצוּ; inf. רָחֹץ, רָחְצָה) *washed himself or another; washed away.* Pu. *was washed.* Hith. *washed himself,* Job 9:30.

רַחַץ m., *washing,* Ps. 60:10.

רָחְצָה f., *washing-place for sheep,* Cant. 4:2; 6:6.

רְחַץ Ch. Ith. *depend on, trust to*, Dan. 3:28.

רָחַק (fut. יִרְחַק; inf. רָחְקָה) I. *was distant.*—II. *kept at a distance, withdrew himself.* Pi. רִחַק *placed at a distance, forsook.* Hiph. הִרְחִיק I. *caused to be distant.*—II. *went to a distance;* inf. הַרְחֵק adv., *afar off.*

רָחֵק m., *one who forsakes*, Ps. 73:27.

רָחוֹק m., רְחוֹקָה f. — I. *a distance, interval.*—II. *distant.*—III. *out of reach.* — IV. *difficult*, Pro. 31:10 (i. e., *brought from afar, precious*); בְּרָחוֹק *afar off;* מֵרָחוֹק *from, at a distance* (of time or space); לְמֵרָחוֹק *at a distance* (time or space); עַד־רָחוֹק *to a distance.*

רַחִיק m. Ch., *distant*, Ezr. 6:6.

מֶרְחָק m. (pl. מֶרְחַקִּים), *distance, distant part.*

מַרְחָק m., *the same;* pl. מַרְחַקִּים.

רָחַשׁ *threw up, bubbled up* (as a spring), Ps. 45:2.

מַרְחֶשֶׁת f., *pot for boiling.*

רַחַת see רוּחַ.

רָטַב (fut. יִרְטַב) *was wet* (with rain), Job 24:8.

רָטֹב m., *moist, fresh*, Job. 8:16. (Arab. the same).

רָטָה, יִרְטֵנוּ; see יָרַט.

רָטַט root not used; Ch. *trembled;* Syr. the same.

רֶטֶט m., *trembling*, Jer. 49:24.

רֻטֲפַשׁ *grew fresh, moist*, Job 33:25.

רָטַשׁ. Pi. רִטֵּשׁ *smote, killed.* Pu. *were killed.*

רִי; see רָוָה.

רִיב (pret. רַב, רַבְתָ, רִיבוֹת; inf. abs. רֹב; inf. const. and imp. רִיב; fut. יָרִיב).—I. *disputed, quarrelled with,* with עִם, אֶת, אֶל, בְּ.—II. *defended,* with לְ.—III. *opposed,* with עַל.—IV. *decided a cause favourably.* Hith. part. מֵרִיב *opposed, contended with.*

רִיב m. (pl. רִיבִים, רִיבוֹת).—I. *controversy, suit.* — II. *quarrel, strife.*

רִיבַי p. n. of a man.

יָרֵב m., *an adversary*, Hos. 5:13; 10:6.

יָרִיב m.—I. *the same.*—II. p. n. of a man.

יְרִיבַי p. n. of a man.

יְרֻבַּעַל, יְרֻבֶּשֶׁת p. n., *titles of Gideon.*

מְרִיבָה f.—I. *strife, contention.* — II. p. n., *a spring in the desert of Sinai.*

רֵיחַ, הָרֵיחַ, רִיחַ; see רוּחַ.

רֵים same as רְאֵם.

רֵיעַ, הָרִיעַ, רוֹעַ; see רֹעַ; רֵעַ, see רָעָה.

רִיפוֹת f. pl., *grain.*

רִיפַת p. n., *one of Japhet's sons, and his descendants.*

רִיק. Hiph. הֵרִיק — I. *emptied.* — II. *made empty, poured out.*—III. *drew a sword, made ready for war*, Gen. 14:14. Hoph. הוּרַק *was poured out.*

רִיק m.—I. *empty.*—II. *an empty, vain thing.*—III. *in vain.*—IV. adv. רִיק, לָרִיק *in vain.*

רֵיק m., רֵיקָה f.—I. *empty.* — II. *hungry, poor.* — III. *unimportant*, Deu. 32:47. — IV. *worthless in character.*

רֵיקָם adv. — I. *emptily.* — II. *empty*

handed.—III. *without cause.*—IV. *without effect.*

רִיר, רוּר *ran;* see רוּץ.

רֵישׁ, רֵישׁ *poverty;* see רוּשׁ.

רֵישׁוֹן Job 8:8; same as רִאשׁוֹן *first.*

רַךְ, רֹךְ; see רכך.

רָכַב (fut. יִרְכַּב; inf. רְכֹב).—I. *rode on a horse, ass,* or *camel.*—II. metaph. of God on the clouds or wind, with בְּ, עַל, accus.; part. רֹכֵב *a horseman.* Hiph. I. *caused to ride.*—II. *carried in a chariot.*—III. *placed upon.* — IV. *caused to be ridden,* Hos. 10:11.

רֶכֶב m. (f. Nah. 2:5). — I. *riding, a rider.* — II. *the upper millstone* (that which rides).—III. *a chariot, chariots.*

רֵכָב p.n. — I. *Rechab,* the father of Jonadab, from whom the Rechabites (רֵכָבִים) were descended. — II. used also of other men.

רְכוּב m., *vehicle, chariot,* Ps. 104:3.

רַכָּב m.—I. *horseman.*—II. *charioteer.*

מֶרְכָּב m.—I. *any carriage to ride in,* Lev. 15:9.—II. *chariots,* 1 K. 5:6.

מֶרְכָּבָה f. (with suff. מֶרְכַּבְתּוֹ; pl. מַרְכְּבוֹת, מַרְכָּבוֹת), *a chariot.*

מִרְכֶּבֶת f., *the same.*

רֵכָה p.n. of a place unknown.

רְכוּשׁ *wealth;* see רכשׁ.

רָכִיל *slander;* see רכל.

רָכַךְ *was timid, gentle.* Niph. *was timid;* fut. יֵרַךְ. Pu. *was softened,* Isa. 1:6. Hiph. הֵרַךְ *rendered timid,* Job 23:16.

רַךְ m., רַכָּה f.—I. *tender, young.*—II. *object of care.*—III. *effeminate.* — IV. *weak, timid, gentle.* — V.

tender-eyed, i.e. having sore eyes, Gen. 29:17.

רֹךְ f., *effeminacy,* Deu. 28:56.

רָכַל *went to and fro, travelled as a merchant;* part. רֹכֵל, f. רֹכֶלֶת *a merchant, dealer.*

רָכָל p.n., a town of Judah.

רָכִיל m.—I. *a busy body.* — II. *slander;* הָלַךְ רָכִיל *he went about tale bearing.*

רְכֻלָּה f., *merchandise* (Ezekiel only).

מַרְכֹּלֶת f., *merchandise,* Eze. 27:24.

רָכַס *tied, fastened.* Ex. 28:28; 39:21.

רֶכֶס m., רִכְסֵי אִישׁ *combinations, artifices,* Ps. 31:21.

רֶכֶס m., pl. רְכָסִים *rugged places,* Isa. 40:4.

רָכַשׁ *acquired, gained* (Genesis only).

רֶכֶשׁ, רְכוּשׁ m., *property, wealth.*

רֶכֶשׁ m., *swift species of horse.*

רָמָה, רָם, see רום; רָם same as רְאֵם, רָאֵם

רָמָה I. *threw.*—II. *shot with a bow.* Pi. רִמָּה *deceived,* lit. *threw down.*

רְמָא, רְמָה Ch. — I. *threw.* — II. *imposed tribute.* Ithpe. *were thrown, placed.*

רִמּוֹן, רִמָּה; see רמם.

רָמוֹת, רָמוּת; see רום.

רְמִיָּה f.—I. *deceit.*—II. *negligence.*

רְמִיָּה p.n. of a man.

מִרְמָה f.—I. *deceit, artifice.*—II. p.n. of a man.

תַּרְמָה f., *deceit, craft,* Jud. 9:31.

תַּרְמִית (תַּרְמוּת) f., *the same.*

רֹמַח m. (pl. רְמָחִים; with suff. רָמְחֵיהֶם) *a spear.*

רַמִּי pl. הָרַמִּים same as הָאֲרַמִּים *the Syrians.*

רַמָּךְ f., *a mare*, Est. 8:10.

רְמַלְיָהוּ p. n., *Remaliah*, the father of Pekah, king of Israel.

רָמַם (pret. pl. רַמּוּ, רֹמּוּ) *was high, lofty*; part. f. רוֹמֵמָה *high.* Niph. (imp. pl. הֵרֹמּוּ; fut. pl. יֵרֹמּוּ) *was raised*, Eze. 10:15, 17, 19.

רִמָּה f., *a worm, worms.*

רִמּוֹן m.—I. *a pomegranate fruit* or *tree.*—II. *an artificial imitation of the fruit.*—III. p. n.: (a) *a city of Simeon;* (b) *a city near Gibeah;* (c) *an idol of the Syrians;* (d) רִמּוֹן הַמְּתֹאָר *a town of Zebulun;* (e) רִמּוֹן פֶּרֶץ *one of the stations of the Israelites.*

רָמַס I. *trampled on, trod on.* — II. *walked in;* part. רֹמֵם *an oppressor*, Isa. 16:4. Niph. *was trodden down*, Isa. 28:3.

מִרְמָס m., *that which is trampled under foot.*

רָמַשׂ I. *move* (as a quadruped).—II. *creep* (as a reptile).

רֶמֶשׂ m. collec.—I. *reptiles.*—II. *small land animals.*— III. *sea creatures,* perhaps *seals*, Ps. 104:25.

רֶמֶת see רום.

רָנָה *rang, rattled*, Job 39:23.

רָנַן (fut. יָרֹן).—I. *sung.*—II. *shouted.*—III. *invited.* — IV. *called for help.* Pi. רִנֵּן I. *sung, rejoiced,* with עַל, בְּ. —II. *sung of, celebrated,* with לְ, אֶל. Pu. fut. יְרֻנַּן *there shall be singing*, Isa. 16:10. Hiph. הִרְנִין I. *caused to sing.* — II. *rejoiced.* Hith. see in רון.

רָנֶן m., pl. רְנָנִים *ostriches*, Job 39:13.

רְנָנָה f., *singing, rejoicing.*

רֹן m., pl. רָנִּים *songs*, Ps. 32:7.

רִנָּה f.—I. *singing, shout of joy.*—II. *a shout* or *cry of any kind.*—III. *a cry for help.*—IV. p. n. of a man.

רֶסֶן m.—I. *bridle, halter.*—II. p. n. a city of Assyria.

רָסַס *sprinkled*, Eze. 46:14.

רִסָּה p.n., *one of the stations in the wilderness.*

רְסִיסִים m. pl. — I. *sprinkling, drop*, Cant. 5:2.—II. *fractures*, Am. 6:11.

רָעָה, רֹעַ, see רוּעַ; רַע, רַע, see רוּעַ; רַע, see רעע.

רָעֵב (fut. יִרְעַב).—I. *was hungry.*—II. *hungered for, was famished.*—III. *suffered from famine*, with לְ. Hiph. הִרְעִיב *allowed, caused to suffer hunger.*

רָעֵב m., רְעֵבָה f., *hungry, famishing.*

רָעָב m.—I. *hunger.*—II. *famine.*

רַעֲבוֹן, const. רַעֲבוֹן m., the same.

רָעַד (fut. יִרְעַד) *trembled*, Ps. 104:32. Hiph. the same.

רַעַד m.,
 רְעָדָה f., } *trembling, awe.*

רָעָה (fut. יִרְעֶה; apoc. יִרַע).— I. *fed.* —II. *consumed.*— III. *devastated.* — IV. *fed on, delighted in.* — V. *associated with.*—VI. *fed cattle.*— VII. *governed a people.* — VIII. *nourished.* — IX. for רָעַע *injured, oppressed;* part. רֹעֶה *a shepherd.* Pi. רֵעָה *became a companion*, Jud. 14:20. Hiph. pres. aff. יִרְעֵם *ruled them*, Ps. 78:72. Hith. הִתְרָעָה *was intimate with, became a companion,* with אֶת.

רֵעֵהוּ רֵעַ, רֵעֶה, רֵעַ m. (pl. with suff.

for (רֵעֵיהוּ).—I. *a friend, neighbour, companion, lover;* אִישׁ...רֵעַ *one... the other.*—II. *thought, will,* Ps. 139:2, 17; see also רוּעַ.

רֵעָה f., pl. רֵעוֹת *female friend, companion.*

רָעָה f., *evil, &c.;* see רַע in רוּעַ.

רֹעָה *breaking;* see רעע.

רְעוּת f.—I. *friend, neighbour.*—II. with רוּחַ *feeding on the wind.*

רְעוּת f. Ch., *wish, will.*

רְעוּ p.n. of a man.

רְעוּאֵל p.n. of a man.

רְעִי m., *pasture,* 1 Ki. 5:3.

רֹעִי m., *a shepherd.*

רֵעִי p.n. of a man.

רַעְיָה f., *female companion, friend.*

רַעְיוֹן m., *desire, pursuit.*

רַעְיוֹן m. Ch., *desire, purpose, thought.*

מֵרֵעַ m. (with suff. מֵרֵעֵהוּ; pl. מֵרֵעִים) *desire, purpose, thought.*

מִרְעֶה m., *pasture.*

מַרְעִית f.—I. *pasturing, feeding cattle.* —II. *a flock.*

רָעַל. Hoph. הָרְעַל *were thrown* (of javelins), Nah. 2:4.

רַעַל m.—I. *trembling, giddiness,* Zec. 12:2.—II. pl. רְעָלוֹת *veils,* Isa. 3:19.

רְעֶלְיָה p.n. of a man.

תַּרְעֵלָה f., *trembling, staggering.*

רָעַם (fut. יִרְעַם).—I. *resounded, roared* (of the sea).—II. *was excited,* Eze. 27:35. Hiph. הִרְעִים I. *thundered.* —II. *caused anger, vexation.*

רַעַם m. — I. *thunder.* — II. *tumult, rage,* Job 39:25.

רַעְמָה f.—I. *rage,* Job 39:19.—II. p.n. of a city of Cush.

רַעְמְסֵס, רַעַמְסֵס (*born of the sun*),

p. n.—I. *the district which forms the eastern boundary of Egypt, called also Goshen.* — II. *a city built there by the Israelites.*

רָעַן. Pil. רַעֲנַן *was green.*

רַעֲנָן m.—I. *green, flourishing.*—II. *prosperous.* — III. *surrounded with foliage,* Cant. 1:16.—IV. *anointed,* Ps. 92:11.

רַעֲנַן m. Ch., *green, flourishing.*

רָעַע (fut. יָרֹעַ; inf. רֹעָה).—I. *broke, broke to pieces.*—II. *crushed.* Niph. fut. יֵרוֹעַ and Hiph. הֵרַע; see in רוּעַ. Hith. הִתְרוֹעֵעַ *was broken to pieces, ruined.*

רְעַע Ch. (fut. f. תְּרֹעַ), *broke.* Pa. the same.

רֹעָה f., *breaking;* שֵׁן רֹעָה *a broken tooth.*

רָעַף and Hiph. הִרְעִיף *flowed, let drop.*

רָעַץ *crushed, overpowered, oppressed.*

רָעַשׁ (fut. יִרְעַשׁ), *was shaken, trembled.* Niph. *quaked* (of the earth), Jer. 50:46. Hiph. I. *shook.*—II. *filled with eagerness* (of a horse), Job 39:20.

רַעַשׁ m.—I. *shaking.*—II. *an earthquake.*—III. *rumbling of wheels.*— IV. *rattling of a horse's hoofs,* Job 39:24.—V. *any tumult,* Job 41:21.—VI. *the rattling of a spear.*

רָפָא (imp. רְפָה, רְפָא; fut. יִרְפָּא; pl. f. תִּרְפֶּינָה). — I. *healed.* — II. *restored to prosperity, delivered from calamity.* — III. *healed,* i. e., *removed transgressions;* part. רֹפֵא *a physician.* Niph. נִרְפָּא (pret. f. נִרְפְּתָה; inf. הֵרָפֵה, הֵרָפֵא; fut.

יֵרָפֵּו .pl.—I. *was repaired* (a vessel). — II. *was healed* (a person or wound).—III. *was rendered wholesome* (water), Eze. c. 47.—IV. *was restored to prosperity*, Isa. 53:5. Pi. רִפֵּא (fut. pl. יְרַפְּאוּ).—I. *repaired*, 1 Ki. 18:30.—II. *healed.*—III. *caused to be cured*, Ex. 21:19.—IV. *made wholesome*, 2 Ki. 2:21. Hith. *get himself cured.*

רְפָאֵל p. n. of a man.

רְפָיָה p. n. of a man.

רְפָאִים p. n., the name of a people inhabiting the country on the east of the Dead Sea, supposed to have been giants; called also יְלִידֵי הָרָפָה . עֵמֶק רְפָאִים *the valley of the Rephaims*, close to mount Moriah.

רִפְאוּת f., *health*, Pro. 3:8.

רְפֻאוֹת f. pl., *bandages, remedies.*

רָפוּא p.n. of a man.

מַרְפֵּא, מַרְפֶּה m.—I. *remedy.*—II. *healing.*—III. *soundness.* See also in רָפָה.

תְּרוּפָה f., *healing*, Eze. 47:12.

רָפַד *supported himself*, Job 41:22; fut. יִרְפַּד. Pi. I. *constructed a couch*, Job 17:13. — II. *refreshed*, Cant. 2:5.

רְפִידָה f., *a throne*; Vulg. reclinatorium, Cant. 3:10.

רְפִידִים p.n., *Rephidim*, a station in the wilderness.

רָפָה (fut. יִרְפֶּה, יִרְף).—I. *hung down* (the hands).—II. *declined* (the day).—III. *sank down* (fuel in the fire), Isa.5:24.—IV. *gave way* (to anger), Jud. 8:3; with מִן. — V. *became weak*, Jer. 49:24. — VI. *desisted.*

Niph. part. נִרְפִּים *became, were idle*, Ex. 5:8, 17, &c. Pi. רִפָּה I. *allowed to hang down*, Eze. 1:24, 25. — II. *weakened* (part. מְרַפֵּא). Hiph. הִרְפָּה (imp.apoc. הֶרֶף; fut. apoc. יֶרֶף) I. *ceased from*, with מִן.—II. *withheld.*—III. *gave up.*—IV. *let go.*—V. *ceased.* Hith. *relaxed himself, was slothful.*

רָפֶה m. (pl. f. רָפוֹת), *weak.*

רָפָה p. n.; see in רפא.

רִפְיוֹן m., *weakness*, Jer. 47:3.

מַרְפֵּא m., *yielding*, Ecc. 10:4; see also in רפא.

רֶפַח p. n. of a man.

רָפַשׂ, רָפַס *trampled down.* Niph. part. נִרְפָּשׂ *disturbed by trampling.* Hith. הִתְרַפֵּס *submitted, humbled himself.*

רְפַס Ch., the same.

מִרְפָּשׂ *water made muddy by trampling*, Eze. 34:19.

רַפְסֹדוֹת f.pl., *floats, rafts*, 2 Ch. 2:15.

רָפַף Po. רוֹפַף *trembled.*

רָפַק Hith. *trembled*, Cant. 8:5.

רָפַשׂ; see רפס.

רֶפֶשׁ m., *mud*, Isa. 57:20.

רְפָתִים m. pl., *stalls for oxen*, Hab. 3:17.

רָצִים, רַץ see רצץ; רָצִים see רוץ.

רָצָא Eze. 1:14; same as רוּץ *he ran.*

רָצַד Pi. *he laid wait for*, Ps. 68:17.

רָצָה (fut. יִרְצֶה, וַתִּרְצ).—I. *approved of, took pleasure in*, with בְּ.—II. *received favourably.*—III. *loved.*—IV. *fulfilled.*—V. *associated with,*

with עִם.—VI. was received favourably; (part. רָצוּי accepted). Niph. נִרְצָה I. was received favourably.—II. was fulfilled, Isa. 40:2. Pi. satisfied by restitution, Job 20:10. Hiph. fulfilled, Lev. 26:34. Hith. made himself acceptable, 1 Sa. 29:4.

רָצוֹן m.—I. approbation, favour (עַל רְ לְרָצוֹן acceptable, well-pleasing).—II. object of approbation.—III. will, pleasure, choice.—IV. uncontrolled will, violence, Gen. 49:6.—V. enjoyment.

רָצַח (fut. יִרְצַח) struck fatally, killed; with or without נֶפֶשׁ; part. רֹצֵחַ homicide. Niph. was killed. Pi. killed habitually, was a murderer by profession. Pu. be killed, Ps. 62:4. תְּרָצְחוּ for תְּרַצְּחוּ

רֶצַח m.—I. crushing, Ps. 42:11.—II. slaughter, Eze. 21:27.

רִצְיָא p.n. of a man.

רְצִין p.n., Rezin, king of Syria.

רָצַע pierced, bored, Ex. 21:6.

מַרְצֵעַ m., an awl.

רָצַף covered, overlaid, Cant. 3:10.

רֶצֶף m.—I. burning coals, 1 Ki. 19:6.—II. p. n., a city of some country subdued by the Assyrians.

רִצְפָּה f.—I. burning coal, Isa. 6:6.—II. an inlaid pavement.—III. p. n., Rizpah, the concubine of Saul.

מַרְצֶפֶת f., the pavement on which the brasen sea stood, 2 Ki. 16:17.

רָצַץ (fut. תָּרֹץ, יָרוּץ).—I. bruised, broke, crushed.—II. oppressed.—III. became broken, burst.—IV. relaxed

himself, Isa. 42:3. Niph. נָרוֹץ was bruised. Pi. רִצֵּץ I. bruised.—II. oppressed. Po. רוֹצֵץ the same; see also in רוּץ. Hiph. bruised; fut. וַתָּרָץ. Hithpo. struggled together, Gen. 25:22.

רַץ m. (pl. const. רָצֵי), small piece of silver, Ps. 68:31.

מְרוּצָה f., oppression, Jer. 22:17; see also in רוּץ.

רַק, רֹק, רְקִי; see רקק.

רְק; see רִיק.

רָקַב (fut. יִרְקַב) became rotten, decayed.

רָקָב m, decay, rottenness.

רִקָּבוֹן m., the same, Job 41:19.

רָקַד leaped, danced. Pi. the same. Hiph. made to leap, Ps. 29:6.

רַקּוֹן, רַקָּה; see רקק.

רָקַח (fut. יִרְקַח) compounded, prepared, Ex. 30:33; part. רֹקֵחַ a compounder of drugs and aromatics. Pu. part. מְרֻקָּחִים compound, ointment, 2 Chron. 16:14. Hiph. threw in spices, Eze. 24:10.

רֶקַח m., perfuming, the preparing of perfumes, Cant. 8:2.

רֹקַח m., ointment, Ex. 30:25, 35.

רַקָּח m., apothecary, perfumer; f. pl. רַקָּחוֹת.

רִקֻּחִים m. pl., perfumes, Isa. 57:9.

מֶרְקָח m., pl. מֶרְקָחִים perfumes, Cant. 5:13.

מֶרְקָחָה f.—I. a pot of ointment, Job 41:23.—II. spices eaten as condiments, Eze. 24:10.

מִרְקַחַת f., perfumery.

רָקִיק, רָקִיעַ, see רקק; רקע see רקע.

רָקַם streaked; part. רֹקֵם s. an embroid-

erer. Pu. *wrought with art* (met. of Christ's mystical body), Ps. 139:15.

רִקְמָה f.—I. *embroidery.*—II. *variety of colours*, Eze. 17:3; dual רִקְמָתַיִם *embroidered on both sides*, Jud. 5:30.

רֶקֶם p. n.—I. *a town of Benjamin.*—II. *of a man.*

רָקַע I. *stretched out* (of God in creation). — II. *stamped on*, 2 Sa. 22:43. — III. *stamped with the feet*, Eze. 6:11. Pi. I. *beat into thin plates.* — II. *covered with a thin plate of gold*, Isa. 40:19. Pu. part. *overlaid*, Jer. 10:9. Hiph. *stretched out*, Job 37:18.

רָקִיעַ m.—I. *the expanse of heaven, atmosphere, sky*, Vulg. firmamentum.—II. *a canopy* (Ezekiel only).

רְקֻעִים m. pl., *plates of metal*, Nu. 17:3.

רָקַק same as יָרַק *spit*, with בְּ; fut. יָרֹק, Lev. 15:8.

רָקִיק m., *a thin cake.*

רֹק m. (with suff. רֻקִּי) *spittle.*

רַק m., רַקָּה f. (Arab. *was thin*) *thin, lean*, Gen. c. 41.

רַק adv. — I. *only.*—II. *certainly*, i. e. *this only.* — III. *except*, with a negative.

רַקָּה f. — I. *the temple* (of the head), Jud. 4:21, 22; 5:26.—II. *the cheek*, Cant. 4:3; 6:7.

רַקּוֹן p. n., a town of Dan.

רַקַּת p. n., a town of Naphtali.

רָשׁ; see רוּשׁ.

רָשׁ רֵשׁ Kal imp., from יָרַשׁ.

רָשָׁה root not used; (Syr. *he gave*).

רִשָׁיוֹן m., *grant, permission*, Ezr. 3:7.

רֵשִׁית *beginning*; see רֵאשִׁית in רֹאשׁ.

רָשַׁם *wrote, decreed*, Dan. 10:21.

רְשַׁם Ch., the same.

רָשַׁע *was, acted, wickedly, unjustly, impiously.* Hiph. הִרְשִׁיעַ I. *condemned.* — II. *declared, proved guilty.*—III. *acted wickedly.*

רָשָׁע m., רְשָׁעָה f. — I. *wicked.* — II. *guilty, faulty.*

רֶשַׁע m. (with suff. רִשְׁעוֹ) *wickedness, impiety, injustice*; pl. רְשָׁעִים.

רִשְׁעָה f.—I. *wickedness.* — II. *fault*, Deu. 25:2.

רִשְׁעָתַיִם p. n.; see כּוּשָׁן.

מִרְשַׁעַת f., *wickedness*, 2 Chron. 24:7.

רֶשֶׁף m. (pl. const. רִשְׁפֵּי).—I. *a burning coal*, Cant. 8:6.—II. *lightning.* III. בְּנֵי ר' *burning arrows*, Job 5:7; רִשְׁפֵי קֶשֶׁת the same, Ps. 76:4.—IV. *burning disease*, Deu. 32:24.—V. *lust*, Cant. 8:6.—VI. p. n. of a man.

רָשַׁשׁ Po. רֹשֵׁשׁ *reduced, subdued*, Jer. 5:17. Pu. רֻשַׁשׁ *was subdued*, Mal. 1:4.

תַּרְשִׁישׁ I. p. n., *Tarshish*, some country far distant from Canaan; אֳנִיּוֹת תּ' probably *merchant ships.* — II. *a precious stone*, probably *the topaz.*—III. p. n. of a man.

רֶשֶׁת Kal inf., from יָרַשׁ.

רָתַח Pi. and Hiph. *boil, caused to boil.* Pu. *was boiled, agitated*, Job 30:27.

רֶתַח m., *boiling*, Eze. 24:5.

רָתַם *bind, yoke*, Mic. 1:13.

רֹתֶם m. (pl. רְתָמִים), *the broom;* in Spanish, *retama.*

רִתְמָה p. n., one of the stations in the wilderness.

רָתַק (Arab. *joined*). Niph. *was bound,* Ecc. 12:6, Kri. Pu. the same, Nah. 3:10.

רַתּוֹק m., *a chain,* Eze. 7:23.

רַתִּיקוֹת (רַתּוּקוֹת) f. pl., *chains,* 1 Ki. 6:21.

רְתֻקוֹת f. pl., the same, Isa. 40:19.

רָתַת (Syr. *he trembled*); see רטט.

רֶתֶת m., *trembling,* Hos. 13:1. •

שׁ

שָׂא Kal imp. and inf. from נשׂא.

שְׂאֹר m., *leaven.*

שְׂאֵת from נשׂא.

שָׂבַךְ same as סָבַךְ, *twist.*

שׂוֹבֶךְ m., *entangled branch,* 2 Sa. 18:9.

שָׂבָךְ m., pl. שְׂבָכִים *ornaments of wreathing,* 1 Ki. 7:17.

שְׂבָכָה f.—I. *network* on the capitals of pillars.—II. *lattice,* 2 Ki. 1:2.—III. *a net,* Job 18:8.

שָׂבְכָא same as סַבְכָא.

שְׂבָם, שְׂבָמָה p. n., a city of the Reubenites.

שָׂבֵעַ, שָׂבַע *was full, satisfied, surfeited,* with בְּ, מִן. Pi. *satisfied.* Hiph. *filled,* with לְ of the person; with בְּ, מִן of the thing.

שָׂבֵעַ m., שְׂבֵעָה f., *full, satisfied, surfeited.*

שֹׂבַע m., *abundance.*

שָׂבַע m., the same; לָשֹׂבַע *to the full.*

שָׂבְעָה, שִׂבְעָה f., the same, Eze. 16:49.

שָׂבַר *looked at, examined,* Neh. 2 13, 15; with בְּ. Pi. *looked to, hoped for* or *in,* with אֶל, לְ.

שֵׂבֶר m. (with suff. שִׂבְרִי), *hope.*

שָׂגָא same as שָׂנָה. Hiph. I. *increased,* Job 12:23. — II. *magnified,* Job 36:24.

שְׂגָא Ch., *increased, became great.*

שַׂגִּיא m., *the Great One* (of God), Job 36:26; 37:23.

שַׂגִּיא m., שַׂגִּיאָה f. Ch.—I. *great.*—II. *much, many.*—III. *greatly.*

שָׂגַב *was exalted.* Niph. I. *was lofty, exalted.* — II. *was secure,* Pro. 18:10. Pi. I. *raised, placed in security.*—II. *made powerful,* Isa. 9:10. Pu. pass. of Pih., Pro. 29:25. Hiph. *was lofty,* Job 36:22.

שְׂגִיב, שְׂגוּב p. n. of a man.

מִשְׂגָּב m. (with suff. מִשְׂגַּבִּי).— I. *a hill, strong place.*—II. *refuge* (of God).

שָׂגָג same as שָׂגָא. Pil. שִׂגְשֵׂג *cause to grow;* according to others, from סוג *he fences,* Isa. 17:11.

שָׂגָה *increased, became great.* Hiph. *increased,* Ps. 73:12.

שָׂדַד. Pi. *harrowed.*

שִׂדִּים p. n., the valley of the Dead Sea, *Siddim.*

שָׂדֶה m. (with suff. שָׂדֵהוּ; pl. שָׂדוֹת; const. שְׂדוֹת, שְׂדֵי).—I. *a field.*— II. *the country.*—III. *any country;* אִישׁ שָׂדֶה חַיַּת *husbandman;* הַשָּׂדֶה *the beasts of the field;* שְׂדֵה מוֹאָב *the land of Moab;* שְׂדֵה אֲרָם *Mesopotamia.*

שָׂדַי sing., the same.

שְׁדֵרוֹת; see סדר.

שֹׁה same as שֶׂה.

שָׁהֵד (Syr. and Ch. סְהַד bare witness).

שָׁהֵד m., eye witness, Job 16:19.

שָׁהֲדוּת f. Ch., testimony, Gen. 31:47.

שַׂהֲרֹנִים crescents; see סהר.

שֹׂוא Kal inf., from נשא.

שׁוֹב; see שׁיב.

שׁוֹבֵךְ; see שׁבך.

שׁוּג same as סוג drove back, 2 Sa. 1: 22.

שׂוּחַ same as שִׂיחַ to meditate, Gen. 24:63.

שׂוּט turn aside, Ps. 40:5.

שֵׂטִים, סֵטִים m. pl., they who turn aside to, Ps. 101:3; Hos. 5:2.

שׂוּךְ hedged with thorns. Pil. שׂוֹבֵךְ the same, Job 10:11.

שׂוֹךְ m., }
שׂוֹכָה f., } a bough, Jud. 9:48, 49.

שׂוֹכֹה p. n., a town of Judah.

שׂוֹכָתִי a Succothite.

מְסוּכָה, מְשׂוּכָה f., a thorn hedge.

שִׂים, שׂוֹם (fut. יָשִׂים, יָשׂוּם; apoc. וַיָּשֶׂם, יָשֵׂם; inf. abs. שׂוֹם; const. שִׂים, שׂוֹם; imp. שִׂים, שֵׂימָה).—I. placed, set.— II. set up.— III. set in array.— IV. placed aside.—V. with עַל, set over.—VI. with עַל, place upon.—VII. with עַל, בְּ, לְ, impute to any one.—VIII. with לְ שֵׁם named.—IX. with שְׁמוֹ placed His name (of the Lord), i. e. the true worship.—X. with or without לִבּוֹ set his heart, considered, regarded, with עַל, אֶל, לְ.—XI. with עַל לֵב or בְּלֵב or אֶל לֵב considered, laid

to heart. — XII. שׂוּם עַל לֵב he considered.—XIII. with לְנֶגְדּוֹ considered, set before him.—XIV. with שׂוּם בְּאָזְנֵי פ׳ he told. — XV. שׂוּם אַף heaped up wrath. (For other idiomatic usages of שׂוּם see concordance.) Hiph. (imp. הָשִׂימִי; part. מֵשִׂים) place, set. Hoph. was placed; fut. יוּשַׂם.

שׂוּם Ch.—I. appointed.—II. with טְעֵם made a decree.—III.with טְעֵם עַל לְ, regarded. — IV. with בָּל לְ endeavoured. — V. שֵׁם דִּי פ׳ named. Ithpe. אִתְּשִׂם I. was made, placed.—II. with טְעֵם was decreed.

תְּשׂוּמֶת f., with יָד a deposit, Lev. 5: 21; [6:2.]

שׂוּר I. governed; fut. וַיָּשַׂר, Jud. 9: 22. Hiph. הֵשִׂיר appointed princes, Hos. 8:4.—II. same as שָׂרָה strove, contended, Hos. 12:5.— III. same as סוּר departed. — IV. same as Ch. נְסַר he sawed, 1 Chron. 20:3; fut. וַיָּשַׂר.

שׂוּרָה f., a row, in rows, Isa. 28:25; (Arab. the same).

שִׂישׂ, שׂוּשׂ (fut. יָשִׂישׂ, יָשׂוּשׂ; inf. abs. שׂוֹשׂ; const. שׂוֹשׂ; imp שׂישׂ) rejoiced, exulted in, with בְּ, עַל.

שָׂשׂוֹן m., joy, rejoicing.

מָשׂושׂ m., joy.

שָׂחַ; see שִׂיחַ.

שָׂחָה swam, Isa. 25:11. Hiph. over-flowed, Ps. 6:7.

שָׂחוּ m., swimming, Eze. 47:5.

שָׂחַט squeezed, crushed, Gen. 40:11.

שָׂחַק I. laughed.—II. with אֶל approved.—III.with עַל laughed at.—IV.

with לְ *despised.* — V. *caused laugh-*
ter. Pi. שָׂחֵק (inf. שַׂחֵק; fut. וַיְשַׂחֵק).
— I. *rejoiced, sported.* — II. *played on*
an instrument, 2 Sa. 6:21. — III.
made sport, Jud. 16:25. — IV. *skir-*
mished, 2 Sa. 2:14. Hiph. *derided,*
with עַל, 2 Chron. 30:10.

שְׂחֹק, שְׂחוֹק m. — I. *laughter.* — II. *sub-*
ject or *object of laughter.*

מִשְׂחָק m., *object of laughter,* Hab.
1:10.

שָׂטָה (fut. יִשְׂטֶה; apoc. וַיֵּשְׂטְ). — 1.
went aside, Pro. 7:25. — II. *went*
astray, Nu. *c.* 5.

שָׂטִים; see שׂוּט.

שָׂטַם *acted fiercely, hardly towards,*
was hated.

מַשְׂטֵמָה f., *hatred,* Hos. 9:7, 8.

שָׂטַן *was an adversary to, opposed;*
part. שֹׂטֵן *an adversary,* Ps.71:13.

שָׂטָן m. — I. *an adversary.* — II. הַשָּׂטָן
the devil, the great adversary.

שִׂטְנָה f. — I. *accusation,* Ezr. 4:6. —
II. p. n. of a well.

שִׂיא; see נשׂא.

שִׂיאֹן p. n., one of the peaks of Hermon.

שִׂיב *was grey-headed.* Part. שָׂב, Job
15:10; Ch. the same.

שֵׂיב m., *grey hairs, old age,* 1 K. 14:4.
שֵׂיבָה f., the same.

שִׂיג m., *retirement,* 1 K. 18:27.

שִׂיד *plastered,* Deu. 27:2, 4.

שִׂיד m., *plaster.*

שֶׂה, שֵׂיָה com. (const. שֵׂה, with suff.
שְׂיוֹ, שְׂיָהוּ), *a sheep* or *goat.*

שִׂיחַ I. *meditated,* with בְּ. — II. *spoke,*

with לְ *with,* or בְּ *of.* — III. *com-*
posed a psalm, sung, with בְּ. Pil.
I. *uttered,* Isa. 55:8. — II. *meditated,*
Ps. 143:5.

שֶׂחַ m., *purpose, design,* Am. 4:13.

שִׂיחַ m. — I. *a plant, bush.* — II. *speech,*
message. — III. *a complaint.* — IV.
sorrow, Job 7:13.

שִׂיחָה f., *complaint, prayer, medita-*
tion.

שִׂים; see שׂוּם.

שְׂכוֹת, שֹׂךְ, שְׂכִּים, שָׂךְ; see שׂכך.

שָׂכָה *root not used;* (Syr. *expected*).

שֵׂכוּ p. n., a place near Ramah.

שֶׂכְוִי m., "*a thunderstorm*" (Lee), Job
38:36.

שְׂכִיָּה f., *objects* (of sight or thought),
Isa. 2:16.

מַשְׂכִּית f. (pl. מַשְׂכִּיֹּות). — I. *figure,*
external image. — II. *imagination,*
internal image.

שַׂכִּין m., *a knife,* Pro. 23:2; (Arab.
the same).

שְׂכִירָה, שָׂכִיר; see שׂכר.

שָׂכַךְ *placed as a covering,* Ex. 33:22.

שֵׂךְ m., pl. שִׂכִּים *thorns,* Nu. 33: 55.

שָׂךְ m. (with suff. שְׂכּוֹ), *a fence,* Lam.
2:6.

שֻׂכָּה f., pl. שֻׂכּוֹת *spears,* Job 40:31.
מְשׂוּכָה f., *a fence,* Pro. 15:19; Isa.
5:5; see שׂוּךְ.

שָׂכַל *was wise, careful, skilful,* 1 Sa.
18:30. Pi. *acted wisely, designed-*
ly, Gen. 48:14. Hiph. I. *looked*
at. — II. *reflected.* — III. *cared for.*
— IV. *acted wisely, was wise.* — V.
prospered. — VI. *made wise, taught,*
with בְּ, עַל, אֶל; part. מַשְׂכִּיל I.
thoughtful, prudent. — II. *a didactic*

poem (title of Psalms); inf. הַשְׂכֵּל, הַשְׂכִּיל *understanding, wisdom*, with accus. לְ.

שְׂכַל Ch. Ith. part. מִשְׂתַּכַּל *considered, looked at*, with בְּ.

שֵׂכֶל, שֶׂכֶל m. (with suff. שִׂכְלוֹ).—I. *understanding, skill.* — II. *estimation, esteem*, Pro. 3:4. — III. *signification*, Neh. 8:8.

שִׂכְלוּת ; see סכל.

שָׂכְלְתָנוּ f. Ch., *understanding, skill*, Dan. 5:11, 12, 14.

שָׂכַר I. *hired.* — II. *bribed.* Niph. *hired himself*, 1 Sa. 2:5. Hith. הִשְׂתַּכֵּר the same, Hag. 1:6.

שָׂכָר m.—I. *reward, hire.*—II. p. n. of a man.

שֶׂכֶר m., *hire.*

שָׂכִיר m., *hired person or thing.*

שְׂכִירָה f., *the act of hiring*, τὸ μισθοῦν, Isa. 7:20.

מַשְׂכֹּרֶת f. (with suff. מַשְׂכֻּרְתִּי).—I. *wages.*—II. *reward*, Ru. 2:12.

שְׂלָו f. (pl. שְׂלָוִים), *a quail.*

שַׂלְמָה trans. for שִׂמְלָה f.(pl. שְׂלָמוֹת).—I. *a garment.*—II. *any cloth.*—III. *clothing.*—IV. p. n., the father of Boaz, who was called also שַׂלְמוֹן.—V. p. n. of a man.

שַׂלְמַי p. n. of a man.

שְׂמֹאול, שְׂמֹאל m., *the left hand or side*; מִשְׂמֹאל *on the left or north*; שְׂמֹאל or עַל שִׂ *on or to the left or north.*

הִשְׂמִיל, הִשְׂמְאִיל Hiph.—I. *went to the left.* — II. *used the left hand.*

שְׂמָאלִית f., שְׂמָלִי, שְׂמָאלִי m., *belonging to the left, on the left.*

שָׂמֵחַ, שָׂמַח I. *was glad.* — II. *expressed joy.*—III. *burned brightly*, with בְּ, עַל, לְ. Pi. שִׂמַּח *made to rejoice*, with עַל, לְ, מִן, בְּ. Hiph. the same.

שָׂמֵחַ m. (pl. const. שִׂמְחֵי, שְׂמֵחִי; f. שְׂמֵחָה).—I. *joyful.*—II. *expressing joy.*—III. *rejoicing in or at*, with לְ.

שִׂמְחָה f. (pl. שְׂמָחוֹת).—I. *joy.*—II. *a festival.*—III. *merriment.*

שְׂמִיכָה ; see סמך.

שְׂמֹאל ; see in הַשְׂמִיל.

שִׂמְלָה f. (pl. שְׂמָלוֹת), *garment*; see שַׂלְמָה I.

שַׂמְלָה p. n., a king of Edom.

שְׂמָמִית f., a species of lizard, Pro. 30:28.

שָׂנֵא (fut. יִשְׂנָא; inf. abs. שָׂנֹא, const. שְׂנֹא, שְׂנֹאת, שָׂנֵאָה) *hated*, with לְ; part. שֹׂנֵא *hater, enemy.* Niph. *was hated.* Pi. part. מְשַׂנֵּא *an enemy.*

שְׂנֵא Ch. part. שָׂנְאִין, *haters.*

שִׂנְאָה f., *hatred.*

שְׂנִיאָה m., f., *hated*, Deu. 21:15.

שְׂנִיר p. n., the name of mount Hermon among the Amorites.

שְׂעִפִּים ; see סעף.

שָׂעַר I. *shuddered.* — II. *feared*, Deu. 32:17, with עַל.—III. *swept, tore away as a tempest*, Ps. 58:10. Niph. *a tempest raged*, Ps. 50:3. Pi. *swept away with a tempest*, Job 27:21. Hith. *raged like a tempest*, Dan. 11:40.

שָׂעִיר m., שְׂעִירָה f.—I. *hairy*, Gen. 27: 11, 23. — II. *a goat* (always with עִזִּים). Pl. שְׂעִירִים I. probably *wild goats*, Isa. 13:21; 34:14.—II. *showers*, Deu. 32:2.

שֵׂעִיר p.n., *Seir*.—I. the district between the Dead Sea and the gulf of Akabah.—II. a mountain of Judah.

שְׂעִירָה p.n., a district unknown.

שֵׂעָר const. שְׂעַר m., *the hair*.

שְׂעַר m. Ch., *the hair*.

שַׂעַר m. — I. *a storm, tempest.* — II. *shuddering, horror*; same as סַעַר.

שְׂעָרָה f., *a tempest*.

שַׂעֲרָה f.—I. *a hair*.—II. *the hair*.

שְׂעֹרָה f., *barley* (the plant); pl. שְׂעֹרִים *barley* (the grain).

שְׂעָרִים p.n. of a man.

שָׂפָה f. (dual שְׂפָתַיִם, שִׂפְתֵי; with suff. שְׂפָתָיו; pl. const. שִׂפְתוֹת). —I. *a lip*.—II. *a language*. —III. *words*.—IV. *brim of a vessel*.—V. *shore of the sea, bank of a river*. —VI. *edge, edging.* — VII. *border of a country*, Jud. 7:22.

שָׂפַח. Pi. *struck with baldness*, Isa. 3:17.

מִשְׂפָּח "*oppression*," Eng. Ver., Isa. 5:7.

שָׂפָם m., *the chin, the beard*.

שָׂפַן *hid, concealed*, Deu. 33:19.

שָׂפַק I. *clapped the hands*, Job 27:23. —II. *sufficed*, 1 Ki. 20:10. Hiph. *bargained with*, Isa. 2:6; with בְּ.

שֶׂפֶק m., *contempt*, Job 36:18.

שַׂק m. (with suff. שַׂקּוֹ; pl. שַׂקִּים).— I. *sack-cloth*.—II. *a sack*.

שָׂקַד. Niph. *was bound, tied*, Lam. 1:14.

שָׂקַר. Pi. *painted the eyes with stibium* (a black powder), Isa. 3:16.

שָׂר; see שׁוּר.

שָׂרַג Pu. *was interwoven*, Job 40:17. Hith. the same, Lam. 1:14.

שָׂרוּג p.n. of a man.

שָׂרִיגִים m. pl., *branches of a vine*.

שָׂרַד *fled, escaped*, Jos. 10:20; (Arab. the same.)

שָׂרִיד m., *one that escapes*.—II. *a remnant*, Isa. 1:9.

שְׂרָד m., *colour*; בִּגְדֵי שְׂ׳ *coloured garments* (Exodus only).

שָׂרָד m., *only*.

שָׂרָה *was a prince, prevailed*, with אֶת, עִם; see שַׂר.

שָׂרָה s. f.; see שַׂר.

שָׂרַי p.n., *Sarai* (afterwards *Sarah*), the wife of Abraham.

שְׂרָיָהוּ, שְׂרָיָה p.n. of a man.

מִשְׂרָה f., *government*, Isa. 9:5, 6.

שָׂרַח p.n. of a man.

שָׂרַט *cut, made incisions*. Niph. *was crushed*, Zec. 12:3.

שֶׂרֶט m., *an incision*, Lev. 19:28.

שָׂרֶטֶת f., the same, Lev. 21:5.

שָׂרִיגִים, see שָׂרַג; שָׂרִיד, see שָׂרַד.

שָׂרַך. Pi. part. f. מְשָׂרֶכֶת *twisting its course, wandering in all directions*, Jer. 2:23.

שְׂרוֹךְ m., *shoe latchet*.

שַׂרְסְכִים p.n. of an Assyrian eunuch.

שָׂרַע, part. שָׂרוּעַ *stretched out, monstrously prolonged* (of a limb). Hith. *stretched himself out*, Isa. 28:20.

שַׂרְעַפִּים *thoughts*; see סעף.

שָׂרַף I. *burned, consumed*.—II. *burned spices at a funeral*. — III. *baked* bricks, Gen. 11:3. Niph. and Pu. *was burnt.*

שָׂרָף m.—I. *a venomous serpent,* probably the coluber cerastes.—II. p. n. of a man.

שְׂרָפִים m. pl., *seraphim, six-winged spirits,* Isa. 6:2, 6.

שְׂרֵפָה f.—I. *burning fire.*—II. *a funeral burning.*

מִשְׂרָפוֹת f. pl. — I. *burning.* — II. מִשְׂרְפוֹת מַיִם p. n., a place near Sidon.

שָׂרַק *combed, hackled flax,* Isa. 19:9.

שֹׂרֵק m., שֹׂרֵקָה f. — I. *a vine of a choice quality.*—II. שֹׂרֵק p. n., a valley between Askelon and Gaza.

שְׂרוּקִים m. pl., *shoots of the vine,* Isa. 16:8.

שָׂרֹק m., pl. שְׂרֻקִּים *bay* (colour of a horse), Zec. 1:8.

שָׂרַר *acted as a prince.* Hith. הִשְׂתָּרֵר *made himself a prince.*

שַׂר m. (pl. שָׂרִים), *prince, ruler, chief, captain.*

שָׂרָה f.—I. *a princess, a woman of rank.* — II. p. n., *Sarah,* the wife of Abraham; see שָׂרַי.

שָׂשׂוֹן; see שׂוּשׂ.

שֵׂת for שְׂאֵת; see נשׂא.

שָׂתַם *shut out,* Lam. 3:8.

שָׂתַר. Niph. *were concealed,* 1 Sa. 5:9.

שׁ

שֶׁ...שָׁ... an abbreviation of אֲשֶׁר, prefixed to every part of speech.

שָׁאַב (fut. יִשְׁאַב) *drew water.*
מַשְׁאָב m., pl. מַשְׁאַבִּים *watering places,* Jud. 5:11.

שָׁאַג (fut. יִשְׁאַג).—I. *roared as a lion.* —II. *shrieked for anguish,* Ps. 38:9.

שְׁאָגָה const. שַׁאֲגַת f. — I. *roar of a lion.* — II. *groan, shriek of anguish.*

שָׁאָה *was desolate* (a city), Isa. 6:11. Niph. I. *was desolate* (a city), Isa. 6:11. — II. *were dashed together,* Isa. 17:12, 13. Hiph. *lay waste,* Isa. 37:26. Hith. הִשְׁתָּאָה *wondered, was in astonishment,* with לְ.

שׁוֹאָה f., Pro. 1:27, Ketib *a storm;* same as שׁוֹאָה.

שַׁאֲהֶם; see שׁוֹא.

שְׁאִיָּה f., *crash, destruction,* Isa. 24:12.

שְׁאֵת f., *desolation,* Lam. 3:47.

שֵׁת f., *noise, tumult of war,* Num. 24:17.

שָׁאוֹן m. — I. *shouting, the noise of waves.*— II. *desolation, ruin.*

מַשּׁוּאוֹת, מַשּׁוֹאוֹת f. pl., *desolation, a desolate place.*

שָׁאַט, שָׁאָט *contempt;* see שׁוּט.

שָׁאט part. from II. שׁוּט.

שָׁאַל, שָׁאֵל (fut. יִשְׁאַל). — I. *questioned, enquired.* — II. *requested, prayed for.* — III. *borrowed,* with מִן, מֵאֵת, מֵעִם, or לְ; שָׁאַל לְשָׁלוֹם *enquired of his welfare, saluted;* שָׁאַל בֵּאלֹהִים *enquired of God.* Niph. *requested for himself.* Pi. שִׁאֵל *asked earnestly,* with בְּ. Hiph. *gave in answer to a request, gave.*

שְׁאֵל Ch., *asked, enquired.*

שָׁאָל p. n. of a man.

שָׁאוּל p. n. of a man, *Saul.* Patron. שָׁאוּלִי.

שְׁאוֹל, שְׁאֹל com., *the abode of the*

soul after death (see אֲבַדּוֹן), with
ה loc. שְׁאָלָה.

שְׁאֵלָה f. (with suff. שְׁאֵלָתִי, שְׁאֶלְתְּךָ,
שְׁאֶלְתָּם), asking, a request.

שֵׁלָה I. same as שְׁאֵלָה. — II. p.n.,
one of the sons of Judah; patron.
שֵׁלָנִי.

שְׁאֵלָא f. Ch., demand, Dan. 4:14.

שְׁאַלְתִּיאֵל, שַׁלְתִּיאֵל p.n. of a man.

מִשְׁאָל p.n., a town of the Levites in
the tribe of Asher.

מִשְׁאָלָה f., prayers.

שָׁאַן. Pil. שַׁאֲנַן was quiet, secure,
wanton.

שַׁאֲנָן m., שַׁאֲנַנָּה f. — I. quiet. — II.
wanton, luxurious. — III. wantonness, pride.

שָׁאַסֶיךָ, שֹׁסֵם; see שָׁסַס.

שָׁאַף I. panted, gasped, Ps. 119:131.
— II. panted for, desired eagerly.
—III. swallowed up, destroyed.

שָׁאַר was left, 1 Sa. 16:11. Niph. the
same. Hiph. left, had left.

שְׁאָר m., the remainder, remnant.

שְׁאָר m. Ch., the same.

שְׁאָר יָשׁוּב (a remnant shall return).
Prophetic name of the son of
Isaiah, Isa. 7:3.

שְׁאֵר m. — I. flesh. — II. any near
relation.—III. a right arising from
marriage, Ex. 21:10.

שַׁאֲרָה f., near, relation, relationship,
Lev. 18:17.

שֶׁאֱרָה p. n. of a woman.

שְׁרִית, שְׁאֵרִית f., remainder, remnant.

מִשְׁאֶרֶת f., kneading trough.

שְׁאֵת; see שָׁאָה.

שֵׁב, with ה parag. שְׁבָה Kal imp.
from יָשַׁב.

שְׁבָא p. n. of a country, probably
Arabia Felix.

שָׁבַב (Arab. kindled).

שָׁבִיב m., flame, Job 18:5.

שְׁבִיב m. Ch., the same.

שְׁבָבִים m. pl., fragments, Hos. 8:6.

שָׁבָה (imp. וּשֲׁבֵה; fut. apoc. (וַיִּשְׁבְּ
carried captive, took prisoners, carried off; part. שְׁבוּיִם m., שְׁבִיּוֹת f.,
captives. Niph. was led captive.

שְׁבוּאֵל p. n. of a man; written also
שׁוּבָאֵל.

שְׁבִי, with pause שֶׁבִי m. (with suff.
שִׁבְיְךָ, שֶׁבְיוֹ (שִׁבְיְכֶם; f. שִׁבְיָה I.
captive. — II. troop of captives. —
III. captivity.

שִׁבְיָה f. — I. troop of captives, spoil.
—II. captivity.

שְׁבִית, שְׁבוּת f. — I. captivity. — II.
captives. שׁוּב שׁ׳ I. turned from
captivity. — II. restored to prosperity.

שְׁבוֹ m., an agate; LXX. ἀχάτης.

שָׁבַח. Pi. שִׁבַּח I. praised, commended.
—II. quieted, restrained, kept back.
Hiph. quieted, Ps. 65:8. Hith.
boast of, glory in, with בְּ.

שְׁבַח Ch. Pa. praised.

שֵׁבֶט, שֵׁבֶט com. (with suff. שִׁבְטִי).
— I. staff.—II. rod (for punishment). — III. sceptre. — IV. dart,
short spear.—V. tribe.

שְׁבַט com. Ch., a tribe, Ezr. 6:17.

שְׁבָט m., the eleventh month of the
Jewish year, corresponding to our
February and March.

שַׁרְבִיט m., a sceptre (Esther only).

שִׁבְיָה, שְׁבִי captive, &c.; see שָׁבָה.

שְׁבִי and שֶׁבִי p. n. of a man.

שְׁבִיסִים m. pl., "sun-like ornaments of the neck," (Schrœder); "cauls," Eng. Ver., Isa. 3:18; sense uncertain.

שְׁבִיעִי ,שְׁבִיעִית; see שבע.

שְׁבִירָה; see שׁבה.

שְׁבִיל m., a path, mode of conduct; (Arab. the same).

שֹׁבֶל m., "locks" (of hair), Eng.Ver., Isa. 47:2.

שָׁבֵל or שָׁבָל f., pl. const. שִׁבֲּלֵי a branch, Zec. 4:12.

שִׁבֹּלֶת f. (pl. שִׁבֳּלִים).—I. a stream of water.—II. an ear of corn.

שַׁבְּלוּל m., a snail, Ps. 58:9.

שֶׁבְנָה ,שֶׁבְנָא p.n., Shebna, the scribe.

שְׁבַנְיָה p. n. of a man.

I. שֶׁבַע, const. שְׁבַע, f. שִׁבְעָה, const. שִׁבְעַת m., seven, the seventh; adv. seventh, sevenfold; שִׁבְעָה שִׁבְעָה by sevens; שִׁבְעָה עָשָׂר m., שְׁבַע עֶשְׂרֵה f., seventeen; dual שִׁבְעָתַיִם I. sevenfold. — II. seventimes. Pl. שִׁבְעִים seventy.

שִׁבְעָנָה m., seven, Job 42:13.

שָׁבוּעַ m. (dual שְׁבֻעַיִם; pl. שָׁבֻעִים, שְׁבֻעוֹת).—I. a week; חַג שָׁבֻעוֹת the feast of weeks.—II. a week of years, Dan. c. 9 & 10.

שְׁבִיעִי m., שְׁבִיעִית f., seventh.

II. שֶׁבַע p. n., (a) a town of Simeon; (b) of a man; (c) שִׁבְעָה name of a well.

שָׁבַע bound by oaths, Eze. 21:28. Niph. נִשְׁבַּע swore, with לְ; swore to, with בְּ; swore by. Hiph. I. caused to swear.—II. adjured.

שְׁבוּעָה ,שְׁבֻעָה f., an oath.

שָׁבַץ. Pi. "embroider," Eng. Ver., Ex. 28:39; sense doubtful. Pu. set (of a precious stone), Ex. 28:20.

שָׁבָץ m., perplexity, 2 Sa. 1:9.

מִשְׁבְּצוֹת f. pl.—I. gold settings (for stones).—II. cloth of gold, Ps. 45:14.

תַּשְׁבֵּץ m., embroidery, Ex. 28:4.

שְׁבַק Ch., left. Ith. was left.

שָׁבַר (fut. יִשְׁבֹּר).—I. broke to pieces. —II. tore (as a wild beast).— III. broke the heart. — IV. broke the power of, destroyed.—V. quenched thirst.—VI. assigned, with חֹק.— VII. from שֶׁבֶר sold corn, Gen. 41:56.—VIII. bought corn. Niph. I. was broken.—II. was torn.—III. was broken (the heart).—IV. was destroyed. Pi. שִׁבֵּר broke with violence. Hiph. I. caused to suffer labour pains, Isa. 66:9.—II. sold corn. Hoph. was broken-hearted, Jer. 8:21.

שֵׁבֶר ,שֶׁבֶר (with suff. שִׁבְרוֹ) I. breaking, fracture.—II. vexation, sorrow.—III. calamity, ruin.—IV. provision, corn.—V. interpretation, Jud. 7:15.—VI. p. n., a place near Ai.

שִׁבָּרוֹן m.—I. breaking, i. e. pain, sorrow, Eze. 21:11.—II. calamity, ruin, Jer. 17:18.

מַשְׁבֵּר m.—I. pains of childbirth.— II. violent pains (of any kind), 2 Sa. 22:5.—III. breakers (of the sea).

מִשְׁבָּר m., the same.

שְׁבַשׁ Ch. Ith., perplexed, Dan. 5:9.

שָׁבַת (יִשְׁבַּת, יִשְׁבֹּת fut.).—I. *ceased.*—II. *rested;* with מִן *from.*—III. *was interrupted,* Neh. 6:3.—IV. *ceased to exist, came to an end.*—V. with שַׁבָּת *kept the sabbath.* Niph. *came to an end.* Hiph. I. *caused to cease.* — II. *interrupted.* — III. *brought to an end.*

שֶׁבֶת m.—I. *ceasing.* — II. *intermission;* see also in יָשַׁב.

שַׁבָּת com. (with suff. שַׁבַּתּוֹ; pl. שַׁבָּתוֹת; const. שַׁבְּתוֹת) *cessation, time of rest, sabbath;* שַׁבַּת שָׁנִים *a sabbath of years.*

שַׁבָּתוֹן m., *rest, a time of rest.*

שַׁבְּתַי p. n. of a man.

מִשְׁבָּת m., pl. מִשְׁבַּתִּים *cessations,* Lam. 1:7.

שֶׁבֶת Kal inf., from יָשַׁב.

שָׁבַת Ch. Kal pret. f., from שׁוּב.

שָׁנָא same as שָׁנָה.

שָׁגַג *erred, committed an error,* Lev. 5:18; inf. בִּשְׁגָם *because of their sin.*

שְׁגָגָה f., *error, unintentional fault.*

שָׁגָה *erred, went astray,* with מִן. Hiph. I. *allowed to err,* Ps. 119:10.—II. *caused to go astray.*

שֵׁגָא p. n. of a man.

שְׁגִיאָה f., *error,* Ps. 19:13.

שִׁגָּיוֹן m. (pl. שִׁגְיֹנוֹת) *a doleful song, lament,* Ps. 7:1; Hab. 3:1.

מִשְׁגֶּה m., *mistake, inadvertency,* Gen. 43:12.

שָׁגַח. Hiph. *looked to.*

שָׁגַל *lay with a woman;* fut. יִשְׁגַּל. Niph. and Pu. pass. of Kal.

שֵׁגָל f., *a queen.*

שֵׁגָל f. Ch., *the same.*

שַׁגָּם Kal inf. with suff., from שׁנג.

שָׁגַע Pu. part. מְשֻׁגָּע *maddened, mad.* Hith. *acted like a madman.*

שִׁגָּעוֹן m., *madness, impetuosity.*

שֶׁגֶר, שָׁגָר m., *offspring, progeny,* Exod. 13:12.

שַׁד, see שָׂדֶה; שֵׁד, see שׁוּד; שֹׁד, see שָׁדַד, שָׂדֶה.

שָׁדַד (יִשָּׁדֵם, יְשָׁדְדֵם fut. with suff.).—I. *attacked, invaded.*—II. *plundered, laid waste, ruined;* part. שֹׁדֵד *invader, plunderer;* שָׁדוּד *destroyed.* Niph. *was laid waste.* Pi. *laid waste, ruined utterly.* Pu. שֻׁדַּד *was laid waste.* Po. *laid waste.* Hoph. הוּשַׁד *was laid waste.*

שֹׁד, שׁוֹד m.—I. *destruction, ruin.*—II. *violence, oppression.*—III. *extorted property,* Am. 3:10.

שַׁדַּי m., *the Almighty* (the name of God as revealed to the Patriarchs); LXX. παντοκράτωρ.

שָׂדָה root not used; (Arab. *was well watered*).

שַׁד m.—I. *teats of an animal.* — II. *breast of a woman;* dual שָׁדַיִם, שְׁדֵי *the breasts.*

שֹׁד m., *the same.*

שִׁדָּה f., שׁ' וְשִׁדּוֹת, Ecc. 2:8, "*musical instruments and that of all sorts,*" Eng. Ver.—*pleasures of every kind* (Ges. and Lee).

שְׁדֵיאוּר p. n. of a man.

שְׁדֵמָה f., *blighted corn;* pl. שְׁדֵמוֹת, שַׁדְמוֹת.—I. *fields.*—II. *corn fields.* Hab. 3:17.—III. *vineyards.*

שָׁדַף *blighted.*

שְׁדֵפָה f., *blight in corn*, 2 Ki. 19: 26.

שִׁדָּפוֹן m., the same.

שְׁדַר Ch. Ithp. *exerting himself*, Dan. 6:15.

שַׁדְרַךְ p.n., *Shadrach*, one of the three holy children.

שֹׁהַם m.—I. *onyx* or *sardonyx.*—II. p. n. of a man.

שׁוֹא m. (pl. with suff. שֹׁאֵיהֶם) *ragings*, Ps. 35:17.

שָׁוְא m.—I. *guilt.*-II. *calamity.*-III. *worthlessness, vanity.* — IV. *falsehood.*

שֵׁו same as שָׁוְא.

שׁוֹאָה f.—I. *a storm.*—II. *destruction.* —III. *a desolate place.*

מְשׁוֹאָה f., *desolation, a desolate place.*

תְּשֻׁאָה f., pl. תְּשֻׁאוֹת *tumult, shouting.*

שׁוֹב, Jer. 42:10, for יָשׁוֹב Kal inf., from יָשַׁב.

שׁוּב (fut. וַיָּשָׁב, יָשֹׁב, יָשׁוּב)—I. *went* or *came back*; with מִן *from*; *turned to, returned*, with עַל, לְ, אֶל, עַד *to.* — II. *turned himself about*, 1 Chron. 21:20. — III. *changed his course of life.* (For many uses with other words which slightly modify these primary meanings, see Concordance.) Pil. שׁוֹבֵב I. *led back.*—II. *restored.*—III. *led astray*, Isa. 47:10. — IV. *refreshed*, Ps. 23:3. Pul. שׁוֹבַב *was brought back.* Hiph. הֵשִׁיב (fut. וַיָּשֶׁב, יָשֵׁב, יָשִׁיב).—I. *brought back.*—II. *restored.*—III. *requited.* —IV. *brought upon a person.*—V. *sent as a tribute* or *atonement.*—

VI. *distributed, assigned.* — VII. *moved away, put aside.*—VIII. *repelled, hindered.*—IX. *recalled, revoked a declaration.*—X. *caused to turn from sin.* — XI. *withheld, withdrew.*—XII. *brought down, reduced.*—XIII. *caused to answer*, Job 20:2. With דָּבָר *answered*; with פָּנָיו *turned away his anger*; with (עַל) אֶל-לֵב *laid to heart, considered*; with פְּנֵי פּ' *turned away, refused.* Hoph. הוּשַׁב *was returned, brought back.*

שׁוּבָה f., *returning*, Isa. 30:15.

שִׁיבָה f., *returning*, Ps. 126:1; see another meaning in יָשַׁב.

שׁוֹבָב m.—I. *a rebellious person.*—II. p.n. of a man.

שׁוֹבֵב m., שׁוֹבָבָה f., *a rebel.*

שׁוּבָאֵל p. n., same as שְׁבוּאֵל.

מְשׁוֹבָב p.n. of a man.

מְשׁוּבָה, מְשֻׁבָה f.—I. *turning away* (from God).—II. *rebellious, backsliding.*

תְּשׁוּבָה f.—I. *return.*—II. *an answer.*

שׁוֹבָךְ p. n. of a man.

שׁוֹבָל p. n. of a man.

שׁוֹבֵק p. n. of a man.

שׁוּג same as שָׁנָה, שָׁגַג.

מְשׁוּגָה f., *error*, Job 19:4.

שׁוּד same as שָׁדַד *laid waste*; fut. יָשׁוּד, Ps. 91:6.

שׁוֹד same as שֹׁד; see שָׁדַד.

שֵׁד m., pl. שֵׁדִים *idols*, Deu. 32:17; Ps. 106:37; LXX. δαιμόνια.

שָׁוָה I. *was equal to, resembled.*—II. *was of equal value or importance.* —III. *was fitting, proper*, Est. 3:8. —IV. *was sufficient*, Est. 7:4. With

אֶל, לְ, בְּ. Pi. שִׁוָּה I. *made level, smoothed,* Isa. 28:25. — II. *made similar,* Ps. 131:2. — III. *made himself like,* Isa. 38:13. — IV. *placed, proposed.* — V. *produced fruit,* Hos. 10:1. Hiph. *made like, compared.* Nithpa. נִשְׁתַּוָּה *being made like,* Pro. 27:15.

שְׁוָא Ch. Pa., *placed, made equal,* Dan. 5:21, with עִם. Ithpa. *was made into,* Dan. 3:29.

שָׁוָה f., *equity,* Job 33:27.

שָׁוֵה p.n., a plain to the north of Jerusalem; שָׁוֵה קִרְיָתָיִם a city of Moab.

שׁוּחַ *went down, sank.*

שׁוּחַ p. n. of one of Abraham's sons; patron. שׁוּחִי.

שׁוּחָה f.—I. *a pit, pitfall.*—II. p.n. of a man.

שִׁיחָה f., *a pit,* Ps. 119:85.

שׁוּחָם p. n. of a man.

שַׁחַת f.—I. *a pit.*—II. *a dungeon.*—III. *a grave;* see also in שָׁחַת.

I. שׁוֹט 1. *spread like water, went to and fro.*—2. *struck, struck into the water,* i.e. *rowed.* Pil. שׁוֹטֵט *ran far and wide.* Hithpal. הִתְשׁוֹטֵט *same as Pil.*

שׁוֹט m.—I. *a whip, scourge.*—II. *calamity.*

שַׁיִט m., *an oar, oars,* Isa. 33:21.

שֵׁטֶט m., *a whip, scourge,* Jos. 23:13.

מָשׁוֹט m., *an oar, rudder,* Eze. 27:29.

מְשׁוֹט m., the same, Eze. 27:6.

II. שׁוֹט (Syr. *despised*); part. שָׁאט *despised* (Ezekiel only).

שְׁאָט m. (with suff. שְׁאָטְךָ), *contempt* (of another), Ezekiel only.

שׁוּל m., *skirt* (of a garment), *train.*

שׁוֹלָל *spoil;* see שָׁלַל.

שׁוּלַמִּית; see שָׁלֵם.

שׁוּם m., *garlick,* Nu. 11:5.

שׁוּנִי p.n., a son of Gad.

שׁוּנֵם p. n., a town of Issachar; שׁוּנַמִּי m., שׁוּנַמִּית f., *a Shunemite.*

שׁוֵעַ, שָׁוַע. Pi. שִׁוַּע *cried out for help, implored,* with אֶל. Pil. and Hiph. see in שָׁעַע.

שֶׁוַע m. (with suff. שַׁוְעִי), *a cry for help,* Ps. 5:3.

שׁוֹעַ m.—I. *affluent,* Job 34:19.—II. *liberal,* Isa. 32:5.

שׁוּעַ m.—I. *safety,* Job 30:24. — II. *affluence,* Job 36:19.—III. p.n. of a man.

שַׁוְעָה f., *cry for help.*

שׁוּעָא p. n. of a man.

תְּשׁוּעָה, תְּשֻׁעָה f., *freedom, safety, salvation, deliverance.*

שׁוּעָל; see שָׁעַל.

שׁוֹעֵר; see שָׁעַר.

שׁוּף (fut. יָשׁוּף).—I. *bruised, shattered,* Gen. 3:15; Job 9:17. — II. *concealed,* Ps. 139:11.

שׁוֹפָךְ p.n., same as שׁוֹבָךְ

שׁוּפָמִי p. n. of a man.

שׁוֹפָר *trumpet;* see שָׁפַר.

שׁוֹק same as שָׁקַק. Hiph. הֵשִׁיק I. *caused to run over,* Joel 2:24. — II. *overflowed,* Joel 4:13. Pil. שׁוֹקֵק *cause to overflow,* Ps. 65:10.

שׁוּק m. (pl. שְׁוָקִים), *a street.*

שׁוֹק com. (dual שֹׁקַיִם), *leg* (of a man or animal); trop. שֹׁקֵי הָאִישׁ *perhaps infantry,* Ps. 147:10.

שָׁק m. Ch., *leg.*

תְּשׁוּקָה f., *desire.*

שׁוֹר (fut. יָשׁוּר).— I. *viewed, beheld, perceived.*— II. *watched* (for good or evil).— III. *went,* Is. 57:9; part. f. pl. שָׁרוֹת *travellers,* Eze. 27:25. See also in שִׁיר.

שׁוּר m.— I. *an enemy* (one who watches for evil), Ps. 92:12.— II. *a wall;* pl. שׁוּרוֹת.— III. p. n., a place in the wilderness; מִדְבַּר שׁוּר *the wilderness of Shur,* between Egypt and Palestine.

שׁוּר m. Ch., *a wall.*

שָׁרוֹת f. pl., *walls,* Jer. 5:10.

שׁוֹר m. (pl. שְׁוָרִים).— I. *an ox.*— II. *a herd of oxen.*

תְּשׁוּרָה f., *a present,* 1 Sa. 9:7.

שׁוּשׁ root not used; (Syr. *alabaster*).

שַׁיִשׁ m., *white marble,* 1 Ch. 29:2.

שֵׁשׁ m.— I. *white marble,* Est. 1:6.— II. *very fine linen.* (See also in its place.)

שׁוּשָׁן m.— I. *a lily.*— II. *an artificial lily.*— III. שׁוּשָׁן עֵדוּת probably the name of a musical instrument.— IV. שׁוּשָׁן p. n.: (a) the city of *Susa* in Persia; (b) a place unknown.

שׁוֹשָׁן m., *a lily;* pl. שׁוֹשַׁנִּים.— I. *lilies.*— II. *musical instruments.*

שׁוֹשַׁנָּה f., the same.

שׁוּשַׁנְכָיֵא Ch., an inhabitant of Susa.

שׁוֹשֵׁתִי Po. pret. from שׁסָה; same as שׁסה.

שׁוּת; see שִׁית.

שׁוּתֶלַח p. n. of a man. Patron. שׁוּתַלְחִי.

שֵׁזַב Ch. Pe. שֵׁיזִיב *delivered, rescued.*

שָׁזַף *beheld, saw.* (See also in שָׁרַף.)

שָׁזַר Hoph. part. שֵׁשׁ מָשְׁזָר *fine twined*

linen (probably wrung out for the purpose of bleaching it).

שַׁח; see שָׁחַח.

שָׁחַד *bribed.*

שֹׁחַד m.— I. *a present.*— II. *a bribe.*— III. *bribery,* Job 15:34.

שָׁחָה *bowed himself,* Isa. 51:23. Hiph. הִשְׁחָה *bowed down,* Pro. 12:25. Hith. הִשְׁתַּחֲוָה (inf. הִשְׁתַּחֲוֺת; Ch. הִשְׁתַּחֲוָיָה; imp. f. הִשְׁתַּחֲוִי; fut. יִשְׁתַּחֲוֶה; apoc. יִשְׁתַּחוּ) I. *prostrated himself;* with לִפְנֵי, לְ *before.*— II. *worshipped.*

שְׁחוּת f., *a pit,* Pro. 28:10.

שְׁחִית f., the same.

שְׁחוֹר same as שִׁיחוֹר; see שָׁחַר.

שָׁחַח (pret. שַׁחוּ, שַׁחֲחוּ; fut. יָשֹׁחַ). — I. *bowed himself, stooped.*— II. *was brought low, humbled.* Niph. the same. Hiph. הֵשַׁח *brought low, humbled.* Hithp. הִשְׁתּוֹחַח *brought low, broke.*

שַׁח m., *having downcast eyes, meek,* Job 22:29.

שָׁחַט (fut. יִשְׁחַט; inf. שַׁחֲטָה). — I. *slaughtered* (an animal).— II. *slew* (a person).— III. זָהָב שָׁחוּט "*alloyed gold*" (Lee). Niph. *was slaughtered.*

שְׁחִיטָה f., *slaughtering, sacrifice,* 2 Ch. 30:17.

שְׁחִין; see שָׁחַן.

שְׁחִים *spontaneous;* see סָחִישׁ.

שְׁחִית, see שָׁחַת; שְׁחִיתָה, see שָׁחַת.

שַׁחַל m., *a lion.*

שְׁחֵלֶת f., some kind of perfume, or pastil; LXX. ὄνυξ, Ex. 30:34.

שָׁחַן (Arab. *fever*).

שְׁחִין m., *inflammation, any burning disease;* שׁ׳ מִצְרַיִם *the ulcer of Egypt.*

שָׁחַף root not used ;(Arab. *was thin*).

שָׁחִיף m., *thin covering of wood*, Eze. 41:16.

שַׁחַף m. LXX. λάρος; *a sea gull*, Lev. 11:16; Deu. 14:15.

שַׁחֶפֶת f., *consumption.*

שָׁחַץ (Arab. *was lifted up*).

שַׁחַץ m., *mightiness, fierceness.*

שַׁחֲצִים p. n., a place in the tribe of Issachar.

שָׁחַק *reduced to dust, crushed, wasted away.*

שַׁחַק m.—I. *dust*, Isa. 40:15.—II. *a cloud;* pl. שְׁחָקִים *clouds.*—III. *the sky.*

שָׁחַר I. *was black*, Job 30:30.—II. *did a thing early, sought early.* Pi. שִׁחַר *sought early*, with אֶל.

שָׁחֹר שְׁחוֹרָה m., f., *black.*

שְׁחוֹר m., *blackness*, Lam. 4:8.

שַׁחַר m.—I. *the dawn;* בֶּן־שַׁחַר *lucifer*, "the morning star." — II. adv. *in the morning.* — III. *rise, origin*, Isa. 47:11.

שַׁחֲרוּת f., *dawn of life, youth*, Ecc. 11:10.

שְׁחַרְחֹרֶת f., *very black*, Cant. 1:6.

שְׁחַרְיָה p. n. of a man.

שַׁחֲרַיִם p. n. of a man.

מִשְׁחָר m., *the dawn*, Ps. 110:3.

שִׁיחוֹר שָׁחֹר m.—I. the name of a river of Egypt, probably the *Nile.* —II. שִׁיחוֹר לִבְנָת a river in Asher.

שָׁחַת. Niph. I. *was spoilt.*—II. *was corrupted*, Gen. 6:11, 12. — III. *was destroyed*, Ex. 8:20. Pi. שִׁחֵת

I. *acted corruptly.*—II. *destroyed.* —III. *broke a covenant*, Mal. 2:8.—IV. *laid aside* (of pity), Am. 1:11. Hiph. הִשְׁחִית same as Pi.; with or without דַּרְכּוֹ *corrupted his way.* Hoph. הָשְׁחַת; part. מָשְׁחָת I. *injured*, Mal. 1:14. —II. *polluted*, Pro. 25:26.

שְׁחַת Ch., part. שְׁחִיתָה *a fault.*

שַׁחַת m.—I. *corruption.*—II. *destruction;* see also שׁוּחַ.

מַשְׁחִית m. (Hiph. part.).—I. *destroyer*, Ex. 12:23—II. *plunderer*, מָשְׁחָת m., *defilement*, Lev. 22:25.

מַשְׁחֵת m., *destruction*, Eze. 9:1.

מִשְׁחָת m., *disfigured*, Isa. 52:14.

שִׁטָּה f.—I. *the pea-thorn;* (Arab. שְׁנַט; Egypt. *shont*); pl. שִׁטִּים *shittim wood, the wood of the pea-thorn.*—II. p. n., a valley of Moab.

שָׁטַח *spread abroad, strewed.* Pi. שִׁטַּח *spread abroad* (the hands in prayer), Ps. 88:10.

מִשְׁטוֹחַ מִשְׁטָח m., *place for spreading nets*, Eze. 26:5, 14; 47:10.

שׁוֹט; see שׁוּט.

שָׁטַף I. *washed off* or *away.*—II. *cleansed by washing.*—III. *swept away* (of a torrent). Niph. I. *was cleansed*, Lev. 15:12. — II. *was swept away*, Dan. 11:22. Pu. *was cleansed*, Lev. 6:21·

שֶׁטֶף שֵׁטֶף m., *washing away, overflowing, inundation.*

שָׁטַר; part. שֹׁטֵר *magistrate, ruler*, Ex. 5:10, 14; Deu. 1:15.

שִׁטְרַי p. n. of a man.

מִשְׁטָר m., *authority, influence*, Job 38:33.

שָׁטַר m. Ch., *sovereignty* (if the reading be correct; some suppose an error for שָׂטַר *side*), Dan. 7:5.

שַׁי m., *offering, present* (always with יוֹבִילוּ *bring ye*).

שִׂיאוֹן p. n., a name of Hermon.

שִׁיבָה; see שׁוּב, יָשַׁב.

שִׁיָה, fut. apoc. תֵּשִׁי *thou forgettest*; LXX. ἐγκατέλιπες, Deu. 32:18; see נָשָׁה.

שִׁיזָא p. n. of a man

שֵׁיזִיב; see שׁוּב.

שַׁיִט; see שׁוּט.

שִׁיחָה; see שׁוּחַ.

שִׁילֹנִי, שִׁילֹה; see שׁלה.

שִׁין, שׁוּן (Syr. *minxit*).

שַׁיִן or שַׁיִן m., pl. שֵׁינִים *urine*.

שֵׁיצָא Ch.; see יצא.

שׁוּר, שִׁיר (וַיָּשַׁר, יָשִׁיר). — fut. I. *sung*; with לְ *to.*—II. *sung of;* part. שָׁרִים, שָׁרוֹת *singers.* Pil. שֹׁרֵר *sounded*, Zep. 2:14; part. *a singer.* Hoph. הוּשַׁר *was sung.*

שִׁיר m.—I. *singing.*—II. *a song.*—III. *instrumental music;* כְּלֵי שִׁיר *musical instruments.*

שִׁירָה f., *a song.*

שֵׁישׁ; see שֵׁשׁ.

שִׁישַׁק p.n., *Shishak*, king of Egypt; LXX. Σεσογχις.

שׁוּת, שִׁית (וַיָּשֶׁת, יָשֶׁת, יָשִׁית; inf. abs. שֹׁת; inf. const. and imp. שִׁית) same as שׂוּם.—I. *placed, laid;* with לְ, עַל *upon;* with עָלָיו *decorated himself:*—also II. *set over, appointed.*—III. *set together, compared,* with עִם.—IV. שִׁ פָּנָיו *looked towards.*—V. שִׁ עֵינָיו

looked out after, Ps. 17:11.— VI. שִׁ לֵב *set his heart upon, regarded,* with אֶל, לְ.— VII. שִׁ יָד עִם *assisted.*—VIII. שִׁ לְנֶגְדּוֹ *looked at, examined,* Ps. 90:8.—IX. *laid up treasure.*—X. *rendered.* Hoph. הוּשַׁת *was required,* with עַל, Ex. 21:30.

שַׁיִת m. (with suff. שִׁיתוֹ) *thorns* (Isaiah only).

שִׁית m., *putting on a dress.*

שָׁתוֹת m. pl., *foundations.*

שֵׁת p. n.—I. *Seth*, the son of Adam.—II. an epithet of the Moabites, Nu. 24:17.

שֹׁךְ, שֹׁךְ Kal inf., from שׁכך.

שָׁכַב (fut. יִשְׁכַּב; inf. שָׁכַב, שְׁכַב; imp. שְׁכַב, שָׁכְבָה.—I. *lay down.*—II. *slept.*—III. *kept his bed.*—IV. *slept with his fathers, died.*—V. *rested* (of the head).—VI. *lay with* (carnally). Pu. *to be laid, to lie.* Niph. I. *placed.*—II. *caused to rest, stopped.* Hoph. *was placed, laid.*

שְׁכָבָה, const. שִׁכְבַת f.—I. *the act of lying with.*— II. *covering of dew,* Ex. 16:13, 14.

שְׁכֹבֶת f., *act of lying with.*

מִשְׁכָּב m. (pl. מִשְׁכָּבוֹת, מִשְׁכָּבִים).—I. *a bed.*—II. *a bier,* 2 Chron. 16:14.—III. *lying in bed.*—IV. *lying with.*

מִשְׁכַּב m. Ch., *a bed.*

שָׁכָה. Hiph. part. מַשְׁכִּים *wandering about lasciviously,* Jer. 5:8.

שָׁכוּל, שָׁכוֹל; see שׁכל.

שָׁכוּר; see שׁכר.

שָׁכַח, שָׁכֵחַ (יִשְׁכַּח) *forgot, disregarded, neglected,* with מִן. Niph. *was forgotten, neglected.* Pi. and

Hiph. *cause to forget.* Hithpa. same as Niph., Ecc. 8:10.

שָׁכַח m. (pl. const. שִׁכְחֵי) *forgetting, neglecting.*

שְׁכַח Ch. Ithp. הִשְׁתְּכַח *was found, was.* Aph. הַשְׁכַּח *found, discovered.*

שְׁכָיָה p.n. of a man.

שָׁכַךְ (inf. שֹׁךְ, שַׁךְ; fut. pl. וַיָּשֹׁכּוּ). I. *stooped.* — II. *abated.* Hiph. הֵשֵׁךְ I. *placed.* — II. *emptied.*

שָׁכַל (fut. יִשְׁכַּל) *lost children, became childless.* Pi. I. *made childless.* — II. *stripped of inhabitants.* — III. *destroyed (of a sword),* Deu 32:25. — IV. *produced an abortion.* — V. *lost fruit, &c., was barren;* part. מְשַׁכֵּלֶת *an abortion.* Hiph. *lost its inhabitants (a land).*

שְׁכוֹל m. — I. *privation of children.* — II. *destitution.*

שַׁכּוּל m., שְׁכֻלָה f. — I. *childless.* — II. *deprived of, without young.*

שִׁכֻּלִים m. pl., *loss of children,* Isa. 49:20.

אֶשְׁכֹּל m. (pl. const. אֶשְׁכְּלוֹת (אַשְׁכְּלוֹת). — I. *a cluster, bunch of grapes or flowers;* (Arab. *bound*). — II. p.n.: (a) of a valley in the south of Palestine; (b) of a man.

שְׁכֲלָל; see כָּלַל.

שָׁכֵם. Hiph. הִשְׁכִּים I. *arose in the morning.* — II. *as soon as he arose.* — III. *came in the morning.*

שְׁכֶם with pause שָׁכֶם m. (with suff. שִׁכְמוֹ). — I. *shoulder, shoulders.* — II. *a load, portion,* Gen. 48:22. — III. p.n., *Shechem,* a city of the Levites in Ephraim; with ה loc.

IV. —שִׁכְמָה, with pause שֶׁכְמָה p.n. of a man.

שֶׁכֶם p.n. of a man; patron. שִׁכְמִי.

שִׁכְמָה f., *the shoulder-blade,* Job 31:22.

שָׁכַן, שָׁכֵן (fut. יִשְׁכֹּן). — I. *lay down to rest, rested.* — II. *continued.* — III. *dwelt.* — IV. *inhabited, was inhabited;* part. שָׁכֵן *inhabiting.* Pi. I. *caused to dwell.* — II. *placed;* שִׁכֵּן שְׁמוֹ *placed his name.* Hiph. I. *caused to dwell.* — II. *fixed.*

שְׁכֵן Ch., Pa., same as Pi. Heb.

שָׁכֵן, const. שְׁכַן m., שְׁכֵנָה, שְׁכֶנֶת f. — I. *inhabitant.* — II. *neighbour, neighbouring people.*

שָׁכֵן m., *a dwelling;* with suff. שִׁכְנוֹ, Deu. 12:5.

שְׁכַנְיָה p.n. of a man.

שְׁכַנְיָהוּ p.n. of a man.

מִשְׁכָּן m. — I. *habitation, dwelling.* — II. *the Tabernacle and Temple.* — III. *lair of beasts.*

מִשְׁכַּן m. Ch., *habitation.*

שָׁכַר (fut. יִשְׁכַּר). — I. *drank wine or strong drink.* — II. *was exhilarated, intoxicated.* — III. *became giddy.* Pi. and Hiph. *made drunken.* Hith. *made himself drunken,* 1 Sa. 1:14.

שִׁכּוֹר, שִׁכּוֹר m., שִׁכֹּרָה f., *drunken, a drunkard.*

שֵׁכָר m. — I. *strong drink (not wine).* — II. *wine,* Nu. 28:7.

שִׁכָּרוֹן m., *drunkenness* (Ezekiel only).

שִׁכָּרוֹן p.n., a place of Judah.

אֶשְׁכָּר m., *rich gift, present.*

שֶׁל; see אֲשֶׁר.

שֶׁל, שַׁלְאָנָן; see שׁלה.

שֵׁלֶב. Pu. part. מְשֻׁלָּבוֹת *joined together* (Ex. 26 : 17 ; 36 : 22).

שְׁלַבִּים m. pl., *edges, borders,* 1 Ki. 7 : 28, 29.

שֶׁלֶג m., *snow.*

הִשְׁלִיג Hiph. "was white as snow," Eng. Ver., Ps. 68 : 15.

שָׁלָה שָׁלוּ (pret. שָׁלַוְתִּי ; fut. יִשְׁלָיוּ ; fut. apoc. וַיֵּשֶׁל). — I. *was prosperous, at ease.*—II. *made prosperous, gave ease to.* Niph. *became negligent,* 2 Ch. 29 : 11. Hiph. *flattered, deceived,* 2 K. 4 : 28.

שְׁלָה Ch., *was at rest,* Dan. 4 : 1.

שַׁל m., *fault, error,* 2 Sa. 6 : 7.

שָׁלָה f. Ch., *error;* same as שָׁלוּת, Dan. 3 : 29. Ketib.

שֶׁלָה 1 Sa. 1 : 17, same as שְׁאֵלָה ; see שָׁאַל.

שָׁלֵו m. (pl. const. שַׁלְוֵי) f. — I. *prosperous, at ease.* — II. *unmindful of God,* Eze. 23 : 42.

שֶׁלֶו, שָׁלֵיו m. — I. *prosperous.* — II. *prosperity.*

שַׁלְו m. (with suff. שַׁלְוִי), *prosperity,* Ps. 30 : 7.

שַׁלְוָה f.—I. *prosperity, ease.*—II. *negligence of God.*

שַׁלְוָה f. Ch., *prosperity,* Dan. 4 : 24.

שָׁלוּ, שָׁלוּת f. Ch., *error, fault, trespass.*

שֶׁלִי m. בְּשֶׁלִי *quietly, privately,* 2 Sa. 3 : 27.

שִׁלְיָה f., *the after-birth,* Deu. 28 : 57.

שַׁלְאֲנָן (from שַׁאֲנָן and שָׁלָה) m., *wholly at rest,* Job 21 : 23.

אֲשֶׁר שִׁילֹה, שָׁלֹה Gen. 49 : 10 ; *quasi* לֹו, i. e., *he whose it is;* "Shiloh," Eng. Ver.

שָׁלוּ, שִׁלוֹ, שִׁילוֹ, שָׁלֹה, שִׁילֹה p. n., a city of Ephraim, where the tabernacle stood ; שִׁילֹנִי *a native of Shiloh.*

שַׁלְהֶבֶת *flame;* see להב.

שִׁלּוּם, שָׁלוֹם, שָׁלוֹם ; see שלם.

שַׁלּוּן p. n. of a man.

שָׁלוֹשׁ ; same as שָׁלִשׁ.

שָׁלַח (fut. יִשְׁלַח ; inf. שְׁלֹחַ, שְׁלֹחַ ; imp. שְׁלַח ; (שִׁלְחָה).—I. *sent* (a person or thing), with לְ, or אֶל, sometimes עַל. — II. *sent word, charge;* with לְ *to;* and בְּיַד *by, by the hand of.*—III. *sent a message to,* with or without דָּבָר.—IV. יָד or בְּ *put forth his hand* (to injure), *laid his hand on,* with אֶל. It has the same meaning without יָד, 2 Sa. 6 : 6. — V. *shoot out arrows.* (For other modifications of the primary senses, see Concordance.) Niph. inf. נִשְׁלֹחַ *to be sent,* Est. 3 : 13. Pi. שִׁלַּח I. *sent.*—II. *sent away.*—III. *allowed to depart, dismissed.* — IV. *set at liberty.* — V. *gave in marriage.*—VI. *sent away, divorced* (a wife). — VII. *put in a place.*—VIII. *put forth* (his hand). —IX. with בָּאֵשׁ *set on fire.* — X. *inflicted a calamity.*—XI. *caused,* Pro. 16 : 28.—XII. *threw, threw off.* —XIII. *cast out, shoot forth.* (See also Concordance.) Pu. שֻׁלַּח *was sent, dismissed, set at liberty, divorced, thrown.* Hiph. with בְּ I. *sent.*—II. *inflicted a calamity.*

שְׁלַח Ch.—I. *sent word, orders.* — II. *put forth* (his hand).

שִׁלּוּחִים m. pl., *divorce* (of a wife), Ex. 18 : 2. — II. *renunciation* (of a

claim), Mic. 1:14. — III. *presents,*
dowry, 1 Ki. 9:16.

שֶׁלַח m. (with suff. שִׁלְחוֹ).—I. *missile.*
—II. *rejection, contempt.*—III. pl.,
shoots, produce.—IV. p. n. of a man.
—V. p. n., *Siloah,* a stream which
ran through Jerusalem; called
also שֶׁלַח.

שִׁלְחוֹת f. pl., *shoots,* Isa. 16:8.

שִׁלְחִי p. n. of a man.

שְׁלָחִים p. n., a town of Judah.

שֻׁלְחָן m. (pl. שֻׁלְחָנוֹת), *table;*
עֲרֹךְ שֻׁלְחָן *spread, provided, a table;*
שֻׁ׳ הַפָּנִים *the table*
of shew-bread.

מִשְׁלָח m.—I. *the sending forth of*
cattle (to graze).—II. (with יָד) *the*
putting out the hand.

מִשְׁלוֹחַ, מִשְׁלָח m., *the same;* I.
and II.

מִשְׁלַחַת f., *the same as* II.

שָׁלַם (fut. יִשְׁלַם) *ruled, had power*
over, with עַל, בְּ. Hiph. I. *allowed*
to rule.—II. *gave authority to, per-*
mitted, with בְּ and לְ.

שְׁלֵט Ch., with בְּ.—I. *ruled.*—II. *had*
power over. — III. *seized.* Aph.
caused to rule.

שֶׁלֶט m., pl. שְׁלָטִים שִׁלְטֵי *shields.*

שַׁלִּיט m., שַׁלֶּטֶת f.—I. *ruler, prince.*—
II. *violent,* Eze. 16:30.

שַׁלִּיט m. Ch.—I. *a ruler.*—II. *that*
which is permitted, lawful; לָא
שַׁלִּיט *it is not lawful,* Ezr. 7:24.

שִׁלְטוֹן m., *power, authority,* Ecc. 8:
4, 8.

שָׁלְטוֹן m. Ch., *authority, ruler,* Dan.
3:2, 3.

שָׁלְטָן m. Ch., *authority, empire.*

שֶׁל, שִׁלְיָה, שָׁלָיו; see שׁלה.

שָׁלִישׁ; שְׁלִישִׁי, שְׁלִישִׁית; see שָׁלַשׁ.

שָׁלַךְ. Hiph. הִשְׁלִיךְ I. *threw into,* אֶל;
on, עַל, בְּ; *to,* לְ; *from,* מִן. — II.
threw down, out, away.—III. *cast*
off (as a plant its leaves).—IV. *ex-*
pelled (a people).—V. with אַחֲרָיו,
אַחֲרֵי נִגּוֹ *cast behind him, de-*
spised. — VI. with עַל יְהוָֹה *com-*
mitted to the Lord. Hoph.
הֻשְׁלַךְ, הָשְׁלַךְ I. *was thrown down,*
out.—II. *was thrown upon the Lord*
(for help), with עַל

שָׁלָךְ m., *the gannet;* LXX. κατα-
ράκτης, Lev. 11:17; Deu. 14:16.

שַׁלֶּכֶת f.—I. *felling a tree,* Isa. 6:13.
II. p. n., a gate of the temple.

שָׁלַל (pret. שָׁלוֹתִי, שָׁלְלוּ; inf. שְׁלֹל;
fut. תָּשֹׁלּוּ, with suff. יִשְׁלוּךְ).—I.
plundered, spoiled.—II. *carried off*
spoil. — III. *scattered,* Ru. 2:16
Hith. אֶשְׁתּוֹלֵל (Ch. for הִשְׁתּוֹלֵל)
spoiled.

שָׁלָל m.—I. *spoil, plunder.*—II. *gain,*
Pro. 31:11.

שׁוֹלָל m., (spoiled) *a captive, captives*

שָׁלֵם (fut. יִשְׁלַם). — I. *was at peace,*
Job 9:4.—II. *was completed.* Part.
שְׁלֹמִי *one at peace with me,* Ps.
7:5; שָׁלוֹם *peaceable,* 2 Sa. 20:19.
Pi. שִׁלֵּם I. *completed.* — II.
restored.—III. *gave in return, re-*
quited.—IV. *performed a vow.* Pu.
I. *was requited.*—II. *was performed*
(a vow). Part. *made perfect,* Isa.
42:19. Hiph. I. *made peace with.*
— II. *made at peace with,* with
אֶל, אֵת, עַם.—III. *completed.*—
IV. *brought to an end.* Hoph.
was made at peace, Job 5:23.

שָׁלֵם Ch., *completed.* Aph. I. *terminated,* Dan. 5:26.—II. *restored,* Ezr. 7:19.

שָׁלֵם m., שְׁלֵמָה f.— I. *perfect, complete, full.* — II. אֲבָנִים שְׁלֵמוֹת *rough, unhewn stones.* — III. אֶבֶן שְׁלֵמָה *hewn, prepared stone,* 1 Ki. 6:7.—IV. *peaceable, at peace,* with עִם.—V. *at peace with God,* with עִם יְהֹוָה.—VI. p. n. of a place, Gen. 33:18.—VII. p.n., *Jerusalem,* Σόλυμα.

שָׁלוֹם m.—I. *peace.*—II. *public quiet.* —III. *prosperity.*—IV. *safety.*—V. *soundness of body.*—VI. *friendship.* Phrases : הֲשָׁלוֹם לְ *is he well?* שָׁאַל לְשָׁלוֹם לְ *enquired after their welfare;* שָׁלוֹם *farewell!* עָשָׂה שׁ' לְ *made peace with them;* קָרָא לְשָׁלוֹם לְ *named peaceable proposals;* עָנָה שָׁלוֹם אֶת *gave a peaceable answer.*

שְׁלָם m. Ch., *peace, safety.*

שֶׁלֶם and pl. שְׁלָמִים m. — I. *peace offering.*—II. *thank offering.*—III. *offering in completion of a vow.*

שִׁלֵּם m.— I. *retribution,* Deu. 32:35. —II. p.n., *a son of Naphtali;* patron. שִׁלֵּמִי.

שִׁלּוּם שָׁלֹם m., *retribution.*

שִׁלֻּמָה f., *the same,* Ps. 91:8.

שַׁלֻּם שַׁלּוּם p.n.—I. *Shallum,* king of Israel.—II. used for other men.

שְׁלֹמֹה p.n., *Solomon,* king of Israel; LXX. Σαλωμών.

שְׁלֻמִי p.n. of a man.

שְׁלֻמִיאֵל p.n. of a man.

מְשֶׁלֶמְיָה שֶׁלֶמְיָהוּ p.n., same as מְשֶׁלֶמְיָה.

שְׁלֹמִית p.n. of a man.

שְׁלֹמִית p.n. of a woman.

שִׁלְמוֹן m., pl. שַׁלְמֹנִים *bribes, penalties,* Isa. 1:23.

שַׁלְמַנְאֶסֶר, שַׁלְמַן p.n., a king of Assyria.

שָׁלַף I. *drew a sword.*—II. *took off a shoe,* Ru. 4:7, 8. — III. *plucked up grass,* Ps. 129:6; אִישׁ שֹׁלֵף חֶרֶב *a man drawing the sword;* i. e., *armed.*

שֶׁלֶף p. n. of some foreign nation, perhaps Σαλαπηνοί.

שָׁלֹשׁ, שְׁלוֹשׁ const. שְׁלָשׁ-, שְׁלֹשׁ; f. שְׁלֹשָׁה, const. שְׁלֹשֶׁת m., *the numeral three;* with suff. שְׁלָשְׁתְּכֶם *ye three;* שְׁלָשְׁתָּם *they three;* שְׁלֹשׁ עֶשְׂרֵה *thirteen;* pl. שְׁלֹשִׁים *thirty, thirtieth.*

שִׁלֵּשׁ Pi. I. *divided into three parts.*— II. *did a thing the third time.*— III. *did a thing on the third day.* Pu. part. I. *threefold.* — II. *three years old,* Gen. 15:9.

שָׁלֵשׁ p.n. of a man.

שְׁלִישִׁי m., שְׁלִישִׁית, שְׁלִישִׁיָּה f., pl. שְׁלִישִׁים I. *third parts.*—II. *chambers third in order, third stories;* f. בַּשְּׁלִישִׁית *a third part;* שְׁלִישִׁיתָה *the third, on the third;* הַשְּׁלִישִׁית *see* מָחָר.

שָׁלִישׁ, שְׁלִשׁ m.—I. *a measure,* probably *the third part of an Ephah.* —II. *abundantly;* pl. שְׁלִישִׁים.— III. *a musical instrument, a trichord* (either harp or lute). — IV. *officers of high rank.* — V. *a peculiar class of soldiers,* LXX. ἀναβάται τριστάται; *their commander was called* רֹאשׁ הַשָּׁלִישִׁים, הַשָּׁלִישׁ *and* רֹאשׁ הַשָּׁלִשִׁי.

שָׁלִשִׁים m. pl., *descendants of the*

third generation, great grandchildren.

שְׁלִשָׁה p. n., a region of Palestine.

שִׁלְשָׁה p. n. of a man.

שִׁלְשׁוֹם ,שִׁלְשֹׁם adv. three days ago; תְּמוֹל שִׁלְשׁוֹם yesterday and the day before, i. e. formerly; כִּתְמוֹל שִׁ׳ as before; מִתְּמוֹל שִׁ׳ heretofore, previously.

מְשֻׁלָּשׁ m., a triad; כִּמְשֻׁלָּשׁ חֲדָשִׁים a triplicity of, i. e. three months, Gen. 38 : 24.

שְׁלָתֶךָ 1 Sa. 1 : 17, for שְׁאֵלָתֵךְ; see שְׁאֵלָה in שָׁאַל.

שָׁם adv., there, thither; שָׁם...אֲשֶׁר where; שָׁם...שָׁם here...there; שָׁמָּה thither, there; שָׁמָּה..אֲשֶׁר whither...where; מִשָּׁם thence; אֲשֶׁר...מִשָּׁם whence.

שֵׁם ,שֶׁם־ m. (with suff. שְׁמִי, שִׁמְךָ; pl. שֵׁמוֹת).—I. a name; בְּשֵׁם פּ׳ in the name of any one.—II. fame, reputation (good or bad).—III. memory.—IV. p. n., Shem the son of Noah.

שֻׁם m. Ch. (with suff. שְׁמֵהּ; pl. שְׁמָהָן), a name.

שִׁמְאֵבֶר p. n., a king of Zeboim.

שְׁמוּאֵל (perhaps for שְׁמוּעָאֵל heard of God), p. n.—I. Samuel, the judge of Israel.—II. used also of other men.

שְׁמִידָע p. n., a son of Gilead; patron. שְׁמִידָעִי.

שַׁמָּא p. n. of a man.

שִׁמְאָה p. n. of a man; שִׁמְאָם the same.

שַׁמְגַּר p. n., Shamgar, a judge of Israel.

שָׁמַד. Hiph. destroyed; inf. destruction. Niph. was destroyed.

שְׁמַד Ch. Aph. to destroy.

שָׁמָה root not used; (Arab. heaven)

שָׁמַיִם, const. שְׁמֵי m. pl.—I. heaven, the sky.—II. toward heaven, the sky.

שְׁמַיִן emph. state, שְׁמַיָּא m. pl. Ch., heaven.

שַׁמָּה ,שְׁמָהוּת; see שׁמם.

שָׁמוּעַ p. n., same as שִׁמְעָא.

שְׁמוּעָה; see שׁמע.

שַׁמּוֹת Eze. 36 : 3, Kal inf., from שׁמם.

שָׁמַט I. gave up a debt.—II. left the land to itself.—III. threw down.—IV. stuck fast. Niph. was thrown down, Ps. 141 : 6. Hiph. gave up, forgave, Deu. 15 : 3.

שְׁמִטָּה f., release, acquittal; שְׁנַת הַשְּׁמִטָּה year of release.

שָׁמַיִם heavens; see שׁמה.

שְׁמִינִית ,שְׁמִינִי; see שְׁמֹנֶה.

שָׁמִיר; see שָׁמַר.

שְׁמִירָמוֹת p. n. of a man.

שַׁמְלַי p. n. of a man.

שָׁמֵם (fut. יִשֹּׁם; pl. יָשֹׁמּוּ; imp. שֹׁם). I. was desolate, laid waste.—II. was astonished; part. שׁוֹמֵם desolate, solitary; שׁוֹמֵמוֹת desolate places. Niph. נָשַׁם was desolate, astonished. Po. part. מְשׁוֹמֵם I. a desolator.—II. astonished, Ezr. 9 : 3, 4. Hiph. הֵשַׁם (fut. יַשִּׁים; inf. הַשֵּׁם; part. מַשִּׁים) I. made desolate, laid waste.—II. astonished. —III. was astonished. Hoph. הָשַׁם or הֻשַּׁם (pl. הֻשַּׁמּוּ) was made desolate. Hith. הִשְׁתּוֹמֵם (fut. תִּשׁוֹמֵם יִשְׁתּוֹמֵם) I. was disconsolate (of the heart).—II. wondered.—III. destroyed himself, Ecc. 7:16.

שָׁמַם Ch. Ith., was astonished, Dan. 4:16.

שָׁמֵם m., שְׁמֵמָה f., desolate.

שְׁמָמָה f.—I. desolation.—II. astonishment.—III. a desolate place.

שִׁמָמָה f.—I. desolation, Eze. 35:7, 9.

שַׁמָּה f.—I. desolation (pl. שַׁמּוֹת).—II. astonishment.—III. p.n.: (a) a brother of David, called also שִׁמְעָא שִׁמְעָה; (b) used also for other men.

שְׁמֵמוּת, שְׁמֹות p.n.; same as שַׁמָּה.

שִׁמָּמוֹן m., astonishment, terrors, Eze. 4:16; 12:19.

מְשַׁמָּה f.—I. astonishment, Eze. 5:15.—II. desolation.

שָׁמֵן or שָׁמַן (fut. יִשְׁמַן) was fat, prosperous. Hiph. I. became fat, Neh. 9:25. — II. made fat, Isa. 6:10.

שָׁמֵן m., שְׁמֵנָה f.—I. plump (of an animal). — II. robust, stout (of a man).—III. nourishing (of food).—IV. rich, fertile, abundant.

שֶׁמֶן m.—I. oil.—II. ointment.—III. richness, delicacy of food, Isa. 25:6. — IV. fertility.—V. prosperity, Isa. 10:27. (עֵץ שֶׁמֶן any resinous tree.)

שְׁמַנִּים m. pl., fatness, Gen. 27:28, 39.

אַשְׁמַנִּים m. pl., "desolate places," Eng. Ver., Isa. 59:10.

מִשְׁמָן m., fatness; pl. מִשְׁמַנִּים fertile places.

מַשְׁמַנִּים m. pl., rich food, Neh. 8:10.

מִשְׁמַנָּה p.n. of a man.

שְׁמֹנֶה f., שְׁמֹנָה const. שְׁמֹנַת m., eight; pl. שְׁמֹנִים eighty.

שְׁמִינִי m., eighth; שְׁמִינִית a musical instrument, probably with eight strings.

שָׁמַע, שָׁמֵעַ (fut. יִשְׁמַע; inf. שְׁמֹעַ; const. שְׁמֹעַ, with ה parag. שָׁמְעָה, with suff. שָׁמְעָתוֹ; imp. שְׁמַע, with ה parag. שִׁמְעָה).—I. heard.—II. hearkened, with בְּ, אֶל, לְ.—III. understood. Niph. I. was heard.—II. was hearkened to. Pi. I. caused to hear, summoned. Hiph. הִשְׁמִיעַ (fut. apoc. תַּשְׁמַע). — I. caused to hear, be heard.—II. proclaimed.—III. summoned.

שְׁמַע Ch., he heard. Ith. he obeyed.

שֶׁמַע p.n. of a man.

שֵׁמַע, שֶׁמַע m. (with suff. שִׁמְעִי, שִׁמְעֲךָ).—I. the act of hearing.—II. report, fame.—III. sound.

שֶׁמַע p.n. of a man.

שֶׁמַע p.n., a town of Judah.

שֹׁמַע m. (with suff. שִׁמְעוֹ), fame.

שִׁמְעָא p.n. of a man; see שַׁמָּה.

שִׁמְעָה p.n., same as שַׁמָּה; patron. שִׁמְעָתִי.

שִׁמְעָה (with art.) p.n. of a man.

שִׁמְעוֹן p.n.—I. Simeon, the son of Jacob and Leah (LXX. Συμεών).—II. used also of his descendants; שִׁמְעֹנִי a Simeonite.

שִׁמְעִי p.n. of a man, Shimei.

שְׁמַעְיָהוּ, שְׁמַעְיָה p.n. of a man.

שְׁמַעַן Kal imp. pl. f. for שְׁמַעְנָה from שׁמע.

שְׁמָעַת p.n. of a woman.

שְׁמוּעָה, שְׁמֻעָה f.—I. a report.—II. a message.

הַשְׁמָעוּת f., a hearing, Eze. 24:26.

מִשְׁמָע m.—I. act of hearing, Isa. 11:3.—II. p.n. of a man.

מִשְׁמַעַת f. — I. *court of hearing,
council.*—II. *subjects,* Isa. 11:14.

שָׁמֵן *root not used;* (Arab. *hastened*).

שֶׁמֶץ m., *a small portion, a hint,* Job
4:12; 26:14.

שִׁמְצָה f., *defeat,* Ex. 32:25.

שָׁמַר (fut. יִשְׁמֹר).—I. *kept watch over,
watched.*—II. *guarded, preserved.*
—III. *kept in mind.*—IV. *attended
to an office.*—V. *took heed.*—VI.
observed, remembered.—VII. *regarded, reverenced.*—VIII. *guarded
against, avoided.* Niph. I. *noticed,
was aware of, perceived.*—II. *was
preserved, delivered.* — III. *took
heed.* — IV. *guarded himself, abstained,* with מִן and מִפְּנֵי; imp.
הִשָּׁמֶר, הִשָּׁמֵר. Pi. *regarded,* Jon.
2:9. Hith. הִשְׁתַּמֵּר *kept, guarded
himself.*—II. *was observed.*

שָׁמִיר m.—I. *a thorny shrub, "*spina
Egyptiaca."—II. *a diamond.*—III.
p.n.: (a) a town of Judah; (b) a
town of Ephraim; (c) of a man.

שֶׁמֶר m., pl. שְׁמָרִים.—I. *sediment,
lees, dregs.*—II. שִׁ מְזֻקָּקִים *clear
wine.*—III. p. n. of a man.

שֹׁמֵר p. n. of a man, and of a woman.

שִׁמְרָה f., *a watch,* Ps. 141:3.

שְׁמֻרוֹת f. pl., *the same,* Ps. 77:5.

שִׁמֻּרִים m.pl., *observance of a festival,*
Ex. 12:42.

שִׁמְרוֹן p.n.—I. a town of Zebulun.
—II. a son of Issachar. Patron.
שִׁמְרֹנִי.

שֹׁמְרוֹן p.n.—I. *Samaria* (Σεβάστη).
—II. *the land of Israel;* שֹׁמְרֹנִי *a
Samaritan.*

שָׁמְרַיִן Ch, p.n., *Samaria.*

שִׁמְרִי p. n. of a man.
שְׁמַרְיָה p. n. of a man.
שְׁמַרְיָהוּ p. n. of a man.
שְׁמָרִית p. n. of a woman; *same as*
שֹׁמֵר.
שִׁמְרָת p. n. of a man.

אַשְׁמוּרָה f., *night-watch;* const.
אַשְׁמֹרֶת; pl. אַשְׁמֻרוֹת.

מִשְׁמָר m. — I. *the act of guarding,
watching.* — II. *keeping guard.*—
III. *imprisonment.* — IV. *a prison.*
—V. *an appointed duty.*

מִשְׁמֶרֶת f. (pl. מִשְׁמָרוֹת).—I. *guarding, watching.*—II. *imprisonment.*

שְׁמַשׁ Ch. Pa., *attended, served,* Dan.
7:10.

שֶׁמֶשׁ com. (with suff. שִׁמְשֵׁךְ), *the
sun,* pl. שִׁמְשׁוֹת *thy pinnacles,*
Isa. 54:12; עִיר שֶׁמֶשׁ *a city of
Dan.*

שִׁמְשׁוֹן p.n., *Samson.* (LXX. Σαμ-
ψών.)

שִׁמְשַׁי p. n. of a man.
שַׁמְשְׁרַי p. n. of a man.
שִׁמְשָׁתַי p. n. of a man.
שְׁנָאָב, שְׁנוּ, שֵׁן; see שׁנן.
שִׁנְאָן, שְׁנָא; see שׁנה.
שֵׁנָא *sleep,* Ps. 127:2; see יָשֵׁן.
שֶׁנְאַצַּר p. n. of a man.

שָׁנַב (Arab. *had a cool mouth*).
אֶשְׁנָב m., *a latticed window.*

שָׁנָה (fut. יִשְׁנֶא, יִשְׁנֶה).—I. *repeated
an action.*—II. *was different,* with
מִן.—III. *was changed.*—IV. *was
disobedient* (part. שֹׁנִים *rebellious*).
Niph. *being repeated,* Gen. 41:32.
Pi. שִׁנָּה, שְׁנָא I. *changed.* — II.
violated a promise.—III. *removed
a person to another place,* Est. 2:9;

with אֶת־טַעְמוֹ *changed his mind,
feigned himself mad.* Pu. fut.
יְשֻׁנֶּא *was changed,* Ecc. 8:1. Hith.
changed, disguised himself, 1 Ki.
14:2.

שְׁנָא Ch.—I. *was changed.*—II. *was
different from,* with מִן. Pa. I.
changed.—II. *made different;* part.
pass. *different.* Ith. *was changed.*
Aph. *changed.*

שָׁנָה f. (pl. שָׁנִים, שְׁנֵי, שָׁנוֹת, שְׁנוֹת).
—I. *a year.*—II. *the produce of a
year;* שָׁנָה בְּשָׁנָה, שָׁנָה שָׁנָה, מִדֵּי
שָׁנָה *yearly;* בִּשְׁנַת שְׁתַּיִם
לְיוֹאָשׁ *in the second year of Joash;*
בִּשְׁנַת שֵׁשׁ מֵאוֹת שָׁנָה *in the six
hundredth year.* Dual שְׁנָתַיִם *two
years;* שְׁנָתַיִם יָמִים *for two years.*

שְׁנָא, שְׁנָה f. Ch., *year;* pl. שְׁנִין.

שֵׁנָה, שֵׁנָא *sleep;* see יָשֵׁן.

שֶׁנְהַבִּים *ivory;* see שֵׁן.

שָׁנִי m., *bright, scarlet colour;* pl.
שָׁנִים.

שְׁנַיִם const. שְׁנֵי m., שְׁתַּיִם const.
שְׁתֵּי f. dual, *the numeral two;*
שְׁנַיִם שְׁנַיִם *apiece;* with suff.
שְׁנֵיהֶם *both of them;* f., *twice,
again;* בִּשְׁתַּיִם *again.* שְׁנֵים עָשָׂר
m., שְׁתֵּים עֶשְׂרֵה f., *twelve.*

שֵׁנִי m, שֵׁנִית f., *second;* f., *again.*
Pl. שְׁנַיִם.

שִׁנְאָן m., " *angels,*" Eng. Ver.;
אַלְפֵי שִׁי *thousands repeated* (Ges.),
Ps. 68:18.

מִשְׁנֶה const. מִשְׁנֵה m.—I. *second.*—
II. *the second rank, second in rank.*
III. *double.*—IV. *a copy.*—V. *of an
inferior kind,* 1 Sa. 15:9.—VI. *a
division of Jerusalem.*

שָׁנַן (pret. שָׁנַנּוּ, שַׁנּוֹתִי).—I. *sharpened*

a sword, &c.— II. *sharpened the
tongue* (of slanderers), Ps. 64:4;
140:4. Pi. *taught assiduously,* with
לְ, Deu. 6:7. Hithpo. הִשְׁתּוֹנָן *was
pained acutely,* Ps. 73:21.

שֵׁן, שֶׁן com. (with suff. שִׁנִּי; dual
שִׁנַּיִם, שְׁנַיִם).—I. *a tooth.*—II. *ivory.*
—III. *the ridge of a rock;* שֵׁן סֶלַע.
— IV. *the prong of a fork.* — V.
p.n. of a place.

שֶׁנְהַבִּים m. pl., *elephant's tooth, ivory.*
(The word is probably a compound
of שֵׁן *a tooth,* and הָב *an elephant;*
from the Sanscrit *ibha.*)

שְׁנִינָה f., *pointed saying, taunt;*
הָיָה לִשְׁנִינָה *he was for a taunt.*

שַׁנְאָב p.n. of a king.

שָׁנַס. Pi. שָׁנַס *girded his loins,* 1 Ki.
18:46.

שִׁנְעָר p.n., one of the names of Babylon and its vicinity.

שָׁסָה *plundered;* part. שֹׁסִים *spoilers.*
Po. שׁוֹשָׁה the same, Isa. 10:13.

שָׁסַס (fut. יָשֹׁם) the same; part. שֹׁאֵם,
with suff. שֹׁאֲסֶיךָ. Niph. נָשַׁם *was
plundered.*

מְשִׁסָּה f., *prey.*

שֶׁסַע שָׁסַע *having a division;* שֶׁסַע
פַּרְסָה or שֹׁסַעַת *having divided
hoofs;* פַּרְסָה הַשְּׁסוּעָה *having a
divided hoof.* Pi. I. *clove,* Lev. 1:
17. — II. *tore asunder,* Jud. 14:6,
&c.—III. *withheld,* 1 Sa. 24:8.

שֶׁסַע m., *division in a hoof.*

שָׁסַף. Pi. שִׁסֵּף *cut down,* 1 Sa. 15:33.

I. שָׁעָה (fut. apoc. וַיִּשַׁע) *looked at favourably, approved,* with אֶל.—II
looked at with attention, with בְּ

—III. *looked to for help*, with אֶל,
עַל.— IV. *looked away from, re-
spited*, with מִן, Job 7:19. Hiph.
imp. הִשְׁעָ I. *looked away from*,
with מִן, Ps. 39:14.—II. *turn away
the eyes*, Isa. 6:10. See also in
שָׁעַע. Hith. fut. apoc. תִּשְׁתַּע *look
about with alarm*, Isa. 41:10; pl.
with ה parag. נִשְׁתָּעֶה *we may look
with alarm, be dismayed*, Isa. 41:23.

II. שָׁעָה *same as* שָׁעַע; imp. שְׁעוּ *be
blinded* (Ges.); " *cry*," from שׁוּעַ,
Eng. Ver., Is. 29:9.

שָׁעָה f. Ch., *an hour*; בַּהּ שַׁעֲתָא *immediately*.

שַׁעֲטָה f., *stamping of hoofs*, Jer. 47:
3. (Arab. *pounded*.)

שַׁעַטְנֵז m., *cloth of a mixture of wool
and flax*, Lev. 19:19; Deu. 22:11.

שֹׁעַל, שַׁעַל (with suff. שַׁעֲלוֹ; pl.
שְׁעָלִים, שַׁעֲלֵי).—I. *palm of the
hand*, Isa. 40:12.—II. *a handful*.

שׁוּעָל m.—I. *a fox.*—II. p. n. of a
man.

שַׁעֲלִים p. n. of a district.

שַׁעֲלַבִּין, שַׁעַלְבִּים p. n., a town of the
Danites; שַׁעַלְבֹנִי *a Shaalbonite*.

מִשְׁעוֹל m., *a narrow way*, Nu. 22:24.

שָׁעַן. Niph. נִשְׁעַן I. *leaned on*, with
עַל.—II. *reclined*.—III. *touched a
boundary* with לְ, Nu. 21:15.—
IV. *depended on*, with בְּ, אֶל עַל.

מִשְׁעָן m., *a support*.

מִשְׁעֵן m., מִשְׁעֵנָה f., *the same*, Isa.
3:1.

מִשְׁעֶנֶת f. (pl. מִשְׁעֲנוֹת), *walking
stick, staff*.

שָׁעַע. Pil. שִׁעֲשַׁע I. *delighted.* — II.

played, Isa. 11:8. Pul. שָׁעֳשַׁע *was
fondled*, Isa. 66:12. Hiph. imp.
הָשַׁע *cover the eyes, make blind*,
Isa. 6:10; see in שָׁעָה. Hithpal.
הִשְׁתַּעֲשַׁע *delighted himself*, with
בְּ.

שַׁעֲשֻׁעִים m. pl., *delights, source of
delight*.

שָׁעָף p. n. of a man.

שָׁעַר Pro. 23:7, "*thinketh*," Eng.
Ver.; *meaning uncertain*.

שַׁעַר m.—I. *value, measure*, Gen. 26:
12. — II. m. (f. Isa. 14:31). — 1.
opening, gate of a city. — 2. *the
people assembled at the gate*, Ru.
3:11. — 3. *the city itself*; with ה
loc. שַׁעְרָה; pl. שְׁעָרִים, שַׁעֲרֵי.

שַׁעֲרַיִם p. n., a town of Judah.

שׁוֹעֵר m., *a porter*.

שֹׁעֵר m., pl. שֹׁעָרִים *blighted figs*, Jer.
29:17.

שַׁעֲרוּר m., f. שַׁעֲרוּרָה *causing to shud-
der, horrible*.

שַׁעֲרוּרִי m., f. שַׁעֲרוּרִיָּה, שַׁעֲרוּרִית *horrible*, Jer. 18:13.

שְׁעַרְיָה p. n. of a man.

שַׁעַשְׁגַּז p. n. of a man.

שַׁעֲשׁוּעִים, שַׁעֲשֻׁעִים; see שָׁעַע.

שָׂפָה (Arab. *became visible*). Niph.
הַר נִשְׂפֶּה *a lofty, conspicuous
mountain*, Isa. 13:2. Pu. שֻׁפּוּ
became prominent (the bones), Job
33:21.

שְׁפָה or שָׁפָה f., *cheese*; pl. const.
שְׁפוֹת, 2 Sa. 17:29.

שְׁפִי in pause שֶׁפִי m. (pl. שְׁפָיִים,
שְׁפָיִם) *elevated, conspicuous place*.

שְׁפוֹ, שְׁפִי p. n. of a man.

שִׁפְחָה f. (pl. שְׁפָחוֹת) *female servant or slave.*

מִשְׁפָּחָה const. מִשְׁפַּחַת f. (with suff. מִשְׁפַּחְתִּי; pl. מִשְׁפָּחוֹת).— I. *a household.* — II. *a family or clan.* —III. *a race or kind.*

שָׁפַט I. *judged.*—II. *decided a cause.* —III. *defended the right of.*—IV. *decided between,* with בֵּין...וּבֵין, בֵּין...לְ.—V. *punished.*—VI. *ruled;* part. שֹׁפֵט *a judge, ruler.* Niph. נִשְׁפַּט I. *was judged,* Ps. 9:20.—II. *reasoned with another, disputed,* with עַל, לְ, עִם, אֶת. Po. part. מְשֹׁפְטִי *my judge.*

שְׁפַט Ch. part. שָׁפֵט *judge,* Ezr. 7: 25.

שְׁפוֹט m. (pl. שְׁפוּטִים) *judgments.*

שָׁפָט p. n. of a man.

שֶׁפֶט m., pl. שְׁפָטִים *judgments, punishments.*

שְׁפַטְיָה p. n. of a man.

שְׁפַטְיָהוּ p. n. of a man.

שִׁפְטָן p. n. of a man.

מִשְׁפָּט m.—I. *deciding, decision, sentence.* — II. *punishment.* — III. *a court of justice.*— IV. *a cause for trial.* — V. *justice, equity.* — VI. *any positive institution; the right claimed upon such institution.*— VII. *custom.* — VIII. *manner, appearance.*

שְׁפִי, שְׁפָיִם, שְׁפִי; see שָׁפָה.

שְׁפָיִם, שְׁפִיפוֹן; see שָׁפַף.

שְׁפִיר, שַׁפִּיר; see שָׁפַר.

שָׁפַךְ I. *poured out.*—II. *shed blood.*— III. *threw up a mound.*—IV. *uttered a prayer.* — V. metaph. *poured out his soul, his heart, his*

anger. — VI. *gave abundantly.* Niph. trop. *was poured out, was shed.* Pu. I. *was poured out.*—II. *slipped.* Hith. הִשְׁתַּפֵּךְ *was shed.*

שֶׁפֶךְ m., *the place of pouring out,* Lev. 4:12.

שָׁפְכָה f., *membrum virile,* Deu. 23:2.

שָׁפֵל (fut. יִשְׁפַּל; inf. שְׁפַל).— I. *was low, was lowered.*—II. *was humbled.* Hiph. I. *brought low.*—II. *sent down,* Isa. 57:9.—III. *cast down, humbled;* שׁ׳ רוּחַ *humble in spirit.*

שְׁפַל Ch. Aph. *humbled, brought low.*

שָׁפָל m., שְׁפֵלָה f.—I. *low.*—II. *low in rank or importance.*—III. *humble.*

שְׁפַל m. Ch., *low in rank,* Dan. 4:14.

שֵׁפֶל m. (with suff. שִׁפְלֵנוּ), *lowly place, condition.*

שִׁפְלָה f., the same, Isa. 32:19.

שְׁפֵלָה f., *low country;* הַשְּׁפֵלָה *the low country,* i. e. the plain between Joppa and Egypt.

שִׁפְלוּת f., *lowness of the hands, inactivity,* Ecc. 10:18.

שָׁפָם p. n. of a man.

שִׁפְמוֹת, שְׁפָם p.n., a town of Judah; שִׁפְמִי *a Shiphmite.*

שָׁפָן m.—I. *the jerboa;* LXX. χοιρογρύλλιος, Lev. 11:5; Deu. 14:7. —II. p. n. of a man.

שָׁפַע (Syr. *inundated*).

שֶׁפַע m., *overflowing, abundance,* Deu. 33:19.

שִׁפְעָה f.—I. *inundation.*—II. *multitude.*

שִׁפְעִי p. n. of a man.

שָׁפַף (Syr. *he crept;* Arab. *a speckled snake*).

שְׁפִיפוֹן m., *a species of serpent*, Gen. 49:17.

שְׁפוּפָם p.n., a son of Benjamin.

שְׁפוּפָן p.n. of a man.

שֻׁפִּים p.n. of a man.

שָׁפַר *was pleasing*, with עַל, Ps. 16:6.

שִׁפְרָה f., *beauty*, Job 26:13.

שְׁפַר Ch., *was fair, pleasing*, with עַל קֳדָם.

שׁוֹפָר m. (pl. שׁוֹפָרוֹת), *trumpet, curved horn*.

שֶׁפֶר m. — I. *pleasantness, beauty*, Gen. 49:21. — II. p.n., a mountain in the wilderness.

שִׁפְרָה p.n. of a woman.

שָׁפִיר p.n., an unknown place.

שַׁפִּיר m. Ch., *pleasing, fine*.

(שַׁפְרוּר) שַׁפְרִיר m., *royal canopy*, Jer. 43:10.

שַׁפַּרְפָּרָא m. Ch., *the dawn*, Dan. 6:20.

שָׁפַת *fixed, placed*.

שְׁפַתַּיִם m. dual, *cooking vessels*.

מִשְׁפְּתַיִם dual, the same.

שֶׁצֶף m., *overflowing*, Isa. 54:8.

שָׁק Ch., *leg*, same as שׁוֹק.

שָׁקַד I. *was sleepless, awake*. — II. *watched, kept watch for*, with עַל. Pu. see next word.

שָׁקֵד I. *almond tree*. — II. *almond*. Hence denom. Pu. part. מְשֻׁקָּדִים *formed like almonds*.

שָׁקָה Niph. *was overflown* (see שׁקע), Am. 8:8. Hiph. הִשְׁקָה (fut. apoc. וַיַּשְׁקְ) I. *gave drink to any one*. — II. *watered the ground*; part. מַשְׁקֶה *giving water*, Ps. 104:13. Pu. *watered, refreshed*, Job 21:24.

שֹׁקֶת f., *drinking-trough*; pl. const. שִׁקֳּתוֹת.

שִׁקּוּי m. (pl. with suff. שִׁקּוּיָי). — I. *refreshment*. — II. *drink*.

שִׁקְוּ or שֶׁקֶו m. (pl. with suff. שִׁקְוּי), *drink*.

מַשְׁקֶה m. — I. *cup-bearer*. — II. *drink*. — III. *a watered country*.

שָׁקָה Kal imp. with ה parag., from נשׁק ; שִׁקּוּץ ; see שׁקץ.

שָׁקַט I. *was quiet, undisturbed*. — II. *ceased*. — III. *remained inactive*. — IV. *was silent*. Hiph. I. *caused to cease*. — II. *was quiet, ceased*, with ל and מִן ; inf. הַשְׁקֵט *rest, tranquillity*.

שֶׁקֶט m., *rest, quiet*, 1 Chron. 22:9.

שָׁקַל I. *weighed*. — II. *weighed in payment, paid*. — III. *estimated, judged*. — Niph. I. *was paid*. — II. *was judged*.

שֶׁקֶל m. (pl. שְׁקָלִים, שִׁקְלֵי). — I. a certain standard weight, *the shekel*. — II. a silver coin of that weight.

מִשְׁקָל m., *act of weighing, weight*.

מִשְׁקוֹל m., *weight*, Eze. 4:10.

מִשְׁקֶלֶת f., *balance*, Isa. 28:17.

מִשְׁקֹלֶת f., the same, 2 Ki. 21:13.

שִׁקְמָה f., pl. שִׁקְמִים, שִׁקְמוֹת *sycamore tree, a species of fig*.

שָׁקַע I. *sank*. — II. *was overflown*. — III. *abated* (of fire). Niph. *was overflown*, Am. 8:8 (Ketib נִשְׁקָה) which see in שָׁקָה.

מַשְׁקָע m., *a pond*, Eze. 34:18.

שְׁקַעֲרוּרֹת f. pl., *hollows, parts corroded*, κοιλάδες, Lev. 14:37.

שָׁקַף Niph. and Hiph. I. *looked*. —

II. *looked down, through, towards.*
—III. *threatened.*

שֶׁקֶף m., *covering, coping,* 1 Ki. 7:5.

שְׁקֻפִים m. pl., *coped, having copings,*
1 Ki. 6:4.

מַשְׁקוֹף m., *lintel, beam over a doorway.*

שָׁקַץ Pi. I. *regarded with disgust.*
—II. *loathed,* Ps. 22:25.—III. *polluted.*

שֶׁקֶץ m., *abominable thing.*

שִׁקּוּץ m., *an abomination.*

שָׁקַק (fut. יָשֹׁק).—I. *ran to and fro.*—
II. *was eager.* Hithpal. *ran to
and fro;* fut. pl. יִשְׁתַּקְשְׁקוּן, Nah.
2:5.

מַשָּׁק m., *running to and fro,* Isa.
33:4.

שָׁקַר (fut. יְשַׁקֵּר) *acted falsely towards,*
with לְ. Pi. שִׁקֵּר with בְּ.—I. *uttered a falsehood.*—II. *acted falsely.*

שֶׁקֶר m.—I. *falsehood.* — II. *a deceitful thing.* — III. עֵד שׁ׳ *false
witness;* לַשֶּׁקֶר *in vain, falsely;*
בַּשֶּׁקֶר, בְּשֶׁקֶר *falsely;* שֶׁקֶר adv.
in vain.

שֻׁקָתוֹת, שֹׁקֶת; see שׁקה.

שֹׁר, שָׁרֵךְ; see שׁרר.

שָׁרָא; see שׁרה.

שַׁרְאֶצֶר p. n. of an Assyrian prince;
see נֵרְגַל שׁ׳.

שָׁרָב m.—I. *drought,* Isa. 49:10.—II.
the mirage, Isa. 35:7 (Arab. the
same).

שְׁרֶבְיָה p. n. of a man.

שַׁרְבִיט *same as* שֵׁבֶט *a sceptre* (Esther
only).

שָׁרָה *set at liberty,* Job 37:3. Pi.
שֵׁרָה *the same,* Jer. 15:11.

שְׁרָא Ch.—I. *untied.*—II. *solved.*—III.
halted, dwelt. Pa. I. *untied.*—II.
began. Ithpa. *was loose.*

שָׁרוֹת, שָׁרָה *walls;* see שׁוּר.

שָׁרָי p. n. of a man.

שִׁרְיָה f., *coat of mail,* Job 41:18.

שִׁרְיָן m., the same.

שִׁרְיוֹן, סִרְיֹן m. (pl. שִׁרְיֹנִים, שִׁרְיֹנוֹת,
סִרְיֹנוֹת).—I. *a coat of mail.*—II.

שִׂרְיֹן p.n., a part of Mount Hermon.

מִשְׁרָה f., *juice;* מִשְׁרַת־עֲנָבִים *juice
of grapes,* Nu. 6:3.

שָׁרוֹת, שָׁרָה; see שׁרר.

שָׁרוּחֶן p. n., a city of the tribe of
Simeon.

שָׁרוֹן p. n., the plain between Joppa
and Cesarea.

שְׁרִיקוֹת; see שׁרק.

שְׁרִירוּת, שָׁרִיר; see שׁרר.

שְׁרִית *same as* שְׁאֵרִית; see שׁאר.

שָׁרַץ (fut. יִשְׁרֹץ). — I. *became numerous.* — II. *produce in great
numbers, swarm.*—III. *creep, crawl,*
Eze. 47:9.

שֶׁרֶץ m. col., *small creatures,* whether
insects, reptiles, or fishes.

שָׁרַק (fut. יִשְׁרֹק).—I. *whistle, or hiss
for, call by whistling,* with לְ.—II.
hiss at in contempt, with עַל.

שְׁרֵקָה f., *derision, scorn.*

שְׁרִיקוֹת f., *hissing, derision,* Jer. 18:16.
—II. *whistling, piping,* Jud. 5:16.

מַשְׁרוֹקִית m. Ch., "*flute,*" Eng. Ver.;
LXX. σύριγγος, Dan. 3:5—15.

I. שָׁרַר (Arab. *made wicked*); part.
שׁוֹרֵר *adversary.*

שָׁרָר p. n. of a man.

II. שָׁרַר (Syr. *was firm*).

שֹׁרֶר m. (with suff. שָׁרֵרֵךְ), the navel, Cant. 7:3.

שֹׁר m. (with suff. שָׁרֵךְ), the same.

שָׁרִיר m., pl. שְׁרִירִים firm, solid parts, Job 40:16.

שְׁרִירוּת f. with לֵב, firmness, obstinacy of heart.

שֵׁרָה f., pl. שֵׁרוֹת chains, bracelets, Isa. 3:19.

שַׁרְשְׁרָה f., a chain.

שַׁרְשְׁרָה f., pl. const. שַׁרְשְׁרוֹת chains, small bracelets, Ex. 28:22.

שֹׁרֶשׁ m. (with suff. שָׁרְשָׁם; pl. שָׁרָשִׁים, שׇׁרָשַׁי).—I. a root.—II. shoot, suckers, Isa. 11:10; 53:2. —III. lowest part of any thing; e. g., sole of the foot, bottom of the sea, &c.—IV. foundation, ground-work; שׁ׳ דָּבָר ground of complaint, Job 19:28.

שֵׁרֵשׁ Pi. denom. rooted up. Pu. שֹׁרַשׁ was rooted up. Poel שֹׁרֵשׁ and Poal שֹׁרָשׁ took root. Hiph. הִשְׁרִישׁ the same.

שֹׁרֶשׁ m. Ch., a root.

שֹׁרֶשׁ p. n. of a man.

שֹׁרְשִׁי (שָׁרֹשִׁי) f. Ch., rooting up, banishment, Ezr. 7:26.

שַׁרְשְׁרוֹת, שַׁרְשְׁרוֹת, see שׁרר.

שֵׁרֵת Pi. שֵׁרֵת.—I. waited on, with אֶת.—II. attended to, with accus.,—III. ל or שׁ׳ בְּשֵׁם יְהוָֹה אֶת־יְהוָֹה performed the service of the sanctuary. — IV. worshipped, Eze. 20:32. Part. מְשָׁרֵת m., מְשָׁרֶת f., minister.

שָׁשָׂה Po. שׁוֹשָׂה; see שָׂשָׂה.

שֵׁשׁ f., שִׁשָּׁה const., שֵׁשֶׁת m., six; pl. שִׁשִּׁים sixty; see also in שׁוּשׁ.

שִׁשָּׁה Pi. gave a sixth part of, Eze. 45:13.

שִׁשִּׁי m., שִׁשִּׁית f., the sixth; in f. a sixth part.

שֵׁשָׁא. Pi. שֵׁשֵׁא caused to walk, led, Eze. 39:2.

שֵׁשְׁבַּצַּר p. n., the Persian name of Zerubbabel.

שֵׁשַׁי p. n. of a man.

שֵׁשַׁי p. n. of a man.

שֵׁשַׁךְ p. n., a prophetic title of Babylon.

שֵׁשָׁן p. n. of a man.

שֵׁשָׁק p. n. of a man.

שֵׁשֵׁר with pause שָׁשֵׁר m., red ochre or red lead; LXX. μίλτος.

שֵׁת, שָׁתָה, שַׁתִּי pret. from שׁוּת.

שֵׁת tumult, see שׁאה.

שֵׁת p. n., שֵׁתוֹת, see שִׁית.

שֵׁת, שָׁתוֹת, see שתת.

שֵׁת Ch., six; pl. שָׁתִּין sixty.

שָׁתָה (inf. שָׁתוֹת, שְׁתֹה, שְׁתוֹ; fut. יִשְׁתֶּה; apoc. יֵשְׁתְּ).—I. he drank. —II. sat at table, banqueted, Est. 7:1.—III. met., experienced.—IV. consumed. Niph. fut. יִשָּׁתֶה, was drunk, Lev. 11:34.

שָׁתָא, שְׁתָה Ch., he drank; pret. with א pros. אֶשְׁתִּיו.

שְׁתִי m.—I. drinking.—II. the warp of a well.

שְׁתִיָּה f., drinking, Est. 1:8.

מִשְׁתֶּה m.—I. the act of drinking.— II. a banquet.—III. the drink itself.

מִשְׁתְּיָא emph. m. Ch., the same.

שַׁתּוּ Ps. 73:9, pret. pl., from שׁתת.

שְׁתַּיִם, see שְׁנַיִם.

שָׁתַל planted a tree.

שְׁתִיל m., pl. שְׁתִלֵי זֵיתִים olive shoots, branches, Ps. 128:3.

שָׁתַם (Copt. to close); שְׁתֻם הָעַיִן "whose eyes were opened," Eng. Ver., Nu. 24:3, 15.

שָׁתַן. Hiph. made water; מַשְׁתִּין בַּקִּיר that ... against the wall; i. e., a very mean man.

שָׁתַק I. became still, was at rest. — II. ceased (of strife), Pro. 26:20.

שְׁתָר p. n., a prince of Persia.
שְׁתַר בּוֹזְנַי p. n. of a Persian.

שָׁתַת same as שִׁית placed.

שֵׁת m. (pl. with suff. שְׁתוֹתֵיהֶם), the buttocks.

ת

תָּא m., a room or chamber; pl. תָּאִים, תָּאוֹת; (Arab. habitation).

תָּא; see תָּוָה.

I. תָּאַב desired, longed for, with לְ, Ps. 119, 40, 174.
תַּאֲבָה f., desire, Ps. 119:20.

II. תָּאַב same as תָּעַב. Pi. part. מְתָאֵב abhorring, Am. 6:8.

תָּאָה Pi. mark, mark out; fut. pl. תְּתָאוּ, Nu. 34:7, 8.

תְּאֵהֲבוּ for תְּאֶהֲבוּ Kal fut. pl., from אהב.

תֹּא, תְּאוֹ m., the Egyptian antelope; antilope oryx (Linn.).

תַּאֲוָה desire; see אוה.

תֹּאכְלֵהוּ Pi. fut. with suff. for תְּאַכְּלֵהוּ, or Kal fut. with suff. for תֹּאכְלֵהוּ, from אכל.

תַּאֲלָה cursing; see אלה.

תָּאַם was double; part. תֹּאֲמִים twins. Hiph. produced twins.

תָּאוֹם m., pl. תֹּאוֹמִים twins; pl. const. תְּאֹמֵי.

תַּאֲנָה, תֹּאֲנָה, תַּאֲנָה; see אנה.

תַּאֲנִים, תְּאֵנָה; see און.

תַּאֲנַת שִׁלֹה p. n., a town of Ephraim.

תָּאַר I. turned, made a circuit. — II. was formed, drawn, used in both senses of a boundary only. Pi. delineated, marked the form of.

מְתֹאָר p. n. of a place, Jos. 19:13.

תֹּאַר m. (with suff. תָּאֲרוֹ, תָּאֳרוֹ).—I. (תָּאֳרוֹ) form, personal appearance. — II. beauty.

תַּאְרֵעַ p. n. of a man.

תְּאַשּׁוּר; see אשר.

תָּאבָה for תֹּאבֶה Kal fut. 2. pers., from אבה.

תְּבֹאֶינָה Kal fut. pl. f., from בוא.

תֵּבָה const. תֵּבַת f. (Coptic an ark, chest; Hierog. the same). — I. Noah's ark. — II. the basket in which Moses was exposed.

תְּבוּאָה; see בוא.

תְּבָאתִי, תְּבָאתָה, תְּבֹאָה for תְּבוֹא; תְּבֹאִי for תָּבֹאי Kal fut. with ה parag., and with suff. תְּבוֹאָתֶךָ for תְּבֹאֶךָ, from בוא.

תְּבוּנָה, תָּבוּן; see בין.
תְּבוּסָה; see בוס.

תָּבוֹר p. n. — I. a mountain of Galilee on the borders of Zebulun and Naphtali. — II. a city of the Levites in Zebulun. — III. a grove of oaks in Benjamin.

וַתֵּבְךְ, תֵּבְךְ Kal fut. apoc., from בכה.

תֵּבֵל, see יבל; תֵּבֵל, see בלל.

תֵּבֵל same as תּוּבַל.

תַּבְלִית; see בלה.

תְּבַלֵל; see בלל.

תֶּבֶן m., *straw.*

תִּבְנִי p. n. of a man.

מַתְבֵּן m., *heap of straw,* Isa. 25:10.

תַּבְנִית; see בנה.

תִּבְעָיוּן Kal fut. pl. with ‍נ parag. from בעה.

תַּבְעֵרָה; see בער.

תֵּבֵץ p. n., a place not far from Sichem.

תְּבַר Ch. part., f. תְּבִירָה *brittle,* Dan. 2:42.

תִּנְבְּהֵינָה for תִּנְבְּהֶנָה Kal fut. pl. f. from גָּבַה.

תִּגְיוּן Hiph. fut. pl. with ‍נ parag. from יגה.

תִּגֶּל Niph. fut. apoc. from גלה.

תִּ׳ פִּלְנְאֶסֶר, תִּלְגַת פִּלֶסֶר, תִּגְלַת פִּלְאֶסֶר, תִּ׳ פִּלְנֶסֶר p.n., a king of Assyria.

תַּגְמוּל; see גמל.

תִּגְרָה; see נגרה.

תּוֹגַרְמָה, תֹגַרְמָה p.n., some country to the north of Palestine.

תִּדְהָר; see דהר.

תִּדִירָא; see דור.

תִּדְמִיעִנִי Pi. fut. pl. with suff. from דמה.

תַּדְמֹר p. n., a city in the Syrian desert, *Palmyra.*

תִּדְעָל p. n. of a king, Gen. c. 14.

תָּהָה (Arab. *a desert*).

תֹּהוּ m. — I. *emptiness.* — II. *a vain thing, nothing.*—III. *desolation.*—IV. *a desert, wilderness.*—V. adv. *in vain.*

תְּהוֹם *the deep;* see הום.

תְּהִי, וַתְּהִי, in pause תֶּהִי, fut. apoc., from היה.

תְּהִימֶנָּ for תְּהִימֵינָה Hiph. fut., from הום.

תְּהִלָה, תְּהִלָּה; see הלל.

תְּהַלָּתֶיךָ for תְּהִלָּתֶךָ; see in הלל.

תַּהֲלוּכָה *procession;* see הלך.

תַּהְפֻּכוֹת, תַּהְפּוּכָה see הפך.

תְּהַתֵּלּוּ Pi. fut. pl. with dag. euphon., from התל.

תְּוָה, תָּו; see תוה.

תּוֹא same as תָּאוֹ.

תּוּב Ch., *returned.* Aph. הָתִיב I. *returned, carried back.* — II. *answered,* with פִּתְגָם.

תֻּבַל, תּוּבַל p.n. of some northern nation, perhaps *the Tibarenes.*

תּוּבַל קַיִן p.n., a son of Lamech, the first artificer in iron.

תּוּגָה; see יגה.

תּוֹדָה; see ידה.

תְּוַהּ Ch., *was amazed,* Dan. 3:24.

תָּוָה Pi. תָּוָה *made marks, scrabbled,* 1 Sa. 21:14. Hiph. I. with תָּו *made a mark,* Eze. 9:4. — II. metaph. *provoked,* i. e. made a painful mark, scratch, wound, Ps. 78:41; Vulg. exacerbaverunt.

תָּו m., *a mark* or *sign,* Eze. 9:4; (Arab. *a mark in the form of a cross,* put upon the necks of camels; hence the Phœnician and Greek letters τ tau).

תּוֹחַ p.n. of a man.

תּוֹחֶלֶת; see יחל.

תָּוֶךְ, const. תּוֹךְ m., *the middle; in the middle, among, within, through;* מִתּוֹךְ *from the midst of;* אֶל-תּוֹךְ *into the midst of;* תּוֹךְ *oppression;* see in תָּכַךְ.

תִּיכוֹנָה m., תִּיכוֹן f., *middle.*

תּוֹכַחַת ,תּוֹכֵחָה; see יכח.

תּוֹלֵדֹת ,תּוֹלָד; see ילד.

תּוֹלָל; see ילל.

תּוֹלָע ,תּוֹלֵעָה ,תּוֹלַעַת; see תלע.

תּוֹמִים same as תְּאוֹמִים; see תאם.

תֹּמֶיךָ for תּוֹמֵךְ Kal part., from תמך.

תּוֹעֵבָה ,תּוֹעֲבַת; see תעב.

תּוֹעָה; see תעה.

תּוֹעָפֹת; see יעף.

תֹּף (Arab. *spit through detestation*). תֹּפֶת f.—I. לְפָנִים 'ת *object of detestation* (one in whose face they spit), Job 17:6.—II. הֹפֶת, with ה parag. תָּפְתֶּה p.n., a place in the valley of Hinnom, near Jerusalem.

תּוֹצָאוֹת; see יצא.

תּוּר I. *go about as a spy, spy out.*—II. *search out, explore.*—III. *travel about*, 1 Ki. 10:15.—IV. *seek after the heart, go astray*, Nu. 15:39, with אַחֲרֵי Hiph. I. *send spies*, Jud. 1:23.—II. *direct aright*, Pro. 12:26.

תּוֹר m.—I. *turn, order*, Est. 2:12, 15.—II. *row, string of beads*, Cant. 1:10, 11.—III. *a turtle dove.*—IV. same as תּוֹרָה *way, manner*, 1 Chron. 17:17.

יְתוּר m., *"that which one discovers"* (Ges.); *"abundance,"* see יֶתֶר (Lee); *"range,"* Eng. Ver., Job 39:8.

תּוֹרָה; see ירה

תּוֹר m. Ch., *an ox.*

תּוֹשָׁב; see ישב.

תּוּשִׁיָּה f.—I. *abundance, wealth.*—II. *abundantly, entirely*, Job 30:22.—III. *security.*—IV. *wisdom.*

תּוֹתָח; see יתח.

תָּזֵז ,הֵתַז; see תזז.

תָּזְלִי ,תֵּאזְלִי for תֵּאָזְלִי Kal fut. 2. pers. from אזל.

תַּזְנוּת; see זנה.

תָּאזְרֵנִי for תְּאַזְּרֵנִי Pi. fut. with suff. from אזר.

תַּחְבֻּלוֹת ,תַּחְבּוּלוֹת; see חבל.

תֹּחוּ p.n., same as תּוֹחַ.

תַּחַז Kal fut. apoc. from חזה.

תֹּאחֵז for תֹּאחֵז Kal fut. from אחז.

תְּחִי fut. apoc. from חיה.

תַּחְכְּמֹנִי p.n. of a man.

תֵּחֵל for תָּחֵל Niph. fut. from חלל.

תְּחִלָּה; see חלל.

תַּחְלֻאִים; see חלה.

תַּחְמָס; see חמס.

תַּחֲנוֹת ,תַּחַן; see חנה.

תַּחֲנוּנוֹת ,תַּחֲנוּנִים ,תְּחִנָּה; see חנן.

תַּחְפַּנְחֵס ,תַּחְפְּנֵס (תַּחְפָּנֵס), p.n.—I. a city of Egypt.—II. תַּחְפְּנֵיס a queen of Egypt.

תַּחֲרָה ,תַּחְרָא; see חרה.

תַּחְרֵעַ p.n. of a man.

תַּחַשׁ m. עוֹר תַּחַשׁ ,עֹרֹת תְּחָשִׁים.—I. a colour of which skins were dyed, probably *blue*; "badgers' skins," Eng. Ver.—II. p.n. of a man.

וַתַּחַשׁ ,תֶּחֱשׁ, Job 31:5; Kal fut. apoc. (חָשָׁה); see חוש.

תָּחַת root not used; (Ethiop. "cast down").

תַּחַת m., *that which is under, below.* Adv. *below;* prep. ὑπό.—I. *under.*—II. *instead of.*—III. *in return for;* תַּחַת אֲשֶׁר *whereas, because that;* 'ת כִּי *because;* (also without כִּי) With suff. תַּחְתֶּיךָ (תַּחְתֶּנִי) ;תַּחְתַּי; (תַּחְתֵּינוּ) תַּחְתֵּיהֶם ,תַּחְתֶּיהָ ,תַּחְתָּיו;

תַּחְתֵּיהֶם‎, תַּחְתֵּיכֶם‎, תַּחְתָּם‎. Comp. מִתַּחַת‎ *from under, under*; אֶל־תַּחַת‎ *under, beyond*; לְ‎ *under.*

תַּחַת‎ p. n.—I. one of the stations of Israel in the wilderness.—II. name of a man.

תַּחַת‎ Ch., תְּחוֹת‎ Ch., } *under.*

תַּחְתִּי‎ m., תַּחְתִּית‎, תַּחְתִּיָה‎ f., *lówer, lowest*; pl. m. תַּחְתִּיִּים‎, f. תַּחְתִּיּוֹת‎ *lowest parts* or *places.*

תַּחְתּוֹן‎ m., תַּחְתּוֹנָה‎ f., *lower, lowest.*

תַּחַת‎ Ch. Aph. fut. from נחת‎.

תֵּחַת‎ Kal fut. f. from נחת‎.

תֵּט‎ Kal fut. apoc. from נטה‎.

תִּיז‎. Hiph. הֵתַז‎, with pause הֵתַז‎ *cut off.*

תִּיכוֹן‎; see תָּוֶךְ‎.

תִּילוֹן‎, תִּלּוֹן‎ p. n. of a man.

תֵּימָא‎, תֵּמָא‎ p. n. of a people of Arabia, and of their country.

תֵּימָן‎; see ימן‎.

תִּימָרוֹת‎; see תמר‎.

תֵּיעָשֶׂה‎, Ex. 25:31, for תֵּעָשֶׂה‎ Niph. fut. from עשה‎.

תִּירֹשׁ‎, תִּירוֹשׁ‎; see ירשׁ‎.

תִּירִיא‎ p. n. of a man.

תִּירָם‎ p. n., one of the sons of Japhet.

תַּיִשׁ‎ m. (pl. תְּיָשִׁים‎), *he-goat* or *ram.*

תָּכָה‎. Pu. תֻּכּוּ‎ *were seated, sat down,* Deu. 33:3.

תֵּכַהּ‎, וַתֵּכַהּ‎ Kal fut. apoc. from כהה‎.

תְּכוּנָה‎; see תכן‎, כון‎.

תּוּכִּיִּים‎, תֻּכִּיִּים‎ m. pl., probably *peacocks,* 1 Ki. 10:22; 2 Ch. 9:21.

תְּכַךְ‎ Ch., *injured, hurt.*

תּוֹךְ‎, תֹּךְ‎ m., *craft, oppression*; see also תָּוֶךְ‎ in תוך‎.

תְּכָכִים‎ m. pl., *oppressions, injuries,* Pro. 29:13.

תַּכְלִית‎, תִּכְלָה‎; see כלה‎.

תְּכֵלֶת‎ f., *violet blue.*

תָּכַן‎ I. *weighed.* — II. *pondered, examined.* Niph. I. *was measured, examined.*—II. *was of just measure, fair, equal.* Pi. תִּכֵּן‎ I. *measured.*—II. *fixed,* Ps. 75:4.—III. *directed,* Isa. 40:13. Pu. *measured, reckoned,* 2 Ki. 12:12.

תֹּכֶן‎ m.—I. *fixed quantity,* Ex. 5:18.—II. *measure, standard,* Eze. 45:11.—III. p. n., a town of the Simeonites.

תְּכוּנָה‎ f.— I. *arrangement, order, structure.* — II. *costly thing,* Nah. 2:10; see also in כון‎.

תָּכְנִית‎ f., *measure, standard.*

מַתְכֹּנֶת‎ f. (with suff. מַתְכֻּנְתּוֹ‎), *measure, proportion.*

תֵּכַס‎ Pi. fut. apoc. from כסה‎.

תְּכֻסֶּה‎ Hith. fut. from כסה‎.

תַּכְרִיךְ‎; see כרך‎.

תְּלָה‎, תֵּל‎; see תלל‎.

תְּלָאִים‎, תְּלָא‎; see תלה‎.

תְּלָאָה‎; see לאה‎.

תְּלָאבוֹת‎, תַּלְאוּבָה‎; see לאב‎.

תְּלַאשָּׂר‎, תְּלַאשָּׁר‎ p. n., a city of Syria or Mesopotamia.

תִּלְבֹּשֶׁת‎; see לבשׁ‎.

תֶּלֶג‎ m. Ch., *snow.*

תִּנְלַגַת‎; see תִּנְלַת‎.

תָּלָה‎ (part. תָּלוּי‎; pl. תְּלוּיִם‎, תְּלָאִים‎).—I. *hung,* with בְּ‎, עַל‎ *upon* (a tree).—II. *"made dependent,"* Job 26:7 (Lee).—III. *placed in sus-*

pense. Niph. *was hanged.* Pi. *hung,* Eze. 27:10, 11.

תָּלָה, וַתֵּלַה Kal fut. apoc., from לתה.

תְּלִי m. (with suff. תֶּלְיֶךָ) *quiver (that which is suspended),* Gen. 27:3.

תְּלֻנּוֹת ; see לון.

תֶּלַח p. n. of a man.

תָּלַל *raised a mound;* part. תָּלוּל *elevated, thrown up,* Eze. 17:22; (הֻתַּל, see הֻתַּל).

תֵּל m. (with suff. תֶּלָּם, תִּלָּהּ).—I. *heap of ruins.*—II. *hill, mound.*—III. תֵּל אָבִיב p. n. of a town of Babylonia.—IV. תֵּל חַרְשָׁא p.n.;. see חָרָשׁ.—V. תֵּל מֶלַח *(hill of salt),* p.n., a place in Babylonia.

תֶּלֶם m., *furrow.*

תַּלְמִי p.n. of a man.

תַּלְמִיד ; see למד.

תָּלֶן Kal fut. apoc., from לון.

תָּלַע. Pu. part. מְתֻלָּעִים *clothed in scarlet,* Nah. 2:4.

תּוֹלָע m. (pl. תּוֹלָעִים) — I. *worm of any kind.*—II. *the worm used in dying scarlet.* — III. *scarlet cloth.*—IV. p.n., *Tolah:* (a) a son of Issachar; patron. תּוֹלָעִי.—(b) a judge of Israel.

תּוֹלֵעָה f., *a worm.*

תּוֹלַעַת f.(with suff. תּוֹלַעְתָּם) *a worm;* שָׁנִי תי, תי שָׁנִי I. *scarlet or crimson.*—II. *the kermes insect whence it was dyed.*

תַּלְפִּיּוֹת f. pl., "*an armoury,*" Eng. Ver.,Cant.4:4; meaning uncertain.

תִּלְאַשַּׂר same as תְּלַאשָּׂר.

תְּלָת f., תְּלָתָא, תַּלְתָּא m. Ch., *three;* pl. תְּלָתִין *thirty.*

תְּלָת m. Ch., the same; שַׁלִּיט תַּלְתָּא and תַּלְתָּא *prince third in rank.*

תַּלְתִּי m. Ch., *third.*

תְּלִיתָי Ch., f. תְּלִיתָאָה the same.

תַּלְתַּלִּים m. pl., *hanging, flowing of hair;* LXX. ἐλάται, Cant. 5:11.

תָּם Ch., with ה parag. תַּמָּה *there.*

תָּמָּה, תֹּם, תַּמָּה, תָּם; see תמם.

תֵּימָא same as תֵּימָא.

תָּמַהּ *wondered, was amazed.* Hith. imp. הִתַּמְּהוּ *be astonished,* Hab. 1:5.

תְּמַהּ m. Ch., *wonder, miracle.*

תִּמָּהוֹן m., *astonishment, terror.*

תַּמּוּז p. n. Syrian idol, perhaps *Adoni*

תְּמוֹל, אֶתְמוֹל adv., *yesterday;* אִתְמוֹל, אֶתְמוּל the same.

תְּמוּנָה; see מין.

תְּמוּרָה; see מור.

תְּמוּתָה; see מות.

תֶּמַח p.n. of a man.

תֶּמַח Hiph. fut. apoc., with י parag. תַּמְחִי, from מחה.

תָּמִיד; see מוד.

תָּמִים; see תמם.

תָּמַךְ I. *took hold of,* with בְּ.—II. *held, held up, supported.*—III. *obtained.*—IV. *apprehended.*—V. *arrived at, reached.* Niph. *was holden,* Pro. 5:22.

תָּמַם (fut. יִתֹּם, יִתּוֹם, יִתַּם; pl. יִתַּמּוּ, with pause יִתָּמּוּ).—I. *was completed, ended.*—II. *was perfect in character, upright.*—III. *ceased, came to an end, finished.* — IV. *wasted away, consumed, destroyed;* עַד תֻּמָּם *until they were destroyed.*

Niph. (fut. pl. יִתַּפּוּ).—I. *was fi-*
nished.—II. *was consumed.* Hiph.
הֵתֵם (fut. יָתֵּם; inf. with suff.
הֲתִימְךָ).—I. *finished, consumed.*—
II. *declared perfect.*—III. *took the*
sum of, counted, 2 Ki. 22:4.— IV.
cause to cease, remove, with מִן,
Eze. 22:15. Hithpa. *showed him-*
self perfect; fut. תִּתַּמַּם, 2 Sa. 22:
26; Ps. 18:26.

תָּמִים m., תְּמִימָה f.—I. *complete.*—
II. *whole, entire.*—III. *free from*
fault, defect.—IV. *integrity.*

תָּם m., תַּמָּה f., *blameless, honest,*
virtuous, pious.

תֹּם, תוֹם־, תָּם־ m. (with suff. תֻּמּוֹ).—I.
completeness.—II. *security, peace,*
prosperity.—III. *innocence, integ-*
rity; pl. תֻּמִּים probably *truth;* see
אוּרִים.

תֻּמָּה f., *innocence, integrity.*

תֹּאֲמִים *double,* contr. for תְּאוֹמִים.

מְתֹם m., *unhurt, sound, soundness.*

תִּמְנָה p. n., *a city of Judah.*

תִּמְנָתָה p. n., *a town of the Philistines;*
תִּמְנִי *a Timnite.*

תִּ׳ סֶרַח, תִּמְנַת חֶרֶס p. n., *a town in*
Mount Ephraim.

תִּמְנַע p. n.—I. *of a woman.*—II. *of one*
of the tribes of Edom.

תָּכֶם; see מסס.

תָּמַם, וַתֵּמֶם Hiph. fut. apoc., from
מסה.

תָּמָר m.—I. *a palm tree;* pl. תְּמָרִים.
—II. p. n. *of a woman.*—III. p. n.
of a town in south Palestine.—IV.
p. n., same as תַּדְמֹר.—V. עִיר
הַתְּמָרִים (*city of palms*), *a name*
of Jericho.

תֹּמֶר m., *palm-tree,* Jer. 10:5.

תִּמֹּרָה f. (pl. תִּמֹּרֹת, תִּמֹּרִים), *arti-*
ficial palm tree.

תַּמְרוּרִים m. pl., *columns,* Jer. 31:21;
see also in מָרַר.

תִּימָרָה f., pl. const. תִּמֲרוֹת *pillars of*
smoke.

תָּמֵר Ex. 23:21, for תָּמֵר Hiph. fut.,
from מרר (same as מרה).

תֹּאמְרוּ for תֹּאמְרוּ Kal fut. pl., from
אמר.

תַּמְרוּק; see מרק.

תַּנִּים, תָּן; see תנן.

תֵּן תְּנָה, תֵּן Kal imp., from נתן.

תִּנְדַּע Ch. Pe. fut., from ידע.

תָּנָה *hired,* Hos. 8:10. Pi. I. *ascribed*
praise to, Jud. 5:11. — II. *cele-*
brated an action, Jud. 11:40.
Hiph. same as Kal, Hos. 8:9.

תַּנּוֹת f. pl., *habitations,* Mal. 1:3; see
also in תַּנִּים.

אֶתְנָה f., *gift, wages of prostitution,*
Hos. 2:14.

אֶתְנִי p. n. of a man.

אֶתְנַן m. (with suff. אֶתְנַנָּה).—I. *fee,*
gift, wages of prostitution.—II.
p. n. of a man.

תִּנְיָן m. Ch., *the second:* f. תִּנְיָנָה,
Dan. 7:5.

תִּנְיָנוּת Ch. adv., *a second time, again,*
Dan. 2:7.

תְּנוּאָה; see נוא.

תְּנוּבָה; see נוב.

תְּנוּךְ see תנך.

תְּנוּמָה; see נום.

תְּנוּפָה; see נוף.

תַּנּוּר m., *a furnace, oven.*

תַּנְחֻמֹת, תַּנְחוּמִים, תַּנְחֶמֶת; see נחם.

תְּנוּךְ m., with אֹזֶן *the lower part of*
the ear.

תַּן or תָּן m., pl. תַּנִּין, תַּנִּים *jackals, or*

other wild animals of the desert; the precise meaning unknown.

תַּנִּים m. sing., for תַּנִּין Eze. 29:3; 32:2.

תַּנִּין m. (pl. תַּנִּינִים).— I. a serpent.— II. any large marine animal.—III. a crocodile.

תִּנְשֶׁמֶת; see נשם.

תֹּסֶף for תֹּאסֵף Kal fut., from אסף.

תָּעֵב. Pi. תִּעֵב I. abhorred. — II. rendered loathsome. — III. was abominable. Hiph. הִתְעִיב I. acted abominably.—II. adv. abominably. Niph. נִתְעָב was abhorred.

תּוֹעֵבָה const. תּוֹעֲבַת f.—I. abomination.—II. impure detestable action. —III. anything polluting.—IV. an idol.

תַּעֲגֶנָה for תֵּעָגֵנָּה Niph. fut. pl., from ענן.

תָּעָה (fut. apoc. תֵּתַע).—I. wandered, went astray.—II. staggered through drunkenness. — III. was in confusion, disorder.—IV. with מֵעַל, מִן, מֵאַחֲרֵי departed from the true worship. Niph. נִתְעָה I. was led astray.—II. was made to stagger. Hiph. הִתְעָה (fut. apoc. יַתַע) I. caused to wander, go astray.— II. deceived, led astray.—III. acted deceitfully.

תּוֹעָה f. — I. apostasy, Isa. 32:6.— II. hurt, injury, Neh. 4:2, 8.

תֹּעוּ תֹּעִי p. n. of a man.

תְּעוּדָה; see עוד.

תְּעָלַת, תְּעָלָה; see עלה.

תַּעֲלוּלִים; see עלל.

תַּעֲלֻמָה; see עלם.

תַּעֲנוּג; see ענג.

תַּעֲנִית; see ענה.

תַּעְנָךְ, תַּעֲנָךְ p. n., a city of the Manassites in the tribe of Issachar.

תָּעַע. Pil. part. מְתַעְתֵּעַ mocking, Gen. 27:12. Hith. part. pl. מִתְעַתְּעִים mocked, 2 Chron. 36:16.

תַּעְתֻּעִים m. pl., mockeries, deceptions, Jer. 10:15; 51:18.

תַּעֲצֻמוֹת; see עצם.

תַּעַר; see ערה.

תַּעֲרוּבָה; see ערב.

תְּפָּים, תֹּף sce תפף.

תִּפְאֶרֶת, תִּפְאָרָה; see פאר.

תַּפּוּחַ m.—I. apple-tree.—II. apple.— III. p. n.: (a) a town of Judah; (b) a town of Ephraim; (c) a town between Ephraim and Manasseh; (d) the name of a man.

תְּפוֹצוֹתִיכֶם Thiphel 1. pers. with suff., from פוץ.

וַתִּפְאֵהוּ, תֹּפֵהוּ for תֹּאפֵהוּ Kal fut. with suff., from אפה.

תְּפִינִים; see אפן.

תָּפֵל (Arab. was unseasoned).

תָּפֵל m.—I. that which is insipid, unsavoury, Job 6:6. — II. insipid, foolish, Lam. 2:14. — III. lime, lime-wash for walls (Eze. only).

תֹּפֶל p. n., a place in the wilderness.

תִּפְלָה f., insipidity, folly.

תְּפִלָּה; see פלל.

תִּפְלֶצֶת; see פלץ.

תִּפְסַח; see פסח.

תָּפַף, part. f. pl. תוֹפֵפוֹת beat the tambourine or drum, Ps. 68:26. Pi. smite the bosom, Nah. 2:8.

תֹּף m. (pl. תֻּפִּים), tambourine, drum.

תָּפַר sew, join together. Pi. the same, Eze. 13:18.

תָּפַשׂ I. laid hold of, seized, with בְּ.

—II. *took in war.*—III. *handle, manage the bow,* &c.—IV. *carry on war.*—V. *set, enchase,* Hab. 2:19.—VI. *administer the law,* Jer. 2:8.—VII. *used the name of God irreverently, perjured himself,* Pro. 30:9. Niph. *was taken, caught.* Pi. *took hold,* Pro. 30:28.

תָּפְתֶּה ,תֹּפֶת; see תּוּף.

תִּפְתָּיֵא Ch. m. pl. emph. *lawyers* or *judges,* Dan. 3:2, 3.

תִּצְלֶינָה for תְּצַלֶּינָה Kal fut. pl., from צלל

תִּקְוָה, see קוה.

תְּקוֹמֵם ,תְּקוּמָה; see קום.

תְּקוֹעַ; see תקע.

תְּקוּפָה, see קוף; תַּקִּיף, see תקף.

תְּקַל Ch., *weighed;* part. pass. תְּקִל; *weighed;* pret. תְּקַלְתָּ *thou art weighed.*

תָּקַן *was arranged, straight.* Pi. I. *set in order.* — II. *made straight* (Ecclesiastes only).

תְּקַן Ch., *the same.* Hoph. הָתְקַן *was set in order, established.*

תָּקַע I. *smote the hands together* (for joy, &c.).— II. *thrust in, stabbed* (of a weapon).—III. *fixed, fastened.*—IV. *pitched a tent.*—V. *threw into the sea,* Ex.10:19.—VI. with שׁוֹפָר ,בַּשּׁוֹפָר *blew a trumpet;* with תְּרוּעָה *blew a horn.* Niph. I. with לְיָד *strikes hands, becomes a surety,* Job 17:3.—II. with שׁוֹפָר *a trumpet is blown.*

תָּקוֹעַ m., *blast with a trumpet,* Eze. 7:14.

תֶּקַע m., *the same,* Ps. 150:3.

תְּקוֹעַ p.n., *Tekoa,* a town of Judah, whence the name מִדְבַּר תְּקוֹעַ *the wilderness of Tekoa;* m. תְּקֹעִי, f. תְּקֹעִית *a Tekoite.*

תָּקַף *overpower, prevail over.*

תְּקַף Ch.—I. *was strong.*—II. *was violent.* Pa. *made strong.*

תֹּקֶף m., *might, power.*

תְּקֹף m. Ch., *the same.*

תְּקוּפָה *circuit;* see קוף.

תַּקִּיף m., *strong, powerful,* Ecc. 6:10.

תַּקִּיף m.Ch., *strong, powerful.*

תַּרְאֲלָה p.n., a town of Benjamin.

וַתֵּרֶב ,תֵּרֶב Kal fut. apoc., from רבה

תַּרְבִּית ,תַּרְבּוּת; see רבה.

תַּרְגֵּל; see רֶגֶל.

תַּרְגֵּם Ch. quadrilitt., *interpreted, translated;* part. pass. מְתַרְגַּם, Ezr. 4:7.

תַּרְדֵּמָה; see רדם.

תִּרְהָקָה p.n., *Tirhakah,* king of Egypt and Ethiopia.

תְּרוּמִיָּה ,תְּרוּמָה; see רום.

תְּרוּעָה; see רוע.

תְּרוּפָה; see רפא.

תֵּרוֹץ Niph. fut., from רצץ.

תִּרְזָה f., name of a tree, *the holly.*

תֶּרַח p.n.—I. a station of Israel in the wilderness.—II. the father of Abraham.

תִּרְחֲנָה p.n. of a man.

תְּרֵין const. תְּרֵי m., תַּרְתֵּין f. Ch., *two.*

תַּרְמִית ,תָּרְמָה; see רמה.

תֹּרֶן I. *mast of a ship.*—II. *flag* or *banner.*

תְּרַע m. Ch.—I. *entrance, door.*—II. *palace* (the porte).

תָּרָע m. Ch., *door keeper.*

תַּרְעֵלָה; see רעל.

תִּרְעָתִי p.n. of a man.

תְּרָפִים m. pl., *Teraphim*; idols of some kind.

תִּרְפֶּינָה, Job 5:18, Kal fut. pl., from רפה.

תִּרְצָה p.n.—I. one of the royal cities of Israel.—II. the name of a woman.

תֶּרֶשׁ p.n. of a Persian.

תַּרְשִׁישׁ; see רשׁשׁ.

תִּרְשָׁתָא, with art., a title of Nehemiah.

תַּרְתָּן p.n., a chief of the Assyrians.

תַּרְתָּק p.n., an idol of the Arvadites.

תִּשָּׂנָא, תִּשֶּׂאינָה for תִּשֶּׂאנָה Kal fut. pl., from נשׂא.

תְּשׁוּמֶת; see שׂים.

תְּשֻׁאוֹת; see שׁוא.

תִּשְׁבִּי p. n. of a man.

תַּשְׁבֵּץ; see שׁבץ.

תְּשׁוּבָה; see שׁוב.

תְּשׁוּעָה; see שׁוע.

תְּשׁוּקָה; see שׁוק.

תְּשׁוּרָה; see שׁור.

תֶּשִׁי, Deu. 32:18, fut. apoc., from שׁיה.

תְּשֵׁם fut., from ישׁם.

תֵּשַׁע const. תְּשַׁע, f. תִּשְׁעָה const. תִּשְׁעַת m., *nine, the ninth*; pl תִּשְׁעִים *ninety*.

תְּשִׁיעִי m., תְּשִׁיעִית f., *the ninth*.

תֵּשְׁתְּ Kal fut. apoc., from שׁתה.

תִּשְׁתַּחוּ Hith. fut. apoc. sing. for תִּשְׁתַּחֲוֶה, from שׁחה.

תִּשְׁתָּעַ Hith. fut. apoc. for תִּשְׁתָּעָה, from שׁעה.

תֵּת, with suff. תִּתִּי Kal inf., from נתן.

תִּתְבָּרַר for תִּתְבָּרַר Hith. fut., from ברר.

תִּתָּה for נָתַתָּה Kal pret., from נתן.

תִּתְחַר Hith. fut. apoc., from חרר.

תִּתֹּם, תִּתָּם Kal fut., from תמם.

תִּתְנַי p.n., a Persian noble.

וַתֵּתַע, תֵּתַע Kal fut. apoc., from תעה.

תִּתְפַּל, 2 Sa. 22:27, transpos. for תִּתְפַּתָּל Hith. fut., from פתל.

תֵּתַצַּב, Ex. 2:4, for תִּתְיַצֵּב Hith. fut., from יצב.

וַתִּתַר, תֹּתַר Hiph. fut. in pause from יתר.